Transforming Agrarian Economies

For Liz and David,
with best wishes,
Tom

TRANSFORMING AGRARIAN ECONOMIES

OPPORTUNITIES SEIZED, OPPORTUNITIES MISSED

Thomas P. Tomich, Peter Kilby,
and Bruce F. Johnston

Cornell University Press
Ithaca and London

First published 1995 by Cornell University Press.

Printed in the United States of America

⊗ The paper in this book meets the minimum requirements
of the American National Standard for Information Sciences—
Permanence of Paper for Printed Library Materials, ANSI Z39.48-1984.

Library of Congress Cataloging-in-Publication Data

Tomich, Thomas P. (Thomas Patrick), 1956–
    Transforming agrarian economies : opportunities seized,
  opportunities missed / Thomas P. Tomich, Peter Kilby,
  and Bruce F. Johnston.
      p.   cm.
    Includes bibliographical references and index.
    ISBN 0-8014-8245-3 (paperback)
      1. Agriculture—Economic aspects—Developing countries.
  2. Agriculture and state—Developing countries. 3. Developing
  countries—Rural conditions. I. Kilby, Peter, 1935–   . II. Johnston, Bruce
  F., 1919–   . III. Title.
  HD1417.T66 1995
  338.1´09172´4—dc20   95-5522

For Nancy, Marianne, and Harriet

CONTENTS

LIST OF BOXES

PREFACE

Can the poorest countries achieve sustained growth while alleviating hunger and other manifestations of mass poverty? The wellbeing of some 60 percent of the world's population depends on the response to this question. These men, women, and children live in the subset of developing countries where the majority of the labor force still depends mainly on agriculture. This book systematically explores the complex challenges of development to identify priorities for action for these CARLs, *c*ountries with *a*bundant *r*ural *l*abor.

The authors have used a combined analytical and historical approach, which is summarized in the Introduction, with the aim of placing agricultural development in its widest context. Intense collaboration has been crucial to this effort. Each of the authors with his special skills made contributions to every chapter.

Collaboration is also the keynote for this book in a longer perspective. It continues a series of collaborative ventures begun by Johnston thirty-five years ago. Building on a 1951 paper analyzing technological change in Japanese agriculture, Bruce Johnston and John Mellor conceptually defined agriculture's "four contributions" to the process of economic development in a 1961 paper that is cited widely to this day. In the 1960s Herman Southworth and Johnston coedited a symposium volume, *Agricultural Development and Economic Growth*, sponsored by the Social Science Research Council, and Johnston examined issues related to structural transformation and labor absorption in papers with Soren Nielsen (1966) and John Cownie (1969). Following work with Kilby in the 1970s, Johnston and William Clark in 1982 published a book focused on the production-oriented, consumption-oriented, and organization programs critical to agricultural and rural development. The treatment of nutrition, health, and population in that book was strongly influenced by Johnston's work in 1974–75 as chairman and rapporteur of the Ninth Session of the Joint FAO/WHO Expert Committee on Nutrition.

Peter Kilby first collaborated with Johnston on a 1972 paper where the focus was on manufacturing—output levels, industry shares, factor intensities—under various patterns of agricultural development. This facet of intersectoral commodity flows was further developed in their 1975 book, *Agriculture and Structural Transformation*, with special attention to the producer inputs of farm equipment and fertilizer. Kilby also helped to extend the structural transformation paradigm through the articulation of technological diffusion in manufacturing, changing market organization, and social structure differentiation in the 1975 book. Over the intervening years, he has continued his research focus on entrepreneurship in developing countries and acquired substantial additional knowledge about the rural nonfarm sector and its interaction with agriculture, the genesis of informal sector technology, and the manufacture of fertilizer and farm equipment. Chapters 2, 6, and 7, which represent Kilby's most important contributions to the present volume, are enriched by those long-standing research interests.

Thomas Tomich is the newest recruit to this ongoing collaborative venture. In a 1984 study of the feasibility of small farm development strategies, he and Johnston deepened the analysis of the farm sector in terms of technology adoption, economies of scale, and farm-size effects. Their follow-up paper in 1985 emphasized a distinction between agricultural strategy and agrarian structure, in recognition not only of the interactions between strategy and structure but also of the crucial differences with respect to policy options. Those endeavors were the starting point for our task of integrating recent empirical evidence, analytical advances, and lessons from experience with the structural transformation perspective of the 1975 book by Johnston and Kilby. A distinguishing feature of the present volume is greater attention to the political economy of development strategy. Tomich introduced the concept of "strategic notions" in an annotated chapter outline for a study of the political economy of agriculture and rural development in 1986. That study grew into this book, and the strategic notions concept became the organizing theme linking our analytical and historical chapters. To the present volume, Tomich also brings the precise delineation of agrarian economies as our "countries with abundant rural labor"; that name and its apt acronym, CARL, however, are from Kilby.

One consequence of collaboration by authors from three different generations of development economists is apparent in our Acknowledgments. Thanks to the wide range of our associates, we have been privileged to draw on the experience, knowledge, and judgment of a large number of colleagues. Without their advice and the pathbreaking work of Simon Kuznets, Kazushi Ohkawa, Hollis Chenery, Yujiro Hayami, and Vernon Ruttan, we could not have undertaken so ambitious a project.

THOMAS P. TOMICH

Cambridge, Massachusetts

PETER KILBY

Middletown, Connecticut

BRUCE F. JOHNSTON

Stanford, California

ACKNOWLEDGMENTS

This book was made possible by financial support from the Agriculture and Rural Development Division of the World Bank's Economic Development Institute (EDI). We were extremely fortunate that J. A. Nicholas Wallis's tenure as chief of that division spanned most of our work. The first stage began when Wallis provided us with support for a study, "The Political Economy of Agriculture and Rural Development." We are also grateful to J. Price Gittinger, who was with EDI at that time, for his encouragement of the initiative. John Malone was our liaison with EDI at the outset. He was succeeded by Richard Manning, who has helped us over many hurdles, substantive and bureaucratic. Wallis, Malone, and Manning gave us a remarkable level of support and patience.

Stanford University's Food Research Institute (FRI) joined EDI as a co-sponsor early in this endeavor. Subsequently, the Harvard Institute for International Development (HIID) also entered into the partnership. We are indebted to Walter Falcon, Director of FRI during most of the book's gestation, and Dwight Perkins, Director of HIID, for the substantial support those institutions provided. Scott R. Pearson, who succeeded Falcon as Director of FRI, has continued to provide critical support in addition to particularly valuable comments on Chapter 11.

Wally Falcon, Nick Wallis, and Richard Manning have been close partners with us in this project. We shudder to think how much time each of them has spent poring over successive drafts of a manuscript that got longer before it got better. Wallis and Manning came through with funds for the editing that all coauthored books need, but few receive. Bruce Ross-Larson and Vince McCullough filled this need superbly. They gave us the breakthroughs in clarity and the reduction in length that we wanted so that the book would be accessible to a wide audience.

FRI hosted Tomich and Kilby during a summer of work with Johnston that was a turning point in completion of the first draft. Greg Binkert prepared a survey of rural finance that was of great assistance in Chapter 5 and made many useful comments on other chapters during that summer. At FRI, Sandra Bernard managed the production of the first draft. Sandra Fraley assisted in getting the enterprise established when it moved to HIID, and Neal Reenan provided helpful research assistance. Tomich is grateful to Clyde Evans for tactical suggestions for getting the job done. Katherine Yost deserves special appreciation for her role in producing a series of "final" versions and managing this increasingly complex undertaking through to completion.

Many scholars and practitioners helped us to shape our views on political economy. During his three years as a resident advisor at the Center for Policy and Implementation Studies in Jakarta, Indonesia, Tomich was privileged to work for an extraordinary practitioner, Ali Wardhana. That work and other advisory assignments undertaken through HIID provided an opportunity to test general propositions against the realities of development problems in Asia and Africa. Carl Gotsch and Michael Roemer, by example and guidance, showed what it takes to be an effective advisor. Tomich is indebted to his colleague Merilee Grindle for her perceptive insights on political economy and her encouragement to cross disciplinary boundaries. William C. Clark gave us an extremely useful assessment of the work at a crucial stage. In an earlier collaboration, which led to their book *Redesigning Rural Development* (1982), Clark provided Johnston with an intensive tutorial on the art and craft of policy analysis and a new appreciation of the importance of organizational issues. Our conversations and correspondence with Grace Goodell also influenced our thinking on these issues.

Kilby would like to acknowledge the Woodrow Wilson Center at the Smithsonian for providing a stimulating environment for his work on Chapters 2 and 6. His colleagues Carl Liedholm and Steven Haggblade enriched those chapters far more than the specific references to their work would indicate. Dennis Anderson and Stanley Lebergott also made valuable contributions to those chapters. Wesleyan University, beyond its generous sabbatical policy, extended two project grants that greatly facilitated Kilby's fertilizer investigation presented in Chapter 7. At an early stage in the work on nitrogen fertilizer, William Sheldrick at the World Bank provided valuable help relating to the technical and economic complexities of that industry.

Johnston has accumulated many intellectual debts in the years he has spent studying agriculture's role in economic development, but he wants to acknowledge especially John Mellor, Yujiro Hayami, Saburo Yamada, and the late Kazushi Ohkawa. He is grateful to Carl Taylor for sharing knowledge acquired during his experience as UNICEF Director in China as well as a lifetime of research and teaching and to Doris Calloway for a continuing tutorial on nutrition. Both Johnston and Tomich benefited a great deal from Reynaldo Martorell's willingness to share his knowledge, especially on the interrelationships between nutrition and child development.

Johnston is indebted to the late William O. Jones and also to Kenneth Anthony and Victor Uchendu for sharing their knowledge and insights concerning tropical Africa. Uma Lele, who directed the World Bank's study of Managing Agricultural Development in Africa (MADIA), invited Johnston to lead a study of U.S. assistance for agricultural and rural development. Research and visits carried out as part of that study were of great value to this work, especially for the preparation of our historical analysis of Kenya and Tanzania, as these were two of the six MADIA study countries.

The Institute of Economics, Academia Sinica, made it possible for Johnston and Tomich to travel to Taiwan to present an early version of the comparison of Taiwan and Mexico. John D. Montgomery and the Pacific Basin Research Center of Soka University of America (working out of the John F. Kennedy School of Government) provided funding that enabled Johnston to do further research on Taiwan's experience in the summer of 1992 and also to participate in a conference in Beijing on agricultural development in China. Funding from the U.S.–Mexico Project initiated in 1980 by Clark Reynolds and Carlos Tello enabled Johnston to make several study visits to rural Mexico and to benefit from the insights of Cassio Luiselli, Heliodoro Diaz, and other members of the Working Group on Agricultural and Rural Development.

We have been able to draw on the experience and judgments of a large number of informal advisors regarding our eight case study countries. Yujiro Hayami commented on our analysis of Japan, and Alan Olmstead, Philip Raup, and B. F. Stanton assisted with aspects of U.S. agricultural history. Carl Taylor, D. Gale Johnson, Alex Inkeles, Alan Piazza, Terry Sicular, Scott Rozelle, Guangseng Wang, Anthony Tang, Qiaolun Ye, and Ramon Myers all helped us to interpret the literature on the former Soviet Union and China. We turned to Merilee Grindle, Andres Antonius, and Leigh Bivings for comments on our analysis of Mexico's experience.

Jyotirindra Das Gupta and David Leonard read and provided comments and encouragement on successive drafts of the manuscript. With them, J. D. Von Pischke, Timothy King, and Emery Roe helped us to recognize the shortcomings of a rough early draft. Will Masters read and provided generous comments on a later version. We have also benefited from comments on portions of the manuscript from Harold Alderman, Nancy J. Allen, Colin Barlow, Robert Bates, Richard Bissell, Howarth Bouis, Burnham Campbell,

Robert Hindle, Jim Ito-Adler, Nathan Keyfitz, Peter Matlon, Leon Mears, Yair Mundlak, Doug Nelson, Pauline Peters, Steven Radelet, Marguerite Robinson, Michael Roemer, Vernon Ruttan, Donald Snodgrass, Peter Timmer, Donald Warwick, and Jerry Wells.

T. P. T.
P. K.
B. F. J.

Transforming Agrarian Economies

INTRODUCTION

Some developing countries have made striking progress in transforming the structure of their economies, in raising productivity, and in reducing poverty. But in fifty-eight countries the majority of the labor force is still primarily dependent on agriculture. These include all of the poorest developing countries, and their 3.1 billion people account for almost 60 percent of the world's population.

Our goal is to present a comprehensive analysis of the state of the art in development strategy for these agrarian economies. Identifying important ideas that have withstood the test of time is central to this task. The relevance of these ideas to any country depends crucially on its stage of structural transformation. This is what led us to concentrate our analysis on the largest (and poorest) subset of contemporary developing countries, the fifty-eight "CARLs" we introduce in Chapter 1. For this reason, too, our pairs of historical comparisons are primarily concerned with the periods when each country fits this class.

Although CARL is an acronym for *c*ountries with *a*bundant *r*ural *l*abor, it is also a proper name, and its roots in ancient usage fit our subject: "carl" was the medieval term for "countryman" or "a man of the common people" and denoted the activities of farmers, workers, and craftsmen. If extended to include women, the economic activities encompassed by this meaning are also those that distinguish CARLs, where agriculture and the rural nonfarm economy predominate.

Why do governments seeking to transform agrarian economies sometimes seize opportunities and act with foresight? Why in other countries—or at other times—do governments not only miss opportunities but also pursue policies that hurt economic and social progress? What can be learned from experience to improve understanding of how countries with widespread, persistent poverty can increase the well-being of their people?

Early in our efforts to understand why some development opportunities have been seized and others missed, we found we had to push beyond the narrow focus on self-interest in the "new" political economy. We have adopted an eclectic view of alternative explanations of policy failures and successes, recognizing that, as with economics, politics involves opportunities as well as constraints. Our approach draws heavily on case studies and comparative historical analyses. This eclecticism was *necessary* because no single theory of political economy encompasses the range of real policy options. It was *useful* because analysis of actual experiences in developing countries demonstrates how strategies that emerge from real-world political economy reflect a mix of individual interests and what we call "strategic notions."

Since the mid-1970's development problems too often have been overshadowed by calls for direct action to alleviate hunger—and, more recently, by environmental issues. Although these are moral imperatives for all, this book will explain why CARLs need to give priority to transforming the structure of their agrarian economies and slowing the growth of their population. Famine relief efforts are rallied (rightly) by the "loud crisis" of starvation, but the effects of famine are minuscule compared with the "quiet crisis" of chronic hunger and persistent poverty. In 1987 more than 5.5 million children under age five died in India, Indonesia, and China alone (Ross and others 1988, p. 8)—deaths due mainly to chronic hunger and disease resulting from mass poverty. In 1974 the call of the World Food Conference for the eradication of hunger by 1985 was no more than rhetoric, albeit well meaning. When scarce resources are wasted on such unfeasible goals, less ambitious but more realistic programs are neglected—and poor people continue to suffer.

The structural and demographic characteristics of CARLs impose harsh constraints on the development options that are feasible. Until a CARL reaches the turning point when the absolute size of its farm population begins to decline, it must give priority to developing the rural economy. This book sets out a development strategy to raise agricultural productivity and expand rural employment—a strategy in which speeding structural transformation is but a part. With technological change, increased specialization, and growth in stocks of capital (human and institutional, as well as physical), longer-term structural and demographic changes make it possible to eliminate hunger permanently. Furthermore, the transformation of an overwhelmingly agrarian economy into a diversified, predominantly industrial, and more productive economy eases the severe resource constraints that poor countries face in coping with environmental problems. But any such strategy needs to be supplemented by programs that give a country's population, rural as well as urban, access to education and basic health services. Moreover, these social programs complement family planning programs and thereby contribute to the slowing of population growth.

THE RURAL ECONOMY IN THE DEVELOPMENT PROCESS

Chapter 1 describes the essence of CARLs in order to come to grips with crucial issues: Why is poverty still prevalent? How can the alleviation of poverty and hunger best be accelerated?

No CARL can eliminate widespread hunger and poverty or muster the economic and scientific resources to deal with environmental problems without structural transformation—from an overwhelmingly rural economy to a diversified, predominantly industrial economy. Chapter 2 describes the patterns in this transformation of economic structure. It also emphasizes that these complex processes depend on technological change and on each nation's history, physical environment, institutions, and human resources.

Patterns of agricultural development during structural transformation are diverse, as Japan and the United States show (Chapter 3). The case study of their transformations from nineteenth-century CARLs to industrial giants in the twentieth century demonstrates the role of strategic notions—the key ideas that enabled policymakers in each of these success stories to act with foresight to seize political and economic opportunities. Indeed, certain strategic notions were crucial in shaping the effective development strategies these two countries pursued. This theme is extended to today's CARLs in the balance of the book.

FROM STRUCTURE TO STRATEGY

Part 2 analyzes sectors within the rural economy, the relationships between the farm and nonfarm rural sectors and between those sectors and the rest of the economy, and the impact of certain macroeconomic and social policies on the rural economy. These economic relationships, in turn, are the basis for assessing prevailing strategic notions and for identifying feasible development strategies.

Agriculture, of course, is crucial in the rural economy, and much attention is given to both the rate and pattern of agricultural development (Chapters 4 and 5). But nonfarm activities and policies that affect interactions between agriculture and industry also are important determinants of employment and income (Chapters 6 and 7). Ultimately, the major strategic question regarding rural nonfarm activities and industrial strategy is the same as it is for agricultural development: What policies can help raise productivity and increase employment opportunities?

Any strategy to develop agriculture and the rural economy needs time. Why not attack the most serious effects of chronic hunger, as in famine relief, by targeting food and other assistance to help those most in need? Famine relief is feasible because the food and money needed to relieve the worst effects are small on a global scale, and the needs are intermittent, often concentrated in regions within countries. Political and logistical problems are the main barriers to famine relief, not food supply and financing.

Chronic hunger is dispersed across more than fifty-eight countries. Raising hundreds of millions out of chronic poverty is a far different problem from staving off famine deaths. Deciding how much direct action is feasible as a means of alleviating mass poverty is complex. The issues need to be placed in a broader context of available options (Chapter 8).

CHOICES AND CONSEQUENCES

Perhaps the most difficult challenge of development in CARLs is to strike a balance between government responsibilities and available resources. Another crucial factor in success or failure is whether opportunities are perceived and acted upon—and whether the "right" opportunities are seized, not just by government, but by farmers, traders, manufacturers, and other economic agents. Research and analysis are useful to guide policy choice; but there will remain large areas of uncertainty, and some choices will prove wrong.

Often policy "mistakes" are simply a matter of some individuals acting out of self-interest at the expense of broader social objectives. But ill-advised actions also result from self-delusion or genuine uncertainty about consequences of particular policies. For example, misguided strategic notions— not just rent seeking—led to waste of billions of dollars in the inefficient quest by many developing countries for fertilizer self-sufficiency (Chapter 7).

Part 3 develops the links between analysis of the rural economy and the political economy of CARLs through historical analyses of development strategy in three pairs of countries: China and the USSR (Chapter 9), Taiwan and Mexico (Chapter 10), and Kenya and Tanzania (Chapter 11). Strategic opportunities and pitfalls depend on circumstances. Each case demonstrates how the interplay between ideas and action affects the opportunities seized and missed under the circumstances of specific countries. These cases illuminate the role of strategic notions—often derived from experience—in shaping policy responses to opportunities and constraints. The conclusion takes a broader look at the forces shaping strategy, demonstrating the role of strategic notions within the complex political economy of CARLs.

Structural transformation takes decades. Yet, there are many pressures to respond to immediate problems. Thus it is especially important that the strategic notions held by policymakers in CARLs be consistent with the constraints and opportunities in their economies, particularly their rural economies. These notions can offer clues about where to invest attention, where to focus effort to learn, and where payoffs to enhanced capacity are likely to be highest. The last thing we wish to do is to promote more "blueprints." Our aspiration is to provide policymakers and others sharing our interest in development with a starting point for focusing, questioning, and revising their strategic notions to improve development outcomes.

PART ONE

THE RURAL ECONOMY IN THE DEVELOPMENT PROCESS

CHAPTER ONE

POVERTY AND THE RURAL ECONOMY

T his book focuses on a particular sub-set of developing countries: coun-tries with abundant rural labor (CARLs). The defining characteristic of these countries is that 50 percent or more of their labor force is engaged in agriculture and other rural activities. Integrally associated with their defining attribute, all CARLs manifest two ad-ditional features: (1) low per capita income and (2) low productivity of farm labor. Most CARLs also have high population growth rates and inequitable distribution of land. Not all of the Third World shares these attributes, Latin America in particular having only three countries where a majority of the labor force is engaged in the rural economy. But all those countries that do possess these structural and demographic features—accounting for almost 60 percent of the world's population—face a distinctive set of problems.

LOW PRODUCTIVITY AND RURAL POVERTY

CARLs by definition are at an early stage of structural transformation—the process by which economic activity and the distribution of labor shift from predominantly agriculture to industry and services (see Chapter 2). For most CARLs, it will be decades before they reach the *structural transfor-mation turning point*, when the absolute size of the agricultural work force begins to decline. Until then, poverty can be alleviated only if productivity and employment in the rural economy are increased. But how?

The Fifty-eight CARLs

In 1990 there were 58 countries, including all the poorest developing countries, where half or more of the work force was primarily dependent on agriculture (see Table 1.1).[1] Broadly, agricultural employment predominates where average income is low. Of 40 countries with a gross national product (GNP) of U.S.$500 or less per capita in 1990, 37 reported that 50 percent or more of the labor force was dependent on agriculture (World Bank 1992b). The three exceptions (Guyana, Sao Tome and Principe, and Maldives) each had a population of less than one million in 1990. Only one country with per capita GNP of more than U.S.$2,500 qualifies as a CARL—Gabon, whose middle-level income stems from its mineral wealth.

The 58 CARLs were home to more than 3.1 billion people in 1990, 59 percent of the world's population. Of the 3.1 billion, 84 percent lived in Asia, with 77 percent in China, India, Pakistan, Indonesia, and Bangladesh. The population density in many Asian countries is exceptionally high, and in Bangladesh and on the Indonesian island of Java population densities are among the highest in any rural area. Diminishing returns to agricultural labor are thus an especially important barrier to increasing productivity.

Only 15 percent of the people in CARLs lived in sub-Saharan Africa in 1990, even though all the region's countries are CARLs, except Namibia and South Africa. This is the one major region where fertility has remained high despite declines in mortality rates. The rate of natural increase there has risen steadily, from an estimated 2.1 percent in 1950 to 2.7 percent in 1965 and 3.1 percent in 1980.[2] For nineteen African CARLs (including Kenya and Tanzania), the projected population growth rate for 1989–2000 is between 3 and 3.9 percent per year (Table 1.1).

Few Latin American countries are CARLs. Agriculture accounts for a majority of the labor force only in Haiti, Honduras, and Guatemala. For most

---

[1] We do not want to suggest that economic development priorities for Indonesia or Pakistan, which both were about to pass below our 50 percent cutoff in 1990, necessarily differ significantly from, say, the Philippines or Myanmar (formerly Burma), each with 46 percent of its labor force primarily engaged in agriculture in that year. Although any cutoff has an arbitrary element, 50 percent—a simple majority—is intuitively appealing as a means to distinguish predominantly agrarian economies. Moreover, China is the only country among our fifty-eight CARLs that is likely to reach its structural transformation turning point before it passes the 50 percent cutoff. There are, on the other hand, a number of pre–turning point countries such as Mexico (Chapter 10) that are not predominantly agrarian.

[2] The *rate of natural increase* is the crude birth rate minus the crude death rate. The rate of population growth is the rate of natural increase net of migration. "Crude" rates simply are the occurrence of a particular vital event divided by the population in question, usually expressed per 1,000. Thus, unlike the total fertility rate discussed in Chapter 8, crude birth and death rates are influenced by the age structure of the population.

Table 1.1.   GNP, share of economically active population in agriculture, and population for 58 CARLs in 1990 and population growth rate projections, 1989–2000

	GNP per capita (U.S. $)	Labor force in agriculture (%)	Population (thousands)	Population growth rate (% per annum, 1989–2000)
GNP/capita $500 or less				
Mozambique	80	82	15,656	3.0
Tanzania	110	81	27,318	3.1
Ethiopia	120	75	49,240	3.4
Somalia	120	71	7,497	3.1
Nepal	170	92	19,143	2.5
Guinea-Bissau	180	79	964	—
Chad	190	75	5,678	2.7
Bhutan	190	91	1,516	2.4
Lao PDR	200	72	4,139	3.2
Malawi	200	75	8,754	3.4
Bangladesh	210	69	115,593	1.8
Burundi	210	91	5,472	3.1
Zaire	220	66	35,568	3.0
Uganda	220	81	18,794	3.3
Madagascar	230	77	12,004	2.8
Sierra Leone	240	62	4,151	2.6
The Gambia	260	81	861	—
Mali	270	81	9,214	3.0
Nigeria	290	65	108,542	2.8
Niger	310	87	7,731	3.3
Rwanda	310	91	7,237	3.9
Burkina Faso	330	84	8,996	2.9
Equatorial Guinea	330	56	352	—
India	350	67	853,094	1.7
Benin	360	61	4,630	2.9
China	370	68	1,139,060	1.3
Haiti	370	64	6,513	1.9
Kenya	370	77	24,031	3.5
Pakistan	380	50	122,626	2.7
Ghana	390	50	15,028	3.0
Central African Republic	390	63	3,039	2.5
Togo	410	70	3,531	3.2
Zambia	420	69	8,452	3.1
Guinea	440	74	5,755	2.8
Sri Lanka	470	52	17,217	1.1
Comoros	480	79	550	—
Mauritania	500	64	2,024	2.8
Other "low income"				
Afghanistan	—	55	16,557	—
Cambodia	—	70	8,246	1.9
Liberia	—	70	2,575	3.0
Sudan	—	60	25,203	2.8
Vietnam	—	61	66,693	2.1

Table 1.1.   (Continued)

	GNP per capita (U.S. $)	Labor force in agriculture (%)	Population (thousands)	Population growth rate (% per annum, 1989–2000)
GNP/capita $500 to $2,500				
Lesotho	530	80	1,774	2.6
Indonesia	570	50	179,378	1.6
Honduras	590	55	5,138	2.9
Zimbabwe	640	68	9,709	2.4
Senegal	710	78	7,327	3.1
Côte d'Ivoire	750	56	11,997	3.5
Swaziland	810	66	788	—
Papua New Guinea	860	67	3,874	2.3
Guatemala	900	51	9,197	2.8
Cameroon	960	61	11,833	2.9
Congo	1,010	60	2,271	3.3
Thailand	1,420	64	55,702	1.4
Botswana	2,040	63	1,304	2.5
Angola	—	70	10,020	—
Yemen	—	56	11,687	3.7
GNP/capita greater than $2,500				
Gabon	3,330	68	1,172	2.8

Sources: GNP per capita and projected population growth rates: World Bank 1992b. Population and agriculture's share of labor: FAO 1992, except for Indonesia, for which data come from the Central Bureau of Statistics, Jakarta.

Note: The World Bank's (1992b) cutoff for "low income" was U.S.$610/capita.

countries in Latin America, structural transformation has already reduced the share of agriculture in the labor force below one-third, for example, to less than 15 percent in Argentina and Chile.

Structural Transformation Turning Point

Rapid population growth in many CARLs means that they have similarities in demography, as well as in economic structure and agricultural productivity. Because there are more young people in CARLs, population growth will persist even if fertility falls sharply because a large proportion of people have yet to reach reproductive ages (Figure 1.1).[3]

[3] Especially in sub-Saharan Africa, AIDS has the potential to alter significantly these medium-term projections of growth in population and labor force because it affects "primarily prime-aged adults in their economically most productive years, who acquire HIV mainly through heterosexual intercourse and young children, who acquire it from their mothers at birth" (Ainsworth and Over 1994, p. 204).

Figure 1.1.   Comparison of age distribution of populations of developing countries and high income countries, 1990 and 2025

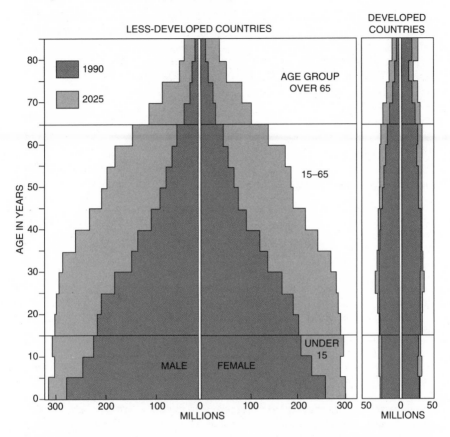

Rapid growth of the population of working age and the size of the rural labor force limit the rate at which workers can be shifted to higher-productivity, nonfarm jobs. Thus, in a mainly agrarian economy (and even with rapid growth in urban industry and services), the relative size of the rural labor force will fall slowly. Consider a simple two-sector model. If the labor force is increasing at 2 percent a year, if agriculture's initial share of the work force is 80 percent, and if nonfarm jobs are expanding at 4 percent a year, it will take 47 years to reach the structural transformation turning point. If the total labor force grows at 3 percent instead, it will take 142 years (Box 1.1).

Poverty and the Rural Economy   13

The timing of the structural transformation turning point—when the absolute size of the agricultural labor force (L_a) peaks and begins to decline—is sensitive to three parameters: (1) agriculture's initial share of the total labor force (L_a/L_t), (2) the rate of growth in the nonagricultural work force (L'_n), and (3) the rate of growth in the total labor force $(L'_t) \cdot L'_a$ can be expressed in the identity:

$$L'_a \equiv \left(L'_t - L'_a\right) \frac{1}{L_a/L_t} + L'_n.$$

In the table, constant rates of change are used in a two-sector framework to show the impact of these parameters on the timing of the turning point.

Initial L_a/L_t (%)	L'_n (%)	L'_t (%)	$L'_n - L'_t$ (%)	L_a/L_t at turning point (%)	Years to turning point
80	4	2	2	50	47
80	4	3	1	25	142
80	5	3	2	40	58
80	6	3	3	50	32
60	5	3	2	40	20

The higher agriculture's initial share, the longer it takes to reach the turning point. For countries such as Kenya or Tanzania, with agriculture's initial share of the labor force at 80 percent and the growth rate of the total work force at 3 percent, it would take 58 years to reach the turning point even with rapid growth of 5 percent in the nonagricultural labor force. For the same growth rates, but with agriculture's initial share at 60 percent, that point is reached in 20 years.

The difference between the growth rates of the nonagricultural labor force and the total labor force $(L'_n - L'_t)$ is the coefficient of differential growth. If L'_n is less than or equal to L'_t, structural transformation will not occur. The greater the coefficient of differential growth, the sooner the turning point is reached. Yet, with 80 percent of the labor force dependent on agriculture and growth in the total work force of 3 percent per year, it still takes 32 years before the agricultural labor force peaks—even with a high rate of growth of 6 percent in the nonagricultural work force.

There are three caveats to these calculations. First, the agricultural sector is assumed to be the residual employer, so rural nonfarm activities and the urban informal sector are ignored. In general, these (diverse) activities share the low labor productivity and low returns to labor that characterize agriculture in CARLs. Second, it is assumed that labor force growth has no impact on the rate of growth in the nonagricultural work force. But in practice, this labor force growth would

Box 1.1. (*Continued*)

generate demand for goods outside the agricultural sector and lead to some expansion in nonagricultural employment (see Chapter 6). Third, rural–urban migration responds to economic stimuli, including intersectoral wage differentials.
Even allowing for these caveats, the message is simple: for most CARLs the structural transformation turning point still is decades away.

Of all CARLs, China, Indonesia, and Thailand have the best hope of reaching the structural transformation turning point before 2000.[4] The absolute
size of the rural labor force of most other CARLs will continue to increase
well into the next century. In Kenya and Tanzania the share of agriculture
will decline from more than 75 percent of the labor force in 1990 to about
two-thirds by 2010, but the size of the agricultural labor force will increase
by 50 to 80 percent (Table 1.2).[5] By 2025 the agricultural labor force in each
country could be twice what it was in 1990. Simply absorbing that many
workers at current wage levels will be a major challenge—let alone expanding
labor demand sufficiently to increase wages in the rural economy.

The number of workers dependent on agriculture will increase even with
more modest rates of labor force growth. India's labor force is projected to
grow at under 2 percent a year for 1990–2000 (Table 1.3). But because two-
thirds of its labor force depended on agriculture in 1990 and growth rates
in the rest of the economy were projected to continue at 2.5 to 3 percent,
India's agricultural labor force may not peak until 2020–25, by which time
it may have grown by more than 60 million (30 percent) over the 1990 level.
Even in countries where agriculture has fallen to almost 50 percent of the
labor force—such as Afghanistan, Pakistan, Sri Lanka, and Guatemala—the
rural work force will continue to increase for years.

In most postindustrial countries the size of the agricultural labor force began
to decline before the relative share of agricultural labor was below 50 percent. But Cownie (1969, p. 303) has shown that, unless the rate of growth
of nonfarm employment is more than twice the rate of growth of the total
labor force, the structural transformation turning point will *come* after the
agricultural share of the labor force falls below 50 percent. In Mexico, for

[4] Policy priorities and opportunities may shift after the turning point. For a review of issues
facing Indonesia as it approaches its turning point, see Tomich 1992a.

[5] The Food and Agriculture Organization (FAO) projections for all fifty-eight CARLs of the
share of the agricultural labor force for 1985–2025 are based on the actual trend in structural
transformation for 1950–80. Then, the shares projected by the FAO were used with International
Labor Organization (ILO) projections of labor force participation rates and the UN's medium
variant population projections to obtain estimates of the size of the labor force dependent on
agriculture and nonagriculture (see FAO 1986 for details).

Table 1.2. Economically active population primarily dependent on agriculture, 1990, with projections for 2000, and 2010, and maximum size attained between 1990 and 2025, for selected CARLs

	Share of labor force (%)			Total (in thousands)			Maximum (1990–2025) total		
								Year	(in thousands)	Total as % of 1990
	1990	2000	2010	1990	2000	2010	Year	thousands)	1990
Tanzania	81	75	68	10,315	12,758	15,891	2025	20,948	203
Bangladesh	69	62	54	23,193	25,221	31,664	2025	34,327	148
Nigeria	65	61	58	26,577	34,259	44,319	2025	66,444	250
India	66	63	60	214,664	243,512	266,164	2020–2025	277,297	129
China	67	60	52	458,428	455,367	417,907	1995	463,070	101
Kenya	77	72	67	7,645	10,438	14,060	2025	20,536	269
Indonesia	50	40	32	35,769	34,884	32,757	1990	35,769	100
Thailand	64	57	50	18,990	19,685	19,171	2000	19,685	104

Sources: For 1990: Same as Table 1.1, except for Indonesia, for which data come from Manning 1992. For projections: UN 1988b.

Note: Countries are listed in ascending order of per capita GNP for 1990.

Table 1.3. Projections of growth rates of economically active population, 1990–95 and 1995–2000, for selected CARLs

	Total labor force		Segment primarily dependent on agriculture		Segment primarily dependent on non-agriculture	
	1990–95	1995–2000	1990–95	1995–2000	1990–95	1995–2000
Tanzania	3.11	3.22	2.27	2.27	5.87	5.86
Bangladesh	2.94	2.83	1.78	1.56	4.97	4.74
Nigeria	2.90	2.99	2.33	2.40	3.90	3.97
India	1.88	1.69	1.37	1.16	2.86	2.64
China	1.33	0.93	0.19	−0.33	3.55	3.01
Kenya	3.69	3.74	3.08	3.07	5.62	5.61
Indonesia	2.20	1.97	0.28	−0.09	3.88	3.49
Thailand	1.70	1.42	0.56	0.17	3.63	3.23

Source: UN 1988b.

Note: The projections in this table are derived from the projections for the absolute size of the labor force and its segments. As a result, they are likely to be even more sensitive to divergences from the underlying assumptions than the aggregate projections presented in Table 1.2. In particular, the projected rates of growth in the nonagricultural segment simply reflect continuation of the trend for 1950–80 in the rate of structural transformation. They do not consider directly the economic factors that will affect the growth in manufacturing and services that will determine these rates in actuality. Thus, they indicate the growth rates necessary for trends to continue and are not economic forecasts.

Countries are listed in ascending order of per capita GNP for 1990.

example, the agricultural labor force fell below half in the 1960s, but the UN projects that its absolute size will grow until at least 2005 (see Chapter 10).

A rate of growth of employment in the nonfarm sectors of more than 4 percent would accelerate the rate of structural transformation (Box 1.1). But history shows that such growth rates are hard to sustain. With the exception of the United States in the three decades ending in 1850 and South Korea with rates as high as 8 percent a year from the 1960s through the mid-1980s, the rate has rarely exceeded 4 percent anywhere for prolonged periods. Countries with a small industrial base, such as Bangladesh, Kenya, and Tanzania, may be able to achieve rates of growth in nonfarm jobs of more than 5 percent a year in the early stages of transformation. But it seems unlikely that these rates could be sustained for decades, much less the 6 percent needed to achieve the structural transformation turning point while their labor force remains predominantly agricultural. Furthermore, the experience of the Soviet Union, reviewed in Chapter 9, demonstrates the human costs and economic hazards of attempting to force rapid industrialization.

The UN (1988b) projections suggest that although 19 of today's 58 CARLs will have less than 50 percent of their labor force in agriculture in 2010, only 11 (including China and Indonesia) will reach their structural transformation turning point before 2025. For the rest (35 of 40 CARLs in Africa, all 3 Latin American CARLs, and 9 of 15 in Asia) there will be continuing growth in the numbers dependent on employment in the rural economy. By 2010 there is likely to be a net increase of over 100 million people (10 percent) in the agricultural labor force of the 58 CARLs, even allowing for declines of about 40 million in China and 1.8 million in Indonesia. Excluding China and Indonesia, the United Nations projects a net increase of 145 million by 2010, more than 30 percent more than those dependent on agriculture and other rural activities in 1990.

Low Labor Productivity in Agriculture

Low productivity is the root of poverty, and there is a large and growing gap in the agricultural labor productivity of rich and poor countries. Between 1960 and 1980, the rate of increase in farm labor productivity in most CARLs has not kept pace with increases in land productivity (Table 1.4). For the twelve lowest-income countries in their analysis (including CARLs such as Bangladesh, India, Pakistan, and Sri Lanka), Hayami and Ruttan (1985, p. 418) found that growth of labor productivity (that is, output per male farm worker) declined sharply from 2.3 percent a year in the 1960s to only 1 percent a year in the 1970s.[6]

An already huge gap in agricultural labor productivity between rich and poor countries is becoming enormous. Consider an extreme example,

---

[6] Hayami and Ruttan restricted calculations to the *male* labor force to improve the cross-country comparability of their results. Because there is great variability in the definitions used to determine whether women members of farm households are or are not included in the farm labor force and even greater variation in actual coverage of women's activities in these surveys, reasonable estimates for a complete cross-country comparison are not available. The statistical and substantive issues of women's labor force participation are considered later in this chapter.

Table 1.4 Agricultural productivity differentials, 1960 and 1980

	Output per male worker in wheat units		Output per hectare in wheat units		Hectares per male worker		Labor force in agriculture,
	1960	1980	1960	1980	1960	1980	1980 (%)
Bangladesh	2.0	1.8	2.51	3.51	0.8	0.5	75
India	2.2	3.1	1.06	1.58	2.0	2.0	70
Egypt	4.4	4.6	6.90	9.18	0.6	0.5	46
Colombia	8.3	17.2	0.79	1.37	10.15	12.5	34
Brazil	9.3	13.2	0.56	0.72	16.7	18.3	31
Mexico	5.1	7.5	0.27	0.52	19.4	14.3	37
Taiwan	7.1	12.4	10.34	18.65	0.7	0.7	18[a]
Japan	10.3	27.8	8.64	12.23	1.2	2.3	11
United States	93.8	285.1	0.80	1.16	117.0	246.6	4

Sources: Data for Taiwan are from *Industry of Free China*, various issues, except agricultural labor force. Other data are from estimates by Hayami and Ruttan 1985 for forty-four countries. The common numerator of "wheat units" was obtained by converting the output of other crops and livestock products into tons of wheat based on their value relative to the price of wheat. See Hayami and Ruttan 1985, pp. 447–65, for details of their computations. Data on labor force in agriculture are from World Bank 1988b, pp. 282–83, except for Taiwan, which is from Chakravarty 1990, p. 141.

[a] The Taiwanese agricultural labor force figure is for 1984, not 1980.

Bangladesh and the United States. Between 1960 and 1980 agricultural labor productivity in the United States increased threefold, whereas output per male worker in Bangladesh declined from 2 to 1.8 "wheat units"—an astounding 158-fold difference in productivity in 1980 compared with 47-fold in 1960.

Both the United States and Bangladesh showed increases in agricultural output of roughly 40 percent in 1960–80. But in Bangladesh over those two decades, there was a 57 percent increase in the male farm work force, from 12.1 to 19.1 million, whereas in the United States the male farm work force declined from 3.8 to 1.7 million. The striking contrasts in the levels and changes in hectares cultivated per male farm worker—up from 117 to 247 hectares in the United States and down from 0.8 to 0.5 in Bangladesh—are attributable entirely to the contrasting changes in the size of the agricultural labor force. Efforts to raise rural incomes must address this problem of low labor productivity resulting from diminishing marginal returns to labor.

Inequitable Distribution of Agricultural Land

Because of the age profile of CARL populations (suggesting many new entrants to the rural labor force) and because of the relatively fixed supplies of agricultural land, typical farms in CARLs, already small, will become smaller. Between 1953–54 and 1971–72 there was a 66 percent increase in the number of farm households in India, but cultivated area increased by only 2 percent (Vyas 1979). The average size of farm holdings fell from 2.5

to 1.5 hectares, and the number of marginal holdings of less than half a hectare more than doubled. According to Kurian (1990), more than 75 percent of Indian farm units were smaller than 2 hectares in 1985–86, and this could rise to 80 percent by the end of this century.

Although the typical CARL farm is small, there is great variation across countries in *agrarian structure*—that is, in the distribution of farms around the mean farm size. The degree of skewness in the distribution of farms by size can range from a *unimodal structure* with most farms clustered around the mean size, to a highly skewed, *bimodal structure* in which most of the land is operated by a few large farms (Box 1.2). This bimodal structure accentuates the tendency toward small farm holdings and disparities in income among rural households.

The rural poor in CARLs, especially in Asia, also include many households with little or no land, although the difference between these "landless" households and those operating small farms may be one of degree rather than of kind (Singh 1983).

Both depend heavily on wages earned in rural labor markets. For example, in the 1970s, nearly two-thirds of the rural labor force in India depended on wages as their primary source of income (although roughly 15 percent worked primarily in nonagricultural jobs) (Singh 1983, pp. 385–86).

Landless households and those dependent on wage labor to supplement their own agricultural production are usually poorer than households with farms of a hectare or more. Estimates for India, Bangladesh, and Pakistan suggest that these poorer, wage-dependent households also are more numerous (Singh 1983, pp. 395–96). In South Asia in 1980 17 percent of rural households were landless. Another 30 percent were "near landless" or marginal farmers who depended on wages to supplement earnings, and those numbers probably are increasing in most CARLs.

HAZARDS, DIVERSITY, AND HOUSEHOLD STRATEGIES

The household is the center of economic decisions in most rural economies. Access to productive resources varies according to the size and age structure of the household, to its members' wealth and power, and to experience, skill, and luck. Households differ according to the quantity and quality of farm land they control, their agricultural and nonfarm activities, and options for use of their time and skills. Wealthy rural households control more resources—land, labor, and capital. Poor households have relatively abundant family labor but limited access to other resources.

Expenditures on chemical fertilizer, hired labor, and farm tools, or on consumer goods and services are constrained by the poor household's limited cash receipts. Farms that do not market any of their production (subsistence farms) have extremely low levels of consumption (as well as production). If

Box 1.2.   Unimodal and Bimodal Patterns of Agrarian Structure

Although the average farm in most CARLs is small, the agrarian structure may be characterized by a subsector of large farms using technologies drastically different from those employed by the majority of small-scale farmers. The range can be seen by comparing the *unimodal* pattern in Taiwan (figure, Panel A) with the *bimodal* pattern in Colombia (figure, Panel B).

Distribution of number of operational units and of area cultivated by farm size.

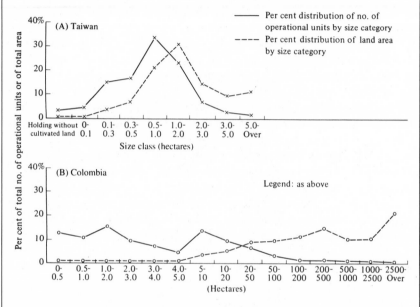

First, contrast the size distribution of land holdings in Taiwan and Colombia. The broken line showing the distribution of agricultural land by size in Taiwan lies only a little to the right of the solid line showing the percentage of farm households in each size category. Although farm units in Taiwan vary in size, most are equally small: four-fifths are within 1 acre of the average size of 3.2 acres (1.2 hectares). In Colombia the distribution of agricultural land by size is radically different from the size distribution of farm operational units. Virtually all farm households are in the size categories of 5 to 10 hectares or less, whereas nearly all of the agricultural land is controlled by a small number of large farms, ranging in size from 50 to 1,000 hectares or more.

Source: Johnston and Kilby 1975, p. 15.

market outlets exist, growth in output translates into growth in marketable surplus and, hence, growth in cash receipts. Thus, the commercialization of farming is really about increasing participation in markets for agricultural goods and for labor.

In poor households investment decisions focus on the allocation of family labor and the division of income between investment in productive assets and immediate consumption. Often investments are subtle quality shifts in the factors of production: acquiring better livestock, planting trees, or adopting new methods of production. These decisions can have a significant impact on production, even if barely perceptible to outsiders.

Hazards of Life in the Rural Economy

Poor households must devote much of their effort and income to obtaining food, and although there is a positive (but imperfect) relationship between income and calorie supply (Table 1.5), chronic hunger is only one result of mass poverty. Poor households also are the most vulnerable to disease and the least able to compensate for income lost owing to sickness or death. Thus, it is inevitable that such households incorporate risk considerations into their decisions, because a failed investment, sickness, or death of an income earner can plunge the family into financial disaster.

Average life expectancy at birth in Japan is 65 percent longer than in Tanzania (Table 1.5). In especially vulnerable groups, such as infants, preschool children, and women in their childbearing years, the hazards of poverty are even starker. Infant mortality in Tanzania or Bangladesh is twelve times the rate in the United States and over twenty times that in Japan. Of one-year-old children in India, Kenya, and Indonesia, more than one in twenty die before reaching age five. In Bangladesh, Tanzania, and Nigeria, this child mortality rate is almost one in ten (see Ross and others 1988). But these are national figures and may understate the magnitudes for rural areas. The World Bank (1990, p. 31) reports that the rural infant mortality rate in India (105) was almost twice the urban rate (57) in the 1980s.

Differences in childhood mortality result from the conditions of poverty: undernutrition, disease, and such other risks as poor sanitation and inadequate public health services. Innocuous childhood illnesses in high-income countries, such as measles, are killers for undernourished children. According to the Commission on Health Research and Development (1990, p. 38), acute respiratory infections, diarrheal diseases, and immunizable diseases kill 9 to 21 million people a year in developing countries, mostly children.

Damage from poverty starts before birth. Low birth weight is a symptom of maternal undernutrition and usually means higher infant mortality and poor growth. More than 40 percent of infants in Bangladesh weigh less than 2.5 kg at birth, compared with 5 percent in Japan. Moreover, the risk of

Table 1.5   Income per capita, daily calorie supply, life expectancy at birth, and rates of infant mortality, low birth weight, and maternal mortality in selected countries

	GNP per capita (1990 U.S.$)[a]	Daily calorie supply per capita (1989)[b]	Life expectancy at birth (1990, years)[c]	Infant mortality rate (per 1,000 live births, 1990)[d]	Babies with low birth weights (%, 1980–88)[e]	Maternal mortality per 100,000 live births (1988)[f]
Tanzania	110	2,206	48	115	14	600
Bangladesh	210	2,021	52	105	47	650
Nigeria	290	2,312	52	98	20	750
India	350	2,229	59	92	30	550
China	370	2,639	70	29	9	130
Kenya	370	2,163	59	67	15	400
Indonesia	570	2,750	62	61	14	300
Egypt	600	3,336	60	66	5	300
Colombia	1,260	2,598	69	37	8	150
Thailand	1,420	2,316	66	27	12	180
Malaysia	2,320	2,774	70	16	10	120
Mexico	2,490	3,052	70	39	12	150
Brazil	2,680	2,751	66	57	8	230
Taiwan	3,897	2,969	73	6	—	19
United States	21,790	3,671	76	9	7	9
Japan	25,430	2,956	79	5	5	15

Sources: (a) World Bank 1992b, pp. 218–19, except Taiwan, which is for 1986 (in 1986 U.S.$) and is from Republic of China 1992. b) World Bank 1992b, pp. 272–73, except Taiwan, which is for 1986 and is from Republic of China 1986. (c) World Bank 1992b, pp. 218–19. (d) World Bank 1992b, pp. 272–73 (e) UNDP 1992, pp. 148–49, except for Japan and the United States, which are for 1985 and are from World Bank 1992b, pp. 272–73, respectively. *Low birth weight* means less than 2,500 g at birth. (f) UNDP 1992, pp. 150–51, except for Japan and the United States, which are for 1980 and are from World Bank 1992b, pp. 280–81.

death during childbirth or postnatally is at least sixty times greater for women in Tanzania or Bangladesh than for women in the United States. The risks in Nigeria may be even greater. Births per woman also are substantially higher in CARLs. For example, a woman in the United States typically would give birth twice in her lifetime, but in Bangladesh five births per woman is usual. Thus, the risks are even larger than these statistics suggest.

Adapting Agricultural Techniques

New agricultural technology has been the most important source of increases in agricultural productivity, but, as discussed in Chapter 4, new techniques also *may* involve greater risk. The 40 percent increase in output per hectare in Bangladesh in 1960–80 and the near 50 percent increase in output per hectare in India (Table 1.4) resulted from new semidwarf varieties of rice and wheat.

The effect on yields of this seed-fertilizer technology (known as the "Green Revolution") is most striking where irrigation projects improved water control. But yield increases do not rest on new inputs alone. Technical know-how must be supplemented by experience, gained over generations and under local conditions, and by farmers' informal trials over successive seasons.

Farmers display remarkable success in working within the bounds imposed by their natural environment and available resources, which span a huge variety of agronomic conditions. They have no choice but to make the best possible use they can of the land available to them. Through a long process of natural and human selection, traditional rice types have evolved that are well suited to physical and economic conditions prevailing in a wide variety of production systems. In many areas farmers have developed varieties that are tall, profuse in their leaf growth, delayed in flowering, and of long duration to maturity. Height provides protection against floods if rains are unusually heavy. Large drooping leaves shade out weeds that would compete for limited nutrients and sunlight. Because there is considerable cloud cover in the tropics during the wet season, late flowering and delayed maturity permit grain formation—the period when greatest photosynthetic activity occurs—to take place after the rains when strong sunlight is available. Beyond a certain minimal threshold, grain yields of typical traditional varieties are relatively insensitive to variations in the level of nitrogen. Indeed, as shown in Figure 1.2, application of nitrogen fertilizer to traditional rice varieties may even lower yield because excessive growth of their stalks will lead to lodging. Nevertheless, these varieties are suited to many farmers' needs because they can accommodate limited ability to finance input purchases and soils with low average nutrient levels while keeping financial risks and yield fluctuations within generally acceptable ranges.

Farmers' adaptation of traditional varieties to adverse growing conditions is as remarkable as the scientific innovations that led to fertilizer-responsive rice varieties. Of course, a great deal of time elapsed while farmers used trial and error to adapt production systems to the specific environments they must work with; scientific research can produce faster results for specific agricultural problems. The power of science lies in meaningful abstraction, rigorous methodology, and the guidelines of theory. In contrast, the experience of farm people embodies the details of complex agricultural production systems. This understanding is particularly important in adapting techniques to adverse conditions and for exploiting unusual local opportunities. Indeed, rather than exemplifying a dichotomy between adoption of researchers' products and adaptation of traditional techniques, it is clear that the role played by farmers is important in adapting the products of scientific research. For example, Bangladeshi farmers make their

Figure 1.2. Yield response of rice to nitrogen, by variety and type of irrigation, synthesized farm-level functions for the Philippines

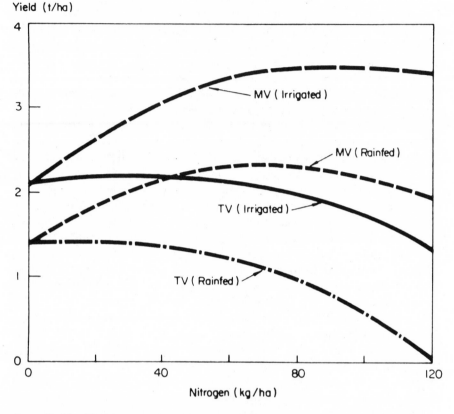

Yield (t/ha)

MV (Irrigated)

MV (Rainfed)

TV (Irrigated)

TV (Rainfed)

Nitrogen (kg/ha)

Source: David and Barker 1978, p. 183. © 1978 The International Rice Institute. Reprinted by permission.

Notes: MV = modern varieties; TV = traditional varieties.

own selections from high-yielding rice varieties (Brammer 1980). Similarly, Franzel (1984) notes the impressive amount of experimentation with maize varieties by Kenyan farmers.[7]

The heterogeneity of environmental conditions and farmers' ability to adapt what they do often defies outsiders' needs to put farm activities into the neat boxes that feature in agricultural surveys. Research might be easier if all farms were operated by a single, male farmer, planting a single crop in

[7] Franzel (1984 p. 207, n. 3) cites one Kenyan farmer who had selected out a purple South American variety that was a parent of a maize hybrid released in Kenya. He preferred the milling quality of the purple variety and also liked it because his chickens did not eat it.

Figure 1.3. Rural household income, by source and farm size, in India, 1970–71

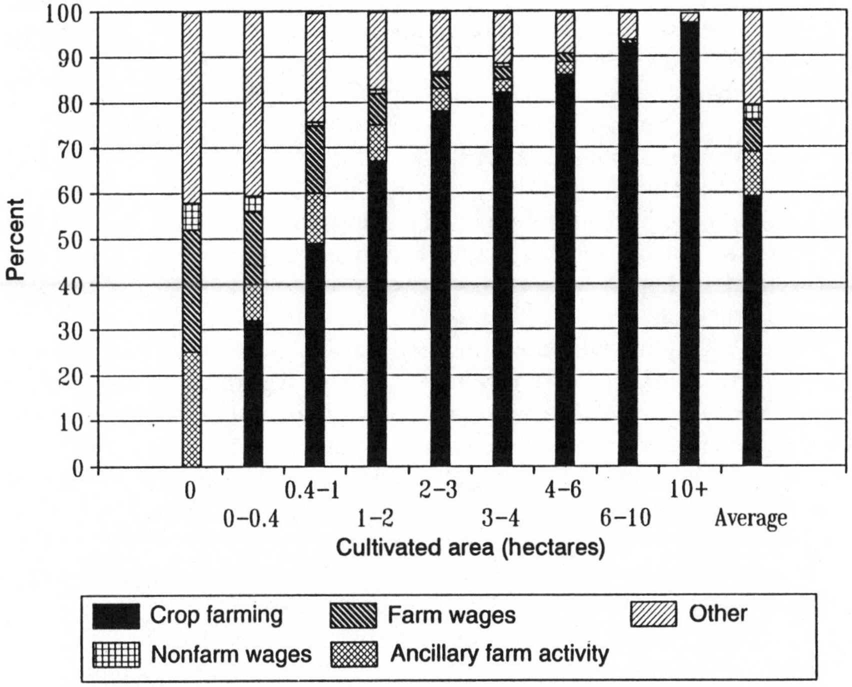

Source: World Bank 1982, Figure 7.1, p. 79.

succession, but this would neither be the best way of employing family labor nor would it be a safe means of ensuring subsistence needs. Indeed, some of the most difficult issues to study—complex intercropping combinations or noncrop options such as livestock—are among the best-adapted and most profitable options available to poor rural households. Diversity in techniques and mixes of crops and livestock activities reflect poor farm households' strategies to cope with heterogeneous conditions, risk, and restricted opportunities to earn income.

Coping with Limited Access to Land

As a consequence of rapid population growth, a growing portion of rural households have little or no access to land, whether access is considered as ownership, tenancy, or reliable employment opportunities in agriculture. The importance of family labor as the dominant factor of production under their control unites households with little land and households with no land. Together, they face a similar set of problems and a limited set of alternatives.

Development strategies designed to alleviate rural poverty must increase the productivity of agricultural labor. But there is a double bind of simultaneously increasing agricultural labor productivity and absorbing a growing rural work force. Opportunities to expand income and employment can come from a variety of sources: raising productivity of a family's own land, wage labor or tenancy on land owned by others, ancillary agricultural activities, such as dairying (Box 1.3.), poultry, and fishing—which are not necessarily limited by access to land—and nonfarm activities, such as processing agricultural products, marketing and trading, and other work in rural services and manufacturing. Neglecting this range of options—particularly noncrop, nonfarm options—overlooks many prospective sources of employment in the rural economy.

Many households with small, marginal farms are almost as dependent on labor markets for sources of income as households with no land (see Figure 1.3). The importance of wage labor in poor rural households' income-earning strategies raises another dilemma in raising agricultural productivity in CARLs. Rural families that own and operate land, provide all the labor, and finance purchases of seeds, chemical fertilizer, and other inputs with their capital will gain many of the benefits from increased yields. But when land and capital are provided by some (often richer) households and labor is provided by other (usually poorer) households, the bulk of the gains could go to landowners rather than the poor. Moreover, a relative shift in income toward richer households could allow them to buy a bigger share of the available land. Thus, even if science can identify technologies that can be adapted widely, there is the possibility that land-poor households could be made worse off. Whether or not this is likely is an issue taken up in Chapters 4 and 5. Nonfarm rural activities also are an important source of income, more so for poor households with little or no land than for households operating medium-size farms (Chapters 2 and 6).

Women's Roles in Coping Strategies

Rural women, as well as men, need to raise their productivity (and so their incomes) in agriculture and other rural activities. Social conventions in many CARLs may keep the role of women and children in agriculture almost invisible. Yet, evidence is mounting of the importance of women's contributions as workers and decision makers in agriculture, nonfarm activities, and rural trade. Although women tend to be particularly active in production of food for home use, weeding, storage and processing of crops, small-scale marketing, and tending livestock, "the division of farm tasks by sex is more rigid in cultural convention than in reality" (Buvinic and Mehra 1990, p. 292). In many CARLs, women are engaged in "male" tasks, ranging from coffee picking in Indonesia to rural construction work in India.

Box 1.3.   Dairy Development in India

The distribution of ownership of buffaloes and cattle is more equitable than that of land in India. Even landless families may own one or more cows or buffaloes. But there are severe bottlenecks in milk marketing, and productivity is low—two reasons for the launch of a national dairy development program, Operation Flood, in 1970, aimed at helping 10 million rural households.

There are three tiers to this program—village producers' cooperatives, district unions, and regional federations that receive technical and financial assistance from two semiautonomous government agencies, the National Dairy Development Board (NDDB) and the India Dairy Corporation (IDC). The NDDB, which began in 1964, served 4,530 village cooperatives and had two million members in 1976. By the mid-1980s, there were 10,000 village cooperatives.

The dairy movement in India is rooted in a dairy producers' cooperative formed in the small town of Anand in 1946. Unlike official "cooperative" programs, this organization "emerged spontaneously as a movement of dairy farmers who organized themselves in an effort to protect and improve their market position." In fact, it was the response to a government scheme to establish a private milk trading monopoly (Alderman and others 1987, pp. 10, 13).

From its earliest years, the organization that became known as the Anand Milk Producers Union Ltd. (AMUL) has been well served by dedicated leadership, with a high priority given to training and service to rural communities. They benefited from economies of scale in pasteurization and the processing of milk products, together with a streamlined system for shipping highly perishable milk to Bombay and other major cities.

A decade of trial and error preceded expansion beyond Gujarat, the state in which the "Anand pattern" originally evolved (Korten 1980). The present system is simple but effective in ensuring regular milk pickups, prompt payment, and accountability to the members. Veterinary services that help reduce the risk of investment in livestock, especially for poor households, also are provided.

Controversy rages over whether Operation Flood successfully replicates the Anand pattern and even whether the circumstances underlying AMUL's success make it impossible to replicate. The risk is that a program with such promise will fall victim to unrealistic and inappropriate goals. Yet, a similar approach in Karnataka (Alderman 1987) indicates that the potential for benefits exists: all farm-size classes appear to gain, including the many landless owners of livestock. But because the share of dairying in total income tends to be largest for farmers with middle-size farms, the absolute size of their gains may be larger than for the landless. Yet, one of the most significant features of the original Anand dairy producers' association and India's National Dairy Development Board is that poor farmers—including those from the lowest castes and, more recently, increasing numbers of women—have acquired the organizational capacity to promote—and defend—their interests.

When household activities also are taken into account, careful surveys usually show demands on the labor of rural women equal to (or greater than) those of men. Few rural women work less than eight hours a day, and some average 12 hours every day. Two time allocation studies in Bangladesh showed that women and men worked roughly the same hours; other studies from Tanzania and Java in Indonesia showed that women worked 20 to 50 percent more hours a day than men; and women appear to put in twice as many hours as men in Burkina Faso and Côte d'Ivoire (Table 1.6).

Demands on women's time, especially in poor households, can mean severe trade-offs affecting family health and nutrition. For example, fuel, food, and fodder gathered from common property, often by women and girls, substitute for goods that otherwise would have to be purchased. But these

Table 1.6. Hours per day spent by women and men on productive activity in rural areas

Country and year of study	Reference	Gender	Home production[a]	Agriculture market and non-market work[b]	Other market work[c]	Un-specified wage work	Total hours worked
Bangladesh (1976 Char Gopalpur district)	Cain 1980	Women	7.65	0.55	0.05	0.45	8.70
		Men	0.90	4.25	1.20	2.40	8.75
Bangladesh (1976, Char Gopalpur district)	Cain, Khanam, & Nahar 1979	Women	5.40	1.71	0.35	0.84	8.30
		Men	1.27	2.80	1.01	3.24	8.32
Indonesia (1972–23, Java)	Nag, White, & Peet 1978	Women	5.61	1.50	4.54	—	11.65
		Men	0.69	4.29	2.64	—	7.62
Indonesia (1972, Java)	White 1975	Women	4.13	2.17	5.67	—	11.97
		Men	0.75	4.24	3.36	—	8.35
Nepal (1972–73)	Nag, White, & Peet 1978	Women	4.86	7.23	0.40	—	12.49
		Men	2.17	6.13	1.88	—	10.18
Nepal (n.d.)	Acharya & Bennett 1981	Women	6.13	3.76	0.91	—	10.80
		Men	1.53	4.33	1.66	—	7.52
Tanzania (1976, Bukoba district)	Kamuzora 1980	Women	3.47	4.24	0.01	—	7.72
		Men	1.13	4.20	0.82	—	6.15
Côte d'Ivoire (1979)	FAO 1983	Women	6.89	1.64	0.13	—	8.66
		Men	0.75	3.14	0.04	—	3.93
Burkina Faso (1979)	McSweeney 1979	Women	3.28	7.43	0.82	—	11.53
		Men	0.12	3.48	2.60	—	6.20

Source: Buvinic and Mehra 1990, p. 294. © 1990 Johns Hopkins University Press; reprinted by permission. Works listed in the Reference column are cited in Buvinic and Mehra 1990.

Note: Reciprocal labor exchange has not been included in this chart.

[a]Home production includes food preparation, child care, hygiene, firewood collection, house construction, attending the sick, and food collection.

[b]Agriculture market and nonmarket work includes hunting and gathering, garden labor, animal care, crop production, rice cultivation, and processing crops for storage or sales.

[c]Other market work includes trading, handicraft production, and food preparation for market sale.

Figure 1.4. Average daily work load of men, women, and children in hill areas of Nepal, 1982–83

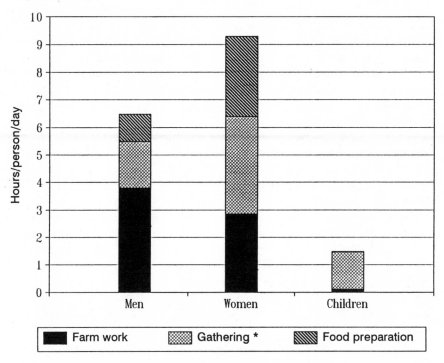

Source: Kumar and Hotchkiss 1988, Abstract, Figure 1, p. 2. © 1988 IFPRI. Reprinted by permission.
*"Gathering" includes collection of fuel, water, and fodder and grazing of livestock.

household tasks can come at the cost of women's opportunities for income-generating work in agriculture and rural, nonfarm activities. A sample of Nepali women, for example, worked an average of 50 to 80 percent more than men, with 40 percent of their time spent on collecting fuel wood and the balance split between farm work and food preparation (Figure 1.4). Because of deforestation, extra time was required for fuel gathering, which cut into women's time for farm work and for cooking.

Another aspect of the subordination of women in the rural economy is the common cultural norm that land is held in the name of adult males, often formalized by land registration programs. Bureaucracies, dominated by males, also tend to overlook women in the design and implementation of development programs.

All this means that poor women have less access than poor men to productive resources other than their labor—and even opportunities to enhance productivity of labor are hampered by barriers to women's access to information, education, and experience. For example, because most extension agents are male, they tend to meet with male farmers and to ignore female farmers, and where property is registered in men's names by convention, it is difficult for women to provide collateral for credit.

In CARLs female-headed households often are among the poorest. In Kenya, for example, 30 percent of households were headed by females according to the Rural Household Budget Survey of 1981–82, but the average proportion of households headed by females decreased with every income decile—from 43 percent for the lowest to 15 percent for the highest (Harvey Herr, personal communication).

It is especially perilous to be poor, female, and young in CARLs. In South Asia, female children tend to receive less health care and have less access to education than their brothers.[8] This bias against women and children (the most vulnerable in rural society) has led to questions about the distribution of benefits of economic development, not just between rich and poor households but between men and women and across generations in the same household (Box 1.4).

The introduction of cash crops and new technology in CARLs should open the way to greater material welfare for all members of a household. However, it also may lead to more responsibility being placed on women for the cultivation of food crops, as the males produce the cash crop—and control the cash income. Only a limited amount of childrearing and housework can be shifted to older children. But technical and economic advance can bring benefits as well. Piped water and the diesel cornmill can shave one to three hours of arduous carrying and pounding from a woman's daily workload (Cairncross 1988). Such advances should permit women to devote time to such commercial nonfarm activities as pot making, spinning, weaving, and brewing, the income from which *they* control.

More than a decade has gone into efforts to create specific income-generating projects for women and to improve their status and prospects for their children. But many such projects degenerate into ill-conceived welfare activities that do little to meet women's needs or enhance their productivity (Buvinic and Mehra 1990). Much more could be accomplished by eliminating administrative barriers to women's full participation in the rural economy. In India, women and girls are responsible for gathering fodder, livestock care, and on-farm milk processing, yet typically have been excluded from membership in dairy cooperatives (see Box 1.3). In Andrah Pradesh, there

[8] Death rates are higher for males than for females from birth until about age 70 in almost all human populations, except certain countries in South Asia. In 1988 the risk of dying by age five was about the same for males and females in India, and female children had a greater risk of dying than male children in Bangladesh, Bhutan, Nepal, and Pakistan (World Bank 1990, p. 240). This reversal in gender-specific death rates is a symptom of discrimination against female children in these societies.

Box 1.4.   Commercialization and Intrahousehold Distribution

Can rising household incomes in poor households worsen welfare for women and children? In many societies women have primary responsibility for food preparation and child care. If agricultural development caused new labor demands that fell mainly on women, they would have to work much harder than they already do, reduce time spent caring for children, or both.

In parts of sub-Saharan Africa women are also the main suppliers of food for the household, whereas income accruing to men's activities can be earmarked for other expenditures. When households willingly shift from production of food for home use to crops for sale, it is unlikely that income will fall, although they may face new risks. In some cultures, however, it is important to consider who in the household has the power to decide about cropping patterns and labor allocation, whether a switch from food crops to cash crops also shifts control of land and its produce from women to men, and if there is a shift in control, whether this affects food consumption and allocation within the household.

Research on agricultural commercialization in the Gambia, Guatemala, India, Kenya, and the Philippines by the International Food Policy Research Institute (IFPRI) indicates that concerns about adverse effects on the welfare of women and children are exaggerated.* Household income rose as a result of schemes to increase crop production for sale, and the additional income increased food consumption without adverse effects on nutrition, even for children. But in most cases, increased income had only a small effect on calorie intake and little, or no, positive effect on children's nutrition. This disappointing outcome must be interpreted with care: rather than an indictment of cash cropping it points to the need for public health programs to reduce the high rates of illness that undermine children's nutritional status (see Chapters 5 and 8).

*See von Braun, Puetz, and Webb 1989 on the Gambia; von Braun, Hotchkiss, and Immink 1989 on Guatemala; Alderman 1987 on India; Kennedy and Cogill 1987 and Kennedy 1989 on Kenya; and Bouis and Haddad 1990 on the Philippines.

is an attempt to break down those barriers through pilot programs aimed at integrating women in dairying as producers, members, and staff of cooperatives, extension agents, and providers of veterinary care. This initiative helped to convince the National Dairy Development Board that it should increase its commitment to women and begin reducing barriers to them in its rules and organization of dairy programs (Chen 1989).

Poor Households and Environmental Stress

In recent years environmental concerns have intensified worldwide, but even the richest countries are struggling to determine priorities and to tackle national problems, let alone global issues. But the debate in rich countries holds few lessons for environmental policy in CARLs. It has been suggested, for example, that "low-input agriculture"—reduced use of fossil fuels, fertilizers, and other purchased inputs—is a more "sustainable" alternative agricultural system (National Research Council 1989; World Resources Institute 1990, p. 98). Sweeping reductions in agricultural inputs may be viable for postindustrial countries such as the United States (where agriculture accounts for less than 2 percent of GDP and employment, the number of farmers is declining, and policies cause costly food surpluses). But for CARLs it would mean lower yields, lower labor productivity, and (possibly) higher food prices.

CARLs must strike a balance on environmental issues. Expanding employment and raising rural incomes require greater agricultural productivity and, so, increasing use of purchased agricultural inputs. Yet, intensification of agriculture, combined with rapid population growth, contributes to land degradation, water pollution, and other environmental stresses caused by, say, the runoff of agricultural chemicals, soil erosion, and destruction of forests.

There is no fixed relationship, however, between agricultural development and environmental stress. Both are influenced by national policies and by investments that seek to increase research capacity and the knowledge needed to shift from resource-based to knowledge-based agricultural systems. Policy failures have resulted in deforestation in Brazil (from ranching subsidies) and in Thailand (from resettlement of farmers displaced by the Nam Pong Reservoir). In each case, policies were bad for the environment, bad for the economy, and did little for agricultural development or poverty alleviation (Panayotou 1990).

The situation is different in Indonesia, where integrated pest management (IPM) shows how ecological considerations can complement good economic policy. IPM for rice reduces environmental stress (because less pesticide is used), lowers risk of crop failure for farmers because IPM provides superior pest control, and (with the ending of pesticide subsidies) saves the government more than $100 million a year (Panayotou 1990). Although classed as a "low-input" approach, IPM relies on higher inputs of technical information on chemical and biological controls and more intensive farm management to substitute for pesticide applications.

Nor is agricultural development the only source of rural environmental stress in CARLs. Unlike in industrial countries, where lower application of many purchased inputs reduces sources of environmental stress, exactly the opposite can happen in CARLs.

Common property resources (forests, grasslands, and water sources that are publicly held or for which access is regulated by rural communities) bear a disproportionate share of the pressure that growing CARL populations place on the rural environment. A study of twenty-one districts in India

(Jodha 1986) shows that the poor people in the sample derived more employment and income from common property than their better-off rural neighbors. Products collected from common property and grazing on common grasslands contributed 10 to 20 percent of average income for landless households and those operating less than 2 hectares in all but two villages; they accounted for less than 3 percent of income for the top 25 percent of landowning households. Few comparative studies are available, but it seems likely that these patterns hold for other CARLs with scarce land and growing populations and that they would be compounded for CARLs with agrarian structures that are more skewed than India's (Chapter 5). Particularly in such cases, however, the local elite may use its political power to usurp control of these valuable resources.

Despite mounting evidence that rural communities can manage common property better than governments (Lipton 1989; Panayotou 1990), these resources are susceptible to degradation from rural population growth precisely because no one has exclusive property rights. As the number of people entitled to use a common resource increases, the returns to all decrease—and population pressure in neighboring communities increases the effort necessary to keep trespassers out.

Take one example: deforestation in Nepal, where 92 percent of the population was dependent on agriculture and other rural activities in 1990 (Table 1.1). "The hill areas of Nepal are a prime example of an area in which low-productivity agriculture is surrounded by rapid environmental degradation as the result of deforestation, and the interaction of the two is promoting further deterioration in both" (Kumar and Hotchkiss 1988, p. 9). Because there are few options to increase low agricultural productivity (and incomes), families have to expand cropped area, which means clearing forests: in the 1970s, 20 to 50 percent of forests were cut in Nepal's hill areas. This increases the time spent (mainly by women) collecting fuelwood from receding forests, which creates a vicious cycle by reducing labor inputs to agriculture and, hence, household income. Kumar and Hotchkiss conclude that increasing agricultural productivity in the higher-potential lowlands of Nepal is the best way to ease pressure on deforestation in the hills.

In CARLs agricultural development causes some environmental stress but also generates solutions over time if it helps to alleviate poverty. As the Nepal experience shows, lack of development of the rural economy holds only problems—not solutions.

Sustainability (that is, preserving a specific stock of natural resources) is the wrong concept for CARLs. The key is to transform the rural economy. CARLs must give priority to policies and programs aimed at development of the rural economy, reduction of population growth rates, and structural transformation (see Chapter 2).

A large share of the labor force dependent on agriculture and other rural activities combined with low labor productivity in agriculture are common to all CARLs. These characteristics explain why, on average, their citizens are poor. Furthermore, the absolute number of men and women who depend on the rural economy will continue to increase and, along with it, so will the absolute number of poor, hungry people. Until CARLs pass the structural transformation turning point, they must contend with the double bind of raising low productivity while simultaneously absorbing additional workers in the rural economy.

The structural and demographic characteristics of CARLs discussed in this chapter raise important questions about whether the rural economy can absorb a growing rural work force and simultaneously provide more productive employment, thereby alleviating poverty and hunger. It has often been argued, however, that these economic concerns miss the point that inequity in the rural economy—especially for CARLs with a bimodal agrarian structure—is not just an economic hindrance but an absolute political barrier to any form of development that benefits the poor.

Most people in CARLs are poor, some are comfortable, and a few are very rich. Local political power is usually distributed in proportion to the ownership of land and other assets. Indeed, power arises from control of such assets. Examples abound where local challenges to these political and economic imbalances have been crushed by force; the threat of violence by the powerful against the weak can be a regular feature of social interaction. Raising productivity on millions of small farms is a formidable task, taking account only of economic and technical factors. Although variation across countries, even from village to village, is substantial, development is more difficult almost everywhere because of the strength of local political forces intent on maintaining the status quo.

Landownership is so concentrated in some Latin American countries, for example, that large landowners may have a great deal of market power in hiring labor, renting land, and lending capital in particular localities. They have the willingness, too, to exercise that power. The persistence of a caste system in India and other Asian countries also poses special problems, as does the low status of women in most CARLs. Providing poor rural people with access to improved opportunities is difficult when they have so little power to influence policies and implementation. But neither despair nor complacency is the right response to these imbalances in local political power in CARLs. Policies and programs can support or undermine poor people's own initiatives to challenge that power.

CHAPTER TWO

STRUCTURAL TRANSFORMATION

How can any CARL raise agricultural labor productivity fifteen-fold or more to the level of Japan and the United States? To lift output per farm worker from three "wheat units" to thirty hinges on the occurrence of three types of change on the farm. These are: (1) the use of new biological-chemical-mechanical inputs in the production process, (2) new technical and organizational knowledge, and (3) access to expanded markets for agricultural produce.

Beyond pointing to various paths that lead out of poverty, structural transformation provides a perspective on the economic, institutional, and demographic factors that constrain policy choices. When three-quarters of the labor force is engaged in agriculture, not only is there a fundamental capital-shortage problem vis-à-vis farm modernization, but also shortfalls in the workings of markets, in the capacity of the government to provide services, and in the productive efficiency of firms are more disabling than when the farm labor force share stands at one-quarter. It follows that many desirable policy choices available in the latter instance lie beyond the bounds of feasibility in CARLs.

THE PROCESS OF STRUCTURAL TRANSFORMATION

The mechanism of economic progress in farming is the same one that operates in every other sector of the economy. That mechanism is *specialization*. Not only is there specialization along specific crop lines among farmers, but also a host of functions formerly carried out by the household is transferred to specialist producers. Increasing division of labor in all economic activity brings with it the opportunity to use machinery whose power, speed, and precision multiplies the yield of human effort. Specialization not only makes possible the introduction of capital equipment, it also facilitates changes to better organization and more productive technologies. The result is augmented productivity of land and capital as well as of labor. As these processes get under way, households shift along the continuum from self-sufficiency to dependence on markets for disposal of their production, for purchase of their raw materials, for opportunities to hire labor and work for wages, for investments and loans, and for other goods and services.

Structural transformation at the sectoral level results from movement toward specialization and market participation at the producer level. Specialization means that new manufacturing and service activities emerge. Formerly small sectors—education, health, financial services—are greatly enlarged. The most dominant change, however, is the proportionate decline in the agricultural sector and the rise of the manufacturing sector. This is in part the result of greater demand for nonagricultural goods with rising incomes,[1] but the more fundamental cause is the transfer of function from generalist producers in the countryside to specialist firms in the towns.

Thus, in countries at the lower end of the income scale members of rural households devote 35 to 50 percent of their time to nonfarm tasks. Gradually such tasks as the making of clothing, utensils, furniture, weapons, jewelry, the processing of crops into food, the construction of buildings and boats are turned over to specialist producers. The transfer of these tasks out of the farm household is not limited to the production of hard goods either: "Fetching water, gathering fuel, educating, litigating, adjudicating, healing, regulating individual conduct, propitiating the deity, waging war, and governing are increasingly turned over to public utilities and oil companies, and to teachers, lawyers, judges, doctors, policemen, priests, soldiers, and congressmen" (Jones 1970, p. 178). In this way the functions of agriculture are gradually pared down to the single activity of producing raw materials.

---

[1] The *relative* decrease of food in the household budget as incomes rise, known as Engel's Law (Chapter 5), is more a consequence than a cause of structural transformation. The higher income elasticity of demand for manufactured goods as a group is also attributable to it being an open-ended set, continually expanding by virtue of the introduction of such new products as television, personal computers, miracle drugs, and the like.

That economic development necessarily implies structural transformation is best illustrated by wealthy agricultural economies that cater to external markets. Examples might be Denmark, New Zealand, and Iowa. What proportion of total output in these "agricultural economies" originates in farming? In 1988 the figures were 5 percent for Denmark and 10 percent for New Zealand (World Bank 1990, p. 183); for Iowa value added on the farm accounted for but 5 percent of the state's output. Farm productivity is high in these economies precisely because of the abundant use of inputs obtained from *outside* the agricultural sector: farm machinery, chemicals, financial credit, transportation, and professional services ranging from those of agronomist to tax consultant. In the United States the value added by these externally supplied inputs to farm cash sales was $99 billion in 1988 against only $52 billion contributed by the land, labor, and capital of the farmer (United States Department of Commerce 1989, p. 49).

High-productivity agriculture entrains industrialization directly; it also fosters it indirectly because the specialized services, differentiated market networks, and financial institutions that serve farming simultaneously lead to increased efficiency in various manufacturing and service activities. Moreover, the roads and other rural infrastructure built initially to facilitate expanded agricultural production also promote the growth of rural nonfarm activities.

Patterns of Structural Transformation

Structural transformation accompanying rising per capita income can be considered along two dimensions, changing output shares and reallocation of the labor force. In both dimensions structural transformation is characterized by *relative* decline in the agricultural sector. But absolute levels of agricultural output and employment will rise throughout much of the prolonged process of structural transformation.

Changing Output Shares. For Tanzania or Bangladesh, agriculture accounts for 35 to 60 percent of the gross domestic product (GDP) (Table 2.1). As productivity and income increase, that share declines sharply. The parallel rise in manufacturing as the most dynamic sector until a middle-income level is attained progresses from 5 to 8 percent and rises to 30 to 35 percent; thereafter it diminishes as the share of educational, governmental, and professional services continue to expand in high-income postindustrial societies. Whatever the particular propellant driving the growth process, every developing country traverses this common pathway of structural change.

It is equally clear from Table 2.1 that the common path can be quite wide. Sectoral shares are influenced by the natural resource endowment, by the size of internal markets, and by economic policies. As an example of the lat-

Table 2.1.   Selected measures of structural transformation, 1990, I

	GNP per capita (1990 U.S.$)	Share in GDP			
		Agriculture (%)	Manufacturing (%)	Services (%)	Other[a] (%)
Tanzania	110	59	10	29	2
Bangladesh	210	44[c]	7[c]	47[c]	2
Nigeria	290	36	7	25	31
India	350	31	19	40	10
Kenya	370	28	11	51	10
China	370	27	38	31	4
Indonesia	570	22	20	38	20
Egypt	600	17	16	53	13
Colombia	1,260	17	21	51	11
Thailand	1,420	12	26	48	13
Malaysia	2,320	21[b]	19[b]	44[b]	16[b]
Mexico	2,490	9	23	61	7
Brazil	2,680	10	26	51	13
Taiwan	7,954	4	34	54	8
United States	21,790	2[c]	17[c]	69[c]	12[c]
Japan	25,430	3	28	56	13

Sources: World Bank 1992b; FAO 1991; Republic of China 1993.
[a]"Other" is comprised of electricity, water, gas, construction, and mining.
[b]For the year 1984.
[c]For the year 1989.

ter, both Japan and Taiwan have far larger manufacturing (and smaller agricultural) sectors than other countries at a comparable income level owing to government policies that favor manufactured exports. The significance of the size of internal markets—permitting the early attainment of economies of scale in manufacturing—can be seen in the abnormally large manufaturing shares for the poor but populous countries of India and China. Conversely the absence of sizeable internal markets has played a role in the moderate manufacturing shares in Kenya and Tanzania.[2]

The natural resource effect on GDP shares is reflected in the makeup of exports. As a country develops, its comparative advantage evolves from resource-intensive commodities to labor-intensive products and finally to capital- and skill-intensive goods. Although the natural endowment strongly influences the level and composition of exports for virtually all CARLs, the impact is most powerful for mineral exporters: the enlarged "Other" category in Table 2.1 for Nigeria, Indonesia, and Malaysia (16–31 percent) is attributable to their petroleum income. Just how important natural re-

[2] Tanzania's exceedingly low share is also the outcome of severe macroeconomic mismanagement that depressed manufacturing output (Chapter 11).

sources can be in determining the level and composition of the GDP has been made transparent by the volatility of energy prices. With the precipitate fall in the price of oil and reduced petroleum production by 1988, Nigeria's per capita output fell to one-third its 1980 high of U.S.$1,040, with an ensuing "expansion" of its agricultural share from 27 to 34 percent—all this with no change in the underlying productivity of domestic factors of production.

In sum, within the broad confines of a common pattern of structural transformation that accompanies the growth in per capita income there is considerable variation around the trend, some of a permanent nature and some transitory.

This pattern is confirmed in the historical experience of contemporary high-income countries. Changing sectoral shares are shown for eight such countries in Figure 2.1. Over the per capita income range of $300 to $11,000 (1985 U.S. dollars), the share of primary production fell from 50 to 60 percent of the GDP to 5 to 10 percent, and that of industry (manufacturing, utilities, construction) rose from 15 to 40 percent. In both cases the historical experience is similar to the relationship derived from a 1960 cross section of high-, low-, and medium-income countries with population above 15 million, as shown by the line marked "large country pattern" (Chenery and Taylor 1968).

The one deviation of the cross-sectional regressions from the historical experience is that the share of primary output tends to fall lower than would be predicted by the cross-sectional estimate. This results from the direction of economic innovation, which has been to substitute manufactured products for those of nature. Thus, detergents, electricity, synthetic textiles, and plastics all meet consumer wants that were served by agricultural commodities 50 or 100 years ago. This trend of substituting away from farm products is likely to continue. Thus, when Kenya reaches a per capita income of $2,000, its manufacturing sector will be larger and its agricultural sector smaller than would be predicted from a 1986 cross-sectional sample.

Although not quite as dramatic as the changing pattern of output, there are also some systematic tendencies for change in its disposition (Syrquin and Chenery 1989). From a level of 73 percent at a per capita GDP of $300, the share of private consumption falls to 63 percent by the $2,000 mark (in 1980 U.S. dollars), whereas gross investment—public and private, domestic and foreign—rises from 18 percent to 25 percent over the same interval. By contrast, the fraction of output attributable to recurrent government expenditures remains more or less constant. As countries advance and become less reliant on the inflow of external resources, the excess of imports over exports drop from an amount equivalent to 5.3 percent of the GDP to 2.5 percent. Finally there are systematic changes in rel-

Figure 2.1. Sectoral output shares in eight countries, 1860–1960 (1985 U.S.$)

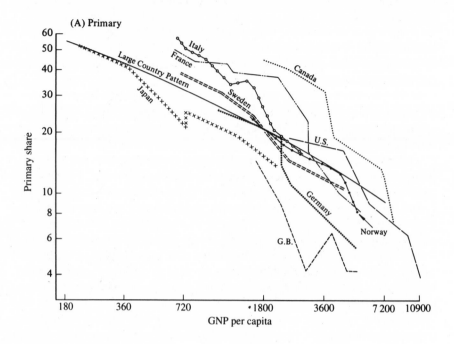

(A) Primary

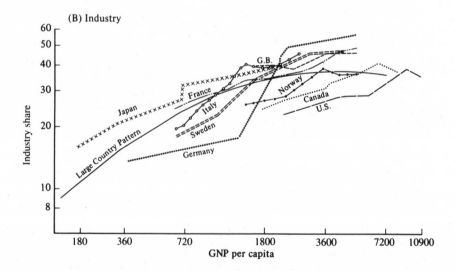

(B) Industry

Source: Johnston and Kilby 1975, p. 38.
Note: 1960 U.S. dollars were converted to 1985 dollars using the ratio CPI (1960):CPI(1985) = 0.2751.

ative prices, with the cost of agricultural and manufactured goods falling with respect to the average price level while those of services of all kinds increase.[3]

Changing Labor Shares. The changing allocation of labor broadly tracks that of output. The share of agricultural labor falls continuously but over a wider range—from 70 to 80 percent to 2 to 6 percent. Hence, measured output per agricultural worker is below the national average until late in structural transformation. The larger the agricultural sector, the greater the deviation below that national average output (Figure 2.2).

Employment shares of all other sectors increase. Initially, manufacturing accounts for a large chunk of nonfarm jobs. As per capita incomes increase, manufacturing shows the highest growth in productivity, which means fewer jobs per unit of output growth than in other nonfarm sectors. This low employment elasticity is mainly the result of increasing capital intensity, which in turn results from a changing mix of industrial products and greater mechanization in existing lines. Policies that avoid subsidies and keep the discipline of comparative advantage in the choice of new industry can significantly raise employment elasticity.

What about employment in other nonfarm sectors? It grows at a faster rate than in manufacturing. Growth in demand is biased toward those sectors where productivity is below the sector average. In construction there is a shift to labor-intensive urban dwellings and away from ports, bridges, and roads. In trade the shift is to retail services and away from less labor-using wholesaling and storage. As the extended family declines and more women enter the labor force, there is a shift from home-supplied to market-supplied personal services—restaurants, domestic services, household repair.

Farming provides the main source of livelihood for over half the population until per capita incomes reach $600 to $800. And, as seen in Table 2.2, per capita output in agriculture tends to rise, although agricultural workers are an ever-shrinking portion of the work force. This flows from the extraordinary advance in measured output per worker: from a low starting point, productivity growth is more rapid in agriculture than in any other sector.

There are, however, five potential labor force measurement errors that affect intercountry comparisons and overstate farm–nonfarm inequality and the rate of productivity growth in agriculture.

First, note the improbably wide variance in the proportion of population counted as economically active in Table 2.2, column 4. Labor force partic-

---

[3] This means that a part of the shift to services in the later stages of structural transformation is an illusion generated by this price effect. The tendency for the prices of nontradable goods to rise relative to tradables at higher levels of per capita income, creating the exchange rate bias in national income comparisons, also means that structural transformation takes place over a narrower range of real income than implied by all of the "nominal" income figures in the tables in this chapter (Syrquin and Chenery 1989).

Figure 2.2. Agriculture's shares in labor force and national output, selected countries and regions, 1960–80

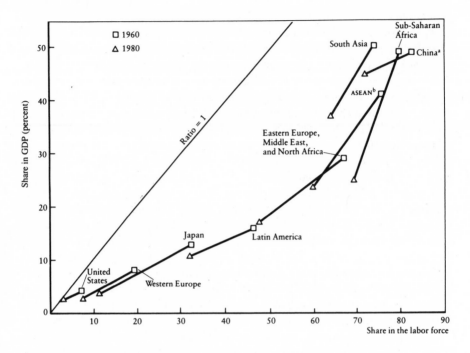

Source: Binswanger and Donovan 1987, p. 24.
[a]Initial data are for 1963.
[b]Data are for the Association of South East Asian Nations (ASEAN), except Brunei.

ipation for the agricultural population ranges over 100 percent between the lowest and the highest, that is, between 28 and 59 percent. Part of this variance is genuine, reflecting differences in age structure and culture (e.g., purdah in Saudi Arabia). Most of the variance, however, results from arbitrary census classification rules of thumb that severely understate women's roles in the rural economy. In Senegal, Mali, and Mauritania the official female participation rate in the rural work force is one-third that of Mozambique, Rwanda, and Benin—that is, 25 percent versus 75 percent (Haggblade, Hazell, and Brown 1989). Moreover, in Thailand everyone above the age of eleven is allocated to the labor force; in many other countries the work force is limited to those between 15 and 59 years of age. Insofar as the participation ratio is overstated, it biases output per farm worker downward (if understated, upward). Thus, although output per capita is 63 percent higher

Table 2.2. Selected measures of structural transformation, 1990, II

	Share of labor force in agriculture (%)	Agricultural output		Labor force participation[a] (%)
		Per capita (1990 U.S.$)	Per farm worker (1990 U.S.$)	
Tanzania	81	53	140	48*
Bangladesh	69	75	376	29
Nigeria	65	116	473	38
India	67	92	364	40*
Kenya	77	89	279	41
China	68	88	219	60
Indonesia	49	127	666	43*
Egypt	41	110	981	28
Colombia	27	208	2,379	32
Thailand	64	179	524	56**
Malaysia	32			42
Mexico	30	238	2,256	35
Brazil	24	281	3,156	37
Taiwan	13	318	6,043	59
United States	2	367[b]	30,969[b]	44
Japan	6	600	18,475	53

Sources: World Bank 1992b, FAO 1991; Republic of China 1993.

Note: Countries are listed in ascending order of GNP per capita, 1990.

[a]Labor force participation measures the proportion of the agricultural population that is economically active, as estimated by the FAO. Where no asterisk appears, the participation rate is approximately the same for both the agricultural and the nonagricultural population. One asterisk indicates that the former exceeds the nonagricultural participation rate by 4 to 6 percentage points; two asterisks indicate 8 percentage points' difference.

[b]For the year 1988.

in Thailand, the measured productivity of Thai agricultural workers is an unlikely 53 percent lower than their Egyptian counterparts.

Second, consider four instances where the participation ratio differs for the agricultural and nonagricultural population. Tanzania, India, Indonesia, and Thailand all have nonagricultural ratios that are 4 to 8 percent lower than the farm participation ratios. If not grounded in fact, this nonagricultural ratio tends to distort relative shares. Again, take Thailand: its output share in agriculture is 12 percent, against an apparent labor force share of 64 percent. This implies that a farm worker produces only one-fifth of average labor productivity in the rest of the economy—an abnormally large difference. As described in Chapter 6, the idiosyncratic Thai census procedure is to classify those households that engage in any farm activity as being agricultural; a more likely count of the farm work force gives a 50 percent agricultural labor force share (World Bank 1989b, p. 117 and annex 5). This revaluation not only raises the nonfarm employment from 36 to 50 percent of the economically active population; it also reduces the implied productivity inequality for agriculture from 0.19 to 0.24.

Although such errors in drawing the line between those who work and those who do not create greater dispersion and can throw into question country comparisons, there is no obvious systematic bias with respect to structural transformation. Not so with the third measurement problem. Because agriculture output consumed by the farm household is often undercounted and valued at imputed prices lower than commercial sales, there is a downward bias—the greater the subsistence element in farm production the bigger the bias. Thus, some of the rise in agricultural output per worker, as structural transformation proceeds, is merely a change in valuation.

But the largest element of the upward bias in the agricultural productivity trend is due to the misclassification of the time that the rural work force devotes to nonfarm activities in the early and middle stages of structural transformation. How misclassification occurs (our fourth and fifth measurement errors), what these activities are, and their magnitude are the subjects to which we now turn.

The Hidden Extent of Rural Nonfarm Activities

Until recently the rural economy was equated with the agricultural economy. The primary function of rural households was thought to be production of food, fiber, and livestock for the home market and one or more crops for export. Household members might be engaged in limited agricultural processing, transporting, and marketing. This conventional view was derived, however, from census statistics that understate rural nonfarm activities. Censuses classify individuals by primary occupation only; other activities are ignored. Moreover, the classification of rural areas as urban (especially the small rural towns that are the hub for much rural nonfarm activity) also understates the importance of nonagricultural pursuits in rural areas (see Box 2.1).

In fact, apart from agricultural processing, a large share of the rural population is engaged in full- or part-time jobs in manufacturing, repair, construction, retail and wholesale trade, restauranting, transport, personal services, and salaried employment in teaching, health services, and public administration. The full-time equivalent employment in rural manufacturing—grain milling, bread, noodles, spirits, clothing, footwear, furniture, metal utensils, fish nets, farm tools, printing, traditional crafts—exceeds total formal sector urban manufacturing employment for 73 percent of the countries for which data are available (Liedholm and Mead 1987). Part-time activities carried on in the homestead, typically by women, include brewing, garment making, and traditional crafts. Petty trading and repair are also frequently part-time. Most of the other activities, located in the larger villages and small towns, are pursued full-time by both men and women.

Box 2.1. Misclassification of the Rural Labor Force and Nonfarm Activity

The minor significance of nonagricultural activities in the rural economy seems to be confirmed, at least for many countries, by the small residual that remained after accounting for the labor engaged in farming and in the production of goods and services in urban areas. UN statistics for 1980, for example, show the residual nonfarm share to be 15 percent for Thailand, 14 percent for Bangladesh, 5 percent for Kenya, 2 percent for Tanzania, and 1 percent for Brazil. For a group of 38 countries, ranging from Argentina to Rwanda, for which agricultural products make up 50 percent or more of exports, the average 1980 rural nonfarm labor force share was just under 5 percent.* For five of these countries the residuals were negative, a phenomenon related to how the rural–urban demarcation line is drawn, as will be discussed.

Such census-based statistics severely understate the size of the rural nonfarm labor force because of two principal causes. The first is that individuals are classified according to their principal occupation only. Secondary occupations are ignored. Where specialization is incomplete, where individuals are involved in a diverse set of activities—farming, trade, transport, an artisan craft—the "principal occupation" criterion can be misleading. As an extreme case, consider a community where all individuals devoted 51 percent of their time to farming and 49 percent to nonfarm enterprises: the labor force would be classified as 100 percent agricultural. As long as agriculture is the principal occupation of a majority of the rural population, this bias to understate the rural nonfarm labor force (and to overstate the agricultural labor force) exists. The second source of underestimation of the nonfarm sector is the arbitrary boundary between rural and urban, and specifically the tendency to misclassify rural areas as urban. It is not often remarked when rural–urban issues are analyzed that UN statistics are not based on a uniform town size dividing line, but rather accept the varying definitions of each country (United Nations 1987b). Thus, the urban population of Japan is defined to be all those living in localities of 30,000 or more, for Nigeria, the boundary drops to 20,000, for Kenya or Honduras it drops to one-tenth the Nigerian figure, and for Peru or Uganda an urban place is any locality of 100 or more! For 42 countries that have a simple locality size boundary between rural and urban, 50 percent have the demarcation at 2,000 persons or lower, whereas only 4 percent place the cut-off at 20,000 or above. But it is the latter that is the appropriate boundary for our problem: small towns, which are the locus of a large share of informal sector nonfarm activities, typically serve the surrounding agricultural community and accordingly are properly assigned to the rural economy.

*Calculated from various appendix tables in World Bank 1988b.

The truest measure of output and employment in nonfarm activities is provided by yearlong rural household income-and-expenditure surveys for a few selected countries (Table 2.3). In these surveys the problems of secondary occupations, seasonality, and nonenumerated enterprises vanish. Farm in-

Table 2.3. Sources of rural household income

	Farm (%)	Nonfarm (%)	Transfers (%)
Botswana (1976)	55.2	32.9	11.9
Kenya (1984)	58.3	33.0	8.7
Zimbabwe (1984)	59.3	22.2	18.5
Philippines (1986)	47.9	39.3	12.8
Korea (1982)	69.8	11.4	18.8
Thailand (1976)	56.0	37.8	6.2
Taiwan (1975)	51.4	40.8	7.8

Note: Figures were assembled by Professor Carl Liedholm.

come includes off-farm agricultural wage earning, as well as commercial and subsistence production of the household. Nonfarm income is understated because it excludes consumption by the farmstead members of nonfarm output. Transfers are mainly remittances from relatives in urban areas but also include government subsidies.

Clearly, the equation of agricultural with rural is incorrect. Among these seven countries, earnings from farming average but 57 percent of household income. Income from nonfarm activities ranges from one-sixth that of farming to more than four-fifths, averaging slightly over one-half. The contrast between this more refined index and the conventional population census measure is striking. The ratio of rural nonfarm to farm activity for Kenya rises from 1 to 16 (5 to 79 percent) to 1 to 2 and from 1 to 5 to 1 to 2 for Thailand.

In conclusion, the size of the rural nonfarm sector has, until quite recently, been severely underestimated in CARLs. This has occurred because of occupational classification procedures employed in population censuses and because of the way the rural-urban boundary has been drawn. The sector is large and diverse. It plays a major role in augmenting rural welfare and can be a significant ingredient in advancing structural transformation. Finally, implied in the underestimation of the nonfarm labor force is an overestimation of that part of the work force devoted to agricultural pursuits.

Natural Resource Endowments Matter Less

In low per capita–income countries, natural resource endowment greatly affects the relative contribution of different sectors to GDP, the type of productive stimuli at work in the economy, and savings and foreign exchange. One natural resource, agricultural land, lies at the center of our subject. The relative endowment of land, in space and quality, has a central bearing on the choice of agricultural strategy. The implications of the land endowment and its distribution across households are considered in detail in Chapters 4 and 5.

Table 2.4. Exploitation of natural resource endowments, 1987–89

	Mining as a percent of GDP	Roundwood production (M³/capita)	Fish catch (kg/capita)
Tanzania	0.2	1.30	15.1
Bangladesh	0.1	0.27	9.0
Nigeria	20.1	0.95	2.5
India	2.0	0.32	4.5
Kenya	0.4	1.53	6.2
China	—	0.25	13.9
Indonesia	13.3	0.99	17.5
Egypt	5.8	0.04	6.1
Colombia	6.2	0.57	2.9
Thailand	2.9	0.70	55.3
Malaysia	10.8	2.82	39.2
Mexico	4.3	0.27	13.3
Brazil	0.9	1.74	6.1
Taiwan	0.4	0.03	67.0
United States	0.8	2.16	25.6
Japan	2.2	0.26	101.4

Sources: World Resources Institute 1992; World Bank 1990; Republic of China 1993; United Nations 1992.

Note: Countries are listed in ascending order of per capita GNP, 1990.

Labor, land, and natural resources constitute the original factors of production. In early development, when the supply of the "produced factor" (capital) is modest and technology rudimentary, natural resources loom large in national output. Later, new technology, capital accumulation, and international trade progressively free the tight relationship between output and resource inputs. Hence, for Holland and Japan, meager natural resources are not a serious handicap to increases in per capita output anymore.

Published data limit country comparisons to minerals, timber, and fish (Table 2.4). Many natural resources must be "discovered": only following investment in search activities, and, then, in specialized infrastructure can the "free gifts of nature" be converted into useful assets. Where the resource commands a high price relative to the cost of extraction, it is an easy matter for CARLs to attract foreign capital and technical know-how. Other natural deposits, such as iron ore or bauxite reserves, may never be converted into economic resources. Extraction and processing of some mineral resources (oil, precious metals, gemstones) usually result in a capital-intensive enclave that provides windfall export income but little stimulus to the economy, no significant input linkages, and few technological or entrepreneurial spillovers.

Because economic development in some CARLs appears to be constrained by limited savings and foreign exchange (to import capital goods and critical intermediate inputs), it is often suggested that structural transformation would be easy if only these bottlenecks could be eased (Chenery 1981, p. 1113; Kreinin 1983, p. 181). Not so. Consider Nigeria and oil.[4] In 1960 windfall revenues from oil were equivalent to 1 percent of the GDP; by 1970 they were 6 percent. Following the two oil price hikes, they rose to 23 percent in 1974–78 and 22 percent of a still larger GDP in 1979–81. These windfalls allowed Nigeria to maintain gross expenditures on capital formation at 23 percent of GDP in 1974–85. However, owing to poor selection and execution of projects and mismanagement of the exchange rate, these investments did not add to productive capacity—and agriculture and manufacturing were eroded by inexpensive imports. When oil revenues were cut by 75 percent after 1981, national income plunged and, for 1974–85 average per capita GDP fell by 3.5 percent a year. The situation was very different in Indonesia, although oil income and capital formation percentages were virtually identical to Nigeria's. There, policies of restraint led to a positive 3.7 percent growth rate in per capita GDP in the same period.

Without the right policies, even the richest endowment of natural resources will not lead to structural transformation. Indonesia's success depended heavily on macroeconomic policies (see Box 5.5), and Nigeria's failure on the lack of agricultural development during the oil boom years of the 1970s.

Because they are less scarce than oil, timber and marine resources command less economic rent.[5] On the other hand their exploitation does save or earn a certain amount of foreign exchange and is often undertaken by domestic entrepreneurs rather than foreign firms. Moreover, the production process is such that extensive use is made of domestic factors of production and inputs from local industries. From the second column of Table 2.3 it can be seen that Egypt and Taiwan have virtually no usable wood resources, whereas Malaysia, the United States, and Brazil benefit from rich endowments. The diversity of the fishery category—from eels to whales, frogs to alligators—and the presence of fish farming and fishing in international waters makes the task of separating the contribution attributable to a nation's natural resources from that attributable to investment and entrepreneurship a difficult one. Among these countries fishing is important for Malaysia and Thailand, with Japan and Taiwan taking the largest catch per capita.

---

[4] The statistics in the remainder of this paragraph are drawn from Pinto 1987, Gelb 1988, and World Bank 1989c.

[5] *Economic rents*, competitively determined returns above the economic costs of labor, capital, management, and inputs required for production and marketing of primary products, should not be confused with *policy rents*, a topic taken up in Chapter 12.

INSTITUTIONAL ASPECTS OF STRUCTURAL TRANSFORMATION

The division of labor among producers cannot proceed without the development of institutions to coordinate their activities. Efficient, competitive markets integrate increasingly specialized producers and consumers of a variety of goods and services. And during structural transformation, markets for labor, land, capital, and financial services multiply in number and in size, with a proliferation of services to buyers and sellers.

Commodity Markets

Markets for agricultural commodities and simple consumer goods can usually be found in early development. As communications with other nations develop, foreign trade brings sizable imports of basic consumer items that are superior substitutes for some local products they displace; machine-made cotton textiles is a notable example. Traded in exchange are one or more primary products, which initially may be produced with underused land and labor. Export production is later augmented by resources once used to produce the import-replaced goods.

As commodity trade increases, its organization becomes more complex and more efficient. Commonly, initial distribution is based on coastal towns, itinerant traders, and periodic markets. Later, it evolves into a highly articulated network, continuous in space and time, encompassing large importers and exporters, commission agents, wholesalers, and a spectrum of retail channels ranging from department stores to hawkers. This merchanting is supported by warehousing, transport, processing, credit, and insurance.

The volume of market exchange rises more rapidly than production of final goods and services. This results from (1) the gradual but uninterrupted transfer of function from the household to the market, and (2) the rising trade in intermediate goods and services that is associated with advancing producer specialization. Thus, the efficiency with which markets operate is a stimulant (or deterrent) to further structural transformation.

Labor Markets

The development of labor markets accommodates differentiation in two directions; specialization by commodity and by skill. In subsistence, household labor produces many items for family consumption. As more goods are purchased on the market, the range of crops and crafts is narrowed. Concurrently, as various functions are transferred out of the household, the nonfarm rural economy begins to emerge, with labor supplied under apprenticeship and for wages.

In some areas the earliest rural labor market emerges in plantations and mines, and in seasonal jobs in cotton ginneries, rice mills, and canneries. In agriculture the evolution of a permanent labor force is determined by agricultural development, landownership, and tenure arrangements (see Chapters 4 and 5). Finally, development of efficient urban labor markets depends on transportation, urban housing, and job information, as well as education.

Labor markets do not just reallocate workers. Wage and salary differences play a central role in the formation of *human capital*—that is, skills and broader characteristics, such as health, that raise the productivity of people. Without human capital to bind together complex technology and organization, structural transformation cannot be sustained.

The development of labor skills depends on other inputs besides pecuniary incentives—education, both general and technical, employer policies, and traditions. Given reasonable education and training, supplies of technical skills respond to market-generated wage premiums. Supervisory and managerial skills are more influenced by sociological factors and tend to develop at a slower pace.

Financial Markets

By increasing the incentive to save and the profitability of investment, financial markets help to raise the level of physical capital formation. They shift investable resources from one sector to another, from areas of limited growth to those of rapid expansion. Efficient financial markets also augment national product and consumer welfare by financing more current business transactions and allowing households more freedom in the timing of large expenditures.

In the subsistence economy, investment by the individual producer is limited by his own ability to save—that is, the household labor time that can be diverted from production for current consumption and from noneconomic activities. Saving and investment are thus combined in the same mutually constraining act. With monetization and development of a market for debt, savings and investment separate, and the geographic boundaries within which investable resources can be mobilized are extended.

Initially in most CARLs, risks are great, competition among lenders is slight, and transaction costs are high. The result: interest rates are high (40 to 100 percent a year), and only the distressed borrow. With economic development, the real cost of lending falls and competition increases.

Consider agricultural lending. With new farm inputs—improved seed varieties, chemical fertilizers—absolute output climbs, raising the margin above subsistence that is available for debt servicing. Other innovations, such as better control of water and more effective plant protection, reduce both the probability of default and the risk premium that the lender charges.

With cadastral and soil surveys dispelling uncertainty about property boundaries and agronomic value, the amount of land given as surety can be lowered, and the costs of contract enforcement are reduced. At the same time demand for agricultural borrowing expands, which spreads risk among different productive activities and increases the number of lenders competing for clients.

Now consider the supply of savings. When borrowing is limited, the savings lent are those of landlords, shop owners, or moneylenders. As the real costs of lending fall and loan demand expands, these lenders are displaced by cooperative societies, banks, and finance companies. These intermediaries have powerful economies of scale in risk spreading, information gathering, and administration. Whereas individual lenders are limited to their own resources, institutions mobilize the savings of countless asset holders.

And so financial deepening advances, as households shift from tangible assets to cash and savings deposits to store wealth. When secure returns are offered to depositors, hoardings of durable commodities and precious metals can be tapped. Households that had never saved because their potential savings capacity fell below the threshold for making a primary loan are now enticed to do so. These new savers are induced to come forward by a steady return on their savings no matter how small, by security of principal provided by diversified lending, and by the right of immediate withdrawal. Just as better information, diminished risk, and lower transaction costs reduce interest paid by borrowers, these same forces result in higher net interest received by savers.

Governmental Influences on Markets

If markets have the potential to mobilize resources for growth, that potential can only be realized through a deft mixture of government support and noninterference.

Financial markets, for example, can only attain requisite levels of predictability after extensive public investment in establishing records and assigning title to real property in all its forms; in operating a legal system that efficiently administers the law pertaining to contract, inheritance, and bankruptcy, and in providing some portion of the formal education required of the lawyers, accountants, and credit analysts who must collect, store, and interpret information. Yet, at the same time and contrary to natural inclination, at the risk of stunting the delicate mechanism of lending and borrowing, governments must abstain from low-interest public lending schemes, abstain from setting interest rate ceilings, and abstain from mandating that scarce loanable funds be targeted to certain industries or classes of borrowers.

Mundane but difficult tasks—such as the collection and dissemination of statistical and technical information and the enforcement of standards in engineering, weights, and measures—are critical government roles in perfecting markets. Likewise, government has a central coordinating, facilitating, and research-sponsoring role to play in the transfer of technology for agriculture (Chapters 4 and 5) as well as industry (Chapter 6).

Government action regarding the spatial location of economic activities also bears on the effectiveness with which markets draw on resources for production. Decisions on transportation systems, public facilities, and other infrastructure help determine the balance of cities versus towns. When non-agricultural activities are located in many regional towns, rather than in one or two large cities, there is greater stimulus to agriculture–industry interaction. Incentives for farmers to increase output are greatly strengthened by access to competitive produce markets in centers where inputs, services, and consumer goods are also available. Close proximity to their clientele similarly enhances the efficiency of public administration and educational institutions. Thus, a measure of urban decentralization—which increases the flow of information between producers and strengthens economic incentives—helps to create a well-articulated economy based on comprehensive market networks.

TECHNICAL CHANGE AND PRODUCTIVITY GROWTH

The evolution of markets that accompanies structural transformation makes three principal contributions to raising per capita national product. First, markets draw into productive use land, labor, and entrepreneurship that might otherwise go untapped. Second, because competitive pricing creates incentives to allocate resources to areas where their return is highest, output per worker tends to increase as a result of the efficient resource allocation. Third, the operation of financial markets results in a more rapid increase in the stock of capital available to assist individual laborers, augmenting their productivity.

Another set of factors raises long-term productivity. "Technical change" encompasses the interconnected elements of new technology, augmented labor skills, and improved organization efficiency.

When research and development become institutionalized, much of the increase in factor productivity comes from applied research that results in specific products or production techniques that fit prevailing factor prices, technical conditions, and consumer tastes. In the past, technical progress was slow and evolutionary, relying on the accidental discovery or the inspired experiments of many small producers. Such was agricultural change in nineteenth-century America and Japan (Chapter 3).

Technical progress in today's CARLs is different. Advances come, for the most part, from drawing on existing knowledge in high-income countries.

Applied technology is embodied in people and in products: its transfer is easiest when the improvement is wholly embodied in the product—such as a sharper tool or electronic calculator—and becomes more difficult when the advance also depends on new skills, restructured organization, and altered relationships with other economic agents. And so, whether the weft of new technology results in outright failure, or a successful enterprise or two, or dissemination across an entire industry depends on the receiving warp of complementary inputs. And the strength and density of that warp are significantly related to the country's progress up the ladder of structural transformation.

New technology is generated in local research institutions and in small and large firms as they modify imported technology. The latter can come in the shape of capital equipment, intermediate goods, patent licenses, foreign technicians, or specialized education. Diffusion of new technology, once introduced, varies greatly. Generally, where techniques are only moderately different from those already mastered, diffusion is likely to be rapid. When local personnel are experienced in a new industry, some are lured to rival firms, and the spread of technology, via imitative competition, is under way. Where the scale and complexity of new technology is vastly greater than existing activities, its transplant has limited impact on productivity.

Government has a critical role to play. Supervised uniform weights and measures, engineering standards, and similar provision of exact knowledge about products and factors of production are prerequisites for applying more advanced techniques. Because private resources are inadequate, government must carry out some adaptive research on industrial processing of local materials, manufacturing techniques, agricultural equipment, and plant varieties. It is not only a question of economies of scale. More often than not the fruits of adaptive research are easily copied by competitors. Unable to capture the full return to their investment, private entrepreneurs curtail research efforts far short of the social optimum. Collective action by farmers for more efficient irrigation, marketing, and seed distribution will often need publicly operated administrative structures. And finally, the success of public education—in imparting general knowledge and forming specific skills—will play an indirect albeit pervasive role in determining the volume of improvements in applied technology.

Technological advance interacts with other sources of productivity growth to affect the organization of the economy and raise per capita income. As a general rule, more productive economies are more complex, refining the production process into a larger number of specialized operations. When a new technology is introduced, the firm as an organization must attain a higher level of knowledge and have command over a wider range of specialized skills. Individual production units grow in scale, employing a larger capital stock and more capital per employee. Cost being but the reciprocal of productivity, superior technology means that cost per unit of output falls.

As division of labor proceeds within the production unit under the influence of newer techniques, those functions that are subject to increasing returns to scale are taken over by specialist producers. The latter, by obtaining a scale of output that permits full cost minimization, can then sell this input to a number of firms cheaper than they themselves can produce it (Stigler 1951). In addition to specialist firms fabricating standardized components or providing wholesaling, purchasing, or maintenance services, the producer network is further expanded by supervised subcontracting with smaller workshops that realize lower cost because of lower overheads and less well paid labor. Thus for the individual firm the proportion of value added to gross output falls and new vertically linked firms emerge as the input-output matrix expands.

ELEMENTS OF SOCIAL CHANGE

The proliferation of firms and public institutions, the emergence of new technologies and marketing relationships, and shifts in individual behavior bring changes to the traditional social structure. The general direction of that change is toward ever-greater differentiation of social roles and institutions, on the one hand, and the emergence of new methods of social integration on the other. For example, the role of village elders is gradually taken over by lawyers, judges, legislators, and family counselors. Some of the new mechanisms of integration that transmit information and supply control are elections, political parties, professional associations, and consumer organizations.

From Kin to Society

The shift of individual loyalties from kin and village to societywide interest groups is difficult and uneven. Old relationships are disrupted, new ones forged. Imported institutions, such as trade unions and parliamentary government, fit poorly—sometimes not at all. Of the many types of social behavior undergoing differentiation and reintegration, political development breaks down most frequently.

Integrating thousands of communities, often with different languages, cultures, and religions, is a herculean task. With migration to cities and towns, there is harsh competition for jobs, wealth, and status. In the search for allies in this struggle, individuals seek advantage by intensifying their ethnic and religious ties. The resultant communal conflict, as well as other dislocations caused by economic change, quickly find expression in the political forum.

The political system must be able to elicit acceptance of national objectives and policies. It also must be capable of organizing and staffing an effective bureaucracy to collect taxes, provide services, and implement government policies. Tensions between their limited governmental capabilities and expanding public expectations generated by the political process have strategic implications for CARLs (see Chapter 8).

A critical ingredient in this process of eliciting acceptance of national objectives and policies is the creation of opportunities for widespread participation in the political system (Goodell 1985). Consider the all too common case in which an economic policy or development intervention is initiated at the top, whether by autocratic leaders or expert foreign advisors. Although they may persist over a long period, when such undertakings are not subject to an iterative process of persuasion, bargaining, and adaptation with those most affected, they often do not succeed. Legal ceilings on rents charged by landlords, irrigation projects, or agricultural cooperatives that are put in place without meaningful consultation are not only likely to be ill-adapted to local circumstances—and hence fail—but also by the lack of predictability that they inject into their surroundings they induce producers to retreat from their comparative advantage to a protective, less efficient diversification of productive activities. In short, actions undertaken by government alone, without the input generated by widespread political participation of the rural population, will (1) shrink the information that flows upward from the grass roots, (2) truncate cooperation beyond parochial boundaries, and (3) curtail entrepreneurial activities. The first two effects mean maladroit policies and projects, and the third means a turning away from specialization toward localized markets as predictability is eroded.

Farewell to Reciprocity

The most basic change in villages that results from integration into large-scale markets is the weakening of reciprocity. Increases in output above minimum subsistence provide households with monetary savings and other liquid assets that can be used for basic consumption needs if local crops fail. For other types of emergencies these savings, plus current income, can purchase essential services previously extended on a nonmonetary basis.

National markets and transport systems allow a food-deficit community to draw on surpluses in distant areas. And modern facilities mean that staple foodstuffs, accumulated in years of abundance, can be stored to supplement reliance on international markets. Because rural market networks are imperfect and take time to adjust to shifts in supply or demand for essential commodities, communal reciprocity disappears only in the late stages of structural transformation.

As the security of reciprocity weakens, incentives for ignoring its commands grow stronger. In a community with no substantial external outlet for the produce of the land, the rewards for expanding output above a certain level are slight. When a community enters a market economy, unlimited production for sale becomes a possibility. Anyone prepared to spurn (or redefine) those ancient canons that apply to heirs of good fortune—expanded obligation to kin and neighbor, to communal celebration, to village improvement, to charity—can now enjoy a material standard of living and bequeath wealth to offspring at heretofore unimagined levels.

The transformation of traditional reciprocal labor arrangements is related to this change. In smallholder communities those who expand output relative to most producers have greater need for outside labor but have less time to reciprocate. Fortunately, enlarged cash sales make possible the payment of money wages, and labor exchange gradually gives way to a wage system. There is a gain in specialization, as some devote themselves fully to management. But communal solidarity is weakened.

In communities where farm land is rented the disruptive effects of new technology and market opportunities are more pronounced. The crop share paid in rent is an important part of the landlord–tenant relationship, whereby the landlord exercises authority in return for providing security for tenants. When new seeds, fertilizers, and irrigation dramatically raise farm yields, the old equilibrium is disrupted. Conditioned by market opportunities, landlords see these gains as accruing to the scarce resources they own. Tenants resist increases in the rental share as a violation of customary norms of distributive justice. This may lead to conflict and, sometimes, eviction and direct cultivation by landlords (see Chapter 5).

As real incomes of most members of a community rise, arbitrary factors dictate that some people (and some communities and regions) will pull ahead of others. Unequal gains flow from the happenstance of being first, good fortune in ownership (of soil, water, location), or the genetic "luck of the draw" in personal energy and ability. Initial wealth is often transformed into permanent economic advantage. Participation in politics that money allows and informal networks create privileged access to scarce resources and, through statutes and administrative practices, raise barriers to would-be competitors.

From Rural to Urban

The differences between agriculture and industry in the organization of production and in the technologies employed have profound implications for social change. The modernization of agriculture, although it entails the same increased use of capital equipment, purchased inputs, and technical knowledge as industry, does not alter the sequential division of labor imposed by nature or alter the social organization of the family farm. Dealings with strangers, novel activities, depersonalized relationships, and new norms are at the periphery rather than the center of the social milieu. In striking contrast, the shift from craft production to large-scale manufacturing means migration to a new place, new society, and new way of working. Spending most of the day away from home, workers have less time for socializing with kin and neighbors. New ideas and activities undermine traditional behavior, and the nature of factory production techniques imposes a fundamentally different organization of work. Factory work must be done among strangers in a largely impersonal setting. Workers perform but a few of the operations of production. Thus, the worker does not control the pace of work, cannot identify with the finished product, and takes little pride in the work.

Social Structure and the Management Factor

Deficiencies in managerial skills are another constraint on the strategic options of countries in the early phase of structural transformation. Such deficiencies in indigenous firms and public agencies limit the speed and efficiency of operations as well as setting a ceiling on the complexity of tasks these organizations can successfully undertake. Unlike the skills of the craftsman, lawyer, doctor, or scientist, whose formal education and on-the-job training result in proficiency levels equal to those attained in industrialized countries, managerial skills fall into a different pattern (Kilby 1972; Strassmann 1968). The managerial shortfall appears to be related to the organization of work in agrarian societies.

The organization of work in the village economy is similar in both manufacture and farming. Apart from small scale and the absence of mechanical power, in both cases the division of labor is *sequential*, with the same individuals carrying out all operations of production. Whether for farmer or craftsman, the need to synchronize the activity of the work force is minimal. Even as farming technology is transformed, the inalterable character of biological growth dictates no change in the seasonal sequence of productive operations—ploughing, harrowing, planting, applying water and nutrients, weeding, harvesting, threshing (Brewster 1950).

Where in farming nature supplies the managerial discipline and product standardization, the situation is very different in manufacture. Here the shift from sequential to *simultaneous* productive operations creates the necessity for a wide range of coordinating, supervising, and controlling functions that had no place in the earlier technology. The appearance of task specialization requires that the work of all groups and individuals within groups be synchronized in time and controlled for standardization, quality, material wastage, and rate of throughput.

Thus as CARLs turn to the operation of large-scale organizations where many activities must be coordinated, they run into difficulties that they do not encounter in farming. Not only is managerial performance frequently hampered by the absence of antecedent roles in traditional production, but also social factors may contribute an additional hindrance. Most of the latter can be traced to role behavior associated with vertically organized status systems. In the case of supervision, foregoing the right to remain aloof from the practical details of a subordinate's task, treating social inferiors as equals in the process of consultation, sharing authority with a person of lower status through cooperative effort—all these things are socially degrading and undermine the supervisor's social worth in his (or her) eyes and those of the supervisor's charges. Superiors cannot acknowledge error or delegate responsibility without diminishing their authority. Normative role expectations by all participants stress compliance over performance in such a setting.

Of course, as structural transformation proceeds, this traditional agrarian heritage is gradually replaced by new learning and a new social inheritance attuned to the present imperatives. But in the meantime, for those private and public organizations that are coordination-intensive, performance is be subject to potential impairment. This impairment takes the form of higher cost and reduced delivery of goods and services as a result of a slower rate of throughput, variation in quality, and wastage of time and materials.

There are several simple but important implications of this analysis for policymakers in countries on the lower rungs of the ladder of structural transformation. Because they are less demanding in their requirements for coordination, small-scale industry and services are able to operate much closer to their production frontiers: strategic choices should favor wherever feasible small over large enterprise. And in the selection of government activities to meet a given need, those options that make the least demand on "the management factor" should be given serious consideration over technically superior services whose delivery requires extensive inputs of coordination and control.

The Demographic Transition

Historically, structural transformation has been accompanied by *demographic transition*. In the first phase of transition mortality rates decline but fertility remains high and the rate of population growth rises significantly. In the second phase rapid population growth ends as fertility declines to levels nearer the greatly reduced mortality rate.

In CARLs rapid population growth prolongs the rural economy's dominant share in the labor force. In earlier times birth and death rates moved during a country's structural transformation in such a way that population doubled over 70 years. For today's CARLs, that may happen in 25 years or less. What has changed?

In Europe before the industrial revolution, the rate of population growth was low—less than one-half of 1 percent a year—because both birth and death rates were high. With the industrial revolution, death rates fell slowly

Table 2.5.   Vital statistics for selected countries, 1920–90

	Crude death rates[a]				Crude birthrates[a]			
	1920	1940	1960	1990	1927	1950	1960	1990
Tanzania	—	—	24	18	—	44	46	48
Bangladesh	—	—	—	14	—	—	—	35
Nigeria	—	—	—	14	—	55	49	43
India	36	27	15	11	—	42	38	30
Kenya	—	—	—	10	—	—	—	45
China	—	—	17[c]	7	—	—	34	22
Indonesia	—	20	21	9	—	52	43	26
Egypt	26	27	17	10	44	44	36	31
Colombia	14	16	13	6	30	37	42	24
Thailand	15	17	8	7	—	46	46	22
Malaysia	37[b]	20	9	5	37	44	41	30
Mexico	25	22	11	5	33	44	44	27
Brazil	—	21	11	7	—	—	42	27
Taiwan	26	18	6	5	44	46	39	17
United States	12	11	9	9	20	24	24	17
Japan	23	16	8	7	34	24	17	11

Sources: Data from United Nations 1988a, Tables 12 and 21; United Nations 1970, Table 12; United Nations 1967, Table 17. For 1990, World Bank 1992b, pp. 270–71, except Taiwan data from Republic of China 1992.

Note: Countries are listed in ascending order of per capita GNP, 1990.

[a]Rates per 1,000. Many of the figures represent a five-year average, sometimes but not always centered on the year shown.

[b]1910.

[c]1953.

as incomes rose and medical knowledge advanced, but birth rates did not decline until 60 to 100 years later. Because the death rate dropped gradually, net additions to the population (helped by emigration) seldom surpassed 1 percent a year. The exceptions were the "empty lands" of North America, Australia, and New Zealand that received immigrants from Europe. There, population growth was 2 to 3 percent per year before tapering off in the first decades of the twentieth century.

In Asia, Africa, and Latin America the pattern has been different: both birth and death rates remained high until after the turn of the century (see Table 2.5). In Japan, for instance, mortality in 1920 was 23 deaths per thousand each year. With a crude birth rate of 34 per thousand, population growth was 1.1 percent per year. Excluding Malaysia, death rates fell by 4 to 9 per thousand in 1900–40: in the following 45 years, death rates have more than halved (by 12 to 15 per thousand) thanks to better public health techniques.[6] This decrease would have been most dramatic in Africa, where

[6] The major public health measures would include immunization against the major epidemics and other diseases, control of malaria, antibiotics, piped water, and, most recently, oral rehydration therapy.

death rates before the control of malaria may have been in the high forties per thousand.

This sharp decline in the crude death rate, when most of the population is rural, is the main reason for rapid population growth in CARLs. Slower growth hinges on changes in the fertility rate. As risks of rural life are diminished and more people move to urban areas, the balance of economic benefits and costs shifts toward smaller families. But there is no simple correlation between income growth and the decline in fertility rates. China and Kenya have similar income levels, yet the natural rates of population increase are 1.5 and 3.5 percent, respectively, in 1990, owing to differences in cultural values and public policy.

HOW STRUCTURAL TRANSFORMATION SHAPES AGRICULTURAL DEVELOPMENT

The degree of structural transformation also places powerful constraints on the development of agriculture. When the primary sector accounts for 50 percent or more of the labor force, there is a limit on the volume of commodity flows from agriculture to other sectors, which sets a ceiling on expansion of farm output. And to the extent that the farmers' cash receipts are held in check, so too is their ability to purchase the externally supplied inputs—tools, transport equipment, fertilizer—that will raise their productivity. By the same token, the limited farm purchasing power is a brake on expansion of nonagricultural sectors. Among those sectors, variation in the disbursement pattern of farm income leads to differential growth rates. The effects of policies on these interactions are a key part of strategy for the rural economy (see Chapter 6).

In countries where agricultural exports are not significant, farm receipts are more or less predetermined by the degree of structural transformation. For example, if 70 percent of the population is in agriculture, an "average" farm family of five has a domestic market of just over two persons; when the farm population is 40 percent, the market is 7.5 persons; and at 20 percent, the market is 20 people. So, for many CARLs the farm sector has a limited domestic market, which implies a purchasing power constraint in early structural transformation.

There are several caveats to this simple model. The income elasticity of demand for food, although less than unity, is positive so that average expenditure per person rises as the share of the nonfarm population increases. A similar bonus results from the growth in demand for agricultural inputs to the relatively fast-growing manufacturing sector. Another source of income for farm households is the growth in nonfarm activities. Finally, the most significant caveat is the degree to which these agricultural economies serve export markets, explored in a later section of this chapter and in Chapter 10 with reference to Taiwan.[7]

Farm Cash Receipts and Disbursements

How are aggregate farm cash receipts affected during structural transformation? Rising marketed shares of farm output and rising per capita consumption of agricultural products mean that the absolute volume of farm receipts (and, so, purchases in other sectors) rises continuously. But as a percentage of GDP, farm purchases fall because of the declining share of primary products in national output. And because the manufacturing sector is small in early development, agriculture's purchases have maximum quantitative impact on industrial development during this period. Finally, with the development of agriculture and the emergence of a technically mature manufacturing sector, average cash expenditures of farms rise sharply, and changes occur in the agricultural inputs and demand for consumer goods.

The impact of agriculture's purchases on other sectors of the economy, as well as the changing input configuration in the farm production function, can be brought into sharper focus by examining the pattern of farm cash disbursements. A fivefold partitioning is employed:

1. Taxes
2. Acquisition of financial assets
3. Payments to factors of production (wages, interest, rent)
4. Current inputs and capital goods employed in production
5. Final consumer goods and services

Ethiopia, Taiwan, and the United States, with agricultural labor force shares of 86 percent, 51 percent, and 7 percent, respectively, in the 1960s, are good examples of early, middle, and late structural transformation (Table 2.6).

---

[7] The foregoing determinants of the rate of growth in farm cash receipts (R'_a) can be summarized in the following expression: $R'_a = w_1 (P'_n + \eta g'_n) - w_2 M'_a + w_3 X'_a$, where P is population, η is the per capita income elasticity of demand for agricultural products, g is per capita income, and M and X represent the value of agricultural imports and exports. The primes indicate annual percentage rates of change, the subscripts a and n denote agriculture and nonagriculture, and the w's are weights that reflect each component's relative contribution to total farm receipts. This formulation requires the simplifying assumption that the terms of trade between agriculture and nonagriculture remain unchanged. Thus, although changes in the international terms of trade are captured in this equation, those in the domestic terms of trade are not. If rises in relative food prices result from failures of food production to keep pace with demand, structural transformation will be impeded so that this is not a sustainable means of increasing cash income.

Table 2.6. Farm cash expenditures on production and consumption: Ethiopia (1967), Taiwan (1967), and the United States (1961) (U.S.$ per farm and percentage breakdown)

Total cash expenditures	Ethiopia[a] $130	Taiwan[b] $1,330	United States[c] $11,939
Taxes	2.7%	4.7%	6.5%
Financial assets	2.6	6.0	4.3
Factor payments	7.7	11.0	11.5
Production expenses	25.3	32.5	45.5
Consumption expenses	61.7	45.8	32.3
Total	100.0	100.0	100.0

Source: Adapted from Johnston and Kilby 1975, pp. 72–73.
[a] Farm size 3.7 to 18.3 acres.
[b] Mean farm size 2.5 acres.
[c] Mean farm size 302 acres.

Taxes and the acquisition of financial assets represent agriculture's public and private savings, from which capital transfers to other sectors. In the three countries the tax take, wholly controlled by policy, ranges from 2.7 to 6.5 percent of receipts. Private savings (acquisition of financial assets) also include equity investment in enterprises outside the household's farming operations. Here the redoubtable Taiwanese, in part helped by a policy of maintaining inflation-adjusted positive rates of interest on time deposits (Tsiang 1987), surpass the far-wealthier American farmer's performance, so that public and private savings combined are about 11 percent in both countries. This compares with 5.3 percent in Ethiopia, where financial markets are nonexistent.

Of factor payments, the bulk of wages and rent are intrasectoral payments, whereas interest on borrowed funds flows to financial asset owners both in and outside the rural economy. In all three countries, farmers rely primarily on family labor and cultivate their own land, hence factor payments are a fraction of total outlays.[8]

The absolute level of production expenditures, agriculture's backward linkages, is a measure of how much farmers are using inputs supplied by specialist producers outside agriculture: 25 percent for Ethiopia, 33 percent for Taiwan, and 46 percent for the United States. The farther up the ladder of structural transformation, the more specialized is the farmer. Compositional differences in these expenditures reflect factor endowments. With more than 30 times the cultivated area of Taiwanese farmers, the Americans rely on land-extensive mechanized techniques; repair and depreciation account for 40 percent of production expenses. Of a much smaller outlay, the Taiwanese

[8] For Ethiopia the principal item is rent (7.5 percent), for Taiwan wages (7.9 percent) and interest (2.1 percent), and for the United States wages (6.5 percent) and rent (3.2 percent).

spent half on fertilizers and chemicals to maximize the yield of their (average) 2.5 acres. For all three, expenditure related to livestock accounted for a quarter or more of production expenses.

Expenditure on manufactured consumer goods and services, "final demand linkages," is an index to the farm family's level of economic welfare. This increases with marketed output, but at a slower pace. Consumption expenditure as a proportion of farm sales falls from 62 percent for Ethiopia to 46 percent for Taiwan to 32 percent for the United States.

There is another (and sizable) intersectoral commodity flow not picked up in farm receipts or expenditures: the value added to the farmer's food and fiber (after sale but before final consumption) by processing, storage, transport, distribution, and marketing. Their value is the difference between farm receipts and farm produce at retail or f.o.b. prices.[9]

Marketing is not important early in the structural transformation when most households produce their own food. When per capita income reaches $275 to $750 and the nonagricultural population grows from roughly 20 to 45 percent, marketed farm produce expands rapidly—on average sevenfold. Growth is more gradual (roughly twofold) as the nonfarm population reaches 70 percent of the total.

What about the influence of farm purchases and forward linkages on manufacturing development in the rural nonfarm and urban sectors? What portion is "lost" to imports? Although these expenditures rise with economic development, they fall as a percentage of GDP. So, early in the structural transformation agriculture has a big effect on manufacturing, as does farm demand on industries producing consumer rather than producer goods. The type of goods and services demanded and the different stimulative effects on nonfarm production and employment are shaped by the agricultural strategy pursued (see Chapter 6).

Farm Cash Receipts and the International Economy

As noted, export markets, and to a lesser extent import substitution, represent an important avenue for enlarging farm income. It is generally held that, owing to terms-of-trade considerations, it will be much more difficult for large countries to sell abroad the same proportion of their agricultural production as achieved by small countries.

As the figures in Table 2.7 indicate, many large countries do indeed have small export shares; Bangladesh, India, China, and Indonesia seem to fit the pattern. Yet, it is not always so. Unfavorable effects on the agriculture sec-

[9] For economies at a per capita income of about $750 and upward (in 1985 prices), the aggregate value of these "marketing services" constitutes a remarkably stable 8 to 9 percent of the GDP. Purchased inputs from other sectors (production expenses) is 2.5 to 3 percent of the GDP, or one-third the value of marketing services (Simantov 1967).

Table 2.7. Openness: Agricultural exports and cereal imports, 1984–86

	Population (millions)	Agriculture's share of GDP (%)	Proportion of farm output sold abroad (%)[a]	Potential for import substitution[b]
Bangladesh	109	48.3	2.6	93
Tanzania	25	58.5	6.7	20
India	816	32.7	2.9	8
Kenya	22	30.7	33.8	27
China	1,088	33.3	4.1	30
Indonesia	175	25.3	8.3	54
Nigeria	110	34.7	0.8	105
Egypt	50	20.0	31.8	1,590
Thailand	55	18.0	51.0	14
Colombia	32	20.0	31.8	315
Brazil	144	12.3	25.9	275
Malaysia	17	21.0	63.6	956
Mexico	84	9.7	13.6	499
Taiwan	20	6.2	32.9	—
Japan	123	3.0	4.0	5,541
United States	246	2.0	42.0	455

Sources: FAO, 1987b; World Bank 1988b.

[a]The value of agricultural exports at the farmgate is assumed to be 60% of the f.o.b. value of agricultural exports.

[b]Kilograms of cereal imports per agricultural worker.

tor's international terms of trade can be offset by several means. One is the achievement of a rate of productivity growth that exceeds the decline in the terms of trade, as in the case of Japan's silk revolution (Box 3.1). Another is diversification of agricultural exports, a strategy so successfully pursued by Taiwan. In other cases, such as Brazilian coffee, the large comparative advantage provided by commodity-specific natural resources provides some room to absorb declines in export prices. Thus, Bangladesh and Nigeria conform to the pattern of China and India, whereas fully one-quarter of Brazil's agricultural production is directed to foreign markets. For the mid-size countries of Egypt, Thailand, Malaysia, and Colombia the shares are even larger.

In some countries import substitution for foods imports can help to expand farm cash sales. The dramatic impact of the seed-fertilizer revolution in India in 1965–75 and in Indonesia (1975–85) was related to import substitution. Both were importing more than 20 percent of their foodgrains. The three-year average of cereal imports per person of the agricultural labor force is a rough index of the potential for import substitution as a way to expand farm cash sales (Table 2.7, Column 4). Comparing Malaysia and Egypt with Tanzania and Thailand suggests that cereal imports (or the lack thereof) are consistent with rapid-growing or slow-growing farm income. In Malaysia more than 60 percent of farm output is exported, a figure in line with its international comparative advantage.

POLICY IMPLICATIONS OF STRUCTURAL TRANSFORMATION

Specialization and technological change are the driving forces that transform an agrarian economy into a diversified and highly productive economy. Although agriculture predominates in early structural transformation, recent research shows that a diverse nonfarm sector also figures large in the unspecialized rural economy of CARLs. In the near term, development strategies for agriculture and rural nonfarm activities are as important for CARLs as industrial strategy is for the "newly industrialized countries" at a later stage of structural transformation.

CARLs cannot eliminate mass poverty without structural transformation, but there is a wide range of successful paths to higher productivity. A country's policy choices matter more than endowments of land, oil, timber, and other natural resources. Without the right policies, even the richest in natural resources cannot sustain productivity growth. With them, they can.

But the "right" policies also depend on a country's stage of structural transformation. So, for CARLs what does the policy dictum "getting prices right" mean, as markets for land, labor, and capital, as well as commodities, are evolving? There is no simple, single answer. Commodity market imperfections arising from poor transport, infrastructure, and communications raise the costs and risks of trade and inhibit the exchange of commodities among regions and in the world market.

CARLs embody the most powerful arguments for and against intervention in markets. Because the evolution of economic institutions, including markets, is both a cause and a consequence of structural transformation, the scope and limits of government policy vary throughout the long process of structural transformation. The plethora of plausible market imperfections, combined with expanding public expectations following social and political change, often propel governments toward intervention. Yet, limited government capacity and inevitable tensions accompanying political development easily subvert the original intent of intervention.

CHAPTER THREE

JAPAN, THE UNITED STATES, AND STRUCTURAL TRANSFORMATION

Even the mighty industrial economies of Japan and the United States were once CARLs, and their experiences hold valuable lessons for countries that today are in early structural transformation. Both Japan and the United States raised agricultural productivity through broad-based development, despite big differences in resource endowments (and history) and, so, in patterns of technological change.

These differences were most apparent before each country's structural transformation turning point. In the United States until 1920 productivity growth followed a labor-saving, land-using pattern. In Japan it was the opposite (that is, labor-using and land-saving) until the 1950s. There were important similarities, too. Both countries were pioneers in government action that increased not only the opportunities for farmers but also their ability to seize those opportunities. So, why and how did these two countries pursue agricultural strategies so well suited to their respective circumstances? And from that, what are the implications for structural transformation in today's CARLs?

JAPAN AND THE UNITED STATES AS CARLS

The United States was a CARL in the nineteenth century. In 1820 agriculture accounted for 80 percent of its labor force. By 1850 it was 55 percent, falling slowly to 40 percent by 1900. Between 1850 and 1900 the total labor force grew from 8.25 to 29 million, due to (then) unusually high rates of natural increase in the population and to immigration, especially between 1880 and 1900. That was the reason why, despite high rates of employment growth in manufacturing and other nonfarm sectors, the agricultural work force rose from 4.5 million to 11.7 million between 1850 and 1900. Indeed, it was not until 1910 that the United States reached its structural transformation turning point—that is, when the absolute size of the farm work force began to decline (see Figure 3.1).

In the 1880s in Japan three-quarters of the labor force (roughly 15.5 million) depended on agriculture, and over the next seventy-five years there was a slow decline in the absolute size of the farm work force. There also was a temporary rise after World War II, as a result partly of the wartime migration of city folk to the countryside (to avoid bombing and food shortages) and partly of the postwar return of Japanese from overseas. In the mid-1950s the farm work force peaked at 16 million before falling rapidly. Thus, Japan's structural transformation turning point is 1955 (Figure 3.1).

Compared with Japan, the United States had abundant and cheap land, but scarce and expensive labor. The differences between the two countries in labor-land ratios and in relative prices of land and labor were influenced by the timing of structural transformation as well as by resource endowments. Thus, arable land per male farm worker in the United States in 1960 was forty-eight times larger than in Japan, whereas in 1880 there was a twenty-one-fold difference. The rapid expansion of crop area in the United States was a major factor in the labor-land differential, but so too was the reduction in farm workers. By 1960 there were 50 percent fewer male workers in U.S. agriculture than in 1880; in Japan the decline was only 25 percent. Those changes in factor endowments caused a widening of the difference in relative factor prices. In 1880 188 working days were required to purchase 1 hectare of arable land in the United States; by 1960 it was 105. In Japan, the labor time needed to buy a hectare increased from roughly 1,600 to more than 3,200 days (Hayami and Ruttan 1985, pp. 165, 480–87).

This difference in factor prices meant that U.S. farmers had less incentive to increase crop yields or maintain soil fertility by manuring. According to the 1852 *Transactions* of Michigan's State Agricultural Society: "But little attention is paid to saving or applying manure; we are aware of its utility, we haul it to our fields if we find time; the low price of lands and high price of labor will not warrant the operation in all cases" (Danhof 1969, p. 260). In fact, fertilizers were not a significant input in American agriculture until the 1930s. But in Japan innovations that raised productivity and output were mainly yield-increasing. Japan drew on Justus Liebig's pioneering work in Germany on plant nutrition, and the technology that emerged was a successful mix of indigenous and borrowed elements.

Figure 3.1.   Total labor force and agricultural and nonagricultural components in the United States from 1820 and in Japan from 1885 (million people)

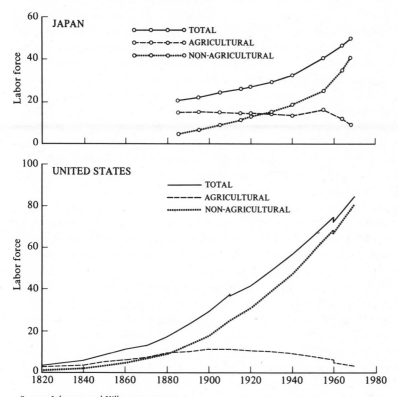

Source: Johnston and Kilby 1975, p. 194.

Despite striking differences in factor endowments, Japan and the United States had remarkably similar rates of growth in agricultural output between 1880 and 1960. Yet, agricultural productivity in the two countries increased in fundamentally different ways, demonstrating that there is no unique path to industrialization.

AGRICULTURAL CHANGE IN THE UNITED STATES

For most of the nineteenth and early twentieth centuries, a major aim of agricultural policy in the United States was to open up virgin land and to create new family farms. Mainly because of the Homestead Act of 1862, roughly one billion acres passed into private ownership—an area about three times bigger than the total acreage now under crops. And easy access to land led to a predominantly unimodal agrarian structure based on family farms (see Chapter 1, Box 1.2). America's South was an exception.

Investment was required to turn virgin land into an economic asset, but much of this was the work of settlers and draft animals that they brought to homesteads. A transport network was crucial in opening new lands—steamboats on navigable rivers and canals. But it was the railroad more than anything that linked expanding farming areas and growing urban markets of the East and, later, overseas. By lowering transportation costs, the expanding transport network played a pivotal role in raising farmgate prices. In the northern states, there were only 73 miles of railroad in 1830. Within a decade there were 3,328 miles and by 1870, 34,776 miles. Foreign investment financed much of the expansion. Immigrants were another inflow of capital, bringing energy, farm know-how, and other skills to the new and growing economy.

In 1910 the farm labor force peaked in absolute size, but 1880 had already marked the end of a long period in which the farm work force increased almost as rapidly as the total labor force. In the 1880s there ceased to be "continuity in the line of settlement," or, as the historian Frederick Jackson Turner put it, "the end of the frontier" (Lebergott 1966, p. 119). More fundamental, however, was the rapid increase in demand for labor in manufacturing, construction, and supporting services, as industry came of age. Moreover, the spread of two-bottom, five-horse ploughs, stationary threshers, and other mechanical innovations made it much easier for agriculture to release labor.

Although the labor force grew rapidly in 1820–90, averaging about 3 percent a year, concern about unemployment was limited to business cycle crises. The absence of serious problems of "labor force absorption" was due to large untapped resources. Thus, domestic demand for farm products, rather than land availability, put the reins on farm income growth.

From Subsistence to Commercial Agriculture

Despite an expanding domestic market in the nineteenth century, foreign markets for agricultural output became increasingly important—cotton exports in the cash economy of the South, and later, grain exports from the Middle West. In 1820 agriculture accounted for 83 percent of total merchandise exports and still stood at 81 percent half a century later.

American farmers and politicians knew that the growth of agricultural output depended on agricultural exports. In 1846 Senator Sidney Breeze said: "Illinois wants a market for her agricultural productions; she wants the market of the world. Ten counties of that state could supply all the home market. We want a foreign market for our produce which is now rotting in our granaries." Agriculture's exports went mainly to Europe, where costs of production of grain and other commodities were higher, despite lower wages. But exports as a source of farm cash income peaked in the last three decades of the 1800s. Domestic urban demand, however, sustained agricultural profitability, and increases in farm cash income transformed semisubsistence agriculture to commercial farming. The proportion of agricultural output sold in urban markets increased from roughly 20 percent in 1820 to 40 percent in 1870 (Danhof 1969).

By mid-century this spreading commercialization was generally thought essential to progress. A writer in the 1850s, commenting on conditions a generation earlier, observed: "The great effort then was for every farmer to produce anything he required within the circle of his own family; and he was esteemed the best farmer, to use a phrase of the day, 'who did everything within himself'." Then, farmers relied heavily on farm-supplied resources and "necessity was converted into a virtue." Moreover, "the disapproval that had long attached to the purchase of anything that could be produced persisted for some time, operating to restrict the amount of specialization that was acquired" (Danhof 1969, pp. 16–17). The extended cash market enabled a farmer to specialize instead of being a "jack-of-all-trades."

Mechanical Innovations and Acreage Expansions

Growth of markets and innovation provided farmers with opportunity and means to expand the cultivated area. It was not until the 1930s that increases in yield per acre began to make a significant contribution to productivity growth.

Inventors, tinkerers, and machinists, working closely with local farmers, were crucial in the design and manufacture of increasingly sophisticated farm equipment, which has been the major factor in raising labor productivity in U.S. agriculture over the past 150 years. Mechanical innovations in 1820–60 in particular led to "more effective application of horse power to every critical task in growing crops" (Danhof 1969, pp. 181, 229). Such progress was due to the ingenuity and persistence of blacksmiths and tinkers and to "the zeal of the widely scattered farmers who purchased the machines as they were offered and operated them under difficult conditions" of poor design and crude construction. Although the specific innovations differ, this process is identical to farm equipment development in Taiwan (see Chapter 6).

Cooperation between farmers and designers and manufacturers of equipment directed inventive activity toward the critical needs of the farms and the elimination of defects in early models (Olmstead and Rhode 1988). Large machinery manufacturers could pour resources into research and development, but small firms, working closely with farmers, had an edge in design.

Much mass-produced, large-scale farm equipment is based on designs of small machine shops that sell rights to large corporations.

Early reductions in labor requirements for harvesting and threshing wheat were dramatic—from 10 to 2 hours per acre for harvesting and 8 to only 1 hour for threshing (Danhof 1944, p. 137). There was a fourfold increase in output per hour of labor in grain production in the United States between 1840–60 and 1900–1910, virtually all due to mechanization (Parker and Klein 1966).

Changes in Farm Size and Agrarian Structure

In 1900 almost half of American farms were between 50 and 175 acres. The most numerous were 100 to 175 acres, which included the quarter-section (160-acre) farms distributed to homesteaders by the U.S. government. This size was most pronounced in the North Central and Western divisions (Figure 3.2, Panels C and E), where most settlement occurred after the Homestead Act. Farms of 50 to 100 acres were the next largest group, accounting for just under 24 percent of farms; less than 1 percent were farms of less than 3 acres or more than 1,000 acres (U.S. Department of Commerce 1902, p. xliv).

In at least four of the five divisions of the continental United States in 1900 there were clear unimodal distributions of land and farms (Figure 3.2). In the North Atlantic and North Central divisions (Panels A and C) these units were mainly owner-operated, the quintessential American "family farm." The huge cattle ranches of Montana, Wyoming, and other western states are responsible for the concentration of larger-size farms in the Western Division (Panel E). As can be seen, the combination of cropland and livestock lends a largely spurious appearance of bimodality. Extensive livestock farming in western Kansas, Nebraska, the Dakotas, and Texas also skews land distributions in the central divisions (Panels C and D). In these semiarid areas intensive crop production is impossible without irrigation and often unsustainable, even with it.

In the South Atlantic and South Central divisions (Panels B and D) the unimodal distribution of farms masks a skewed distribution of landownership. Cash tenancy and sharecropping were common, and the typical farm was smaller than in the rest of the United States. In 1900 most farms in the South were 20 to 50 acres, including the typical tenanted cotton farm, "40 acres and a mule." Where soils were heavier, one mule power limited planting and, so, farm size to 20 acres. After the Civil War the breakup of plantations and leasing of subunits shifted the agrarian structure of the South. Average farm size in the South Atlantic division fell by more than 70 percent from more than 375 acres in 1850 to 108 acres in 1900 (U.S. Department of Commerce 1902, p. xxi).

Mechanical innovations that changed the shape of American agriculture evolved in response to the increase in the cost of labor relative to machinery. That and economic developments led to an increase in average farm size without much change in the family farm. Between 1930 and 1970 there was a rapid decline in the farm work force and in the number of farms, whose average size rose from 157 to 374 acres. But labor inputs per farm changed little. In 1930, it was 1.42 years of family labor plus 0.49 years of hired labor; in 1970, it was 1.36 years of family labor and 0.48 years of hired labor (Kislev and Peterson 1982, p. 588).

Until World War II large-scale crop production was confined mainly to California and Florida, accounting in 1929 for only 5 percent of total production. By 1964 it was 44 percent, and in 1982 13.4 percent of farms (with sales of over $100,000) accounted for 72.5 percent of all sales (Krause and Kyle 1970, p. 749; Raup 1985, pp. 7, 8).

Peculiarities of the American South

The American South is the exception to the broad-based agricultural change in the United States. The advent of railroads and the influx of immigrants largely bypassed the South (and its plantations) in the nineteenth century. Indeed, it remained isolated from these developments until 1940.

Before the Civil War the South's economy was based on slavery, and its legacy was the persistence of a low-wage labor market and an abundance of labor bottled up in southern agriculture. Not until the growing demand for labor during World War II did the South begin to experience the rising cost of labor that characterized the rest of the American economy for most of the nineteenth and twentieth centuries.[1]

The end of slavery changed the organization of plantation agriculture. Most land came to be cultivated by tenants or sharecroppers. Hiring laborers indirectly as tenants was most profitable for landlords because tenant families had an incentive to work hard on their own plot whereas the problems of shirking were great with large labor gangs on plantations. Wages of black and white farm laborers were similar, but discrimination against blacks meant that more whites could climb the "agricultural ladder," moving from wage laborer to sharecropper or tenant and, perhaps, even to owner-cultivator.

The South's isolated low-wage labor market was weakened during World War I, when many black and "poor white" families moved to the North and established a foothold for later migrants. The New Deal legislation of the 1930s raised the lethal blow to this repressive system that wartime labor demand delivered in the 1940s. Minimum wage legislation had little impact in

[1] Gavin Wright (1986) describes the transition in the South from the political economy of an isolated, low-wage labor market to a region actively attracting northern industry.

Figure 3.2.   Distribution of number of operational units and of area of farms by size for five divisions of the continental United States, 1900

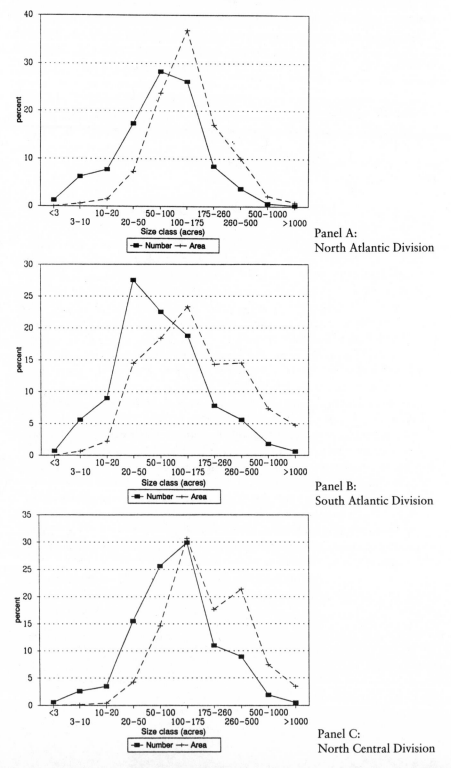

Panel A:
North Atlantic Division

Panel B:
South Atlantic Division

Panel C:
North Central Division

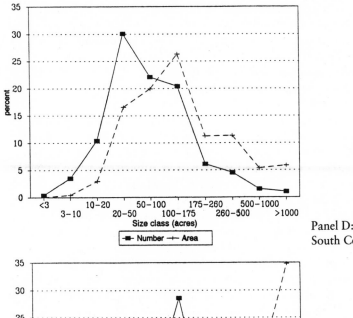

Panel D:
South Central Division

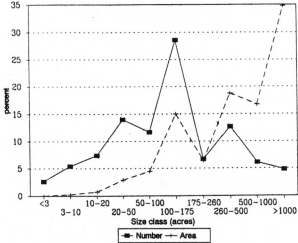

Panel E:
Western Division

Source: U.S. Department of Commerce 1902.

Key: *Number of farms* means number of farm operating units. *Area* is "improved area," including crop-land, permanent pastures, permanent meadows, orchards, and vineyards.

Notes: The North Atlantic Division includes Maine, New Hampshire, Vermont, Massachusetts, Rhode Island, Connecticut, New York, New Jersey, and Pennsylvania; the South Atlantic Division includes Delaware, Maryland, the District of Columbia, Virginia, West Virginia, North Carolina, South Carolina, Georgia, and Florida; the North Central Division includes Ohio, Indiana, Illinois, Michigan, Wisconsin, Minnesota, Iowa, Missouri, North Dakota, South Dakota, Nebraska, and Kansas; the South Central Division includes Kentucky, Tennessee, Alabama, Mississippi, Louisiana, Texas, Oklahoma, and Arkansas; the Western Division includes Montana, Wyoming, Colorado, New Mexico, Arizona, Utah, Nevada, Idaho, Washington, Oregon, and California.

the North but was surprisingly effective in raising wages for unskilled workers in the South. More important, however, the New Deal also provided for the payment of acreage allotments to restrict production and raise prices. This had the unintended effect of encouraging landowners to terminate tenancies. By shifting to direct cultivation, landowners eligible for these allotments could retain the whole subsidy rather than share it with tenants as the federal law required.

The end of the long isolation of the southern economy had dramatic effects, particularly on the pace of technological change. With a tightening labor market, there was a push to perfect a mechanical cotton picker. In 1950 only 8 percent of the United States cotton crop was mechanically harvested; by 1964 it was almost 80 percent, reaching 100 percent in 1972 (Wright 1986, p. 244). With swift mechanization came a sharp decline in the agricultural labor force between 1930 and 1969. In 1930 white tenants and sharecroppers numbered 1.1 million; in 1969, 118,000. For blacks, the decline was from about 700,000 to only 18,000 (Wright 1986, p. 245).

The Mississippi Delta typifies the sequence of changes from farm mechanization in the South (Day 1967). In 1940–49 there was an increase in off-farm demand for labor and in cotton acreage that offset the effects of labor-saving techniques on aggregate labor demand. For land preparation tractors replaced mules, which were still used for interrow cultivation. Picking of cotton and maize was done by hand. In the next stage there was complete mechanization of preharvest operations, except for some hand weeding of cotton and maize, and harvesting, except for hand picking of cotton. Finally, mechanical cotton pickers were adopted, and cropping became less labor-intensive, when, for example, soybeans replaced cotton and maize.

The effect of early technological change was to push sharecroppers off the farm, but not yet out of the region. Seasonal demands for labor increased, and by ending sharecropping contracts landowners created a "conveniently located labor pool that could be inexpensively transported to surrounding plantations and farms" (Day 1967, p. 442). In later mechanization, cotton pickers and chemical weed control pushed labor out of agriculture and the region. Between 1940 and 1949, the labor input per unit of output declined from 33.5 to 19.4 hours per hundredweight; by 1957 it was only 2.4 hours.[2]

The exceptionally rapid pace of agricultural change in the South was possible because of the technological advances already made and adopted elsewhere in the United States—just as today's CARLs can borrow existing technology. The accelerated pace of change in the South after 1940 contrasts

[2] Paradoxically the Freedom Summer of 1964 and other changes set in motion by the Civil Rights movement, accelerated labor-saving innovations. These changes raised the cost of hiring farm labor as perceived by the farm operator above the actual cost as determined by the prevailing wage rate. They also weakened the force of noneconomic considerations that previously slowed the rate of adoption (Gotsch 1972, p. 340).

sharply with the earlier, slower, trial-and-error progress in the rest of the United States. Innovations, such as herbicides, had been developed elsewhere, and the research and development techniques already evolved reduced the time required for technological problem solving.

AGRICULTURAL CHANGE IN JAPAN

In Japan yield-increasing innovations were more important (and occurred earlier) than in the United States. In the Meiji period (1868–1912) there were attempts to mechanize with farm equipment developed in the United States and England. This failed because the machinery had been designed for agricultural economies with scarcer farm labor and larger fields. Only in sparsely populated Hokkaido did the imported equipment find a place.

Early Research and Biochemical Innovations

Much of Japan's early innovation success was based on seed-fertilizer combinations that later epitomized the "Green Revolution." In the pre-Meiji period some Japanese farmers had developed relatively high-yielding, fertilizer-responsive crop varieties, as well as simple improvements in cultivation techniques. But severe restrictions on internal movement and communications had limited their spread countrywide. With the Meiji Restoration yields increased substantially as the proven techniques and varieties spread throughout the country.

Use of commercial fertilizers had begun to expand as early as 1880 thanks in part to German advisers who brought knowledge of Liebig's work on plant nutrition.[3] Organic fertilizers—fish meal and soybean cake—were the first major commercial fertilizers, but farm-supplied manure and compost continued to be significant nutrient sources for some time. In the 1920s chemical fertilizers became available in bulk and at prices competitive with the cost of organic fertilizers (commercial and on-farm). By then, the use of manure and compost required farm labor that could be applied more profitably in other ways.

Organized agricultural research in Japan probably dates to 1882, when Tokitaka Yokoi, director of the Fukuoka Agricultural Experiment Station, developed a technique of placing rice in salt water to separate sound from immature seed—a simple refinement of a practice that Yokoi had observed

[3] The German agricultural advisers Oskar Kellner and Max Fesca, who came to Japan in 1881 and joined the faculty of agriculture at Komaba, brought knowledge of agricultural chemistry and soil science. It is almost certain, too, that they were familiar with the first publicly supported agricultural experiment station established in Germany (at Mockern, Saxony) in 1852.

among a few innovative farmers. This was the start of the distinctive synthesis known as the "Meiji Technology." Researchers at experiment stations directed the extension activities of agricultural associations, ensuring that research was relevant and widely applied.

Research techniques gradually became more sophisticated. A project to improve rice varieties by pure line selection initiated in 1905 was followed by one for artificial cross-breeding. But a major step was in 1925, when an "Assigned Experiment System" established a nationally coordinated crop-breeding program to make efficient use of the few agricultural scientists with training and skills for crop breeding (Hayami 1975, pp. 65, 144–46). Such selection and breeding of high-yield, fertilizer-responsive varieties of rice fostered an efficient "fertilizer consuming rice culture" (Ogura 1963).[4]

There are strong complementarities between improved varieties, increased use of fertilizers, and adequate water control. In the Meiji period therefore, public investment, legislation, and local institutional innovations to improve the land infrastructure became increasingly important (Hayami 1975, chap. 7). There were also more projects to improve water control by realigning fields and irrigation channels and providing drainage for individual fields (Hayami 1975, pp. 71–74). Simple mechanical innovations that reduced labor bottlenecks (such as the rotary foot-pedal thresher that reduced the seasonal labor peak at harvest) were of far less importance than in the United States.

Growth in Agricultural Exports and Farm Cash Receipts

Productivity increases in Japan's sericulture were important because silk earned foreign exchange to finance the imports of machinery and raw materials essential to development (Box 3.1). Moreover, silk and silk fabrics were produced almost entirely from indigenous resources, whereas cotton textiles required sizable imports of raw materials. Between 1868 and 1930 silk (and fabrics) averaged 42 percent of merchandise exports.

With the rapid expansion of silk (and fabric) exports world prices fell, but the effect was offset by increases in productivity. Thus, technical advances sustained the profitability of sericulture until the emergence of nylon as a competitor—and more profitable alternatives in Japanese agriculture. But it is doubtful that any alternative could have made more efficient use of Japan's resources or generated such foreign exchange in the sixty years to 1930.

[4] Semidwarf, fertilizer-responsive varieties of wheat were also developed. One variety (Norin 10) was introduced to the Pacific Northwest of the United States shortly after World War II. It was the source of the famous Gaines variety, the origin of genes for the varieties that led to large increases in wheat yields in Mexico (Chapter 10) and that played a crucial role in Asia's "Green Revolution."

Box 3.1.   Japan's Silk Revolution

Thanks to research and technological innovations, there was a spectacular increase in productivity in Japan's silk industry between the 1880s and the 1930s. The seventeenfold increase in the output of raw silk was more than twice the increase in cocoon production, which in turn was nearly twice the increase in the acreage of mulberry trees, whose leaves are food for silkworms. Research at the Tokyo Imperial University in 1909 led to the development of hybrids between Chinese and Japanese silkworms that were less susceptible to disease and spun larger cocoons. As a result, the yield of raw silk per metric ton of cocoons rose from about 75 to almost 140 kg between 1908–12 and 1938–42.

Moreover, because of improvements in fertilization, the production of mulberry leaves rose. Productivity was further enhanced by better methods of handling leaves. There was progress, too, in hatching and rearing the silkworms. Artificial hatching was especially significant because an autumn crop of cocoons then became almost as important as the (naturally hatched) spring crop. This was the main reason for a 60 percent rise in cocoon production between 1911–20 and 1931–40, despite an increase in mulberry acreage of less than 25 percent. The more striking increase of nearly 150 percent in the output of raw silk of more than 1 million farm households in the same period owed much to increased specialization and efficiency in producing silkworm eggs, organizational innovations (such as forward-purchasing contracts between large silk breeders and farmers or associations of sericulturists), and other measures that increased efficiency and standardized quality.

Unimodal Agrarian Structure in Japan

The distribution of farms by size in Japan has been remarkably unimodal, and until the late 1960s, there was little change in their number (Table 3.1). Between 1880 and 1960 agricultural and overall economic development generally benefited greatly from agricultural strategies that fostered widespread increases in productivity and output among Japan's small-scale farmers. Postwar land reform had remarkably little effect on the size distribution of farm operational units, but it did change landownership—and that had sweeping economic and political consequences. The most apparent was the increased purchasing power among most of the rural population, when former tenants no longer had to make large rental payments.

Agriculture's Role in Development

Japanese agriculture propelled economic development. Agriculture's rising productivity financed investments in infrastructure and in new manufacturing, commercial, and transport enterprises that became dominant

Table 3.1. Number and size distribution of Japanese farms for selected years, 1908–70

Years	Number of farms (millions)	Percentage distribution by size class (ha)[a]					
		<0.5	0.5–1	1–2	2–3	3–5	>5
1908	5.4	37	39	20	6	3	1
1920	5.5	35	33	21	6	3	2
1940	5.4	33	33	25	6	2	1
1960	6.1	38	32	24	4	2	1
1970	5.3	38	30	24	5	2	1

Source: Hayami 1975, p. 9.
[a]May not add to 100 because of rounding.

elements in the Japanese economy. Taxation, especially in the nineteenth century, was used to transfer resources from agriculture to the more rapidly growing sectors. In 1873 the new land tax was set at 3 percent of the market price of land—roughly 30 percent of the yield for irrigated rice land and 20 percent for dry land (Hirschmeier and Yui 1975, p. 83). Unlike a tax on output, this did not undermine production incentives, but it probably increased farmers' incentives to raise yields.[5] Indeed, agriculture accounted for 85 percent of tax revenues in 1888–92 and for still some 40 percent in 1918–22.

From 1887 to 1936 investment by government, excluding military expenditure, was about 30 percent of gross domestic fixed capital formation. Such investments were mainly in extending and improving railways, establishing "model" factories, and subsidizing the merchant marine. The reverse flow of funds to agriculture was limited, although funding of agricultural research, rural infrastructure, and some other public goods and services was of strategic importance.

In intersectoral flows of private capital in Japan there was a net outflow from agriculture. Deposits of farmers in cooperative banks and other financial institutions were much larger than borrowings by farmers (Kato 1966, pp. 8–11). In the Meiji period the substantial savings by agricultural landowners played a big role in establishing and operating financial institutions and in launching many small-scale rural factories.

---

[5] Such a tax would have been impractical in the land-abundant United States, especially on the frontier where administrative capacity was patchy. Nineteenth-century U.S. agriculture was taxed indirectly, however, through import tariffs that raised the domestic price of industrial goods relative to farm products. As will be discussed, the "unequal treaties" imposed on Japan capped import tariffs and, as a consequence, shielded Japanese agriculture from the adverse effects of import-substituting industrialization strategies.

Table 3.2. Indices of output, inputs, and total factor productivity in the United States and Japan, 1880, 1920, and 1960

	United States			Japan		
	1880	1920	1960	1880	1920	1960
Output (net of seed & feed)	100	180	340	100	205	334
Total inputs	100	184	193	100	119	174
Total factor productivity	100	98	176	100	172	192

Source: Adapted from Hayami and Ruttan 1985, pp. 480–87.

AGRICULTURAL PRODUCTIVITY GROWTH

From 1880 to 1960 the 2.4-fold increase in output in the United States was just slightly greater than in Japan (see Table 3.2). The increase in total inputs was also faster in the United States, however. Thus, in Japan, the 92 percent rise in total factor productivity (net output per unit of inputs) was greater than the 76 percent increase in the United States. There are striking differences in the timing of high and low rates of growth in Japan and the United States. From 1880 to 1920 there was rapid output growth in Japan, but growth in input use was limited. In the United States the growth of output was slower, but the increase in use of inputs was more rapid. In the next forty years, the picture was reversed (Figure 3.3).

These contrasting patterns were magnified by changes in total factor productivity, which increased by more than 70 percent in Japan between 1880 and 1920 but declined slightly in the United States. Conversely, in 1920–60 there was an 80 percent increase in factor productivity in the United States that explains most of the increase in output. In Japan the rise in factor productivity was slightly more than 10 percent.

Differences in types of inputs (not just levels) are at the heart of these contrasting patterns of productivity growth. In Japan the growth of factor productivity in 1880–1920 followed a *labor-using, land-saving pattern of agricultural development*, built on yield-increasing innovations that intensified agricultural production on scarce land. Stagnant factor productivity in the United States during the same period reflects horizontal expansion on to new land in a *labor-saving, land-using pattern of agricultural development* based on new mechanical technology, not on rising crop yields.

Saving Labor and Using Land in the United States, 1880–1920

Arable land in the United States more than doubled between 1880 and 1920, but output per hectare fell, partly because of shifts to areas of lower rainfall. But public policy and farmers' efforts were aimed mainly at expanding the cul-

Figure 3.3. Changes in total output, total input, and total productivity in the United States and Japan, 1880–1980

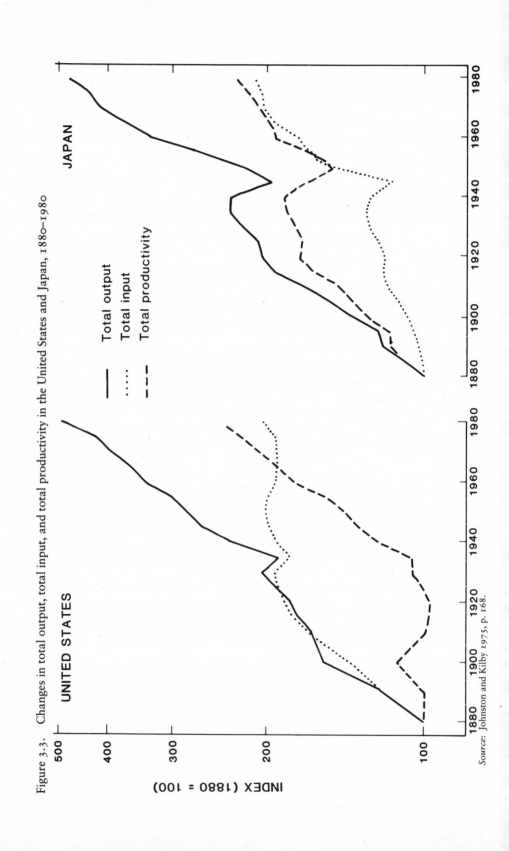

tivated area and the acreage cultivated per worker. Moreover, plant-breeding strategies in the United States were not very effective. The emphasis was on protective research (for example, in developing rust-resistant wheats to maintain yields), and scant attention was given to developing fertilizer-responsive crop varieties. In fact, because of this low-caliber scientific research, yield-increasing innovations in the United States were neglected until the 1930s.

Faster Productivity Growth in the United States, 1920–1940

America's history of steady or declining yields ended with an average annual increase of 1.4 percent in 1920–40 and a still higher 2.1 percent in 1940–60. Hybrid varieties of maize and the increasing use of fertilizer that began in the mid-1930s were mainly responsible. Between 1940 and 1950 fertilizer per hectare of cropped land in the United States rose from 11 to 25 kg. In 1960 it was 49 kg, but that was only slightly above Japan's 45 kg per hectare used in 1915 and less than a fifth of the 272 kg per hectare used in 1960.

Average increases in U.S. farm output of 1.9 percent a year in 1940–60, when the rise in total inputs was a mere 0.1 percent, resulted partly from a buoyant economy that enabled the large nonfarm sector to absorb workers from agriculture at 3.7 percent a year. In 1960–80 the decline in the male farm work force, at 3.8 percent annually, reduced the labor force in 1980 to 1.8 million, down from 4 million in 1960 (Hayami and Ruttan 1985, pp. 120, 167, 480). In addition, with yield increases averaging a record 2.1 percent a year, output per male worker tripled.

Using Labor and Saving Land in Japan, 1880–1960

Thanks to an emphasis on yield-increasing innovations, agricultural output per hectare in Japan in 1880 exceeded levels reached 80 years later in Bangladesh, India, Pakistan, and the Philippines (Table 3.3). But because agricultural land was limited relative to Japan's large agricultural work force, output per worker in 1880 was only slightly above the 1960 levels of Bangladesh and India and below those for Pakistan and the Philippines. By 1960 Japanese productivity had increased more than fourfold and was three to five times higher than for those four countries. Driven by increasing output per hectare between 1880 and 1960, labor productivity in Japan rose continuously, except for stagnation in 1920–40 (Box 3.2). Because of limited increases in cultivated land and small declines in the work force over those 80 years, increases in area cultivated per worker contributed much less.

In Japan between 1950 and 1960 farm output increased by 4.4 percent a year helped by an increase in power tillers from 89,000 to 514,000 in 1955–59 (Tsuchiya 1969, p. 156). Net and gross value added in agriculture

Table 3.3. Labor and land productivities and man-to-land ratios in Japan and selected Asian countries

	Agricultural output per male farm worker (wheat units)	Agricultural output per hectare of farmland (wheat units)	Agricultural land area per male worker (ha)
Japan			
1878–82	2.5	2.9	0.9
1898–1902	3.4	3.6	0.9
1933–37	7.1	5.5	1.3
1957–62	10.7	7.5	1.4
Other Asian countries, 1960			
Bangladesh	2.0	2.5	0.8
India	2.2	1.1	2.0
Pakistan	3.1	0.9	3.5
Philippines	3.3	2.1	1.6

Source: Japan figures are from Hayami 1975, p. 8; data for other Asian countries are from Hayami and Ruttan 1985, p. 120.

Notes: *Output in wheat units* is the gross agricultural output net of intermediate products, such as seed and feed, with individual products aggregated by their price relative to the price of a ton of wheat. *Agricultural land area* includes pasture land. Also see note 6 of Chapter 1.

grew at 4 and 4.2 percent, respectively.[6] Yield increases were based on plant breeding and other biological advances, as well as new industrial inputs, such as vinyl sheeting used to cover rice seedlings to allow earlier transplanting and to reduce frost damage.

THE POLITICAL ECONOMY OF AGRICULTURAL DEVELOPMENT

Before the structural transformation turning points in the United States and Japan, the initiatives of their governments, of farmers, and of other rural entrepreneurs were remarkably apt for the conditions—and remarkably successful in furthering agricultural development and economic growth. Why? The induced-innovation model provides a basic explanation that fits the contrasting patterns of productivity growth in Japan and the United States (Box 3.3).

As Hayami and Ruttan write, "A common thread of the success in both countries . . . was the capacity to develop agricultural technology to facilitate the substitution of relatively abundant factors for scarce factors in accordance with market price signals" (1985, p. 197). This process has been

[6] After 1960 the pattern of change was reversed. With the rapid decline of Japan's farm work force from the mid-1950s, the area cultivated per worker almost doubled, whereas the increase in yield per hectare in 1960–80 was just over 40 percent. As a result output per male worker increased 2.7 times. But analysis of contemporary Japanese agriculture by Van der Meer and Yamada (1990) suggests that economic performance since 1960 has been poor.

Box 3.2.   Stagnation in Japanese Agriculture, 1920–40

Between 1920 and 1940 agricultural progress and economic transformation in Japan were seriously retarded. During the 1920s, especially, the rate of increase in agricultural output was slow in comparison with earlier decades, and there was a sharp reduction in the rate of increase in total factor productivity in the 1930s as well as in the 1920s.

By 1920 considerable structural transformation had taken place, and the non-farm sectors weighed much more heavily—48 percent of the total labor force compared with only about 25 percent in the 1880s. Hence, the agricultural work force would have begun to decline significantly in absolute size during the 1920s if the growth of nonfarm employment had continued at the fairly rapid rates that prevailed during the earlier decades. In fact, nonfarm employment grew at only 1.8 percent a year during 1920–40; and much of the increase in the off-farm labor force was in self-employment in low-productivity service activities.

Slow growth of farm output and the limited decline in the farm labor force were the principal factors accounting for the sharply reduced growth of factor productivity in 1920–40. The most obvious factor limiting the growth of demand for farm output in Japan was the expansion of food imports from Taiwan and Korea, which satisfied most of the increase in demand after 1920. High prices, which provoked the rice riots at the end of World War I, gave rise to concern about the country's "food problem" and led to the adoption of vigorous measures to expand rice production in Taiwan and Korea, which were then Japanese colonies. This resulted in rapid growth of rice exports to Japan, and the "food problem" quickly gave way to an "agricultural problem"—concern with the low prices and depressed economic conditions affecting Japanese agriculture. The price of rice declined at an average annual rate of 2 percent between 1920 and 1935, and domestic production grew at a rate of only 0.4 percent, reducing farm cash receipts from this major crop (Hayami and Ruttan 1971, pp. 221–26).

decisive in the response of the private sector in each country, but it is easy to overstate the role of relative prices in government decisions on agricultural research and other public programs.[7] Although the appropriate response (by farmers, farm-input suppliers, other rural traders, scientists, and administrators) to changes in relative prices is a necessary condition for agri-

[7] Hayami and Ruttan recognize that market forces are only part of the story. In a monograph with Thirtle, Ruttan quotes Paul David's observation that neoclassical analysis is a "system of thought which in its pure form happens to be fundamentally ahistorical, if not actually anti-historical." They go on to recognize the need "to come to grips with historically contingent events" in order to understand the process of technological change (Thirtle and Ruttan 1986, p. 130). The factor prices at the heart of the Hayami-Ruttan induced innovation model have the advantage, however, of being quantifiable. From an analytical perspective, a disadvantage of strategic notions (Box 3.4) as a complementary perspective is that policymakers' beliefs are neither quantifiable nor even observable with any certainty. This problem is unavoidable in analysis of development strategy (see Chapter 12).

Box 3.3.   The Induced-Innovation Hypothesis

The idea of *induced technological innovation*, introduced by John Hicks in his *Theory of Wages*, is that prices of labor, land, and other factors of production influence patterns of productivity growth and in particular that changes in relative factor prices induce innovations that save scarce, expensive factors and use the abundant and inexpensive. The resulting *bias of technological change* is the shift in factor proportions, the ratio of land to labor, for example, measured at constant factor prices. Of course, a cost-reducing innovation may mean that use *per unit* of output decreases simultaneously for several factors. Nevertheless, as shown in the two-factor framework of the figure (with labor and land as the factors), such changes also can alter factor proportions.

In the figure unit-output curves T^1, T^2, T^3, and T^4 represent cost-saving technologies compared to unit-output curve T^0. The five points A^0, A^1, A^2, A^3, and A^4 are the least-cost combinations of land and labor for their respective technologies at prevailing factor prices (indicated by the slope of either of the lines DE or FG). But although total factor costs of one unit of, say, wheat are the same at points A^1, A^2, A^3, and A^4, the cost to produce one wheat unit is higher at A^0. To demonstrate, first, compare A^0 and A^1. Less labor and land are required—in equal proportions—to produce a wheat unit at A^1 than at A^0. The move from A^0 to A^1 lowers total costs but does not change the land-labor ratio. Thus, the move from A^0 to A^1 (a shift in technology from T^0 to T^1) is *neutral*, or *unbiased*. The cost-saving shift from A^0 to A^2 also reduces use of both factors per wheat unit, but the reduction in land is much greater than the drop in labor. In Hicksian jargon T^2 is a *land-saving, labor-using innovation* relative to T^0 because, measured at constant prices, the land-labor ratio falls. Similarly, T^3 is a *labor-saving, land-using innovation* relative to T^0 because the land-labor ratio rises in a shift from A^0 to A^3. The labor-saving bias is even stronger for T^4, the only case in this example where cost-saving innovation lowers yields relative to T^0 (with prices held constant).

Extensions of the induced-innovation hypothesis by Hayami and Ruttan (1971, 1985) show that economic efficiency of any path to productivity growth in agriculture depends on factor endowments. The contrasting patterns of Japan and the United States epitomize this: the land-saving bias in Japan dovetails with its limited land endowment, and the labor-saving bias in the United States fits its abundant land and relatively expensive labor. Work by Hayami and Ruttan (1971, 1985) and other country studies provide support for the hypothesis at the aggregate level.

Microeconomic mechanisms underpinning this aggregate hypothesis are clearest for the labor-saving, land-using pattern. Because land was relatively cheap and labor scarce in the United States, the scope for cost reduction was greatest through animal-powered (and later machine-powered) technology that substituted for human labor. Potential profits inspired efforts to meet this demand for innovative, labor-saving farm implements in nineteenth-century America. Thus, relative factor endowments, expressed through market prices, steered innovation and adoption toward a labor-saving bias.

Box 3.3   (*continued*)

Biases of technological change with two factors of production, labor and land

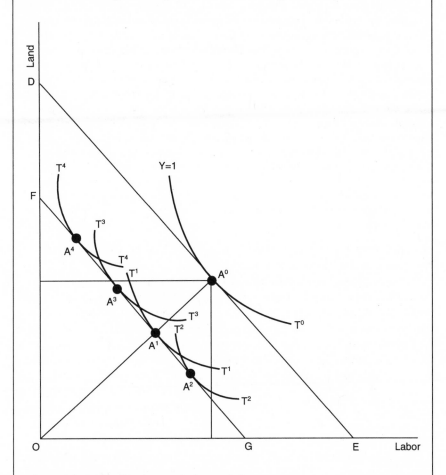

Source: Adapted from Binswanger and others 1978, Figure 2.1, p. 19.

Private rewards for innovation depend on patents, copyright, and legal redress for infringements. It was hard for many early U.S. inventors to capture the profits from mechanical innovations. For seed-fertilizer technology underlying land-saving productivity growth in Japan and particularly for agronomic practices (information about timing and placement of fertilizer, for example), it is often impractical to charge adopters. Thus, market mechanisms alone generate inadequate innovative activity.

Box 3.3 *(continued)*

Hayami and Ruttan have drawn attention to *induced institutional innovation*, especially when inducement mechanisms fail through markets. Incentives for research on agronomic practices, for example, could be met by public funding of agricultural research institutions. But the success of such efforts is not ensured in the absence of the market test that directs innovative activity toward an appropriate bias. Ruttan and Hayami (1990, p. 103) suggest that the appropriate response of research scientists in public institutions depends on their interaction with farmers. In short, agricultural scientists must view farmers as their clients. This client-driven ideal seems to have prevailed in the United States and Japan. Unfortunately, institutional incentives, social conventions, and misguided strategic notions (Box 3.4 and Chapter 4) can make it difficult to achieve this ideal in CARLs, especially where a bimodal agrarian structure creates a small but powerful group of large-scale farmers who set the research agenda.

This box draws heavily on Binswanger and others 1978, pp. 18–22, and Hayami and Ruttan 1985.

cultural development, the relative prices of land, labor, and capital also are outcomes of institutions and policies.

There are long lags between a decision to establish, say, an agricultural research institute and the time when it contributes to agricultural innovations. The development of such institutions also influences the technological innovations ultimately produced. If, for instance, Japanese policymakers had persisted in borrowing farm equipment from the United States and the United Kingdom, the development path might have been rockier and closer to those followed by the U.S.S.R., Mexico, and Tanzania (Chapters 9, 10, and 11). Instead, Japanese policies favored broad-based efforts to increase yields. Similarly, a different rural economy would have emerged in the United States if the plantation system of the South, instead of the family farms of the Northeast, had been the model for westward expansion.

Agricultural change in both Japan and the United States was based on far-sighted policy decisions that influenced (rather than responded to) relative factor prices.[8] Inevitably, this involved trial and error but also "the derivation of aspirations from experience rather than from imitation" (Bruton 1983, p. 44). So it is necessary to distinguish between *modernization* (that is, borrowing prototypical means and prescribed ends) and an indigenous policy process that generates both changing preferences about outcomes and changing capacities to produce outcomes. Although the Meiji reformers have

[8] This is all the more remarkable because these decisions were made without the methods required to analyze these choices and their consequences (such as project appraisal techniques and computable general equilibrium models).

been portrayed as "rational shoppers" for organizational models, their efforts to establish public institutions (such as police and postal services) depended as much on Japanese innovation as state of the art elsewhere in the world (Westney 1987).

Agricultural development in the United States and Japan was shaped by several "strategic notions" (Box 3.4). These influenced the interrelated development of (1) science, experimentation, and increasingly productive agricultural technologies, (2) interacting development institutions, and (3) education and other aspects of human capital formation. Unlike in some of today's CARLs, there never were serious doubts among policymakers in either country about the feasibility or desirability of broad-based agricultural development.

Strategic Choices in the United States

Five types of institutions interacted to transform U.S. agriculture (Bonnen 1987): (1) farmer organizations, (2) land grant colleges and universities, (3) the Department of Agriculture, (4) private markets and firms that provided purchased inputs to farmers as well as marketing farm products, and (5) local, state, and national political institutions. Not all groups had a voice in this coalition. Sharecroppers pushed off Southern farms in the 1950s, for example, and until recently farm laborers in the Southwest and urban consumers. Nor was there absence of conflict: witness farmers' complaints about railroads' monopolistic freight pricing. But because of the unimodal structure of U.S. agriculture and the abundance of land in the nineteenth century, the institutions that served farmers broadly served the interests of most of the rural population.

These institutions played a pivotal role in the political economy of U.S. agricultural development through systemwide decision making by consensus (rather than command), through the articulation of teaching, research, extension, and farm groups in the system, and through decentralized decision making. Although articulation of the system of institutions is necessary for coordinating functions, decentralization allows adaptations to location-specific farming environments and responses to political, social, and cultural variations.

There were two chance elements in the evolution of these developmental institutions. First, land grant colleges preceded the nationwide system of experiment stations. As a result, the colleges played a key role in agricultural research, as well as teaching, unlike the usual arrangement whereby research is assigned to a branch of the ministry of agriculture. Second, when the Congress set up an extension service in 1914 the land grant colleges were already a potent political force in command of teaching and research, so that it was logical to add extension as a third function.

Box 3.4.   Strategic Notions

Agricultural development strategy depends on chance alignments of economic circumstances, political interests, and organizational capacities, on perceptions of those alignments as opportunities, and on actions to seize them. Policymakers can have only a notion of the policies and programs that will catalyze development. These *strategic notions* combine personal perception of "facts" (derived from limited information) with ideas of varying concreteness. The beliefs underlying anyone's strategic notions derive from personal experience and interpretation of others' experiences, as well as cognitive processes influenced by education. Moreover, because they are derived from similar backgrounds and experience, strategic notions are likely to be shared by many of a country's policymakers.* Strategic notions about agricultural development also draw on experiences in other nations—some widely beneficial, others destructive.

Strategic notions incorporate visions of future prospects and influence preferences about alternative states of the world. Ideas of a desirable pattern of agricultural development might emphasize either of two strategic views: focusing on a small subsector of large, mechanized farms, or stressing broad-based growth in productivity among an increasing proportion of farms, including the small ones that predominate in CARLs. Each is a strategic notion regarding agrarian structure and agricultural development. Other examples of strategic notions include beliefs about the appropriate roles of markets and government, about trade-offs between economic growth and equity or the environment, about potential contributions of rural financial institutions and other nonfarm rural enterprises to economic growth, about the appropriate bias of technological change, whether based on underlying notions of induced innovation (Box 3.3) or modernization, and about a wide range of other beliefs regarding development problems and opportunities in the rural economy. Such notions fall far short of precise views of the world. They are not mental models. But the potential for inconsistency, even irrationality, in strategic notions does not nullify their importance.

*There are similarities between our concept of strategic notions and Douglas North's "consensus ideology." He refers to "the constructions of reality (ideology) that individuals develop to contend with their environment." (North 1981, p. 205). He emphasizes that ideology encompasses a comprehensive way of perceiving the world; it economizes on information costs and also incorporates a judgment about the fairness of institutions and exchange relationships. "Consensus ideologies evolve when the individuals of a universe have similar experiences; divergent ideologies stem from divergent and conflicting perceptions of reality" (p. 205). Elsewhere, he refers to "the decline of large-scale integrated ideologies such as Marxism" and notes "that with the modern fall in information costs ideologies have become more fragmented and partial," which adds to the similarity between his view of ideology and our concept of strategic notions (p. 58n).

Land grant colleges were set up under the Morrill Act of 1862, which provided grants of federal land to help finance state colleges of "agricultural and mechanical arts." Congressman Morrill's earlier bill had failed, largely because the congressional leaders from the South were opposed to public support of education, especially federal support for higher education.[9] But the outbreak of civil war was a strategic moment. Southern opponents had left Congress and created the opportunity for public action. In 1862 Congress also passed the Homestead Law, allowing any citizen to file for 160 acres of unappropriated public land and to obtain title after farming the land for five years.

Moreover, in 1803, when Ohio became a state, one section (out of 36) in each township was reserved for local public schools. That became the usual pattern. Roughly 77 million acres in states admitted to the Union were reserved for such schools, usually a one-room school house with a young teacher responsible for grades one through eight (Cochrane 1979, pp. 38–43, 236–37). In addition to inducing states to establish land grant colleges, land grants induced entrepreneurs to build transcontinental railroads.

Viewing these events as strategic moments when opportunities were seized, it is easy to explain the success of the U.S. agricultural development strategy. Demands on government were modest because grants of public land were easier than raising tax revenues to finance equivalent subsidies. Public policy was guided partly by Thomas Jefferson's notion of an "agrarian economy" based on owner-operated family farms. It was also influenced by Adam Smith's *Wealth of Nations*, particularly his view that government should be responsible for setting up and running "certain public works and certain public institutions, which it can never be for the interest of any individual, or small group of individuals, to erect and maintain."

So, huge federal landholdings were used to finance the two most strategic interventions—fostering public education and railway construction. Moreover, prevailing attitudes—whether called the "protestant ethic," "functional activism," or the "enterprise creed"—contributed to and reflected a social and economic climate favorable for economic growth (Tweeten 1987). Finally, the unimodal agrarian structure of the United States meant, at least in the nineteenth century, that government employees came from a rural society similar to that of the people they served—and often gave more than lip service to being "public servants."

Strategic Choices in Japan

Japan was the first non-Western country to industrialize. How and why did it succeed despite unfavorable initial conditions, including the classic problem of "too many people on too little land"? In the Meiji period (1868–1912) the promotion of education and of institutional, technical, and

[9] Emphasis on the value of education can be traced to the Puritan colonists of New England. Their emphasis was originally on religious dogma, but education became increasingly strong. New Englanders carried their faith in education as they settled the West, and universal primary education characterized most rural areas with the exception of the South (W. Cochrane 1979, pp. 235–37).

economic change reflected the resolve of the Japanese government and people "to secure first the independence and then the fullest possible economic and military development of their country" (Sansom 1950, p. 441). The watchword of the period—"A Rich Country and a Strong Army"—sums up a strategic notion that shaped the development of economic policy under the Meiji leaders, just as ideas of Thomas Jefferson and Adam Smith affected events in the United States.

In the early Meiji period the interests of landlords and industrial capitalists regarding agricultural policy coincided because both stood to benefit from increase of agricultural output (Yujiro Hayami, personal communication, 1987). Agriculture still had a strong comparative advantage in food production, and industrialists saw its development as a source of food for factory workers; landlords would benefit from increased yields. But interests conflicted on agricultural prices. Unlike in many of today's CARLs, the Meiji agricultural strategy favored productivity growth that served broader national interests—including the rural majority—rather than cheap food policies catering mainly to urban interests.

Conditions probably were conducive to pursuit of these broader interests. There was a strong, progressive government, and Japan also had an unusual culture. The Emperor was the "divine" heir of the Japanese, and traditional family loyalties were extended to include the Emperor and, so, the nation. There was a conscious and effective effort to develop patriotism and strengthen loyalty to the Emperor, summed up in the slogan, "Revere the Emperor and Expel the Barbarians." This slogan with its xenophobic sentiments (at a time when the forced opening of Japan by Commodore Perry and his U.S. squadron of "Black Ships" was but one of many ominous gestures by foreign powers) helped to unite the opposition that brought an end to the Tokugawa shogunate (Sansom 1950, p. 298). Ironically, the nationalistic response to the "unequal treaties" imposed on Japan by the United States and other foreign powers also led the Meiji reformers to search for new institutional models outside Japan, at least in part to renegotiate the treaties (Westney 1987, pp. 18–19).

In Japan's "aristocratic revolution" the warrior class "did not merely surrender its privileges. It abolished them. There was no democratic revolution in Japan because none was necessary: the aristocracy itself was revolutionary" (T. C. Smith 1960, p. 370). Smith's analysis runs like this. The long period of stability under the Tokugawa shogunate had profoundly altered the feudal society. Warriors became administrators; the feudal aristocracy were bureaucratized, weakening bonds and status rewards based on ascription, replacing them with ability and performance. Real power passed to the lower echelons because of the increasing complexity of administration. Moreover, the ties of the warrior class to the land were weakened. Apart from some 250 large lords (daimyo), support of the samurai came in payments in cash or kind. "Only the great lords had to be deprived of their power, and the deed was sooner done because their powers had come to be exercised, in fact, by officials who might trade them for similar powers within a vastly larger organization" (p. 377). A new and higher loyalty to the Emperor also sanctioned transfer of power to a central government.

Moreover, the "public spirit" engendered by Confucian education (and its values and attitudes) affected not only the higher reaches of government and business but also cooperation at the village level (Dore 1965a). Sansom (1950, p. 185) says that Confucian tradition had "inculcated in the whole nation habits of discipline and obedience" with the result that "the most sweeping transformations were accomplished with relative ease, because the mass of the people were schooled in respect for men blessed with courage, trained in public affairs, and moved by a high sense of duty." DeVos (1965) and Dore (1965a) both stress the importance of Confucianism on the individual's capacity for self-improvement in fostering attitudes conducive to economic progress. DeVos (1965, p. 578) also argues that because of Confucianism and other influences on family structure "socialization, within the Japanese family, inculcated in many Japanese a type of self-motivated achievement orientation" that "made it possible to adequately man the operation of the society that was being self-consciously guided toward gaining a position of eminence in a world that was then exclusively dominated by Western states."

Confucianism and its respect for learning also shaped strategic notions in education. The many private schools at the time of the Meiji Restoration were a big advantage. It was the positive view of education that "prompted the new central government in the early 1870s to institute compulsory education as one of its first acts of reform" (Dore 1964, p. 235). Popular demand for education made it easier to require local governments to meet most of the financial burden.

But a radical modification of attitudes was also needed to create an education system appropriate to economic growth. There was a shift to practical and technical. The preamble to the Education Code of 1872 is fascinating as a precursor of contemporary discussions of investment in human capital. "Every man," it says, "only after learning diligently according to his capacity will be able to increase his property and prosper in his business. Hence knowledge may be regarded as the capital for raising one's self; who then can do without learning?" (quoted in Kikuchi 1909, p. 68).

In feudal Japan "it was held that the purpose of education was not to fill a young man's mind with useful facts but to make him virtuous by teaching him the wisdom of gods or sages and so forming his character" (Sansom 1950, p. 453). In his influential book *The Encouragement of Learning*, Yukichi Fukuzawa epitomizes the attitude of the Meiji reformers. A prolific writer and intellectual who promoted the spread of knowledge about the

Western world and its ideas, Fukuzawa emphasizes the value of a practical education. He is scornful of the traditional scholar as "a man who has penetrated deeply into the classics and history but cannot carry out a business transaction—such people as these are nothing but rice-consuming dictionaries, of no use to their country but only a hindrance to its economy" (quoted in Sansom 1950, p. 454).

The rapid increase in elementary schools, "technical supplementary schools" (that stressed topics useful to agriculture), and middle schools imparted technical knowledge, strengthened the decision-making capabilities of farmers, and made them receptive to innovations. Better education benefited all—those who were to enter farming and, through training, the rural youths who were to move into jobs in industry, commerce, and government.

As in the United States, the unimodal agrarian structure in Japan meant that many agricultural scientists and professionals came from farm households and began their education in a rural schoolhouse. Moreover, Japan's political leaders and government officials regarded agricultural improvement of great importance and supported agricultural research and extension. Prefectural governors and village leaders promoted county fairs and agricultural meetings, and prizes were awarded for improved farming practices and new farm enterprises, such as sericulture.

In addition to actively fostering education, research, and construction of infrastructure, the Meiji government also helped to develop technical and entrepreneurial capacities, including the establishment of "model factories" that pioneered new industrial activities. Economic progress depended on many entrepreneurs, including five million farm operators responding to market-determined prices. Subsidies stimulated some enterprises, but markets generally were not distorted by policy interventions, and prices were allowed to act as a spur to efficiency.

Agriculture provided much of the capital for expanding manufacturing and other nonagricultural sectors, and government reliance on the land tax was important in early Meiji. But Ohkawa and Ranis (1985, p. 11) stress that, even before World War I, "there was a gradual shift in how investment funds flowed—from government reliance on the land tax to finance infrastructural investment and provide subsidies to the private sector, to the channeling of private agricultural saving, later supplemented by industrial profits, through a growing financial intermediation network." Most important, Japan "followed a policy of flexible, market-determined interest rates, permitting, at the same time, a positive inducement to savers, an efficient allocation for borrowers, and an effective defense against inflationary pressures" (pp. 11–12). But Japanese policymakers sometimes deviated from broadbased development. The allocation of credit to borrowers during 1920–31 discriminated against small- and medium-scale firms and, in particular, affected nonfarm job opportunities (Box 3.5).

Box 3.5.   Japan's Macroeconomic Policies and Nonfarm Employment in the
Interwar Period

Inappropriate economic policies in Japan and economic uncertainty and problems abroad undermined growth of nonfarm employment in the interwar years
(Kaneda 1988, p. 55). In 1918 Japan found itself with large foreign exchange and
gold reserves—and an inflated cost, price, and debt structure. Because of prevailing strategic notions about the gold standard, the financial authorities were
determined to return the yen to prewar parity with the dollar and the pound sterling. To achieve that, the yen was pegged at a rate higher than its equilibrium
price, and tight monetary policies were applied during most of the 1920s. Indeed,
Japan's exchange rate was consistently overvalued in 1920–32.

   To overcome the effects of overvaluation on the competitive position of Japanese
exports, both industry and government adopted policies aimed at the "rational-
ization" of industry, including emphasis on production in larger and more capital-intensive enterprises. In Japan banks have played a dominant role in financing
industry. So, because of the close links between the banks controlled by the
zaibatsu—the large financial-industrial conglomerates, such as Mitsui and
Mitsubishi—and large-scale, capital-intensive firms in the "modern" sector of industry, those enterprises fared well in the rationing of available credit. But small-
and medium-scale firms in the "semimodern" sector bore the brunt of the tight
money policies (Lockwood 1954, p. 293; Okhawa 1965).

   Thus, the slowing down of investment and growth was felt mostly by industries that were labor-intensive and that might otherwise have offered a major outlet for surplus farm labor and mitigated the financial hardship, unrest, and social
tension that prevailed in rural Japan during the 1920s and 1930s. Studies of the
emergence of extremist groups suggest that there is an important relationship between this damming up of population in the countryside and the successful seizure
of power by the militarist clique that carried Japan into World War II (Scalapino
1953, pp. 270, 389–92).

The development strategy pursued during the Meiji period was not just
induced by the response of farmers, entrepreneurs, administrators, and scientists to relative prices (Inukai and Tussing 1967). Japan's first "development plan," embodied in a report entitled *Advice for the Encouragement of
Industry* (*Kogyo Iken*), was completed in 1884. It consisted of thirty volumes
of description and analysis of economic conditions and a detailed statement
of policies and targets for ten years. There was emphasis on mobilization of
labor and entrepreneurial skills in small-scale rural enterprises: sericulture,
sake brewing, tea, leather, weaving, spinning, wood products, and so on.
Stressed, too, was improving productive techniques in indigenous industries
in the belief that, with guidance and technical assistance, these small-scale,
dispersed enterprises would foster overall economic development. Thus, the

report states: "Manufacturers are to be directed to postpone the establishment of a factory with big machines, and at present to pay more attention to the improvement of machines which they now use" (quoted by Inukai and Tussing 1967, p. 61). Some activities, said the report, would have to be more capital-intensive, but meantime, indigenous industries and relatively abundant labor would make their contribution to the expansion of output and provide complementarities to emerging large-scale enterprises: "The planners understood that Japan had to become an industrial and military power by her own resources and that virtually her only resources were her indigenous industries and abundant labor. If development was to occur, it had to reflect the planning of the government elite, but it was the people themselves who had to do the practical innovating and work" (Inukai and Tussing 1967, p. 65).

Policymakers' vision of broad-based development strategy is illustrated in the official response to agitation in the 1880s to reduce the new land tax. *A Treatise on the Strategy of Agricultural Development (Konoronsaku)* rejected the argument for a tax reduction, advocating "more positive measures to develop agriculture such as agricultural schools, experiment stations, itinerant lectures, and agricultural societies" to reduce the burden on farmers (Hayami and Ruttan 1971, p. 164). In fact, the tax was reduced a bit, and the "more positive measures" were also implemented.[10]

Undoubtedly, there was a willingness and ability to consider alternative patterns of development, which suggests that a conscious decision was made to pursue a broad-based strategy for agriculture and the rural economy and to seize opportunities for increases in productivity.

Since reaching its structural transformation turning point in the mid-1950s Japan has joined Western Europe and the United States in implementing agricultural price support programs and protectionist trade policies to ease adjustment problems in the agricultural sector (see Box 3.6). Demands by farmers for government intervention through trade protection and price supports appear to be a universal for countries with high per capita income: the decline in demand growth for food is accompanied by increasing capacity to produce food because well-developed research institutions generate rapid technological change. Government subsidies to U.S. agriculture ran at tens of billions of dollars a year in the 1980s, for example. Adjustment problems in Japan, however, have been especially acute.

---

[10] A land ordinance promulgated in 1884 reconfirmed the high rate of land tax but allowed landowners "some alleviation of their tax burdens" (Ogura 1963, p. 125). It is also noteworthy that from 1868 to the early 1880s agriculture and indigenous small-scale firms received little attention; official policy gave uncritical encouragement to industry and establishment of "model factories." But during the 1880s the Meiji leaders responsible for economic policy faced up to those problems, carried out detailed studies, and came up with practical recommendations based on intimate knowledge of the existing situation (Inukai and Tussing 1967, pp. 52–55).

Box 3.6. Delayed Restructuring of Japan's Agriculture

Japan's structural transformation turning point, reached in the mid-1950s, also marked an increase in productivity of labor and of real wages in agriculture (Minami 1968). Rapid industrial progress since the 1960s has been paralleled by a sharp shift in comparative advantage away from agriculture to industry. In 1960 agriculture accounted for 30 percent of employment; in 1985, its share had fallen to 8 to 9 percent. But the decline in agriculture's share of the GDP was even steeper, from 14 percent to only 3 percent. In the United States the decline in agriculture's share of the GDP between 1960 and 1985 was from 5 to 3 percent, but its share in employment fell from 10 to 3 percent (Van der Meer and Yamada 1990, p. 134).

The Japanese government's response has been to maintain agricultural protection and support prices of farm products, especially rice, at high levels, sometimes as much as eight times world prices. In 1960–80 the *nominal rate of protection** for farm products more than doubled, from 41 to 84 percent, thanks to restrictions and price support policies embodied in the Agricultural Basic Law of 1961. It is no accident that this law came in the wake of Japan's structural transformation turning point.

Such policies helped farm households get incomes that compare favorably with nonfarm households. Thus, agricultural policies since 1960 have been minimizing (or postponing) social tensions and political costs that would have resulted had market forces been given free rein to respond to the abrupt shift in comparative advantage from agriculture to industry.

Structural transformation, which gives rise to strong demand for the government to intervene, also reduces the political cost of supplying such policies. In Japan rice accounted for more than 10 percent of consumer expenditure in urban households in 1959 but had fallen to 4.3 percent in 1969, even though agricultural prices increased by about 80 percent in the 1960s, against a 2 percent rise in manufacturing prices (Hayami 1972; Anderson and Hayami 1986).

For 85 percent of farm households farming is now done on a part-time basis. By 1986 farming accounted for only 13 percent of income, with off-farm income making up nearly two-thirds, and grants and pensions comprising the remainder. Even in 1960 farming accounted for only half the income of farm households, and about two-thirds of all farm households were part-time (Van der Meer and Yamada 1990, p. 135).

Farm folk and their organizations had great political power in postwar Japan (George and Saxon 1986; Hayami 1988). Policies that encourage part-time farming have political advantages, despite substantial economic disadvantages. Maintaining high rice prices is politically attractive because rice is grown by most farm households, and as the staple food, it is central to widely held concerns about

*The *nominal protection coefficient* is the ratio of the domestic price to the world price. The *nominal rate of protection* is the nominal protection coefficient minus 1 and usually is converted to a percentage. For the sake of comparison, the average nominal rate of protection for food products in the European Economic Community increased from 33 to 36 percent between 1960 and 1980. In other words, food items were 36 percent more expensive on average in Europe than in the world market in 1980. As noted in the text, food averaged 84 percent above world market prices that year in Japan.

Box 3.6.   (*continued*)

food security. In addition, rice is an easy crop for Japan's part-time farmers to grow.

Agricultural cooperatives that handled collection and rationing during and following World War II have been retained but modified to support farm prices. As a result, cooperatives have been "favored by the government with privileges, regulations, backing of marketing cartels, and in several cases even with monopoly rights" (Van der Meer and Yamada 1990, p. 140). Moreover, the government and especially the cooperatives "have aimed continuously to keep as many people in farming as possible. This has gradually resulted in a farm sector and farmers' organizations mainly consisting of part-time farmers. Not only have agricultural interests a strong power within the political system, but within the farmers' organizations the interests of inefficient small farms tend to dominate" (Van der Meer and Yamada 1990, p. 158).

High farm prices have encouraged overuse of variable inputs and overinvestment in capital. Thus, artificially high prices are an obstacle to the restructuring needed to reverse growing inefficiency in Japanese agriculture. In 1980 and 1984 net value added was actually negative (Van der Meer and Yamada 1990, p. 125).

The effects of Japan's structural transformation in reducing comparative advantage of agriculture does not apply uniformly to all products. The comparative disadvantage is especially great for land-intensive crops, such as rice and other cereals and for pasture-based rearing of livestock. "Japanese farmers produced little more than 10 kg paddy per hour in the early 1980s in contrast to US farmers who produced about 500 kg" (Van der Meer and Yamada 1990, p. 154). For products such as vegetables, fruits, milk, and other livestock products based on purchased feed, efficient labor-saving techniques can be introduced on very small farms. For example, horticultural farms in the Netherlands average only 2.5 ha of horticultural crops but have labor productivity three to seven times higher than that of such farms in Japan.

Are the United States and Japan Special Cases?

Public decision making has to contend with uncertainty and conflicting bureaucratic and political interests, but culture also influences development. For example, the homogeneity and "oneness" of the Japanese distinguishes Japan from many CARLs, especially where independence resulted in countries comprising groups that shared little more than a common colonizer. Look at the lack of national integration in countries of sub-Saharan Africa with their numerous ethnic groups. Sharp social divisions in many Latin American countries also appear to impair the national unity and mutual interests that were favorable factors in Japan.

But were political conditions in the United States and Japan uniquely favorable for policymakers to set policies and build the public institutions that generated such success? The myths of Washington, Jefferson, and Lincoln have obscured the political controversies of their time. Similarly, the success of contemporary Japan has contributed to the mystique of the Meiji reformers. In fact, politicians had to overcome conflicting political forces and institutional problems. Key policies on land settlement and public education in the United States were finally put in place during the Civil War. Indeed, the war's effect on Congress created those opportunities. The "treatise on the strategy for agricultural development" and the *Kogyo Iken* "development plan" were both prepared following a tough period when Japan had a "disturbed economy." During its first decade the Meiji government faced over 200 peasant uprisings and four samurai revolts (Sproat and Scott 1975, pp. 17–18).[11] If anything distinguishes the United States and Japan from today's CARLs, it is *not* the free hand of their leaders to institute economic policy in a political vacuum.

Japan and the United States are not alone in their capacity to raise agricultural productivity. Indonesia, a country of extraordinary cultural diversity and independent only since the late 1940s, has done so—and at a faster pace. Productivity in Indonesia rose from 2.4 to 4 wheat units per male agriculture worker[12] between 1960 and 1980, an increase almost identical to that from 2.3 to 3.9 in Meiji Japan over the thirty years to 1910 (Booth 1989, pp. 1244–45). As Booth (1989, p. 1246) has shown, growth in rice yields on Java between 1970 and 1983 "was as great as that which occurred in Japan between 1880 and 1948, and in Taiwan between 1913 and 1955" (Table 3.4).

Strategies pursued in Japan and the United States have been effective in promoting agricultural development and structural transformation, but there has been much variation in the economic outcomes of public decision making. There is a striking contrast between Japan's agricultural protectionism of the past thirty-five years and the enlightened policies that shaped agricultural development in Japan in the late nineteenth and early twentieth centuries. The rise of that protectionism is a textbook illustration of public choice theory: the power of groups with a vested interest in protectionist policies is greater than the political power of groups that opposed those distortionary policies that reduce economic efficiency and arouse the ire of Japan's trading partners (Anderson and Hayami 1986; Hayami 1988).

Although public choice theory, along with economic and demographic changes, explains the political economy of protectionism, it does not explain government actions and strategies during the Meiji period. The choice of those far-sighted and appropriate policies was strongly influenced by the

[11] There was even opposition from within the Meiji reformers. Westney (1987, p. 4) reports that "the first [Meiji] minister of justice, Eto Shimpei, who fought hard with the bureaucrats of the Finance Ministry for the resources to build a centralized system of courts and judicial police in the early 1870s, resigned from the government in 1873 over foreign policy issues. In 1876 he led a samurai uprising in Southwestern Japan and was condemned to death by one of the courts he had been instrumental in creating."

[12] See Chapter 1, note 6.

Table 3.4.　Rice yields in Japan, Taiwan, and Java (t/ha)

Year	Yield	Yield index
Japan		
1880	2.00	100
1910	2.62	131
1948	3.28	164
1969	4.38	219
Taiwan		
1913	1.35	100
1955	2.22	165
1970	3.14	233
Java		
1970	1.81	100
1983	3.01	166

Source: Booth 1989, Table 10, p. 1246. © 1989. Reprinted by permission of Elsevier Science Ltd., The Boulevard, Langford Lane, Kidlington OX5 1GB, U.K.
Note: Yields are five-year averages centered on year shown.

prevailing nationalism and concern for the public good by leaders who were "moved by a high sense of duty" (Sansom 1950, p. 185). Dore (1965b, pp. 124, 130) also recognizes that many Meiji leaders were motivated by self-advancement and wealth. But in the final analysis "the rhetorical ethic did have its restraining effect. . . . Policy was always the result of a dialectic between the ideal and private interest, never guided solely by the latter."

Tension between private interests and the public good also has been a theme in United States history. Despite sharp differences between Thomas Jefferson or Thomas Paine and Alexander Hamilton or James Madison, "all were agreed that a republic needed a government that was more than an arena within which various interests could compete"; and "republican government, they insisted, could survive only if animated by a spirit of virtue and concern for the public good" (Bellah and others 1985, p. 253).

To understand the political economy of development is to identify factors that determine how "the tension between private interest and the public good" will be resolved. The outcome is affected by the "civic virtue" exemplified by leaders such as George Washington "forming the new nation, ruling without excess, and retiring to ordinary life"; but political vision also "plays an indispensable role in providing understanding of the present and of the possibilities for change" (Bellah and others 1985, pp. 254, 270, 271). Similarly, Dore (1965b, p. 130) emphasizes that "Meiji leaders were trained in the calculation of the consequences of political action, in the difficult art of subordinating immediate to long-term objectives, and in the habit of evaluating consequences and objectives in the light of abstract principles."

To be sure, corruption and rent seeking were prevalent in both countries. Their adverse effects on development were, however, limited because most decision making in the economic arena was guided by market-determined prices rather than government intervention. Masayoshi Matsukata, finance minister in Meiji Japan, articulated his understanding of the comparative advantage of public and private initiative with unusual clarity. In his memorandum proposing the central bank that was founded in 1882, he pointed out that, although "government should not take immediate concern in trade and business matters . . . financial matters which have a direct bearing on the well-being of the community at large . . . must be undertaken by the government. . . . The establishment of a central bank is just such a policy" (as quoted by Haru Matsukata Reischauer [1986, p. 96]).

IMPLICATIONS FOR TODAY'S CARLS

Lessons drawn from experience in the United States or Japan are likely to be misleading for contemporary CARLs unless attention is given to the big differences in the timing of their structural transformation. The important implications for contemporary CARLs derive from the experience of the two countries prior to reaching their structural transformation turning points—1910 for the United States and 1955 for Japan. Although significant decline in the size of Japan's farm work force dates only from 1955, agriculture's share in the total labor force had declined to less than 50 percent in 1930 (Table 3.5). Although that was much larger than the 22 percent share of agriculture in the United States labor force in 1930, it was well below the corresponding figures for Taiwan and Mexico, which were "late developing" relative to the United States and Japan. It was emphasized in Chapter 1 (see especially Box 1.1) that the rate of structural change in the occupational composition of a country's labor force is determined by agriculture's initial weight in the total labor force and the rates of growth of the total labor force and of nonfarm employment. The limited decline in agriculture's labor force share in Taiwan and Mexico in 1930 (and even 1960) reflected the large increases in their rates of growth of population and labor force that resulted from very rapid reductions in infant and child mortality (Chapters 8 and 10). The delayed onset of structural transformation is even more evident in contemporary CARLs such as Kenya and Tanzania, also included in Table 3.5. As late as 1985 the share of agriculture in their total labor force was higher than in the United States in the 1820s or Japan in the 1880s.

In Japan and the United States strategic decisions on education, agricultural research and other support services, and investments in rural infrastructure fostered different patterns of agricultural development. Japan faced a scarcity of agricultural land, whereas the United States had new land available for settlement until late in the nineteenth century. For both, however, national and local policies and technologies adopted by farmers were ap-

Table 3.5.   Percentage of total labor force in agriculture in the United States, Japan, Taiwan, Mexico, Kenya, and Tanzania

Country	1900	1930	1960	1970	1985
United States	40	22	8	4	3
Japan	66	48	31	20	8
Taiwan	71	68	56	37	18
Mexico	67	69	54	44	33
Kenya	—	—	—	85	79
Tanzania	—	—	—	90	83

Sources: Reproduced from Johnston and Kilby 1975, pp. 454ff., except for 1970 and 1985 figures that are from FAO 1988, Table A.1, and for Taiwan figures for 1970 and 1985 that are from Republic of China 1988. (In recent years the figures for Taiwan refer to the employed labor force age 15 and over instead of 12 and over; on that basis the 1960 share is reported as 50 rather than 56 percent.)

Note: In Japan 75 percent of the labor force worked in agriculture in 1880. For the United States, agriculture's share of the labor force was 80 percent in 1820 and 55 percent in 1850.

propriate to their prevailing structural and demographic conditions and the different physical environments for agriculture.

Strategic decision makers were influenced by realism, idealism, and pragmatism. In Japan the realism of the Meiji reformers was to recognize that virtually the only resources available were existing small-scale farms and indigenous industries and an abundance of labor; and hence there was an emphasis on productivity increases through the development and widespread use of labor-using, land-saving technologies suited to the needs of small farms and small- and medium-scale manufacturing firms. In both countries idealism was evident in the faith in education and efforts to inculcate the "ideals of service, stewardship, and cooperation" invoked in the late nineteenth century by President Charles William Eliot of Harvard and a group of leading Bostonians (as quoted by Bellah and others 1985, p. 260). Pragmatism was there, too, in the emphasis on government's catalytic and facilitating role in economic development. Moreover, emphasis on creating a favorable policy environment and government initiatives to provide public goods and services (such as education, agricultural research, and infrastructure) limited the opportunities for officials to exercise the arbitrary authority that encourages rent-seeking behavior (see Chapter 12).

Strategic notions always provide a simplified understanding of a complex reality; the consensus and action that are facilitated may be for good or ill. Economic policies that resulted in retarded growth in Japan in 1920–31 (Box 3.5) and had such adverse effects on agriculture and on the growth of nonfarm jobs were strongly influenced by a commitment to return to the Gold Standard at the pre–World War I parity with the dollar and sterling. Recent political acceptance of Japan's agricultural protectionism has been helped by the strategic notion of self-sufficiency based on concerns about food security. These agricultural policies created politically powerful interest groups in the agricultural cooperatives that have been given responsibility for implementing programs of protection and price support. Cooperatives and the politically powerful part-time farmers have stubbornly resisted even reforms that would promote the long-term interests of the agricultural sector. Consumers, too, lose because agricultural prices would be much lower if the labor-saving innovations now appropriate in Japan's high-income economy were encouraged rather than stifled. The most important implications for today's CARLs, however, derive not from the dilemmas of political gridlock in high-income economies but from the experience of the two countries prior to reaching their turning points (1910 for the United States and 1955 for Japan).

Three features of the "Japanese model" are significant for CARLs, and each has a parallel in the U.S. experience. First, Japanese agricultural output increased within the existing small-scale farming system. Yet, the image of "modern" agricultural development for many is the "U.S. model" of labor-saving, land-using mechanization, which was possible only because of extraordinary land endowment. It was not feasible in Japan until after its structural transformation turning point, when the number of workers per hectare of agricultural land began to fall as a result of the declining farm work force.

Japan's land-saving, labor-using pattern during its early development is feasible for CARLs despite their rapid labor force growth. Although Japan's labor force growth was slower, there was less cultivatable land per male agricultural worker in Japan in 1901 than there was in Taiwan or on the Indonesian island of Java in 1971 (Table 3.6).[13] Taiwan's labor-using, land-saving pattern of agricultural development, which was initiated during the period of Japan's colonial rule, made it possible to reduce "underemployment" in agriculture despite a 70 percent increase in the farm labor force between 1930 and the mid-1960s (see Chapter 10). The examples of Japan and Taiwan notwithstanding, a common misinterpretation of the "U.S. model," together with misinterpretation of earlier experience in England by Marx and others, have given rise to a widely (and incorrectly) held notion that economies of scale are important in agriculture. Strategic notions about scale of production and farm size are pivotal to agricultural development strategy for CARLs (Chapter 4).

Second, most farmers in Japan and the United States were involved in increases in agricultural productivity. Thus, the growth of output was characterized by widespread use of technological *innovations* and new *inputs* that increased productivity of labor and land. There were different technologies in Japan and the United States, but broad-based agricultural development

---

[13] The rapid decline in agriculture's share of the labor force in Japan from 76 percent in 1880 to 52 percent in 1920 was facilitated by modest population growth of 1 to 1.5 percent during Japan's demographic transition, which is similar to the growth rates during the demographic transition in Western Europe.

Table 3.6. Hectares of cultivated land per male agricultural worker in Japan, Taiwan, and Java

Year	Japan	Taiwan	Java
1901	0.62	—	0.72
1911	0.66	0.78	—
1931	0.78	0.84	0.95
1951	0.79	—	—
1961	1.02	0.69	0.73
1971	1.44	0.63	0.64

Source: Booth 1989, Table 4, p. 1238. © 1989 Pergamon Press. Reprinted by permission.
Notes: Data for Java refer to 1905 instead of 1901 and 1930 instead of 1931. Data for Taiwan refer to 1913 instead of 1911 and 1937 instead of 1931.

strategies and unimodal agrarian structures were mutually reinforcing in each case. This, and the U.S. model of owner-operated farms, have inspired the strategic notion that land reform is a prerequisite to broad-based development (Chapter 5). The Japanese land reform after World War II helped to establish a unimodal pattern of landownership about the time Japan reached its turning point (1955). But this unimodal structure of operating units was achieved through tenancy and despite a highly skewed distribution of landownership throughout the crucial period of its agricultural growth.

Third, there was concurrent growth in agriculture and industry. Their interactions had profound implications for growth, and there is potential for CARLs to foster these beneficial interactions (Chapter 6). *Private initiatives* were central to this process in Japan and the United States, but *selective government initiatives* to build key *public institutions* and *infrastructure* were decisive in each country. And neither country adopted price policies that substantially distorted producer *incentives* until after its structural transformation turning point.

Innovative behavior that produced new agricultural inputs is, perhaps, the main contrast in their experiences. Market incentives were sufficient to induce the private sector to produce a stream of mechanical innovations that drove laborsaving, land-using development in the United States. Especially in early agricultural change in Japan, however, government programs to develop public capacity for agricultural research accelerated the development and adoption of fertilizer-responsive seeds and agricultural practices that were the basis for the labor-using, land-saving pattern. Government action in the latter case is crucial to the seed-fertilizer technology. Farm machinery and fertilizer are also distinguished by the linkages from producing these crucial inputs (see Chapters 6 and 7).

Public investment in irrigation and drainage increases land productivity and is more important to the land-saving pattern of countries such as Japan than for the United States. In each case, however, public policy promoted the development of transport infrastructure to integrate domestic and world markets, thereby raising incentives to produce commodities, such as wheat and silk, for export. Better transport also lowers the cost of purchased inputs in rural areas for farmers and nonfarm rural entrepreneurs.

Direct government initiatives to borrow technology and organizational designs and to promote rural nonfarm activities in Japan contrast with the decentralized approach in developmental institutions of the United States. This is partly because of cultural differences, but the diversity of agronomic conditions and ethnic mix of the United States meant that decentralization was indispensable if programs were to be appropriate to local conditions. Different institutions accommodated the relative homogeneity of Japan. There, the successful strategy for agriculture depended on the development of indigenous technical knowledge through participation by farmers in agricultural research and development. Witness the Meiji practices of cooperation between experiment stations and farmers to screen indigenous techniques and of hiring veteran farmers as instructors at agricultural colleges (Okhawa and Hayami 1989).

The strategic notions that supported Japanese and U.S. initiatives for public education run deep in each culture, a commitment to education that is shared by many contemporary CARLs. The success of land grant agricultural colleges in the United States and their counterparts in Japan depended on a complementary commitment to primary education in rural areas. Beyond the direct effect of basic education on farmers' capacity to assess new technology and to seize new economic opportunities (T. W. Schultz 1975; Jamison and Lau 1982), these primary school systems produced a stream of rural people who received further training. Unlike in many CARLs, agricultural researchers and rural civil servants in Japan and the United States were often raised in farm households. As a result, they understood the needs and potential of family farms, even (in Japan) very small-scale farms. Thus, the success of Japan and the United States in implementing broad-based agricultural strategies derives partly from unimodal agrarian structures and investments in education.

The most fundamental of the notions that influenced agricultural development strategies in Japan and the United States was the conviction that government and private initiatives can, and should, be complementary. Both *laissez-faire* and *dirigisme* were rejected, in contrast to contemporary ideology and much of the advice given to CARLs over the past forty years. Instead, policymakers in both countries tried to balance the role of government and the economic activity of private firms.

The decisions and foresight of Japan's leaders cannot be explained entirely (or even predominantly) by their response to relative prices. But government's interventions did *not* distort relative prices during the Meiji period. Ohkawa and Ranis (1985, p. 13) remark, "Perhaps luckily, Japan did not at first have the tariff autonomy required to construct import-substitution, hot-house conditions for its industries." The "unequal treaties" that Japan signed with the United States and European powers in the years after Commodore Perry limited the import duties that Japan could impose—a maximum of 5 percent in 1865–99. So Japan was spared many of the adverse effects on resource allocation and economic efficiency that have often resulted from distorted incentives in contemporary CARLs, especially those that led to underpricing and preferential allocation of capital and foreign exchange. More important, decisions about research priorities and choices that determined the long-term pattern of technological change were not distorted by inappropriate price signals.

This comparison of innovations, inputs, infrastructure, institutions, initiative, and incentives in Japan and the United States has focused on the "Six I's," which by design or default are elements of any agricultural development strategy. They are discussed more fully in Chapter 5. Their relevance extends beyond agriculture to encompass a broader strategy for development of the rural economy in CARLs (Part 2).

PART TWO

FROM
STRUCTURE
TO STRATEGY

CHAPTER FOUR

SMALL FARMS IN A BROAD-BASED AGRICULTURAL STRATEGY

M ost CARLs, with scarce agricultural land and large labor forces, are better suited to the labor-using, land-saving pattern of agricultural development seen in Japan. This is a far cry from ill-conceived strategic notions about the advantages of large farms, which led to costly mistakes and missed opportunities for many CARLs. That does not mean that all farms should be uniformly small, but as long as rural wages are low, as they are in CARLs, such farms are more productive and provide more jobs. Any efficient agricultural strategy for a CARL must be "broad-based," meaning that it increases productivity among a large and growing proportion of these small farms. But there are obstacles and dangers.

Given the diversity of farming (even locally, let alone regionally and nationally), how can a strategy be developed to raise productivity on so many small farms? And if farmers' techniques are already well adapted to local farming systems and conditions (Chapter 1), what scope is there for raising productivity, anyway? Even if it can be raised through science, do poor households have the means to benefit? Or will the new technology be monopolized by the rich? And will scarce resources be spread too thinly to have much impact?

Despite these questions and the great variation in answers within and among poor countries, some elements of a broad-based strategy make sense for all CARLs.

Land, especially cropland, is scarce in most CARLs. So, with rising populations, the trend well into the twenty first century will be toward less cropland per agricultural worker and even smaller farms. That alone should caution all but a handful of CARLs against pursuing a land-using, labor-saving strategy based on the experience of the United States.

Hectares of agricultural land per agricultural worker—the basic measure of the balance of land and labor—vary enormously from country to country (Table 4.1). In 1990 densely populated Bangladesh, India, Indonesia, Egypt, and Taiwan had less than 1 hectare per worker; the (then) USSR had over 30 hectares, and the land-rich United States almost 150 hectares for each worker.

There are caveats to such comparisons. Labor force estimates usually undercount women workers in agriculture and often misclassify the rural labor force, considering only the primary occupation. Moreover, land endowments across countries and regions should really be assessed by taking into account things such as soil fertility and climate, although land quality is even harder to aggregate into meaningful national summaries than it is to quantify.

Comparing only cropland (arable land and land under permanent crops but excluding permanent pasture) reduces disparities between countries—but not by much. China comes out worst, with only 0.21 hectare per agricultural worker. Tanzania, Kenya, Bangladesh, India, Indonesia, Egypt, and Taiwan also had less than 1 hectare per worker in 1990. The United States had more than 65 hectares of cropland for each worker. Part of the Bangladesh–United States farm labor productivity differential (Chapter 1) springs from the more than 160-fold difference in cropland per worker.

Narrowing the comparison further to only irrigated land, the 1-to-55 cropland ratio between Japan and the United States falls to 1 to 9. This is because only 10 percent of U.S. cropland is irrigated; in Japan it is more than 60 percent. Irrigation, common elsewhere in Asia, is important because it increases the number of crops that can be grown each year. It also raises the average yield for each crop planted, and it attenuates the risk of variations in rainfall always present in nonirrigated farming. On average, more than 35 percent of cropland is irrigated for fifteen Asian CARLs. One-quarter is irrigated in India, about one-third in Bangladesh and Indonesia, and (according to the Food and Agriculture Organization [FAO]) 50 percent of China's cropland was irrigated in 1990.

Contrast the figures on Asia's irrigation with sub-Saharan Africa and Latin America. The average proportion of cropland irrigated was 5 percent for the three Latin American CARLs and 4 percent for the 34 CARLs in sub-Saharan Africa (for which data are available) of which only nine have irrigation on more than 5 percent of cropland. Madagascar and Swaziland head this list,

Table 4.1.   Endowments of land and labor in CARLs and other selected countries, 1990

Country	Agricultural land/ agricultural labor force (ha/worker)	Cropland/ agricultural labor force (ha/worker)	Irrigated land/ agricultural labor force (ha/worker)	Irrigated land/ cropland (%)
Tanzania	3.72	0.33	0.01	4
Nigeria	2.72	1.22	0.03	3
Kenya	5.30	0.32	0.01	2
40 CARLs in sub-Saharan Africa	6.32	1.01	0.04	4
3 CARLs in Latin America	2.24	1.14	0.06	5
Bangladesh	0.42	0.39	0.13	32
India	0.84	0.79	0.20	25
China	1.08	0.21	0.10	50
Indonesia	0.94	0.62	0.21	35
Thailand	1.21	1.17	0.23	19
15 CARLs in Asia	1.05	0.45	0.16	35
13 CARLs in Asia (excluding China and Indonesia)	1.00	0.78	0.23	30
All 58 CARLs	1.79	0.54	0.14	26
Egypt[a]	0.44	0.44	0.44	100
Colombia	15.88	1.88	0.18	10
Malaysia	2.18	2.16	0.15	7
Mexico	10.62	2.65	0.55	21
Brazil	18.27	4.49	0.20	5
Taiwan[a]	0.80	0.80	0.44	55
USSR	31.89	12.23	1.13	9
United States	149.79	65.94	6.52	10
Japan	1.37	1.20	0.74	62
World	4.40	1.31	0.22	16

Sources: Table 1.1 and FAO 1992, except for Taiwan, Republic of China 1991.

Notes: Taiwan data are for 1987. *Arable land* encompasses land under annual crops (double-cropped areas are counted only once), temporary meadows for mowing or pasture, market gardens, cultivation under glass, and fallow land. *Cropland* comprises arable land plus land under permanent crops, such as tree crops. *Agricultural land* includes cropland and permanent pastures. Data on irrigated land are available for only 34 of the 40 CARLs in sub-Saharan Africa.

[a]Denotes the absence of permanent pasture.

with 30 percent irrigated, followed by the Sudan (15 percent), Somalia (11 percent), Mali (10 percent), Senegal and Zimbabwe (8 percent), the Gambia (7 percent), and Mauritania (6 percent). In Kenya, however, only 2 percent of cropland is irrigated, in Nigeria 3 percent, and in Tanzania 4 percent. For most of sub-Saharan Africa the average amount of irrigated land per agricultural worker is minuscule, and rainfed crops are the rule.

The ratio of large animals to pasture area gives a rough suggestion of the extensive nature of livestock subsectors (see Table 4.2). Feedlots notwithstanding, there is less than one large animal for every 2 hectares of pasture land in either the United States or the USSR. Colombia, Mexico, and Brazil—each with pasture accounting for over three-fourths of agricultural land—illustrate the extensive nature of ranching in much of middle-income Latin America with ratios of large animals to pasture below 1.

Egypt is at the opposite extreme of pasture land endowments. Egypt's agriculture, where virtually all land is irrigated cropland, supports a large population of cattle, buffaloes, horses, mules, donkeys, and other livestock, large and small, with negligible pasture. In crowded Egypt—as in India and Bangladesh with ratios of twenty and forty large animals per hectare, respectively, pasture land is not the base for livestock production. Instead fodder is raised on arable land, gleaned as crop byproducts, gathered along roads, canals, and from common property, or purchased and brought to animals. Such intensive livestock raising—and its demands for labor—is nevertheless a profitable alternative for households with little or no land. Tending large livestock, dairying, and raising small animals—sheep, goats, and (where culturally acceptable) pigs—as well as poultry are important economic activities for Asian women and children.

The endowment of pasture per agricultural worker in the forty sub-Saharan CARLs appears much more generous than in the CARLs of Latin America and Asia. However, comparison of area alone masks fundamental disadvantages in range quality, climate, and the prevalence of pests and diseases that severely constrain livestock populations in large sections of sub-Saharan Africa. There also is huge variation within the region. The endowment of pasture land per agricultural worker in Nigeria is not too different from that of China. But Botswana's endowment (over 120 ha/worker according to the FAO) is the greatest among CARLs by far and surpasses even that of the United States. Mauritania is next among CARLS at 94 hectares per worker, followed by Chad with 30 hectares per worker. But don't swap the Montana ranch for pasture in the Sahel.

In pasture and livestock, Tanzania is representative of sub-Saharan Africa. Permanent pasture accounts for over 90 percent of agricultural land, there are well over 3 hectares of pasture per agricultural worker, and Tanzania has a ratio of about four large animals for every three workers in agriculture. This ratio of large livestock per agricultural worker suggests that animal traction

Table 4.2. Pasture land, labor, and livestock in CARLs and other selected countries, 1990

Country	Pasture/ agricultural labor force (ha/worker)	Pasture/ agricultural land (%)	Large animals/ pasture (no./ha)	Large animals/ agricultural labor (no./worker)	Small animals/ agricultural labor (no./worker)
Tanzania	3.39	91	0.38	1.27	1.31
Nigeria	1.51	55	0.32	0.49	1.21
Kenya	4.98	94	0.37	1.86	1.83
40 CARLs in sub-Saharan Africa	5.04	84	0.27	1.34	1.96
3 CARLs in Latin America	1.10	49	1.55	1.70	1.12
Bangladesh	0.03	6	41.51	1.07	0.52
India	0.06	7	22.63	1.27	0.80
China	0.87	81	0.31	0.27	1.19
Indonesia	0.33	35	1.23	0.40	0.64
Thailand	0.04	3	13.92	0.57	0.26
15 CARLs in Asia	0.59	57	1.06	0.63	1.07
13 CARLs in Asia (excluding China and Indonesia)	0.22	22	5.40	1.19	0.93
All 58 CARLs	1.25	70	0.59	0.74	1.20
Egypt[a]	0.00	0	Undefined	1.37	1.38
Colombia	14.00	88	0.69	9.62	2.16
Malaysia	0.01	1	31.59	0.38	1.27
Mexico	7.98	75	0.57	4.56	3.42
Brazil	13.78	75	0.81	11.17	4.84
Taiwan[a]	0.00	0	Undefined	—	—
USSR	19.66	62	0.34	6.69	11.91
United States	83.84	56	0.43	36.07	23.51
Japan	0.17	12	7.30	1.23	3.10
World	3.09	70	0.45	1.41	2.33

Sources: Table 1.1; FAO 1992; World Resources Institute, 1992. Data on livestock are three-year averages for 1988–90 from World Resources Institute 1992 based on FAO data.

Notes: *Large animals* comprise mainly cattle but also include domestic buffaloes, camels, horses, mules, and donkeys. *Small animals* include domestic sheep, goats, and pigs. Poultry are not included.

[a] Denotes the absence of permanent pasture.

and smallholder livestock production potentially could play roles in Tanzania and other countries of sub-Saharan Africa similar to their contributions to agricultural productivity in South Asia, where ratios of livestock to agricultural labor are similar and both cropland and, particularly, pasture are scarcer.

In summary: land—especially cropland—is scarce in CARLs. No CARL in Asia, Latin America, or sub-Saharan Africa had more than 3 hectares of cropland per agricultural worker in 1990 save two: Afghanistan (3 ha/worker) and Botswana (5 ha/worker). The weighted average for all fifty-eight CARLs was less than 0.6 hectares of cropland per agricultural worker. Regional averages ranged from less than one-half ha/worker for the fifteen Asian countries that account for 84 percent of the population of CARLs to 1 ha/worker for the sub-Saharan CARLs and 1.1 ha/worker for the three in Latin America (Table 4.1).

There is little scope for expanding cropland in most CARLs. And, as discussed in Chapter 1, the rural labor force for the group is projected to grow until at least 2010. Thus, the trend into the next century will be toward lower ratios of cropland per worker and smaller farms (also see Alexandratos 1988). Taking the Asian CARLs as a group, the balance of land and labor is declining toward the ratio of 0.4 hectare of cropland per agricultural worker—the level Japan reached in 1955, when its agricultural labor force peaked.[1]

On average, the CARLs of sub-Saharan Africa and Latin America have relatively more cropland and much more pasture per worker than their Asian counterparts. Rapid population growth in many African countries will narrow that gap over coming decades, however. Moreover, the average for the sub-Saharan CARLs of almost 5.5 hectares of agricultural land (cropland plus pasture) in 1987 is a far cry from almost 40 hectares per agricultural worker in the United States at the time of its structural transformation turning point in 1910.[2] That sixfold difference, which would be magnified if adjusted for land quality, should caution all but a handful of CARLs regarding the appropriateness of the U.S. model for them. The few plausible exceptions all are in sub-Saharan Africa; these are examined in more detail later.

STRATEGIC NOTIONS ABOUT SMALL FARMS

In farming bigger does not necessarily mean better—and certainly not for CARLs. Agricultural development in both Japan and the United States followed a broad-based strategy for productivity increases (involving most farms), but the Japanese example has not been embraced by enough contemporary CARLs. Instead, erroneous notions about the advantages of large-

[1] Calculated from Hayami and Ruttan 1985, Table C.3, p. 486.
[2] Calculated from labor force data in Lebergott 1966 and land data from Hayami and Ruttan 1985, Table C.2, p. 480.

scale farming have led to costly mistakes and missed opportunities. These notions have derived from impressions of agriculture in the United States and other countries that have passed their structural transformation turning points or from Marxist-Leninist theory, which underlay Soviet agricultural strategy.[3]

Belief that economies of scale are prevalent in agriculture is a widely held strategic notion. It underpins the view that a *dualistic strategy*, emphasizing new technology on large-scale farms, is better than a broad-based approach (see Box 4.1). Such ideas for CARLs emerged under colonialism but have carried over, to a surprising extent, beyond independence. The emphasis on economies of scale in the Stalinist model of agricultural development (Chapter 9) was especially influential in the 1950s and 1960s when many CARLs were gaining independence.

An extension of these ideas is that mainstream economic analysis is irrelevant to traditional, peasant farms. This often is reinforced by beliefs that farmers operating small-scale plots are bound by tradition, fatalism, and a "subsistence mentality," making them incapable of responding to price changes and disinterested in profitable new production techniques.[4] That small-scale farmers use much of their produce for their own consumption is valid in predominantly agrarian economies; U.S. farmers were "subsistence-minded" until the 1840s. Yet, if taken to an extreme (as Stalin did), this leads to the mistaken notion of little or no linkage between small-scale farms and the rest of the economy, fostering development strategies that put industrialization first and ignore agriculture.

Confusion about fragmentation, private property, and efficient scale of agricultural production clouds thinking on agricultural strategy in China

[3] Lenin and, especially, Karl Kautsky pioneered the extension of Marx's view of political economy to a development strategy including agriculture. The subsequent emphasis on economies of scale in agriculture and the superiority of large farm units in Marxist-Leninist thought can be traced to Kautsky's seminal work, *The Agrarian Question*, which appeared in 1899. Although Kautsky's political views were repudiated in 1914 by other Marxists, his ideas about agricultural economics continued to have major influence, albeit anonymously. Through their implementation in Stalin's collectivization drive (Chapter 9) and subsequent emulation in other countries, Kautsky's notions far outlived his personal reputation in Marxist-Leninist circles (see the Preface to Kautsky 1988 by H. Alavi and T. Shanin). Alain de Janvry (1981) provides a useful synthesis of Marxist-Leninist views on agrarian structure and strategic options.

[4] Rogers (1969) provides an example of some of the views that were current in the 1960s. Bates (1988) supplies a critique that is still relevant because, as he observes, "anyone who works in present-day developing areas knows that, despite overwhelming evidence to the contrary, significant elites and especially intellectuals remain convinced that peasant farming provides an inadequate foundation for development" (p. 507). He also argues that regardless of ideological pedigree, notions about the superiority of large farms are rooted in eighteenth-century commentary on the economic rivalry between England and France. Bates (p. 510) concludes that reassessment of the historical data refutes the notion that the larger scale of English farms provided an advantage over its rival. (See also Johnston and Kilby 1975.) Marx, of course, was among those influenced by the prevailing misinterpretation of English agricultural development.

Box 4.1.   Some (Useful) Jargon

In *dualistic strategies*, productivity growth is restricted to a narrow range of farms, usually (the minority of) large farms, although the concept could apply to any strategy that uses a disproportionate share of scarce resources (land, capital, or administrative capacity) and is limited to a few (large or small) farms. Definitions of "small," "medium," or "large" are not essential to these concepts; what matters most for efficiency and equity is the proportion of farms and of rural work force ultimately involved in productivity growth.* In keeping with faith in economies of scale, dualistic strategies often are based on agricultural mechanization and other labor-saving, capital-using technologies that cannot spread to the majority of small farms.

Broad-based strategies are associated with divisible innovations, such as seed-fertilizer combinations and simple implements. These technologies tend to spread among farms of various sizes and to complement, rather than displace, the large and growing rural labor force of CARLs. No development strategy can be broad-based if it fails to expand opportunities for greater productivity for women as well as men.

A broad-based strategy seeks to include most small and medium farms, which are invariably the vast majority. If most farms are under 5 hectares, innovations adopted by the small farm majority can have a significant impact on agriculture in the aggregate. Larger farms are not necessarily excluded nor should farms be of uniform size. Indeed, in Taiwan, a classic example of broad-based development, there is substantial variation in farm size.

One of the errors of nineteenth-century land settlement policy in the United States—in what was otherwise a successful broad-based strategy—was its inflexibility about farm size. Land grants were 160 acres in the arid plains of the Far West, the same in the central prairies. As Lockeretz (1984, p. 159) points out, this failure to incorporate the ecological variation of such a vast country into policy choices created an unsustainable agrarian structure in some regions, which in turn contributed to the Dust Bowl of the 1930s.

Just as small farms should not be uniformly small, different farms and different regions do not develop at the same rate. Some environments are so hostile that the most realistic opportunities for inhabitants lie in migration or in non-farm activities. If, for example, a country has distinct regions of semiarid grassland and irrigated cropland, distributions of farms by size should (and will) differ between them. So will the opportunities for agricultural development. In general, the greater the number of such *recommendation domains* (Byerlee and others 1982) within a country, the more complex the process of setting strategic priorities. Although it may often make sense to begin with high-potential areas, the arid and semiarid regions of, say, Kenya and Tanzania are areas where less well-endowed farming systems loom too large to be ignored.

*Our nomenclature was influenced by the contrast between *focus strategies* and *dispersal strategies* introduced by Barlow and Jayasuriya (1984b) to compare tree crop development programs in Indonesia. In an earlier book Johnston and Kilby (1975) used the term *unimodal* to describe both a broad-based strategy and the unimodal agrarian structure associated with such a strategy.

Strategy affects the distribution of benefits and the timing of opportunities within localities just as it cuts across regions. Intentional or not, dualistic strategies are exclusive. Smaller groups enjoy an organizational advantage in seeking policy rents, and dualistic strategies promote such groups. Thus, dualism will concentrate benefits and accentuate political and economic inequalities. Broad-based strategies are *inclusive*. The United States and Japan show that powerful vested interests emerge even in broad-based strategies, but a dualistic strategy would appear to hasten the formation of such groups.

(Lin, Yao, and Wen 1990, pp. 490–93). In a story on China's dilemma over future reform, *The Economist* reported: "The government is toying with several solutions to the stagnation of agricultural growth expected in the next few years. Ideologically, it favors 'scale farming,' a disguised form of recollectivization, and is nervous of the sensible alternative—the creation of large, and more efficient, private farms" (June 15, 1991, p. 35). Predictably, William Hinton, an adherent of Maoist strategy, favors recollectivization and argues that mechanization is "the only way to redress the balance" between agricultural labor productivity in China and in the United States (Hinton 1990, pp. 112 and 120). He suggests tractors of 40 to 100 horsepower, rather than the 15-horsepower "walking" two-wheel and small four-wheel tractors that abound in China (Hinton 1990, p. 116). It is startling (then again, perhaps not) that *The Economist* shares Hinton's muddle about economies of scale. Neither gives serious attention to promoting productivity growth among small farms, something grasped by Japan's Meiji reformers 100 years ago.

Support for economies of scale in agriculture lives on elsewhere, despite the ebb of Marxist-Leninist ideology and proven pitfalls of dualism. Keith Hart, for example, argues that only through mechanization and by establishing "large, capital-intensive estates" can agriculture in Africa contribute to economic development; otherwise, it is "faced with the prospect of a dozen Haitis" (Hart 1982, pp. 157–58, 165). And in this spirit, Nigeria has subsidized mechanization to promote large-scale food production. But such persistent misunderstandings of the economics of farm size have weakened the effort to overcome the decline in African agriculture (Delgado 1988; Eicher 1990).

Traditional notions about economies of scale are behind strategies that invariably favor large farms and neglect smaller ones. To this day, most policymakers and intellectuals in sub-Saharan Africa and Latin America are skeptical about the potential of small farms. The view is influential in Asia, despite abundant local evidence to the contrary. Officials in international organizations are not immune to the appeal of bigness. Even *The Economist* lapses.

Look at the evidence from research spanning more than thirty years. T. W. Schultz's *Transforming Traditional Agriculture* (1964) played a major role in the revision of thinking about smallholder decision making and helped to reinstate mainstream economic analysis as a tool for studying agriculture in CARLs. The basic notion is that economic rationality, at the root of neo-classical economics, governs the decision making of traditional farmers. Like their counterparts in small, privately managed firms throughout the world, small-scale farmers in CARLs make economic decisions that are consistent with their interests. Now, the predominant notion among agricultural economists is that smallholders are "poor but efficient." Traditional agriculture is poor but efficient because it is static: farmers have identified optimal allocations through long trial and error.

Ironically, even this hypothesis has been used to promote a dualistic strategy. Lipton (1968, p. 348) relates a revealing comment from a 1965 television interview with a former minister of agriculture about agricultural strategy for India's Fourth Five-Year Plan: "Peasants on unirrigated land, he argued, had learned to make the best use of their resources in thousands of years of unchanged environment; outlays must be concentrated on the 10 percent of farmers with the best prospects of raising their output."

The minister neglects technological change and so misses Schultz's point. Raising productivity in traditional agriculture depends on new high-payoff inputs. But once these are introduced, it is not certain that the efficiency of traditional agriculture will be maintained. Later, T. W. Schultz (1975) pointed out that during transitions from one efficient equilibrium to another, different farmers adjust at different rates according to, among other things, education and experience.

Once productivity of traditional agriculture has been raised by new technology, smallholders may be less poor, but will they still be efficient? And can broad-based development strategies really achieve the efficient expansion of agricultural output necessary to feed growing populations? Or should policymakers focus efforts on large farms?

THE ECONOMICS OF FARM SIZE

Let's start with a clarification. *Economics of farm size* so far has been used to mean *economies and diseconomies of scale* and *economies and diseconomies of farm size*. These must be treated separately. *Economies and diseconomies of farm size* refer to the effect of farm size on changes in input and output relationships. *Economies and diseconomies of scale* (or increasing and decreasing returns to scale) apply only to the relationship between proportional changes in *all* inputs and the resulting effect on output—that is, the output effects of multiplication of production activities without changing relative input proportions (see Box 4.2).

Different intensities of labor, land, or capital use by farm size result from economies and diseconomies of farm size; they are not scale effects. Economies or diseconomies of farm size can (and do) exist even in the absence of pure scale effects.

The Scale of Agricultural Production

Economies and diseconomies of scale do exist in agriculture; very large and very small farms tend to rent out land. The crucial question is: does scale matter significantly over the size range that includes most farms? Put another way, at what size are significant scale economies exhausted and do diseconomies begin?

Scale economies in agriculture arise from agricultural activities involving indivisible (or "lumpy") inputs and integrating agricultural production with other economic activities that embody significant scale economies. Tractors are lumpy inputs: the economies of scale in tractor ownership result from fuller use when the farm size approximates the tractor's capacity. Tractor hire services can be a substitute for ownership, but because of critical timing requirements and scheduling difficulties, they are not a perfect substitute. But although the tractor itself is subject to economies of scale as a source of power, there is nothing intrinsically indivisible about agricultural cultivation activities. Alternative, divisible technologies exist. When capital is relatively scarce and the opportunity cost of labor is low, human- or animal-powered implements are likely to be more socially efficient than tractors for many tasks, although not all. Nevertheless, increases in the number of tractors in a CARL are more likely to result from subsidies (for tractors, fuel, or interest rates) than social efficiency (see Box 4.3).

Is managerial capability a lumpy input because it is embodied in an individual? Clearly, a superior manager can have a greater impact on output when managing a large farm. This, however, must be balanced against potential diseconomies in the scale of management in agriculture. Agricultural management is likely to be superior when decision making is decentralized and decisions are made by many owner-cultivators or tenants, because such farmers have intimate knowledge of their land and of other resources. Moreover, shirking and poor performance increase as farm size increases—and so do costs to control them.

Only a few crops—sugarcane, tea, and palm oil—require close coordination between production and processing, which is characterized by economies of scale. Shipping and marketing of perishable crops—for example, bananas for export—also involve economies of scale. In most of these cases, pro-

Box 4.2.   Returns to Scale

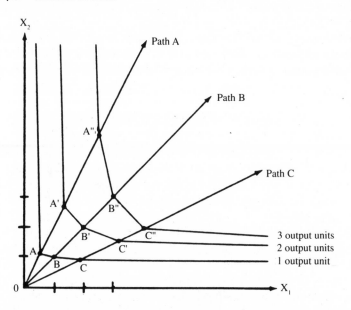

Portions of a two-input, single-output production function depict different scale effects to isolate the technical nature of scale economies. Each kinked curve links the combinations of inputs X_1 to X_2, yielding a specific level of output. Increasing either input increases total output. Scale effects with only two inputs are defined as the effect on the level of output of proportional changes in both inputs. Graphically, this corresponds to tracing a straight-line path away from the origin and observing the relationship between quantities of inputs and output. Ratios of input X_1 to X_2 are 1:2, 1:1, and 2:1 for Path A, Path B, and Path C, respectively. This (unusual) production function was drawn to depict decreasing, constant, and increasing returns to scale in a single graph. These effects can be seen by considering the length of segments connecting different output levels.

> For Path A: $OA < AA' < A'A''$
> For Path B: $OB = BB' = B'B''$
> For Path C: $OC > CC' > C'C''$

Because it is necessary to more than double inputs on Path A to increase output from 1 to 2 units, Path A exhibits diminishing returns to scale. By a similar reasoning, Path B exhibits constant returns to scale (doubling both inputs doubles output), and Path C represents increasing returns to scale. These effects are purely technical. However, manifestation of the technical effects depends on economic decisions regarding efficient input combinations.

Source: Johnston and Tomich 1984.

duction is well-suited to a small farm, and the associated activities involving economies of scale can be profitably organized through group arrangements without affecting the organization of agricultural production. Taiwan provides one example: independent small-scale producers supplied most of the sugarcane for its mills. Malaysia's experience suggests that a similar approach is feasible for palm oil (Barlow 1986). And the Kenya Tea Development Authority efficiently meshes smallholder tea production with timely, large-scale processing.

The colonial legacy of large-scale, vertically integrated producers, processors, and marketers of export crops has contributed to the idea that huge "agribusinesses" are more efficient producers than small farms. This is not necessarily so. Take the large-scale producers of "plantation crops" (sugarcane, coconuts, bananas, and pineapples) in the Philippines. They were exempt from agrarian reform (at least before the Aquino regime) because of presumed economies of scale. Yet, the myth of scale economies in producing and marketing Philippine coconuts, other tree crops, and sugarcane has been debunked (by Hayami, Quisumbing, and Adriano 1990). For sugarcane, yields on farms of more than 50 hectares are higher than for those under 10 hectares—but so, too, are production costs. Furthermore, these larger farms have preferential access to subsidized credit. Thus, their higher yields do not provide conclusive evidence of greater economic efficiency. In fact, it is likely that the Philippines' small-scale sugarcane growers are more socially efficient because they make greater use of abundant labor and economize on scarce capital.

As with coconuts, there are no important yield differences between large and small farms producing bananas or pineapples in the Philippines (Hayami, Quisumbing, and Adriano 1990). The economics of exporting fresh bananas and canned pineapples, however, are complicated by the quality control and uniformity necessary to compete in major export markets, such as the United States and Japan.

The domination of these exports by a few vertically integrated multinational corporations gave the Philippines a competitive advantage over the small-scale production and decentralized handling of these commodities in Taiwan. Although Taiwan lost most of its fresh banana export market to the higher-quality Philippine product, it remained competitive in low-priced canned pineapples until the early 1970s (Ranis and Stewart 1987). Marketing links and brand-name recognition of the U.S. and Japanese multinationals exporting from the Philippines may have been decisive in increasing exports. But these advantages arise in distribution; they are not incompatible with small-scale production. If there is an economic advantage of large-scale production of perishables for export, it probably lies in producing large quantities of uniform fruit. This, in turn, may depend on strict measures to control pests and diseases, as well as close coordination of har-

Box 4.3. Production Efficiency

Graphs of production processes using two inputs to produce a single output are used here to simplify the definition of *economic efficiency*, which comprises *technical efficiency* and *allocative efficiency*. Technical efficiency and allocative efficiency are both necessary components of economic efficiency. The distinctions apparent here are true also for complex agricultural production processes.

Technical efficiency is an engineering concept. Comparison of the technical efficiency of two producers requires that they have the same access to technical information and input supplies. The following graphs plot technically possible combinations of two inputs to produce a unit of output. Figures A, B, and C depict different technical relationships between inputs. In Figure A, inputs X_1 and X_2 can be substituted freely; so, only the cheaper of the two inputs will be used. The technology in Figure B is the opposite: substitution between X_1 and X_2 is impossible, and the proportion of X_1 and X_2 employed will not be affected by price.

The curves in Figure C represent two technologies with substitution possibilities characteristic of agricultural production. Smoothly bending unit-output curves indicate diminishing marginal rates of substitution (more and more X_1 must be substituted to replace X_2, or vice versa). Figure C establishes the technical superiority of producers operating at point 1 or 2 relative to point 3. A producer at point 1 uses less of each input to produce a unit of output than a firm at point 3. A firm at point 2 uses the same amount of X_1 as a firm at point 3, but less X_2 is used. Points 1 and 2 are technically superior to point 3, which is technically inefficient. If no feasible points lie closer to the origin on Figure C, points 1 and 2 are both technically efficient. Figure C only shows that point 1 uses more X_2 and less X_1; point 2 uses more X_1 and less X_2. But Figure C *does not* contain enough information to determine which of the two technically efficient points is economically efficient.

Allocative efficiency means making production decisions so that the marginal costs for additional inputs and investments equal the revenue expected from the resulting increase in production. Appropriate use of this criterion depends on knowledge of the actual prices experienced by producers. It also presumes that all decision makers seek to maximize profits and that they can do so instantaneously.

Figure D adds input price information to the technical relationships of Figure C. If all producers face the prices of inputs X_1 and X_2 indicated by the solid lines, the slope of the lines identifies the allocatively efficient input proportions in Figure D. Point 3 is allocatively efficient, but not technically efficient. Point 2 is technically efficient, but not allocatively efficient: it uses too much X_1 at these prices. Only point 1 is economically efficient because it is both technically efficient and allocatively efficient at these prices.

If prices in Figure D change such that X_1 becomes relatively cheaper and X_2 relatively more expensive (as depicted by the dashed price line in Figure D), efficiency evaluations change. At these prices point 3 is inefficient (technically and allocatively), point 1 is no longer allocatively efficient (meaning it is no longer economically efficient), and point 2 attains economic efficiency. In response to these price changes, an economically efficient producer initially operating at point

Box 4.3. (continued)

1 would shift to point 2. The ability to allocate—and reallocate—is the essence of allocative efficiency.

Assessment of economic efficiency is complicated by market imperfections (for example, transaction costs and risk) and by policy distortions that mean that market prices do not reflect true economic scarcities. *Financial efficiency* means that production decisions are economically efficient when evaluated at *market* prices. *Social efficiency* means that production decisions are economically efficient when evaluated at *economic* prices; that is, the marginal *economic* costs of additional inputs and investments equals the marginal economic value of the expected production increases. In short, financial efficiency and social efficiency are distinguished by reference to the prices used. With perfect markets and in the absence of policy-induced distortions, the measures are identical because market prices reflect economic scarcities. Financial efficiency and social efficiency diverge to the extent that market imperfections—including those leading to farm-size effects—and government policies cause differences between economic values and the costs farmers face.

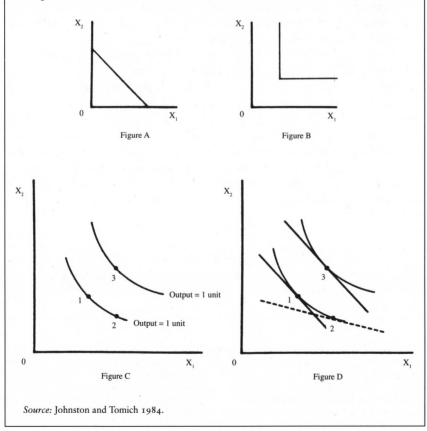

Figure A

Figure B

Output = 1 unit

Output = 1 unit

Figure C

Figure D

Source: Johnston and Tomich 1984.

vesting and handling. But even these are not unassailable examples of economies of scale. Thailand, where small-scale contract growers are conspicuous, has overtaken the Philippines in canned pineapple (Hayami and others 1990, pp. 142–43).

Like sugarcane in the Philippines, yields on large coffee estates in Kenya and big tobacco plantations in Malawi are higher than on smallholdings. But they had no advantage over smallholders in financial efficiency: higher production costs offset higher yields (Lele and Agarwal 1989). Indeed, Kenya's coffee smallholders are more efficient—financially and socially—than the estates. The economics of tobacco production in Malawi is more complex, but tobacco smallholders may make better use of domestic resources—that is, they are more socially efficient—than estates.

For agriculture in India (and in other developing countries) most evidence is consistent with a study of about 1,000 Indian farms (Bardhan 1973) suggesting that returns to scale are constant or decreasing in most districts. In general, this study shows no advantage in efficiency or output for large farms. It concludes that the inverse relationship between output per hectare and farm size is mainly the result of the inverse relationship between farm size and inputs of labor and other nonland inputs.

Generally, economies and diseconomies of scale are unimportant in agriculture in CARLs, with returns to scale as constant or slightly decreasing. Analyses by Kawagoe, Hayami, and Ruttan (1985) and by Hayami and Ruttan (1985, p. 157) suggest that scale economies exist in high-income countries, but that agricultural production in CARLs is neutral with respect to the scale of farm operation.[5] And evidence indicates that large farms in CARLs have no advantage over small farms in *financial* efficiency. Indeed, small farms often are more *socially* efficient than large ones, and contrary to popular opinion, large farms that have higher yields than small farms are the exception, not the rule.

Farm Size and Factor Intensity

Small farms are not simply scaled-down models of large farms. Systematic differences in output and input intensities result from farm-size effects and have important policy implications. The notion that bigger farms are better (or best) in CARLs is inconsistent with the evidence:

---

[5] An extension of this analysis by Lau and Yotopoulos (1989) using a more flexible specification suggests the plausible conclusion that the quantity of machinery (measured in tractor horsepower) per farm is at the heart of this change in agricultural technology in the course of structural transformation. They conclude (p. 266) that although agriculture may display increasing returns to scale in countries such as the United States and Japan that have passed their structural transformation turning point, CARLs are likely to display decreasing or constant returns to scale in agriculture.

- There is an inverse relationship between farm size and output.
- There is no necessary relationship between farm size and the adoption of technology.
- There is an inverse relationship between farm size and employment.

Much evidence points to a decline in output per unit area as the total area of a farm increases—the famous "inverse relationship" between farm size and output (see Figure 4.1). Berry and Cline (1979) summarized data for a number of developing countries, including Brazil, Colombia, the Philippines, Pakistan, India, and the Muda River area of Malaysia, and found that land productivity on smaller farms was higher than on larger farms. Similarly, a study of FAO farm-management data for developing countries in Asia, Africa, and Latin America found a strong negative relationship between farm size and output for all but three countries (Cornia 1985); likewise for Bangladesh (Hossain 1977) and Indonesia (Booth 1979; Keuning 1984).

There are two qualifications to the inverse relationship. The first is related to an inverse relationship between farm size and land quality. But attempts to control land quality in the Philippines (Roumasset 1976) and Colombia (Berry and Cline 1979) simply weaken the relationship; they do not reverse it. Second, the relationship may also be weakened by technological change, as shown in analysis of farm survey data for India from 1968–69 to 1970–71 (Bhalla 1979) and a study of Bangladesh (Hossain 1988). Deolalikar (1981, p. 275) even asserts that "the inverse relation is true only of a traditional agriculture." For India, that view is supported by Singh's (1990, pp. 101–07) survey of empirical studies. Of thirteen studies of India *before* high-yielding varieties, eight support an inverse relationship, three are ambiguous, and only two suggest a productivity advantage for large farms; for another 11 studies based on data from the early years of India's Green Revolution, that is, the 1960s to the mid-1970s, Singh (1990) reports that only two supported an inverse relationship, two were ambiguous, and seven suggested that it no longer held. Evidence that the relationship is reversed (as in Roy 1981) appears to have been a phenomenon of the early phases of technological change, however.

If productivity growth were restricted to large farms for long enough, the inverse relationship could be overturned, more so if investment in infrastructure, price policies, and other elements of agricultural development strategy also favored large farms. Indeed, the dualistic strategy Mexico followed from 1940 to 1970 was almost a blueprint for undermining the inverse relationship (Chapter 10).

But technological change on small farms can keep pace with overall productivity growth in agriculture, sustaining the inverse relationship. Studies of farms in India's Haryana State by Carter (1984) and of new high-yielding wheat varieties in the Indian Punjab (Sidhu 1974) indicate that the relationship persisted after the spread of new varieties. So does a study of rice

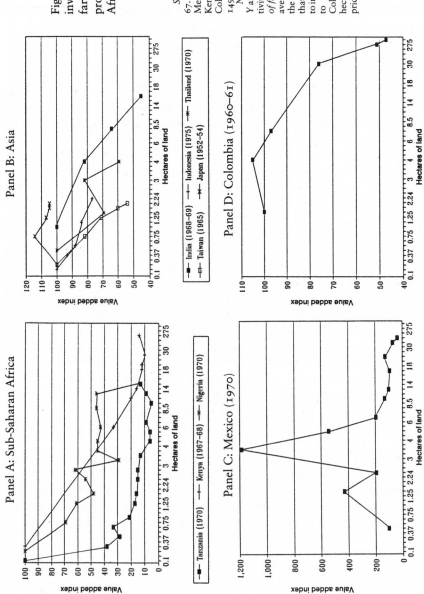

Figure 4.1. Examples of the inverse relationship between farm size and total factor productivity from sub-Saharan Africa, Asia, and Latin America

Sources: Indonesia: Keuning 1984, p. 67. Tanzania, Nigeria, Thailand, and Mexico: Cornia 1985, pp. 520–23. Kenya, India, Taiwan, Japan, and Colombia: Berry and Cline 1979, pp. 59, 149, 173, 195, 197, 201.

Notes: The value added index on the Y axis is an index of total factor productivity (with smallest farm unit = 100). *Size of farm operating unit* refers either to the average size of farms for that size class or the midpoint of the reported range for that size class. Data for Indonesia refer to irrigated rice only. Data for Kenya refer to settlement schemes only. Data for Colombia are value added per "effective hectare," which is adjusted for land prices.

Figure 4.2.   Rice yields for high-yielding and traditional varieties on Java, Indonesia (1976)

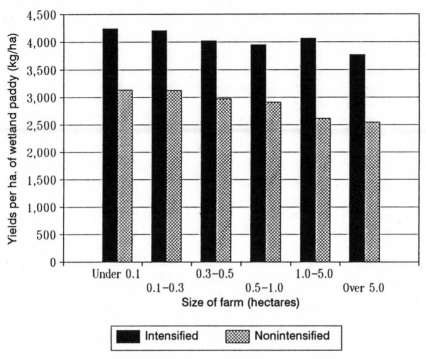

Source: Booth and Sundrum 1984, p. 124.

farmers in the Philippines (Herdt and Mandac 1981) and evidence for rice farmers on Java (Figure 4.2). So, although the inverse relationship may weaken (or even reverse) during the early days of adoption of new technology, small-scale farmers can catch up and ultimately surpass larger farms (Lipton and Longhurst 1989, pp. 141–44).

Farm Size and New Technology

There is often a lag in the adoption of technology on small farms relative to large farms, possibly because of risk aversion, lack of education, and im-perfections in credit markets and access to information.

Poor farmers may be conservative in production decisions, because failure to achieve expected profits could threaten household subsistence. This, it has often been argued, means that large (that is, wealthier) farms are better able to adopt new techniques, because they are less concerned with risk. But this presumes (implicitly) that new techniques are riskier than traditional methods.

Research on rainfed areas in India's semiarid tropics and elsewhere nevertheless suggests that the riskiness of new techniques and higher-yielding varieties has been overstated and that the ability of small-scale farmers to manage risk has been underestimated (Walker and Ryan 1990, Chapter 8). First, there are a significant number of cases where new farming techniques provide higher expected yields and *lower* risk. For example, Walker and Ryan (1990, p. 223) cite a study in northeastern Thailand where no trade-off between expected returns and risk was found in 44 of 47 comparisons of cropping activities. And from their extensive Indian data set, they "could cite only a handful of cases where risk played a prominent role in the adoption of improved practices, technologies, or cropping systems" (Walker and Ryan 1990, p. 262).

Choices were clear-cut in most cases. Either new varieties (or techniques) were unlikely to outperform local ones unless weather was exceptionally good, so few farmers adopted them, or they were more profitable under all but the most adverse circumstances, and only a severely risk-averse farmer would forgo the new technology. Although experimental measurements of risk aversion are of limited reliability, most Indian farmers who participated in these studies displayed moderate to intermediate risk aversion in simulation games. More important, they revealed, through their decisions in the real world, that they could identify strategies that allowed them to use new techniques and varieties at an acceptable risk through gradual, informed selection among new varieties, adaptation of new practices, and diversification of activities.

The skills and experience of small-scale farmers, too, are often overlooked as potentials for adaptive capacity. Small-scale farmers can gain experience through limited on-farm experiments before moving to whole-hearted commitment to a new technology. Indeed, the great advantage of a sequence of divisible innovations epitomized by improved seed-fertilizer combinations is precisely that such an incremental adoption process is facilitated. Comparing the adoption of specific innovations shows that only for lumpy inputs have large-scale farmers done significantly better than small-scale farmers. Of thirty villages in Asia, large farms (more than 3.1 hectares) were the major adopters of tractors, but farms under 1.1 hectare had faster and higher adoption of modern varieties, fertilizer, and pesticide (Figure 4.3); likewise, in a review of agricultural development in South Asia (Singh 1990, p. 200) and in an International Maize and Wheat Improvement Center (CIMMYT) study of new wheat varieties and other technology in the Mexican Altiplano (Byerlee and Hesse de Polanco 1982).

There appears to be no intrinsic long-run productivity disadvantage for small farms, but the distribution of gains between large and small farms depends on the timing of adoption. An analysis of twenty-three studies of the effect of education on agricultural efficiency showed that primary education was more likely to have a positive effect under technological

Figure 4.3. Relative adoption behavior by farm size and type of technology (Cumulative percentage of farms in three size classes adopting specific innovations. Farms in thirty selected villages in Asia.)

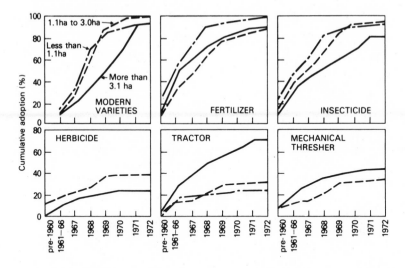

Source: Pinstrup-Andersen 1982, Figure 6.2, p. 130. © Longman Group Ltd. Reprinted by permission.

change, supporting Schultz's hypothesis (Lockheed, Jamison, and Lau 1980).[6] Thus, more primary education in rural areas may reduce the lag between adoption on large and small farms. This is why notions regarding education were emphasized as part of broad-based development strategies in the United States and Japan (Chapter 3) and why similar attention is given to education in the case studies of China, Taiwan, Mexico, Kenya, and Tanzania (Part 3).

Increases in rice yields in Indonesia, which helped it move from being the world's biggest importer to self-sufficiency by 1985, would have been impossible without widespread technological change on small farms (Figure 4.4). High-yielding varieties accounted for more than three-fourths of rice planted in Indonesia by 1981 (Dalrymple 1986a, p. 50). Indeed, the spread of high-yielding varieties of rice across South and Southeast Asia (from 13,800 hectares in 1965–66 to 35.7 million hectares or roughly 45 percent of the planted area in 1982–83) was due to widespread adoption on small, as well as large, farms. In new wheats, the spread has been more dramatic. In India, high-yielding wheat rose from 4.2 percent of wheat area in 1966–67 to more than 75 percent by 1982–83. For all South and Southeast Asia, the

---

[6] They also noted that four to six years of primary schooling might represent a threshold for the positive effect of education.

Small Farms in a Broad-Based Agricultural Strategy　129

Figure 4.4. Yields of irrigated rice in Java, Indonesia, 1968–90

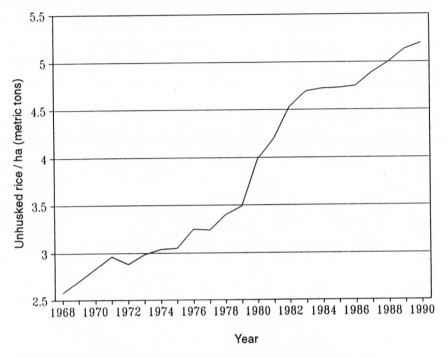

Source: Booth 1988, p. 140, and Central Bureau of Statistics, Jakarta, Indonesia.

area planted to high-yielding varieties already covered almost 80 percent of wheat area by 1982–83 (Figure 4.5).

Patterns of adoption are uneven, but not because of differences in attitudes of farmers. In their article on "Impediments to Technical Progress on Small versus Large Farms," Perrin and Winkelmann (1976, p. 893) emphasized that "the most pervasive explanation of why some farmers do not adopt new varieties and fertilizer while others do is that the expected increase in yield for some farmers is small or nil, while for others it is insignificant due to differences (sometimes subtle) in soils, climate, water availability, and other biological factors." Indeed, a detailed investigation of Plan Puebla in Mexico showed that recommendations were not adopted because they simply did not make sense for the soil conditions on many farmers' plots (Gladwin 1979). The adoption of hybrid maize in Kenya is another example (see Chapter 11).

In studies of Asian agricultural development in the early 1970s there were fears that in areas where the new technology proved feasible, it was being monopolized by larger landholders, who might then use profits to buy up smaller farms and polarize rural society further. This has proved far too pessimistic.

Figure 4.5. Area planted with higher-yielding rice and wheat in South and Southeast Asia, 1965–66 to 1982–83

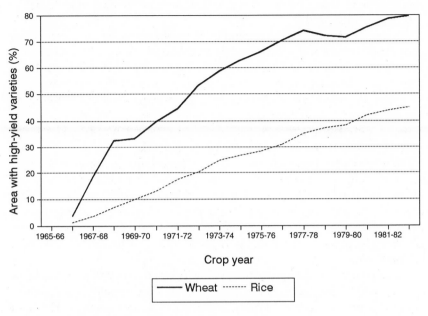

Source: Dalrymple 1986a and 1986b, Table 4.6, p. 87.

Despite real disadvantages, many small farms can adopt high-yielding seeds and fertilizer if new varieties can be adapted to their farming conditions. The eviction or displacement of smallholders has been caused not by new varieties and fertilizer but by technological change coupled with mechanization subsidies and other policies that promote a bimodal distribution of farms (see, for example, Lipton and Longhurst 1985, pp. 36–37; Singh 1990, pp. 191–95).

Farm Size and Labor Inputs

As agricultural labor forces continue to increase, it is important to look at employment-generating prospects and, so, at farm size and labor use. Job opportunities are vital because a growing share of the rural labor force in CARLs are landless laborers or members of farm households that depend on wage labor as their primary source of income (Chapter 1).

Studies in India and other Asian countries made during the early years of the Green Revolution confirmed higher labor use on small farms. In Taiwan, labor per hectare has been inversely related to farm size. In Japan, this inverse relationship with inputs has been reversed as the expansion of employment opportunities in the economy increased the opportunity cost of farm labor, moving Japan into a labor-saving, capital-using phase. But as late as 1975 in Japan there was a strong and steady reduction in labor use as farm size increased.

This inverse relationship has significant implications for the demand for labor in agriculture and, so, for income distribution in rural areas. In general, differences in labor use are substantial among farms of different sizes. Japan in 1952–54, Taiwan in 1965, and Colombia in 1960–61 showed a strong inverse relationship for countries at, or near, the structural transformation turning point (Figure 4.6). In both Japan and Taiwan agricultural labor was almost entirely family labor, although before the post–World War II land reforms much of it came from members of tenant households.

The relationship between farm size and hired labor is not as well established, but there is much evidence that even small farms hire labor. The Indonesian islands of Java and Bali are perhaps typical (Figure 4.7). Labor hiring, substantial even in the smallest category, is higher for some larger size categories. For India hired labor per acre actually decreases with farm size (Bhalla 1979, p. 165, and Figure 6.2). Kenya shows an even more pronounced decline (Collier 1989).

The introduction of high-yielding rice varieties in the Philippines was associated with a big reduction in family labor and, initially, a more-than-equivalent increase in hired labor (Roumasett and Smith 1981). The same pattern has been reported for Bangladesh (Hossain 1988). A related effect was found in another set of studies: when farm household income went up because of higher output prices, family labor inputs decreased (Singh and others 1986, p. 163).

When labor-saving innovations for land preparation (power tillers) and for weeding (herbicides) were adopted in the Philippines, the increase in labor hiring was reversed. This was induced "by the falling cost of mechanical power and herbicides relative to animal power and labor" (Roumasset and Smith 1981, p. 416). This transition to capital-using, labor-saving technologies would have happened eventually, as it did in Japan.

One big aim of development is to raise returns to labor by increasing labor (demand) through labor-using, land-saving productivity growth. Unfortunately, the rise in labor demand in rural areas is often cut short by the premature onset of capital–labor substitution induced by macroeconomic distortions (Chapter 5).

Farm-Size Effects

Markets for factors of production may be imperfect or nonexistent in CARLs because of incomplete information, high transaction costs, risky prospects, and costly enforcement or difficult supervision of performance.

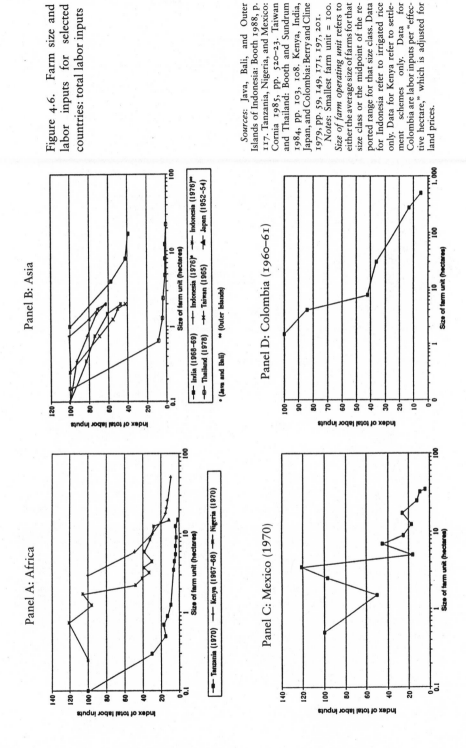

Figure 4.6. Farm size and labor inputs for selected countries: total labor inputs

Panel A: Africa

Panel B: Asia

Panel C: Mexico (1970)

Panel D: Colombia (1960–61)

Sources: Java, Bali, and Outer Islands of Indonesia: Booth 1988, p. 117. Tanzania, Nigeria, and Mexico: Cornia 1985, pp. 520–23. Taiwan and Thailand: Booth and Sundrum 1984, pp. 103, 108. Kenya, India, Japan, and Colombia: Berry and Cline 1979, pp. 59, 149, 171, 197, 201.

Notes: Smallest farm unit = 100. *Size of farm operating unit* refers to either the average size of farms for that size class or the midpoint of the reported range for that size class. Data for Indonesia refer to irrigated rice only. Data for Kenya refer to settlement schemes only. Data for Colombia are labor inputs per "effective hectare," which is adjusted for land prices.

Figure 4.7.   Farm size and hired labor inputs for selected countries

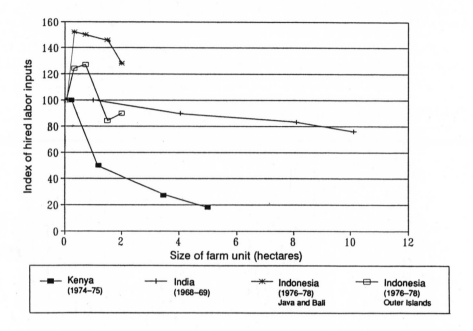

Sources: Kenya: Collier 1989, p. 751. India: Berry and Cline 1979, p. 165. Java, Bali, and Outer Islands of Indonesia: Booth 1988, p. 117.

Notes: Smallest farm unit = 100. *Size of farm operating unit* refers to either the average size of farms for that size class or the midpoint of the reported range for that size class. Data for Indonesia refer to irrigated rice only.

These imperfections have different impacts on farms of varying sizes, including differences in costs.

The considerable diversity in the three broad factors of production—land, labor, and capital—interacts with market imperfections to bring about farm-size effects.[7] Land productivity is affected by, for example, soil quality and rainfall and labor productivity—not only by the size of the work force but also by such things as health, nutritional status, education, experience, and motivation. Similarly, capital assets differ greatly in potential risks and returns. Relationships among people with different claims on factors (landlords and tenants, employers and employees, borrowers and lenders) are obscured by access to information. Workers know more about their skills than potential employers. Sellers of land, livestock, or used equipment are more aware of its qualities than potential buyers. Borrowers have a better idea about their ability to repay than their creditors. Because knowl-

[7] This section draws heavily on the synthesis of behavioral and material aspects of production relations by Binswanger and Rosenzweig (1986).

edge can be withheld or disguised, exchanges of information may be hampered even for simple transactions because of conflicting interests. In complex, longer-term transactions (sharecropping, for example), imperfect information leads to problems of monitoring and enforcing agreements ("moral hazard"). So, imperfect information, risk, and attendant transaction costs affect rural markets for labor, land, and capital, and these effects tend to differ by farm size.

The main diseconomies of farm size come from hiring costs and incentive problems. Because family members have a claim on residual production, rather than receiving a fixed wage, their self-interest is to maximize farm profits by working hard and using their initiative.

In hiring two forces drive up employers' costs and drive down laborers' remuneration. Workers incur costs in searching for a job and in forgone production in the family farm household. Employers incur hiring and screening costs, as well as supervisory costs that increase with the number of hired workers. So, the inverse relationship between farm size and intensity of labor may be due to diseconomies of size arising from supervisory costs.

In addition, because the number of distinct decisions rises with farm size, decision-making skills are subject to diseconomies of farm size as a direct result of the heterogeneity of natural resources and the diversity of the resource-management tasks in agricultural production processes. These managerial diseconomies lead to incentives to substitute capital equipment for labor supervision, pressure reinforced by economies of farm size in borrowing.

Preferential access to credit and reduced costs of capital are, perhaps, the most important economies of farm size. These reflect economies of scale in lending because average costs to lenders are inversely related to the size of loans and because credit limits are directly related to collateral requirements. Land is particularly suitable for use as collateral (but only when property rights are well defined). As a result, landowners enjoy special advantages that extend beyond (and derive from) their relative wealth. Owners of small plots, tenants, and rural wage laborers have limited access to credit and pay higher interest. The negative relationship between farm size and cost of capital in India reflects differing interest charges by credit source as well as farm-size effects (Figure 4.8). Here, large farms have preferential access to government programs that provide subsidized credit, and small-scale farmers depend primarily on village moneylenders and other high-cost sources.

Capital market imperfections spill over into land markets. In particular, the value of land as collateral becomes embodied in land market prices (but not in rents), raising land prices above the present discounted value of land productivity. This makes land purchases more difficult for landless people who also need land to get credit. The evidence that points to an inverse re-

Figure 4.8. Cost of capital by farm size, India, 1970–71

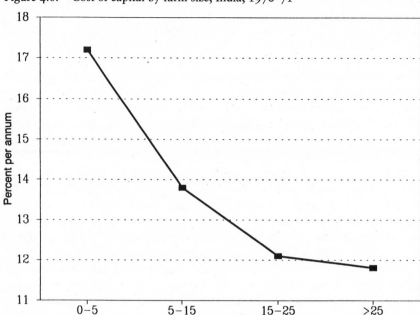

Source: S. Bhalla in Berry and Cline 1979, Table A.5, p. 160. © 1979 Johns Hopkins University Press. Reprinted by permission.

lationship between farm size and output indicates that in countries where labor is relatively abundant, diseconomies typically outweigh economies of farm size. The inverse relationship of farm size to output arises from factor market imperfections and leads to systematic differences in inputs and outputs across farm units of different sizes. Together, these farm-size effects also create a tendency for smaller operating units to adopt relatively labor-using and capital-saving technologies (Box 4.4).

TECHNOLOGICAL CHANGE IN ASIA AND SUB-SAHARAN AFRICA

History, politics, and culture are important factors in the distribution of farm sizes and patterns of agricultural development. The size distribution was often established in colonial times, along with institutions to support the status quo. It is hardly surprising, then, that there is economic and social inequality. In many countries, paternalism, bureaucratic practices, and disparaging attitudes toward small-scale farmers are major obstacles to agricultural development.

Asian Agricultural Development Successes

Agricultural development in Asia has been especially encouraging despite meager land endowments. In addition to the Japanese and Taiwanese successes (Chapters 3 and 10), progress in South Korea has been spectacular. In all three, economic transformation was helped greatly by broad-based agricultural development. In China, although incomes are still low, remarkable progress has been made in eradicating acute poverty and improving the health and nutrition of the masses. For China, too, agricultural development has, for the most part, involved broad-based productivity growth similar to that of Japan and Taiwan (Chapter 9).

South and Southeast Asia have benefited most from the spread of high-yielding, fertilizer-responsive varieties of rice and wheat. Semidwarf wheats have been largely limited to areas of controlled irrigation in northern India and in Pakistan, although there has also been a surprising spread of high-yielding varieties in rainfed areas of northern Pakistan and Bangladesh. The impact of the high-yielding varieties of rice has been wider but uneven. Rainfed and deep flooding areas (much of Bangladesh and Thailand) have benefited little from semidwarf rices, although some second- (and later-) generation varieties have extended the area where higher-yielding varieties have had an impact.

In South and Southeast Asia, rainfed and dryland rice covers a larger area than irrigated rice fields, around which the population is concentrated (Huke 1982, p. 7). Initially, innovation was concentrated on the relatively homogeneous environment of irrigation. This enabled scientists to develop varieties suitable to irrigation in many countries. Potential yield increases were large and reliable, diffusion of new varieties rapid, and the returns on research investment enormous: 84 percent for the International Rice Research Institute (IRRI) and 74 percent in 1975 for national research programs in Asia (Evenson 1978, p. 238).[8]

Many of the most populated countries in Asia have made much progress in broad-based agricultural development. The rapid stream of innovations has disturbed the "traditional" equilibrium, and farmers have increased inputs to move toward a new equilibrium. But many farmers are still fine-tuning production decisions. Soon after Indonesia reached self-sufficiency in rice, for example, production was threatened by pests. It became clear that pesticides were being overused. In Java in the late 1980s evidence showed

[8] The growing supply of agricultural scientists, social scientists, agricultural administrators, and other specialists has been a significant positive factor in much of South and Southeast Asia. Rapid expansion of agricultural research programs since the mid-1960s would not have been possible without well-trained and increasingly experienced scientists and administrators. Development of India's agricultural universities during the 1960s benefited substantially from economic and technical assistance. Parallel developments have occurred in many other countries in South and Southeast Asia.

Box 4.4. Farm-Size Effects and Capital-Labor Ratios

Relationships between farm size (measured in land area) and relative quantities of capital and labor inputs depend on at least three inputs to the production process: land, capital, and labor. Even a simple three-input, one-output graphic representation, such as Figure A, is difficult to interpret. To compare production

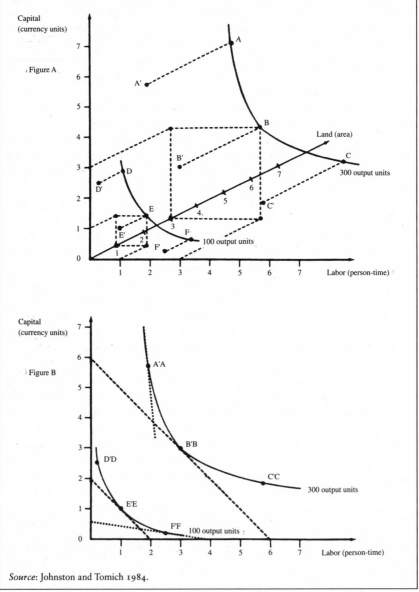

Source: Johnston and Tomich 1984.

possibilities for farms in two size categories (1 unit and 3 units of area), imagine that the curves in Figure A are projected on to the plane formed by the labor-capital axes. Points A, B, C, D, E, and F are projected to points A′, B′, C′, D′, E′, and F′. This "side view" representation corresponds to the two-dimensional graph in Figure B.

Without farm-size effects and under ideal economic conditions, costs of capital and labor are the same regardless of farm size. This is depicted by the two parallel cost lines (with arbitrarily chosen slope) indicated by the broken lines in Figure B. The economically efficient point for small farms, at E′E, and for large farms, at B′B, corresponds to an identical capital-labor ratio regardless of farm size.

Farm-size effects arise because capital and labor costs vary by farm size, as depicted by the dotted cost lines in Figure B. Financial institutions' economies of scale in lending, the collateral value of land, and other imperfections in credit markets decrease capital costs for large farms relative to average levels. At the same time, costs of transactions and monitoring increase the effective cost of labor as hired labor increases relative to fixed management capacity. The steep cost line tangent to point A′A represents the shift in unit costs experienced by large farms from farm-size effects: capital is relatively cheap and labor is relatively more expensive at the farm level. Conversely, the relative disadvantage in credit markets and greater intensity of management attention per unit area on smaller farms leads to a flatter line tangent to the curve for small farms at point F′F. Relative to average unit costs, capital is costlier, and hired labor is cheaper on small farms.

Figure B illustrates the fact that farm-size effects make smaller farms more labor-using and capital-saving than large farms. So, factor proportions can differ systematically by farm size, even if all farms are financially efficient and if all farms have equal access to technology.

Source: Johnston and Tomich 1984.

---

that phosphate fertilizer on irrigated rice could be cut by at least 25 percent without reducing yields. Such fertilizers are a small part of production costs for farmers but were a large slice of fertilizer subsidy costs. And as for pesticides, official recommendations and price policies contributed to inefficiencies on the farm. Indonesia is addressing these problems, but such technical and allocative inefficiencies characterize "post–Green Revolution" agriculture in large areas of Asia (Byerlee 1987). The problems of widespread adoption of higher-yielding varieties (and concomitant levels of other inputs) present new challenges to improve farmers' management skills and to develop institutions that can generate the information farmers need and supply it in a form farmers can use.

The sketchy data that are available suggest that food production in sub-Saharan Africa failed to keep pace with the growth of population in the 1970s and 1980s. Future prospects are even more disturbing. African countries face a formidable long-term problem in their transition from resource-based agricultural growth to science-based agriculture, in which increases in factor productivity become major sources of expanded output.

Hopes that Africa would quickly follow Asia in a Green Revolution have been dashed because of agroclimatic conditions and continuing weaknesses in national agricultural research. In addition, there is scant incentive for farmers to invest in the labor-using, land-saving innovations developed for Asia in areas where land is still abundant.

In 1990 eighteen sub-Saharan CARLs had more than 5 hectares of agricultural land per agricultural worker (Table 4.3). But population growth is shifting some countries toward relative labor abundance and land scarcity. For example, Nigeria, Africa's most populous country, has only 2.7 hectares per worker, and the agricultural work force in 2025 will be at least twice as large as it was in 1990—and still growing.

Already, 21 countries containing most of the people of sub-Saharan Africa have high population densities or will by 2025 (Binswanger and Pingali 1988, p. 88). To standardize differing climates and soils, comparisons are based on *agroclimatic population density* and *agroclimatic labor density*, respectively, the projected population and agricultural labor force, each divided by agricultural production potential measured in kilocalories. This yields results that are likely to hold despite uncertainty in the underlying projections.[9] By this measure most countries of sub-Saharan Africa will have a higher agricultural labor density than India by 2025 (see Figure 4.9).

Nine African countries, including Kenya and Nigeria, have mixed climates with large areas of good soils and reasonable rainfall and hold almost half of sub-Saharan Africa's population. By 2025 they will have a suitable agronomic base and sufficient population densities for land-saving, labor-using technologies to make sense.

The climate in another nine countries (about 9 percent of the sub-Saharan population) is arid or semiarid. Without irrigation (limited by the physical environment and high capital costs), cropping potential is severely constrained. The extreme case is Botswana: it has an agroclimatic population density comparable with those of Egypt and Mexico despite having one of

[9] Aside from the problems in interpreting population and labor force projections (Chapter 1), estimates of agroclimatic population densities and agroclimatic labor force densities depend crucially on projections of calorie production in agriculture. Higgins and others (1982) review the assumptions and complex methodology used for these estimates.

Table 4.3. Projections of population density by climate, selected countries

Climate category/ country	Agricultural land/ agricultural labor force in 1990 (ha/worker)[a]	Cropland/ agricultural labor force in 1990 (ha/worker)[b]	Projected population density in 2025 (pop./ kcal)[c]	Projected population growth (1989– 2000) (%/year)[d]	Projected agricultural labor force in 2025 as % of 1990[e]
Humid lowlands					
Congo	20.09	0.33	Low	3.3	209
Zaire	2.63	0.91	Low	3.0	207
Equatorial Guinea	4.18	2.88	Low	—	102
Liberia	9.12	0.56	Low	3.0	214
Malaysia*	2.18	2.16	Low	2.3	59
Guinea-Bissau	4.01	0.95	Low	—	150
Mixed rainfall					
Gabon	14.69	1.30	Low	2.8	98
Central African Republic	5.66	2.27	Low	2.5	96
Angola	11.36	1.19	Low	3.0	194
Zambia	18.84	2.81	Low	3.1	264
Cameroon	5.76	2.64	Low	2.9	126
Madagascar	9.39	0.78	Low	2.8	173
Chad	32.75	2.18	Low	2.7	113
Côte d'Ivoire	6.56	1.45	Low	3.5	135
Mozambique	7.07	0.47	Medium	3.0	189
Sudan	24.96	2.62	Medium	2.8	102
Tanzania	3.72	0.33	Medium	3.1	206
Nigeria	2.72	1.22	High	2.8	245
India*	0.84	0.79	High	1.7	129
Mauritania	94.62	0.49	High	2.8	225
Kenya	5.30	0.32	High	3.5	266
Arid or semiarid					
Mali	13.54	0.88	Medium	3.0	202
Swaziland	6.71	0.99	High	—	153
Botswana	126.86	5.09	High	2.5	189
Mexico*	10.62	2.65	High	1.8	90
Egypt*	0.44	0.44	High	1.8	131
Somalia	20.89	0.49	High	3.1	155

Sources: Climatic classifications: Binswanger and Pingali 1988, Table 2, p. 87; (a) and (b), FAO 1992; (c), Binswanger and Pingali 1988, Table 2, p. 87; (d), World Bank 1992b; (e), United Nations 1988b.

Notes: Mixed rainfall includes countries with intermediate rainfall and countries with high- and low-rainfall regions. Within climate categories, countries are ranked by ascending projected population density in 2000 (Binswanger and Pingali 1988). Columns 1 and 2, see Tables 4.1 and 4.2. Column 3, low density means less than 100 people per million kilocalories of potential production by 2025; medium density means 100 people per million kilocalories of potential production now or by 2025; high density means 250 people per million kilocalories of potential production now or by 2025.

*Denotes countries not in sub-Saharan Africa.

Figure 4.9. Agroclimatic labor density for selected countries, estimates for 1980 and projections to 2000 and 2025

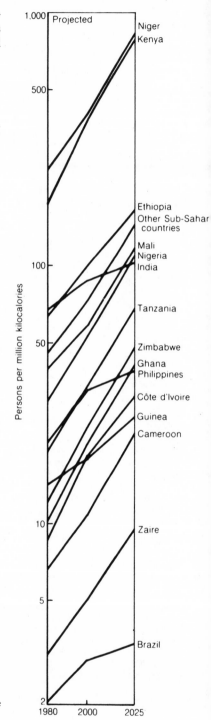

Source: Binswanger and Pingali 1988, Figure 1, p. 86.

the world's highest ratios of agricultural land per agricultural worker (Table 4.3). Here, as well as in Niger and Somalia, extensive livestock production may continue to be the most suitable farming system. But arid and semi-arid countries also face intense population pressure on meager land resources.

Thirteen CARLs (20 percent of the sub-Saharan population but only 3 percent of that for all CARLs) will have low agroclimatic population densities until at least 2025. All of the low population density CARLs had more than 4 hectares of agricultural land per worker (except Zaire), but not one had as much as 3 hectares of cropland per worker. And among the five with over 10 hectares of agricultural land per worker—Congo, Gabon, Angola, Zambia, and Chad—pasture accounted for 85 to 98 percent. Shifting cultivation is especially likely to persist in the Congo, Zaire, Equatorial Guinea, Liberia, and Guinea-Bissau because intensive cropping is difficult to sustain on the fragile soils of the humid lowlands (Binswanger and Pingali 1988, pp. 88 and 95).

National research is exceptionally difficult in Africa because of the diverse areas of rainfall—from humid forest and transitional zones (where soils are fragile and home to tsetse flies that spread sleeping sickness) to semiarid regions, where rainfall is marginal and erratic.

Moreover, Africa has not benefited as much as Asia from the sustained efforts of external donors for institution building. Foreign aid per capita was high in sub-Saharan Africa in the 1980s but not before donor countries, especially the United States, had moved away from an earlier emphasis on long-term institution building.

Because many sub-Saharan countries have small populations, the tax base and supply of trained personnel for national research systems is grossly inadequate. The wide variation in agroclimates and fragmented farming systems call for regional experiment stations serving several countries because similar climates spread across different countries and diversity within a country is great. But maintaining regional cooperation between countries is extremely difficult. Experience with the International Agricultural Research Centers and colonial regional research programs show the importance of foreign aid in negotiating cost-sharing and related arrangements. But such aid needs to be more effective.

Aid inflows increased by roughly 20 percent a year in current prices during the 1970s but created many problems. Ill-advised and poorly coordinated policies and programs of both bilateral and multilateral donor agencies contributed to the poor performance of African agriculture during the 1970s and 1980s (World Bank 1981, p. 130, and 1984; Lele 1992).

Another common problem in Africa has been the need to respond to food shortages with inadequate and ill-prepared crash programs. For example, state farms in Ghana, Tanzania, Ethiopia, and Mozambique were motivated by the Marxist belief that there are economies of scale in agriculture and that it would be easier to buy grain for urban areas from state farms rather than from small-scale farmers. Concentrations of capital, foreign exchange, and expertise in large state farms means that most farmers are deprived of inputs and supporting services; in such cases pessimistic prophesies about small farms increasing productivity, output, and sales are self-fulfilling.

Sub-Saharan governments often assume responsibility for marketing food crops, distributing inputs, and other essentially commercial activities that are difficult for bureaucracies to manage effectively. Administrative capacity in sub-Saharan Africa is less than in other developing regions because opportunities for education and administrative experience were limited until the postindependence period that began in the 1960s.

EFFICIENCY, EQUITY, AND TECHNOLOGICAL CHANGE

Incorrect notions about economies of scale and economies of farm size work against the labor-using agricultural development that is necessary for the efficient use of CARLs' large (and growing) rural labor force. Major barriers to an adequate rate and appropriate bias of technological change stem from the lack of strong national research systems to generate innovations suited to the needs of farms, small ones in particular.

The contrasting agricultural productivity growth in Japan and in the United States highlights a key strategic notion: the social efficiency of patterns of development depends on a country's land, labor, and other factors of production. Both the United States and Japan raised productivity through broad-based strategies, but their transitions from resource-based to science-based agriculture were different. In Japan it was a labor-using, land-saving pattern that raised crop yields. In the United States it was a land-using, labor-saving technology that increased the area farmed by a single family. Both were efficient paths, given the (then) factor endowments of each.

For most Asian CARLs, the route to a high-productivity agriculture is a land-saving, labor-using pattern similar to those of Japan and Taiwan. But specific innovations and inputs in Japan and Taiwan are not the answer for all farming systems in all CARLs in Asia, and even less so for the CARLs of sub-Saharan Africa and Latin America.

The extreme range of conditions of African agriculture makes it difficult to generalize about an appropriate pattern for the transition. Some of Africa's farming systems are extensive, shifting cultivation befiting labor-scarce, land-abundant rural economies, but this balance is changing. A land-saving, labor-using pattern of growth will suit the majority of Africa's rural population by 2025. But differences in land quality, especially limited irrigation potential and reliance on rainfed cropping, tree crops, and pasture, mean that opportunities to increase productivity in Africa differ fundamentally from those seized in the seed-fertilizer revolution in irrigated areas of Asia.

Population pressure on a frail land base is especially severe in the arid and semiarid regions of sub-Saharan Africa. There, the question of appropriate factor-saving bias of technologies needed to sustain land productivity and to conserve scarce moisture is particularly complex. For example, moisture-saving technologies tend to be labor-using, but techniques differ significantly depending on peak season demands for labor inputs (Matlon 1990; Sanders and others 1990).

A land-using, labor-saving bias is likely to be appropriate for the foreseeable future in thirteen African CARLs, but land in these countries is of neither the quantity nor the quality of that in the United States in the nineteenth century. Furthermore, African labor productivity is low, and most farms are small, even where land is abundant. In the Zairian Basin, for example, the average household plants only about two-thirds of 1 hectare, though more land is available (Tshibaka 1989). There, land farmed by a household could double or triple (and, so, incomes), even with average farm size still under 5 hectares.

Fortunately, there are opportunities for substitution over many input combinations, enabling choice of technologies that are appropriate to factor endowments. In all CARLs, even those with abundant land, this includes fuller, socially efficient use of the growing rural work force, coupled with economizing on scarce capital. In short, alleviating rural poverty through broad-based strategies that involve small farms is consistent with a socially efficient path for agricultural development—*if* a stream of innovations is available for small farms.

Institutional Requirements

There is little hope that CARLs can increase productivity without making the transition from a resource-based to a science-based agriculture. The potential contributions of publicly funded agricultural research institutions have been shown by the rapid diffusion of semidwarf varieties of rice and wheat in Asia.

The varietal improvements of IRRI and CIMMYT, the first of the International Agricultural Research Centers, had an unusually broad impact because of the breakthrough in identifying the genes that determine photoperiodism (that is, the effect of day length on growth) in rice and wheat. But this "Green Revolution" was limited mainly to controlled-irrigation areas. Even then, research was needed to determine agronomic practices for local conditions. Moreover, even under similar environments for irrigated rice, local variations in soil structure and in soil organic matter can cause substantial variations in yields (Herdt and Mandac 1981, p. 398).

Small Farms in a Broad-Based Agricultural Strategy 145

Most countries that benefited from high-yielding rices and wheats managed to create indigenous scientific capacity for adaptive research and development. They were then able to use imported prototypes of genetic material, equipment, scientific know-how, and methodologies and instrumentation for experimental work, as well as organizational designs and management procedures, to adapt plant and animal varieties to local ecological and socioeconomic conditions. This capacity for location-specific research is especially important for widespread increases in productivity and output among a country's small farms.

The lack of national research systems in many CARLs also results from failures to devise research and extension methods to foster technological progress in the diverse, rainfed environments of many countries. Japan and Taiwan could generate a stream of innovations adapted to their small farms because of the homogeneous irrigated agriculture in both countries. But there was still a need for adaptive research. Witness the time required to evolve techniques for growing *japonica* varieties of rice under Taiwan's semitropical conditions and to develop high-yielding, fertilizer-responsive *indica* varieties (Chapter 10). But once appropriate techniques and varieties had been identified, diffusion was rapid and widespread because environmental and socioeconomic conditions were homogeneous.

Most of today's CARLs face problems in generating an appropriate stream of innovations for small farms, despite being able to draw on a larger pool of scientific knowledge and experimental methods. This is partly because research has been biased toward the needs of large farms (de Janvry and Dethier 1985). The limited relevance of experiment station research to the needs of small farms is accentuated by the extreme heterogeneity of rainfed farming systems, especially in Africa. Devising and institutionalizing techniques to exploit the potential benefits from marrying experiment station research and knowledge of local farmers therefore deserve special emphasis under rainfed conditions (S. Biggs 1989; Chambers and others 1989; Tomich 1992b).

CHOOSING THE PATH OF PRODUCTIVITY GROWTH

The anti–small farm biases in the political economy of many CARLs reinforce the economic misconceptions underpinning policymakers' preference for dualism. Moreover, owners and managers of large-scale private farms have a vested interest in perpetuating policies that give them preferential treatment. Although they often stress the traditional notion extolling the virtues of large farms, they may be motivated more by an interest in maintaining their managerial positions in public agricultural enterprises. Another premise is that because state farms are more easily controlled, they are believed to be more reliable than small ones as a source of food supplies for urban areas. Finally, the ruling regime may view as a threat a situation where most of the population consists of individual farm households (see case studies in Part 3). Policymakers in Japan and the United States do not appear to have had serious doubts about the feasibility (or desirability) of broad-based agricultural development. The lesson from patterns of innovation and input use suited to their contrasting resource endowments is that there are many socially efficient paths to agricultural productivity growth. But it is not enough to borrow techniques, imitate institutions, and mimic initiatives from other countries (see Part 3). Taiwan (like Japan) avoided premature mechanization, but countries such as the USSR, China, Mexico, and Tanzania have all fallen prey at various times to the notion that "modern" agriculture is synonymous with the mechanization of large farms.

The false strategic notion that economies of scale are important in agriculture underpins the overemphasis on trade-offs between equity and efficiency, as well as the skepticism about broad-based agricultural development. Ill-conceived notions that understate small-scale farmers' abilities to make efficient production decisions and to master new techniques have cast further doubt on the development potential of small farms. In fact, as long as rural wages are low, as in all CARLs, small farms make more productive use of scarce resources than do large farms. Furthermore, small farms have the capacity to use new technology, if it has an appropriate bias.

The labor-using, land-saving bias of Japanese agricultural development is appropriate for many Asian CARLs. As structural transformation proceeds, capital and alternative employment opportunities become more abundant, and wages rise along with labor productivity. Then, the pattern of growth shifts to capital-using, labor-saving technology. But efficient sequences of productivity growth are likely to occur only if market prices for labor, land, and capital reflect relative scarcities. Efficient sequences also depend on governments supplying the infrastructure necessary to support development and building institutions, such as agricultural research organizations, that pursue goals consistent with underlying comparative advantage. Thus, the pattern of growth depends not only on a country's initial factor endowments but also on its policymakers' choices (see Chapter 5).

The labor-using, land-saving pattern is a window of opportunity for simultaneously increasing labor productivity and employment in agriculture in most CARLs where land is scarce. Even the few sub-Saharan countries with abundant land share the challenge. This opportunity is important, at least until the structural transformation turning point is reached.

There is a risk that policymakers in CARLs will choose dualistic strategies and opt for the capital-using, labor-saving technology used in countries that have passed their structural transformation turning point, partly because of differing definitions of "small farm." Even the World Bank has contributed to the confusion. In a report on sub-Saharan Africa, the Bank (1989a, p. 93) argues for "medium- and large-scale" farming—citing plantations in Côte d'Ivoire, Kenya, and Malawi—in addition to smallholders. But in much of sub-Saharan Africa, a "medium-size" farm has 5 to 15 hectares and typically has more in common with small farms than with the technology and economics of large ones.

Take maize production in Eastern and Southern Africa (CIMMYT 1990, p. 14). Small-scale hand-hoe cultivators operate 1 to 3 hectares and account for 45 percent of planted area. "Medium" farms, using animal traction, cultivate plots of 1 to 10 hectares and cover 50 percent of maize area. Only 5 percent is heavily mechanized maize production on large farms of 50 to 100 (or more) hectares. Within agroclimatic zones, appropriate innovations could spread among small- and medium-size maize farms with potential to involve most farmers in broad-based productivity growth. In contrast, innovations suited to large maize "estates" are unlikely to spread to the other 95 percent of farms.

CHAPTER FIVE

AGRICULTURAL STRATEGIES AND AGRARIAN STRUCTURE

For most CARLs redistribution of land could have a great beneficial effect on agricultural development but is often blocked by the political economy. Such reform would promote a unimodal agrarian structure, which offers big advantages in employment, income distribution, and linkages through demand for agricultural commodities. Fortunately, land reform is not the only path to a unimodal structure, nor is it a prerequisite for a broad-based strategy in most CARLs. In fact, a broad-based strategy can promote a unimodal structure. But this requires that policymakers avoid policies favoring large farms over small ones. Even then, a broad-based strategy alone cannot eradicate poverty and hunger, nor can it compensate for bad macroeconomic policies.

INEQUITABLE LAND DISTRIBUTION

Data on the distribution of farms by size mask big variations from village to village and across farming systems and regions (Figures 5.1 and 5.2). Moreover, large landholders often conceal how much land they own and smaller holdings may be missed by censuses. But even if data were perfect, the striking contrasts among countries would not be eliminated.

Types of operating units include owner-cultivated farms, sharecroppers, other tenancies, and part-tenants (farmers with some land they own and some they rent or sharecrop). Often, landownership is more concentrated than the distribution of operating units.[1] But it is the number and types of operating units (tenancies, etc), not landownership, that is crucial to agricultural development strategy because operating units are the locus of most production decisions.

Strategy and Structure

The relative social efficiency of small farms discussed in Chapter 4 may be offset by *differentiating factors* resulting from government policies that give large farms a differential (and artificial) advantage over smallholdings (Okhawa, 1972). Because these factors have a differential impact on the productivity—and, so, profitability—of farms by size, they also affect the agrarian structure that emerges with technological change.

These differentiating factors are the hallmark of a dualistic strategy, which promotes polarization of farms into a bimodal structure either by encouraging the concentration of landownership through the skewed distribution of income from growth or by making the operation of large farms more attractive than renting parcels out to tenants. Sometimes these shifts can be rapid, as in the American South when mechanization and social changes led landlords to evict sharecroppers and concentrate on owner operation with hired labor. Rapid or not, a shift toward bigger farms is hard to reverse, especially if it involves mechanization. Indeed, mechanization "is the most distinctive differentiating factor because of its associated economies of scale" (Okhawa 1972, p. 290).

In broad-based strategies, there are no differentiating factors, and economic forces are set to work through conscious policy decisions to promote a unimodal structure of operating units. In this vein, it is important that agricultural research programs generate divisible innovations that are neutral to scale. Such innovations (for example, biological and chemical inputs, such as fertilizer-responsive seeds) are feasible and profitable for small farms. Large farms' greater access to institutional credit may be a major differentiating factor, even when innovations are divisible, because of the need to finance complementary inputs, such as fertilizers (Okhawa 1972). But farm-size effects (Chapter 4) mean that smaller farms will have a comparative advantage over larger farms in employing labor-using technologies as long as wage rates are low. If such a stream of technologies is produced, large-scale

[1] In some cases, though, as in Egypt, tenancy leads to a greater concentration of units because more area is rented to mid-size operators from owners of very small holdings than is rented out by larger landowners (Abdel-Fadil 1975, pp. 14–15).

landowners will probably find it profitable to rent out land rather than operate it themselves in large parcels. In this way, broad-based strategies can promote a unimodal distribution of operating units.

This choice exists even for some CARLs, such as Kenya, with a bimodal agrarian structure. Since the decade before independence, Kenya's policies and programs have promoted broad-based development among most (including small) farms. But there is growing concern that the political climate in Kenya may lead to greater dualism (see Chapter 11).

Extreme Bimodality

Landownership is so concentrated in some Latin American countries that land barons may have considerable market power in hiring labor, renting land, and lending capital in particular locales. Of the three Latin American CARLs, Guatemala and Honduras show extremely bimodal structures (Figure 5.1). In Guatemala in 1979, two-thirds of the land was run by 2 percent of the farms. In Honduras in 1974, over half the land was operated by roughly 3 percent of farms. Haiti shows less skewness for 1971, but data reported to the FAO may not be reliable.

In Latin America the economic power of the (few) big landlords and their links with other elites give them sufficient political power to block the redistribution of land. Land reform has also been compromised by legislation that stresses the social function of landed property, which means that "owners who are making more productive uses of their land are less vulnerable to losing it to reform beneficiaries" (Eckstein and others 1978, p. 8). Ironically, large farms are seen as fulfilling this social function when they mechanize. But renting land to be cultivated intensively with labor-using, land- (and capital-) saving technologies is regarded as "antisocial"; in fact, renting out land increases the likelihood that it will be redistributed—one reason Latin Americans have less access to tenancies than Asians.

Landlords may also exert control of the labor market, which helps to explain why large landowners are unwilling to give workers the option of becoming tenants. Even if tenancy were permitted, the interlinkage of labor, land, and capital market transactions through tenancy contracts could leave tenants little better off than wage laborers when landlords have substantial power in factor markets. Where local factor markets are controlled by an elite and where this applies to most rural communities, prospects for broad-based development will be bleak. Then, urban migration may offer the best hope for the rural poor, but this comes at a high price—in greater social and economic problems in urban areas.

Apart from Guatemala, Honduras, and Haiti, Latin American countries already have much less than half their labor force in agriculture and are no longer CARLs (Chapter 1). In Mexico, for example, only about a third of

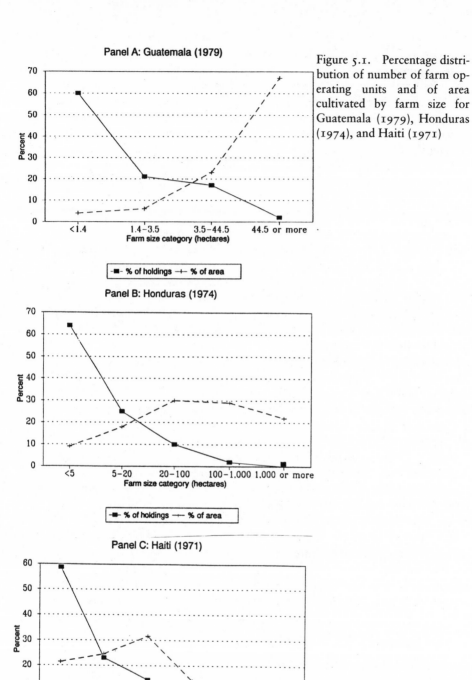

Figure 5.1. Percentage distribution of number of farm operating units and of area cultivated by farm size for Guatemala (1979), Honduras (1974), and Haiti (1971)

Panel A: Guatemala (1979)

-■- % of holdings -+- % of area

Panel B: Honduras (1974)

-■- % of holdings --+-- % of area

Panel C: Haiti (1971)

-■- % of holdings --+-- % of area

Sources: Guatemala: von Braun and others 1989, Table 3, p. 22. Honduras: Grindle 1986b, Table 5.13, p. 97. Haiti: FAO 1981, Tables 2.3 and 3.3.

the labor force works in agriculture, and the agrarian structure remains bimodal despite successive attempts at land reform. The subsector of large, capital-intensive farms that emerged as a product of Mexico's dualistic agricultural strategy attained sufficient political and economic clout to block significant new land redistribution initiatives. Indeed, de Janvry and Sadoulet (1989, p. 1407) conclude that attempts to implement redistributive land reforms failed throughout Latin America in the 1960s and 1970s because governments pursued dualistic strategies that sought first to raise productivity on larger farms. In any event, the opportunity to alleviate rural poverty during structural transformation has been missed in Mexico (see Chapter 10).

Intermediate Cases

Many CARLs fall between unimodal and bimodal distributions of farm operating units. In these intermediate cases, such as Haiti, India, and Kenya, land reform could promote a unimodal structure and narrow the inequalities in the rural economy. But in most countries where land redistribution would be socially and economically desirable, it is not politically feasible. As Galbraith said in 1951, "The world is composed of many different kinds of people, but those who own land are not so different—whether they live in China, Persia, Mississippi, or Quebec—that they will meet and happily vote themselves out of its possession" (quoted in Dorner and Thiesenhusen 1990, p. 66).

Redistribution of landownership is not the only way to change agrarian structure. India is a good example of an intermediate between the unimodal and bimodal extremes (Figure 5.2). Policymakers in India (and other CARLs) can shift toward either extreme through policies and programs that affect the willingness of "large-scale" farmers (10 to 50 hectares) to rent out land to some of the (majority of) farmers operating less than 5 hectares.[2] Even in other countries of Asia, where "big" landowners have 10 to 20 hectares, the scope for renting is substantial.

---

[2] Asian landowners, like their Latin American counterparts, use violence to maintain their privileged positions in the rural economy. Robinson (1988) documents how rural elites in the Indian state Andhra Pradesh systematically employed violence to enforce their power in labor and credit markets. Beatings were routine; however, among the most serious sanctions a landlord could apply to a landless family was to cut them off from work and credit (M. Robinson 1988, p. 31). Yet, where there are a number of landlords in a village, as is usual in Asia, collusive practices are undermined by individual landlords' incentives to circumvent traditional norms in order to attract more or better laborers. Traditional systems include sanctions against landowners offering better terms for employment, credit, or tenancy and against workers seeking jobs and loans outside the village. But in India since the 1970s gradual change in rural politics, social reforms pressed by the central government, and expansion of economic opportunities have weakened the restrictive practices that bound landless workers to specific landowners in the past.

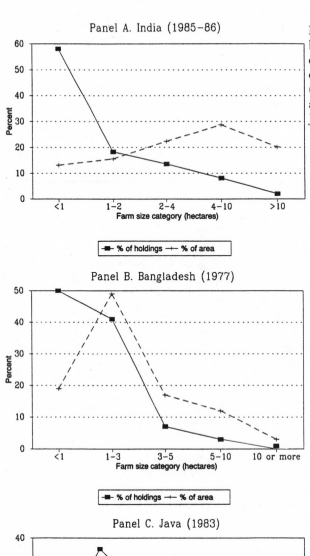

Panel A. India (1985–86)

Panel B. Bangladesh (1977)

Panel C. Java (1983)

-■- % of holdings   -+- % of area

Figure 5.2. Percentage distribution of number of farm operating units and of area cultivated by farm size for India (1985–86), Bangladesh (1977), and the Indonesian Island of Java (1983)

Sources: India: Kurian 1990, p. A-179. Bangladesh: Booth and Sundrum 1984, Table 6.5, p. 139. Java: Booth 1988, Table 2.21, p. 58.

Note: Data for Java refer only to holdings that have a foodcrop component.

Land Tenancy: Efficiency, Not Equity

Is a unimodal structure of ownership and therefore land redistribution a precondition for broad-based agricultural development? No. Broad-based strategies may not be feasible in, say, many Latin American countries without land reform, but such strategies were feasible in Japan, Taiwan, and Korea *prior* to the redistribution of land after World War II and *despite* the concentration of landownership. The reason? Large landowners found it profitable to rent land in small plots to tenants so that the size distribution of *operational* units was unimodal. True, income distribution in rural areas was unequal, but landowners and tenants shared an interest in investments in agricultural research, irrigation, and other infrastructure that helped technological progress based on divisible, yield-increasing innovations. The later land reforms resulted in more equal distribution of income and reinforced the unimodal distribution of farms, but they were *not* a necessary condition for broad-based development.

The relative efficiency of land-tenure arrangements is a pivotal issue if a unimodal agrarian structure is pursued through short-term tenure contracts, rather than restructuring landownership. Farm-size effects on production decisions (that is, declines in output and labor use per unit area with increasing farm size) seems to hold under many circumstances, regardless of the tenure arrangement.

But there is credible evidence on either side of the debate about the relative efficiency in sharecropping. Social and cultural norms (whether neighbors collude with shirking sharecroppers or report them to landlords) and legalities (whether the law favors landlords or tenants) affect landlords' ability to monitor sharecroppers' activities and enforce agreements and to structure incentives to ensure efficient land use (see Box 5.1). In Asia, where sharecropping is prevalent, there is evidence of only "very minor differences" in input and output intensities between sharecropped and owner-cultivated farms of the same size (Binswanger and Rosenzweig 1984). This suggests that problems of incentives, monitoring, and enforcement had little empirical significance and that the farm-size effects outlined in Chapter 4 are likely to hold for sharecropping. Moreover, "not a single study of the adoption of high-yielding varieties that adjusts for farm-size effects has shown serious adoption lags on tenanted or sharecropped farms or plots" (Binswanger and Rosenzweig 1984, pp. 27–29).

Another study nevertheless found a big negative impact of sharecropping on output and labor input per unit area between owned, fixed-rent, and part-tenant sharecropping in six villages of India's semiarid tropics (Shaban 1987). In this study, perhaps the best-conceived empirical research on the topic, sharecropped plots displayed much lower output and labor use intensities than the owner-cultivated plots of the same household, even after allowing

Box 5.1   Land Reform: Theory and Practice

Given the skewed landownership in CARLs, land and labor can be combined in proportions more appropriate to relative factor endowments through three factor-market transactions: land sales, wage labor, or land tenancy. Sales are rare because most land-poor people do not have the means to acquire land and landowners have little incentive to sell it.

Tenancy combines landlords' land with tenants' labor. It also combines landowners' advantages in credit markets with small-scale tenants' advantages due to diseconomies of farm size in labor hiring and management. Land tenancy can be through fixed rents (paid in kind, cash, or labor) and rent paid as a share of production (that is, sharecropping or share tenancy).

Sharecropping has been the most controversial in theory and practice. Until the publication of Cheung's seminal article in 1968, sharecropping generally was thought of as economically inefficient as well as unjust: inefficient because it discouraged tenants from applying optimal inputs, and unjust because of the large rental share received by landlords. It is now recognized that share tenancy involves more than a land transaction. It is also a credit system and a way to share risk and minimize transactions costs in labor hiring and supervision as well as to decentralize production management decisions.

These interlinked transactions show how sharecropping can be mutually beneficial for landlords and sharecroppers. Transaction costs and imperfect information are important factors underlying the willingness of landlords and tenants to accept share rent arrangements. The diseconomies of farm size in labor hiring and supervision can so affect input and output decisions that landowners gain by dividing their land into smaller plots operated by tenants, rather than hiring labor to operate a big farm themselves. These imperfections in labor markets also mean that landless people with management skill can often do better as sharecroppers than as wage laborers while incurring less yield risk than tenants paying fixed rent in cash or kind.

Furthermore, as Braverman and Stiglitz emphasized (1986), profit-sharing and cost-sharing combine incentives for tenants to adjust input levels (in response to weather, for example) while allowing landlords to reap some benefit from on-the-spot management decisions in ways that are not available through wage labor or fixed-rent contracts. And because owners of large farms enjoy economies of farm size in access to credit, capital market transactions linked to land tenancy allow landlords and tenants to split the difference between costs of capital to mutual gain. Interlinking increases the scope for mutual benefits by reducing transaction costs, including searching, monitoring, and enforcement. Indeed, the efficiency of sharecropping over other tenure arrangements hinges on these costs: if monitoring and enforcement costs are sufficiently low, production decisions under sharecropping will approximate those under fixed rental contracts or owner-cultivation. Land tenure regulations adopted when land redistribution is

This box draws heavily on Binswanger and Rosenzweig 1986, Hayami and Kikuchi 1982, Hayami 1991, and Tomich 1991a. See also Newbery 1975, Roumasset 1976, and Bardhan 1980.

Box 5.1 *(continued)*

not politically feasible are usually intended to establish rent ceilings, to secure tenure, and to abolish sharecropping. The goal of land tenure reform is to give tenants some, but not all, property rights in land by mandating formal changes in contracts. Politically, this seems to be an attractive compromise: tenants (usually middle-income farmers with a strong political voice) gain new rights, and landlords retain some claim to each plot of land.

But this view of land-tenure reform is misleading because it overlooks both the mutual advantages of existing tenancy contracts and actions open to landlords, including eviction of tenants. The problems governments face in monitoring and enforcing compliance with land tenure regulations are more daunting than a landlord's costs of coping with imperfect information about performance of a few tenants. The lack of reliable information and the ease with which landlords can wield political power to influence policy implementation broaden the scope for unintended effects and abuses. For example Singh (1990, p. 297) concludes that India's legislation to fix rental ceilings "prompted evictions of tenants or voluntary surrenders of land and, where tenancy continued, led to informal agreements with much greater insecurity for tenants. These measures displaced more tenants in the 1950s than the much criticized displacements in the name of mechanization or the Green Revolution in the 1960s and 1970s." And as Hayami (1991) points out, agricultural economists share in the blame for the prevalence of counterproductive tenancy regulations because the conventional wisdom once was that tenancy reform was a second-best alternative to redistributive land reform.

for differences in irrigation and plot value. This suggests limitations on landlords' abilities to monitor tenants and enforce contracts—or both. As Shaban notes (1987, p. 908, note 21), India's land-to-the-tiller laws lead landlords in the six villages to choose short-term contracts that undercut the enforcement effectiveness of eviction while reducing the risk of appropriation. So, these comparisons do not provide a test of the relative efficiency of sharecropping in the absence of land-tenure regulations and when successive renewals are the norm.

Despite some unresolved questions, an earlier summary statement by Berry and Cline (1979, p. 30) still seems valid: "The possible distortions of sharecropping have received a great deal of theoretical attention. However, both the ambiguous theoretical conclusions and the inconclusive empirical evidence on the subject suggest that it is of considerably less importance for policy purposes than the issue of productivity in relation to farm size." Furthermore, landlords and tenants freely choose to sharecrop, as they do in the semiarid tropics of India (Walker and Ryan 1990, p. 175), suggesting that it is more mutually beneficial than alternatives. Today the prevailing view is that "significant inefficiency of share tenancy is expected to arise only when the scope of contract choice is institutionally restricted" (Otsuka, Chuma, and Hayami 1992, p. 2007).

But the incentives for investing family labor to improve the productive capacity of land are lessened when tenants do not have security of tenure. Thus, although there may be short-run efficiency under tenure, long-run growth potential is more problematic. In a study of squatters on public land in Thailand, Feder and Onchan (1987) concluded that land-improving investments were significantly affected by insecurity of ownership despite relatively low risk of eviction. (See also Feder and others 1988.) With private land, however, it often is in the landlord's interest to invest funds to enhance land productivity—even if tenants' incentives to devote cash and labor to investments are inhibited by insecurity of tenure.

Where, as in most CARLs, there are inverse relationships between farm size and output, and labor use and concentration of political power blocks land redistribution, tenancy (including sharecropping) can be a *relatively* efficient way to combine land and labor in agricultural production. Sweeping redistribution of land would be more equitable, and if post-reform property rights were as secure as in Japan and Taiwan, redistribution could increase investment in land. But for most CARLs persistent efforts at land reform in the face of powerful political opposition may be counterproductive. This is especially so if land-tenure reform that puts a ceiling on rents and proscribes share tenancy is advocated as a substitute for land redistribution (see Box 5.1). Such strings attached to tenure reform encourage big landlords to opt for direct cultivation, rather than renting out smaller plots to tenants.[3]

Abundant Land

Where land is scarce (that is, in most CARLs) and where most of the land is operated by large farms, the average farm size for the great majority of farm households will be much smaller than already is inevitable. For this reason alone, broad-based and dualistic strategies tend to be mutually exclusive in all but a few CARLs. Even where land is abundant, the two strategies can still be mutually exclusive, although not necessarily so.

Malaysia's population, land endowment, and climate make its agroclimatic population density comparable to Africa's land-abundant countries (see Table 4.3). And the expansion of treecrops by Malaysia's estates did not preclude expansion of smallholdings. Initial expansion of rubber by small-

---

[3] Land taxes could be useful in augmenting government revenues for infrastructure investments and other development programs while reducing interfarm and interregional inequalities in income even if land redistribution is not feasible. Yet, there also is considerable doubt as to whether even a flat-rate land tax would be politically feasible under such circumstances. And an attempt to make a land tax progressive according to farm size would have even less chance of success in countries where landlords are sufficiently powerful to block land redistribution.

holders was a spontaneous response to the opportunities demonstrated by big estates earlier in the twentieth century, but broad-based strategies were eventually necessary (and effective) in expanding smallholder rubber. Key elements of that strategy included research on production and processing, schemes for replanting rubber with higher-yielding varieties, and more rapid settlement of new land.

Other elements of Malaysia's success (of broad-based strategies for smallholders, coupled with expansion on large private estates) are unlikely to be shared by many CARLs. Specifically, the trade-offs in the allocation of scarce resources of investment capital, government funds, and trained personnel between smallholder development and private estates were not serious, because capital for the estates came mostly from overseas investors. And, especially in the early development of rubber and oil palm, much managerial and technical expertise also came from abroad.

Indonesia's results in the 1970s and 1980s are more likely outcomes for most CARLs. Despite its successful broad-based strategy for rice, Indonesia opted for a strategy to transfer production techniques from large-scale rubber plantations to smallholdings.[4] After more than a decade, this strategy had failed to generate widespread increases in rubber productivity, even though land availability was not a serious problem in Indonesia's Outer Islands. More than 85 percent of Indonesia's smallholders did not benefit because the development schemes of that period were so management-intensive. Indeed, it could take more than 60 years for those schemes to cover even the present population of rubber producers (Barlow and Jayasuriya 1984b). The projects were well-funded by Indonesian oil revenues and loans from the World Bank and other organizations. But they stretched the management capacity of Indonesia's public agencies and led to a complete withdrawal of advisory services to ordinary smallholders. Moreover, improved planting materials were restricted to project participants.

Much broader coverage could be achieved by distributing planting materials to smallholders through publicly supported nurseries, as well as disseminating agronomic information to help them to realize more of the potential of higher-yielding rubber varieties through their own initiative (Barlow and Jayasuriya 1984b; Barlow and others 1991; Tomich 1991b). This would initiate a learning process, and as many more farmers

---

[4] Barlow and Jayasuriya (1984b) distinguish between focus and dispersal strategies in assessing Indonesia's smallholder treecrop development schemes. In their dichotomy, a focus strategy is characterized by (1) attempts to transfer a capital-intensive technological package directly from estates to smallholders, (2) emphasis on achieving economies of scale, and (3) intensive public sector management requirements. In a manner analogous to a dualistic strategy for the agricultural sector as a whole, a focus strategy for smallholder treecrop development inevitably restricts program benefits to a minority of farms. Their dispersal strategy is based on government efforts to promote the spread of relatively labor-using, capital-saving technology that is better suited to smallholders' initial resource constraints.

acquire the knowledge, skills, and cash income, yields would gradually be raised. Eventually, many Indonesian smallholders would progress to cash- and skill-intensive techniques to further increase yields and profits. This has happened in Malaysia, which is much further along the path of structural transformation.

ADVANTAGES OF UNIMODAL AGRARIAN STRUCTURE

Policymakers often believe that when small farms are included in development strategies, there must be a sacrifice of economic efficiency for equity. Attention to the social advantages of broad-based development may have contributed to this common (but mistaken) notion. In fact, broad-based strategies to promote a unimodal agrarian structure offer bigger economic, as well as social, advantages in CARLs than the dualistic approach.

More Efficiency, More Equity

Because of low agricultural productivity in most CARLs, there almost always is potential for development. True, it may be difficult to realize that potential in some areas because of deficiencies in agricultural research, extension, output marketing, and input distribution. Conversely, some small farms may have exceptional opportunities to expand output rapidly and at relatively low cost because of past investments in roads, irrigation, and other infrastructure and because profitable technologies adapted locally are already available.

Broad-based strategies that promote a unimodal agrarian structure nonetheless have big economic advantages because of the fit between the resource requirements for such strategies and the resource endowments of CARLs. Specifically, economies and diseconomies of farm size mean that the increases in productivity of most farms will be accompanied by a more socially efficient use of labor than if growth were confined to a few large farms.

Because of trends in relative factor endowments (and the double bind of increasing agricultural labor productivity and demand for rural labor), socially efficient expansion requires technology that is capital-saving and labor-using, even for land-abundant CARLs. Where land is scarce, as in most CARLs, socially efficient technological change would be relatively land-saving, too. Farm-size effects lead small farms to favor labor-using and capital-saving agricultural technologies (Chapter 4). The resources of these poor, but typical, households resemble the relative factor endowments of the rural economy. As they strive to subsist, these households intensify use of abundant family labor and conserve scarce capital.

Technological change brings uneven changes in factor productivity and input demand, a situation that means variations in relative prices of land, labor, and capital during economic development. Consequently, the incentives and benchmarks for social efficiency of production techniques are determined during agricultural development. Rather than a distinct efficient point, determined by resource endowments and maintained by prices in a static economy, a changing economy can follow alternative paths.

Economies and diseconomies of farm size reinforce subsequent demand for agricultural labor under the socially efficient growth path corresponding to a unimodal agrarian structure. In contrast, farm-size effects encourage substitution of capital for labor among large farms in a bimodal structure. Thus, instead of a single efficiency-equity trade-off, policy decisions should be viewed as choices among development paths that are financially efficient but differ in social efficiency of use of national labor, land, and capital. These differences matter, particularly in the equilibrium levels of wages and food consumption in the rural economy.

Expanding Employment

The big advantage of a unimodal, rather than bimodal structure of operating units in furthering both economic and social aims is in the more rapid expansion of employment opportunities (within and outside agriculture). The explanation? The fostering of labor-using and capital-saving technologies. That they increase farm output efficiently by fuller utilization of CARLs' large (and growing) farm work force is also the key to minimizing agriculture's needs for scarce capital.

With the highest rural population density in Asia, the Indonesian island of Java has faced a tough task in absorbing its growing rural labor force. According to Booth and Sundrum (1984, pp. 129–30), "the densely settled regions of Indonesia have coped with growing population pressure . . . by a leveling down of the size distribution of farms. Over time, an increasing proportion of farms thus fall into the small sizes with higher rates of labor use." This may be the best course for Java. In rice growing in Indonesia, the shift toward smaller farms raised agricultural output and labor demand, helped by production incentives from agricultural price policies and investments in irrigation. Certainly, households that depend primarily on agricultural wages benefit from greater labor demand under a broad-based strategy.

Linkages in the Rural Economy

Land accounts for as much as half the value added in agriculture in CARLs. Although land reform is the most powerful means of redistributing income in the rural economy, it is unlikely to happen in most CARLs. Nevertheless, because the inverse relationship between farm size and labor inputs appears to hold for many tenure relationships (as long as the opportunity cost of labor is low), a unimodal pattern of operational units can also improve income distribution. This can occur, albeit more modestly than with land redistribution, to the extent that greater demand for agricultural labor supports rural wages.

One of the main lessons of the Green Revolution and subsequent research has been to confirm that the distributional effects of technological change depend heavily on the social and institutional environment. Thus, few generalizations can be made about the effects of agricultural development on income distribution.[5] Although the direct effects of agricultural development have not relieved rural poverty as quickly as hoped, agricultural productivity increases through technological change are a necessary ingredient of development strategy. Indirect effects, operating through complex linkages within the rural economy are controversial, but the available evidence indicates that these have important benefits for rural employment and income distribution.

Direct Effects on Income Distribution. Often, most gains from technological change go to landlords and owner-operators, rather than tenants and hired laborers. This can happen even when the technology is land-saving and labor-using because it raises yields of scarce land while the supply of labor is increasing faster than the rise in demand. Even so, the distributional bias toward landowners is greater under a dualistic strategy.

Even if better-off households obtain a bigger share of the direct income gains, greater demand for labor resulting from broad-based strategies means that wages can rise (or fall less) with employment increases. In contrast, dualistic strategies help to depress wage rates by reducing the demand for labor while its supply is increasing—and if demand falls, wages fall, too.

The distributional biases that occur when land is scarce and labor abundant are not reasons to avoid technological change. Indeed, if the rural labor supply grows and other things remain stagnant, including technology, wages will fall anyway.

Analysis by Hayami and Kikuchi (1982) of the effects of labor force growth in two Javanese villages demonstrates how "the wage rate is bound to decline, the return to land to rise, and the income position of laborers and tenants to deteriorate relative to that of landowners when the rate of growth of the rural labor force exceeds the rate of growth in demand for labor" (Hayami and Ruttan 1985, p. 345). It is also demonstrated that this is not an inevitable outcome of technological change. In the village with technological stagnation, the returns to land increased at the expense of labor's share. In the other village (with significant technological progress), the labor input per hectare increased more than 40 percent, mainly because of an in-

---

[5] Quizon and Binswanger (1983) and Lele and Mellor (1981) provide formal analytical treatments of these complex issues.

crease in multiple cropping and of the adoption of new varieties. These higher labor inputs led to a rise in wages and an increase in labor's share of production—all because increasing demand for labor exceeded labor force growth.

Patterns of Demand for Food.   One of the most firmly established generalizations in economics is Engel's Law: the higher a household's income, the lower the relative share of food in its total expenditure. In CARLs roughly two-thirds of disposable income will be spent on food by average households.[6] (That declines to about 20 percent in high-income countries.) When incomes increase, poor households also spend more of that extra income on food than higher-income households. As a general rule, a 10 percent increase in income of poor households leads to an 8 percent rise in food expenditures, with 50 to 70 percent of the extra income spent on food (Alderman 1986).

In CARLs poor households spend much of their income on foodgrains and also on other starchy staples, such as cassava, sweet potatoes, and plantains. The ratio of starchy staples to total calories can be as high as 80 percent in CARLs. As incomes increase, the share of these starchy staples in total calorie intake declines (Bennett's Law). With high incomes, diets shift toward meats, dairy products, and nonstarchy fruits and vegetables. Income growth among lower-income households will have a greater impact on demand for major grains than would the same growth in higher-income households.[7]

The rural poor often depend on wage labor as a primary source of income because they have little access to land—and, so, are net purchasers of grain. Because foodgrains take such a large chunk of the poor's incomes and marginal expenditures, grain prices are as important in the distribution of real income as demand for agricultural labor and rural wages.

Income gains for the rural poor as consumers (rather than producers) of foodgrains are among the most important impacts of agricultural development, especially when aggregated at an international level (Lipton and Longhurst 1989). The substantial net benefits from technological change in rice production in Colombia, "accrued to consumers, with the lowest-income households capturing a disproportionate share" (Scobie and Posada

---

[6] Thorough reviews of patterns of demand for food by income class can be found in Poleman (1981), Timmer, Falcon, and Pearson (1983, Chapter 3), Alderman (1986), and Chaudhri and Timmer (1986).

[7] As countries reach the structural transformation turning point, there is likely to be an explosion in derived demand for feedgrains resulting from expanding demand for meat and dairy products. Meat from grain-fed livestock represents 3 to 10 times its weight in feedgrains (Poleman 1981, p. 29). In the mid-1970s direct consumption of grain was higher in India (128 kg/capita/yr) than in the United States (63 kg/capita/yr), but total grain consumed per capita in the United States was 4.5 times Indian per capita consumption because of feedgrain demand (Chaudhri and Timmer 1986, p. 62).

1984, p. 384). Here, there is no distinction between rural and urban consumers, so it is hard to generalize about countries with different structural and demographic features. Contrary to what one might expect from a hasty interpretation of Engel's Law, Colombia illustrates the importance of the demand side of the market for foodgrains. When there is little scope for grain exports or substitution for grain imports, expansion of domestic demand can play a key role in absorbing production increases and maintaining incentives for further expansion of agricultural output. Conversely, without growth in domestic foodgrain production or imports to meet demand from increases in population, the rising cost of these wage goods can be an important constraint to the expansion of nonagricultural employment and, thereby, slow down structural transformation (Lele and Mellor 1981).

Much work remains to be done on the direct effects of agricultural development on income distribution in CARLs. But another potential advantage of a unimodal structure of operating units is that it contributes (through greater demand for labor and the consequent pattern of income distribution) to demand that matches the growth in agricultural output from the higher-yielding grain varieties that have played a major role in agricultural development. This has clear social benefits too: hungry people eat more. It is also this interaction between rural labor markets and foodgrain markets, along with technological change, that could shift the rural economy out of a low-productivity, low-wage, low-food-consumption trap onto a development path that combines relief of hunger and poverty with rising productivity (Mellor and Johnston 1984).

Although the increase in total farm output is likely to equal (or exceed) growth under a dualistic strategy, growth in marketed output in broad-based strategies could be slower because of the greater increase in food consumption by the landless and small farm households. Nevertheless, raising food consumption among these low-income families is an important development aim; increasing marketable surpluses while the poor stay hungry is not.

Linkages and Indirect Effects of Agricultural Growth. When grain farmers' incomes increase, they have more money to buy agricultural inputs, such as fertilizer and farm equipment. These purchases raise agricultural output yet again and, sometimes, stimulate economic activity outside agriculture. The backward linkages of agricultural growth are considered in Chapters 6 and 7.

Increased grain output also stimulates agricultural processing and marketing of agricultural products, new mills, warehouses, and jobs. These linkages can have substantial economic effects. In a study of the impact of high-yielding rice in South India, Hazell and Ramasamy (1991) found that for every rupee of increased value added in agriculture, there was an additional 0.87 rupee of value added in the nonfarm economy. This indirect effect derived about equally from backward and forward linkages (agricultural demand for inputs, marketing, and processing) and from consumption linkages (the effect of higher income on consumer demand).

In CARLs most incremental income goes to consumption rather than to investment or working capital for additional inputs. In a narrow interpretation of economic development, lack of physical capital is seen as the primary constraint to growth—and increases in consumption are seen to conflict with development. This not only confuses ends and means but also overlooks important growth linkages from consumption.

Increased consumption from the spread of higher-yielding foodgrains can generate many jobs, even if most of the first-round income gains go to higher-income rural households (Mellor 1976). Large yield increases from new grain varieties generate small increases in tenants' and laborers' incomes and large increases for landlords and owner-operators. For example, in India only 5 to 15 percent of first-round income growth went to laborers (Mellor and Lele 1973, p. 37). Because of demand patterns, the greater the concentration of income gains among high-income households, the larger the consumption linkage effects outside the foodgrain sector. So, if attention is restricted to the direct impact of technological change on labor demand in grain production, important employment effects are overlooked.

Higher-income rural households spend more extra income on meat, dairy products, and nonstarchy fruits and vegetables than low-income households. And expenditures on these increase faster than income growth in CARLs because average income elasticities of demand are greater than 1. Furthermore, producing these commodities often is labor-intensive but requires small amounts of land and capital. Thus, these commodities can be well suited to low-income rural households with little land and abundant family labor. Vegetables and fruit can be grown in garden plots and benefit from close attention and management, for which family labor is better than hired labor. In fact, the diseconomies of farm size in their production can be greater than for grains, giving smallholders a further advantage.

In countries such as India, dairying can offer substantial opportunities for employment of family labor (Chapter 1). The main hurdle is the initial cost of a young cow or female buffalo and also the risk of loss to diseases or theft. Almost everywhere, however, even poor households can begin livestock production with poultry, sheep, or goats. Even larger animals do not need to graze in pastures (Chapter 4). Indeed, it is likely that fodder will be gathered by family members and then brought to animals that are kept at home. Furthermore, because a cow or female buffalo is a valuable asset, it is likely to be kept near the house and carefully tended, usually by women or children. These home-based activities can provide income opportunities for women that are acceptable, even where cultural norms discourage their participation in wage labor.

THE "SIX I'S" OF AGRICULTURAL STRATEGY

Although it may be tempting to seek easy and quick solutions to hunger and poverty through large-scale farms and other dualistic strategies, it will result only in frustration and a waste of resources. For CARLs the best course is broad-based development. The main concerns of policymakers should be to provide innovations, inputs, incentives, infrastructure, institutions, and initiative—the "six I's"—necessary for this pattern of development to occur.[8]

Innovations and Inputs

Poor national agricultural research programs are among the most serious obstacles to widespread increases in productivity on small farms. Effective national research systems depend on increasing the number of indigenous, well-trained agricultural scientists and on allocating human and financial resources to attain a critical mass of research effort directed at the major crop and livestock systems in principal farming regions.

Often, political leaders and policymakers little appreciate the potential returns from agricultural research. Yet, that has changed in some Asian countries, especially India and Indonesia, where the rapid spread of high-yielding varieties of rice and wheat generated greatly increased support for agricultural research.

Successful research programs are self-reinforcing. Success builds public awareness, especially among farmers, that productivity can be increased greatly by appropriate innovations. Thus, politicians and policymakers are influenced indirectly by the popularity of research, as well as the high returns being realized in rural areas.

The big problem for national research is that it must be aimed at needs of small-scale farmers operating under widely differing agricultural environments, especially in rainfed areas. Farming systems research was developed as a response to this problem. The International Maize and Wheat Improvement Center (CIMMYT) and other advocates of farming systems research have emphasized the need for "on-farm research with a farming systems perspective" and efforts to identify promising "components" for farmers to fit into their farming systems (Byerlee, Harrington, and

[8] Four of the "Six I's"—inputs, infrastructure, institutions, and incentives—were used as an expositional device in the 1986 Food and Agriculture Organization (FAO) report, *African Agriculture: The Next Twenty-Five Years*. William Omamo, a Kenyan agricultural economist and former minister of agriculture, added "initiative" as a fifth "I" in his opening statement at an Agricultural Sector Study Workshop of the African Development Bank held in Abidjan February 1–2, 1989. The addition of "innovation" as a sixth "I" is related most obviously to the emphasis on induced innovation of Hayami and Ruttan (1971, 1985) discussed in Box 3.3. Streeten (1983) also uses this device: his "Five I's" are inputs, institutions, infrastructure, information, and incentives.

Winkelmann 1982). The emphasis on problem solving and on farmers' needs in this approach strengthens linkages in national research systems between commodity programs and adaptive research, between research and extension, and between research and policy analysis (Byerlee and Tripp 1988). But given the acute scarcity of qualified scientists for farming systems research, there is urgent need for better ways of exploiting the combined benefits of experiment station research and local knowledge and management capacity of farmers, as they apply new technologies to their specific environment. The economic value of research can be enhanced by efficient information flows that tap this on-farm experience.

Increasing effectiveness of research deserves priority because appropriate innovations can be self-spreading. Nevertheless, returns to investment in research can be enhanced by also increasing the effectiveness of agricultural extension—but only if there is something useful to extend. In the words of one extension specialist, "most extension field services have been a complete waste of time" (Roling 1982).[9] Moreover, extension agents tend to focus on large farms rather than smallholdings (and men rather than women), which means that extension programs can contribute to factors that differentiate across farms.

Agrarian structure can be important in determining agricultural research priorities and the bias of technological innovations. In a bimodal structure, big landowners can ensure that priorities go to labor-saving, capital-using innovations, even though they are inappropriate for most farms. Take rubber production in Southeast Asia. Research programs generated innovations and inputs suitable to capital-intensive rubber production on the large-scale plantations that sponsored research (Barlow and Jayasuriya 1984a). A similar, inappropriate bias in agricultural research has been documented by de Janvry (1978) for Argentina. (For other cases, see Sanders and Ruttan 1978, Chambers 1983, and Hayami and Ruttan 1985, p. 362.)

Conversely, broad-based productivity growth (through divisible technology such as higher-yielding, fertilizer-responsive seeds or trees) can build broad political support for research on these technologies. Furthermore, government sometimes can use technology as "a surrogate for asset redistribu-

---

[9] An effort by Birkhaeuser, Evenson, and Feder (1991) to assess the social returns to agricultural extension was hampered by the limited number of empirical studies. They concluded (p. 645) that "it was not possible to establish empirically the conditions that are conducive to effectiveness, although common sense can suggest a number of these, such as a continuous flow of research-generated improved technology or availability of complementary inputs." The Training and Visit (T and V) system promoted by Daniel Benor and the World Bank has been the most widely diffused approach to improving the effectiveness of extension systems. By avoiding tasks other than extension and by the deployment and in-service training of field workers, the system "seems to go a long way to rationalize the use of existing extension resources" (Roling, p. 106). However, this "contact farmer" approach may not be effective in achieving broad coverage of small farms.

tion" (de Janvry, Sadoulet, and Fafchamps 1989).[10] For example, much of the debate about agricultural strategy in the Philippines is concerned with land reform. Meanwhile, smallholder foodcrop producers continue to lose opportunities to be tenants as land shifts into large-scale production of export crops. Reorienting agricultural research to accelerate yield increases of smallholder crops such as maize would help slow, if not reverse, this process (Bouis and Haddad 1990).

The international network of agricultural research centers, which have yielded high returns, cannot substitute for national research systems but can increase the payoff to parallel investments in national programs. Foreign aid in research is important because national research systems cost much in foreign exchange to strengthen—for example, paying for overseas graduate training and foreign expertise (see Taiwan and Mexico, Chapter 10). Perhaps more fundamental is foreign assistance in strengthening local institutions of higher learning and improving graduate degree training in the agricultural sciences, agricultural economics, and other disciplines needed to staff agricultural research institutes.

Incentives

National capacity to produce technological innovations and high-payoff inputs, physical infrastructure, and development institutions all affect farm profits, the main incentives for private initiative. But these effects take years, even decades, to be realized; some incentives (through market-determined prices) nevertheless have an immediate impact on farmers' decisions about production and investment. Government intervention (or lack of it) in prices and markets for agricultural outputs and inputs are key features of development strategies.

"Getting prices right" need not always mean that domestic prices are linked to prices in world markets—but it usually does for agricultural commodities. Cogent arguments can be made for intervention in a few crucial prices.[11]

---

[10] De Janvry, Sadoulet, and Fafchamps (1989) also provide a formal model of the effects of agrarian structure on the rate and bias of technological change.

[11] See, for example, Timmer, Falcon, and Pearson (1983). Most governments appear to have a strong preference for stabilizing food prices; such costly schemes suggest that these preferences are rooted deeply in politics and society. There is no consensus, however, regarding the "optimal" degree of price stabilization from an economic standpoint (see Newbery and Stiglitz 1981; Kanbur 1984; Timmer 1989). In practice, "stabilization" almost always affects average prices as well as price variation—and it is the price level that is the focus of this section as well as our consideration of costs and benefits of consumer food subsidies in Chapter 8. Typically, the relevant policy question is not the optimal rate of stabilization but how to minimize trade-offs (in terms of budgetary costs and economic distortions) for a given degree of stability. Pinckney (1988) elaborates practical techniques for judging trade-offs across costs and benefits, which is taken up again in Chapter 11 regarding Kenya.

In CARLs, however, even managing prices for key commodities is beyond the capacity of most governments, much less comprehensive intervention in most commodity prices. As Timmer (1987) points out in his review of intervention in rice markets since the mid-1960s, the most important lesson of the Asian experience is the need for "flexibility in the face of uncertainty." The rub, of course, is that this is a great weakness of bureaucracies—and a corresponding strength of markets.

Yet, it is usually political expedience, not economic logic, that drives interventions to set agricultural prices. Too often they distort the terms of trade against agriculture and stifle incentives for production and investment in the rural economy. Efforts to offset these distortions in incentives through, say, input subsidies can introduce differential effects by farm size, with large farms reaping the greatest benefits.

Egyptian policy from the 1960s to the mid-1980s is a prime example of "getting prices wrong"—of cheap food policies and an attempt to tax agriculture to finance public sector-led industrialization. Direct transfers from the agricultural sector resulting from Egypt's price policies alone accounted for more than 10 percent of agricultural gross domestic product (GDP) in eight of the ten years 1974–83 and were more than 38 percent in 1975 (Dethier 1989, p. 217). And that was even before accounting for the effects of an overvalued exchange rate. Intervention, which focused on major tradables, such as cotton, wheat, and rice, also induced farmers to shift toward relatively unregulated nontradables, such as livestock fodder and fresh vegetables. So cockeyed was Egypt's policy that there were times in the 1970s when the market price of wheat straw made it more valuable to farmers than the grain, requisitioned at official prices.

In Taiwan a price policy for rice and fertilizer resulted in a net tax on agriculture, but much of this revenue was reinvested to develop rural infrastructure. Combined with profitable innovations flowing from Taiwan's research institutions, this allowed farm profits to grow, despite the unfavorable prices. There is considerable scope for debate on pricing, but maintaining farm profitability through prices and other determinants of incentives is a necessary condition for broad-based agricultural development.

Malawi's development strategy shows how differentiating factors can do little to ease poverty and damage economic prospects when policies, especially pricing, favor large-scale agriculture to the detriment of smallholders' incentives. Malawi's dualistic strategy was "predicated on the notion that smallholder agriculture . . . was not an appropriate engine of growth. Rather, the estate sector was viewed as a means of generating needed revenues and foreign exchange, with the smallholder subsector providing cheap labor and wage goods in support of this strategy" (Sahn and Arulpragasam 1991a, p. 44).

The estates received preferential access to land, credit, and support services and were free to export tobacco to the world market. Smallholders had to sell products (maize, the main smallholder crop, as well as tobacco, rice, groundnuts, and other crops) to ADMARC, the agricultural marketing board, at artificially low prices. In the 1970s this led to a rapid expansion of estates, which became dependent on cheap labor and capital; among smallholders, population pressure and alienation of land for estates reduced farm size in land-scarce Malawi. Productivity growth was slow partly because of neglect of smallholders in government development initiatives (Kydd and Christiansen 1982). When this strategy proved unsustainable in the 1980s, adjustment was made more difficult by the neglect of smallholders in virtually every aspect of agricultural strategy (Sahn and Arulpragasam 1991b).

Imperfections in commodity markets in CARLs mean that there can be a role for marketing and price policy. But this should be to improve imperfect markets in the short run and promote long-term market development, not to replace markets with bureaucracies. A broad-based strategy is unlikely to be successful unless the scarce resource of administrative capacity is concentrated where government action is indispensable. This means that mainly private firms should carry out agricultural marketing, which can be performed more efficiently by relying on price and market mechanisms rather than the calculation and control of government agencies (see Box 5.2). This strategic notion of market-oriented pricing is a crucial element of broad-based development.

Such a strategy is not the same as *laissez-faire*. When market imperfections are identified, selective interventions can improve markets rather than replacing them with state-administered bureaucracies. These interventions can include investments in transportation, communication, storage, or other market infrastructure.

Jones's (1984) analysis of the effect of deficiencies in road systems and market information on food marketing in sub-Saharan Africa, for example, stresses the problem of spatial arbitrage: "The picture of free African markets that emerges is a set of two-level systems, each focusing on a different consuming center, with adjustments at the margins of the supply areas but with long-distance arbitrage only when supplies within the separate areas fall badly out of balance" (Jones 1984, p. 126). This suggests not only that public investment in transport infrastructure is an important complement to price policy, as discussed later, but also that government can play an important role in providing market information as a public good.

Before transport infrastructure is well established, a marketing agency may be needed to undertake long-distance trade to shift supplies between major markets, but this should be a complement to, not a substitute for, private traders. For example, BULOG (Indonesia's Agency for Management of Food Logistics) paid a floor price for yellow maize in one of Indonesia's Outer Islands, where farmers previously grew only white maize for own consumption. After a few years, enough yellow maize was being marketed to

Box 5.2.   The Basic Case for Reliance on Markets to Allocate Agricultural Goods

Markets and prices deserve special attention in agricultural development strategy because agricultural production and marketing can be undertaken by small independent operators. Indeed, small farms and local trading firms in agriculture are quintessentially private enterprises. Yet, the restrictive statist view of development opportunities is manifested in the artificial distinction between formal markets—those influenced by government and presumed to be relatively efficient—and informal markets beyond official control and presumed to be partially formed and inefficient. Notions that free markets are imperfect and presumptions that monopoly power allows traders to exploit farmers are often invoked in an effort to justify direct government interventions in agricultural markets.

The burden of proof must rest with those who think that agricultural prices are too important to be left to market forces. The statist obsession with imperfections of market institutions creates its own paradox: markets with heavy government intervention tend to be the least efficient. Furthermore, government control of agricultural product prices typically reduces farmers' income in CARLs (but not in higher-income countries).

Evidence from many countries has demonstrated the efficiency advantages of decentralized decision making by private enterprises for the rural economy in general and for agriculture in particular. The diversity of the rural economy in CARLs—and of physical environments, together with the complex interactions among resource endowments, technology, institutions, history, and cultural heritage—make it impossible to draw up an ideal plan and an optimal set of policies and programs for realizing agricultural planning targets.

attract private traders. Even though these traders offered lower prices, they cut into BULOG's market share by offering farmers better payment terms and greater convenience. The remarkable aspect of this tale is that the marketing agency resisted the usual bureaucratic urges to increase subsidies or impose a ban on private trade (Peter and Carol Timmer personal communication, 1990).

Indonesia also provides a rare example of substantial input price subsidies that did not lead to rationing and black markets. But this success in meeting growing fertilizer demand in the late 1970s and 1980s even at two-thirds or less of the world price depended on two factors that other CARLS are unlikely to share. First, the country's comparative advantage in nitrogen fertilizer production (Chapter 7) meant that supplies were adequate to meet domestic demand. Second, and more important, increased demand coincided with Indonesia's oil windfall, so there was enough funding to cover the budgetary costs of subsidies to meet demand at the official price.

Even so, there may be a similar role for state-owned agencies in other CARLs to market fertilizers, or other new inputs, if initial demand is not sufficient to attract private suppliers. But this should be only transitional toward a more efficient market, which can occur only if public agencies and private firms eventually compete on equal terms. Even then, there are plenty of pitfalls (Box 5.3).

Infrastructure

Rural infrastructure—roads, ports, irrigation, drainage, telecommunications, and electrification—has fallen from favor in development strategies because, it was thought, benefits would be monopolized by better-off farmers. But in most CARLs infrastructure will not be developed sufficiently unless government takes a hand. So massive are the financial requirements for many projects that the private sector is unlikely to undertake them alone.

Investments in rural roads provide a rare opportunity for policymakers to please almost everyone: reducing transport costs lowers marketing margins, allowing consumer prices to fall and producer prices to rise without squeezing private traders' incentives. Transport accounts for 20 to 40 percent of fertilizer marketing margins in developing countries (Mittendorf, Lee, and Trupke 1983). Moreover, public works projects generate significant off-farm rural employment.

Efficient transport becomes increasingly important in the transition from traditional, resource-based to science-based agriculture. Purchased inputs, such as higher-yielding seeds and fertilizer, must be distributed on time and in large quantities, as more smallholders adopt the new technology. Furthermore, the initial surge in marketed surplus resulting from new technology can swamp an inadequate transport system, as happened in Pakistan in 1969 (Falcon 1970, p. 701). As a result, "large, uncovered piles of rice accumulated at railheads, and prices to farmers fell substantially."

Factor market imperfections are less tractable than deficiencies in commodity markets, but infrastructure investments can play a positive role here, too. As the ratio of arable land to population and labor force shrinks, the intensity of land use and the returns to land increase. Hayami and Ruttan (1985) stress that productivity expansion through more intensive land use can be helped by public investments in infrastructure to enhance the quality of existing land. Investments in land quality, such as irrigation and transportation systems, can complement the farms' labor-using, land-saving technological change.

For big projects substantial benefits from investment in infrastructure result from broader effects on regional income, employment, and investment that are more difficult to measure than direct effects, such as yield increases on a single farm from irrigation. In a pathbreaking effort to measure these benefits, Clive Bell and Shantayanan Devarajan (Bell, Hazell, and Slade 1982,

Box 5.3   Misguided Marketing in Mexico's CONASUPO

In early 1972 a team of young economists and agronomists drew up a blueprint for a marketing initiative by CONASUPO, a powerful Mexican government agency for purchasing, importing, and distributing grain and other food products. Their "theoretical explanation for the growing marginalization of the subsistence sector . . . began with the assumption that in order for a traditional farmer to pass to the modern agricultural sector, it is necessary for him to produce a surplus, to retain the use of the surplus, and finally to invest it productively [but] the problem is that any surplus produced by the Mexican peasant is extracted by individuals and groups who make their livings by exploiting him" (Grindle 1977, p. 84).

The team's analysis led to a policy statement calling for a "transformation of subsistence agriculture in Mexico," with a key role for a CONASUPO initiative in the rural economy: "The federal government, by means of deliberate and programmed activity, should intervene more decisively in rural areas to provide a change in the impact of market forces on the peasants" (quoted in Grindle 1977, p. 89). There was a big expansion in CONASUPO's marketing and distribution in rural areas, including in grain reception centers from 1,131 to 2,434 in 1973–75. Those centers were to receive, weigh, analyze, and pay for the grain that farmers delivered to CONASUPO. Some 1,500 analysts at the reception centers received training in a program that included "extensive efforts to promote their 'social conscience' . . . to prevent a reoccurrence of corrupt practices" (Grindle 1977, p. 115).

There is little evidence that CONASUPO was able to bring about "change in the impact of market forces on the peasants." In fact, the CONASUPO diagnosis was based more on casual observation than on careful analysis of the performance of marketing in rural areas. Moreover, there has been a tendency to ignore problems that commonly arise with administered prices—for example, and in Mexico a serious one, the delay in revisions of official prices. This often means that administered product prices lag behind increases in prices of farm inputs and therefore fail to provide an adequate incentive to producers.

Some studies of food marketing systems in developing countries have concluded that most alleged imperfections are not supported by the evidence, although imperfections may be found in remote areas where there is little competition among traders. (See, for example, Jones 1972 and Lele 1974). Those conclusions probably need to be qualified for Mexico. Allegations that local bosses (*caciques*) forcibly prevent the entry of potential competitors to preserve the power of privileged merchants have a ring of plausibility, especially given the frequency with which *caciques* resort to violence. It should not be overlooked, though, that a government-operated channel for buying and selling commodities has considerable market power, which means that some officials are likely to seize opportunities for underpaying farmers or overcharging consumers. Indeed, the officials who benefited from the earlier system also were likely to be the same who benefited from the CONASUPO system.

These pitfalls of intervention in agricultural marketing are not unique to Mexico. Indeed, the patterns in the CONASUPO case are the rule, not the ex-

Box 5.3   (*continued*)

ception, for CARLs. It is never easy to inculcate a social conscience that will dissuade officials from collecting monopsony rents if the opportunity exists, and few CARLs have the institutional capacity needed to credibly enforce sanctions against such abuses of power.

---

p. 216) estimated that the social rate of return to the Muda irrigation project in Malaysia exceeded 20 percent and that the main beneficiaries were the poor. But there are many other examples where irrigation investments have not been socially profitable; in sub-Saharan Africa particularly, such projects are expensive, and social benefits have been low or negative (Binswanger and Pingali 1988; Pearson, Stryker, and Humphreys 1981).

A common notion is that Africa simply "must" expand irrigation, but physical limitations—lack of water, poor drainage—restrict areas in which irrigation makes economic sense. A better notion for Africa (and elsewhere) would be that irrigation deserves a look—but that look should be close and hard.[12] Without careful preappraisal "the farmers' promised banquet may turn out to be simply an engineering picnic" (Carruthers and Clark 1981, p. 1).

There is another important caveat: costs of maintaining infrastructure are often overlooked, especially in externally funded projects in sub-Saharan Africa. Governments have had to face unanticipated—and unmanageable—recurring expenses on roads and other projects. Aid agencies are reluctant to provide operating costs because they "fear that such aid will enable the recipient to postpone measures . . . that would make an activity financially self-sustaining" (Gray and Martens 1983, p. 113). As a result, investments have deteriorated rapidly and benefits have been cut short because governments did not have enough funds to cover recurrent costs. Transport and irrigation projects both are susceptible to this myopia, but irrigation runs into additional problems resulting from the frequent failure to realize that investment in irrigation in arid climates such as Egypt (or much of South Asia) must be coupled with equally costly drainage projects if benefits are to be sustained.

Rather than more aid, what is needed in infrastructure investment is more attention—by donors and recipients—to priorities, costs, and financial capacity. Gray and Martens argue that the operating cost problem will be solved in the long run by economic growth and an expanded tax base. Another approach is to devolve management responsibility to local organizations with a stake in project benefits and presumably an incentive to raise local funds or mobilize labor to ensure that benefits continue.

[12] An important beginning has been made in a study summarized by Moris and Thom (1987).

Institutions and Initiative

The balance between public intervention and private initiative is the most delicate for institutions. Public policy initiatives need a pragmatic, pluralistic approach to seizing opportunities as they emerge. But care is needed to avoid crowding out private initiative, both individual and collective. In the United States rural people organized themselves for many economic, social, and political purposes—ranging from water districts, ranchers' associations, and marketing cooperatives to 4-H clubs, churches, and political clubs. These were effective complements to state and national institutions, such as land grant colleges and agricultural extension services. Likewise, Japan had its distinctive local institutions (Chapter 3). Local organizations exist in contemporary CARLs as well, including Indian villagers' organizations for managing common grazing land and irrigation (Wade 1987).

Occasionally, outside efforts are needed to promote such organizations. The Taiwanese irrigators' associations, which grew from unlikely roots as instruments of control during the Japanese colonial period have emerged as participatory organizations since World War II. Unfortunately, more typical of experience in CARLs is the destruction of local irrigation organizations and the stultifying effect on individual initiative that resulted from the Dez irrigation project in the Shah's Iran (Goodell 1986). This is symptomatic of the incompatibility of centralized bureaucratic control and local participation. Much work has to be done on how best to promote institutions necessary to the operation of markets and the provision of public goods and, at the very least, how national initiatives can avoid undermining reasonably effective organizations that exist in CARLs. A note of caution, however: some local institutions that allocate and enforce property rights are simply instruments of the local elite.

Translating concern into public policies to redress local imbalances in political and economic power has often proven illusory. Rural credit programs have been a mainstay of public policy initiatives to undermine the presumed market power of landlords and village moneylenders. Paradoxically, as discussed in the next section, the main result has been to create differential access to cheap credit by farm size, with (as usual) larger ones benefiting most.

There is even controversy about what would seem to be a fundamental institutional requirement: a system to record property titles and certify boundaries. Establishing secure property rights in land is important for a broad-based agricultural strategy. It facilitates the transfer of ownership and fosters investments to raise land quality. And it makes it safer for landlords to rent out land to tenants. In Kenya Collier (1983, 1989) has argued that the insecurity of property rights of the larger landowners, the high costs of monitoring tenants because many landlords are absentees, and their limited recourse for enforcement of contracts have thwarted the emergence of land tenancy institutions and thereby inhibited more efficient combinations of land and labor.

Aside from land redistribution, which seems unlikely, land registration might be a means of promoting efficient factor markets. But the costs of formal registration are substantial, even in sub-Saharan Africa, as stressed by Feder and Noronha (1987) and Migot-Adholla and others (1991), and indigenous systems already provide relative security of property rights for many farmers (but not necessarily large-scale farmers), and informal recognition of individual property rights is increasing. Thus, the social gains from formal titling may still be small. On the other hand, a formal effort to establish land titles can act as an invitation to powerful individuals to use the system to alienate land from smallholders with legitimate but informal rights. Investments in agricultural research and in rural infrastructure deserve higher priority, particularly if it is probable that formal land titling will be implemented unfairly and, as a consequence, further differentiate farms by size.

Perhaps the apparent pitfalls in remedying institutional shortcomings of factor markets are the reason why governments have a penchant for intervention in commodity markets. The proliferation of crop authorities, doing what could be better done by the private sector, has often been a source of costly inefficiency in marketing and has led to a diversion of scarce administrative capacity away from essential tasks. Public initiatives should avoid commercial activities and concentrate on public goods, such as the institutional framework for markets to function efficiently and fairly.

But direct involvement of a public agency in commercial activities can occasionally yield significant economic benefits. A notable example: the Kenya Tea Development Authority (KTDA), performs a useful role in tea processing which is characterized by economies of scale (Chapter 11). By seizing opportunities beyond the grasp of individual smallholders, the KTDA catalyzed rapid expansion of tea production. It is important to note, however, that the organization of the KTDA recognizes the smallholders' capacity to organize tea production at the farm level and restricts itself to activities in which economies of scale are important, such as dissemination of new technology and coordination of the timely delivery of tea leaves to processing factories. The KTDA has performed a valuable role in making investments in "tea roads" and in organizing the collection and processing of tea leaves that made it possible for some 140 thousand small-scale farmers to raise their incomes by undertaking tea production. This happened despite the long-held belief that tea could be produced efficiently only by plantations. India's National Dairy Development Board is another example (Box 1.3) of a successful public initiative in an essentially commercial activity that embodied a clear vision of the comparative advantage of small-scale producers vis-à-vis the larger organization.

The contrasts between, say, BULOG's public initiatives to make a market in yellow maize and Malawi's tobacco development policies illustrate the need for a clear vision of the advantages of broad-based strategies and the pitfalls of dualism. There is a near-universal need to strengthen policy-oriented research and analysis in CARLs. This strengthening is needed to evaluate price policies, infrastructure investment proposals, institutional reforms, and other options for increasing productivity—and, thereby, to promote a consensus on agricultural policy choices.

BULOG's success with public initiatives is no accident. "BULOG had to pursue its two policy mandates—stabilize the price of basic food grains and ensure their supply—over twenty years in frequently changing circumstances. That it was successful at doing this was a result of substantial investment in technical and managerial staff. Its own growing competence and reputation meant that BULOG became a powerful bureaucratic actor itself, and an effective proponent of the policies it was charged with pursuing" (Thomas and Grindle 1990, p. 1168).

Policy analysis is needed, too, to address environmental issues, the role of women in agriculture, and other unanticipated issues that will emerge with agricultural development in CARLs. This will require not only increases in the quantity, but also the flexibility of analysts if they are to accommodate a changing policy agenda. An especially important and difficult challenge is to make this policy research and analysis less vulnerable to political shifts—to ensure that such research will receive sustained support and have an impact on the policy process, while maintaining independence from political imperatives.

LIMITATIONS OF AGRICULTURAL DEVELOPMENT STRATEGY

Does broad-based agricultural productivity growth alone provide sufficient income growth and employment to alleviate poverty and hunger? No, not alone.

Employment and Population Growth

Rural wages will remain low as long as the rural labor force is growing as fast as (or faster than) the expansion of employment opportunities. This situation hits the landless dependent on wage employment. At the same time, landlords can increase the already-large crop share that tenants have to pay.

Even labor-using agricultural technologies can absorb only so much of a growing rural labor force when there is little or no possibility for expanding the area under cultivation. Growth in agricultural employment is unlikely to exceed 2.4 to 3 percent annually, even where growth in agricultural output has been exceptional, say, 4 to 5 percent a year (Mellor 1986, p. 70).

Higher rates of employment growth are probably possible only through falling wages, even with labor-using technological change, because of diminishing marginal returns. Furthermore, divisible, labor-saving chemical and mechanical innovations from Japan and Taiwan may be spreading fast to other parts of Asia (Jayasuriya and Shand 1986). Thus, rapid wage increases are unlikely to be realized from the direct effects of agricultural development alone.

Expanding the employment opportunities in manufacturing and service activities using labor-intensive technologies is critical in providing employment opportunities for a rapidly growing labor force. Initially, it can reduce the effects of diminishing returns in agriculture. Subsequently, more rapid growth of employment outside agriculture accelerates the structural transformation turning point. But policies to promote nonfarm productivity growth and employment can (see Chapters 6 and 7) complement or conflict with agricultural development.

Poverty Alleviation and Human Nutrition

Agricultural development and other policies for productivity growth and employment are not quick fixes for rural poverty. Because of distributional biases, the process of reducing rural poverty will be time-consuming. Moreover, alleviating undernutrition will be slow. Increasing income of the poor appears to raise calorie consumption at less than half the rate of increases in food expenditures (Alderman 1986, p. 39). More surprising, studies often show that increases in calorie intake do not translate into significant improvements in health indicators, especially among preschool children (Behrman, Deolalikar, and Wolfe 1988; Bouis and Haddad 1990; Kennedy and Cogill 1987). These results have caused a reevaluation of the emphasis on calorie sufficiency in food policy research. They have also renewed policy interest in selective public health measures and nutrition education.

If a 10 percent rise in income leads to only a 1.5 percent increase in calorie consumption and households have an average 15 percent calorie deficit, income would have to double just to close the gap (Chaudhri and Timmer 1986, p. 19).[13] Yet, the interrelated objectives of improving the health and survival prospects of infants and preschool children and of slowing population growth are too important to be neglected, even in CARLs facing severe financial constraints. Policy options for assisting young children and their mothers can contribute to the success of agricultural development strategies in raising rural wages and to the acceleration of the process of structural transformation because they help to reduce population growth rates and, thereby, hasten the structural transformation turning point (Chapter 8).

---

[13] An analysis of data from rural South India even suggested that increases in income had little, if any, effect on nutrition (Behrman and Deolalikar 1987).

Macroeconomic Policies and Development Strategy

None of these efforts can succeed, however, unless there are parallel improvements in macroeconomic management. Macroeconomic policies in many CARLs have had adverse effects on agricultural development and the rural economy generally. Policies that distort relative prices undermine economic efficiency and tend to promote large farms at the expense of smaller farms and the rural work force. Fiscal imbalances often mean there are inadequate budget allocations for essential agricultural support services, notably agricultural research and rural roads.

The indirect effect of macroeconomic policies—primarily the exchange rate, as discussed in Box 5.4—often has a further depressing effect on agricultural incentives in developing countries and dominates the direct effects of sectoral price policies (Krueger, Schiff, and Valdes 1988).

The combined effects of import-substituting industrialization strategies, overvalued exchange rates, and negative real interest rates can render even the best agriculture sector policies moot. They also tend to discriminate against the smaller-scale, labor-intensive firms that are the basis of hope for agriculture–industry linkages to promote nonfarm employment (Coxhead 1992; Haggblade, Liedholm, and Mead 1986).

Macroeconomic policies that allow large farms to acquire tractors and other machinery at artificially low prices have especially adverse effects on the prospects for broad-based agricultural development. Imports of industrial machinery, tractors, and other capital goods are often at low, or zero, tariffs because of the erroneous belief that this is a good way to promote capital formation. Faced with stagnating agricultural production, governments are especially prone to allow duty-free imports of tractors and tractor-drawn equipment. An overvalued exchange rate means that their price in local currency is already artificially low. When large farmers also have access to subsidized credit, the incentive to invest in inappropriate capital-using, labor-displacing technologies is huge. And therein are two of the principal distortions resulting from ill-advised macroeconomic policies—artificially low interest rates and overvalued currencies.

Not only do these distortions encourage the capital-intensive technologies in the near term, but because of distorted price signals and biased research, they induce a pattern of innovations ill-suited to a country's resource endowment.

Rural Capital Markets

A widely shared strategic notion among development specialists as well as policymakers in CARLs is that market failures are extensive in the financial sector. Informal financial markets have high interest rates and

Box 5.4 Managing the Exchange Rate

The rate of exchange between the domestic and foreign currencies is a linch-pin of the economy. Its influence on product prices across the economy parallels the impact of the wage rate and the interest rate on the cost side. To state it precisely, the exchange rate is the price of foreign exchange. It aligns domestic product prices with the world economy, thereby determining the relative profitability not only of exports but also of import substitutes and nontradables. In our context, whether agricultural exports are strong or weak, whether food production leads or lags population growth, these outcomes will be fundamentally conditioned by movements in the exchange rate.

When the exchange rate deviates from its equilibrium value—roughly, a price of foreign currency that produces a balance in the current account—misallocations result, and economic growth is curtailed. Are such deviations frequent? Do they tend to be random in direction? In the face of ubiquitous pressures to maintain short-run consumption, the evidence suggests that among many CARLs there is a bias for monetary authorities to err in one direction. Unlike the response to a nonequilibrium exchange rate movement that undervalues the local currency (and hence makes imports more expensive), prompt corrective measures are not always taken in the case of an overvaluation. A dramatic example of the importance of managing the exchange rate is found in a comparison of Nigeria and Indonesia during the oil exporters' commodity boom of 1973–81. After the first quintupling of the oil price, both countries' foreign exchange earnings surged manyfold. In Nigeria for 1974–78 there was a windfall of foreign exchange equivalent to 23 percent of non-oil GDP. For Indonesia the comparable windfall was 16 percent. The second price hike of 1979 lead to another windfall for 1979–81 equivalent to about 22 percent of non-oil GDP in both countries (Gelb 1988, pp. 62–65). After 1981 oil revenues fell off sharply. The GDP grew in both countries during the oil boom; in the decade that followed, the GDP grew at an average annual rate of 5.4 percent in Indonesia while that of Nigeria contracted at a rate of −0.4 percent per year (World Bank 1991, p. 206). In 1970 Nigeria's per capita GNP was 185 percent of Indonesia's; by 1989 it stood at exactly 50 percent of Indonesia's $500 per person.

These dramatically different outcomes are attributable in large measure to Indonesia's more skilful management of its exchange rate and its inflation-adjusted cousin, the "real exchange rate." While Nigeria's nominal exchange rate was allowed to appreciate in the late 1970s, Indonesia devalued. While Nigeria's public spending consistently exceeded its soaring public revenues after 1974, Indonesia ran, on average, budgetary surpluses (Gelb 1988, chaps. 12 and 13).

After the initial cheapening of foreign exchange as its supply surged in 1974–78 in both countries, Indonesia's devaluations and prudent spending policies brought its prices back into line with those of its trading partners (see table). By contrast, the prices of Nigerian agricultural and manufactured goods were allowed to move in dollar-equivalent values to ever-higher, more uncompetitive levels.

Box 5.4 *(continued)*

Nigeria attempted to protect its manufacturing sector from inexpensive imports by quantitative import restrictions. But an overburdened licensing system could neither deal with such complexities as the need for spare parts (with the consequence that the sector operated at a low-level of capacity use) nor fend off system-defeating illegal issuance of import licenses to high-placed politicians and bureaucrats. Thus, manufacturing as a proportion of non-oil GDP stagnated.

As for agriculture, it was twice-taxed by Nigeria's foreign trade regime: to the undermining competition from imported rice, wheat, and other foodstuffs was added the burden of higher-priced domestically manufactured inputs and consumer goods. The little development spending directed to agriculture went to ill-fated large-scale, capital-intensive parastatal farms that provide a classic example of the misguided quest for economies of scale described in the previous chapter. Indonesia, by contrast, strengthened the capacity of smallholder farming by spending on irrigation and feeder roads and by promoting high-yielding rice varieties. The net result was that Indonesia's agricultural output advanced, led by its food production. The reverse occurred in Nigeria (see table).

In sum, although agriculture's development is directly shaped by a wide range of sector-specific interventions, an overvalued exchange rate can short-circuit carefully constructed sectoral strategy. No doubt a longer list of right and wrong policy decisions contributed to the divergent outcomes. But skillful management of the exchange rate and of the margin between public revenues and public expenditures was clearly at the core of success in Indonesia, just as inept handling of these two policies was the source of disorder in Nigeria.

Movements in the real exchange rate

	Nigeria	Indonesia
1969–72	100	100
1974–78	129	133
1979–81	163	104
1982–83	194	109
1984	287	92

Agricultural output per capita

	Nigeria	Indonesia
1969–72	100	100
1974–78	91	109
1979–81	91	123
1982–83	84	127

little or no long-term credit. This, it is presumed, shows that moneylenders are monopolistic exploiters of farmers and rural laborers. A second strategic notion has been that credit is a crucial constraint to the adoption of new technologies and, so, to improved agricultural output. By supplying rural credit at favorable terms, it was hoped that agricultural production would increase. It was further assumed that the rural poor would be the main beneficiaries because otherwise they have to pay high interest rates to moneylenders. Therefore, credit allocation by government quotas and incentives has frequently been considered to be essential in promoting rapid economic growth.

Development banks and other financial institutions are often directed to make credit available at artificially low interest rates, programs that often have been supported by international donors. This creates excess demand for the credit available from institutional lenders, and ceilings on deposit interest discourage saving. The inevitable result is administrative rationing of loans from institutional sources. The bigger and more influential farmers receive the lion's share, while the overwhelming majority must turn to high-cost credit from village moneylenders and other traditional sources—or, more often, do without.

In Costa Rica in 1974 the largest 10 percent of agricultural loans accounted for roughly 80 percent of all such lending by banks—even less equally distributed than farm land (Vogel 1984, pp. 138–39). For Brazil the ratio of loans to gross product value in 1975 was only 0.05 for farms with less than 10 hectares, and 0.36 for those with more than 10,000 hectares. After the expansion of credit at highly subsidized rates, that ratio rose sharply to 0.75 for large farms but only to 0.06 for the small ones (Sayad 1984, p. 149). Subsidized rural credit programs were intended, ostensibly, to improve small farmers' access to credit, but they have been a serious and costly failure in many countries.

Indeed, the general conclusion is that artificially cheap credit has been ineffective, inefficient, inequitable, and ultimately detrimental to economic growth:

Clearly, charging low interest rates on formal loans and paying even lower interest rates on savings deposits is the most harmful policy in rural financial markets. . . . Low interest rates have two important effects on lenders and borrowers. First, they inflate the demand for loans and increase the tightness with which lenders ration credit; the result is almost always to concentrate cheap loans in the hands of relatively few people. . . . Small and new borrowers and those who have weak collateral are rationed out of credit markets under these conditions. The net result of this rationing process is increased concentration of incomes and ownership, and inefficient allocation of resources. . . . The second major effect of low interest rates is on household savings, especially among low- and middle-income households. Low interest rates deny these households the alternative of holding their savings in financial form. . . . As a result, the ability of an economy to encourage financial savings is reduced and capital formation is retarded. (Von Pischke and others 1983, p. 427)

Positive interest rates in real terms are necessary to encourage people to put savings into the financial system, instead of accumulating nonfinancial savings, such as precious metals, inventories, consumer durables, and real estate.[14] Financial savings can be lent to entrepreneurs for investment, enhancing economic growth. Indeed, if the countryside is served by an efficient banking system, growth in the rural economy can be stimulated. Financial institutions can be much more efficient than traditional lenders in carrying out financial intermediation. And, maybe, it is possible to establish viable rural banking institutions (Box 5.5).

Financial sector policies, such as lending regulations and interest rate policies, have a big impact on the rural economy and agricultural development. Cheap credit policies discriminate against small farmers and promote capital-intensive farming, processing, and manufacturing technologies that limit the expansion of employment in the countryside. And rationing, corruption, and red tape severely limit small-scale farmers' access to subsidized credit programs. It is essential, too, for policymakers to take a broader view of financial intermediation, including the mobilization of savings and lending to rural nonfarm enterprises, as well as to farmers.

HARD TO ACHIEVE, EASY TO LOSE

If agricultural innovations and new inputs are to contribute to broad-based productivity growth, they must be able to spread to many of a country's farms, including a growing percentage of the small farms that inevitably predominate in CARLs. The advantages of a unimodal agrarian structure—for employment opportunities in agriculture and patterns of demand for agricultural products—make this structure superior to a bimodal structure for CARLs.

The economic advantages of a unimodal agrarian structure are hard to gain, easy to lose. Such a structure could be achieved by redistributing

---

[14] The price of capital represented by interest rates has distinctive characteristics. The notion of a "market-clearing price" freely determined by forces of supply and demand and totally unfettered by government regulations is flawed in credit markets because of the pervasiveness of adverse risk selection and moral hazard (McKinnon 1988; Stiglitz and Weiss 1981). Von Pischke (personal communication, November 1989) notes, however, that "market failure in finance is basically a subjective concept. . . . So practitioners should be warned that claims of market failure tend to be to some degree erroneous and usually self-serving professionally."

Box 5.5   Rural Banking Reform in Indonesia

The General Rural Credit Program (*Kredit Umum Pedesaan*) is exceptional on three counts. First, it is the largest rural credit program in Indonesia, and perhaps in the world, with $310 million outstanding at the end of 1988. Second, rather than loans being earmarked for specific activities such as rice production, almost any profitable economic activity is eligible. Third, unlike in traditional programs, the interest rate is set to cover the cost of funds plus a margin for operating costs and loan losses of the Peoples' Bank of Indonesia, the state bank responsible for implementation. Thus, the bank has a commercial interest in the program's success.

General Rural Credit, launched in January 1984, grew out of the collapse of a traditional credit program, which had been introduced in the 1970s as part of Indonesia's rice intensification drive. In the earlier program loans were made to finance rice production inputs at a subsidized interest rate (12 percent a year in nominal terms) that was less than the rate paid on savings deposits. Thus, the People's Bank had little financial incentive to expand credit and a disincentive to raise rural savings. Targeted credit may have played a constructive role in the early years of the push to raise rice yields. But between 1975 and 1983 the number of farms participating fell by 60 percent, and the share of credit repaid fell to 80 percent or less. As arrears mounted, losses to the People's Bank were on the order of $30 million a year. Despite these problems, one accomplishment of the credit program for rice intensification stands out: through it Indonesia established the infrastructure for a rural banking system, often where no formal lending institution existed before. The key component was the village branches of the People's Bank. Although not established everywhere, these had the potential to serve one-third of Indonesian villages.

When the credit program for rice intensification collapsed in 1983, more than 3,600 village branches and roughly 13,000 employees had little or nothing to do. This was a crucial turning point for the development of rural banking in Indonesia. One response would have been to close these offices and transfer the staff elsewhere in the People's Bank.

Instead, the Ministry of Finance and the People's Bank seized the opportunity to effect a reform of rural banking in which General Rural Credit was a central element. It also created opportunities to expand rural savings programs that had been neglected by the bank because of the disincentives created by subsidized credit. Rural banking reform was a "response to problems and opportunities that had arisen, informed by the lessons of experience both in Indonesia and elsewhere" (Snodgrass and Patten 1991).

The key to reform was the strategic notion that generalized rural credit at commercial rates could better meet rural people's needs than subsidized credit, which was formally targeted to socially desirable ends but was unsustainable in practice.

On this and other points, Indonesian proreform policymakers were on the cutting edge of research results and international practice. Higher interest rates of

This box draws heavily on Snodgrass and Patten 1991.

about 30 percent a year, required to put the program on a sound financial footing, were controversial. But falling oil prices in the early 1980s probably helped shift the balance in favor of the reform as funds were no longer available to subsidize large rural credit programs.

In any event, the rapid growth of the General Rural Credit Program shows that it was both feasible and attractive for rural people to borrow at commercial rates. Furthermore, savings have been growing in tandem. By January 1989 the People's Bank had opened more than 5.1 million accounts, and rural savings were projected to exceed the amount of credit outstanding.

These changes also transformed rural banking from a threat to solvency into a profitable activity for the People's Bank. As a result, rural banking gained attention at the highest levels of the institution, and institutional initiatives were created to expand rural banking services. The reform was not just a matter of a policy shift. In a complex organization such as the People's Bank, the incentives must be right not only for the organization but also for people working at various levels in the organization.

---

landownership—if it were politically feasible.[15] Broad-based strategies provide a more realistic option to promote a unimodal structure of operating units by creating economic incentives for landlords to rent out plots to tenants, but this process will be slow. Unfortunately, counterproductive land tenure regulations and other policies that lead to eviction of tenants or a premature transition to labor-saving, capital-using technology can promote a quick shift toward a bimodal structure. And once these shifts occur, they are difficult to reverse.

Broad-based agricultural development often is compromised by differentiating factors that favor the few farms that are large. For example, policies intended to overcome agricultural stagnation (from inadequate allocation of resources for the infrastructure and institutions to support broad-based development and from the disincentives of price distortions) commonly lead to corrective measures that benefit only large-scale farms. This preferential treatment of big landholders worsens the problem of fostering widespread increases in productivity among the majority of farmers.

---

[15] In Japan and Taiwan (and also South Korea) land reform was feasible because of special circumstances. Moreover, transitional effects on output were trivial because the reforms affected only the size distribution of landownership, not the size distribution of farm operational units.

CHAPTER SIX

LINKS BETWEEN
AGRICULTURE
AND INDUSTRY

H ow does the pattern of agricultural output affect the development of other sectors of the economy? In the words of Chapter 5, what are the different linkages between agriculture and these sectors and their indirect effects in a broad-based strategy, compared with a dualistic strategy?

AN OVERVIEW

For this purpose it is useful to conceive of agriculture as linked to three spatially separate economies or "sectors"—the local rural nonfarm economy, the more distant urban economy, and the international economy. Between agriculture and each of these is a two-way flow of commodities, of financial resources (taxes, savings, remittances, aid), and of labor. Except to the extent that the rural household is operating in both the farm and local nonfarm economies, these flows take place through markets. Their volume and direction are best seen in farm cash disbursements (see Chapter 2).

The flow of commodities from agriculture may be to all three sectors (for example, rice in Thailand) or to only the international sector (say, chrysanthemums in Tanzania) or only the local nonfarm economy (for example, fresh milk).[1] As to the inward flow to agriculture, each of these economies can supply a bundle of goods and services that is partially unique and partially substitutable for those supplied by one or both of the other sectors. For example, a cocoa farmer may buy an inexpensive machete from a local blacksmith, a more costly one made in an urban factory, or a premium-grade import from Sheffield, England. The farmer cannot buy chemical fertilizers produced in the local nonfarm economy; but it is only there that one can purchase repair services for farm equipment. The commodities in which the local nonfarm economy is the sole supplier are characterized by considerable customization or transport costs; they are sometimes referred to as *nontradables*.

Different patterns of agricultural expansion lead to different patterns of commodity flows among the three economies. If production functions were the same everywhere and all factors of production were fully employed in each sector, the choice of agricultural strategy would have little external significance. But this is not so. Production techniques in the rural nonfarm economy, relative to the urban economy's, are "despecialized" and therefore small-scale, labor-using, and sparing of imported inputs and material capital.

The two sectors equally differ in supply elasticity: because of less reliance on scarce imported equipment and intermediate goods and greater dependence on low opportunity cost labor, indirect "multiplier" effects are more pronounced in the rural nonfarm sector. By contrast, expenditure directed at large-scale urban industry is more likely to encounter import or physical capacity constraints, with the demand stimulus being diverted from quantities to prices.

In summary, the hypothesis to be explored in this chapter is that in agriculture's interactions with other sectors of the economy there is a mechanism—based on a differing mix of production inputs and of consumption goods—analogous to the one that operates within agriculture itself. Just as expanding agricultural output generates more employment through direct and secondary effects under a broad-based strategy, so too do the production and consumption links associated with this expansion generate more employment and a higher share of income for workers in the nonagricultural sectors. The success of such broad-based expansion is strongly influenced by the range of low-price substitute and partial substitute commodities that the local nonfarm economy is able to supply vis-à-vis the other two sectors whose products are better suited to the dualistic pattern.

---

[1] The mandatory forward link to transport means that there are no pure *agricultural* exports.

ADAPTING TECHNOLOGY TO FACTOR ENDOWMENTS

Differences in technology are a central constitutive element of each of the three sectors. The effective incorporation of new technology consonant with changing resource endowments is a necessary condition for structural transformation. Success depends on how well the two individual domestic sectors perform in borrowing, adapting, and diffusing new technology in the complex process described in Chapter 2. For the rural nonfarm sector, this, in turn depends on *the range of intermediate production techniques* offered to producers in that sector. For the urban industrial sector, where borrowed technology takes precedence over adapted technology (and where protective tariffs and quotas may insulate it from international competition), the critical aspect of performance is likely to be *avoidance* of technology transfer incongruent with comparative advantage. Avoiding inappropriate import substitution is essentially a political economy problem; how to generate a wide range of intermediate technology choices is less well understood, involving nondiscrimination against the small-scale sector in a number of policy areas over a substantial period.

In the area of technology transfer, the central fact for a late-developing country in the twenty-first century is the existence of a massive inventory of proven technologies. Drawing on this inventory creates potential for growth in factor productivity and gross domestic product surpassing that seen in Europe and the United States before World War I. Yet, the outcome is far from certain; inappropriate selection from the technology shelf quickly leads to excessive dualism, high cost, and stunted growth.

How do CARLs draw on this off-the-shelf technology? Where it is embodied in capital equipment, as in manufacturing, CARLs have access to the most advanced technical know-how only in a form that is inappropriately capital-intensive (figure in Box 6.1, Point T in panel C).[2] Other available technologies that are better suited to local factor proportions are less productive (that is, older). The implication is that a sizable portion of labor available to manufacturing at the going wage rate may not be absorbed and remains unemployed or is shunted into other sectors, where it lowers the returns to labor and contributes a smaller marginal product. The transfer of inappropriate new technology slows the growth in nonfarm employment and so delays structural transformation.

---

[2] The mapping of technological progress in the figures in Box 6.1 in terms of productivity is the mirror image of the inward-shifting isoquants of Box 3.3. The emphasis here is less on the bias of technical progress—it is assumed to be neutral or labor-saving—than on which portion of the isoquant of each period becomes embodied in machinery and equipment that producers subsequently use.

Box 6.1. Managing the Technology Backlog

Consider the production of any commodity—a yard of cloth, a chair, a loaf of bread. With existing scientific knowledge and machine-building know-how, a society has at any point in time the capability of constructing many equipment packages with different levels of capital intensity per worker (K/L) to produce the good. In the figure, Panel A depicts two such hypothetical ex ante production functions for 1900 and 1990. For any amount of capital per worker (or more exactly, capital services per worker-hour) output is in every case higher in the later years: advances in technical knowledge continually raise the productivity of all inputs and thereby shift the production function upward.

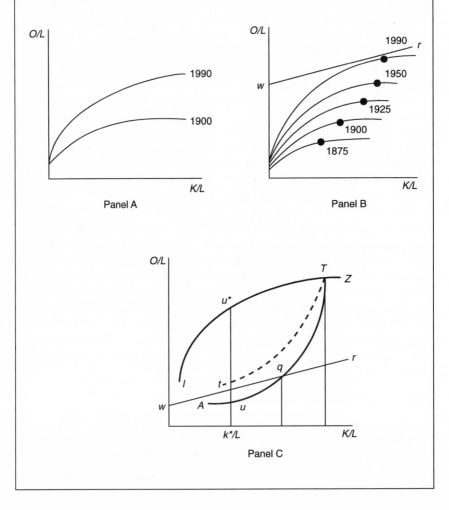

Panel A

Panel B

Panel C

Box 6.1. (*continued*)

In the real world of scarce resources, not all factory design possibilities mapped out in the ex ante production function are brought to the blueprint stage or even investigated. Given the relative prices of capital and labor, only one technique will minimize production costs (several, if we allow for regional variation). Thus, only a few commercially feasible production techniques, representing a narrow range of factor proportions, are actually embodied in equipment by the capital goods industry. This narrow range of equipment is what is available to investors. Moreover, moving forward in time, the available production processes become progressively more capital-intensive. This is depicted in Panel B, where a single technique (large dot) is developed from the menu of technological possibilities in each period and the embodied capital-labor ratio rises with each newer vintage.

The secular trend of rising capital intensity in production techniques available to investors, in industrial countries and CARLs alike, is a result of technical progress and systematic changes in factor prices as a byproduct of economic growth in the high-income, industrial countries. Specifically, capital is cheapened relative to labor in high-income countries as (1) higher levels of per capita income and growth of financial intermediation lead to increased savings and lower interest rates, (2) technical advances in the production of capital goods lower the cost of capital equipment, and (3) widespread increases in labor productivity lead to higher wages. The prices of labor and capital are introduced into the analysis by the line *wr* (shown only for the most recent year). The wage rate is the point of intersection on the O/L axis, and the price of capital is the slope of the line.* If product and factor markets are competitive and free of externally imposed distortions, the tangency point between the factor price line and the production function will identify the least-cost production technique that will become embodied in capital equipment.

Panel C illustrates the situation faced by a technology-borrowing country. The lower its degree of economic development, the smaller will be the capital endowment per worker, that is, the distance of K^*/L from the origin. The term K^*/L represents the level of capital intensity consistent with full employment (any point to the right entails unemployment). The schedule *ITZ* represents the range of capital-labor proportions theoretically available to produce the commodity using the latest knowledge. In fact, without a capital goods industry with research and development, only the relatively capital-intensive technique *T* is available to the borrowing country. The range of effective choice lies along *AT*, the embodied technology from the previous periods.**

The line *AT* thus represents the "technology shelf" from which developing countries can actually borrow. If the equipment embodying all older designs are avail-

---

*The equation of the line is $O/L = w + r(K/L)$, where w is the marginal product of labor and r is the marginal product of capital.

**The line *AT* intersects the tangency points of each historical period. It links rather than envelops the tangency points so that the profit-maximizing point of this quasiproduction function is at the right-hand intersection of the output-capital price line with *AT*. *AT* may be either concave or convex relative to *IT* depending on changes in the rate of scientific progress in the past. As derived from panel B, it shape implies a more rapid rate of progress in recent decades.

Box 6.1. (*continued*)

able and known to investors, the price line will intersect AT at q. To the extent that older equipment is unavailable or unknown to the investor, the actual choice will lie closer to T and be associated with even greater unemployment. The older vintage technology at u is consistent with full employment, but its productivity is insufficient to be economically viable, that is, it falls below wr. The dotted schedule tT represents the potential for local producers to mold production techniques in a labor-using direction. These adaptive innovations of "de-specialization" and "labor addition," in essence, shift AT leftward. With respect to the influence of policy, to the extent that the wage rate exceeds the scarcity value of labor or that the interest rate undervalues the opportunity cost of capital, the profit-maximizing capital-labor ratio will be shifted to the right, reinforcing the likelihood of inappropriate choice.

The exposition of choice of technique with two homogeneous factor inputs catches but one important facet of the technology transfer problem. In the real world technical input requirements are numerous and specific. A given production process calls for particular labor skills, raw materials of uniform specifications, and a minimum (perhaps very large) scale of output. Even electricity voltage, water impurities, and climate are production inputs. Take climate: because of temperature and humidity factors, cocoa butter produced by existing technologies is a "different" (that is, lower-quality) product when made in the tropics, the home of the cocoa bean. Technical attributes such as these mean that in borrowing production techniques and undertaking research in new technology, a much broader range of circumstance than just the interest rate and wage for unskilled labor must be taken into account.

So, how can CARLs acquire advanced technology that is not lethally inappropriate? There are three ways. First, and most ambitious, is to reembody existing scientific knowledge in a form that is well-suited to the factor proportions and environmental circumstances of today's CARLs (panel C in Box 6.1, shift from u to u^*). Second, and most common, is to modify a borrowed production technique to raise its labor intensity without sacrificing all of its higher total-factor productivity (figure in Box 6.1, movement to a point on Tt). Third, when neither the first nor the second is feasible, is to abstain from local production and rely on imports.

Embodying Scientific Knowledge

The Case of Agriculture. The most dramatic example of research that aimed at, and achieved, a new embodiment of existing scientific knowledge in a form appropriate for labor-abundant countries is to be found in agriculture. High-yield cereal crops for the tropics required many input alterations. Here, the adapted technology raised the productivity of land as well as that of labor and capital.

In CARLs traditional cereal varieties had been selected over generations to produce a stable, if modest, yield in areas of low soil fertility and wide variations in weather. Because of this successful adaptation, these varieties were ill-suited to benefit from chemical fertilizers, which became economically affordable in the late 1950s. For wheat and rice these extra nutrients simply added to leaf and stalk growth. Drawing on the biological knowledge used to develop high-yield varieties for temperate climates, agricultural scientists (in publicly supported research institutes) in Mexico, Taiwan, and the Philippines created a new varietal plant architecture that radically shifted the farmer's production function (panel C in Box 6.1, from u to u^*).

These new varieties were designed to reduce the land-labor input ratio, by raising yields more than labor productivity. Varieties were bred that were short, with sturdy straw and narrow erect leaves. The plants have a high capacity for tillering (stems per plant), are insensitive to day length, and have a short growing season. The short sturdy straw means the plants are resistant to lodging, despite a doubling of the grain-to-straw ratio. The leaf configuration minimizes the shaded area, allowing greater plant density. With uninterrupted photosynthesis, the crop matures in a fixed time after planting; early maturity opens the way for double, or even triple, cropping. With complementary inputs, the yield increases of the new varieties were 150 percent or more.

How does this reduce the land-labor input ratio? In two ways. The new technology is not totally embodied in the seed and fertilizer. Higher soil fertility and narrow leaves improve conditions for weed growth: more labor must be used for weeding. Moreover, planting is best done by transplanting seedlings in straight rows at even intervals, instead of broadcasting the seed; this increases labor per cropped acre by as much as 100 percent. And when a second or third crop is added, even more labor is needed.[3] Thus the new technology is land-saving and labor-using. Because wheat and rice supply over half the food calories consumed in CARLs, the Green Revolution was truly a revolution.

The Case of Manufacturing. Unlike in agriculture, there have been no such stunning reembodiments of scientific knowledge in appropriate production for industrial products.

Many technology development centers have been established in the past twenty-five years, sponsored by national governments, bilateral donor

[3] As well as more labor inputs, the new irrigated rice technology requires greater precision in farm management—in higher plant population, control of planting depth, deeper plowing, the use of checkrow markers, more careful placement and timing of fertilizer applications, and more exact water control. The shorter growing period requires an adjustment in the seasonal organization of farm activities.

agencies, international bodies, and private voluntary organizations. These centers have focused on agricultural machinery, construction, selected manufacturing technologies, and small-scale industry products. Their mission has been to develop their own prototype equipment or promote those developed in small engineering firms in the private sector. Because public agencies need not recover the cost of product development, they are in a position to pursue radical redesign, an area of endeavor where the low probability of success and problems of capturability rule out commercial initiative. Ironically, the technology centers have overwhelmingly directed their efforts at the same incremental modification of existing products that is done far more successfully by private entrepreneurs.

Two examples, both in agricultural equipment, demonstrate the difference between failure and success, Jean Nolle's "Tropiculteur," and the International Rice Research Institute's (IRRI) axial-flow rice thresher. The reembodiment of scientific principles is modest in both cases, but they represent two of the most ambitious "appropriate technology" mechanical undertakings in the past thirty years.

First developed in Senegal in 1955 by a French agricultural engineer, the wheeled toolcarrier can be used for ploughing, seeding, weeding, and transport.[4] It consists of a two-wheeled steel chassis, onto which can be fitted a range of tools, including plough, ridger, tine harrow, seeder, fertilizer applicator, weeder, or groundnut harvester. Most toolcarriers can be used as carts, some for carrying water. They can be adapted for spraying chemicals, logging, and even mowing. Most are designed to be pulled by two oxen, using a steel or wooden drawbar, although they can be used with buffalo, horses, and donkeys. There are many variations in height and wheeltrack. Some have manually operated lift systems for better headland turning and transport between field and homestead. Some have three-point linkages and others eyebolt clamps, and some depend on adjustments requiring wrenches.

In 1960 the British National Institute of Agricultural Engineering developed its own animal-drawn toolcarrier and promoted it in a number of African countries. In the late 1970s the International Crops Research Institute for the Semi-Arid Tropics (ICRISAT) adapted Nolle's "Tropiculteur" and encouraged its subsidized distribution in India. With encouraging reports about the wheeled toolcarrier in the 1970s and 1980s, batch production was begun in Brazil, with smaller numbers produced in Honduras, Nicaragua, and Mexico. As late as 1988, development and promotion were continuing in at least twenty developing countries on three continents.

Paul Starkey of the University of Reading, who evaluated the status of

[4] The following treatment of the wheeled toolcarrier is based upon Starkey 1988.

wheeled toolcarriers for the German foreign aid agency GTZ, estimates the total investment in designing, promoting, and producing wheeled toolcarriers over the past thirty years at $40 million. As to its success, he concluded:

It would appear that in the thirty years up to 1987, about 10,000 wheeled toolcarriers of over 50 different designs had been made throughout the world. Most were distributed through subsidized credit schemes; few were bought by farmers for realistic prices (in 1988, $1,000 to $2,500 depending upon attachments). The number of wheeled toolcarriers used by farmers as multipurpose implements for several years seems to have been negligible. The majority have been abandoned or used as carts. Farmer rejection has been apparent since the early 1960s, yet as recently as 1987 the majority of researchers, agriculturalists, and decision-makers in national programs and aid agencies were under the impression that wheeled toolcarriers were a highly successful technology.

Wheeled toolcarriers have been rejected because of their high cost, heavy weight, lack of maneuverability, inconvenience in operation, complication of adjustment and difficulty in changing between modes. By combining many operations into one machine they have increased risk and reduced flexibility compared with a range of single purpose implements. Their design has been a compromise between the many different requirements. In many cases for a similar or lower cost farmers could use single purpose ploughs, seeders, multipurpose cultivators and carts to achieve similar results with greater convenience and less risk. (Starkey 1988, p. 10)

The scale and duration of the wheeled toolbar failure is unusual. Yet, in its major attributes the experience is all too typical: an appealing and widely publicized concept, field testing limited to the optimal environment of the research station, little ex post evaluation. The intensive iterative process involving farmers, actual field conditions, and local equipment fabricators so critical in agricultural development in Japan and America was absent.

How different for the axial-flow thresher. The newly established agricultural engineering unit (Small Farm Machinery Development Program) at IRRI in the Philippines first turned to designing a rice thresher in 1967. Because of the dramatic success of the new high-yielding varieties and their labor-using bias, it was feared that labor bottlenecks at peak periods, especially harvesting and threshing, would hamper multiple cropping, precluding the full gains from the Green Revolution (IRRI 1986, pp. 373–89).

After working with conventional threshing principles, IRRI's design engineers decided in 1970 to try the axial-flow concept. Originally developed by Japanese engineers for rice milling machines, it had never been employed successfully in threshers. Following IRRI's breakthrough, it has since been incorporated in large combine harvesters in North America and Europe.

In contrast to the conventional principle of a single pass over a threshing drum, with axial flow the rice passes around the drum in a spiral fashion

Table 6.1. Reduction in labor requirements by using a rice thresher

Philippines	Labor days/ton	Thailand	Labor days/ton
Foot treading	7.7	Buffalo treading	4.9
Hand beating	5.5	Tractor treading	2.4
Portable axial-flow thresher	0.8	Large axial-flow thresher	1.3

Source: Duff 1987, p. 19.

three or four times. There are a number of important gains. Cylinder speed can be reduced, requiring less power while threshing is more thorough and does less damage to the grain. The prolonged exposure results in separation from the straw without the use of bulky straw walkers. The machine is simple and compact. Following extensive testing in the Philippines in 1972–73, plans and prototypes were released to private manufacturers there in 1974. The TH3 had a capacity of 1 ton of paddy per hour and cost $1,700; in 1975, a smaller portable version (the TH6) was introduced, with a capacity of 400 kg per hour and a price of $500. By the end of that year, the machines were being produced in five countries.

An important modification to the IRRI design by Philippine manufacturers was the replacement of the rotary grain separating-and-cleaning mechanism with a flat oscillating screen, which improves efficiency and compactness. Other changes included more powerful engines, spring suspension, and rubber tires. In Thailand, where farms are larger and contract threshing is more extensive, private manufacturers greatly increased its scale, as well as making alterations to suit local crop and weather conditions.

The reduction in labor requirements and drudgery is great, particularly in the Philippines where foot treading and hand beating prevailed (Table 6.1). The effect of the new thresher is to reduce total labor requirements in harvesting and threshing by about 20 percent and to raise the profitability of rice growing.

Molding Production Techniques

Far more common than reembodiment of technological principles is the modification of borrowed techniques. In large-scale manufacturing factor proportions can be pushed in a labor-using direction in two ways, by "labor addition" and "despecialization." In small-scale manufacturing, this can be achieved only by despecialization. Where the policy environment is supportive and the entrepreneurial base is strong, factor proportions are altered, and with great frequency. Achieved through a wide variety of mundane arrangements, the aggregate effect can be the difference between success and failure in drawing on the technology backlog.

Large-Scale Manufacturing. *Labor addition* simply means adding more labor to the equipment in such a way as to increase its output. Labor addition takes two forms. The first is to alter a machine or production process so that additional labor inputs can be applied at each point in time. In Meiji Japan the latest British and American spinning equipment was run at faster-than-designed speeds, and more people were employed to deal with the larger number of broken threads (Ranis 1972). A variant of this practice was to spin the breakage-prone short-staple Indian cotton rather than the more expensive American cotton. In spinning (and weaving) Japanese machine minders were four times the number employed in an identical plant in America. In silk reeling the Japanese employed more than twice the number of operatives as the Italians, again with greatly enhanced capital productivity. Similarly, alterations in U.S. electronics technology, when transferred to Taiwan, involved accelerated operation and manual repair of defective pieces, with more workers used in inspection and maintenance.

The second form of labor addition is multiple-shift operation. Because the useful life of buildings and many nonmoving machinery parts is a function of time rather than use, an increase in the hours of operation does not lead to a proportionate increase in capital consumption. A reduction in idleness of production facilities is also a reduction in the capital-labor ratio: the same stock of capital equipment can provide employment for two or three times the labor force as under a single shift.

Both economic policies and social preferences impinge on the entrepreneur's ability and willingness to exploit a capital investment more fully. With high urban unemployment, labor for a second and third shift is easily recruited. More difficult to recruit are supervisory and managerial personnel: they are generally not in excess supply, and social status factors may dampen their enthusiasm for shift work.[5] Clearly, differences in culture and the intensity of the entrepreneurial drive come to bear at this point. From plant visits, Ranis suggested that multiple shifts were more prevalent in Taiwan and South Korea than in other Asian countries (Ranis 1972, pp. 22–24). But evidence of the entrepreneurial factor can be seen more clearly in West Africa in the longer hours of factory operation there among Lebanese and Greek firms in comparison with their European and African counterparts in the same industries.

The second way in which the capital-labor ratio is lowered in large-scale manufacturing is by *despecialization*. This, the most common factor substitution in CARLs, takes two forms.

[5] The studies summarized by Winston (1971a) show that in developed countries reluctance of employees to switch to shift work is greatest among the more educated: "One suspects that this is due largely to social status and expectations which are likely to be even more pronounced in hierarchical traditional societies and especially ones with a colonial background in which social status and shift work rarely went hand-in-hand."

Despecialization through the substitution of *manual operation* is most easily seen in auxiliary production processes—that is, receiving and preparing materials, assembling components, packaging, and loading. These activities frequently account for a large proportion of factory space and labor. They also offer considerable possibilities for substituting semiskilled labor for capital. The variability of factor proportions in these auxiliary activities is partly explained by their limited effect on product quality (hence, less need for precision) and by the fact that many of them were originally manual operations. In CARLs not only will the substitution of semiskilled labor in these processes provide more jobs and reduce costs, but also it may reduce minimum plant size.

A 1970 field study in Kenya (Pack 1972) looked at food processing and other light industries. It found that British firms had substituted manual operations for conveyor belts, fork-lift trucks, and filling-labeling-capping machines employed in their home factories. Where mechanization was retained in these peripheral activities (for example, unloading pineapples), the decision was related to quality control. In most industries surveyed, more than half the labor force was engaged in auxiliary operations. These labor substitutions were in response to low wages and the desirability of introducing more factor divisibility; for example, replacing a single and underused high-volume machine by workers whose number could be varied according to the desired output.

In the core manufacturing process, despecialization consists of using earlier vintage capital goods. This involves less modification and more direct drawing on the technology shelf, trading off scientific knowledge for a more appropriate embodiment. Whether the lower wage rate in CARLs is sufficient to offset the disadvantage of a less specialized operation depends on the enhancement of productivity from the additional knowledge embodied in the most recent equipment.[6]

Spinning, weaving, bleaching, and printing of cotton textiles have frequently used older vintage equipment. Around 1900 manually operated weaving looms in low-wage countries (for example, Japan and India) were often competitive with power looms; in contrast, cottage industry techniques were quickly crushed in competition with mechanized spinning. Different rates of technical progress in the next half-century reversed this: in the 1950s and 1960s, labor-using 1930 vintage spinning and printing equipment was compatible in low-wage countries with low-cost production, whereas only the most recent design automatic looms could similarly qualify. For many of the products demanded in CARLs, earlier vintage equipment is superior, as well as more labor-using.

---

[6] In terms of panel C in Box 6.1, it depends on the curvature of *AT*. That higher productivity is reflected in the price of the competing import.

Equipment of older design has several advantages for CARLs. First, such equipment usually permits lower output than more recent equipment. Second, the skill levels required for servicing are lower, although more maintenance may be needed. Third, older equipment is less demanding on such complementary inputs as raw material uniformity, temperature and humidity tolerance, and voltage constancy. Fourth, the introduction of new and improved movable parts (most used machinery is reconditioned before export) can sometimes greatly increase productivity over the original design.

Second-hand equipment also has drawbacks. The matching of equipment between processes often requires technical ingenuity; standardized spare parts are no longer available and must be made to order; and being less automated, the equipment needs more supervision on the factory floor. Moreover, price determination for second-hand equipment occurs in a highly imperfect market: sellers typically possess more knowledge about the value of the equipment to the purchaser than the buyer does about its cost to the seller. All this means that only CARLs with a well-developed light engineering industry, adequate supplies of supervisory personnel, and an ability to search in a number of overseas markets can benefit from extensive use of second-hand machinery.

Technical Rigidity. There are some industries where the inherent nature of the productive process precludes significant factor substitution, irrespective of the relative cost of capital and labor.[7] Oil refining, smelting, iron and steel, paper, cement, and continuous-process chemical industries are all examples. In these cases, in the absence of natural protection from high ocean transport costs, the efficient choice is to import.

In a careful empirical investigation, Forsyth, McBain, and Solomon analyzed 181 manufacturing industries for technical flexibility. They identified eight fundamental physical barriers that inhibit the substitution of labor for capital:

1. The use of high or low process temperatures
2. The presence of liquids or gases
3. The application of fluid pressure on materials in process
4. The need for high-speed operation
5. Close manufacturing tolerances
6. High load factors
7. Handling of indivisible, heavy materials
8. The presence of special hazards

---

[7] This is described in panel B of the figure in Box 4.3.

Interestingly, of the 181 industries, nitrogenous fertilizers, agriculture's largest backward linkage (see Chapter 7), ranked fifth, being subject to seven of the eight barriers (Forsyth, McBain, and Solomon 1982, p. 65). As will be seen, widespread domestic production of nitrogen fertilizers flows from an ill-conceived strategic notion, strongly held within CARLs and the donor community.

Small-Scale Manufacturing. Among small-scale producers technology is modified by despecialization in two ways, by product variation and process simplification. *Product variation* can run from minor qualitative differences (for example, wrapped and unwrapped bread) to essentially different products (fashion leather shoes instead of tire-rubber sandals). Associated with such product variation are differences in scale of operation, capital intensity, and other input requirements. For example, in Kenya in 1990 an armchair made in a small-scale workshop sold for U.S.$14 whereas the same model (but constructed from seasoned wood, squarely joined, and flush with the floor) sold for more than U.S.$90 from major furniture manufacturers.

Sometimes minor variations in product quality can be associated with different capital-labor ratios. Thus, in 1965 a study of Nigerian bread baking showed that variation in crust color was the only difference between loaves baked in a wood-fired peel oven and bread baked in an automated electric reel oven. In addition to oven choice, there are options regarding dough brake, bread pans, wrapping methods, and financial control. Producers competing in the same market had capital-labor ratios (in 1985 prices) ranging from $1,950 to $4,500 per worker (Kilby 1965, pp. 46–51).[8]

Process simplification is frequently (but not always) associated with *product variation.* Process simplification usually happens when an inventive local mechanic or technician successfully copies an imported machine but does so in a way that permits the use of cheaper local materials, fewer quality control procedures, and less skilled labor. Although the machine is usually less efficient than the original design, it is a successful innovation because the efficiency loss is confined to performance characteristics (for example, specification tolerances, speed of operation) that are not essential in CARLs. One example of process simplification is the slow-speed diesel engine produced in India and Pakistan until the mid-1970s. The engine was the main energy source for tubewells and low-lift canal water pumps in areas where there was no electricity, and it played an important part in South Asian agriculture. Based on the English Ruston and Blackstone horizontal single-cylinder engines designed around 1890, it used cheaper fuel and had a longer life and fewer breakdowns than the high-speed engines of the Lister type.

[8] The submarket is for wrapped, high-quality bread. The largest producer had the lowest capital-labor ratio.

The horizontal engine was first imitated in India by three big engineering firms in the 1930s (Government of India 1961; Smith 1970). From the mid-1950s a second round of imitation occurred as small-scale workshops entered the market and captured an increasing share of sales. It was these small producers, under the spur of competition, who effected process simplifications that reduced the price of the machine without impairing its functions. By substituting scrap for pig iron at the foundry stage, they reduced raw material costs by 50 percent. Design changes were also made in the fuel pump, lubrication system, governor, and atomizer.

Of the four modes of altering input proportions, product variation and process simplification have had the greatest impact on labor absorption, on economizing capital and foreign exchange, and on providing low-cost goods. In short, product variation and process simplification constitute the applied technology of the informal sector.

THE RURAL NONFARM ECONOMY: THE KEY LINK

In the rural economy, nonfarm activities account for a large share of output and employment, ranging from 40 to 80 percent of that of agriculture. Such nonfarm activities encompass agricultural processing, small-scale manufacturing and craft activities, repair, construction, retail and wholesale trade, restauranting, transport, personal services, and salaried employment in teaching and public administration. Excluded for purposes of this chapter is nonfarm production for own consumption. Off-farm agricultural wages and the renting out of land are allocated to agricultural income.

Nonfarm activities give rise to household income in three ways: part-time activities carried on in the homestead, full- or part-time occupation in a separate enterprise, usually in a larger village or small town, and wages earned in such an enterprise.

A national random survey of 11,000 households in Thailand provides a detailed picture of the rural nonfarm sector there (Table 6.2). Thailand does not have a single town size as the dividing line between rural and urban. Urban areas are those of 50,000 people or more, plus towns of 10,000 or more that have sufficient tax revenue to maintain municipal services and "communes." Rural areas include villages and "sanitary districts" of 10,000 or more that cannot yet sustain all municipal services. Finally, a farm household is defined as one that has a crop or livestock enterprise. Given this liberal definition, households whose main income may come from nonagricultural activities are classified as farm households. (It is this same definition that results in the overestimate of Thailand's agricultural labor force noted in Chapter 2.)

Table 6.2. Nonfarm employment and income in Thailand, 1976–77

	Urban areas		Sanitary districts		Rural villages	
Population (in 1,000s)	5,244		4,225		26,358	
Economically active (in 1,000s)	2,877		2,776		20,166	
Primary occupation (%)						
Farming	3.7		55.9		85.8	
Forestry and fishing	1.0		0.9		1.2	
Nonagricultural	95.3		43.2		13.0	

Type of household	Farm	Nonfarm	Farm	Nonfarm	Farm	Nonfarm
Households (%)	4.6	95.4	52.7	47.3	82.7	17.3
Income (baht, in 1,000s)	42.77	41.85	25.02	29.99	17.66	19.64
Sources of income (%)						
Farm	29.5	1.7	50.5	3.4	61.5	8.3
Other agricultural	2.3	2.1	8.1	4.4	9.1	11.6
Nonfarm	68.2	96.2	41.4	92.2	29.4	80.1

Source: World Bank 1983b, p. 26.

Notes: Sanitary districts are localities that have reached 10,000 persons but have not yet developed other urban characteristics. The baht is equivalent to 5 U.S. cents. "Other agricultural" income includes agricultural wages and land rent.

Thailand was strikingly rural in 1977, with 78 percent of the labor force located in villages, 11 percent in the semiurban sanitary districts, and only 11 percent in urban areas.[9] However, the share of nonfarm activities in rural areas is surprisingly high—39 percent in villages and 68 percent in sanitary districts, for a weighted average of 44 percent. In all households, the share of nonfarm income rises, along with household income, from village to sanitary district to urban area. At 17,660 baht, farm households in the village enjoy an income equal to two-fifths that of the urban household. Unexpectedly, nonfarm rural households have higher average incomes than farm households, 19,640 baht compared with 17,660 baht. Can it be inferred that the landless household is not necessarily worse off in Thailand than the average farm household?

Nonfarm Income and Income Inequality

Land is the farmer's principal productive asset, and the size of holdings has commonly been used as a variable to stratify rural households into income classes. In five countries (in Asia and Africa) there is an inverse relationship between size of landholding and the share of nonfarm income in total rural household income (Table 6.3). For the smallest landholding

[9] Thailand's labor force participation rate is higher in rural than in urban areas (Table 2.2), which is also evident from the first two rows of Table 6.1. The 13 percent "primary occupation" versus the 39 percent income share for village nonfarm activities confirms that the primary occupation statistic systematically understates nonfarm output (Chapter 2).

Table 6.3. Size of landholding and relative importance of nonfarm income in total household income

Country	Size of holding (acres)	Nonfarm income share in total household income (%)	Total household income ($)
Korea, 1980	0.00 – 1.23	74	3,005
	1.24 – 2.47	39	3,450
	2.48 – 3.70	28	4,321
	3.71 – 4.94	23	5,472
	4.95 +	16	7,401
Taiwan, 1975	0.00 – 1.23	70	2,768
	1.24 – 2.47	52	3,442
	2.48 – 3.71	44	3,701
	3.72 – 4.94	39	4,570
	4.95 +	26	5,566
Thailand, 1980–81	0.00 – 4.10	88	1,362
(4 regions)	4.20 – 10.20	72	974
	10.30 – 41.00	56	1,613
	41.00 +	45	1,654
Sierra Leone, 1974	0.00 – 1.00	50	587
	1.01 – 5.00	23	404
	5.01 – 10.00	14	546
	10.01 – 15.00	12	770
	15.00 +	15	927
Northern Nigeria, 1974	0.00 – 2.46	57	479
	2.47 – 4.93	31	377
	4.94 – 7.40	26	569
	7.41 – 9.87	15	769
	9.88 +	24	868

Source: Liedholm and Kilby 1988.

categories in each country, nonfarm income accounts for more than 50 percent of household income.

Is nonfarm income sufficient to reduce income inequalities in rural areas? Because of nonfarm income, total income for rural households with the least land in Sierra Leone, Northern Nigeria, and Thailand exceeds the incomes of those with somewhat larger farms. This "vertical J-shaped" relationship between total household income and landholdings is, perhaps, not unexpected in Africa, where land is not a limiting factor. It also holds in some parts of Asia, such as in Thailand and Japan, although not in Korea and Taiwan.

These general findings question the notion that farm size is a good proxy for total rural household income or an indicator of who are the rural poor. Complex factors bearing on farming, nonfarm enterprises, and off-farm trading and employment opportunities determine rural household income levels. Although this heterogeneity complicates the task facing policymakers in dealing with the rural poor, it also means that there are wider opportunities to be developed.

Relating total nonfarm income share to total rural household income quintiles or terciles (from low to high) in Sierra Leone, Nigeria, and Thailand, reveals the "vertical J-shaped" relationship again (Table 6.4). Rural nonfarm income is thus relatively important at both ends of the income distribution spectrum. For low-income rural households wages from working on other's farms and service activities predominate; for high-income households, the predominant sources are administrative and manufacturing activities, which tend to have higher entry barriers and yield higher returns than other nonfarm activities or agriculture.

What is the net effect of nonfarm income on overall income inequality in rural areas? The results from two African studies as well as from Thailand indicate that including nonfarm income with farm income reduces the rural Gini coefficient in each case. Gini coefficients for per capita farm income alone were 0.43 in Sierra Leone and 0.32 in Nigeria, compared with coefficients on combined farm and nonfarm incomes of 0.38 and 0.28, respectively (Matlon and others 1979). In rural Thailand the Gini declines from 0.58 when only farm income is considered to 0.38 when all the sources for the rural household's income are included.[10] The available evidence, albeit limited, does suggest that rural nonfarm income reduced rural income inequalities in several countries.

Rural nonfarm activities also help to smooth household income over the year. An analysis of the monthly income of 424 rural households in Thailand reveals, for example, that the variability of total household income was substantially less than that of net farm income over the year.[11]

Are rural nonfarm enterprises efficient users of economic resources? If some nonfarm enterprises generate more real output per unit of resources expended than large urban counterparts, agricultural and other policies that enhance these activities increase both output and employment.[12] Comparisons of small and large enterprises using partial-efficiency measures, particularly the output-capital ratio, have yielded a mixed picture of the relationship between capital productivity and size.[13] Moreover, only

[10] Calculated from data on 424 rural households collected by the Thai Rural Off-Farm Employment Project (see Narongchai and others 1983 for details).

[11] The coefficient of variation computed for net farm income was 2.07, but was only 0.64 for total household income, which includes nonfarm income sources (computed from monthly data generated by the Thai Rural Off-Farm Employment Project—see Narongchai and others 1983).

[12] Employment would increase if the labor-capital ratio of smaller firms exceeded those of the larger ones. Most empirical studies show that small rural enterprises are more labor-intensive than their larger-scale counterparts in the aggregate. At the industry-specific level, the same results hold, although with exceptions, such as Korea (see Liedholm and Mead 1987 for details).

[13] See, for example, Page and Steel 1984 and Liedholm and Mead 1987 for a review of the evidence.

Table 6.4. Percentage of rural household income earned from farm and nonfarm sources by income class

	Income class	Farm (%)	Nonfarm (%)
Sierra Leone, 1974	Lowest tercile	80.3	19.7
	Middle tercile	81.2	18.8
	Highest tercile	80.0	20.0
Northern Nigeria, 1974	Lowest quintile	76.6	23.4
	Middle quintile	78.0	22.0
	Highest quintile	61.4	38.6
Thailand, 1980–81	Lowest quintile	37.5	62.5
(4 Regions)	Middle quintile	44.0	56.0
	Highest quintile	34.9	65.1

Source: Liedholm and Kilby 1988.

rarely are rural and nonindustrial enterprises specifically examined in these analyses. And all such studies based on partial-efficiency measures suffer one significant drawback: if some resource other than the one included in the measure has a nonzero opportunity cost, it may well yield incorrect results.

Comprehensive economic efficiency measures, such as total factor productivity and social benefit-cost analysis, overcome this problem.[14] Ideally, all scarce resources are explicitly included and are evaluated at their "shadow" or "social" prices that reflect scarcity values. Unfortunately, only a few such studies exist (Ho 1980; Cortes, Berry, and Ishag 1985) and none consider rural nonfarm enterprises explicitly.

Liedholm and Mead (1987), however, recently used a social benefit-cost measure to compare the relative efficiency of small rural manufacturers with larger scale urban ones in Sierra Leone, Honduras, and Jamaica.[15] The key

[14] For a detailed discussion of these measures, see Biggs 1986.

[15] Following the approach suggested in Cortes, Berry, and Ishag 1985, the ratio of the enterprise's value added to the cost of capital and labor, both valued at their shadow or "social" prices, was used to measure economic efficiency. More specifically, the social benefit-cost ratio (SBC) is calculated on the basis of the following formula: $SBC = VA/(r_s K + w_s L)$, where VA = value added; r_s = shadow or "social" price (interest rate) of capital; K = total fixed and working capital; w_s = shadow or "social" price of labor; and L = total labor hours, including family and apprentice hours. A ratio greater than 1 means that the activity or enterprise has a positive effect on the *total output* of the economy, and a ratio less than 1 means that it has a negative effect. If actual rather than "social" prices are used to evaluate value added, however, the ratio can only be used to compare the productivity of enterprises in the same sector.

The primary data were generated from the detailed small-scale industry surveys conducted by Michigan State University and host country researchers. Approximately 495 rural manufacturing firms were surveyed in Honduras (see Stallmann 1983), 200 in Sierra Leone (see Chuta and Liedholm 1985), and 150 in Jamaica (see Fisseha 1982). *Small-scale* refers to firms employing 50 (or fewer) people, and *rural* refers to localities with 20,000 inhabitants or less. Hundreds of rural firms in each country were interviewed twice weekly over a twelve-month period to obtain daily information on revenues and costs. Information on large enterprises was obtained from the worksheets for the industrial censuses in Sierra Leone and Honduras and

finding, as reported in Table 6.5, is that the small manufacturers use fewer resources per unit of output than large counterparts in most industry groups. In eight of the twelve industries, the social benefit-cost ratios are higher for rural small-scale enterprises. The larger enterprises prevail only in apparel in Jamaica and Honduras and in shoes and furniture in Sierra Leone. Moreover, in all but two industries, the social benefit-cost ratios for small rural nonfarm enterprises exceed 1.

A weakness of this analysis is that output and purchased inputs were valued by using domestic, not world, prices. Fortunately, enough data were available from Sierra Leone to compute social benefit-cost ratios at *world prices*. This showed that at world ("social") prices, small manufacturing enterprises in Sierra Leone are more efficient than their larger counterparts in all industries, except shoes (Liedholm and Kilby 1988).

To summarize, although "despecialized" rural manufacturing enterprises are technologically less efficient than their relatively capital-intensive, large-scale urban competitors, advantages of "product variation" and the absence of inefficiency-breeding protective subsidies means that in practice they frequently are more economically efficient. Access to foreign exchange at the official exchange rate, import duty relief on imported capital equipment, loan capital at low interest rates, and quotas or protective tariffs on competing imports are the differentiating factors that divert production toward capital-intensive urban manufacturers. Putting an end to these discriminatory policies in Sierra Leone and other CARLs would raise economic efficiency in all sectors. It would raise total employment, and most probably it would increase the relative size of the rural nonfarm economy.

Intersectoral Commodity Flows

What is the quantitative significance of commodity flows from the non-farm economy to rural households relative to those from the urban and the international economy? The flows are production inputs, forward linkages, and consumer items. Of production inputs, the largest (chemical fertilizers) does not originate in the rural economy; a portion of farm equipment does.

---

from the National Planning Agency's Industrial Survey in Jamaica. The small-scale enterprise surveys were both conducted in 1979; the large-scale surveys covered 1977 in Jamaica and 1975 in Honduras. The economic conditions in these countries did not differ markedly between these periods, however.

In calculating the social benefit-cost ratios, the "shadow" social price of capital was assumed to be 20 percent, and unpaid family labor was valued at the average price for *skilled* labor in small-scale industry. The actual wages paid to all workers in large enterprises were included at 80 percent. For a justification of these adjustments, see Haggblade, Liedholm, and Mead 1986. Because world prices for outputs and material inputs were not available for Honduras and Jamaica, domestic prices were used; this means that efficiency comparisons had to be limited to large- and small-scale rural enterprises in the same product group with similar mixes of output and purchased inputs.

Table 6.5. Social benefit-cost ratios (domestic prices)[a] for various large- and rural small-scale industry groups in Africa and Latin America

Country/enterprise group	Rural small-scale groups[b]	Large-scale groups[c]
Africa		
Sierra Leone, 1974–75		
Bakery	1.86	1.03
Apparel	1.78	0.53
Shoes	1.65	2.00
Furniture	0.81	0.87
Metal products	1.63	1.61
Latin America		
Honduras, 1979		
Apparel	0.82	0.89
Shoes	1.27	0.54
Furniture	1.44	0.84
Metal products	1.21	0.74
Jamaica, 1979		
Apparel	1.00	1.79
Furniture	2.51	1.36
Metal products	1.87	1.58

Source: Kilby and Liedholm 1986.
[a]Gross output and purchased input values used to compute value added (numerator) are evaluated at actual (domestic) prices; hired labor costs are evaluated at actual wages paid for small- and at 0.8 of actual wages for large-scale groups. Unpaid family (including proprietor) is valued at skilled wage rate for small-scale industry in each country (Le. 0.16 per hour in Sierra Leone, Lm. 0.71 per hour in Honduras, and J$ 1.50 per hour in Jamaica). Capital was evaluated at a shadow interest rate of 20 percent in each country. For a rationale for these particular shadow rates, see Haggblade, Liedholm, and Mead 1986.
[b]Small-scale firms employ less than fifty persons.
[c]Large-scale firms employ fifty persons or more. With one exception, these firms are located in large urban areas.

The size of these sales will depend on the level of farm mechanical inputs (very low in Africa, moderate in Asia and Latin America) and on the pattern of agricultural development. By contrast, the size of forward linkages do not vary greatly between a unimodal or a bimodal pattern. These linkages consist of processing, storage, transport, and distribution of food and fiber after it leaves the farm. The rural nonfarm economy's share in these linkages is primarily in food processing and distribution.

Although localized forward linkages give rise to more value added than comparable agricultural inputs, the latter (particularly farm equipment) can have a direct impact on agricultural productivity. Other nonfarm activities, such as trading and transport, stimulate farm output by reducing marketing costs. Farm equipment inputs, however, can directly affect yield per acre and output per person.

The largest share of rural nonfarm output (60 to 80 percent) goes to consumer goods and services (Table 6.6). The large component spent on food reflects modest levels of per capita income. As expected, the expenditure

Table 6.6. Rural household expenditure patterns

	Sierra Leone	Northern Nigeria	Muda, Malaysia	South India
	Average budget share (%)			
Locally produced				
Food	71.4	75.3	46.4	63.0
Nonfood	10.2	8.4	18.1	17.4
Regional imports				
Food	3.1	5.4	20.3	12.3
Nonfood	15.3	10.9	15.3	7.4
	Expenditure elasticities			
Locally produced				
Food	0.93	0.93	0.53	0.77
Nonfood	1.75	1.34	2.05	1.77
Regional imports				
Food	0.35	1.07	0.65	0.98
Nonfood	0.98	1.16	1.66	1.17

Source: Haggblade, Hazell, and Brown 1989, p. 1188. © 1989. Reprinted by permission of Elsevier Science Ltd., The Boulevard, Langford Lane, Kidlington OX5 1GB, U.K.

elasticities are uniformly higher for "nonfood." Unexpected, perhaps, are the uniformly higher elasticities for "nonfood" produced in the rural nonfarm economy vis-à-vis "imported nonfood."

Included in "locally produced nonfood" are tailor-made clothing, footwear, metal products, hats, wooden furniture, pottery, and mats; firewood; schooling and medical care; domestic servants, laundering, and hairdressing; eating and drinking out; repairs, improvement and construction of homes; and transport.

African spending supports far less rural nonfarm activity than do Asian spending patterns. This is partly attributable to lower incomes but also to poor transport networks and few big rural towns. In Malaysia and South India the villagers have easier access to more consumer goods and services in rural towns than their African counterparts, who are further from market centers and have limited means of transport (Haggblade, Hazell, and Brown 1989). In Africa, therefore, investment in rural infrastructure is a priority.

In nonfood, the highest elasticities are associated with services: for transport in Sierra Leone, it is 1.38, and for personal services and ceremonial outlays, 2.38. By contrast, the elasticity for manufactured products of small-scale producers is 0.76. In Northern Nigeria and Muda (in Malaysia), the figures for housing construction and repair are 1.40 and 3.02, and for transport 1.67 and 1.48, respectively.

Table 6.7. Expenditure elasticities of rural households for various small- and large-scale enterprise products

Products	Scale	Sierra Leone (1974)[a]	Bangladesh (1980)[b]
Food			
Bread	Small	+0.69	+1.14[c]
Clothing			
Dresses and pants (tailoring)	Small	0.72[c]	+0.96[d]
Dresses and pants (clothing)	Large	+0.59	—
Dresses and pants (imported)	Large	+1.49	+0.29
Lungi	Small	—	+1.61[c]
Lungi	Large	—	+1.00[c]
Sari	Small	—	+2.00[c]
Sari	Large	—	+0.63[d]
Sari (synthetic)	Large	—	+1.74[c]
Wood			
Furniture	Small	+1.61[c]	+2.00[c]
Metal			
Agricultural tools and utensils	Small	+0.50	+1.06[c]
Agricultural tools and utensils	Large	+0.89	+1.29[c]
All small-scale industry		+0.76[c]	—
All large-scale industry		+0.33	—

Sources: Sierra Leone: King and Byerlee 1978; Bangladesh: BIDS 1981.
[a]In Sierra Leone, data from 203 rural households were fitted into a modified form of a ratio semilog inverse expenditure function.
[b]In Bangladesh, data from 444 rural households were fitted into a semilog expenditure function with the values in the table estimated at mean expenditure levels.
[c]Estimated coefficients significant at 1 percent level.
[d]Estimated coefficients significant at 5 percent level.

Although they are not as high as those for services, measured elasticities for many locally manufactured goods are sizable and bear comparison to the "import" competition (see Table 6.7). Despite the very modest range of incomes over which these elasticities were calculated, demand for locally made products in these communities will for some time exceed that for sophisticated products from abroad or from large urban factories.

The Elasticity of Supply. The extent to which these demand projections for rural nonfarm output are realized depends on the supply response. For short-run supply elasticity, evidence from the Michigan State and other surveys suggests that "excess capacity" of 20 to 40 percent exists in rural nonfarm enterprises in most developing countries. Although there may be periodic shortages of raw materials and working capital in some activities, the overwhelming cause of excess capacity is insufficient demand. So the short-run supply curve may be highly elastic.

For the long-run elasticity, the potential constraint is blocked entry, with the primary candidates being capital and specialized skills. For most activities, initial capital requirements fall between $50 and $900 and are usually financed from personal savings and loans from family and friends. Hire-purchase is available for rice and maize mills and other fee-for-service processing equipment. Even where capital requirements are much higher, there is usually sufficient access to finance for some individuals in the rural economy so that a bottleneck does not long remain. A similarly optimistic conclusion emerges for skill barriers: formal educational requirements are low; specific skills are formed by apprenticeship and learning by doing in gestation periods ranging from six months to three years.

Some Amendments.   Cross-sectional observations taken at one point in time generate a wealth of reliable data pertinent to narrowly defined questions in a way that other methods cannot match, but they usually fail to capture the effect of those elements subject to systematic change over time. There are several such omitted time trends that modify projections derived from the cross-sectional elasticity coefficients. The broad effect of these amendments is to lower predicted manufacturing output and to raise further the predicted expansion of services.

As structural transformation proceeds, the rising cost of labor will alter relative prices, affecting particularly low-value cottage industry and petty trade. In more specialized, full-time manufacturing, the initial range of rurally supplied goods will be larger or smaller, depending on craft traditions and entrepreneurial endowment (it tends to be larger in Asia and Latin America than in Africa). But as per capita income rises, there is a shift in location in all countries from village to regional town and metropolitan area. Although the rural producer has an advantage in less expensive labor and premises, improving rural roads progressively diminishes protection against urban competitors. At the same time, the more gifted rural entrepreneurs are attracted to towns, where larger markets promise higher entrepreneurial returns; economies of agglomeration yield further advantages in the availability of more skilled labor and of cheaper and diverse raw materials. Production in the towns, while carried out in units four or five times the size of the rural producer, is still comparatively small-scale and labor-intensive.

If there is large-scale public investment in the infrastructure of regional towns, many entrepreneurs will locate there, and output will not be lost to the larger rural economy. But as entrepreneurs do migrate to urban areas and urban-based substitute goods (plastic utensils, synthetic textiles) replace traditional products, the demand for rurally produced manufactures will fall. These changes are not captured in the expenditure coefficients.

Expenditure studies may also underestimate nonfarm transport and trading activities, because most of these are embedded in the price of the consumer good. As there is a shift away from village-produced goods, the share of these marketing services will rise. Hence, inferences from household expenditure underestimate the growth in aggregate rural nonfarm services.

Table 6.8. Agricultural technical advance and nonfarm activity: The supply-side impact (640 Bangladesh rural households, 1981–83)

Type of agricultural technology[a]	Return per hour (taka)	Hours per week	Household income (taka)
Traditional			
Farming	5.1	46.5	237
Nonfarming[b]	4.4	35.5	156
Cottage industry	4.4	—	—
Wage labor	2.8	—	—
Trade	2.3	—	—
Services	11.4	—	—
New (traditional region = 100)			
Farming	129	108	140
Nonfarming[b]	159	71	112
Cottage industry	190	19	37
Wage labor	106	59	62
Trade	295	72	213
Services	104	130	135

Source: Hossain 1988, pp. 95, 120, as reported in Haggblade and Liedholm 1992.© 1988 IFPRI. Reprinted by permission.

[a]Traditional versus new technology-using regions are demarcated by access to irrigation, use of modern rice variety (60% vs. 5%), fertilizer consumption, and other agricultural practices.

[b] Nonfarm wage labor includes earth hauling, construction, transport and "other" employment.

Supply-Side Effects from Agriculture

What happens when the technical advance is uneven between agriculture and nonfarm production? It is tacitly assumed in cross-sectional analyses that the rate of advance is uniform. The "seed-fertilizer revolution" is an obvious instance to the contrary. Mahabub Hossain has made a promising start at capturing the supply-side effects when labor productivity rises sharply in farm activity but is relatively unchanged in nonfarming. He surveyed 16 villages in two farming regions, where only one region had adopted the new biochemical technology. That region also had a more developed rural infrastructure (see Table 6.8).

The top panel shows hourly earnings in farming and nonfarming, along with hours worked and income per week for eight villages in the nonadopting region. The second panel shows the same for eight villages in the "progressive" region, expressing each variable as a percentage of that in the first region. The returns per worker in "progressive" farming are 29 percent higher, with households devoting more time to farming and less time to nonfarming.

The higher opportunity cost of labor in the progressive region alters the composition of nonfarm activities toward more remunerative services, with a contraction in low-return cottage industry, wage-labor earth hauling, and petty trade. While the hours per week fall by 29 percent, the income from now more valuable nonfarm activities is 12 percent higher than in the 320 matched households in the traditional farming region.

The first wave of new technology, with emphasis on biochemical innovations, is labor-using and therefore tends to bid up wage rates, given a less than perfectly elastic labor supply. Even though this will probably be associated with a contraction in the share of nonfarm activities, it benefits the landless and poor households who have their own labor to sell.

The second phase of new technology sees a greater emphasis on labor-saving innovations—herbicides for weed control and mechanical inputs for soil preparation and harvesting—so that growth in demand for agricultural labor may lag the growth in the rural labor force. Then, returns to labor in agriculture may stagnate or decline. In employment, the proportionate size of the nonfarm economy is likely to rise, with expansion in the low-skill, low-yield activities. It is then that technical progress in nonfarm activities—both in higher productivity and in new goods and services—has a key role in sustaining the returns to labor, not only in its own sector but in the larger agricultural sector as well.[16]

FARM EQUIPMENT: A STRATEGIC LINKAGE

Although quantitatively less important than chemical fertilizer, the purchase of farm tools and machinery by a modernizing agricultural sector is a significant backward linkage to the manufacturing sector. But it is their technological dimension that gives these expenditures their true significance. In manufacturing, agricultural equipment is a large portion of output of the metal-working industry in a CARL. Thus, the organizational and technological developments experienced in the production of farm implements can affect the country's capacity to produce other capital goods and to embody in these goods technology adapted to the economy's relative factor endowment. In agricultural development these capital inputs strongly influence productivity and farm income by their cost, the variety of tasks they perform, and the technology (design efficiency) they place at the farmer's command.

The "Bare Essentials" Principle

Because farming has many producers and undifferentiated products, earnings beyond wages and land rent are typically held to a minimum by competitive forces. This limits the money available for capital equipment and

---

[16] Haggblade, Hammer, and Hazell 1991 and Haggblade and Liedholm 1992 provide a comprehensive analysis of the returns to labor in the nonfarm sector, making assumptions about the rate and bias of technical change in agriculture, rates of population growth, and expenditure elasticities. The discussion in the text owes much to these two articles.

puts pressure on the farmer to buy the cheapest tools for the job, particularly when much farm equipment is used for only a few weeks in each year. We term this the *"bare essentials" principle*. The following statement by a team of agricultural engineers in Taiwan in 1953 describing animal and manually powered equipment, mostly in the $5 to $50 range, gives witness to this phenomenon:

Farm implements in Taiwan are comparatively cheap and this is due to the farmers' purchasing power. Manufacturers often have to sacrifice quality in order to maintain a low price. If sturdy and highly efficient farm implements are to be made, their prices will have to be raised; farmers because of their financial stringency, will not be able to buy these implements even if they are aware of their good performance. In other words, the farmers in Taiwan should be temporarily satisfied with the minimum serviceability of implements available. (Ma, Takasaka, and Yang 1955)

This pressure to find the cheapest implement is usually described in terms of the level of purchasing power. In fact, even where purchasing power is high (for example, in the United States) but the farm product markets are competitive, narrow profit margins above minimum costs forces the farmer to be price conscious about equipment. Look at Taiwan in 1970, when average farm income was roughly triple its 1953 level and labor scarcity had brought about much mechanization. In explaining why power tillers (price: $900–1,500) had not spread more rapidly (24,640 units as of 1969), the Joint Commission on Rural Reconstruction's (JCRR) farm machinery specialist stated:

In spite of the increasing demand for farm equipment by Taiwan farmers, prices of farm machines, especially power tillers produced by local manufacturers are generally beyond the financial capacity of the average farmer. . . . It is doubly hard to market farm machinery among the farmers with their low purchasing power. (Peng 1970, pp. 3–4)

A sudden and discontinuous increase in farm cash receipts overrides the "bare essentials" principle. Witness what happened in the Punjab in India and Pakistan in 1963–75. Two years of drought resulted in a 50 percent rise in grain prices and high food imports. With new seed varieties, the stage was set for a rapid expansion of output at unusually high prices and reduced costs. Cash receipts rose quickly, and net farm income increased even more rapidly. During this disequilibrium interval the farmer makes a higher income by investing in equipment that enables rapid production increases rather than equipment that minimizes unit cost. Augmented profits also provide higher purchasing power for farm equipment. The result is a shift in demand away from human- and animal-powered equipment toward tractors, tractor-drawn equipment, and combine harvesters. Government lending programs unintentionally encouraged this trend. Most new equipment is not produced by the same firms as before: the gap in manufacturing processes is too great. There is a sharp rise in scale of output, capital intensity, and in import content. Thus, in India, of the seven major tractor manufacturers in 1985 only one (Swaraj) was a native firm; in Pakistan both tractor assemblers were associated with foreign firms, and after fifteen years, except for one Massey-Ferguson model, import content was still 70 percent (Mohan and Rizk in IRRI 1986).

On the supply side the absence of significant economies of scale or other barriers to entry operates in the same direction as demand preferences to promote the ready supply of low-priced farm tools. Most farm implements can be manufactured on a small scale; even the production of 14-hp two-wheel tractors and diesel engine pumpsets can be set up with a modest investment in fixed plant through the use of subcontractors and the purchase of standardized "trade" components and subassemblies. Most metalworking skills can be learned on the job; only the largest firms serving the quality market employ craftsmen with technical training. As long as above-normal profits are being made, the number of producers increases as experienced workers leave employers to set up on their own. This fission process intensifies competition and leads manufacturers to reduce costs.

Beyond the temporal pattern of user demand, however, the changing variety of farm tools and their efficiency are strongly influenced by an "ingenuity factor" that is not constant across countries. Because many basic principles of design for agricultural equipment had been worked out by the late nineteenth century, agricultural engineering research seeks to adapt known designs to different crop requirements, local circumstances, and factor prices.

With a few exceptions, public-sponsored agricultural research units have had only modest success in developing prototypes that are widely adopted. The real success has come from small engineering workshops. Their inventiveness and ability to sustain prolonged interaction with the farm user is a key ingredient to an evolutionary pattern of agricultural development.

Farming Tasks and Farming Tools

In this section, taking Taiwan as our exemplar, we examine the role that tool design can play in promoting an evolutionary agricultural development that both incorporates yield-increasing technical possibilities and makes full use of the farm labor force. The outstanding feature of Taiwan's farm implements is the degree to which each has been designed to a special task and a specific environment. An example is the harrow, one of eight tools used in secondary tillage. In 1952 there were nine kinds of harrows: the comb harrow, three knife tooth harrows (standard, bent frame, flexible tooth), two spike harrows, the bamboo harrow, the pulverizing roller, and the stone roller.[17] Since 1952 the animal-drawn tined tiller and the disk harrow have been added. One of these harrows, the standard knife tooth, has twelve regional variants. Width, length, material, and number of teeth, shape of tooth blade, and method of affixing teeth are adapted according to local topography, field size, soil structure, and available construction materials. Similarly, basic types of hoes—earth opening, hilling, weeding—are found in six zonal varieties that differ in weight, dimensions, and angle of blade according to climate, soil conditions, and crop requirements.

Progressive evolutionary agricultural modernization implies a growing inventory of farm tools. One-fourth of the 1952 stock of implements had been introduced in the preceding 30 years. Of 40 new implements, 12 performed new yield-increasing tasks, for example, the check row spacing marker and the sprayer. Sixteen new tools performed the same work as before but faster, for example, the potato-slicing machine, duster, and manure fork. The remaining items did a superior, yield-increasing job or superior and faster work. Of the 40 tools, 19 were labor-saving. Most new implements cost more than those they displaced.

Because the cost of materials is the major component of manufacturing costs, prices of implements tend to vary according to weight. Nearly two-thirds of the implements weighed less than 10 pounds; and the average price for half of the 160 items was less than $20 at 1985 prices. Most animal-drawn implements were $40 to $200.

Many new and more expensive items came into use in the twenty years after 1952. There was a sharp increase in pumpsets for irrigation and drainage, and most were small centrifugal pumps driven by a 5-hp diesel engine. These portable, low-lift pumps were initially imported from Japan but are now made by fifteen or so Taiwanese firms that also export them. The rapid spread of sprayers, which began in 1955, was also based initially on imports from Japan; and mist blowers and dusters, introduced from Germany in the early 1960s, were soon manufactured locally. An artificial grain dryer, introduced in 1966, greatly reduces losses due to fermenting, sprouting, and molding where harvesting must be done in the rainy season. After experimenting with American prototypes, which proved either too heavy or too costly, the Provincial Department of Agriculture and Forestry adapted a Japanese design utilizing a kerosene burner and an electric blower.

[17] A richly detailed survey of some 160 farm implements was undertaken in 1952 by Professors Ma, Takasaka, and Yang, *Farm Implements Used in Taiwan Province.* Our treatment of post-1952 developments is based on our own field observations and various papers by a Joint Commission on Rural Reconstruction specialist on farm machinery, T. S. Peng, "The Development of Mechanized Rice Culture in Taiwan," 1969, and "Present Problems and the Future of Agricultural Mechanization in Taiwan," 1971.

During this period, partial mechanization to break emerging labor bottlenecks was ubiquitous. Threshing and winnowing were speeded up by adding a small gasoline or electric motor to replace the foot pedal and hand crank. The winnower was further improved by adding bearings in the revolving mechanism and an auger elevator for moving the grain into the hopper. Small electric motors replaced the human arm as the motive power for the sweet potato slicing machine.

In the 1950s the power tiller was introduced. Taiwan's JCRR began to experiment with 2- to 10-hp American and Japanese two-wheel tractors in 1954, and by 1956 it was evident that an adapted Japanese rotary-type diesel engine tiller was best suited to Taiwan. Its spread was gradual, associated with the provision of technical know-how to the farmer and repair services. The average of hours of tiller use rose from less than 450 hours a year in 1960 to 828 hours in 1969; at the same time, the work done per hour rose. (For example, the hours to prepare 1 hectare of paddy were reduced from 19.4 in 1965 to 14.7 in 1969.) These changes increased the social profitability of the power tiller when Taiwanese agriculture experienced, for the first time, a shortage of farm labor.

From the 1970s onward the scarce factor in Taiwanese agriculture was labor. Average farm size increased, and the number of farm households fell. Cropping intensity also diminished somewhat, and mechanical inputs, substituting for labor, proliferated. There was also a rapidly growing use of power rice transplanters, rice combine harvesters, and power tea harvesters. Power tillers peaked in 1981 at just under 94,000, while four-wheel tractors rose from under 1,000 in 1974 to over 10,000 by 1987.

Structure of the Farm Equipment Industry

Producers of farm equipment can be divided into three subsectors. Simple traditional tools are made mainly by rural carpenters and blacksmiths. Improved implements, light processing equipment, irrigation pumps and motors, and some tractor-drawn implements are fabricated by light engineering workshops in towns near or in farming areas. Tractors, combines, and other large items are produced by large firms (which we will call tractor manufacturers). The relative size of these three subsectors varies with economic development and with the pattern of farm holdings. In the United States and Europe, tractor manufacturers are dominant, and the artisan subsector is small or nonexistent. In much of Africa rural artisans produce almost all farm equipment, except for imported items and a few implements that are turned out by stamping presses in relatively large workshops. Asia and Latin America are somewhere in between, with no sector dominant.

Until the mid-1970s rural craftsmen were the dominant sector in India and Pakistan, but in Taiwan they have come to be a very small sector. Village artisans typically work adjacent to the family dwelling and employ capital of around $150 to $300. The smithy will include a small brick forge with hand bellows, anvil, hammer, chisels, and tongs; the carpenter has saws, adzes, files, hand drills, chisels, mallet, and hammer. There is no formal quality control for raw materials, forging temperatures, or product specifications; the outcome depends solely on the judgment and skill of the individual. The artisan has a few years of primary education at most and no technical training other than traditional apprenticeship. Even so, remarkable technical results are often achieved—for example, the double-layered blade of the self-sharpening Taiwanese hoe and harvesting sickle.[18]

The rural artisan is not usually an entrepreneur: production is made to order with the customer paying for materials in advance. These artisans are the principal repairers of all farm equipment, except tractors and power tillers. Payment, particularly for repairs, may be in kind, although the trend is toward cash. In only two items (the Persian wheel and the improved ox cart) is there specialization by commodity; these producers are in towns.

In light engineering, the largest sector in most Asian countries, the scale of output and employment is larger. Firm size ranges from five to 100 employees. There is division of labor between casting, forging, machining, and assembling. Power tools such as lathes, drill presses, and grinders, are used, as are hand tools. Components and product specifications tend to be more uniform, although in the absence of jigs, fixtures, and quality controls, true interchangeability of parts is not achieved. Batch production is for a general market, and some less-expensive items are sold wholesale to distributors.

There are some common elements in workshop and artisan production. The early urban firms are often established by progressive blacksmiths and traders involved in selling farm tools. In both technical training is imparted through experience and apprenticeship. Most entrepreneurs come from the journeymen ranks; with no significant capital requirements, a rise in demand encourages enterprising employees to set up on their own. The industry thus tends to be highly competitive and profit rates low. Like the rural artisan, urban workshops are seldom wholly specialized in agricultural equipment; they manufacture other products, such as band saws, oilseed expellers, cotton gins, electric fans, textile looms, and lathes.

A study in Pakistan provides a comprehensive view of that country's workshop sector in 1982 (Nabi 1988). Serving a farm labor force of 14 million workers, there were some 600 firms producing tubewell engines, tractor implements, tractor-powered threshers, trailers, and sugarcane and chaff cutters. Located in clusters in each of five regional towns, firms ranged in size from 2 to 62 employees, with 40 percent engaging less than 5 workers and

---

[18] A brief resume of a 1969 UNIDO survey of farm equipment manufacturing for twelve Asian countries is given in Swammy-Rao 1971.

10 percent engaging more than 20. Thirty-one percent of the entrepreneurs had no formal schooling (including that of the largest firm), and 18 percent had 10 years or more. Only 5 percent of the entrepreneurs had some formal technical education, while none of the workers had so benefited; in short, technical knowledge is acquired by apprenticeship and learning by doing. Extensive subcontracting relationships, as well as the fission process by which new firms are established, are channels by which superior know-how passes from larger to smaller producers.

Tractor manufacturers constitute the third segment of the farm equipment industry. They produce the most sophisticated agricultural machinery that is fabricated domestically. There are a few large firms with capitalization of several million dollars or more. Most of them have, as a technical collaborator and minority partner, a well-known international manufacturer whose machine they produce—for example, Massey-Ferguson, Ford, Yanmar, Kubota, Iseki, and Mitsubishi.

In Pakistan some firms assemble tractors, with local content averaging about 35 percent. In India, there are thirteen such firms, with local content making up over 75 percent. The technology of these firms is much the same as that found in light engineering workshops. However, tractor manufacturers employ industrial and design engineers, trained technicians, and use sophisticated testing equipment and interchangeable parts. Moreover, unlike the workshops, they sell their product through dealership networks and provide after-sales service, which contribute to a high investment requirement. To supervise and coordinate production and marketing calls for substantial managerial organization.

The skills, capital, and entrepreneurial organization needed for tractor manufacture provide high barriers to entrance for domestic businessmen. This potential for monopoly and consequent high-priced, poorly serviced tractors has not come to fruition. Rivalry among Japanese, European, and American producers for a footing in areas with long-term potential (even if not initially profitable) has provided healthy competition. For their local partners, these multinationals have approached large light engineering firms already producing and selling agricultural implements, reputable merchandisers of hard goods, or, where they have developed their own distributional network, the government.

The success of the farm equipment industry in providing effective inputs for agriculture is determined in significant measure by the interconnections among the three subsectors. In addition to the competitive interplay of price, quality, and service of substitutable implements in the product market, these interconnections include specialization of function in intermediate components and flow of personnel, designs, and manufacturing techniques between subsectors. The degree to which these interconnections develop depends on the temporal continuity of the industry's growth and on governmental policies. The former is related to the pattern of change of farm purchasing power, as well as the general state of development of light engineering. The policy factor includes procedures for licensing scarce raw materials, price control, methods for promoting new implements, and various tax and subsidy policies.

One of the most interesting linkages between the subsectors is the satellite (or ancillary) system. Although subcontracting is a feature of engineering, automotive, and electrical industries in industrialized countries, their potential for transmitting advanced technology to many indigenous firms is magnified in developing economies. Several examples from the 1970s indicate the scope of this type of subcontracting. The China Agricultural Machinery Company is Taiwan's largest power tiller manufacturer (in which Yanmar and Iseki are the technical partners). It purchased from 17 satellite firms components that accounted for about 20 percent of the price of their machine; in earlier years such purchases had been as much as 40 percent. Two years after starting power tiller production, Krishi Enterprises in Hyderabad had developed ancillary relations with 32 small firms. Escorts, India's largest tractor maker, subcontracts to 200 firms, of which three-quarters employ 20 to 50 workers.

Unlike specialist firms that produce standardized parts used by many manufacturers, the ancillary workshop makes interchangeable components built to the specifications of the contracting company. The primary company supplies the ancillary with technical drawings, jigs, fixtures, a prototype, and raw materials where they are licensed, as with steel alloys in India. The primary firm sends a full-time adviser during the start-up period; afterward, it provides technical assistance through the regular visits of quality control inspectors.

The primary company initiates an ancillary system because it minimizes investment, both in fixed capital for productive facilities and working capital for raw materials. Because of cheaper labor (lower wages, more apprentices) and fewer management overheads, the ancillary supplies the item cheaper than the contractor could. In addition to learning, the subcontractor is provided with those things most sorely lacked—design, quality control, and a market outlet. Although the ancillary is vulnerable to abuse (for example, delayed payment), many small metalworking firms (more than half in India) continue such arrangements, which suggests mutual benefits inherent in the system.

Although most Asian governments enforce diminishing import content for licensed manufacturers, only India specifies the minimum share of inputs from ancillaries. This is important. Primary firms tend to reduce subcontracting as accumulated earnings relieve earlier capital scarcity. They do so to adjust production more promptly to unanticipated changes in the market. The higher cost of internal production is offset by smaller inventories and reduced fluctuation in return on investment. While desirable for the primary firm, this cutting back on ancillaries sacrifices a greater social benefit through diminished transmission of technical and managerial know-how to small firms.

The more progressive and better educated entrepreneurs in workshops also obtain new designs from publicly supported research institutions. The firms that obtain technical drawings from the research institutes are among the largest (usually more than sixty employees) and most capital-intensive firms in their subsector. Because of little or no distribution network and of an inability to cover the market, these producers are unable to protect innovational profits from imitators within the workshop sector. This has induced progressive firms to specialize in producing CKD (complete knockdown) component sets for wholesale distribution to local blacksmiths who assemble, retail, and provide after-sales service. An arrangement of this sort, especially in Taiwan but gaining momentum in India, not only permits the progressive firm to cover the market better and to economize on working capital, but also hastens the transfer of improved technology and design to the artisan sector.

NOURISHING LINKAGES

Agriculture is linked to the rural nonfarm sector, to the urban sector, and to the international economy. These links entail commodity flows, capital flows, and labor flows. Equally important, but far more difficult to measure, is a flow of knowledge between sectors.[19]

Agriculture's commodity sales to and technology-embodying inputs purchased from the two spatially distant sectors are a central element in structural transformation. Given employment and equity objectives, it is the intensity of the interaction between agriculture and the rural nonfarm economy that is of particular importance for the CARL.

---

[19] The recent growth literature, highlighting the importance of externalities and other increasing returns phenomena, is consonant with the themes of this book. (See, for example, Murphy, Shleifer, and Vishny 1989a and 1989b and Romer 1986 and 1992.) We would argue, however, that the economies of scale associated with large modern manufacturing establishments—implying the desirability of a "big push" industrialization effort as suggested by P. N. Rosenstein-Rodan and Ragnar Nurkse four decades ago—are less important than the knowledge-spillover externality. The latter is far more likely to occur when, as in Taiwan (Chapter 10), growth in national output results in large measure from the burgeoning of small- and medium-scale enterprise. Shleifer (1990) points to externalities associated with new investment, when a firm is successful in initiating a new process, machine, or product that is copied by others in the same industry: "A particularly important instance of imitation occurs when a firm's employees themselves break out and start their own firms based on knowledge they have acquired by doing and by watching." This is precisely the "hiveing-off" process that has long been recognized by those who study the emergence of new firms. In contrast, large-scale firms tend to be capital-intensive, technologically sophisticated, and few in number. Here there will be few opportunities for generating externalities.

On the demand side, the potential size of aggregate links from the farm sector are fixed by but a single determinant, the level of agricultural production. So the relevant government actions to maximize growth elsewhere in the economy are precisely those macro and sector-specific policies, delineated in Chapter 5, that influence the growth in farm output itself. Apart from farming's "forward linkages" (the processing, transporting, and marketing of food and fiber), the mix between sectors varies with the pattern of agricultural expansion. Given the procurement preferences of small- and medium-size farm households for both consumer goods and production inputs, their purchases are less oriented toward the urban and international economies than those of large estate farms. In short, policies that promote a unimodal pattern of farming will promote the growth of labor-using small enterprises both in the village and in the rural town.

How efficient these linkages are depends critically on the supply response. Here, the single most important intervention is the construction of rural roads and infrastructure for regional towns. The former undermines local monopolies and reduces the delivered cost to the farmer of consumer goods, equipment, and construction materials. By building up regional towns, with their economies of agglomeration, the most able rural manufacturing entrepreneurs are afforded supplier networks and larger markets than are available in the village setting. Their migration to the major cities is thus avoided, retaining in the rural economy both employment and a localized growth pole.

Government programs can strengthen the small producer directly by encouraging schemes that provide working capital loans and by taking measures to upgrade the quality of apprentice training and to disseminate best-practice production methods. Schemes to provide large fixed capital loans to small enterprise have had but a mixed record, but there has been great success with short-term working capital lending. Typically operated by private voluntary organizations, these programs have used streamlined delivery systems to supply credit for very small operators in manufacture, services, and commerce in the rural nonfarm sector. Bangladesh's Grameen Bank is well-known. A far larger program in Indonesia, servicing more than five million borrowers annually, not only earns a large surplus but also is government-operated (Box 5.5).

The most pervasive, indirect influence for strengthening the supply response is pricing policy. Just as in farming, small manufacturers should have the same access to critical spare parts, high-performance imported raw materials, and other production inputs as the most favored large producer. Instead, they are often relegated to an uneven playing field with respect to the cost of loan capital, denied access to a key technology-embodying import owing to foreign exchange rationing, or forced to bear higher import tariffs than capital-intensive urban competitors, and such policy-created market imperfections weaken any linkages achieved. This attenuation results from the artificially higher cost imposed on rural nonfarm and other small producers and from a constriction in the range of technology options that can be exploited.

Heavily subsidized import-substituting industrialization not only tends to undermine employment-generating links between agriculture and other sectors of the economy, but it also retards the growth of the economy in more direct ways. For such industries the appropriate choice of technology may well be reliance on the international economy. Unhappily, a major input linkage from agriculture has provided one of the most dramatic examples of the ill-starred import-substituting development strategy, the case of chemical fertilizer, to which we now turn.

CHAPTER SEVEN

FERTILIZER PRODUCTION: STRATEGIC PITFALL?

C ARLs face peculiar opportunities and pitfalls because they trail other nations as they ascend the ladder of structural transformation. Like agriculture, manufacturing industries have technological biases (see Box 6.1), but in some, as discussed in the preceding chapter, there is dramatically less scope for substitution of labor for capital than in agriculture. Two major industrial inputs to agriculture span the range of possibilities. In farm equipment, product variation and process simplification offer wide scope for substitution. In fertilizer production the freedom to vary capital-intensive input coefficients is almost nil, and economies of scale are massive. So, all but a few CARLs can import chemical fertilizer far cheaper than they can produce it. Yet, many still choose to invest in fertilizer capacity.

AN OVERVIEW

Since the advent of the Green Revolution in the mid-1960s, chemical fertilizers have had a central place in transforming farm production in developing countries. Their fertilizer consumption has risen from 4 million nutrient tons in 1960 to 20 million by 1975, the year of the "fertilizer crisis," to 64 million tons by 1990. Expenditure on fertilizer exceeds that for all other agricultural purchased inputs combined—high-yielding seed, irrigation, farm equipment. Hence, the way in which fertilizer is acquired and delivered to farmers is an important element in agricultural strategy.

Fertilizer production has few linkages with other sectors and has yet to be associated with any significant technological externalities. On the other hand, owing to the sheer magnitude of fertilizer use, a country's fertilizer policy has macroeconomic consequences. In practice, the public sector is extensively involved in its production and distribution: in importing it or investing in plants to produce it, and in delivery to the farmer at prices that are below cost and on credit only partially repaid. In the instance of India, direct budgetary fertilizer subsidies at the retail level, to take but one of the cost elements, have exceeded $1 billion per year.

Thus, fertilizer has sizeable fiscal and foreign exchange ramifications. And because of its capital-intensity, and hence the very large volume of financial resources preempted by initiating local production—"make or buy" decisions have allocation consequences far beyond the agricultural sector.

The extraordinary growth of fertilizer consumption (9 percent a year over the past thirty years) lies at the heart of the Green Revolution. It is the conventional view that new semidwarf plant varieties, which appeared in the 1960s and whose yield was highly responsive to chemical nutrients, were the driving force behind that revolution, with fertilizer playing a complementary but passive role. Quite the contrary. Without the continuous fall in the real price of fertilizer over the past 100 years, there would have been no Green Revolution. Between 1910 and 1957 the real price at the farmgate was halved, and since 1957 it has been halved again (see Figure 7.1).

What has caused this dramatic price fall? The cost of electricity, a large input of production until the mid-1960s, declined sharply between 1930 and 1960. More economical methods of packaging and transport and a shift to higher analysis fertilizer materials (for example, from ammonium sulphate, with 21 percent nitrogen, to urea, with 46 percent) has reduced the cost of distribution. The major savings, however, have come from a stream of discoveries in applied chemistry and mechanical engineering relating to the production of superphosphates, phosphoric acid and, above all, ammonia. Just as these technological advances played a major role in the Green Revolution, so they had a decisive impact on international cost advantage in fertilizer production. Curiously, despite the major consequences for resource allocation, comparative advantage has received little attention.[1]

---

[1] This chapter focuses on the *availability* of fertilizer. Should it be imported or produced locally, and if so, how? The *efficiency of fertilizer use* is a subject of perhaps equal importance. Because it is made up of many components, all of which lack dramatic visibility, efficiency of use tends to receive less attention than availability. In most developing countries, starting from a given level of fertilizer availability at the factory gate or ocean port, only a fraction of the potential output response is achieved. The foregone potential (from 20 to 80 percent) is a result of storage and transportation losses, lack of detailed scientific knowledge as to specific crop responses across intracountry agroclimatic environments, and a shortfall in knowledge of specific fertilizer mixes, late delivery of fertilizer to the farmer, and fertilizer–crop price relationships that lead to misallocation of nutrients between crops.

Figure 7.1. The real price of fertilizer, 1910–1990 (U.S. data)

Source: U.S. Department of Agriculture.
Note: Price of fertilizer/consumer price index: 1910–14 = 100.

International specialization leads to higher real incomes. Producing for world markets reduces some risks, but it gives rise to new ones. Thus, most countries—rightly or wrongly—seek self-sufficiency in basic foodstuffs, irrespective of comparative advantage. How far back should that self-sufficiency reach? To farm equipment? To the steel from which it is made? To fertilizer, which may add 2 to 10 percent to food output? To the bag in which it is shipped? The answer is a fine judgment of political economy. It entails weighing the certain increased cost of local production against the uncertain benefit of avoiding a transitory price spike or possible nonavailability of the import, as in the "fertilizer crisis" of 1974–75. Like an insurance policy, there may also be distributional issues: who are the principal beneficiaries and who pays the premium.

CARLs are likely to pay only a small premium for self-sufficiency for commodities where production involves sizable local inputs of labor or raw materials; where there is a mature technology refined into standardized labor operations and supervisory routine; where requirements for infrastructure are modest; where the optimum scale of production (hence market transportation radius) is not overlarge; and where the price of purchased inputs and final product are not volatile. Two additional factors also favor import substitution: a sizeable share of ocean transport in the cost of the competitive import, and plant construction costs that do not greatly exceed those in the exporting country.

In all but a few CARLs the balance of these considerations—technological complexity, feedstock endowment, infrastructure, capital intensity—would seem, on an a priori basis, to weigh heavily against home production of chemical fertilizer. Notwithstanding, government officials in many countries, with the active support of aid donors, have chosen to allocate billions of scarce investment dollars in the pursuit of self-sufficiency.

After a period of some twenty years of investing in factories, the production of nitrogen, phosphate, and potassium fertilizers in developing countries had by 1967 reached 4.7 million nutrient tons. This accounted for 54 percent of fertilizer consumption in those countries. By 1990 production had risen tenfold to 51.7 million tons, with the coverage of local consumption rising to 80 percent. This 51.7 million tons represented 30 percent of world production.

What kind of financial resources have these investments required? Table 7.1 sets out production capacity by country for nitrogen as it was in 1976 and 1990. Assuming a conservative investment cost per ton of $1,200, there has been an investment of more than $37 billion since 1976 ($24 billion excluding China). If we consider all existing capacity and add in an estimate for the production of phosphate and potassium, total Third World fertilizer investment is in the neighborhood of $80 billion.

Before proceeding to an empirical evaluation of how successful these investments have been, it will be helpful to outline the major technological developments that have reshaped the industry over the past four decades in question.

TECHNOLOGY

The focus is on the production of nitrogen, which accounts for well over half of all fertilizer materials. The technology of manufacture consists of a series of processes that first produce hydrogen and nitrogen from basic inputs (air and a carbon feedstock), then synthesize ammonia from these elements, and finally convert the ammonia to nitrogen fertilizer. The basic process by which ammonia (NH_3) is synthesized from elemental nitrogen and hydrogen was developed early in this century by two German chemists, Fritz Haber and Carl Bosch. As shown in Figure 7.2, the manufacture of nitrogen fertilizers is divided into four steps, of which the first three pertain to ammonia. The first step is the production of hydrogen from superheated steam and some form of carbon feedstock. The carbon combines with the oxygen of the water, thus freeing the hydrogen ($H_2O + C \Rightarrow CO + H_2$). In

Table 7.1. Nitrogen capacity in developing countries (thousands of metric tons)

	1976	1990
Egypt	369	967
Algeria	272	816
Libya	—	544
Sub-Saharan Africa[a]	75	450
South Africa	701	690
China	7,517	18,423
India	2,981	8,748
Indonesia	288	2,683
Pakistan	345	1,150
Bangladesh	233	826
North Korea	454	871
South Korea	627	488
Taiwan	334	305
Malaysia	43	315
Other Asian[b]	263	734
OPEC Gulf states[c]	1,308	3,244
Turkey	125	696
Syria	41	313
Brazil	27	1,021
Mexico	547	2,469
Trinidad	376	1,394
Venezuela	29	650
Cuba	36	321
Other Latin America[d]	309	345
	17,300	48,463

Source: International Fertilizer Development Center 1992.
Notes: By order of importance in 1990:
[a]Nigeria (272), Zambia, Zimbabwe, Madagascar (46), excluding South Africa.
[b]Thailand (244), Vietnam, Burma, Afghanistan (58).
[c]S. Arabia (835), Kuwait, Qatar, Iran, Iraq, UAR, Bahrain (272).
[d]Colombia (151), Peru, Argentina (78).

the second step, shift conversion, the resultant mixture is compressed and, with the aid of a catalyst, freed of carbon monoxide and other impurities. The third and final step in ammonia production is the Haber synthesis in which three volumes of hydrogen are reacted with one volume of nitrogen, obtained from the air, at elevated temperature and pressure in the presence of an iron catalyst to obtain NH_3.

As shown in Figure 7.2, once produced, the ammonia is converted into a fertilizer product in one of the following ways: in a water solution (anhydrous ammonia) or reacted with sulfuric acid (ammonium sulfate), with nitric acid (ammonium nitrate), or with byproduct carbon dioxide (urea). Because urea is now the dominant form of nitrogen fertilizer, it is the focus of this chapter. (Urea is produced in the reaction $CO_2 + 2NH_3 \Rightarrow CO(NH_2)_2 + H_2O$.)

Figure 7.2. The production of ammonia and its relationship to nitrogen and phosphate fertilizer end-products

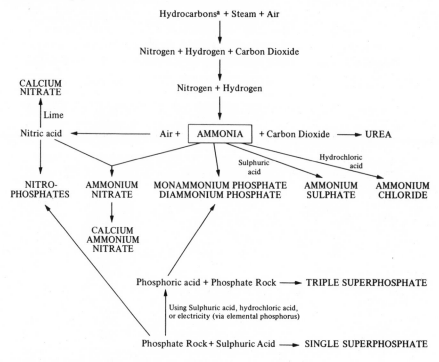

Source: Johnston and Kilby 1975, p. 104.

Notes: [a]Hydrocarbon feedstock can be natural gas, ethane, liquefied petroleum gases (LPG), or light naphtha for the reforming process. With heavier hydrocarbon feedstocks, partial oxidation processes would have to be used, which require higher capital costs than the reforming process.

CAPITALS indicate products used as fertilizer materials.

Each of these processes has been subject to a continuing stream of technical advances.[2] In the production of hydrogen there have been changes to cheaper feedstocks and to more efficient processes. In the case of feedstock, coal was displaced by oil distillates in the 1940s, and they in turn were replaced with natural gas in the late 1950s. There have been parallel advances from the original water–gas process to partial oxidization to steam reforming. Catalyst improvements—first the introduction of chromium and more recently a second-stage copper–zinc catalyst—have raised the efficiency of carbon monoxide removal and hence the yield of hydrogen.

The effect of all these technical advances is reflected in the long-term downward trend in the real price of fertilizer over most of the century. As can be

[2] Much of the material is drawn from Slack 1968, chap. 8, and Boswell and others 1985.

seen in Figure 7.1, the impact of the seminal innovation (the Haber-Bosch process) appears about 1918–25; the downward trend recommences in about 1940 and continues until the surge in energy prices in 1973. The jump in energy prices was shortly followed by a sharp escalation in the equipment and engineering cost of plant erection of over 100 percent in the rush to make new investments, which only slackened by about 1983–84. But by 1985 the real price of fertilizer was once again reaching new lows, with energy-saving technical progress being one of the factors at work.

The advances in nitrogen fertilizer technology since World War II are summarized in Table 7.2. For CARLs, these advances have a twofold effect. One is to lower the real cost of fertilizer to the farmer, providing a key component in the engine of agricultural advance. A second, negative, consequence is the erosion of economic efficiency of already-established producers whose technology is increasingly obsolete.

The most dramatic obsolescence-creating development was in 1963 when the centrifugal compressor replaced the complex, maintenance-intensive reciprocating compressor in ammonia synthesis for nitrogen fertilizer production. This innovation tripled optimum plant scale, more than doubling investment requirements. With a considerably lengthened plant life, capital depreciation per ton was cut in half. The new compressor cut natural gas requirements from 38 to 34 thousand British thermal units (MBTU) per ton of ammonia (Henderson, Perkins, and Bell 1972, pp. 23 and 30).

OPEC price hikes in 1973 and 1979 pushed fertilizer technology toward a refinement and integration of processes aimed at conserving energy in natural gas-based plants and to reexplore coal-based technology. More efficient energy use, by high-pressure steam generation and preheating combustion air to the reformers, has resulted in a 15 percent savings in fuel and feedstock at an additional plant investment cost of 6 percent. With respect to coal, the greater process complexity of two state-of-the-art plants commissioned in India in 1981 translated into double the investment requirement per ton; they can cover cost only if they operate at 100 percent of capacity

Table 7.2. Advances in production technology: nitrogen fertilizer, 1945–90

Change in feedstock	Year	Changes in process engineering	Year
Coal to naphtha	1940s	Partial oxidation to steam reforming	1950s
Naphtha to natural gas	1950s	Piston to centrifugal compressor	1960s
		Gas separation to carbonate oil recycle	1960s
		Catalyst improvement	1960–70s
		Energy-saving process design	1970–80s

and obtain coal at one-third the market price. These plants took eight years to build and have operated at less than 30 percent of capacity.

For an efficient large-scale ammonia plant (based on 1985 technology) in both capital cost and the amount of energy required, natural gas has an overwhelming advantage over coal and fuel oil and a moderate one over naphtha (see Table 7.3). Where natural gas is flared or otherwise has a low opportunity cost, it is even cheaper per BTU. Thus, most exporters of nitrogen fertilizers—Russia, Romania, the United Arab Emirates (UAE), Canada, Indonesia—have huge reserves of natural gas with very low opportunity costs.

In summary, rapid advances in fertilizer technology have resulted in significant and continuing reductions in the real price of fertilizer. This is an unmixed blessing for CARLs that rely primarily on importation. By contrast, for countries that established significant production capacity in the 1950s, 1960s, and, less damagingly so, in the 1970s, the full benefit of cost reduction was not captured. This loss resulting from the use of obsolescent feedstocks, processes, and scale of plant is *in addition to* losses that these countries might suffer owing to the absence of comparative advantage (high-price inputs, below-capacity operation).

COMPARATIVE ADVANTAGE: THE EVIDENCE, 1950–70

Despite the a priori case against import-substituting fertilizer production, the governments of CARLs, strongly supported by donor agencies, have felt that such investments were economically desirable. And they produced feasibility studies showing high rates of return to justify their decisions. We now have four decades of evidence—the actual costs of construction and operation of these plants—with which to test the realism of the "engineering assumptions" employed in these feasibility studies.

We divide our examination into two periods. The 1950–70 period was characterized by "greenfield" investments (construction of full supporting infrastructure along with the factory) and rapidly changing technology. The 1970–90 period, considered in the next section, is one of expansion on existing sites, a more modest pace of technical advance, and rising prominence of OPEC-based producers.

Pakistan

Investigation into fertilizer production in Pakistan began in 1949 in response to post-partition concerns about self-sufficiency and saving of foreign exchange. In 1950 plans were drawn up by the West Pakistan Industrial Development Corporation for a small ammonium sulphate plant at Daudkhel (Table 7.4). It was based on local coal and gypsum because nei-

Table 7.3. Capital costs and energy requirements for alternative processes

	Investment cost (natural gas = 100)	MBTU per ton of ammonia
Coal	200	45
Fuel oil	160	37
Naphtha	115	35
Natural gas	100	32

Source: Sheldrick 1987, p. 65.

ther naphtha nor natural gas was then available. A Belgian engineering firm contracted to build the factory, and finance was provided under U.S. foreign aid. Construction started in December 1952 and was scheduled to be completed in three and a half years. The cost, including processing gypsum, was to be $12.8 million. Another $0.5 million was allocated to the colliery 26 miles away. In fact, construction took over five years, and the cost surged to $19.1 million, a 49 percent overrun. Much the same happened at Pakistan's second public sector plant at Multan.

In both cases the ex ante estimate omitted import duties, working capital, railway extension, staff training and insurance; the price of equipment and the number of European contractors were underestimated. At Daudkhel, further outlays went to shore up sinking foundations and to modify gasifiers because the coal used was of a lower quality than tests had indicated.

Similarly, at Multan the gas quality was lower and decarbonization and desulphurization plants had to be introduced. When the ammonia plant could not produce at the required output, another 60 ton-a-day unit had to be installed at a cost of $12.6 million. During trials in 1961 leakages in the production line and excessive overconsumption of catalysts meant more work, more time (another two years), and additional interest charges ($2.9 million).

Pakistan's most efficient investment during this period was the private sector Esso plant at Dharki. Like Multan, it used reciprocal compressor technology in ammonia production and was based on natural gas, discovered in the mid-1950s and early 1960s. Although it was also subject to sharply rising equipment prices, its completion was on time and at an investment cost per ton almost half that of Multan.

Table 7.4. Pakistan's early experience with fertilizer production

Construction start-up	Feedstock	N-capacity (tons, in 1,000s)	Months	Cost overrun (%)
Daudkhel, 1958	Coal	11	64	49
Multan, 1963	Gas	73	66	48
Esso-Dharki, 1968	Gas	81	24	80

India

Although in many ways India's experience in the 1950s and 1960s paralleled that of Pakistan, it differed in that India made a major effort to develop (through two public sector companies) its capacity to design, manufacture, and construct fertilizer plants (see Table 7.5).

All public sector plants have cost more than original estimates.[3] Gestation periods averaged more than five years. Roughly two years were needed to let contracts, acquire land, and arrange licenses. Building the factories took much longer than in the private sector (Table 7.5, column 3). Problems were legion and included unfulfilled time schedules of contractors and equipment manufacturers, delays in issuing foreign exchange licenses, unjustified technical risks, defective work and equipment, explosions, unexpected feedstock impurities, and assorted technical difficulties (Merrett 1972). For the two private plants for which there is information (Kota and Kanpur), speedier execution seems to be explained by more careful project planning, by greater reliance on imported capital goods and expert foreign contractors (hence, higher foreign exchange content), and by less encumbered, more determined entrepreneurial follow-through.[4]

Taiwan

Much of the 1970 capacity in Taiwan had been achieved by expanding existing facilities (Yuan 1964). For three big public sector projects the gestation period was five years or more. By contrast, the private sector's $23 million urea project at Miaoli holds the record for Asia's shortest gestation period. The agreement between Mobil Oil, Allied Chemical, and the Taiwanese Fertilizer Corporation (TFC) was signed in August, 1961. Planned by Allied, and engineered by the Badger Company, construction started in July, 1962, with start-up 15 months later. This was accomplished despite a

---

[3] Bhagwati and P. Desai 1970, p. 163. Detailed accounts of the fertilizer investment experience can be found in Merrett 1972 and Robert Repetto 1971, chap. 3.

[4] In addition to the high cost of investment from the inefficiency of plant construction, an additional burden for public sector plants has been generous investment in housing and townships. "Evidently, all the projects have been lavish with the use of land. At Sindri there is one house constructed per acre of land, the argument being that land is cheap. Even at Trombay [adjacent to a large urban area], the Fertilizer Corporation of India (FCI) has provided housing to 97 percent of its workers. The cost of township formed 12.6 percent of total project cost at Sindri and 12 percent at Nangal" (Bhagwati and Desai 1970, p. 81). Not only are public sector undertakings more prone to build townships when they are not necessary, but because of overstaffing, the townships are larger than they would otherwise be. And this in turn gives rise to higher non-capital costs as well: 11 percent of the government firm Fertilizers and Chemicals Alwaye (FACT) and FCI labor force is employed in staffing schools, hospitals, and other municipal services (Merrett 1971, p. 81).

Table 7.5. Investment cost per ton of nitrogen capacity, India, 1958–70

Plant	Start-up	Feed-stock	Years under construction	Investment (millions of rupees)	Workers employed	Ammonia plant (tons/day)	Nutrient capacity (thousand tons/year) N	P₂O₅
Public sector							N	P₂O₅
Alwaye	1947	Naphtha	4	393	6,428	355[a]	92	36
Sindri	1951	Coal	5	469	7,139	463[a]	117	—
Nangal	1961	Electricity	3	312	3,284	307	80	—
Rourkela	1963	Off-gas	—	—	1,708	—	120	—
Trombay	1965	Naphtha	4	456	2,107	350	90	45
Neyveli	1966	Lignite	6	388	1,594	285	70	—
Gorakhpur	1969	Naphtha	5	349	2,013	350	45	—
Namrup	1969	Natural gas	6	243	2,074	200	45	—
Private sector								
Varanasi	1959	Coal	—	55	—	40	10	—
Ennore	1963	Naphtha	—	84	756	66	16	10
Baroda	1967	Naphtha	—	630	1,624	950[a]	230	55
Visakhapatnam	1968	Naphtha	—	487	945	325	85	75
Kota	1969	Naphtha	2	464	1,199	450	120	—
Kanpur	1969	Naphtha	3	610	992	830	207	—

Sources: Data from Fertilizer Association of India 1973; and AID 1970.
[a] In two plants.

United States longshoremen's strike and a typhoon.[5] Ingenious planning and faultless execution were rewarded with an extremely low investment cost and trouble-free operation.

An Evaluation

Table 7.6 brings together roughly comparable investment costs per ton in the three Asian countries and a composite figure for seventeen U.S. firms. The latter represent single-train urea plants based on natural gas ammonia facilities, using the centrifugal compressor technology.[6] Computational

[5] A full chronicle of this project is provided by a series of articles in *Industry of Free China* 20(11), November 1961. In 1970, in response to political pressures generated by a farm recession, the government reduced the ex-factory price of urea to $95 per ton, which was under Miaoli's cost. Under these circumstances TFC was obliged to buy out Mobil-Allied.
[6] The data for the United States were collected in a careful investigation by a team of researchers at Michigan State University. See Henderson and others 1972, Tables A-1, A-8, A-30, and B-2.

Table 7.6.   Investment cost per ton of nitrogen capacity, 1950–70

Plant	Start-up	Investment cost[a] ($ millions)	Domestic content (%)	Investment cost at SER[b] ($ millions)	Investment cost per ton[c] (1970 $)
United States					
Average 17 firms	1967	40.1	100	40.1	169
Pakistan					
Daudkhel	1958	19.1	40	15.3	2,227
Multan	1963	53.8	35	44.4	800
Esso-Dharki	1968	45.5	46	35.0	459
Taiwan					
Mobil-Allied	1963	23.0	43	23.0	296
India					
Public sector					
Sindri	1951	98.5	40	78.8	1,452
Nangal	1961	65.5	54	47.9	1,095
Neyveli	1966	81.5	52	60.3	1,430
Namrup	1969	32.4	70	24.8	683
Private sector					
Kanpur	1969	81.3	65	63.9	335
Kota	1969	61.9	50	51.6	467

[a]Converted to dollars at official exchange rates: Pakistan rupee, $1 = 4.76 Rs; Indian rupee, $1 = 4.76 Rs prior to 1967 and 7.5 Rs after. The investment cost of Mobil-Allied was reported in dollars.

[b]Investment cost when domestic content was revalued at shadow exchange rates (SER): Pakistan rupee, $1 = 9.52 Rs; Indian rupee, $1 = 9.52 Rs prior to 1967 and 11.25 Rs after. No overvaluation in the case of the new Taiwan dollar.

[c]SER investment cost adjusted for inflation and divided by tons of nitrogen capacity.

procedures were such as to understate the Pakistan and Indian investment costs.[7]

The range in investment cost is not the 1.4 or 1.5 multiple of the U.S. standard assumed in the ex ante feasibility studies; rather, it is typically four to eight times the $169 norm. For those plants above $1,000, much of the explanation is related to obsolescent technology in ammonia production involving coal, lignite, or water electrolysis. Among later Asian plants, private sector projects have been less expensive, particularly so for the 1963 Mobil-Allied investment. The Esso-Dharki factory is closest in vintage to the U.S. composite; yet, the investment cost is 2.7 times higher. The superiority of the U.S. facility is partly due to advanced technology, the scale of output, and the lower delivered cost of equipment and engineering services. Centrifugal compressors were not used in India or Pakistan until 1971.

[7] There are two sources of underestimation. Many projects received loans on which no interest charges were levied during construction. Second, the choice of shadow prices for domestic content (extremely low as an average for the periods they cover) and the assumption that local purchases were completely free of foreign exchange content also introduce a downward bias.

In this early (1950–70) period comparative disadvantage in creating output *capacity* placed these countries under an extreme handicap before production ever commenced. Equally, comparative advantage in *production* was undermined by high input prices and low capacity utilization derivative from a host of operational problems—electricity interruptions, unavailability of railcars, labor strikes, diversion of feedstock, breakdowns.[8] Although private sector plants fared better, "the vagaries of electric power supply, railway transportation and coal supply, all of which are in the public sector, affect the efficiency of operations of *all* fertilizer plants, both public and private" (T. N. Srinivasan in Segura 1985, p. 60). In 1971–72 average utilization in forty developing countries was 56 percent for nitrogen plants and 52 percent for phosphate plants. Thus, the already-high capital cost rises another 40 to 60 percent per unit of achieved output.

At a minimum estimate, the cost of production of fertilizer in Pakistan, Taiwan, and India ranged from 50 to 110 percent above the cost of imports. In most other developing countries it was even higher. Clearly, during these two pioneering decades movements toward self-sufficiency exacted an extraordinarily heavy toll.

COMPARATIVE ADVANTAGE: THE EVIDENCE, 1970–90

Conditions in the period 1970–90 have been far more favorable. National governments, public sector engineering companies, international engineering firms, and aid donors have all benefited from twenty years of learning. The pace of technological change has slowed, and most investments are not "greenfield" but expansions at existing sites.

The eleven projects in the sample for the last two decades (Table 7.7) are drawn from World Bank–financed ventures that had been up and running for at least four years at the time of their evaluation. They were rigorously screened when the loan application was made and are in countries that are "among the largest and more industrially advanced of the Bank's clients" (World Bank 1986a, p. i). Two of them rank among the most successful industrial projects ever financed by the Bank. Thus, the performance of this group should be considerably more favorable than for the industry at large.

Pakistan

The Bank's first loan was to the private Dawood-Hercules venture in Pakistan, a large natural gas-based plant employing the new centrifugal compressor technology. With the Fluor Corporation as the general contractor,

[8] For a discussion of operational efficiency and the cost of production during this period, see Johnston and Kilby 1975, pp. 344–48.

Table 7.7. Eleven fertilizer projects, 1971–83

Plant	Start-up[a]	Months under construction	Investment cost (millions of current $) Esti-mated[b]	Actual[b]	FE (%)[c]	Nutrient capacity (N, tons, in 1,000s)	Overrun Time (%)	Cost (%)	Cost per ton[d] N-capacity (1984 $)[e]	Utilization 1983 (%)	1984 (%)
Dawood-Hercules (Pakistan)	1971	19	78.4	84.1	55	169	8	7	1,741	94	100
Gorakhpur (India)	1976	41	16.0	23.0	50	62	37	44	1,146	56	59
PUSRI III (Indonesia)	1977	39	192.9	178.3	81	262	-3	-8	1,217	103	113
Nangal (India)	1977	55	91.5	154.5	30	226	92	68	1,294	79	88
Multan (Pakistan)	1979	53	84.4	235.7	58	186	121	179	2,310	81	82
Sindri (India)	1979	56	174.5	187.8	30	226	36	7	1,589	78	78
Talkha II (Egypt)	1980	61	123.5	194.7	69	262	103	58	1,623	67	67
FERTIMEX-Bajio (Mexico)	1980	60	45.2	71.1	22	—	35	57	—	67	31
PUSRI IV (Indonesia)	1980	29	186.0	142.5	80	262	-12	-23	1,220	105	106
FERTIMEX-ISTMO (Mexico)	1982	78	81.1	205.2	21	—	90	153	—	—	—
Ashuganj (Bangladesh)	1983	91	249.4	433.3	57	243	90	74	2,625	52	71

Sources: World Bank, following reports: 1345, Pakistan Dawood-Hercules Urea Project; 3582, Multan Fertilizer Expansion Project; 4455, Egypt-Talkha II Fertilizer Project; 5382, Mexico-Fertilizer I Project; 5419, PUSRI III and IV; 6073, Sustainability of Projects.

[a] Start-up refers to the start of operations for the completed project.

[b] Estimated and actual investments are both in current dollars.

[c] Foreign exchange content.

[d] Cost per ton of N-capacity is: cost adjusted to 1984 dollars divided by annual nitrogen capacity (330 days/year). The percentage of utilization is taken from the World Bank Documents listed in Sources.

[e] N-capacity is calculated as 46% of urea capacity, 22.5% of NP capacity, and 25% of CAN capacity.

this project was planned in 1968 with construction beginning in 1969 and start-up in 1971. The $84 million urea facility set a record for the Indian subcontinent, with a cost overrun of only 7 percent. Moreover, from the third year, the plant was running at or near full capacity.

The Bank's second effort in Pakistan was less successful. In 1974 a major expansion of the public sector plant at Multan was planned. The pre-1963 reciprocal-compressor technology would be replaced with a 910-ton-per-day (tpd) centrifugal compressor, and nitrophosphate would be added to the product mix. Construction was completed in July 1978, twenty-nine months behind schedule and 179 percent over budget. The cost overrun was due to the usual public sector viruses: poor planning and over-optimism.[9] Unfortunately, that was not all. Because of design flaws, capacity of the NP plant was scaled down from 220 to 180 tpd. Even then, it did not reach 80 percent capacity utilization until the fifth year of operation. Moreover, because of the low quality of the imported Jordanian rock phosphate (used to minimize foreign exchange costs) and of the failure of the licensor adequately to adapt its process to this type of rock, the nutrient content of the nitrophosphate is 15 percent below standard.

Mexico

Like Pakistan's and India's, Mexico's fertilizer industry is comparatively well developed. All thirteen plants are government owned. The two urea ventures here (Bajio and Istmo) were limited to the "fourth stage," converting ammonia and carbon dioxide from nearby PEMEX plants. They experienced construction delays of 43 percent and 90 percent, respectively. Both projects encountered major problems with local contractors. At Bajio the construction firm lacked the technical know-how to complete the final 40 percent of the work; at Istmo the engineering contractor was to blame. Loss of skilled workers, delays in delivery of detailed specifications from equipment suppliers, and shortages of structural steel could be linked to Mexico's construction boom.

But the principal cause of underperformance was FERTIMEX's overall project management. Their lack of competence can be traced to insufficient experience with large projects, shortage of qualified technical personnel, and management turnover. When the project was already under way, it was decided to double capacity at Istmo, requiring major modifications in off-site

---

[9] The specific elements of the overrun were (1) sharply higher-than-estimated inflation (world and Pakistan) after the 1973–74 oil crisis; (2) inaccurate estimation of civil construction requirements, such as relocating roads and railroad at the plant site, the alterations to existing buildings, exclusion of cost of purchase of construction equipment that was thought available for rental, the underestimation of land required for expansion; (3) underestimation of equipment cost by engineering firms; and (4) additional inflation resulting from the longer-than-projected implementation period.

arrangements. A change in top management after the 1976 national elections did not help. Nor did frequent changes in departmental structure and administrative procedures and an unwillingness to delegate authority to sub-project managers or to accept advice from outside experts. The results? Late placement of orders and contract payments, insufficient inspection of materials and equipment prior to shipment to the site, and lack of control over design changes and work by local contractors.

The economic impact of all of this was to raise investment costs by 57 percent for Bajio and 153 percent for Istmo. According to the Bank's ex post calculations, these plants still had a positive economic rate of return of 16 percent. In fact, correction for underestimation of the major input price and for overestimation of the price of urea discloses that both projects experienced very large negative rates of return.[10]

India

The first of three expansion projects in India, started in December 1971, was a naphtha-based plant built in the mid-1960s at Gorakpur. Originally "overdesigned," with surplus capacity in some sections, it was expected that selective investments would increase production capability by 60 percent at a unit cost well below that of a new plant. Delays in equipment delivery and depreciation of the rupee against the yen were the principal causes of overruns (see Table 7.7). Since startup in 1977 the expanded plant has never operated above 61 percent of capacity and has averaged about 50 percent. Its standby capacity was well matched to the downtime required for maintenance and equipment failure. Thus, the World Bank concluded in its 1986 "Sustainability Report" that "the additional investment has not led to a measurable increase in output and consequently the economic rate of return for the expansion is negative" (World Bank 1986a, p. 47).

Like Gorakpur, the Nangal and Sindri projects represented "debugging"/ expansion projects at existing plants run by the Fertilizer Corporation of India (FCI). However, they used more advanced technology and, owing to shortage of naphtha, were based on gasification of heavy fuel oil. Moreover, in both instances, the government was determined to curtail India's dependence on foreign technical know-how by making maximum use of local technological capabilities. As in the two Mexican plants, this is reflected in the extraordinarily low foreign exchange content of these investments (Table 7.7).

Following its loan commitment for the Nangal expansion, the Bank spent four years wrangling with the Indian government over which production

---

[10] On the basis of actual market prices for urea and ammonia, the gross value added was sufficient to cover variable costs in only two of five years; in no year was value added sufficient to cover combined fixed and variable cost. Nor can there be any case for savings of foreign exchange: the ammonia intermediate is otherwise exported.

technology should be used to produce nitrogen.[11] Construction finally began in 1972 on a 900-tpd ammonia plant, with a partial oxidation process for the production of nitrogen. Of the nitrogen output, 600 tons were to be used in a new single-train 1,000-tpd urea plant and the remaining 300 tons to be diverted to old units to produce calcium ammonium nitrate. The existing electrolysis plant and 310-tpd ammonia unit were to be shut down.

The Nagal expansion was completed two years behind schedule, with a cost overrun of 61 percent. Delays in the detailed engineering, late delivery of equipment, and damage to the urea reactor during shipment were the main reasons. Partly because of FCI's (and the contractor's) inexperience with large fuel oil–based plants, problems arose in stabilizing production. That, together with a defective boiler and raw-material shortages, resulted in capacity utilization of less than 50 percent until 1982. The project's economic rate of return (ERR) was further reduced because the old electrolysis and ammonia units continued to run.[12]

The Sindri expansion was virtually identical in feedstock, process design, and scale to that of Nangal, but it greatly benefited from Nangal's experience. The overrun was smaller in both time and cost. Sindri also relied more on Indian equipment. In the final Nangal compromise, foreign engineering firms were responsible for the basic design of the ammonia and urea plants, FCI for the detailed engineering and procurement of equipment. At Sindri a big Indian firm, which had assembled imported components for the three turbocompressors for Nangal, insisted that it would manufacture the components as well. The compressors were sophisticated, and the Indian company had never manufactured such equipment. The Bank, which felt that such a decision was not prudent, eventually withdrew finance for those items. In the event, there were problems, and a supervisor from the foreign licensor was brought in to complete the work.

Sindri's capacity utilization did not reach 80 percent during any of its first six years. Fuel inputs per unit of product have been well above design norms. Although there has been downtime because of the railway's failure to deliver the requisite fuel oil feedstock and because of excessive ash in the coal, the major problem has been mechanical.

[11] Indian authorities wanted to base the process on free oxygen from an existing water electrolysis plant, which entailed linking subprocesses (for which FCI already held licenses) that had not been previously used in an integrated form. The Bank opposed this plan because gasification technology was changing rapidly. FCI had no commercial experience with the process, which involved higher capital and operating costs than the orthodox process based on heavy fuel oil. The specific partial oxidation process employed was that recommended by the Bank. FCI's preferred low-pressure process was implemented in two other plants with which the Bank was not associated. These two, Durgapur and Cochin I, have had a history of technical problems, and neither have achieved acceptable capacity utilization.

[12] Because the electrolysis unit was charged only one-quarter of an economic price for its electricity, its operation is highly profitable. On the other hand, when thermal power is priced at true scarcity value, the ammonia cost is twice the c.i.f. import price.

Six other new large gas-based urea plants in India (private and public) all are achieving high capacity utilization but, owing to high capital cost of $2,150 per ton of capacity, the economic cost of production far exceeds c.i.f. price of imports (Pradahn 1988). This effect also holds for six public sector plants built in the 1970s, but for these the problems are high rates of feed-stock consumption and average capacity utilization of 62 percent.

The average capacity utilization of the Indian fertilizer industry was 68 percent in the 1970s and 73 percent in the 1980s. To this handicap was added dependence on high-cost feedstocks, with natural gas accounting for only 42 percent in 1989, up from 13 percent in 1980 (*Agro-Chemicals* 1990, p. 33).

Indonesia

So far, the evidence against public sector fertilizer plants, accounting for nearly 90 percent of all Third World output, is damning. However, one (in Indonesia) is among the most successful industrial projects ever financed by the Bank (World Bank 1985b).

The government-owned P. T. Pupuk Sriwijaya (PUSRI) is Indonesia's largest fertilizer manufacturer. PUSRI I began production in 1964, with an initial expansion completed ten years later. Work started on PUSRI III in April 1974 and on PUSRI IV in June 1975, with completion times of 39 and 32 months, respectively. The projects were finished ahead of schedule, 15 percent under cost, and quickly reached full capacity. What was different about PUSRI III and IV?

They came on the heels of the just-completed PUSRI II. Experienced management was in place, and the same contractors for the urea and ammonia plants (Kellogg and Mitsubishi, respectively) could be used without a lengthy qualification process. Likewise, expatriate consultants from the earlier project were reemployed as legal advisers, technical advisers, marketing consultants, and financial management consultants. Moreover, the two new plants were identical; any problems encountered in PUSRI III were rectified before PUSRI IV.[13] A bonus/penalty clause gave contractors an incentive for early completion. A "master letter of credit" short-circuited long delays in approvals from customs and the Central Bank that were normal in Indonesia then—and are prevalent in most other developing countries.[14]

---

[13] PUSRI III included a number of infrastructural items (storage tanks, electricity-generating unit, bagging plant) to serve the entire complex. In PUSRI IV the major extraplant component was a training center for the national industry.

[14] The normal procedure was for each procurement package to have a letter of credit for foreign exchange purchases, whether or not these funds came from the Central Bank. After long delays encountered in PUSRI II, a "divisible, irrevocable, transferable master letter of credit" for part of total project cost was approved by Bank Indonesia and issued by an Indonesian bank in favor of PUSRI's consultants through their foreign banks. Individual letters of credit and the documents of purchase were returned to Indonesia and debited against the authorities. Following the post-procurement review, the master letter of credit was resupplied with another advance against the total foreign exchange allocation to the project.

There was comprehensive training for hundreds of individuals in Indonesia and overseas; assignment of supervisory personnel to the head office of the engineering firms in Houston and Tokyo; and a large training center in Indonesia with courses (using sophisticated simulators) given by the ammonia and urea contractors, by vendors' service personnel, and by management consulting firms.

Uniquely, PUSRI deferred to overseas contractors and the World Bank on virtually all matters of technology, training, and project management. Thus, project execution had more in common with Mobil-Allied or Dawood-Hercules than with Multan or Bajio. There was no attempt to achieve either foreign exchange savings or ex ante low cost investment at the risk of something other than the best outcome.

Did Indonesia take to heart the thirty years of errors by its neighbors and redefine the public sector paradigm? Probably. It has five state-owned companies working closely with foreign technical partners and efficiently running a dozen large ammonia–urea plants. But there have been a few failures. The 1984 Kaltim I plant, built against all advice on floating barges, had to be relocated on land at a cost overrun of almost 200 percent. Indonesian officials say that they want greater local participation in plant design and engineering; yet, the government continues to abide by loan covenants of the Japanese and American Export-Import Banks reserving much control on these matters to overseas firms. Although this aspect is not unique to Indonesia, the industry is subsidized (charged $1 or less per MBTU of natural gas compared to the liquified natural gas f.o.b. export price to Japan of $2.50–3.50). Even so, with self-sufficiency and urea exports of half a million tons, the Indonesian public sector record is remarkable.

An Evaluation

The major performance characteristics of the nine projects of the past two decades are summarized in Table 7.7. Two additional Bank projects are included. Talkha II was a public sector expansion in Egypt; its construction saw the familiar range of snarls and ultimately ended up with heavy reliance on foreign contractors. As of 1986, annual utilization had not exceeded the 76 percent achieved in the second year. Ashuganj is a greenfield project located in Bangladesh's natural gas fields. A public sector undertaking involving a large consortium of donors, it too has failed to achieve high rates of utilization.

The cost per ton of capacity in 1984 dollars is shown in the ninth column of Table 7.7. The high domestic content of the Indian plants generally results in lower cost. The higher figure for Dawood-Hercules vis-à-vis the other private investments is the difference between a greenfield and an expansion project.

The variation in observed investment costs is less than in the 1950–70 period. Here the differences are two- and threefold as against four- to sixfold.

How much of this improvement is due to selection bias, because of the Bank's unwillingness to support lower-quality projects, cannot be known. But some improvement would be consistent with "learning by doing" and the absence of abrupt technological change.

Despite the improvement, as seen in Table 7.8 fertilizer production in these countries is still far from achieving competitive capital costs. The investment cost per ton of capacity shown in the first column is lower than the comparable figures in Table 7.7 owing to adjustment for overvalued exchange rates. The second column factors in that part of operational efficiency reflected in capacity utilization. The final column expresses this as a percentage of the comparable U.S. investment cost. Even the most efficient Indonesian plants have a capital cost 100+ percent higher than the American benchmark. For the eight-country sample average, the figure is 246 percent above the U.S. average. To this disabling handicap with respect to capital cost should be added, in many cases, a higher per-unit consumption of fuel and feedstock.

THE POLITICAL ECONOMY OF FERTILIZER INVESTMENT

The political dimension is a puzzle. Given powerful a priori reasons why most CARLs could expect to be at a severe comparative disadvantage, why in the 1950s and 1960s did they invest their limited funds in fertilizer production? And why, given over thirty years of dismal performance, have they persisted over the past twenty years in this costly mistake?

An examination of official documents on the earliest fertilizer projects in India, Pakistan, and Taiwan suggest that systematic assessments of comparative advantage were not undertaken. Instead, given available feedstock and a local market of sufficient size, it was decided that it would be desirable to move toward self-sufficiency in this basic agricultural input. Self-sufficiency and the conservation of scarce foreign exchange have continued to underpin the rationale for fertilizer investments in the forty years since.[15]

[15] A statement by the Executive Director of the Indian Fertilizer Association illustrates both the argument and its highly charged opacity: "Because of the lower price of imports, it is sometimes suggested that importing would be cheaper than increasing production at high-cost plants. This conclusion is not valid. India cannot base its long-term supplies on temporary declines in international prices. Second, developing countries like India face acute shortages of foreign exchange. Long-term planning has to be aimed at achieving a reasonable degree of self-sufficiency to conserve foreign exchange, particularly when raw materials are available indigenously. Finally, the increase in the average cost of production is the result of output from recently commissioned plants and of the steep increase in input prices. It is inappropriate to compare the costs of production at these newer plants with imports coming from old plants. Similarly, the prices of inputs are not comparable. For instance, the price of gas, particularly in the Gulf countries, is very low as compared to India, as is true for naphtha and fuel oil" (Pratap Narayan, "Fertilizer Pricing in India," in Segura and others 1986, p. 151). It would be hard to find a more succinct statement of comparative *dis*advantage than that given in the executive director's last two sentences.

Table 7.8.   Investment cost per ton of nitrogen (1984 $, at parallel market exchange rate)

Plant	Per ton of capacity	Per ton produced	Per ton produced (U.S. = 100)
U.S. average	501	496	100
Dawood-Hercules (Pakistan)	1,280	1,320	266
PUSRI III (Indonesia)	1,210	1,120	225
Nangal (India)	868	1,040	210
Multan (Pakistan)	2,063	2,531	510
Sindri (India)	1,066	1,367	276
Talkha II (Egypt)	1,353	2,019	407
PUSRI IV (Indonesia)	1,213	1,150	232
Ashuganj (Bangladesh)	1,959	3,185	642

Note: The cost per ton of capacity is adjusted downward for the overvaluation of its domestic currency content, using parallel market exchange rates from *International Currency Yearbooks*. The cost per ton produced is calculated by dividing capacity by the 1983–84 utilization level. The U.S. average is based on fifty plants, roughly 75 percent of the industry, with data supplied by the Fertilizer Institute.

Following the OPEC price spike of 1974–75, one aspect of self-sufficiency was raised to an independent argument: a local fertilizer industry provides farmers with insulation against the volatility of world markets for this critical production input, with all that implies for food security.[16]

More than thirty years of experience provide ample evidence to refute these arguments. That the record has gone largely unexamined suggests that other forces are at work. Economic nationalism? These large technologically advanced plants have been heralded by governments and the local press as important aspects of industrialization. They are particularly attractive to those countries such as India or Mexico that have stressed basic industries and heavy engineering as critical elements in their development strategy.

Other motives may be more selfish, advantaging one group at the expense of the whole country. In this, fertilizer is not unique. First, investment in a

[16] These points were reiterated in 1984 at an international seminar on fertilizer pricing with participants from ten nations. Despite the potential for higher costs, they held that domestic industry as a source of supply was preferable to imports. "Furthermore, other factors such as utilization of local resources, search for self-reliance, industrial policy and regional development imperatives are always considered by governments when analyzing the feasibility of local production" (Segura and others 1986, p. 15).

nitrogen or phosphate plant creates a strong locality benefit in employment during construction and a small amount of direct employment thereafter. Second, because most fertilizer plants are publicly owned, investing in local production rather than importing expands the public sector. An increase in its size vis-à-vis the autonomous market enhances the power, patronage, and economic control of elected officials and civil servants—the very individuals asked to make an impartial decision.

The third and most narrow localization is the opportunity that such investment creates for collecting "rent." Because of its financial scale ($100 million to $400 million), because no two designs and costs are the same, and because of catch-all "cost overruns," fertilizer plants are uniquely suited to illegal multimillion dollar markups.[17]

Donor Delusion

But perhaps the decisive factor in the plethora of uneconomic fertilizer plants in developing countries has been the role of international donors. They have actively supported the drive to fertilizer self-sufficiency. It began with the United States in the early 1950s and has since been taken up by the World Bank, regional development banks, the Food and Agriculture Organization (FAO), and the United Nations Industrial Development Organization (UNIDO). In 1970 the World Bank established a special division to help would-be borrowers to perfect loan applications, to assist in international contracts, and to set up management systems to control the complex process of plant construction.[18] Between 1969 and 1985 the Bank lent $3.4 billion for Third World construction of fertilizer plants.

After the 1973 OPEC price hike, some UN agencies and the Bank formed the Commission on Fertilizers. Each year the commission publishes five-year world supply and demand projections, with recommendations on new capacity to be located in the less developed countries. It also regularly publishes a report (in essence, a generic feasibility study) estimating investment costs and rates of return for nitrogen and phosphate plants, given various feedstocks and needed infrastructure investment.

---

[17] Junaid Ahmad, Walter Falcon, and Peter Timmer, whose experience is in Pakistan, Bangladesh, and Indonesia, suggest the overcharge is around 20 percent, "split between the supplier and the government officials responsible for accepting bids" (Ahmad and others 1988, p. 42). In the Middle East the markups may be considerably higher (Strassmann 1989).

[18] The Bank's 1970 decision to support fertilizer investment on a major scale was not related to price volatility or comparative advantage. Rather, it seems to have implicitly accepted the notion of self-sufficiency: "The heavy involvement of the Bank in expanding fertilizer production arose from the increased attention given at the time to world food production and agricultural development as the green revolution required not only the new high-yielding seed varieties but also additional complementary inputs such as fertilizer" (World Bank 1986a, p. i). The alternative of relying on inexpensive imports appears not to have been considered.

It is at the level of the feasibility study that donor bias is most critical. In World Bank feasibility studies "engineering optimism" takes precedence over "behavioral realism" with respect to investment costs (often assumed to be 40 percent above the U.S. benchmark) and capacity utilization (assumed to be 90 percent). But systematic optimism is also present in estimating future input and output prices.[19] The most critical price projection, which has maximum impact on value added and the profit margin, is that of the finished product. In making such projections, a roughly equal number of estimates might be expected to lie above and below the ex post actual price.

As seen in Table 7.9 these projections have been systematically and substantially higher than the actual prices, providing false justification for many fertilizer investments. And the pattern is much the same in the pre-1979 period.[20] These overestimations meant that many approved projects could not have succeeded, even with a "perfect performance" in investment cost and operational efficiency (for example, Bajio).

Another piece of the puzzle is support from some academics (and opposition from none). These are mainly agricultural economists who emphasize the volatility of world fertilizer prices. They support substantial autarky to ensure a stable input price, as well as macroeconomic stability in balance of payments and government budget.[21] Empirical studies, perhaps influenced

---

[19] Little and Mirrlees (1990, pp. 358–63) document the inflation in estimated ERRs in World Bank appraisal reports that first occurred in the mid-1970s during the McNamara administration. Working from a sample of 2,000 investment projects, mostly in the public sector, the average ERR rose from 17 percent in 1968 to 29 percent in 1980. Ex post ERRs, calculated several years after project completion, remained constant at 13 to 17 percent. Consistently upward-biased price projections are identified, interestingly, as a key ingredient in this process.

[20] At the Eleventh Session of the Fertilizer Commission in April 1990, William Sheldrick, a central figure in the IBRD/FAO/UNIDO working group, said: "At one time, particularly during the 1970s, when many large fertilizer plants were being appraised, urea price projections were made on the basis that in a constantly increasing market, prices would have to rise to justify new investments. They were also made on the basis that gas prices in the developed countries would increase with increasing oil prices up to about $5 per mbtu, whereas natural gas in the plant being appraised would stay at a much lower opportunity cost of about $1. Many plants were approved on the basis that urea prices would rise to $250 per ton and more. Undoubtedly, this approach, which now appears naive and over-optimistic, resulted in some cases of uneconomic plants being built and aggravated the situation of oversupply and low prices that has basically prevailed since about 1979" (Sheldrick 1990, p. 3).

[21] See for example Ahmad and others 1988. Although Ahmad, Falcon, and Timmer stress that domestic cost of production must be "reasonable" and that some imports are desirable to make up shortfalls in local output, their general conclusion is that instability resulting from total reliance on imports "may dampen the entire growth process as well as threaten the political survival of any government that attempts such a strategy" (p. 44). From the other side, T. N. Srinivasan has questioned the volatility of fertilizer prices when deflated by a suitable index of crop prices and pointed out that home production and subsidized retail fertilizer prices are not the appropriate policy instruments for the intended goals. Nevertheless, noting that policymakers *perceive* a volatility problem, that self-sufficiency is an unquestioned goal, and that the state is already deeply involved in production and distribution, the author limits his attention to moderate reforms of the system as it now exists (Segura and others 1986, chap. 2).

Table 7.9. World Bank price projections for project evaluation (bagged urea, f.o.b. Western Europe, $ per ton)

	Actual price	Projected prices				
		Sindri (5/79)	PUSRI (11/80)	Talka (6/81)	Bajio (12/82)	Ashuganj (5/86)
1979	146	160	—	—	—	—
1980	222	155	215	—	—	—
1981	217	155	211	230	—	—
1982	160	160	216	236	208	—
1983	124	175	233	251	221	—
1984	171	185	251	268	247	—
1985	136	195	270	285	280	—
1986	107	195	273	288	294	133
1987	117	195	276	291	294	152
1988	155	195	278	294	294	166
1989	137	195	281	297	318	180
1990	144	195	284	300	318	192

Note: These long-term projections are made and revised at regular intervals by the International Economics Department of the Bank. They are used in both the Appraisal Report and the Project Performance Audit Report.

by the obscure and convoluted financial arrangements that shroud most fertilizer ventures, have tended to be limited to the application of programming models based on ex ante data.

Of course, the most important fail-safe mechanism should have been ex post evaluation studies of each of these costly investments. Valid studies on the economic rate of return of these projects have simply not been undertaken—either by the public investors or by the donors. Determined optimism shut out reality. World Bank "Completion Reports" and "Performance Audit Reports" ostensibly undertake rate of return analysis, but as they invariably utilize the same optimistic ex ante prices employed in the original feasibility study—even when actual prices are available—their results are invalid.

This syndrome was most dramatically revealed in the major 1986 *Review of Experience in the Fertilizer Subsector*. In this retrospective policy study the Bank explicitly rejected the use of actual prices! It did so on the grounds that actual prices were beyond the control of those who implement projects—thus confusing the evaluation of implementation with the evaluation of projects.[22] The finding that five of seven of our projects, for which the calculation could be made, had economic rates of return ranging from 15 to

[22] "For the purpose of recalculating the ERRs, the Project Completion Report estimates have been adjusted by replacing projected data with actual production and inputs for the years through 1984, and modifying projections for subsequent years on the basis of recent operating experience. [However] No *adjustment has been made to economic prices of either inputs or outputs as given in the Project Completion Reports; they are beyond the control of each project*" (italics added) (World Bank 1986, p. viii).

42 percent provides implicit justification for further investments.[23] At actual prices, only two projects at best would have positive rates of return. So, this second error, resulting from the organizational imperative in the World Bank to make large project loans, precluded donors from learning from their first mistake. Optimism was sustained.

WHY CARLS SHOULD IMPORT FERTILIZER

In 1950–70 nitrogen fertilizer production in developing countries was more costly than importing. This stemmed from technological obsolescence and the absence of comparative advantage. In 1970–90 there was more moderate, less disruptive technical advance, but still a large comparative disadvantage. This disadvantage is rooted in the inherently more costly process of creating technically sophisticated industrial capacity in developing countries, in the higher cost of finance of each dollar needed to create this capacity, and in managerial and infrastructural shortcomings that lead to its less than full utilization.

Two of these factors can be translated into differences in comparative cost. By deriving investment cost per ton of urea (from Table 7.8) and by taking industry norms reported by Sheldrick (1987, p. 46) on such "fixed costs" as labor, administration, maintenance, and insurance, a cost function can be constructed.[24] Assuming uniform plant life (twenty years), cost of capital (a conservative 10 percent), and cost of natural gas ($1 per MBTU), a unit cost schedule can be drawn (Figure 7.3). Based on the sample of nine firms, this schedule isolates the handicap, relative to imports, imposed by high cost capacity and less than full utilization.

All of the plants are producing at an economic cost well above the world price (Figure 7.3). And this is likely an underestimate. If the opportunity cost of finance is greater than 10 percent, if natural gas has other uses with a higher payback than $1 per mbtu, or if the plants consume more fuel and feedstock per unit of output than plants in exporting countries, then the true cost of each ton of urea exceeds imports by more than the $40 to $150 shown.

Given that the insurance premium entailed in a policy of self-sufficiency is so high, what of the benefits this insurance policy is intended to provide? The first benefit is protection against price volatility. However, for twenty-seven of the past thirty years, the *maximum point of price variation* for nitrogen

---

[23] The economic rates of return as calculated were: Talkha II at 15 percent, Gorakpur at an unspecified negative return, Sindri at negative 2 percent, Multan at 19 percent, Bajio at 19 percent, PUSRI III at 32 percent, and PUSRI IV at 42 percent.

[24] The unit cost function (UC) employed is as follows: $UC = g + 1/Cu[FC + IC(1 - S/N_y + IRR)]$, where g = cost of energy per unit of output; FC = fixed cost of labor, administration, maintenance, and insurance; IC = investment cost; S = end-of-life salvage value at discounted present value; C = plant capacity; N_y = factory's lifespan in years; IRR = rate of return on total capital employed; u = proportion of capacity utilized.

Figure 7.3. The economic cost of production (circa 1984–88)

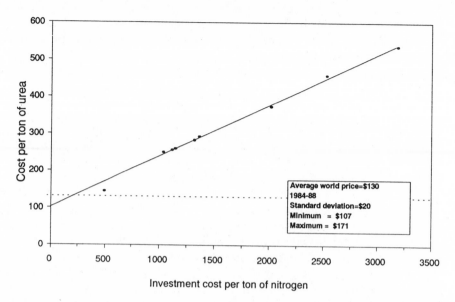

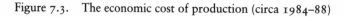

fertilizer fell *below* the cost of domestic manufacture in CARLs. Clearly, volatility is less of a financial burden than the "solution" of self-sufficiency.[25]

The second intended benefit is avoidance of an absolute shortage, with its disruptive impact on the national food supply. Given the highly dispersed world fertilizer industry, and the immunity of its feedstock to the short-term vagaries of weather or economy, a significant shortage is unlikely. Indeed, the sole instance cited is the so-called "fertilizer crisis" of 1974. Yet, both production and consumption of fertilizer *rose* in 1974 (FAO 1978). With widespread drought and rising prices of food and energy, international donors endorsed the existence of a "fertilizer crisis" at the World Food Conference of 1974. In so doing, they fueled speculation that drove the price of urea to $360 per ton by the year's end. As donors have recently acknowledged, there was no shortage, and by July 1975 the price was back to $140.[26]

[25] Regarding the two brief periods of OPEC price hikes, speculative frenzy drove the price of urea up some 400 percent from its 1972 low (1972–74) and again by 52 percent in 1979–80. However, if the urea price change is deflated by the rise in crop prices, the true increase to the farmer is on the order of 150 percent and 27 percent, respectively.

[26] In his 1990 paper William Sheldrick states: "[It was] the psychological reaction to a perceived food and fertilizer shortage that made urea fertilizer prices increase by more than 200 percent in 1974. Certainly there would have been no great shortage of nitrogen fertilizers at the time if offtake had been in a reasonable and orderly manner. A post-examination today would indicate that as far as nitrogen supply/demand balance was concerned, the balance is as tight now as it was then. . . . Certainly, in retrospect information available to the World Food Conference of 1974 was far from perfect, and in particular, failed to account for the large amount of new capacity then being built" (Sheldrick 1990, p. 20).

The final intended benefit of self-sufficiency is conservation of foreign exchange. Calculation of the foreign exchange savings entails estimating the foreign currency content of domestic output and subtracting it from the c.i.f. cost of imports. The foreign exchange portion of domestic production is made up of directly imported inputs used by the manufacturer and its supplier industries, plus the indirect opportunity costs for those local inputs that might have earned, or saved, foreign exchange elsewhere (for example, naphtha, skilled labor). Inputs that have no foreign currency opportunity cost are such items as unskilled labor, insurance, indirect taxes, and feedstocks that would not otherwise be used (for example, flared natural gas). Such calculations were carried out by I. M. D. Little and his associates for India in the 1960s (OECD 1968, chap. 4). They estimated that 64 percent of variable inputs and 70 percent of investment and other fixed overheads have a foreign exchange opportunity cost. In calculating it they assumed an 80 percent utilization rate; the actual rate was 68 percent. At no time during the 1960s (including 1965–66 when import prices were high) did the Indian fertilizer industry save foreign exchange. On the contrary. Domestic production of 1 ton of nitrogen fertilizer involved a greater sacrifice of foreign exchange than did direct importation.

In sum, given the low nontradable content of fertilizer, it is clear why the decision to undertake domestic production does not conserve foreign exchange. When the world price of fertilizer rises above the cost of domestic manufacture, the avoided domestic price increase is just offset by a loss in foreign exchange elsewhere—higher import costs of fuel or petrochemical products or lowered export earnings. The balance-of-payments deficit is unaffected by the decision to be self-sufficient.

The Gains from Specialization

What are the gains to be reaped by turning away from self-sufficiency? With fertilizer priced at true opportunity cost, there is an indirect gain in allocational efficiency, as producers and consumers in adjacent markets obtain better information. Then, there is the direct gain from redeploying resources to the production of other goods.

To obtain a rough idea of this direct benefit it is necessary to estimate (1) the quantity of investment resources freed up for other uses, and (2) the difference in the likely average economic rate of return in those uses compared to fertilizer production. Projected construction needs over the next decade include 25 million nutrient tons of new capacity, plus replacement of 20 million tons of obsolete and worn-out plants; of this, 60 percent is likely to be in developing economies (Sheldrick 1990, p. 23). Investment per ton is estimated at $1,430 on the assumption of an even split between "greenfield" sites ($1,650) and "expansion" sites ($1,200). The resources thus freed up are $38.6 billion. The likely ERR for new fertilizer investment is between –5 and +5 percent; the rate for alternate uses is perhaps 12 percent.[27] Even this rough calculation suggests that investing in line with comparative advantage and importing fertilizer will increase national incomes by $2.7 billion to $6.6 billion.[28] If the same were applied to investment in phosphate fertilizer, another 20 percent would be added to these figures.

Can a case be made that the very largest countries are an exception? Specifically, are potential terms of trade effects from their entrance into the import market sufficient to offset the high cost of local manufacture? There have indeed been upward price movements when India or China has made unusually large purchases, but they have lasted but a few months at most, and in no case was the increased fertilizer import price equal to their cost disadvantage in manufacture. On the basis of the past thirty years one can say the expected benefit of this strategy has been very small while the expected cost has been large.

The evidence should give pause to any CARL considering an import substitution strategy for fertilizer. Their relative endowments of labor, capital, and management put most CARLs (even most large countries with abundant low-cost feedstock) at a comparative disadvantage in fertilizer production. Small purchasers lack even a theoretical basis for concern about the effects of their policies on world prices. Moreover, smaller countries do not have the scope for the repeated, costly process of learning by doing.

Taiwan's Mobil-Allied provides a best-case scenario for the typical CARL, where inputs must be imported. Even though plant installation was exemplary, investment costs per unit of capacity were high in Taiwan, because of restricted scale. Importing raw materials for reexport of fertilizer to achieve economies of scale does not make sense for CARLs: transport costs for these bulky raw materials are prohibitive. Mexico, another middle-income country shows that investment in fertilizer production can be uneconomic even with domestic feedstock.

Indonesia's success, at least with nitrogen, is the exception that proves the rule. By eschewing typical public sector policies, by maximum reliance on foreign equipment and on foreign technical know-how, Indonesia was able to convert its abundant feedstock endowment and large market into a comparative advantage; even exports have proved profitable. Most CARLs lack Indonesia's natural gas and market size. These CARLs should import rather than expand production.

Choosing autarky (or even self-reliance) creates a fertilizer industry of a few large producers, and hence, prone to rent seeking. Certainly, costly huge projects are prime opportunities for corruption. And the creation of vast public enterprises gives rise to organizational interests that resist reform.

---

[27] The World Bank typically assumes 15 percent for this purpose.
[28] Calculated as $38.6 billion times 0.07 and 0.17, respectively.

Almost without exception, fertilizer policies have overemphasized self-sufficiency and underemphasized comparative advantage. The notions underpinning costly investments were not confined to domestic policymakers; they were shared—indeed promoted—by technical experts in the World Bank and elsewhere.

CHAPTER EIGHT

FISCAL BALANCE AND SOCIAL PROGRAM PRIORITIES

Too often, "poverty-oriented" and "growth-oriented" development strategies are depicted as mutually exclusive. They are not. Spending on education and health not only has direct benefits to individuals but also contributes to economic growth and accelerates structural transformation. Yet, governments in many CARLs assume responsibilities and provide public consumption beyond their capacity to finance and administer such programs. The result, often, is rapid inflation and a large foreign debt, which adversely affect economic growth and social programs. Allocation of public resources needs to seek a balance among investments in physical, human, and social capital because mounting imbalances between government commitments and available resources lead to macroeconomic crisis.

Achieving and maintaining such a balance depends on the demands on resources and the government's capacity and willingness to mobilize such resources through, for example, taxation and foreign aid. CARLs face a particularly difficult challenge in balancing pressing social needs with their limited fiscal resources and administrative capacity. Striking this balance depends crucially on the mix of interventions included in public initiatives. Adjustment within the public sector should involve not only reducing expenditure in line with available resources but also reprogramming those expenditures and redirecting administrative effort to better meet development objectives.

In this world of limited resources, complementarities inevitably coexist with competitive relationships. Nowhere is that more apparent than in the tensions that exist between the need for fiscal balance, so as to avoid the distortions that result from double- (or triple-) digit inflation, and the need to invest in enhancing the quality of human resources through education and public health programs. To be sure, there are also important complementarities among public investments in agricultural research, in extension programs, and in rural roads. But these agricultural sector investments do not carry the same risk of exploding bureaucracy and fiscal hemorrhage associated with certain social programs.

Judgments concerning the allocation of funds for social programs are especially important—and difficult. Governments may easily aggravate their problems of fiscal balance by creating perceived "entitlements" to expensive, open-ended social programs, such as food subsidies, that ill serve development objectives. Reversing such decisions is costly, politically and socially. But there is also a considerable risk of allocating too little to some other strategic social programs, thereby missing promising opportunities to advance both the social and economic goals of development. Even CARLs, with their severe resource constraints, are well-advised to support certain public health activities that are extremely cost-effective and that produce positive externalities. Moreover, there is potential for synergy among the positive externalities arising from social programs for education (especially for females), child survival, and voluntary family planning.

ECONOMIC STABILITY AS A PUBLIC GOOD

Economic stability is determined by the fiscal, monetary, and other macroeconomic policies of government and is therefore unavoidably a public good (see Box 8.1). In the 1950s and 1960s, inflationary finance often was advocated to mobilize resources and speed up development. The trade-off was put in these terms: "If it is impossible to increase taxation, and the alternative is between creating capital out of credit, and not creating it at all, the choice one has to make is between stable prices or rising output" (W. A. Lewis 1954, p. 403).

Since the worldwide increase in inflation in the 1970s, a new consensus has emerged that emphasizes the adverse effects of inflation. Nobel Laureate Lewis also provides a good statement of the new consensus: "The principal lesson we have all learned, LDC and MDC ["less developed country" and "more developed country"] alike, is that inflation is a terrible scourge. But how to avoid it in face of all the pressures is yet to be seen—pressure for higher real wages, for more public services, for more housing, and so on. Such pressures did not exist a century ago. In the twentieth century, governments have undertaken to provide a rising standard of living, at say 5

Box 8.1. Private Goods and Public Goods

Musgrave and Musgrave (1984, p. 50) distinguish four categories of goods and services (see table).

| | Exclusion | |
Consumption	Feasible	Not feasible
Rival	1	2
Nonrival	3	4

In *rival consumption*, consumption by one individual precludes consumption by any other. In the *nonrival* case, consumption by one individual does not reduce opportunities for others to consume that good or service.

Private goods and services are cases of rival consumption. The benefits of consumption of private goods are *internal* to the consumer (for example, consumption of food or fertilizer).

Public goods and services are nonrival in consumption. Public goods and services include positive *externalities* (for example, the benefits of national security and economic or political stability). *Externalities* are costs or benefits that are not reflected in market prices; they may be associated with production or consumption.

Feasible *exclusion* means that individual consumption can depend on the consumer paying the full cost of the good or service. If exclusion is infeasible, people can benefit without bearing the full costs.

In case 1, consumption is rival, all benefits are internal, and all costs can be internalized. This is the ideal case of private goods: the prices generated in a competitive market for these goods or services result in allocation such that no individual can be made better off without making another worse off. Case 2, often called the "free rider problem," is one case of market failure: individuals capture all benefits but can avoid bearing the costs.

Case 3 and case 4 are central to public policy choices. In either case, consumption in nonrival. Indeed, the marginal cost of consumption is zero. Therefore, infeasibility of exclusion (in case 4) does not matter, and cases 3 and 4 are commonly treated together as public goods or services. In general, markets will fail as sources of public goods because, although the costs of these goods and services would be borne by individuals, the benefits are widespread. This is the standard case in which government expenditure on public goods and services results in net welfare gains relative to the market.

percent a year, whereas in fact they do not know how to reach 2 percent" (W. A. Lewis 1988, p. 22).

High rates of inflation are not only the result of ill-informed policies; they also are the consequence of real social pressures. High inflation often leads to overvaluation of the exchange rate and to large changes in relative prices of products and factors of production. It is usually the direct cause of negative real interest rates, and by compounding uncertainty, it discourages private investment and other long-term commitments.

Difficulties in Reaching Consensus on Priorities

Recognition of the importance of economic stability as a public good needs to be accompanied by awareness of the reasons why it is so difficult to reach a workable consensus on development priorities that is necessary to maintain a balance between government responsibilities and resources. Commitment to import-substituting industrialization and certain other strategic notions widely held by development specialists and policymakers in CARLs have contributed to the ill-advised macroeconomic policies and the dubious priorities for social service programs that have had such adverse effects on development of the rural economy.

After World War II, policymakers in most developing countries advocated import-substituting industrialization as an overriding priority for public investment and management. At that time, the strategic notion of import-substituting industrialization was an understandable reaction, especially in Latin America, to the great depression of the 1930s. Foreign exchange earnings of developing countries, which had been dependent on primary product exports, dropped precipitously—more than 60 percent in 1929–32 (Little, Scitovsky, and Scott 1970, p. 31). The strategic notion of import-substituting industrialization has had great appeal ever since.

Import-substituting industrialization was pursued through protectionism with little consideration given to its effect on factor proportions, industrial efficiency, or relationships between manufacturing and other sectors of the economy. That (and financial, fiscal, trade, and exchange rate policies) encouraged the growth of inefficient, capital-intensive manufacturing firms such as the fertilizer plants analyzed in Chapter 7, while discouraging agricultural development and a sustainable expansion of domestic industry.

It is now recognized that development involves not only physical capital but also human and social capital. CARLs face a difficult task in establishing efficient social and economic mechanisms to maintain and increase stocks of capital per head and for keeping "the rate of return on them roughly in alignment" (H. Johnson 1969, p. 9). Decentralized decision making, together with market-determined prices, offers advantages as an allocation mechanism. But balanced accumulation of capital in its various forms also requires investments in public goods (such as agricultural research, rural roads, education, and public health programs) that depend on the fallible judgment of government decision makers.

The limited administrative capacity of CARLs, as well as severe financial constraints, highlights the importance of setting priorities for investments in human resources and in building educational, research, and other key institutions (see Box 8.2). But an "optimal" allocation of resources for investments in human and social capital is inherently difficult. It is hard to quantify benefits, especially because there are complementary, as well as competitive, relationships among those activities. Moreover, subjective decisions to invest in human resources increase the pressure to make excessive allocations for other programs that do not merit high priority. As will be discussed, food subsidy schemes, which tend to be (or become) extremely costly, are an example of an intervention that is often popular but that generally does not merit priority in CARLs.

Foreign Aid and the International Environment

Foreign economic and technical assistance can ease resource constraints in CARLs. However, it is difficult to provide foreign aid that realizes that potential. Indeed, such assistance can have adverse effects—for example, in diverting attention away from a country's efforts to mobilize domestic resources for development.

Furthermore, the contrasting treatment of agriculture in the developed and developing world has had damaging effects on agriculture in CARLs (Thorbecke 1988; Tyers and Anderson 1992). The United States, Japan, and other postindustrial countries often provide substantial protection for farmers (see Chapter 3). In contrast, many CARLs discriminate against agriculture through policies that keep the domestic price below the world price. As a result, depressed domestic prices and low prices for agricultural imports are disincentives for domestic production. Moreover, the surpluses that accumulate in the postindustrial countries are periodically eliminated, thus leading to artificially low world prices. Large surpluses, especially in the United States and the European Community, influence foreign assistance toward food aid. This serves a valuable purpose in meeting emergency food needs. But it has a twofold risk: local consumers may grow to prefer imported cereals over domestic staples, such as maize, millet, and sorghum, and the flow of food aid may be unreliable.

Macroeconomic management in CARLs is complicated by other factors. Significant amounts of their export earnings come from primary products subject to volatile world prices. Take oil prices. A barrel of crude oil cost $2.21 in 1971. It rose to $3.56 in 1973 and jumped to $10.24 in 1974. After rising to $16.77 in 1979, it reached $27.60 in 1980, reached $32.03 in 1981, before dropping to $26.44 in 1985 and collapsing to $11.60 in 1986 before a modest recovery to $16.65 in 1987. Coffee, cocoa, copper, and other primary commodities have seen similar peaks and troughs. According to the International Monetary Fund's (IMF) *International Financial Statistics*, rice prices quoted in Bangkok, Thailand, rose sharply from $130 per metric ton

Box 8.2. Political Economy of Public Goods and Services

Distortion of prices and government involvement in activities that can be handled better by the private sector have received the bulk of the attention in the recent literature on political economy. There are, however, parallel effects of these choices on a government's capacity to provide public goods and services essential for agricultural growth. Indeed, adverse economic effects of misdirected investment and inefficient production induced by distortion of prices are compounded by the government's resulting incapacity to provide essential public goods and services.

Governments frequently assume costly operational responsibilities for marketing agricultural commodities that exceed their administrative capacity. At the same time, they neglect fundamental responsibilities, such as improving (or at least maintaining) transport facilities, communications, and related infrastructure essential to the efficiency of that marketing, as well as other economic activities. Consequently, economic development falls short of what could be generated through the initiative of farmers, private traders, local machine shops, and other entrepreneurs.

In contrast to the zero-sum political game favoring consumption of private goods by a few and excluding all others, public goods (such as information about improved timing and placement of fertilizer) are opportunities to build broad-based political support. Government efforts that generate and disseminate weather forecasts, new technology, and other useful information; that contribute to macroeconomic stabilization; that control natural hazards (through flood, fire, and disease control); and, up to a point, investments in infrastructure, are all public goods that often yield high social returns. For example, public investment in agricultural research shows real rates of return of well above 10 percent, including those in sixteen developing countries (Ruttan 1982). This suggests massive underinvestment in agricultural research. Yet, these studies—and the results that in many countries can be seen firsthand in farmers' fields—are making policymakers aware of the priority that agricultural research deserves in development budgets and of the political value of such programs.

Public goods and services, too, are influenced by powerful interest groups. In agricultural research, there have been biases favoring, for example, large rubber plantations in Malaysia (Barlow and Jayasuriya 1984a). Pressure can also come from the bureaucracy: rents in the construction of water projects and regulation of access to water lead to widespread overinvestment and rent seeking in irrigation systems in the United States as well as India (Repetto 1986; Wade 1985).

Nevertheless, in CARLs public goods and services merit the highest priority for the use of limited administrative capacity, policy analysis, and public finances. Government initiative is required because there is no effective alternative to provide adequate public goods and services as part of an agricultural strategy. Agricultural research, basic education, public health, and physical and social infrastructure simply will not reach socially optimal levels without financial and administrative support from public agencies. Most important, it is possible under many regimes—witness the United States, Japan, China, Taiwan, India, and Indonesia.

in 1971 to $541 in 1974 at the time of the world food crisis. Two years later the price had fallen to $254, to rise again to $483 in 1981 before dropping to $293 the following year.

There were, too, unprecedented fluctuations in the value of the U.S. dollar in the 1970s and 1980s. It cost 0.43 pounds sterling in 1974, appreciating to 0.59 pounds in 1976. In 1980, it was worth only 0.42 pounds but then rose to 0.87 in 1984 before falling to 0.53 pounds in 1987. Since the U.S. dollar has been the de facto "numeraire" of international payments, such fluctuations introduce much uncertainty into international trade and finance.

Since the early 1970s many things, including unproductive investments and a sharp rise in real interest rates, caused a serious debt crisis in Latin America and many African countries. In 1970 only a few countries had a ratio of annual debt payments (interest plus amortization of principal) to export receipts of 12 percent. As of 1980, total debt service as a percentage of exports of goods and services was nearly 24 percent in the middle-income countries, but the average was down to just over 20 percent in 1991, mainly because of significant reductions in some Latin American countries. Among the low-income countries, debt service as a percentage of exports averaged about 10 percent in 1980 but then rose sharply to 21 percent in 1991 (World Bank 1993, pp. 284–85; Thorbecke 1988, p. 13).

From Stabilization to Structural Transformation

CARLs face a difficult challenge: how to combine stability with rapid growth, structural transformation, and elimination of malnutrition, high mortality and morbidity rates among children, illiteracy, and other manifestations of poverty.

The ideas and policies that emerged in Taiwan in the 1950s (Chapter 10) produced rapid economic growth with macroeconomic stability, greater equality in income distribution, dramatic declines in mortality and births, and the virtual eradication of malnutrition. According to S. C. Tsiang, an architect of those economic policies, "two popular misconceptions in development policy that were highly fashionable among academic circles" were replaced by two policies that were critical to rapid economic growth and improvement in income distribution.

A shift from a protectionist import-substitution strategy toward an equilibrium exchange rate and trade liberalization "induced a vast shift of labor supply from land-intensive agriculture, towards those labor-intensive industries in which Taiwan obviously had superior comparative advantages" (Tsiang 1987, p. 36). The shift from agriculture, which was subject to "the relentless law of diminishing returns," to labor-intensive industries made possible "a large net increase in the marginal productivity of labor and, hence, in the real wage rate" (pp. 28, 36). However, along with the rapid increase in the share of manufacturing in trade and in gross domestic product (GDP), there was a shift in agriculture toward land-saving products, including technically demanding ones, such as canned asparagus and mushrooms, which rapidly replaced traditional exports of sugar and rice.

In 1950 Taiwan abandoned the low interest rate policies that were then fashionable, raising the interest rate on savings deposits to roughly the rate of inflation, then around 100 percent. Tsiang emphasizes that "the abandonment of the artificial, government-enforced low interest rate policy in Taiwan enabled it to avoid the selection of excessively capital-intensive and labor-saving methods of production, or those industries using such methods of production" (p. 36). This shift to a policy of interest rates high enough to induce a flow of savings into financial institutions was remarkably effective in expanding the supply of investable funds. In the early 1950s adjustments of interest rates were made to expand domestic saving and to avoid a resurgence of inflation (Tsiang 1987, pp. 29–33).

PRIORITIES FOR SOCIAL PROGRAMS

There is now general acceptance of the proposition that expenditures on education and health are investments that contribute to economic growth in addition to their value to the direct beneficiaries. It is also recognized that enhancing the quality of human resources through investments in education and health, including improved nutrition, represents an important pathway out of poverty, especially for those with little access to land and other assets. There has, however, been a lack of consensus concerning the government interventions that merit priority in economies where poverty is severe and pervasive and government resources are exceedingly scarce.

In the 1970s there was considerable enthusiasm for a "basic needs approach" and "integrated rural development" (see Box 8.3). The analysis in preceding chapters, the historical experience examined in Chapter 3, and the discussion yet to come in Part 3 emphasize the importance of broad-based development strategies that expand opportunities for productive employment and raise returns to labor, thereby making possible widespread increases in food consumption and progress in satisfying other basic needs. Experience in Taiwan is especially interesting in illustrating the importance of an integrated *perspective* that directs attention to the need for an appropriate sequence of government interventions to foster increases in agricultural productivity, investments in rural infrastructure, the strengthening of educational institutions, and public health measures

Box 8.3. Basic Needs and Integrated Rural Development

In the 1970s the international development community became enthused about a "basic needs approach." Some needs are indeed more "basic" than others. Clearly, the well-being of a country's population depends on much more than average income. In addition to distribution of income, much depends on the composition of the goods and services that comprise the national product. Education and health services are important ingredients of the quality of life, and they depend on social service programs. Moreover, well-conceived programs to give the rural (as well as urban) population access to education and basic health services merit priority as public goods because they create positive externalities that affect human capital formation and economic growth. However, such social service programs need to be supplementary to, rather than substituting for, a broad-based agricultural development strategy.

The notion of "integrated rural development," also promoted by the development community in the 1970s, was useful in focusing attention on *rural* development. It helped to counter a tendency toward "urban bias" and corrected a narrow, production-oriented view of agricultural development. A focus on *rural people* directed attention to the importance of their access to education, health, and family planning services, as well as income and employment generated by rural nonfarm activities.

In practice, most integrated rural development programs achieved little because attempts to integrate administratively diverse activities cause problems of coordination that exceed the implementation capacity of CARLs. There are exceptions. India's Integrated Rural Development Program enabled landless and marginal households to augment incomes by using family labor for milk production. The administrative challenge was great—access to credit for the purchase of a cow or buffalo, strengthening veterinary services, and supporting institutional reforms for collection and marketing of milk. The challenge was manageable, however, because of India's high administrative capacity and the availability of a workable "model" evolved by the AMUL or Anand Milk Producers Union Ltd (see Box 1.3). That Indian program is a good example of a successful program that conforms with the World Bank's peculiar definition of "rural development" as a "strategy designed to improve the economic and social life of a special group of people—the rural poor"; but in general the "rural development" projects supported by the Bank have not performed well (World Bank 1975, p. 3; World Bank 1988a).

that achieve broad coverage of a country's rural as well as urban population.

In the decades since World War II there has been greatly increased public spending on education and public health programs in most developing countries, influenced by growing recognition that such programs merit priority as quasi-public goods.[1] Some oil-importing countries were forced to reduce total government expenditures and the shares going to social programs following the oil price hike of 1973. Similar pressures were faced by oil importers and exporters alike in the debt crisis of the 1980s. Reductions in the shares of education and health were especially large in Mexico (an oil exporter) in the mid-1980s as a result of its debt crisis. But by 1990 the share of central government expenditure for education had recovered to nearly 14 percent (Table 8.1). For health a 1.9 percent share in Mexico in 1990 was still much below the 4.5 percent share in 1972, although the reduction in central government expenditure was partly offset by an increase in state-level outlays for health (see Box 10.1).

There are few clear patterns over time in shares of total government expenditure in Table 8.1. Central governments' relative share of gross national product (GNP) drops slightly in some countries with rapid economic growth (Indonesia and Thailand between 1980 and 1990), but shows remarkable resilience in most cases. Egypt—notorious for its bloated bureaucracy—is the only example among these of significant compression in central government (from almost 54 percent of GNP in 1980 to 40 percent in 1990). To be sure, some sub-Saharan CARLs saw significant government retrenchment in the 1980s. But cutting central government expenditure is difficult and slow, as shown by the United States as well as Kenya and Bangladesh.

The most obvious pattern in Table 8.1—and one of the most important for our purposes—concerns the relative shares of central government expenditures going to education and health. For all the developing countries in the table (except Brazil), central governments' expenditures on education exceed those for health. Indeed, public education budgets often are two to three times the size of health budgets (as in Tanzania, Bangladesh, Kenya). This developing country pattern is the reverse of the United States, where health care entitlements for the elderly combined with an aging population are one of the forces driving up public expenditures on health relative to education. In contrast, it is preschoolers who suffer a disproportionate share of the high morbidity and mortality in CARLs. Fortunately for these countries, it is much less expensive to improve the health and lengthen the lives of young children than the elderly.

The fiscal question "how much is enough?" is complicated for social programs because there are no simple causal linkages running from program expenditures to human capital and welfare or even to gross indicators of

---

[1] Education, health, and nutrition are *quasi-public* or *mixed goods and services* because benefits are neither purely private nor purely social. Mixed goods also include child survival programs that ultimately produce pecuniary externalities in labor markets (Birdsall 1988). If reductions in infant and child mortality lead to reduced fertility, the fall in population growth leads to a smaller labor force in fifteen to twenty years. Other things being equal, workers will benefit from higher wages.

Table 8.1. Central government expenditures for education and health, 1972, 1980, 1990

	Total expenditures (% of GNP)			Expenditure for education (%)			Expenditure for health (%)		
	1972	1980	1990	1972	1980	1990	1972	1980	1990
Tanzania	19.7	28.8	—	17.3	13.3	—	7.2	6.0	—
Bangladesh	9.2	10.0	15.0	14.8	11.5	11.2	5.0	6.4	4.8
Nigeria	9.1	—	—	4.5	—	—	3.6	—	—
India	10.5	13.2	18.2	2.3	1.9	2.5	1.5	1.6	1.6
Kenya	21.0	26.1	31.4	21.9	19.6	19.8	7.9	7.8	5.4
Indonesia	15.1	23.1	20.4	7.4	8.3	8.4	1.4	2.5	2.0
Egypt	—	53.7	40.2	—	8.1	13.4	—	2.4	2.8
Colombia	13.1	13.5	15.1	—	19.1	—	—	3.9	—
Thailand	16.7	19.1	15.1	19.9	19.8	20.1	3.7	4.1	6.8
Malaysia	26.5	29.6	31.3	—	—	—	—	—	—
Mexico	11.4	20.9	18.4	16.4	18.0	13.9	4.5	2.4	1.9
Brazil	29.1	20.9	36.0	8.3	0.0	5.3	6.7	8.0	7.2
United States	19.0	21.7	24.0	3.2	2.6	1.7	8.6	10.4	13.5
Japan	12.7	18.4	16.7	—	—	—	—	—	—

Sources: World Bank 1992b, pp. 238–39; World Bank 1993, pp. 258–59.
Note: Data were not available for China or Taiwan.

education opportunity and health status, such as enrollment rates and life expectancy. What is certain, however, is that increasing emphasis on funding and implementation of certain social programs can bring better living standards over time. Between 1965 and 1990 there has been impressive expansion in school enrollments, especially for females, and increases in life expectancy at birth in developing countries (Table 8.2).[2]

Table 8.3 shows how little is spent on health in developing countries. Except for the United States, total health expenditures cluster between 2 and 6 percent of GDP. The average for sub-Saharan Africa and Asia (except China, India, and Japan) is 4.5 percent of GDP. The average total health expenditure per capita in 1990 was U.S.$24 for sub-Saharan Africa, U.S.$11 in China, U.S.$21 in India, and U.S.$61 for the rest of the developing countries in Asia compared to over U.S.$1500 per capita in Japan.

Private expenditures account for about half of total health expenditures among the developing countries listed in Table 8.3. Public sector expenditures on health were only U.S.$5 per capita in India, U.S.$7 in China, and U.S.$24 for the rest of developing Asia; the average was U.S.$13 per capita for sub-Saharan Africa. As additional attention was given to health in Thailand, the fivefold differential between education and health in 1972 narrowed to a threefold difference in 1990 (Table 8.1). But even with that, pub-

[2] Moreover, some of the most significant increases in educational coverage and life expectancy occurred prior to 1965.

Table 8.2. Educational enrollment and life expectancy at birth, 1965 and 1990

	Percentage of age group enrolled in primary school		Percentage of age group enrolled in secondary school		Females per 100 males enrolled in primary school		Females per 100 males enrolled in secondary school		Life expectancy at birth in 1965 (years)		Life expectancy at birth in 1990 (years)		Change in life expectancy at birth (years)	
	1965	1990	1965	1990	1965	1990	1965	1990	Male	Female	Male	Female	Male	Female
Low-income economies[a] (excluding China and India)	50	79	10	28	58	76	34	66	44	45	54	56	10	11
Tanzania	32	63	2	4	60	98	33	74	41	45	46	49	5	4
Bangladesh	49	73	13	17	44	81	14	49	45	44	52	51	7	7
Nigeria	32	72	5	20	63	76	43	74	40	43	49	54	9	11
India	74	97	27	44	57	71	35	55	46	44	60	58	14	14
Kenya	54	94	4	23	57	95	38	78	46	50	57	61	11	11
China	89	135	24	48	65	86	47	72	53	57	69	71	16	14
Indonesia	72	117	12	45	82	93	—	82	43	45	60	64	17	19
Egypt	75	96	26	82	64	80	41	76	48	50	59	62	11	12
Colombia	84	110	17	52	102	96	57	100	57	61	66	72	9	11
Thailand	78	85	14	32	89	95	68	97	54	58	63	68	9	10
Malaysia	90	93	28	56	84	95	—	104	56	60	68	72	12	12
Mexico	92	112	17	53	91	94	53	92	58	61	66	73	8	12
Brazil	108	108	16	39	98	—	93	—	55	59	63	69	8	10
Taiwan	b	b	b	b	—	—	—	—	—	64[c]	71[d]	76[d]	—	—
United States	100	105	—	92	92	95	—	—	67	74	73	80	6	6
Japan	100	101	82	96	96	95	101	99	68	73	76	82	8	9

Sources: World Bank 1992b, pp. 274–75, 280–81; World Bank 1993, 294–95, 300–301.

[a]Low-income economies as defined by the World Bank in 1992.

[b]1978. The World Development Report reports that 67% of all children of primary school age were enrolled in 1960, including 47% of female children in that age group; 37% of all children of secondary school age were enrolled in 1960 but no breakdown by gender is given. Between 1965 and 1984, the total number of students in secondary education increased from 1.6 to 6.8 million. Enrollment in higher education rose from 238,000 to 1.5 million over that same period (Taiwan Statistical Data Book).

[c]1960. 1978 World Development Report; average for men and women.

[d]Taiwan Statistical Data Book 1987. Data are for 1985.

Table 8.3. Health expenditure and official development assistance (ODA), 1990

	Total health expenditures (% of GDP)	Total health expenditures (U.S.$/ capita)	Private sector health expenditures (U.S.$/ capita)	Public sector health expenditures (U.S.$/ capita)	ODA for health (U.S.$/ capita)
Sub-Saharan Africa	4.5	24	11	13	2.5
Asia (excluding India, China, and Japan)	4.5	61	37	24	0.9
Tanzania	4.7	4	1	3	2.1
Bangladesh	3.2	7	4	3	1.2
Nigeria	2.8	9	5	4	0.6
India	6.0	21	16	5	0.3
Kenya	4.3	16	6	10	3.5
China	3.5	11	4	7	0.1
Indonesia	2.0	12	8	4	0.9
Egypt	2.6	18	11	7	2.1
Colombia	4.0	50	28	23	0.8
Thailand	5.0	73	57	16	0.7
Malaysia	3.0	67	38	29	0.1
Mexico	3.2	89	45	45	0.8
Brazil	4.2	132	44	88	0.6
United States	12.6	2,763	1,535	1,228	n.a.
Japan	6.4	1,538	385	1,154	n.a.

Source: World Bank 1993, pp. 210–11; see pp. 197–98 for explanation of the disaggregation of private and public expenditures.

Note: "n.a." means not applicable: these are donor countries.

lic sector expenditures on health in Thailand came to only U.S.$16 per capita in 1990 (Table 8.3).

Official development assistance (ODA) plays a significant role in financing public sector health expenditures in some countries, most notably in Africa. The figures for ODA for health in Table 8.3 omit many transfers under the auspices of nongovernmental organizations, so they understate assistance. Nevertheless, it is clear that even if ODA were doubled, public expenditures for health programs still would be in the range of U.S.$15–25 per capita for most developing countries and considerably less for some, including Tanzania, Bangladesh, Nigeria, India, and Indonesia.

In Tanzania aid flows accounted for over half of total health expenditure (public and private) as compared to about 1 percent in Thailand. Private outlays for health in Thailand in 1990 were more than three times as large as public health expenditures. Even though public expenditures for health in Tanzania were three times as large as private health expenditure, the 1.1 percent of GNP devoted to public health expenditures in Thailand permitted a much greater per capita outlay than the 3.2 percent of GNP devoted to public health expenditure in Tanzania (World Bank 1993, p. 210). As a result of rapid economic growth in Thailand and stagnation and decline in Tanzania, there is now nearly a sixteenfold difference in per capita GNP in the two countries.

The purpose here is *not* to argue for reallocation of central government funds from education to health. (With age structures heavily weighted toward young people, it is understandable and appropriate that CARLs would have large public sector education budgets.) Instead, our purpose is to emphasize that the health budget is a small slice of central government expenditure that, for a given country, tends to have a relatively stable share of GNP. In large part, more public spending for social programs will follow economic growth. In the meantime, the resources available for social programs (especially public health) in most CARLs are lean indeed.

Education and Human Capital Formation

In his review of the literature on investments in education and its social and private returns, T. P. Schultz (1988, pp. 543–630) emphasizes that an "educational explosion" has narrowed the gap in educational opportunities between high- and low-income countries. In most developing countries, too, the wide gap between educational attainment of women and men has narrowed at the primary and secondary levels (see Table 8.2). This is especially important because reductions in fertility and in child mortality are both linked to female education.

There is concern, however, that rapid expansion of schooling in many countries has meant a decline in quality. There seems to be only limited agreement about the most cost-effective ways to improve quality and even less about the optimal trade-offs between "quantity" and "quality."

Consensus seems to have been reached concerning the validity of the economic interpretation of the expansion of educational opportunities that is stressed by both T. W. Schultz (1980) and T. P. Schultz: economic returns to education are reflected in the enhanced ability of workers and entrepreneurs (and farmers are both) to identify and seize new opportunities. T. P. Schultz (1988, p. 575) draws on country studies to make regional estimates of the average social and private rates of return. In all cases, the estimated private returns are higher than the social returns, reflecting that a major part of educational expenditures are publicly financed. Both social and private returns are highest from primary education. In Asia the social returns of 12 and 14 percent, respectively, for secondary and higher education, are probably close to the social opportunity cost of capital. For primary education, however, the estimated private returns (18 percent) are higher than the social returns. At 27 and 35 percent, the social returns to primary education in Africa and

Latin America are above the Asian level and about twice as high as the estimated social returns to higher education. At 19 percent, the social returns to secondary education in both Africa and Latin America are also substantially below the returns to primary education. Estimated private returns to secondary and higher education in those two regions are around 30 percent, much above the estimated social returns.

Despite problems in estimating returns to education and other forms of human capital, both private and public investments in education are rewarded by substantial returns. In Tanzania and Kenya, Knight and Sabot (1990, p. 21) find strong evidence of the economic returns of education: "Literate and numerate workers are more productive, and education and reasoning ability are valuable to workers mainly because they allow them to acquire skills that increase their productivity. Our analysis strongly supports the human capital interpretation of education–wage relationships, although not to the complete exclusion of other influences."

Because many of the economic returns to education result from individuals identifying and profiting from new opportunities, there are bound to be major interactions between educational returns and technological change or other opportunities to profit from reallocating resources (T. W. Schultz 1975; Welch 1978). Returns to investments in rural schooling tend to be high in situations where research is generating new production possibilities whereas in stagnant situations the returns to education are low (T. P. Schultz 1988, p. 605; Jamison and Lau 1982).

This complementarity also influences returns to investments in higher education in agriculture and veterinary science. A principal return to investments in agricultural higher education comes from the direct and indirect contributions of local agricultural colleges in strengthening national research programs. The involvement of university faculty members and graduate students can make a big contribution to ongoing research while providing critically important training for future researchers.

Hard Choices on Health and Nutrition

Although there is considerable agreement concerning the importance of investments in education, there has been a serious lack of consensus with respect to government policies related to health, nutrition, and population. Part of the problem stems from technical uncertainty (see Box 8.4). But good health and nutrition are both of such fundamental importance as basic human needs that special difficulties arise in making decisions about what is feasible as well as desirable, given the severe resource constraints in CARLs.

There has been a tendency for many bilateral and multilateral agencies and nongovernmental organizations (NGOs) to focus on hunger and malnutrition as particularly serious manifestations of poverty. Often, this has

Box 8.4. Changing Views on Nutritional Requirements

It is often assumed that minimum nutritional needs can be defined with precision. In fact, assessing nutritional status and requirements is complex. Energy requirements, for example, depend not only on age, body size, sex, physical activity, and the presence, or absence, of infectious or parasitic diseases. There are also sizeable biological differences in people that affect nutritional requirements, even though their measurable characteristics are the same. Children have the greatest potential for "adapting" to restricted food intake. In addition to restricting activity, they adjust through a slower rate of growth. These adaptive responses also are warning signs of higher risks of sickness and death. Such adaptation may also mean a reduction in body size as adults, which may be costly.

For an exceptionally competent evaluation of nutritional status based on survey data and estimates of nutritional requirements, see Calloway and others 1993. This paper also provides a concise summary of some of the major conclusions of an important collaborative research support program (the Nutrition CRSP). Field studies carried out in Egypt, Kenya, and Mexico provided a wealth of data on food intake, socioeconomic and anthropometric characteristics, morbidity, performance on cognitive tests, and other indicators of nutritional status. The study provides further evidence of the danger of trying to impose the judgments of "experts" on household decisions concerning food consumption. All three of the country studies point to the nutritional value of a diet that includes at least modest quantities of animal products: "Nutritional enhancement associated with animal products appears to be due to their contribution of specific nutrients and their higher digestibility, to the replacement of foods that contain interfering substances and, perhaps for small children, increased energy density of the diet" (Calloway and others 1993, p. 383).

This finding points to another swing in the pendulum of expert opinion. In the early 1970s the "protein gap" view of the world food problem was discarded because of recognition that much of the protein deficiency being observed was a result of inadequate intake of energy, causing protein to be "burned" for energy rather than performing its distinctive functions. That lesson was so well learned that sometimes poor households have been criticized for "wasting" money on costly animal products when their energy needs were not being fully met. It appears that the trade-offs were more complex than was appreciated by many outside experts.

led to emphasis on direct government action. In famine situations there is no substitute for emergency distribution of food, and it is often possible to mobilize international relief to meet such needs. At times, a widespread preference for granting relief in the form of commodities—particularly food— seems to also influence foreign aid policies related to chronic hunger. Thus, a Presidential Commission on World Hunger in the United States concluded that priority should be given to "assuring that people who are poor need not be hungry as well" and, accordingly, endorsed food stamp programs as an approach that "enables needy people to buy additional food while stimulating rather than depressing demand for local supplies" (Presidential Commission on Hunger 1980, pp. 40–41).

That report was issued when there was still a good deal of enthusiasm for "multisectoral nutrition planning" following the 1974 World Food Conference when a universal declaration had been adopted calling for the eradication of hunger by 1985. In 1978 a similarly ambitious declaration of Health for All by 2000 was adopted at the Alma Ata International Conference on Primary Health Care. Although the Alma Ata declaration also displays a measure of rhetoric, its time scale of twenty-two years was somewhat more realistic than the World Food Conference's eleven-year target for the eradication of hunger. More fundamentally, cost-effective technologies are available that have been remarkably successful in achieving rapid reductions in infant and child mortality. So, in spite of the resource constraints they face, CARLs should give high priority to *selective* investments in public health measures.

Furthermore, a number of these selective public health interventions provide major nutritional benefits. Disease can be as serious a cause of undernutrition as inadequate food intake, especially for young children. For example, diarrheal diseases and measles, which each contribute so much to high child mortality in CARLs, also undermine the nutritional status of the children who survive. Low availability of food makes it difficult for these children to catch up after the nutritional setback of each bout of disease, making them more susceptible to subsequent infection and also increasing their risk of death from subsequent illnesses. Oral rehydration therapy (ORT) for diarrhea, vaccination against measles, and public health education to improve sanitation and thereby reduce exposure to infection, all can help break this vicious cycle of hunger and disease. Unfortunately, "nutrition programs" too often have focused exclusively on raising food intake while ignoring the link between disease and malnutrition. Yet, it is this heavy disease burden that probably lies behind the surprising finding that rising household incomes alone can have so little impact on the nutrition of preschoolers in low-income countries (Box 1.4).

The Rise and Fall of Multisectoral Nutrition Planning

Multisectoral nutrition planning contributed to enthusiasm for urban-oriented food subsidy programs, school lunch programs, and other schemes for supplementary distribution of food. For CARLs, this is particularly unfortunate because food subsidy and distribution schemes are costly.

Costs of Food Subsidies. In Egypt, Sri Lanka, and Mexico food subsidies have amounted to 5 percent of GDP, and they have accounted for 15 to 25 percent of total government expenditures in Bangladesh, Egypt, Sri Lanka, and Pakistan (Valdes 1988, p. 84). In many countries the fiscal costs of subsidies increased in the early 1970s as governments attempted to protect consumers from the effects of rapid increases in food prices. Since 1977, when Sri Lanka shifted from a general to a targeted food subsidy, the cost has declined from 15 to 5 percent of total government expenditure; but in Egypt in the first half of the 1980s food subsidies cost around $2 billion annually, or 16 to 18 percent of total government expenditures (Pinstrup-Andersen 1988a, p. 12; Valdes 1988, p. 84). Compared to the shares of central government expenditures for health and education, the 15 to 25 percent of government budgets spent on food subsidies in countries such as Egypt and Sri Lanka was large indeed.

When food subsidies are financed by monetary expansion, they result in an inflationary increase in prices and, eventually, currency depreciation leading to further increase in the general price level (Siamwalla 1988, p. 328). Moreover, in countries with explicit subsidies, "there is a temptation for governments to try to reduce fiscal costs by transferring part of the cost to farmers" (Valdes 1988, p. 78). Thus, implicit subsidies financed by imposing low prices on farmers often have big negative effects on producer incentives and the well-being of rural households.

How do we explain such huge spending on food subsidies and other such schemes, when the "actual results have been discouraging" (Kennedy 1988, p. 152)? Part of the explanation is that hunger is seen as a particularly shocking manifestation of poverty. Subsidized food policies have also been encouraged by the availability of food aid and by support of some agencies and NGOs in developed countries that focus on hunger. Public opinion surveys in donor nations show that support for foreign assistance to eradicate hunger is far stronger than for economic and social development. The notion of direct action to eradicate hunger by distributing food has a straightforward humanitarian appeal as well as attracting support from farm groups and other protagonists of food aid.

The Political Economy of Food Subsidies. Much of the support for food subsidies and food distribution schemes can be explained by politics within developing countries. Usually, the most powerful political interest groups are civil servants, the military, urban labor, and sometimes industrial interests. They have a direct interest in cheap food, and, as in Egypt, it may be regarded as a "right" to be defended by protests, including riots, by "politically influential or potentially volatile groups" (Hopkins 1988, p. 125).

The problem of targeting is unavoidably difficult for food distribution schemes. In his introduction to a recent book on *The Political Economy of Food and Nutrition Policies,* Per Pinstrup-Andersen reports that "multisectoral nutrition planning has failed as a planning and implementation tool" largely because of "the failure to explicitly consider political economy issues" (1993 pp. xiii, xiv). In his concluding chapter, Pinstrup-Andersen suggests that the "leakage" that normally occurs in nutrition programs ostensibly aimed at providing cheap food for the poor should be used to ensure the political sustainability of such programs rather than being viewed as something to be deplored. Thus, he recommends that consideration be given to

a two-pronged targeting of the nutritionally vulnerable and a large enough subset of the politically powerful to assure sustainability, leaving the rest of the urban population to pay market prices for food. . . . Narrow targeting on the poor and powerless generally does not generate much political support, and some past programs, such as the Colombian food stamp program, targeted themselves out of existence. (Pinstrup-Andersen 1993, pp. 227, 229)

The price of such political sustainability, however, often is an unsustainable drain on the government budget that can destabilize the economy and does not promote economic growth. Although food, next to air and water, is the most basic of human needs, it is nonetheless a private, not a public good.

An Emerging Consensus for Selective Public Health Interventions

Each CARL will differ regarding the precise set of public health problems that merit priority. Local research can provide guidance in setting priorities and designing programs. In some isolated mountainous areas, for example, goiter and mental deficiency (from a lack of iodine) are serious problems for which iodization of salt is an exceptionally cost-effective solution. Similarly, effective nutrition education must be based on awareness of specific deficiencies that can be corrected by improved understanding. For example, many mothers in Indonesia used to expel and discard the colostrum secreted at the onset of lactation. A carefully designed nutrition education program achieved considerable success in replacing the common view that colostrum was "dirty" and the cause of illness with understanding that it contains antibodies that confer considerable immunity against infection during the critical postnatal period.

Support has been growing in developing countries and among donor agencies for assigning a high priority to certain public health programs that merit priority everywhere. These programs are characterized by their cost-effectiveness and by embodying a mix of public and private benefits. Immunizing a child against measles, for example, slows transmission of the disease and thus confers a positive externality. Similarly, information programs for promoting improvements in personal hygiene, in environmental sanitation, and in diet through nutrition education are essentially public goods. Control of flies, mosquitoes, and other carriers of disease, or promoting the use of latrines, reduces the risk of spreading infectious diseases, thereby conferring communitywide benefits. Furthermore, provision of cost-effective health services to the poor is likely to be viewed as a socially acceptable approach to poverty reduction (see World Bank 1993, pp. 5 and passim) that is not as susceptible to the pressure to expand benefits that bloats the cost of food subsidies.

There is now a wealth of evidence showing that public health measures can be cost-effective in reducing mortality and morbidity. The methodologies available tend to be especially powerful in reducing infant and child mortality. This is important for CARLs because children account for a large percentage of the total population: 46 percent of the population in the countries of sub-Saharan Africa is under 15 compared to 19 percent in the high-income, postindustrial countries. The concentration of deaths among small children is even more pronounced: it is estimated that children under age five accounted for half of all deaths in sub-Saharan Africa in 1990 but less than two percent of all deaths in high-income countries (World Bank 1993, pp. 200–202).

The sharp contrasts that have emerged among developing countries in mortality rates for infants and young children to a large extent reflect the extent to which their governments have seized opportunities to introduce cost-effective health measures. As of 1960, the estimated under-five mortality rate in sub-Saharan Africa was just over 250 per thousand live births, and the rates in Asia were not a great deal lower: an estimated 235 in India, 210 in China, and 182 per thousand for the rest of Asia (excluding Japan). Between 1960 and 1990 China's child death rate fell dramatically to an estimated 43 per thousand, and in India and the rest of Asia under-five mortality in 1990 was only a little over half the level in 1960. In sub-Saharan Africa, the reduction in the weighted average death rate for children under five was only from 251 to 175 per thousand, although in Zimbabwe and Kenya estimated child mortality was down to 58 and 83 per thousand by 1990 from 159 and 203 in 1960, respectively.

The interventions that have made such a major contribution to those dramatic declines in death rates for infants and young children include immunization programs, oral rehydration therapy for diarrheal diseases, nutrition and hygiene education, and environmental sanitation. Although such preventive and promotional activities can be affordable even in CARLs, their design and implementation are not easy. Physicians typically have a bias toward curative care, and health professionals find it difficult to decide on priorities and on the sequencing of interventions so that programs are manageable and affordable. Perhaps it is a belief that health professionals are not capable of facing up to the need for trade-offs between coverage and quality that prompts economists such as Timmer (1988, p. 335) to question the appropriateness of what he assumed would be "massive investment in human capital through nutrition, health, and family planning services in the countryside."

A 1979 article by Walsh and Warren was a notable exception to the common failure of health professionals to assess priorities and recognize trade-offs between coverage and quality. They argued that *selective* primary care should focus on "the infections causing the greatest amount of most readily preventable illness and death: diarrheal diseases, malaria, measles, whooping cough, schistosomiasis and neonatal tetanus" (Walsh and Warren 1979, p. 969). Except for schistosomiasis, all the infections in their "high-priority group" affect infants and small children more than adults. These should receive priority not only because they are widespread and serious but because they are easy to prevent or cure. Respiratory infections and malnutrition (along with a half dozen other health problems) are the "medium-priority group": they have high prevalence and high morbidity or mortality, but they are more difficult and costly to control. There are, however, a few preventive measures against specific nutrient deficiencies, notably of iodine and vitamin A, that merit high priority because they are so cost-effective. More recently, antibiotic treatment for pneumonia has been shown to be cost-effective as a curative intervention (Carl Taylor, personal communication 1993).

Although it is difficult to design public health programs to give mothers and children access to the most cost-effective health services, a number of countries have succeeded in both rural and urban areas. In part, this is a result of a concerted effort by WHO, UNICEF, bilateral agencies, and a number of NGOs to mobilize support and action focused on the most cost-effective interventions. An example is UNICEF's GOBI, *G*rowth monitoring, *O*ral rehydration therapy, *B*reast feeding, and *I*mmunization. GOBI is usually linked with FFF (*F*emale education, *F*amily spacing, and *F*ood supplements).

Among the activities embraced by UNICEF's emphasis on GOBI, questions have been raised about the value of growth monitoring unless much attention and resources are devoted to planning, training, supervision, and management of the measurement of children so that conscientious recording of an individual's growth can enhance the effectiveness and utilization of child health services (Gerein and Ross 1991).

And among UNICEF's three "F's," the priority for food supplementation is not as clear as the importance of female education and voluntary contraception to space births (family spacing) discussed later in this chapter. It would be clearer—albeit at the expense of alliteration—to refer to most of the "food supplements" advocated by UNICEF as "nutritional supplements." Nutritional supplements are specifically aimed at, for example, preventing low-birth-weight babies and preventing vitamin A deficiency. Some specific types of nutritional supplementation, such as supplements of iron (and perhaps zinc and folacin) to reduce the prevalence of low birth weight, merit priority because newborns of poorly nourished women who receive supplements show big improvements in birth weights that are associated in turn with reduced infant mortality and improved physical and mental development (Martorell and Gonzalez-Cossio 1987).

In addition to causing blindness, vitamin A deficiency also substantially increases the risk of infant and child mortality and morbidity. Giving infants and small children a massive dose of vitamin A three times a year is a cost-effective health intervention, although nutritionists increasingly argue that promoting home production of leafy green and yellow vegetables and fruit (such as papaya) and improved child feeding practices are better ways of increasing intake of vitamin A, iron, vitamin C, and other essential nutrients.

In contrast to the specificity of nutritional supplementation, "food supplementation" connotes more general feeding, such as school lunch programs, aimed at alleviating protein and energy malnutrition. While feeding of mothers and children may appear attractive as a direct intervention to alleviate hunger of vulnerable groups, food is fungible within the household. The net increase in intake for target groups often is substantially less than the food that is distributed (even if feeding occurs at clinics or schools) because it is partially offset by reduction of food consumed within the home. Although usually not as expensive as unrestricted food subsidies, such feeding programs can be costly and often involve substantial administrative burdens. So, among the seven GOBI-FFF interventions, growth monitoring and food supplementation are two that CARLs might well choose to phase in at a later date.

The priorities suggested in the pioneering analysis by Walsh and Warren and that are incorporated in the essence of UNICEF's GOBI-FFF have been confirmed by an ambitious joint effort by the World Bank and WHO to quantify the impact of about 100 diseases and injuries. The approach adopted in that exercise was to estimate the "global burden of disease" by combining the losses represented by premature death with the loss of healthy life from illness or other disability. These were then used to calculate comparable measures of the cost-effectiveness of specific interventions in terms of dollars per "disability-adjusted life year" (DALY) saved (World Bank 1993, p. 60). Although there are complications, the approach is useful in orienting priorities toward health problems that cause a significant disease burden and for which cost-effective interventions exist.

An important finding of the World Bank/WHO research reinforces arguments for giving priority to interventions aimed at improving the health and survival prospects of infants and small children. For example, on the basis of data from two urban areas in sub-Saharan Africa and a rural district in Bangladesh, it was estimated that immunization of small children against measles was able to prevent the disease at a cost of only about $15 per case prevented. The estimated cost per death averted was roughly $500, and the cost per DALY saved was only $15 to $20. And eight of the nine childhood diseases that account for at least 80 percent of the ill-health of young children can be addressed by interventions costing less than $100 per DALY saved. Comparable estimates of the cost-effectiveness of vitamin A supplementation for children under age 5 indicate a cost per death averted of only

$50 and a cost of just $1 per DALY saved. Another important finding is that cost-effective measures—including improved access to information on family planning and contraceptives, prenatal care, and childbirth and postpartum clinical services—exist to deal with several of the main threats to women's health during their childbearing years (World Bank 1993, pp. 9–10, 62–64; see also Jamison and others 1993).

Based on these studies of disease burden and cost-effectiveness, the World Bank estimated that the cost of a package of high-priority health services in developing countries would be U.S.$12–22 per capita per year in 1990. Of this, U.S.$4–7 is for public health programs, and the balance is for certain clinical services, including prenatal and delivery care (World Bank 1993, pp. 68, 106, 117). Inevitably, the World Bank's judgments on costs and contents of these health packages will be controversial. It is striking, nevertheless, that the limited health expenditure levels for developing countries presented in Table 8.3 would be, in many cases, adequate to purchase the package of public health programs and clinical services identified by the Bank as meriting priority in low-income countries. Note, too, that the costs are a fraction of those associated with food subsidies.

There are promising opportunities for technological progress to expand the range of cost-effective interventions, although the continuing spread of AIDS poses an enormous challenge. It remains to be seen whether medical research will achieve scientific breakthroughs capable of curing AIDS or of easing the task of slowing its spread. The World Bank (1993, p. 99) has rightly stressed that AIDS deserves special attention because failure to control the epidemic early results in more damaging and costly consequences in the future. The prospects for research advances to increase the effectiveness of selective primary health care are, however, considerably more promising. The powerful new tools of molecular biology and genetic engineering increase prospects for more effective and new vaccines for control of major tropical diseases.[3]

Some program innovations are also promising. The Expanded Immunization Program, initiated by WHO in collaboration with UNICEF, is aimed at rapid spread of vaccination for children. It has helped to reorient health services, and there has been rapid expansion of coverage. It is estimated that by 1990 coverage by immunization programs for polio, DPT (diphtheria, pertussis, and tetanus), and measles had reached 80 percent of all small children compared to coverage of less than 5 percent in 1977 and 20 to 30 per-

---

[3] A special Programme for Research and Training in Tropical Diseases was initiated in 1976 under the sponsorship of the United Nations Development Program (UNDP), the World Bank, and the World Health Organization (WHO). It mobilizes resources for research and development in new and improved methods for the control of major tropical diseases, including vaccines, drugs, diagnostic tools, and control of disease vectors (Commission on Health Research for Development 1990, pp. 62–64).

cent in 1983 (World Bank 1993, pp. 72–73). Effective implementation must, however, keep pace with technological breakthroughs. For example, unless the use of sterile needles can be assured, vaccination campaigns could spread hepatitis, AIDS, and other bloodborne diseases.

Extending Coverage of Rural Health Programs. Needless to say, it is essential for such cost-effective measures to reach rural, as well as urban, people. Since 1977 the expansion of public health facilities and medical personnel in Thailand has been especially rapid in rural areas. It has included an emphasis on "preventive and promotive services, as well as those highly public in nature" (Vuthipongse 1989, p. 40). Significantly, only a decade after the Declaration of Health for All by 2000 adopted at the Alma Ata International Conference on Primary Health Care in 1978, village health volunteers served over 90 percent of Thailand (p. 52). Important, too, has been health education, a community-based approach in which "government officials were reoriented to catalyze community action and provide training" and "appropriate and sustained development of institutional capacity" (pp. 52, 56). In contrast, a Tanzanian health specialist (at the same Takemi Symposium on International Health) was critical of his government and donors for Tanzania's excessive dependence on external resources to maintain its health services (Muhondwa 1989). Thailand's under-five mortality rate declined from 149 to 36 (per thousand live births) between 1960 and 1990 whereas the estimated decline in Tanzania was from 242 to 165.[4]

The limited success of rural health programs in many countries is linked to a reluctance to charge fees and an unwillingness or inability to promote community participation. Such involvement can contribute to the success of rural health, nutrition, and family planning programs. Individuals give priority to curative care, and community health workers find that dispensing a few drugs is less demanding than preventive and promotional activities. But active participation of local groups, such as village health committees, promotes community recognition that preventive and educational activities are the most cost-effective use of scarce resources.

Local participation is also needed to mobilize local resources, including fees, to cover part of the cost of a village health program. David Pyle (1981, pp. 231–32) reports that local officials responsible for a Community Health Worker Program in India were against charges, claiming that the local people would not pay even small amounts for health services. But Pyle reports that virtually all villagers that he interviewed said that they would. He emphasizes that this would also increase the villagers' sense of involvement in the program and the accountability of the village-level worker to the local community.

---

[4] For total fertility the contrast has also been large: a decline in Thailand's total fertility rate from an estimated 5.5 births per woman in 1970 to 2.3 in 1991 whereas the total fertility rate in Tanzania was virtually unchanged at 6.3 compared to 6.4 in 1970. For reasons discussed later, these contrasts in child survival and fertility are not simple coincidences.

The Fertility Transition

The determinants of changes in fertility are complex. They include biological factors (notably postpartum amenorrhea, which reduces conception among lactating women), as well as the economic, social, and attitudinal factors that influence access to contraceptives and the desire to use them.

In 1971 Dudley Kirk advanced the conclusion that once developing countries enter the phase of the demographic transition when birth rates begin to decline, the rate of decline of fertility seems to be "enormously speeded up" as compared with countries that experienced the demographic transition earlier. Cleland and Wilson (1987) confirm Kirk's conclusion and suggest that "ideational" factors, such as changes in attitudes and social norms, explain why declines in fertility, observed in the second phase of the demographic transition, are so abrupt.

In their review of the fertility transition in Europe, Knodel and van de Walle (1986, p. 411) emphasize that fertility declines took place under many social, economic, and demographic conditions. They note that "a cursory reading of western experience" can lead to the conclusion that "development is the best contraceptive." But they point out that "the steady and irreversible increase in the practice of family limitation" that occurred under a variety of social and economic conditions "suggests that the idea of controlling the number of children born rather than leaving it to fate has a wide appeal, once the possibility of control is realized." And they stress that prior to the onset of fertility decline "the practice of fertility limitation was largely absent (and probably unknown) among broad segments of the population" (Knodel and van de Walle 1986, pp. 390, 392, 411). They further emphasize that the timing of such declines was influenced strongly by culture and language, independent of socioeconomic conditions.[5]

The World Fertility Survey (forty-one countries) and other data for developing countries also reveal subnational differentials based on race, religion, or language. Cleland and Wilson (1987, p. 24) stress that "within culturally homogeneous populations, birth control and resulting marital fertility decline spreads to all sectors within a remarkably short period of time [which] implies that the fundamental forces of change operate at the societal level" (p. 24). Hence, Cleland and Wilson (1987, p. 25) conclude that much of the explanation for observed fertility trends "must lie in social or psychological elements, such as aspirations, knowledge, attitudes or social norms which are capable of rapid transformation."

But what are the important societal factors affecting when the demographic transition enters the second (declining fertility) phase? Per capita income and other economic factors stressed in the "household demand"

[5] They cite as one example the contrast between the French- and Flemish-speaking regions of Belgium.

models of fertility offer useful insights about determinants of change (Birdsall 1988). But because income per capita changes only slowly, it does not explain the sharp declines in fertility typical of the second phase of the demographic transition. Two factors stand out as being particularly important in bringing about the changes in knowledge, attitudes, and practice that characterize the fertility transition: improved survival prospects for infants and small children and increases in female education.

The Child Survival Hypothesis. Surprisingly, the first factor, the so-called child survival hypothesis, has been controversial. It is true, of course, that the increases in population in recent decades have been due to big declines in mortality and delayed (and limited) declines in fertility. But the persuasive formulations of the child survival hypothesis do not argue that reducing child mortality will automatically and promptly lead to declines in fertility. The argument is rather that the effectiveness of health and family planning activities can be enhanced if a concerted, programmatic effort is made to accelerate progress in reducing infant and child mortality *and* to increase parental awareness of the improved survival prospects, thereby facilitating adoption of the novel practice of limiting family size (Taylor 1977).

A synthesis by Easterlin of "the economics and sociology of fertility" shows why improving the survival prospects of infants and small children and increasing parental awareness of the improved prospects is a promising intervention for accelerating the reduction in fertility. It focuses on changing relationships between the number of children who survive and parents' demand for children.[6] Before a country has begun the demographic transition, there is no "problem" of unwanted children. Because of high infant and child mortality, the "potential supply" falls short of the number desired. Traditional practices, such as no intercourse during lactation, hold expressed fertility below the biological maximum, but there is no conscious action to limit fertility. In fact, traditional values and attitudes, such as childbearing as the major source of status for women, reinforce a large-family norm prior to the transition.

As child-survival prospects improve, Easterlin argues, a threshold is reached as parents become aware that the potential number of surviving children exceeds the desired number of children. Reaching that threshold marks the transition to a desired family size that reflects conscious decisions by parents.[7] "Excess supply" will also be influenced by changes that reduce the desired number of children, such as the economic benefits and costs of rearing children when child labor is reduced and more children attend school.

---

[6] The original presentation of the synthesis is in Easterlin 1975; but see also Easterlin 1978; Easterlin and Crimmins 1985; and Easterlin, Pollak, and Wachter 1980.

[7] Carl Taylor (personal communication, December 1993) suggests that recent data indicate that there is often a dramatic fall in fertility after the infant mortality rate falls to about 60 per thousand.

Focusing on the impact of improving child survival prospects in reaching the fertility threshold is especially important because, as noted, interventions are available that are capable of achieving further reductions in infant and child mortality rapidly and at low cost; and their feasibility has been shown in countries as diverse as Sri Lanka, Costa Rica, and China. However, many CARLs are failing to seize that opportunity because of neglect, faulty design, or weak implementation of rural health and family planning programs.

Potential for Rapid Changes in Fertility and Child Survival. Taken as a group, the forty-one countries (excluding China and India) that were classed as low-income economies in 1990 had the same 2.5 percent per year rate of natural increase in population in 1990 that prevailed in 1965 (Table 8.4). Although this suggests unrelenting, rapid population growth, there have been substantial reductions in the underlying birth and death rates. (The rate of natural increase is the difference between the crude birth rate and crude death rate converted to a percentage.) And some countries have made much more progress than others in reducing mortality and bringing birth rates in balance with lower death rates. None are more worthy of note in this regard that the world's two largest countries. India's rate of natural increase fell from 2.5 percent per year in 1965 to 1.9 percent in 1990. China's deceleration was even faster, from 2.8 to 1.5 percent. On the other hand, rates of natural increase for the three sub-Saharan CARLs in the table all started above the average for these low-income countries in 1965 and accelerated.

Rates of natural increase and the underlying crude rates serve better as indicators of population growth than of underlying fertility and mortality because they are sensitive to the age composition of the population. For example, crude birth rates will be high wherever the women of childbearing age are a large share of the population even if each woman has relatively few children. The estimates of changes in total fertility rates (TFRs) and under-five mortality rates in Table 8.4 give a more useful basis for assessing the widening differentials that have emerged among countries since the 1960s.[8]

Except for Kenya's exceptionally high TFR of 8, the rates in 1965 for the developing countries in Table 8.4 range from 5.5 to 6.9 births per woman. Kenya's TFR declined considerably to 6.5 in 1990, below Mexico's TFR of 6.7 in 1965. Mexico's rapid decline over 25 years to a TFR of 3.3 in 1990 holds some optimism for Kenya's future. Moreover, Mexico's fertility de-

[8] The *under-five mortality rate* is the probability of dying before age five years per 1,000 live births. Thus, it incorporates the infant mortality rate, which is the probability of dying by age 1 per 1,000 live births, and what is conventionally called the child mortality rate, the probability of dying by age five per 1,000 children who survive to their first birthday. Obviously, the higher the probability of dying, the lower the probability of survival until age five. Occasionally, the term "child mortality" will be used in this chapter to refer to under-five mortality. The *total fertility rate* is the number of children a woman would bear if (1) her lifetime fertility corresponded to the prevailing age-specific rates, and (2) she lived to the end of her reproductive years. The other demographic measures used in Table 8.4 are defined in Chapter 1.

Table 8.4. Population growth, fertility, and mortality for selected countries

	Rate of natural increase (%/year)		Crude birth rate (per 1,000)		Crude death rate (per 1,000)		Total fertility rate (births/woman)		Under-5 mortality rate (per 1,000 births)	
	1965	1990	1965	1990	1965	1990	1965	1990	1960	1990
Weighted average for low-income countries[a] (excluding China and India)	2.5	2.5	46	38	21	13	6.4	5.2	251[b]	175[b]
									182[c]	97[c]
Tanzania	2.6	3.0	49	48	23	18	6.6	6.6	242	165
Bangladesh	2.6	2.1	47	35	21	14	6.8	4.6	251	137
Nigeria	2.8	2.9	51	43	23	14	6.9	6.0	204	191
India	2.5	1.9	45	30	20	11	6.2	4.0	235	127
Kenya	3.2	3.5	52	45	20	10	8.0	6.5	203	83
China	2.8	1.5	38	22	10	7	6.4	2.5	210	43
Indonesia	2.3	1.7	43	26	20	9	5.5	3.1	214	111
Egypt	2.4	2.1	43	31	19	10	6.8	4.0	256	56
Colombia	3.2	1.8	43	24	11	6	6.5	2.7	132	21
Thailand	3.1	1.5	41	22	10	7	6.3	2.5	149	36
Malaysia	2.8	2.5	40	30	12	5	6.3	3.8	106	20
Mexico	3.4	2.2	45	27	11	5	6.7	3.3	148	38
Brazil	2.8	2.0	39	27	11	7	5.6	3.2	179	69
Taiwan[d]	3.3	1.3	40	18	7	5	6.3	2.8	—	—
United States	1.0	0.8	19	17	9	9	2.9	1.9	31	11
Japan	1.2	0.4	19	11	7	7	2.0	1.6	37	6

Sources: World Bank 1992b, pp. 270–71; World Bank 1993, pp. 200–201.
[a]Countries (other than China and India) with GNP per capita of U.S.$600 or less in 1990 as listed in World Bank 1992a.
[b]Weighted average for thirty countries in sub-Saharan Africa.
[c]Weighted average for sixteen countries in Asia, excluding China, India, and Japan.
[d]Taiwan's TFR shown for 1965 is an estimate for 1953–58 (JCRR 1961, p. 56). Taiwan's TFR shown for 1990 is an estimate for 1975 (World Bank 1978, p. 105). Taiwan's crude birth and death rates and rates of natural increase are for 1960 and 1985 (Republic of China 1988, p. 5).

cline is not unusual. Taiwan's fell from an average TFR of 6.3 for 1953–58 to 2.8 in 1975 and the TFRs in China, Thailand, and Colombia fell from 6.3–6.5 to 2.5–2.7 from 1965 to 1990. Those twenty-five years saw drops in TFRs of one-third or more even in India, Egypt, and Malaysia (where TFRs were 4 or less by 1990).

Some of the changes in mortality rates for children under age five are even more striking, as are the differences between countries. For example, whereas there was less than a twofold difference between Malaysia's 106 per thousand and Nigeria's 204 per thousand in 1965, by 1990 the differential was nearly tenfold (20 versus 191). Under-five mortality in China fell from 210 per thousand in 1960, not greatly below the 1960 rate in Tanzania, to 43 per thousand in 1990, less than one-fourth the estimated rate in Tanzania in that year.

Female Education, Child Survival, and Fertility Decline. Declines in fertility are associated with rising levels of female education. Especially notable is the fact that as early as 1984 China and Sri Lanka, two low-income countries with significant reductions in fertility, had rates of female enrollment in secondary schools of 31 and 64 percent, respectively, compared to an average of 15 percent for thirty-five low-income countries (excluding China and India) in 1985. The correlation between declines in fertility and in child mortality and the association of those declines with relatively high levels of female education are also apparent in the two African countries that, together with Kenya[9] (Chapter 11), have recently entered the fertility transition (Table 8.5).

Numerous studies have emphasized the important interactions between the level of a mother's schooling and the level of fertility and the survival prospects of infants and small children. Field research by Robert LeVine and his associates sheds light on the role of female education in the complex interactions that appear to lead to the interrelated outcomes of improved child health and reduced fertility. Analysis of survey data for samples of urban and rural households in Mexico focuses on evidence of effects on mothers' aspirations, attitudes, and beliefs and on maternal behavior related to the care of infants and small children. Their findings suggest that women who went further in school may well have acquired an increased desire and capacity "to seek and use public health information facilitating child survival and family planning" (LeVine and others 1991, p. 483). Moreover, they find evidence that increased schooling that enhances the "verbal responsiveness" of mothers to their children seems to change the nature of the mother–child relationship in ways that influence the health

[9] See Table 8.4 for changes in fertility and under-five mortality in Kenya. For secondary school enrollment, 19 percent of Kenyan females in that age group were enrolled in 1990. That figure is low relative to Botswana and Zimbabwe (and many Asian countries), but it was much higher than the level in all but four other countries in sub-Saharan Africa: Cameroon, Ghana, Madagascar, and Nigeria (World Bank 1993).

Table 8.5. Correlation between fertility, mothers' education, and child survival

	Total fertility rate (births/woman)		Under-5 mortality (per 1,000 births)		Females in secondary education (% of age group enrolled)
	1970	1991	1960	1990	1990
Zimbabwe	7.7	4.7	159	58	46
Botswana	6.9	4.8	—	45	47

Source: World Bank 1993.

and survival prospects of their children and also their own attitudes and practices affecting family size." In LeVine's words, "Women's attendance at school initiates a cumulative process over the generations that contributes to the demographic transition."

It would be a serious mistake to assume that only formal education has a significant impact on the changes in attitudes and behavior that lead to improved child health and lower fertility. Successful family planning programs are invariably associated with effective information, education, and communication (I, E, and C) activities. In fact, "development communication" broadly defined to include nonformal education, distance learning, and social marketing has become a powerful tool in the implementation of broad-based development strategies.[10] Furthermore, these programs are not expensive.

Enhancing the Effectiveness of Family Planning Programs. The receptivity of various audiences to messages aimed at promoting family planning (or other types of behavioral change) will almost certainly be influenced by the extent to which they have been involved in dynamic processes of technological and economic change. For example, Eva Mueller (1971) and others who have studied the rapid spread of family planning in Taiwan in the 1960s argue that rising aspirations among the great majority of farm households engendered by widespread agricultural progress meant that families quickly embraced a number of new attitudes and practices—adopting new plant varieties and other innovations, investing in better education for their children, purchasing new inputs or consumer goods that were previously beyond their reach, along with conscious action to limit family size.

The presence (or absence) of well-designed and well-implemented family planning programs is one of the most significant contrasts between countries that have achieved big reductions in fertility and those that have not. Socioeconomic development and family planning programs operate synergistically: they have more than simply additive effects on fertility (Bongaarts, Mauldin, and Phillips 1990; Mauldin and Berelson 1978).

---

[10] A recent publication of the U.S. Agency for International Development (AID 1993) provides a useful summary of progress over the past twenty-five years in improving the concepts and methodology of development communication.

That has not stopped some from challenging the view that family planning programs can accelerate the fertility transition. For example, the Caldwells (1988) have argued that because of family structures and (essentially religious) attitudes toward fertility, there is little demand for limiting family size in sub-Saharan Africa, and the "Asian Family Planning Model" is not suited to that region. Subsequently, Professor Caldwell (1991, p. 272) has put forward a more nuanced view. He has emphasized that the onset of fertility decline in Africa is likely to occur at lower levels of child mortality than elsewhere. Accordingly, he argues that it is especially important in Africa to link family planning with intensive maternal and child health programs. However, in Asia, too, "deep gloom pervaded the early stages"; and, as late as 1961, the prevailing view in Taiwan was that its farm families were deeply traditional and that its culture made it unlikely that a family planning program would be effective, except with a few educated and "westernized" people (Freedman 1987, p. 59). Nonetheless, remarkably rapid success was achieved with the family planning program (see Chapter 10), as in Indonesia.

An abrupt policy change and a new program in Indonesia in the early 1970s led to increases in family planning that cannot be explained solely by the influence of socioeconomic change. In Java and Bali the percentage of married women using contraceptives increased from 3 to 50 percent in 1971–81. It seems beyond doubt that the government program "speeded the process, especially as it has affected the rural poor" (McNicoll and Singarimbun 1982, p. 33).

The Matlab Project in rural Bangladesh was designed to challenge "the widely accepted view that economic development and improvements in well-being are pre-requisites to demographic change" (Phillips and others 1988, p. 313).[11] Behind the Matlab Project was the idea that in developing countries many couples (maybe a majority) "are most appropriately characterized by ambivalence in their attitudes toward family size and contraception." But an intensive service program can "create demand for services leading to contraceptive adoption when it might otherwise not occur . . . [because] the outreach worker of the program provides the social support that enables women to bypass the sociocultural controls against family planning" (Phillips and others 1988, pp. 322, 323).

Since late 1977 young married women, who are full-time employees of the Project and residents of the 70 villages they serve, have visited all eligi-

---

[11] Matlab District is the site of a field research station of the International Centre for Diarrhoeal Disease Research. It has advantages as a field site for population policy research because of the accurate and complete demographic data collected since the mid-1960s. The comparison area receives the usual services of the government's health and family planning program. Thus, a comparison can be made between the impact of the government program and the intensive outreach system in the project area. The criticism that such experiments always succeed can be countered. The Matlab Project was preceded by a Contraceptive Distribution Project that ensured an ample supply of contraceptives but failed to induce a sustained increase in family planning.

ble women in the Matlab Project area. Modern contraceptive use increased from 7 percent to 20 percent in three months, rose to 33 percent at the end of eighteen months, and then between 1983 and 1985 reached a plateau of 45 percent. In another 87 villages in an area with similar social, economic, and demographic conditions, contraception increased only slightly and has remained at low levels.

There is likely to be a big discrepancy between social and private calculations of costs and benefits of additional children. For example, rapid growth in the number of, say, landless laborers, will be a powerful factor depressing returns to labor. But families may see an advantage in more children to contribute to household income as wage laborers. It is possible, however, that such "supports for high fertility erode under conditions of worsening poverty." However, poverty-based demand for contraception is likely to remain latent without a strong family planning program "that provides couples with support for fertility regulation" (Phillips and others 1988, pp. 327, 329).

Those conclusions from the Matlab Project are controversial. There is, however, wider evidence that well-designed family planning programs make a difference and that improvements in income are not a prerequisite for fertility decline. Economic pressure can also motivate couples to reduce family size. Thus, a specialist in the World Bank's Population and Human Resources Department asserts "that the fertility decline has begun in Sub-Saharan Africa," in part because "stagnation or even declines in incomes have made people become more sensitive to the economic costs of children, and this has led to substantial reductions in family-size preferences in parts of Africa" (Cochrane 1991, pp. 261, 269). She also emphasizes the need to reject "the false dichotomy over whether it is demand or the supply of family planning programs that matters. It is clearly both and there is interaction between the two elements" (Cochrane 1991, p. 265).

Moreover, the quality of family planning programs makes a difference in the impact on the fertility transition. Program performance can be strengthened by (1) ensuring strong political support, (2) adapting its design to fit the local social structure and norms, (3) supplementing clinic services with outreach activities that enhance accessibility of contraceptive supplies and information, and (4) providing good-quality services, including a choice of contraceptives, and competent and caring personnel who can provide follow-up information about side effects and alternatives (Bongaarts, Mauldin, and Phillips 1990, p. 307).[12] Experience in Kenya (Chapter 11) is a recent

[12] Although it is administratively difficult—and potentially expensive—there are important advantages in integrating family planning with health services. Caldwell (1991) and Cochrane (1991) both argue that it is especially important in sub-Saharan Africa to link family planning efforts with mother-and-child health programs. Such links also strengthen the capacity of health services to achieve broad coverage in order to slow the spread of AIDS by detecting HIV infection, by promoting contraceptive methods that prevent infection, and by treating pelvic infections that increase the spread of AIDS among heterosexual couples.

reminder that time is required to achieve reasonably competent implementation of family planning activities in association with public health programs.

WHICH "GROWTH-ORIENTED" STRATEGY?

The contrasting experience of Taiwan and Mexico (Chapter 10) suggests that the key question is not whether a country pursues a growth-oriented strategy: poverty cannot be eradicated without economic growth. Rather, the question is, which *type* of growth-oriented strategy? A broad-based strategy, with strong growth linkages to decentralized industrial development and with reliance on labor-using, capital-saving technologies, can lead to rapid growth and reduce poverty. However, there are cogent reasons for selective interventions to improve the health and survival prospects of infants and small children. They can reduce infant and child mortality rates more rapidly than would occur through income growth alone. Linking those health activities with appropriately designed efforts to spread family planning can lead to rapid declines in fertility and slow the explosive population growth of some CARLs. In addition, progress in bringing down shockingly high maternal mortality rates through cost-effective interventions to make pregnancy and delivery safer is complemented by declines in fertility that reduce the frequency with which women confront the risks of child birth.[13]

Rapid population growth (above 2 percent per year) sharply increases the time required for CARLs to reach the structural transformation turning point (see Chapter 1). The situation is extreme in Kenya and Tanzania because of the unusually rapid growth of their populations (Chapter 11). But the implications are general: policies that foster fertility reduction, thereby slowing rapid growth in the population and labor force, complement policies for expansion of output and employment opportunities.

Cost-effective technologies for reducing mortality and morbidity among small children merit high priority because they improve survival prospects and also because they enhance the health and productivity of children in later years. Malnutrition in the first three years of life may impair the cognitive as well as the physical development of children. However, it is the *interaction* of malnutrition and a poor social environment that is a powerful influence on cognitive development. For example, the syndrome of malnutrition, frequent illness, and apathy not only affects the exploratory activity of infants and small children but also influences the stimulation that they receive from

---

[13] It is estimated that "about one in 50 women in developing countries dies as a consequence of complications of pregnancy and childbirth, compared with only one in 2,900 in the established market economies" (World Bank 1993, p. 113). See also Table 1.5.

their mothers and others.[14] Moreover, reaching a threshold in the reduction of infant and child mortality increases acceptance of family planning.

Thus, *some* social programs, such as public health interventions targeted at young women and their children, offer ways to alleviate the worst effects of poverty for the most vulnerable among the rural population. Experience demonstrates that this can be done ahead of the slower process of structural transformation necessary to eliminate the root causes of mass hunger and poverty. Furthermore, the same programs also can accelerate the demographic transition, thereby hastening the structural transformation turning point.

Clearly, political pressures in CARLs can favor social programs—exemplified by food subsidies—that mainly transfer money from the national budget or rural families to much-less-needy urban residents. The budgetary imbalance from massive public transfers for cheap food either proves unsustainable as part of a macroeconomic crisis or, if sustained, crowds out public investments needed for more fundamental social and economic objectives.

The economic case for seizing opportunities to raise productivity and to expand employment through broad-based development strategies has been presented throughout the chapters of Part 2. Too often, however, a few large farms are favored to the detriment of the majority of farms; redistributive land reform is infeasible, and the political compromise, land tenure reform, makes things worse for tenants and laborers; money continues to be wasted on inefficient fertilizer factories; ill-conceived credit programs foster labor-displacing mechanization; and, as discussed in this chapter, costs of food subsidies balloon while public health budgets stay lean.

Why do some governments appear to act with foresight and seize the most promising opportunities whereas others pursue strategies detrimental to economic and social progress? Certainly, a part of the answer is that the social structure associated with poverty tends "to produce a particular type of politics, which is the type least likely to set a high premium on so generalized an objective as national development" (Leys 1971). Often, a preoccupation with staying in power appears to be the principal concern of political leaders and policymakers. So, for example, priority is often given to costly food subsidy schemes because they serve the interests of the government's urban-based support coalition.

Moreover, the exigencies of a world of sometimes abrupt change and incomplete knowledge often can be seen to take precedence over the pursuit of the strategies reviewed in Part 2. Whether it was a desire to cushion consumers from a sudden fourfold increase in the cost of food or fuel or to ex-

---

[14] See Ricciuti 1979 and Johnston and Clark 1982, pp. 53–54, for summaries of the evidence and relevant literature.

ercise countervailing power against an emerging monopsony position for Del Monte or Dole, the scope for government action reaches well beyond the narrow assumptions of a perfectly competitive economy. Thus, the starting point for policymakers in most CARLs is extensive regulatory intervention, more or less control over the money supply, the interest rate, and the exchange rate, government spending that ranges from 15 to 45 percent of GDP, and a political economy where almost any policy change that is beneficial for broader objectives also redistributes income.

Given these initial conditions, what are the prospects that a CARL can adopt the "right" strategy? It was emphasized in Chapter 3 that strategic choices in Japan and the United States, during the periods when each was a CARL, were shaped by strategic notions that fostered broad-based agricultural development. The experience of the six countries examined in Part 3— China and the Soviet Union, Taiwan and Mexico, and Kenya and Tanzania—is highly diverse. Again, however, we find clear evidence of the impact—for good or ill—of strategic notions held by political leaders and others who shaped decisions affecting development outcomes.

PART THREE

CHOICES AND CONSEQUENCES

CHAPTER NINE

CHINA
AND THE
SOVIET UNION

Collectivization is a disastrous strategy for agricultural development. Stalin's swift collectivization of Soviet agriculture between 1929 and 1935 institutionalized many barriers to agricultural growth. The economic and human costs were enormous and unnecessary. Farm output fell sharply, farmers slaughtered their livestock rather than allow them to be confiscated, and millions of people died in the famine of 1933. Handicraft production and small-scale industries were casualties as well, accentuating the fall in rural living standards. And later reliance on "command farming" and a "campaign approach" merely led to waste and inefficiency. The dramatic changes associated with the collapse of the Soviet regime have been followed by a spate of literature on the shortcomings of a Soviet-type command economy.[1]

China's approach to collectivization apparently managed to avoid many of the problems in the Soviet Union—or so it was believed until the late 1970s. Data emerging since Mao Tse-tung's death in 1976 show that collectivization in China also handicapped agricultural development. And further contradicting the previous easy assessment was the remarkable upsurge in agricultural production and in rural nonfarm activity in China following

[1] See, for example, the summary by Ericson (1991) that introduces a symposium on economic transition in the Soviet Union and Eastern Europe and the survey of agriculture and the transition to the market by Brooks and others (1991).

the agricultural reforms that began in 1978. The reforms strengthened individual incentives, decentralized decision making, and enlarged the scope for initiative in the rural economy. China's experience—given its economic, structural, and demographic features—is more relevant to problems confronting other contemporary CARLs than is the Soviet Union's. In 1985 three-fourths of China's work force depended on agriculture, compared with only one-fifth in the Soviet Union.

In the USSR, the economic strategy not only thwarted agricultural productivity growth but also destroyed the social and institutional basis for agricultural development, making reform exceedingly difficult. China's strategy at least allowed the social basis for broad-based development to survive. China's collectivization left intact the essence of its small farm system and other rural institutions, providing a foundation for growth once policymakers accepted the need for agricultural policy reform. Strengthening that foundation, China expanded access to primary education, public health, and family planning services and invested in rural infrastructure.

These two cases are important because of their influence on the strategic notions that policymakers hold in many CARLs. Failure to acknowledge errors—much less to learn from them—is one of the striking features of both. The totalitarian regimes of Stalin and Mao inhibited communication to maintain control, but this also smothered the flow of information about the consequences of policy choices.

COLLECTIVIZATION OF SOVIET AGRICULTURE

Stalin's collectivization and subsequent agricultural strategies featuring collectives or state farms (in Cuba, Egypt, Ethiopia, Mexico, Tanzania, and elsewhere) conforms to a tenet of Marxist-Leninist ideology—that large farms are economically superior to small ones. Soviet decision makers also assumed that the peasantry was inimicable to the society they were trying to build (see Box 9.1).

A crisis in urban grain supplies was the catalyst for Stalin's collectivization. As in many contemporary CARLs, priority was given to supplying cities and industrial centers. But forced collectivization was also seen as a way of controlling the rural population (Lewin 1968; Nove 1971). Indeed, Stalin was determined to eliminate the independent peasant population, which he saw as a threat to the regime, especially the richer peasants, or Kulaks.

Agriculture in Soviet Economic Development

"Steel was a final good to Stalin, and bread an intermediate one," said Abram Bergson (quoted in Tang 1967, p. 1118). Collectivization was an integral part of Stalin's accelerated industrialization. Its emphasis was on heavy

Box 9.1. Marxist-Leninist Notions and Soviet Agriculture

Until 1954 collective farms accounted for more than 90 percent of agricultural output in the Soviet Union. They were based on cooperative use of resources in a village or villages. Major decisions were made by a manager, but the state constantly interfered in the farm's internal affairs (Kahan 1964, p. 254). Members were obliged to render labor services. Remuneration was based on "work points" that determined their share of output after the share claimed by the state and after production costs and taxes. Each family was assigned a small plot that was farmed intensively to supplement food and income. The state farms, which became increasingly important after 1954, were organized like industrial enterprises and relied on hired labor and more extensive use of farm machinery than the collective farms.

Invoking Lenin to supply the rationale for collectivization, Joseph Stalin summarized agricultural strategy in a 1933 report on the First Five-Year Plan:

The party proceeded from the fact that in order to consolidate the dictatorship of the proletariat and to build up socialist society it was necessary, in addition to industrialization, to pass from small, individual peasant farming to large-scale collective agriculture with tractors and modern agricultural machinery, as the only firm basis for the Soviet power in the rural districts. . . .

Lenin said: There is no escape from poverty for the small farm (V.I. Lenin, *Selected Works*, Vol. VI, p. 370). . . .

Lenin said: . . . It is essential to adopt joint cultivation on large model farms. Without that there can be no escape from the chaos, from the truly desperate condition, in which Russia finds herself (V.I. Lenin, *Selected Works*, Vol. VI, p. 371).

Proceeding from this, Lenin arrived at the following fundamental conclusion: Only if we succeed in proving to the peasants in practice the advantages of common, collective, cooperative, artel [traditional Russian collective labor] cultivation of the soil . . . will the working class, which holds the state power, be really able to convince the peasant of the correctness of its policy and to secure the real and durable following of the millions of peasants (V.I. Lenin, *Selected Works*, Vol. VI, p. 199).

In this connection, the object of the Five-Year Plan in the sphere of agriculture was to unite the scattered and small individual peasant farms, which lacked the opportunity of utilizing tractors and modern agricultural machinery, into large collective farms, equipped with all the modern implements of highly developed agriculture. . . .

The party has succeeded in converting the U.S.S.R. from a land of small peasant farming into a land where agriculture is run on the largest scale in the world.

These strategic notions have been remarkably resilient. Stalin reiterated many of the same ideas in a speech introducing the Fourth Plan in 1946 (*New York Times*, February 10, 1946). Indeed, it was not until the 1980s that the failure of this strategy was acknowledged.

The terror at the heart of Stalin's strategy of revolution and social control engendered its own genre of black humor. On one occasion, Stalin published a critique of the Soviet collectivization drive that elicited a number of letters that took issue with his conclusions. In his "Reply to Collective Farm Comrades," Stalin (1942, p. 175) wrote: "It was my duty to reply to the letters in private correspondence; but that proved to be impossible, for more than half the letters received did not have any return address (the writers forgot to send their addresses)." But a much later exchange suggests, as Stalin must have known, that the addresses were omitted deliberately. Dixit and Nalebuff (1991, p. 17) offer the following parable: "Kruschev first denounced Stalin's purges at the Soviet Communist Party's 10th Congress. After his dramatic speech, someone in the audience shouted out, asking what Kruschev had been doing at the time. Kruschev responded by asking the questioner to please stand up and identify himself. The audience remained silent. Kruschev replied: 'That is what I did, too.' "

industries to produce "the means of production" that were considered the key to rapid growth. Agriculture was simply a source of food and raw materials for industry and an expanding urban population, as well as a foreign exchange earner to finance essential imports. This strategy of surplus extraction also meant that agriculture should make a maximum contribution to domestic saving; and, therefore, the reverse flow of inputs and consumer goods to agriculture should be an absolute minimum.

Rock-bottom prices for grain delivered against compulsory quotas and payments in kind for services provided by the Machine Tractor Stations represented a huge flow of resources out of agriculture—in effect, saving forced on the peasantry. In 1936 the compulsory procurement price for wheat was 15 rubles a ton, but this was sold to state mills at 107 rubles a ton. Thus, the "turnover tax" was 92 rubles a ton, almost nine-tenths of the wholesale price (Nove 1969). This was the principal means by which the rural population was forced to finance a large part of the rapid industrialization initiated in 1928 with the first Five-Year Plan. Moreover, the urban population was assured of food supplies. In years of shortage, the needs of industrial workers were met by reductions in the already-low consumption by farm households.

Rapid industrialization, collectivization, and other measures lowered the standard of living of the rural population. But did agriculture make a large net contribution to the capital requirements of other sectors? Statistics are sketchy, but Millar (1970) suggests that the net capital flow from agriculture was probably modest because the reverse flow into agriculture, including budget grants to the Machine Tractor Stations and interest-free grants to state farms, nearly offset the expansion of agriculture's sales. In short, the "surplus" extracted from the rural economy at great human cost was, to a large extent, recycled into inefficient large-scale agriculture rather than invested productively elsewhere. The immediate economic cost included decline in total factor productivity in agriculture between the late 1920s and late 1930s (Karcz 1967; D. G. Johnson 1971), and the economic costs of this strategy increased with time.

Since Stalin's death in 1953 there has been a large increase in the flow of resources into agriculture to overcome his legacy of poor agricultural performance. In 1950 agriculture's share in total investment was 10 percent; since the early 1970s it has been 30 percent (Ofer 1987, p. 1804). But apart from two periods, 1952–58 and 1964–70, the results have been disappointing.[2] There was slower growth in output in the 1970s despite "a decade of unprecedented levels of agricultural investment, a doubling of fertilizer availability, and significant improvement in the relative income position of farm people" (D. G. Johnson 1983, p. 19).

Shortcomings in Soviet development strategies have now become more apparent. In agriculture, "it is clear that the economic payoff fell far short of expectations in the 1930s and that the Soviet Union is still paying dearly for the decision to collectivize and for the way the decision was implemented" (Ofer 1987, p. 1803). The impressive industrial growth in the Soviet Union in the 1950s seemed to vindicate the low priority given to agriculture. However, Stalin's strategy was not a basis for sustained growth even in the industrial sector. Later, there was a decline in growth of income per capita and of manufacturing. Early industrialization took place when the dominant technological advance in industrialized countries "was concentrated in heavy industry and machinery, energy, and raw materials" (Ofer 1987, p. 1823). These activities were well suited to the institutional capacities and structure of the Soviet system; hence, problems of centralized planning and a command economy did not become serious until later.

Adverse Effects of Central Planning and Collectivization

There are many reasons for the secular decline in Soviet growth (Ofer 1987, pp. 1814–16). As in any country, the Soviet Union's increases in output are limited by the rate at which new inputs of land, labor, and capital can be added. Hasty implementation of crash programs also led to inefficient investment, which undermined sustainable growth and led to yet greater use of inputs in pursuit of output targets. On top of that, the growing complexity of the economy made it increasingly difficult to translate goals into detailed production plans. Moreover, expanding military spending absorbed a vast amount of scarce resources, both human and material. Finally, material incentives were weakened by inability to fulfill targets for consumer goods, whose production was cut first when growth faltered.

[2] From 1952 to 1976 the annual growth of agricultural output by six-year period, based on three-year averages centered on the specified year, were for 1952–58, 6.7 percent; 1958–64, 1.5 percent; 1964–70, 4.5 percent; and 1970–76, 1.6 percent (D. G. Johnson 1983, p. 18).

The adverse effects of Soviet strategy on technological change have been even greater because the structure of incentives and centralized decision making hindered development and the adoption of innovations. The USSR's inability to follow industrial rivals toward an "information-intensive economy" with emphasis on electronics, computers, and communications magnified the shortcomings of the Soviet system.

Often, machinery and other inputs were unavailable because state-run manufacturers lacked the awareness, incentive, and capacity to respond to the diverse needs of Soviet farms (Nove 1983, p. 89). In the 1960s and 1970s there was a continuing failure to increase agricultural productivity (D. G. Johnson 1983; Brooks 1983). Despite high investment in Soviet agriculture in the USSR's final decades, the decline in the share of agriculture in its labor force (from 34 to 20 percent in 1965–85) was less than the 14 to 7 percent for nineteen industrial market economies (World Bank 1987b, p. 265). Since payments to collective-farm members were a residual, there was little incentive for managers to economize on labor use.

Soviet reforms faltered in late 1990 partly because major cities were threatened with chronic food shortages. Yet, forecasts for grain production were favorable. The problem was not the endemic inefficiency in agricultural production but the inability to get crops from farms to consumers. Because of the repression of private trade for more than 70 years, there were few experienced entrepreneurs to step in when state-operated food distribution networks collapsed. These institutional weaknesses are compounded by poor transport systems. Neglect of marketing infrastructure is another result of Soviet strategic notions, in particular the Marxist distinction between "productive" and "unproductive" investments. The latter included "all investments in services such as housing, urban infrastructure, and consumer services as well as in public administration, banking and other business services" (Ofer 1987, p. 1807). Those shortcomings continue to plague agriculture in the former republics of the USSR.

CHINA'S EVOLVING STRATEGY

For nearly a decade after the victory over General Chiang Kai-shek and the Kuomintang, the policies of Mao Tse-tung resulted in increasingly drastic changes, culminating with rural communes in 1958. Policy shifts away from pragmatism reflected the interruptions by Mao's radicalism—the Great Leap Forward (1958–60) and the Cultural Revolution of 1966–76 (Perkins and Yusuf 1985, pp. 4, 90). The undercurrent of pragmatism was due to the long and intimate association of Mao and other Communist leaders with China's peasants, especially when the party headquarters were located in Yenan, a remote rural area. During "nearly two decades of skillful guerrilla campaigning in the 1930s and 1940s, the Communists became adept at organizing and leading the peasantry" (Perkins and Yusuf 1985, p. 88). In contrast, Stalin, Lenin, and most Soviet leaders had weak links with Russia's farm population. Indeed, Lenin and Stalin saw their agricultural strategy as "war" against the peasants.

Land Reform and Collectivization

Redistributive land reform by China's Communist leaders had many objectives. But a major one was to break the power of the rural gentry. Landlords, roughly 3 or 4 percent of the population, were treated harshly. Takeover of their land and other property was accomplished by intimidation, beatings, and even murder. William Hinton, who was in a Chinese village in 1948, observed "the brutality of the old system echoed again and again in the convulsions of its demise." At times, even "families that rented out small plots of land, hired some labor, or loaned out modest sums at high interest were called rich peasants and attacked as such" (Hinton 1966, pp. 141–43).

The Communist Party tried to ensure that most land went to the poorest rural families, regarded as the natural base of party support. Between 1950 and 1952 roughly half of the arable land was redistributed among 300 million or so peasants. Also redistributed to them were animals, tools, cash, and other assets. The share of rural income of the lowest 20 percent of the rural population may have nearly doubled, from 6 to 11 percent. This is the main reason for China's relatively equal distribution of income within rural regions. Later collectivization preserved that intraregional equality in income distribution. However, there is still substantial interregional inequality (Perkins and Yusuf 1985, pp. 108 and passim).

Collectivization began immediately after land reform. The first step was "mutual aid teams" of 8 to 10 families. Next came "elementary agricultural producers' cooperatives" of 20 to 25 families. This was followed by "advanced producers' cooperatives" of 150 to 200 families, in which most of the land, implements, and labor were pooled, although some individual ownership rights were retained.

Collectivization came quickly after land reform, primarily to consolidate the party's control in the countryside. The need "to prevent the rise of an independent class of wealthy peasants . . . was widely accepted within the party" (Perkins and Yusuf 1985, p. 75). It was also believed that it would be easier to mobilize surplus rural labor and so increase capital formation and agricultural production.

The same political and economic objectives were behind the decision in 1958 to merge the advanced producers' cooperatives into some 26,000 huge rural communes (averaging about 5,000 households). The three-tier structure of the communes (organized into brigades and production teams) strengthened the regime's control over economic and social decisions. There was massive mobilization of rural labor: tens of billions of days were devoted to rural construction projects. Yet, the results have been disappointing, in part because most of the easier sites had been developed earlier. Furthermore, "many projects were carried out on the basis of poorly conceived designs and frequently did as much harm as good" (Perkins and Yusuf 1985, p. 51).

In line with the Marxist-Leninist view, China's leaders in 1958 believed that the communes would enjoy economies of scale and adopt modern farming technologies more rapidly and more successfully than would small peasant farms.[3] Collectivization was expected to increase and maintain income equality among the rural population. Ability to supply urban centers was also a big consideration. Finally, just as producers' cooperatives were regarded as superior to privately owned family farms, collective ownership was regarded as a still higher form of ownership, and the pooling of land and resources in a large rural commune was viewed as an advance toward "all-people" or state ownership.[4]

So optimistic were Mao and his colleagues about the economic gains that many lower-level cadres submitted inflated estimates of production. This accounts for the delay in recognizing the disastrous results from the whirlwind rise of the rural communes in 1958 (Ashton and others 1984). Tragically, grain continued to be extracted from the countryside to feed the urban population and to export: China's net grain *exports* were 4.2 million tons in 1959 and 2.7 million tons in 1960. Later, it was discovered that production had fallen to 165 million tons in 1959 and 139 million tons in 1960, compared to 180 million tons in 1955 (Jamison and Piazza 1987, p. 472; Walker 1984, p. 160). In 1961, 4.5 million tons of grain had to be imported to supplement domestic production, still only 143 million tons.

In the meantime, the worst famine in history killed at least 23 million (and maybe 30 million) people between 1959 and 1962.[5] China's national aver-

---

[3] China established some state farms. In 1979 they accounted for less than 2 percent of the farm labor force and for about 4 percent of the cultivated area. They are mainly for treecrops, such as rubber and tea (Lardy 1983, p. 100).

[4] William Hinton was a technical volunteer who worked in China between 1947 and 1953 to promote large-scale, mechanized agriculture. Echoing the Soviet notions in Box 9.1, he recalls Mao's view that "under the conditions existing in China, only a fundamental shift in productive relations in the countryside—a shift from individual to collective agriculture—could lay the groundwork for an all-round development of productive forces, provide a market for China's growing industries, supply these industries with raw materials, and make possible the introduction of tillage machinery, electricity, pumps, and modern techniques of all kinds into the Chinese countryside" (Hinton 1970, p. 219).

[5] As in other CARLs, China then relied heavily on calories and other nutrients from grain, potatoes, and other "starchy staples." Hence, there was almost no scope for offsetting reductions in food supplies by direct human consumption of grain normally destined for feeding livestock. Deaths in the Soviet Union associated with collectivization of the 1930s would have been greater without the slaughter of livestock and an increase in direct human consumption of starchy staples normally fed to livestock. Nevertheless census data that became available only after the collapse of the USSR indicate that at least 6 million people perished in the 1930s as a result of liquidation of the Kulaks, collectivization, and the 1932–33 famine (Livi-Bacci 1993).

Figure 9.1. China's death rate and average per capita food energy availability, 1953–65

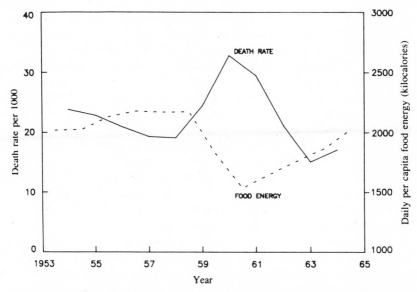

Source: Ashton and others 1984, Figure 1, p. 623. © 1984 The Population Council. Reprinted by permission.

age daily calorie availability in 1960 was only about 1,500 (Figure 9.1). In contrast, Ethiopia's, at 1,735, was the lowest in 1980, and only four other countries had average daily calorie availabilities below 1,800 (see Ashton and others 1984).

In December 1962 a secret resolution of the Central Committee of the Chinese Communist Party summarized the painful lessons of collectivization, emphasizing that "we should obtain agricultural products by economic rather than by administrative means" (as quoted in Walker 1984, p. 163). Drastic changes were made to decentralize decision making and to restore producers' incentives. The average size of communes was reduced, and, by 1980, their number had doubled. More important, farm management was shifted from the commune to the brigade or, in most cases, the production team of some thirty to forty farm households. Policies on private plots were liberalized, and rural markets were again permitted (Perkins and Yusuf 1985, p. 79).

Nevertheless, Mao's preference for direct planning and reliance on "administrative means" for China's agriculture continued. His "rejection of international comparative advantage" was "extended to China's domestic economy as well" (Lardy 1983, p. 49). This bias, which prevailed before 1978, was reinforced by the weakness of China's transport system. Policies that discouraged specialization and exchange had adverse effects on resource allocation and productivity. Moreover, China's poorest provinces suffered most from Mao's emphasis on regional self-sufficiency.

Agricultural Policy Reforms since 1978

Reforms in China since 1978 had a remarkable impact on production. Under the "responsibility system," production teams were subdivided into individual households, which contracted with production teams to deliver fixed amounts of specified products or to carry out particular tasks (Perkins and Yusuf 1985, pp. 80–83). And since 1984, land rights to households were typically granted for 15 to 30 years to strengthen private incentives for land improvement (Lardy 1986, p. 326). Communes have now disappeared, replaced by township and village administrative units.

The reforms doubled growth in grain production, dramatically improved total factor productivity, and increased rural nonfarm activity (Figure 9.2). Between 1957–78 and 1978–84 the annual increase in grain production rose from 2.1 to 4.9 percent. Increases for other crops were even greater, for example, from about 1 percent to nearly 15 and 19 percent a year, respectively, for oil-bearing crops and cotton (Lardy 1986, pp. 326–27). Moreover, the rise in farm income has been reinforced by rapid expansion of rural nonfarm employment and income.

Improved incentives and efficiency contributed to increases in crop output after 1978. Decollectivization meant that members of a household were the direct beneficiaries of their own hard work, initiative, and managerial decisions. Higher quota prices and other policy changes that have raised producer prices have also improved incentives. Jettisoning the policy of local self-sufficiency allowed increased specialization and productivity gains from more efficient use of resources.

All of these changes accelerated the growth of rural farm and nonfarm output because they "have stimulated latent entrepreneurial impulses of a kind that have been very strong in China in the past" (Barnett 1986, p. 9). Tapping the energy and enterprise of millions of rural households is behind China's dynamism in recent years.

To avoid a sharp increase in urban food prices, government subsidies on cereals and edible oil increased fivefold between 1974–78 and 1983. The 20 billion yuan spent on those subsidies in 1983 was a heavy fiscal burden, and, as a result, budgetary outlays for agriculture have been reduced sharply (Lardy 1986, pp. 328–33; see also D. G. Johnson 1987, p. 29). These reductions were offset by increased private investment financed from higher farm incomes. However, additional income was used primarily for increased consumption and private investment in housing because of uncertainty about continued reform. Such uncertainty had less effect on outlays for current inputs, and there was an increase in use of chemical fertilizers—from an esti-

Figure 9.2. Index of China's total factor productivity in agriculture, 1952–87

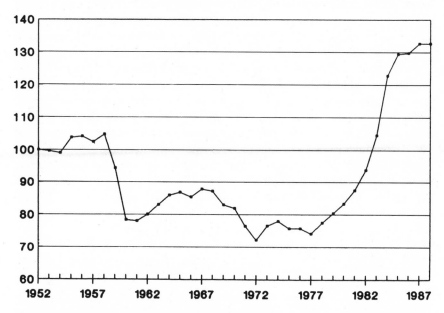

Note: Lin (1990) presents several estimates of changes in total factor productivity, but argues that Wen's estimates on which this figure are based are probably the most accurate available. Furthermore, as Lin notes, the broad patterns of change suggested by the various estimates are very similar.

mated 65 kg (in nutrient weight) per hectare in 1977 to 178 kg in 1984. That (and some improvement in the balance of applications of nitrogen, phosphate, and potassium) helped to increase crop yields and output (Stone 1986, p. 455; Lardy 1986, p. 331).

In fact, growth in production has slowed considerably since 1984. In 1985–89 growth of agricultural output averaged 3.5 percent, compared to more than 6.5 percent in all but one of the preceding six years; crop production fell in 1985 and 1988. This slowdown was due mainly to declines in farm product prices and increases in prices of farm inputs (Sicular 1990). (The fiscal burden of subsidies was reduced by cutting the prices paid to farmers for commodities bought by the government.) Moreover, government policies allowing private nonfarm enterprises, together with credit policies that diverted funds from farming to nonfarming, encouraged an outflow of labor and other resources from agriculture.

Growth of domestic fertilizer production also slowed in 1985 and 1986, along with a sharp decline in fertilizer imports. And because of frequent policy changes (and pressure on fertilizer manufacturers to hold down prices that was tighter than the pressure on their input and transport prices), fertilizer makers have diversified into less-regulated products. Moreover, farmers are applying less manure and weeding less "because the value of their labor in off-farm and non-foodcrop farming activities is much higher than it was a decade ago" (Stone 1989).

Nevertheless, China's experience since 1978 is strong evidence that incentives and decentralized decision making help to expand agricultural production and to increase total factor productivity. With rural communes came a fall in total factor productivity, followed by stagnation until 1978 when it rose rapidly (Figure 9.2), which is not surprising. Members of communes receive remuneration according to "work points" or something similar that is only loosely based on their contribution to the group. Incentives to work hard and exercise initiative are few, unlike a situation where rewards are linked directly to performance.

Contradictions in Maoist Strategies

China's leaders were committed "to serve the rural poor," and they have seen "their future and the future of the policies they believe in as being intimately tied to the prosperity of the countryside" (Perkins and Yusuf 1985, p. 5). However, there was an equally strong commitment to an industrial state supporting modern military forces. This led in the 1950s to a Stalinist development strategy, with emphasis on heavy industry, such as steel and machinery. And that continued to be the dominant strategy until Mao's death, despite rhetoric about "agriculture as the foundation."

Unlike the Soviet Union, China was able to implement a self-reliant strategy for agriculture that expanded output by labor-using, capital-saving technologies and minimized the flow of scarce resources into agriculture. "The choice of a self-reliant strategy was deliberate. The government budget directly controlled nearly a third of national product, and industrialization proceeded rapidly throughout the three decades, but these resources were directed mainly toward the machinery and steel sectors, not agriculture" (Perkins and Yusuf 1985, p. 194).

China's version of an "industrialization first" strategy resulted in a unique urban bias. After rising from 12.5 to 15.4 percent in 1952–57, the increase in the urban share of population to 17.9 percent in 1957–78 was slight. This was due to a virtual ban on migration from rural to urban areas. Since then, controls have been relaxed.[6] However, the ability to enforce that ban is striking evidence of the government's capacity to implement policies.

[6] The large reported growth of the urban population from 241 million in 1983 to 382 million in 1985 (or 38 percent of the total) is, however, misleading. In 1984 the Chinese redefined "urban," and a large, but unknown, part of the increase results from this reclassification (Perkins 1988, p. 639).

Prohibition of migration meant that there was no need to increase compulsory grain deliveries to feed city dwellers (Walker 1984, p. 182). At the same time, self-reliance for rural areas meant that agriculture had to support a bigger rural population—up 57 percent in 1957–82 to 859 million, which compares with a 46 percent urban increase to 145 million. With limited scope for expanding the cultivated area, efforts to increase rural incomes faced a severe resource constraint.[7] Moreover, only a fraction of government investment went to agriculture—14.6 percent of capital construction in 1965, compared to 50.8 percent for heavy industry.[8] Because of this investment bias to urban heavy industry and infrastructure, the increase in urban demand for labor was steeper than the growth in the urban work force (restricted by the migration ban). As a result, there was a rapid rise in the capital intensity of urban production. In addition, more urban residents, particularly women, entered the labor force to meet the increased demand for labor. It is not surprising, then, that urban family incomes rose more rapidly than the incomes of rural families (Perkins and Yusuf 1985, pp. 124–28).

Effects of Self-Reliant Strategy on Rural Industry. As in most Asian countries, there is a tradition of rural nonfarm activity in China. However, "one of the unique features of China's efforts to increase agricultural production has been the degree to which required inputs have been supplied by small-scale enterprises located in the countryside near those who use their products" (Perkins and Yusuf 1985, p. 61). That applies especially to the policy of "walking on two legs" that encouraged, for example, small-scale rural iron and steel plants, normally suited to large-scale urban production.

With rural communes in 1958 came a rapid, but fragile, expansion of collective nonfarm enterprises.[9] Diversion of labor to nonfarm activities probably contributed to the disastrous decline in agricultural production in 1958–61. By 1963, many nonfarm enterprises had been abandoned, but, with renewed ideological and financial support, there was again rapid growth after 1969. Output of commune industry doubled in value between 1971 and 1975 and, again, in 1975–1979 (Travers 1986, pp. 378–79). By 1982 these enterprises accounted for 11 percent of industrial output, compared to 3 percent in 1971. They produced more than 90 percent of lime, sand, and gravel and 75 percent of bricks and tiles and accounted for one-third of hydroelectric capacity and one-sixth of coal output (Travers 1986, p. 381). But economic effects of self-reliance vary substantially by industry. The small-scale rural iron and steel plants have been especially questionable because

[7] However, expansion of irrigation and drainage and, especially, tubewell development on the North China Plain beginning in 1965 led to significant increase in irrigated area.

[8] The share of investment allocated to heavy industry rose from 34.3 to 51.6 percent between 1952 and 1957; it was not until 1981 that heavy industry's share fell below 50 percent.

[9] Perkins and Yusuf (1985, pp. 61–65) provide a concise summary of China's rural industry, commerce, and services. See also Perkins and others (1977), Travers (1986), and Wong (1986a, 1986b).

of economies of scale and of inadequate local supplies of raw materials. China's contrasting experience in rural production of cement and fertilizer is summarized in Box 9.2.

Rural industries successfully expanded output of simple items—farm tools, small hand-operated machines such as threshers and insecticide sprayers, and small machines for processing farm products (Wong 1982, pp. 142–43). Locating such industries in rural areas conserved scarce engineering skills for large-scale, urban plants, and the available rural labor had a low opportunity cost. In China "the state has assigned noncrop enterprise the particular role of absorbing surplus rural labor" (Travers 1986, p. 385). (The rural labor force had increased from 110 million in 1957 to 333 million in 1982.)

China's small-scale farm machinery plants are flexible and responsive to the location-specific demands of customers, unlike the farm machinery industry in the Soviet Union. However, decentralized production of more sophisticated farm machinery—small diesel engines and single-axle power tillers, for example—was less successful (Wong 1982). The bulk of output came from a few urban factories; most of the small-scale plants were operating below their break-even point, partly because of "enormous difficulties in coordinating the supply and assembly of the large number of inputs required" (Wong 1982, p. 143). More fundamentally, small-scale rural manufacture of sophisticated farm machinery is impractical because of the required engineering precision, strict specifications for raw material, and high-quality control of the final product (see Chapter 6). These can only be achieved by a tightly controlled, medium- to large-scale firm, with investment in testing equipment and employees with scientific training. All are found in large cities.

Improvements in Well-being in Rural China

In the past forty years the well-being of China's rural population has improved despite virtually no increase in per capita food supplies between 1957 and 1977. During Mao's Great Leap Forward and Cultural Revolution, there was much death and suffering, avoidable tragedies, and infringements of human rights. Even so, there are positive lessons from rural China's progress in increased access to education, improved health and nutrition, and in slower population growth in a country where pressure of population on limited good agricultural land is a major problem.

Education. In 1949 only about 25 percent of children of primary school age were enrolled. By 1958 it was 67 percent, or 86 million children. Another 8.5 million children attended secondary schools, which were concentrated in large towns and cities; so, perhaps only 10 percent of rural children of secondary school age were enrolled, compared to 17 percent nationally (Perkins and Yusuf 1985, pp. 172–73).

Box 9.2.   China's Rural Cement and Fertilizer Plants

In the late 1970s small rural plants accounted for two-thirds of China's cement production and over half of the production of nitrogen fertilizer. Given the low value per ton of cement, substantial rural demand (for dams, lining canals, and many other projects), and China's weak and expensive rural transport system, the advantages of dispersed production using abundant, local raw materials outweighed the higher quality and economies of scale possible with larger, centralized cement plants.

China's small-scale fertilizer plants played a major role in the remarkably rapid increases in the production and use of chemical fertilizers.* In the late 1950s when China was largely cut off from world trade and high-technology investment, the Ministry of Chemical Industries pioneered a scaled-down fertilizer plant (annual capacity: 800–2,000 tons of nitrogen). It could produce low-analysis, ammonium bicarbonate fertilizer (17 percent nitrogen) from coke, and later anthracite. By 1979 there were 1,540 such plants, accounting for 54 percent of total output, or 5.6 million tons of nitrogen.

Even though China's intermediate technology achieves competitive investment costs per ton of capacity, coal consumption per ton of output has been high. That and frequent stoppages (capacity utilization is 50–70 percent) translate into production costs that are double or triple those of China's large-scale plants, based on natural gas. The large plants use efficient centrifugal compressors to produce ammonia, which is converted to urea containing about 2.5 times as much nitrogen as ammonium bicarbonate.

China's small, coal-based fertilizer plants employ obsolete technology—the partial oxidation and reciprocating piston compressors (see Chapter 7). There have been problems with the rudimentary equipment, and the poor quality of coal has meant the purchase of high-cost coal from other provinces (even other countries) for 75 percent of the small plants. Electricity shortages and delays in coal delivery have added to the problems. Another hitch is that, unlike urea, ammonium bicarbonate is unstable; losses in transport and storage are sizeable, raising the effective cost of fertilizer even more.

Unlike cement, technological advantages and massive economies of scale in large fertilizer plants offset the limited advantages of rural production of fertilizer. China's small-scale plants were an expensive, second-best approach to offset policy-induced distortions stemming from rural self-reliance, underinvestment in transport infrastructure, and inefficient allocation of industrial investment and foreign exchange.

Many less efficient rural small-scale fertilizer plants have been closed, but in 1982 ammonium bicarbonate still accounted for 53 percent of total nitrogen produced—and that despite an 80 percent increase in urea production in 1978–82. By then, urea production reached nearly 3.2 million nutrient tons, as thirteen large-scale plants approached full capacity. Should China's small-scale fertilizer plants continue operation? They accounted for 57 percent of China's ammonia production in 1988. Whatever the fate of these fertilizer plants in China, it is not something other countries should emulate.

*This treatment of small-scale fertilizer plants draws heavily on Wong 1986a and Stone 1986.

According to the 1964 census, China's population was about 700 million, of which 240 million people had received some education, although mostly only primary. The 1982 census showed that a little more than 600 million (out of one billion) had received some education, and 41 percent beyond primary education. In 1964 32 million had entered junior middle school; by 1982 the number was 178 million. Striking was the increase from 9 million to 66 million in 1964–82 in those attending senior middle school. The increase in the university-educated was more limited—from 3 million to 6 million (Banister 1986, pp. 178–79).

Rural Health Programs, Infant Mortality, Family Planning. It is useful to examine China's efforts to promote health, to reduce infant and child mortality, and to bring a halt to population growth as a set of interrelated activities.[10] When the Chinese Communist Party took control of the mainland in 1949, decades of war had increased already-high levels of mortality and chronic illness. Industry and national defense were the government's priority, not health. Between 1950 and 1956, it never allocated more than 2.6 percent of spending to health. Nevertheless, through inexpensive mass programs for the prevention of disease and the promotion of environmental sanitation, life expectancy increased from forty to fifty-one years between 1953 and 1957 (Banister 1987, pp. 52, 116). There was also a rapid fall in infant and child mortality.

Of all initiatives in the Great Leap Forward, commune health centers, founded in 1958–60, probably had the most lasting and positive impact. In the short run, however, health deteriorated disastrously because of the widespread famine. Both the crude death rate and infant mortality more than doubled between 1957 and 1960 (Banister 1987, p. 116). Many health centers were closed in the early 1960s for lack of money; but, as the rural economy recovered, medical facilities were rehabilitated, and cost-sharing schemes were devised. With the Cultural Revolution, commune clinics were upgraded into rural hospitals, and brigade health stations were established. There was a large increase in paramedics (commonly, but inaccurately, called "barefoot doctors"), who staffed the brigade health centers. More affluent production teams had their own paramedics. Costs were held down by concentrating on immunizations and other preventive measures including the promotion of hygiene and environmental sanitation (see Taylor, Parker, and Jarrett 1988). Of the government's health budget, 60 percent went to rural

[10] There appears to be agreement among demographers that China's censuses in 1953, 1964, and especially 1982 provide detailed and high-quality data that make possible "a reasonably plausible account of demographic trends" (Ashton and others 1984, p. 618). Thus, Ashton and his associates (1984) and Banister (1986, 1987) agree that high death rates for the famine years 1959–61 imply about 30 million "excess deaths." There are, however, significant differences in the estimates of year-to-year changes in the respective reconstructions. Data since 1982 appear to be much less reliable.

Table 9.1. Infant and child mortality in China, 1955–1985

	1955–60	1960–65	1965–70	1970–75	1975–80	1980–85
Infant mortality[a]	179	121	81	61	41	39
Child mortality[b]	77	47	36	23	16	17

Source: Ross and others 1988, pp. 229, 231.
[a]Deaths before age one per 1,000 live births.
[b]Number of children per 1,000 that reach age one who die before age five.

areas. Families made a modest contribution to the cost of cooperative medical insurance, so bringing treatment "within the reach of the great mass of rural inhabitants" (Perkins and Yusuf 1985, p. 141). By 1964, health conditions had improved markedly. Life expectancy was fifty-seven years, well above the pre–Great Leap peak of fifty-one years of 1957.

Infant and child mortality are sensitive indices of health conditions. These showed a dramatic decline in 1960–65, because the 1955–60 figures included the drastic rise in infant and child mortality during the 1959–61 famine (Table 9.1). Even so, the decline since then has been dramatic and compares favorably with that of other developing countries.

In Ethiopia, for example, estimated infant mortality of 180 per 1,000 in 1955–60 was about the same as the famine-inflated figure for China. But the 1980–85 estimate of 155 per 1,000 was four times as high as in China. For child mortality the contrast is even greater. For 1980–85, an estimated 126 of every 1,000 children that reached age one in Ethiopia died before age 5, approximately eight times the rate for China. The contrast with Kenya, which has been among Africa's most successful in reducing infant and child mortality, is less striking but still considerable. Kenya's infant mortality rate in 1980–85 at 80 per 1,000 was roughly twice as high as China's, and child mortality was three times as high (Ross and others 1988, pp. 228–31).

Unlike health policy, population policy in China has been marked by abrupt shifts. Mao Tse-tung took an orthodox Marxist view. He believed "that China's large population would be an asset because it meant abundant labor and labor was the source of all wealth" (Aird 1986, p. 187). However, when the 1953 census showed a population 100 million larger than expected, that orthodox view was temporarily reversed.

A family planning program was initiated in 1956, but this was overtaken by the rural communes and the Great Leap Forward in 1958. A second program got under way in 1962, but that, too, was interrupted—by the Cultural Revolution. Since 1969 family planning has been promoted vigorously and, all too often, with much coercion.

Emerging Problems. By 1978 most couples were having only two or three children, and the total fertility rate fell to 2.7, down from 6 in the 1950s (Banister 1987, pp. 182, 230). That was achieved by a "pervasive organizational structure" of many family planning workers and peer pressure. Policymakers then reacted strongly to demographic analyses, showing a huge bulge at the young adult age. Since this meant that China's population would continue to grow for decades, a policy of one child per family was adopted to bring the rate of natural increase down to zero by the year 2000. There were special benefits for one-child families and penalties for those with more. The government also encouraged local officials to resort to coercion if necessary (Box 9.3), although foreign health specialists in China say that since the mid-1980s such strongarm tactics, including forced sterilizations and late abortions, have been reduced significantly (Carl E. Taylor, personal communication, August 1990). Indeed, there is now a tendency to speak unofficially of a one-male child policy.

Undoubtedly, some of China's development problems will be eased by the slowing of natural increase. The remarkable rise since 1977 in per capita food production, for example, is due partly to the decline in the rate of natural increase from 2.6 percent in 1965 to, perhaps, 1.1 percent in 1985 (World Bank 1987b, p. 256). This sudden reduction in fertility will not be an unmixed blessing, notably because of its long-term effects on the age distribution of the population. It seems that central government officials may have come to recognize the adverse effects on China's age structure resulting from the one-child family policy so that, as noted, there may have been some de facto relaxation of that policy.

Post-1978 reforms, and the rapid rise in rural incomes, have had mixed effects on rural health services. Many "barefoot doctors" have undergone additional training to qualify as "rural doctors," but some have shifted to other, more profitable activities. Before 1978, rural health services were labor-intensive, with little capital equipment. For example, for lack of refrigeration in rural areas, vaccines were "distributed in a rush-relay system going from the vaccine institute to end use in three days. The rural doctor picked up vaccine by bicycle at the township or county center and rushed back to his village where he had arranged for the children to be waiting" (Taylor and others 1988, p. 230).

Even so, much was achieved, although there were big provincial variations. For immunization against measles, for example, coverage ranged from 53 percent in Guangdong Province to 94 percent in Beijing, and for DPT from only 17 percent in Gansu Province to 92 percent in Beijing (Taylor and others 1988, p. 230). In 1985 the government committed itself to reach 85 percent of children aged under one year. As part of that program, it planned national coverage with refrigeration equipment to keep vaccines at the right temperatures throughout distribution.

Access to rural health services deteriorated following the weakening (or collapse) of cooperative medical schemes and health stations established by communes and production brigades. The most serious impact seems to

Box 9.3. The One-Child Family Policy and China's Missing Females

Some demographers, including Banister (1987), say that coercion led to an increase in female infanticide. An analysis by Hull (1990) of a "One Percent Survey of China" in 1987 provides clear evidence of a change in the sex ratios of births and young children that *might* be a result of an increase in female infanticide. Hull emphasizes, however, that the rising sex ratios in 1982–87 might also be due to gender-specific abortion or widespread concealment of births of female children. Because female infanticide is illegal and now widely and severely condemned in China, there is obviously no direct evidence of its extent. Likewise, the State Family Planning Commission prohibits the use of procedures to determine the sex of a fetus for purposes of aborting female fetuses, but there are reports of government concern that ultrasound examinations especially are being used for that purpose. Hull finds it difficult to believe that missing female births and young female children are concealed from interviewers and local officials. But an unpublished paper by Susan Champagne (1989, p. 1) suggests that evasions are common and "are linked to the rural reforms which have given rise to freedom of mobility, proliferation of free markets, and possibilities for free enterprise." (Champagne draws on 200 interviews in 1987–88 of peasants, urban residents raised in the countryside, and urban residents with rural relatives carried out in sixteen provinces, municipalities, and autonomous regions. She also made extensive use of PRC periodicals and newspapers.) Johansson and Nygren (1991) verify Hull's conclusion that the *reported* sex ratio in China is much higher than normal in the 1980s but present data from a two-per-thousand survey that indicate adoptions account for about half of China's "missing" girls. (Adoption data were not available to Hull.) Overrepresentation of females among adopted children and underreporting of female births may together explain much of the high sex ratio. Johansson and Nygren (p. 50) conclude: "That female infanticide does occur on some scale is evidenced by reports in the Chinese press, but the available statistical evidence does not help us to determine whether it takes place on a large or a small scale."

have been on preventive services. There were problems, too, in remunerating rural health workers in maternal and child health programs. It is difficult to generalize; however, "the implementation of child health activities seem to have slowed down in recent years in less economically-advanced and remote areas, in spite of the genuine overall concern and policy statements which emphasize the importance of child health care. Since health care policy is highly decentralized, local financing arrangements vary greatly as each commune seeks to guarantee essential curative services and maintain health programs" (Taylor and others 1988, p. 228). Although the communes are now townships and brigades are villages, both often retain some institutional arrangements of the commune system. Yet, post-reform, little was done to ensure a smooth continuation of public health. As a result, makeshift arrangements have evolved, with much local variation in effectiveness and coverage.[11]

LESSONS FROM CHINA AND THE USSR

The Soviet Union and China have concealed policy records and details of decision making, which makes it difficult to draw confident conclusions from their experiences. Even so, many (sometimes chilling) insights into their policies and the consequences have emerged, especially after reforms in each country in the 1980s and the collapse of the USSR in 1991.

The Verdict on Collectivization

Collectivization and central planning handicapped development in the USSR. This affected all of the Six I's—innovation, institutions, inputs, incentives, initiative and infrastructure—that fostered agricultural development in Japan and the United States (see Chapter 3). In China the picture is more complex, but the negative lessons of collectivization are also strong.

The dramatic growth in agriculture and rural nonfarm enterprises in post-Mao China demonstrate the benefits of producer incentives and individual initiatives with decentralized decision making. Many other factors contributed to the remarkable expansion of China's agricultural output after 1978, including favorable weather and rapid increase in chemical fertilizer application. However, there seems to be broad agreement about the results:

The effects of the decollectivization that has taken place in China have been extraordinary. Chinese agriculture has grown far more rapidly in recent years than anyone believed possible. There has not only been a great increase in the overall value of agricultural output; a very significant diversification of agricultural production has taken place, with increased attention to crops other than grain and to animal husbandry, fisheries, and other non-crop activities. Moreover, so-called "sideline" activities have greatly expanded, and there has been a rapid growth of both local industries and commerce in rural areas. During the recent period, agriculture has been the most dynamic sector in the entire Chinese economy—something few would have predicted before the new policies were introduced. (Barnett 1986, pp. 7–8)

[11] Dreze and Sen (1989) cite estimates by Banister of rising infant mortality as evidence of a collapse of rural health activities. According to Banister's reconstruction of changes in infant mortality between 1978 and 1984, there was a rise from 37 to 50 per thousand. But that apparent increase was entirely due to an alleged increase in infant mortality among females from 38 to 67 per thousand; infant mortality among males continued to decline from 37 per thousand in 1978 to 34 per thousand in 1984 (Banister 1987, p. 116). But as discussed in note 10, available demographic estimates for recent years may be seriously flawed.

The Institutional Legacy. The concentration of population, labor force, and economic activity in rural China is an important reason why reform progressed with surprising speed. Entrepreneurial impulses among peasants, suppressed for decades, were not extinguished and emerged with vigor with decentralized decision making. Dramatic increases in incomes have generated broad support for economic reforms, especially among the rural population. Per capita income of urban families increased by 43 percent between 1978 and 1983, but in rural households, it doubled (Dernberger 1986, p. 37).

Progress in large-scale urban enterprises was limited in China, as was the pace of change in the USSR. It was in China's favor that its rural economy is large and the rural population had not been bureaucratized in the way that its urban sector (and most of the Soviet economy) had been.

Nevertheless, the massacre in Tiananmen Square in June 1989 and the repression of popular demands for political change raise serious doubts about prospects for economic and political reform. Bureaucratic opposition is a particularly important obstacle to further reform. "A decline in bureaucratic control means a decline in bureaucrats' power. If the new system makes bureaucratic skills built up over decades obsolete, those being made obsolete will fight reform" (Perkins 1988, p. 626). Such opposition is probably even more entrenched in the Soviet Union, where bureaucratic control has existed longer and is more comprehensive. Thus, academician Vladimir Tikhonov, a chief architect of Gorbachev's attempt at rural *perestroika*, speaks of "128 million bureaucrats" opposed to perestroika in the countryside (Laird 1988).

Japan's Development and China's Strategic Options

The Soviet Union remained faithful to Marxist-Leninist agricultural notions because its vast land endowment allowed decades of effort aimed at raising output by expanding the cultivated area. However, with that option virtually exhausted by the 1950s, China has laid the foundations for broad-based agricultural development, which bear significant similarities to the pattern followed by Japan (Chapter 3). Ironically, these similarities also extend to Taiwan, which repeated key elements of the Japanese pattern (Chapter 10).

Japan and Taiwan employed broad-based agricultural development strategies that resulted in a unimodal agrarian structure and a labor-using, land-saving pattern of gradual, widespread productivity increases on small farms. Except for short (and disastrous) experience with large farms when communes were first established, most of China's farm *operational* units were always small. Even before post-Mao reforms, the production team (of thirty to forty families) managed cultivation of thirty to forty hectares. Therefore, agricultural output could be expanded by labor-using, land-saving technologies that relied on yield-increasing, *divisible* innovations as adopted in Japan and Taiwan: chemical fertilizers, high-yielding, fertilizer-responsive varieties of rice and other crops, and improvements in water management.[12] By 1977 improved high-yield, fertilizer-responsive varieties were being grown on 80 percent of the area devoted to rice (Lardy 1986, p. 331). The similarities are more obvious since the 1978 reforms, which led to the dismantling of communes and renewed emphasis on family farms as key decision-making units in agriculture.

Another similarity is China's priority in expanding and improving the rural infrastructure, notably irrigation and drainage. As in Japan and Taiwan, the better irrigation and control of water has been an important complement to the seed-fertilizer innovations. However, development of a national transportation system in China has been limited. Indeed, the emphasis on rural industries in China was partly a response to high transport costs (see Box 9.2).

Similarities between strategic options for agricultural development in Japan, Taiwan, and China also extend to rural, small-scale industry. In China the agricultural reforms broke the constraints on trade imposed by the self-reliant strategy. They established the legitimacy of sideline occupations, including private work in manufacturing, construction, transport, and commerce. China's farm population responded quickly. Between 1978 and 1983 the contribution of those nonfarm activities to farm household income rose from 8 to 19 percent. And by 1983 rural nonfarm employment reached 67 million, with jobs in collective nonfarm enterprises accounting for less than one-half. Even so, the share of nonfarm income was below those of comparable CARLs, suggesting scope for further shifts.

China's rural industries appear to have been the most dynamic force in the economy. Output from rural industry increased by 266 percent in 1982–86, and nonfarm rural employment reached 120 million (*The Economist* 1987, p. 10). The same article also emphasizes the complexity of the evolving system, noting that China has neither a planned nor a market economy but one dominated by "a system of bargaining between factory managers and government officials at every level of the bureaucracy" (p. 15). A striking feature has been the speed with which opportunities have been identified and initiatives taken, despite the system's complexity.

China, Japan, and Taiwan all attached importance to developing the quality of rural human resources by expanding education and access to health

[12] Although China's policymakers have talked expansively about "complete mechanization of farm activities within a few years," Perkins and Yusuf (1985, pp. 59–60) stress the "air of unreality" about many mechanization targets. In any event, while expansion of rural mechanization since the early 1960s has been rapid, it has not realized the Marxist-Leninist vision of large-scale, mechanized agriculture.

services. It is unfortunate, however, that a serious effort to promote family planning in China was not launched until twenty years after Communist control of the mainland. And it is deplorable that, since the One-Child Family Campaign began in January 1979, coercion has been used for sterilizations and abortions. The experience of Taiwan, Costa Rica, South Korea, and others suggests that similar results could have been achieved without coercion (see Chapter 10), especially if China's policymakers had faced up to the problems of rapid population growth more quickly.

CHAPTER TEN

TAIWAN
AND
MEXICO

Taiwan provides an outstanding example of success in promoting equitable growth through a broadbased strategy of agricultural development. In the 1960s Mexico was also widely regarded as an agricultural success story. There were, however, some expressions of concern at the time that Mexico's dualistic agricultural development strategy had bypassed the great bulk of the country's farmers (Johnston 1966, pp. 285–87). The abrupt transition during the second half of the 1960s from a sense of progress to concern with stagnation and inequality is well captured in these "before and after" statements:

Rural Mexico seemed to be able to play the dual role of absorbing an increase in population and of producing food and raw materials for the rest of the economy. The labor that was left over was easily and conveniently absorbed in the expanding urban economy. The record-breaking achievements in agriculture and industry, the phenomenal growth of the cities in general and of Mexico City in particular, and the expansion of the middle classes were all part and parcel of the "Mexican miracle" . . . In the 1960s, even such visible shortcomings of the process as the urban squatter settlements were considered to be temporary phenomena. (Alba and Potter 1986, p. 55)

By the late 1960s that optimism had been replaced by somber concerns about stagnation and inequality:

There was a widespread realization in government, professional, and academic circles that the long period of sustained economic growth and stabilizing development
fell far short of what had been expected. The system had failed to transform the
growth process and break the cycle of social and economic unevenness, and the supposedly transient conditions of subsistence agriculture and urban marginality threatened to become permanent. (p. 59)

The dualistic strategy pursued in Mexico (also Brazil, Colombia, and several other Latin American countries) reinforced the bimodal agrarian structure of those countries and has not been effective in eliminating widespread
rural poverty or in contributing to sustainable growth in industry (Grindle
1986b; de Janvry 1981).

Taiwan's greater success in reducing rural poverty cannot be explained by
more natural resources. Taiwan epitomized the Asian dilemma of "too little land and too many people" with no more than 0.84 hectare of land per
male agricultural worker between 1913 and 1971 and population growth
in the 1950s approaching that of Kenya and Tanzania in the 1980s (Chapter
11). Mexico has more cropland per rural worker (more than 3 ha/male agricultural worker as late as 1987) and is well endowed with valuable natural
resources, such as petroleum.

The physical environments of Taiwan and Mexico are vastly different,
however, notably in the much greater extent of rainfed agriculture in Mexico.
In the late 1980s 25 percent of Mexico's agricultural land was suitable for
crops (of which only 1 hectare in five was irrigated), and 75 percent was
permanent pasture (FAO 1988). In Taiwan virtually all agricultural land is
suitable for crops, with over one-half irrigated. However, Mexico has much
more pasture land, and its irrigated land per worker compares favorably
with Taiwan's. For geographical as well as historical reasons, irrigated land
in Mexico has been concentrated in the sparsely populated north. Public
investment that harnessed the rivers flowing from the mountains through
arid plains in that region and private investment in large, mechanized farms,
led to a rapid expansion of irrigated land that affected only a minority of
Mexico's farm workers. Despite continued growth in the agricultural labor
force in Mexico, *average* irrigated land per male worker was greater (about
0.6 ha/male worker) in the late 1980s than in Taiwan when its rural work
force peaked in the 1960s (0.5 ha/male worker).

Mexico's public investment failed to have a broader impact on agricultural
development because of political factors and strategic notions. Taiwan's success in raising rural incomes was helped by a reduction in fertility, which slowed
population growth and hastened its structural transformation turning point.
Mexico's farm work force continues to grow, despite agriculture's shrinking
share of national income. But, as discussed later, the demographic differences
and their impact on labor force growth also were influenced by policy choices.

The contrasting experience of Taiwan and Mexico is especially interesting because of the role of redistributive land reform in the two countries. In Taiwan the incentive effects of land reform contributed to the acceleration of yield increases after 1952, but, as will be discussed, the reform was not a necessary condition for the success of Taiwan's broad-based strategy. Indeed, the foundations of that strategy were laid during the fifty years of Japanese colonial administration that began in 1895. Mexico, which conducted the largest redistributive land reform in Latin America, missed its opportunity for a unimodal agrarian structure. The real puzzle is to explain Mexico's bimodal agrarian structure and dualistic development strategy when a rural-based revolution included land reform as a fundamental goal.

STRUCTURAL TRANSFORMATION AND POPULATION GROWTH

When mortality began to decline in Taiwan and Mexico, the fall was more rapid than in, for example, Japan and the United States, which experienced demographic transition before medical advances that made possible rapid reductions in death rates (see Figure 10.1). The initial steep fall in mortality in Mexico was due to abnormally high death rates during the Revolution. Because of an earlier fall in mortality, Taiwan's labor force in the 1930s was already increasing at 2.3 percent a year. In the 1950s, Taiwan's rate of natural increase was 3.2 to 3.8 percent. In addition, there were one to two million refugees from Mainland China. In the 1930s Mexico's labor force grew by less than 1 percent per year, but by the 1950s and 1960s the rate was more than 3 percent.

Taiwan reached its structural transformation turning point in the mid-1960s; at the same time agriculture's share fell below half of its labor force. The decline in its farm work force since has been accelerated by a fall in growth of its total labor force, which reflects a reduction in population growth fifteen years earlier, and the growth in nonfarm jobs. However, in Mexico, the decline in fertility did not accelerate until the late 1970s, so rapid growth of Mexico's population of working age will continue for some time: its total labor force could grow at 3 percent a year between 1985 and 2000 (World Bank 1987b, p. 265). As in Taiwan, agriculture's share of the labor force fell below 50 percent in the 1960s. Unlike in Taiwan, the farm work force has grown by 50 percent since, from six million in 1960 to, perhaps, nine million in 1990, which suggests that its structural transformation turning point will come after 2005 (United Nations 1988b, p. 220; see also Chapter 1, Box 1.1.). Differences in policy choices (more than in natural resource endowments) lie at the heart of Mexico's and Taiwan's contrasting structural transformation paths since the 1960s.

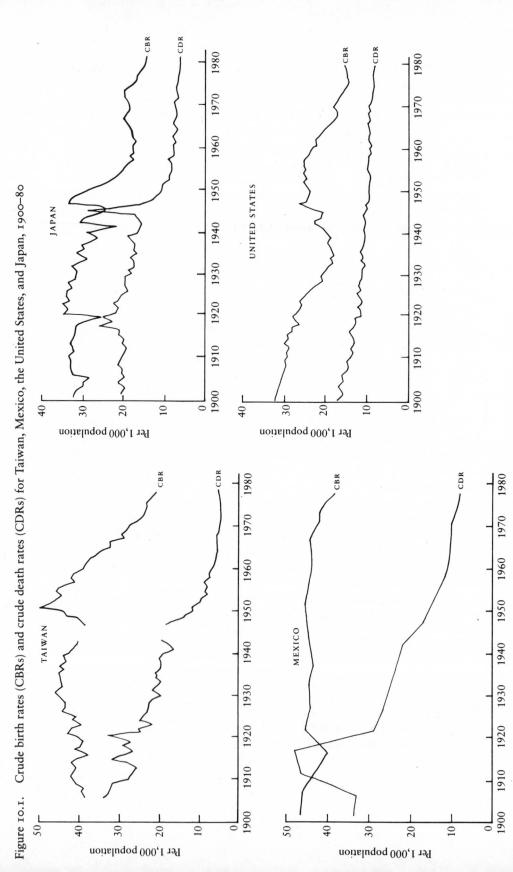

Figure 10.1. Crude birth rates (CBRs) and crude death rates (CDRs) for Taiwan, Mexico, the United States, and Japan, 1900–80

Source: Johnston 1987, pp. 34–35. © 1987 by Board of Trustees, Leland Stanford Junior University. Reprinted by permission.

Table 10.1. Changes in farm output and various inputs in Taiwan, 1911–15 and 1956–60 (index numbers unless otherwise indicated)

Period	Total farm output	Cultivated land area	Cropped area	Farm labor force	Labor inputs in working days
1911–15	100	100	100	100	100
1956–60	337	127	196	149	198

	Working days			Fertilizer consumption (1,000 metric tons)	Total current inputs[a]
Period	Per cultivated hectare	Per cropped hectare	Per worker		
1911–15	195	167	117	50.8	100
1956–60	305	170	155	663.5	512

Source: Lee 1971.

[a] In contrast with Japan, livestock feed has long been an important component of current inputs in Taiwan. It accounted for 57 percent of current inputs in 1911–15 and 41 percent in 1956–60 when fertilizer represented 45 percent of the total.

TAIWAN: THE JAPANESE PATTERN REPEATED

Agriculture in Taiwan, even more than in Japan, shows the potential for increasing output by widespread use of yield-increasing innovations on small farms. Crop production grew at an average of 3.5 percent a year before, and after, World War II; and factor productivity increased at 2.5 percent in 1920–39 and at about the same rate in 1951–64 (Christensen 1968, pp. 16, 21; Lee 1971, p. 49.)

Farm output rose 3.4 times between 1911–15 and 1956–60, whereas cultivated land increased by only about 27 percent (Table 10.1). The cropped area almost doubled as a result of an increase in the index of cropping intensity from 116 in 1911–15 to 180 in 1956–60. And with the introduction of higher-yielding varieties and a thirteenfold increase in fertilizer consumption, yields also rose substantially.

Because growth of Taiwan's labor force accelerated in the 1930s and in the 1950s and 1960s, there was a substantial increase in the size of the farm work force, even though its share of the total labor force had fallen from 68 to 53 percent. However, Taiwan's broad-based strategy significantly reduced underemployment, despite the limited scope for enlarging the cultivated area. Between 1911–15 and 1956–60, the farm work force increased by about 50 percent, but the labor input in working days almost doubled because of an increase in cropped area (through multiple cropping). The average number of working days per cropped hectare was virtually unchanged.

The number of farm households doubled between 1930 and 1960, and the average farm size fell from roughly 2 hectares to 1. Only about 6 percent of farms, other than a few sugar plantations, were larger than 3.25 hectares; most were close to the average size (see Box 1.2). Yield-increasing innovations affected most farm households, and net farm income per acre was consistently higher in the smaller ones (JCRR 1966, p. 219). After Taiwan reached its structural transformation turning point in 1964 (when the farm work force peaked at 1.8 million), the reduction in cultivated land per farm worker was reversed. At the same time, the shift toward mechanization accelerated. Between 1960 and 1973, power tillers increased in number more than tenfold, from about 3,700 to more than 38,000 (Shen 1976, p. 4). By 1973 agriculture's share in the total labor force was less than a third, and rising wages had reduced multiple cropping, with a greater reliance on labor-saving equipment.[1] By 1988 the farm work force was 1.1 million, only 14 percent of the total labor force (Republic of China 1989a, p. 16). There were 916,000 farm households in 1979; in 1985 there were 780,000. Full-time farm households, which had accounted for almost half the total in 1960 and 30 percent in 1970, had fallen to only 15 percent of all farm households in 1985.

The decline in agriculture's share of exports was dramatic, from 92 to 22 percent between 1955 and 1970. Sugar and rice still accounted for 76 percent of all exports in 1955, but a mere 3 percent in 1970. By then, agricultural exports were dominated by new, higher-value products—canned asparagus and mushrooms, pineapples, and bananas. Between 1955 and 1970 the share of industrial products grew from 8 to 78 percent of total export proceeds, which had increased twelvefold during the twenty-five-year period (Republic of China 1985, p. 203). Partly as a result of these increases in industrial exports, the nonfarm labor force grew rapidly from 1952.

Japanese Colonial Initiatives, 1895–1945

In the first few years of administration, subsidies from Japan paid for much expenditure on administration and development in Taiwan. However, like European colonial powers, Japan developed local sources of revenue, which soon covered the costs of colonial administration and investment.

Japan and Taiwan had much in common, unlike other colonial relationships. Rice was the staple food of both, and labor-intensive, small farms predominated in both. Thus, the transfer of agricultural technologies and Japan's colonial policies initiated the pattern of labor-using, land-saving productiv-

---

[1] Multiple cropping also peaked in 1964 when the index of cropping intensity reached 190. By 1988 the index was 136, reflecting the decline in the farm work force and the rising opportunity cost of labor (Republic of China 1989a, p. 64). Thorbecke (1979, pp. 147–49) provides a useful compilation of annual figures for inputs between 1946 and 1975. The number of tractors in 1965 was 425. In 1973 there were 749, rising rapidly to 1,323 in 1975.

ity growth among Taiwan's small farms. Japan's emphasis on developing Taiwan as a supplier of rice and sugar continued until the 1930s. This left Taiwan well endowed with the prerequisites of broad-based development, including agricultural research institutions and rural infrastructure. "It was the combination of its practical knowledge of local institutions, its attention to details, and its painstaking supervision of research and extension work, that made the government so influential in guiding Taiwan's agricultural development" (Ho 1971, p. 318). Undoubtedly, Japan's effective administration and the responsiveness of the Taiwanese were helped by the cultural, social, and economic similarities between the Japanese and Taiwanese.

Even Japan's approach to colonial finance helped to lay the foundations for Taiwan's agricultural development. The first major step was in 1898— a land survey initiated to identify ownership. This, admittedly, was for tax purposes, but it also laid the groundwork for Taiwan's redistributive land reform in the 1950s by creating a reliable record of ownership and tenancy.

Agricultural Innovations and Inputs

Underlying agricultural productivity growth in Taiwan has been the support given to research since the early colonial years. In 1903 the Japanese created a Central Agricultural Research Bureau and experiment stations in the major regions. Research and other agricultural programs employed high-caliber specialists from Japan, and many made their careers in Taiwan. Thus, colonial administration incorporated major "technical assistance" with continuity in personnel.

The research institutions established by the Japanese survived the end of colonial rule. This was possible because by the beginning of the 1930s a third of Taiwanese children of primary age were in school, and during that decade appreciable numbers were being trained in agricultural vocational schools and universities in Japan and Taiwan to work in agricultural research and extension programs. With the retrocession of Taiwan to the Republic of China following World War II Chinese scientists and agricultural administrators from the Mainland moved into senior positions previously occupied by Japanese. But many Taiwanese, who had acquired training and experience during the period of colonial rule, contributed to the continuity in research.

Rice, which accounted for half of the total value of agricultural output, was at the center of agricultural research. Despite similarities between Taiwan and Japan, special problems had to be overcome to replicate Japanese success in raising rice yields. Varietal improvements based on the native *indica* led to some increase in yields, but the first significant progress followed the adaptation of *japonica* rice from Japan. It took roughly ten years to adapt japonicas and to develop agronomic practices to grow them in tropical Taiwan. By 1932 roughly a third of the rice area was planted with japoni-

Table 10.2.   Indices of area, yield, and production of rice and sugarcane in Taiwan, 1901–70 (1901–10 = 100)

Period	Rice			Sugarcane		
	Area	Yield	Production	Area	Yield	Production
1901–10	100	100	100	100[a]	100[a]	100[a]
1911–20	112	104	117	323	95	306
1921–30	128	120	154	371	164	608
1931–40	152	145	220	387	298	1,155
1941–50	150	125	187	361	197	710
1951–60	180	168	302	306	303	927
1961–70	180	222	401	310	326	1,015

Sources: JCRR 1966, pp. 23 and 47; Republic of China 1972, pp. 49–52.
[a] 1902–10 = 100.

cas. Then, in 1957 stiff-strawed, fertilizer-responsive *indica* varieties were developed with yield characteristics similar to japonicas.[2]

Research programs in Taiwan generated a stream of other profitable innovations, adapted not only to the physical environment but also to the needs of small farms. For example, relay-interplanting systems (that is, planting crops, such as sweet potatoes, melons, and vegetables, in succession with rice) intensified cropping and increased farm incomes, despite the reduction in farm size after World War II.

Not all advances came from public research institutions. Many simple mechanical innovations of private entrepreneurs increased farm productivity. Moreover, enlarged production of farm equipment contributed to the growth of rural-based manufacturing (Chapter 6).

Growth in Output of Rice and Sugar.   The increases in area, yield, and production of rice and of sugarcane, the second most important crop, are summarized in Table 10.2. The large expansion of Taiwan's rice production during the 1950s and 1960s was absorbed by increased domestic demand resulting from the influx of population from the Chinese mainland and a high rate of natural increase. The increase in crop area resulted mainly from increased double cropping, although there was some shift of acreage from sugar to rice.

Sugarcane, Taiwan's second biggest crop, was expanded faster before World War II, because Japan viewed Taiwan as its source of sugar. Subsidies and inducements encouraged cane production by Taiwanese farmers and the setting up of sugar mills by Japanese corporations. By 1929 exports reached 750,000 tons and provided most of Japan's sugar supplies. The threefold in-

[2] One of these varieties, Taichung Native No. 1, was introduced on a large scale in other countries in Asia and in tropical Africa. Under more humid conditions, notably in India, Taichung Native No. 1 encountered serious disease problems; but a dwarf *indica* variety from Taiwan was one of the parents of IR-8, the first improved variety released by the International Rice Research Institute.

crease in cane yields between 1902–10 and 1931–40 benefited greatly from cane breeding in Java and Barbados in the late nineteenth century. By 1930 most cane acreage in Taiwan was planted with the high-yielding POJ varieties developed in Java after 1910. Although processing became a large-scale industry, cane production was mainly done on Taiwan's small farms.

Taiwan and Java epitomize the divergent outcome that technological change can produce under different agricultural strategies. On Java, the home of the POJ sugar variety, the Dutch colonial administration effectively banned small-scale sugarcane production in 1923 by prohibiting mills from buying cane from smallholders (Elson 1984).[3] The widespread adoption of POJ varieties by smallholders in Taiwan, however, demonstrates how higher-yielding sugar varieties could be part of a broad-based strategy that reinforced a unimodal agrarian structure.

Labor-Using, Land-Saving Productivity Growth, 1952–66. The average productivity of labor in agriculture (Y/L) can be expressed as the product of the land–labor ratio (A/L) and output per unit of cultivated land (Y/A) (where Y is net output of agriculture, A the input of cultivated land, and L input of labor). Moreover, the rate of change in output per worker (Y/L) is roughly equal to the sum of the rates of change in area cultivated per worker (A/L) and in yield (Y/A). For 1901–50 and 1952–66 Taiwan's average rates of change were:

Period	Y/L	A/L	Y/A
1901–50	1.2	0.4	0.8
1952–66	3.3	−0.8	4.1

Thus, during Japanese rule yield increases were twice as important as increases in area cultivated per worker. In 1952–66 extraordinary yield increases permitted an increase in labor productivity despite a decline of more than 25 percent in the cultivated area available per worker (Figure 10.2).[4]

[3] The Sugar Syndicate, an association of large-scale sugar plantations in colonial Java, pressed for this restriction with the argument that "to keep the cultivation up to standard . . . two things are necessary: intellect and capital. The industry has both of these at its disposal, the native farmer as yet has neither" (quoted in Elson, p. 217). This is spurious. It camouflaged the Syndicate's concern about expansion of profitable, small-scale sugarcane production. Such expansion could interfere with European firms' efforts to secure land from Javanese smallholders under unfair terms. Thus, the restriction grew out of the political economy of the bimodal agrarian structure in colonial Java. Its consequences reinforced that structure.

[4] See Thorbecke (1979, p. 153) for a fourfold partitioning of annual change in labor productivity for 1946–75. Agricultural reversals are not unique to sub-Saharan Africa of the 1980s; Taiwan had setbacks too. The isoquants in Figure 10.2 are an index of average labor productivity (with 1926–30 = 100). War and the influx of Mainland Chinese in the 1940s set agricultural labor productivity back thirty years: the figure for 1946–50 was below that for 1916–20. Reconstruction, new investment, innovation, and agrarian reform brought labor productivity within 5 percent of prewar levels by 1950–55. By 1956–60 labor productivity was 17 percent higher than in 1936–40.

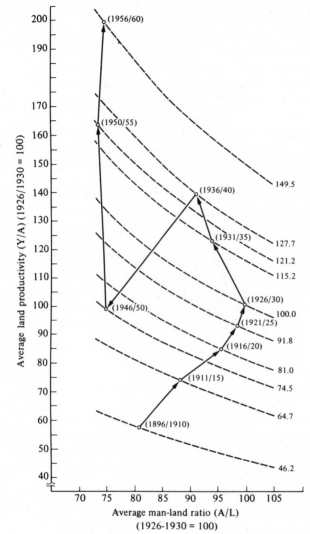

Figure 10.2. Growth path of agricultural labor productivity in Taiwan, 1896–1960

Source: Reproduced from Cristina M. Crisostomo and others, "The New Rice Technology and Labor Absorption in Philippine Agriculture" (paper prepared for the Conference on Manpower Problems in East and Southeast Asia, Singapore, May 22–28, 1971). It was adapted from T. H. Lee 1971.

Investment in Rural Infrastructure

Another major colonial development in Taiwan was the creation of the infrastructure that supported broad-based development. Fixed capital outlays by the Japanese administration averaged about 25 percent of government expenditures (which grew rapidly with tax receipts). Of this spending, half or more went to the construction and improvement of railways, harbors, and roads. By the 1920s most of the island had access to inexpensive transport (Ho 1971, p. 314).

Another priority of Japan's development policy in Taiwan was the extension of irrigation, drainage, and flood control. When Taiwan was ceded to Japan in 1895, irrigation was primitive and limited. Irrigated land increased from about 32 percent of the cultivated area in 1906 to 64 percent in 1943 (Ho 1971, p. 319). Investment in irrigation rose sharply during the 1920s, accounting for almost 15 percent of total investment in Taiwan. Since World War II there have been further improvements in irrigation design and management and in land improvement. Better water control for agriculture was a precondition for the widespread use of new varieties and the rise in cropping intensity.

Large-scale irrigation projects were carried out by the colonial government, but grants, loans, and technical assistance to irrigation associations for small-scale systems were more important. These associations organized, partly financed, managed, and maintained local irrigation systems. A network of agricultural associations also enabled the government to carry out an effective extension program at low cost. Many extension workers and technicians were employed by those associations. Government subsidies covered only a part of their salaries; the rest was paid by the farmers, which made the extension agents directly accountable to the farmers they served.

Land Reform in the 1950s

The redistribution of land in the early 1950s began with a "Farm Rent Reduction Program" in 1949, followed by government land sales in 1951 and by the "Land to the Tiller Program" in 1953 (Wu 1988).[5] Landlords were forced to sell land in excess of a ceiling (3 hectares for medium-grade paddy land). They were compensated in bonds that were denominated in rice and sweet potatoes as a hedge against inflation. The increase in incentives of this postwar land reform contributed to the impressive advances in yields after 1952 (C.-C. Chen 1967; Wu 1988).

The episode provides evidence that redistributive land reform can reinforce a broad-based development strategy by establishing a unimodal distribution of farm *ownership* units. Many (e.g., de Janvry 1981, p. 257) attribute Taiwan's success to the redistributive land reform.

A unimodal agrarian structure was, however, established during the Japanese colonial period. In 1905 Japanese land reform in Taiwan terminated the land rights of 40,000 top-level landlords (*ta-tsu hu*), compensat-

[5] The farm rent reduction, which limited farm rents to 37.5 percent of the major crop, affected more than two-fifths of farm households, and about 20 percent of farm families benefited from the government's sale of land owned by Japanese nationals (Thorbecke 1979, pp. 173–74).

ing them with government bonds. So-called "tenant landlords" became the legal owners and assumed responsibility for land tax. Even so, landowner-ship remained skewed, with 10 percent of farm households owning about 60 percent of the cultivated land (Myers and Ching 1964, p. 559). But scrupu-lous collection of a fixed land tax was an incentive for landlords to make land more productive.

As in Japan, Taiwan's strategy was broad-based development of small farm *operational* units and labor-using, land-saving productivity growth. In both countries ownership was skewed prior to the postwar land reforms; but large landowners rented out most of their land in small plots to tenants. More eq-uitable landownership from land reform reduced disparities in income distri-bution as former tenants became owner-cultivators. But this simply reinforced a unimodal agrarian structure, already well established through tenancy.

Contemporary CARLs should recognize that Taiwan's redistributive land reform was performed under unique circumstances. The Kuomintang (Chinese Nationalist) administration of General Chiang Kai-shek had just gone through what John Brewster calls a "catastrophic learning experience" in their defeat by the Communists and expulsion from the mainland. One painful lesson was the need for support of the farm population (Brewster 1967). Moreover, the administrators of land reform were Chinese from the mainland, and the landlords obliged to sell were Taiwanese, which mini-mized conflicts of interest. Such conflicts are serious in a country, such as India, where many officials and members of parliament and of local leg-islative bodies own land that would be affected by redistributive land re-form. Moreover, Taiwan's program was influenced by officials administering the U.S. aid program in Taiwan who were familiar with the successful land reform in Japan after World War II.

Incentives and Farmers' Response

Farmers in Taiwan have long been receptive to innovations. For exam-ple, Taichung Native No. 1, a new rice variety, had been adopted by 90 percent of farmers in Ta-Chia District, near Taichung, within two years of its introduction in the late 1950s. And the rapid expansion of exports of canned mushrooms and canned asparagus in the 1960s is evidence of readi-ness to acquire technical knowledge to seize profitable new opportunities. Willingness to change was helped by farmers' positive experience with pre-vious innovations, even if some were forced on them.

In the early years of colonial rule Japanese police enforced local adoption of new varieties and cultivation practices. By the 1930s Japanese officials shifted to "encouragement," promoting new varieties through fertilizer sub-sidies and free seed. Later, under the Kuomintang, a rice-fertilizer barter scheme was enforced through a government monopoly on fertilizer. Farmers were obliged to deliver rice at an unfavorable price in exchange for fertilizer. It was, in effect, an inefficient agricultural tax because it maximized the disincentive to use a highly productive input. In 1964–65, for example, Taiwanese farmers paid some 60 percent more for ammonium sulphate than farmers in Japan and in the United States. Even so, fertilizer use and crop yields increased.

Neither the land tax and the coercion of the Japanese nor the price distortions of the Kuomintang's fertilizer-rice barter scheme frustrated the development of Taiwan's agriculture. Either policy would have undermined production incentives had there been no stream of innovations and no investments in infrastructure that drove productivity growth and reduced marketing margins, and, so, sustained increases in after-tax farm income.

Intersectoral Capital Flows

Rapid expansion of farm output in Taiwan helped overall economic growth and rapid structural transformation: by releasing labor for industry; by supplying food for a growing nonfarm work force; and through agricultural exports to finance imports of industrial equipment. Fundamental, however, was the way in which increases in agricultural output helped to finance investments outside agriculture.

The net capital outflow from agriculture (including terms-of-trade effects) was slightly more than 30 percent of the value of agricultural production in 1911–15 and was still 21 percent in 1931–35, by which time the real value of output had increased by 150 percent. Moreover, most of the net real capital outflow was a net outflow of funds, specifically, land rent, interest, and taxes, and net transfers through financial institutions.

T. H. Lee's pioneering studies provide long-run estimates of farm output, sales and purchases, and resource transfers to nonagricultural sectors (Table 10.3). Despite a rise in the farm population from 2.1 million in 1911 to 5.2 million in 1960, output per man grew at an annual 1.8 percent, achieved with limited external purchases of capital goods. The rise in crop yields, which was the major contributor to labor productivity growth, was associated with an elevenfold increase in chemical fertilizers, the major item in current inputs.

The most striking feature of Taiwanese agricultural development is the marketed share (the second row of Table 10.3). That share of total production measures the degree to which agriculture stimulates growth in the rest of the economy. "The more of an economy's productive activities are carried out through market transactions and the more savers hold financial rather than real assets—so the more likely savings will be moved through financial institutions into uses in which their real return is highest" (Wade 1990, p. 63). In that respect Taiwan has been well ahead of other develop-

Table 10.3. Intersectoral resource flows in Taiwan, 1911–69 (millions of Taiwan dollars at 1935–37 prices)

	1911–15	1921–25	1931–35	1936–40	1950–55	1961–65	1966–69
Agricultural output	162.9	238.0	361.4	422.5	513.3	801.6	1,044.9
Marketed share (%)	56.3	63.8	71.7	71.4	58.0	60.6	61.9
Resource transfer share (%)	30.5	26.1	24.8	21.1	22.0	13.4	13.8
Total farm cash sales	91.6	151.7	259.3	301.6	297.8	485.8	646.8
Percentage breakdown							
Sales to nonfarm households	32.6	26.7	23.2	22.6	46.4	40.6	42.5
Sales to foreign countries	16.9	23.2	34.4	32.3	5.5	7.4	8.2
Sales to processors	50.5	50.3	42.4	45.1	48.1	52.0	49.3
Total	100.0	100.0	100.0	100.0	100.0	100.0	100.0
Total farm purchases	42.1	92.6	169.8	212.5	185.0	378.5	502.4
Percentage breakdown							
Current inputs	18.3	27.4	32.3	31.6	32.2	32.6	35.6
Fixed capital	2.3	7.9	5.6	3.6	3.3	10.4	15.6
Consumer goods	79.4	64.7	62.1	64.7	64.5	57.0	48.8
Total	100.0	100.0	100.0	100.0	100.0	100.0	100.0

Source: Data from Lee 1971; and T. H. Lee, "Strategies for Transferring Agricultural Surplus under Different Agricultural Situations in Taiwan" (paper prepared for the Japan Economic Research Center Conference on Agriculture and Economic Development, Tokyo and Hakone, September 1971). The five-year periods omitted here for brevity are included in the original sources.

ing countries since the early 1960s. Indeed, monetization of Taiwan's economy dates from Japanese rule.

Between 1911–15 and 1936–40 Taiwan's agricultural exports (at constant prices) increased fourfold; and in 1938 Japan took 80 percent of foreign sales. In the early 1920s, when the nonagricultural population was only 30 percent, agricultural exports contributed twice as much to farm cash earnings as did domestic sales. Exports, thus, lifted the ceiling on output expansion that would otherwise have been imposed by the small nonfarm population. In 1921–25, for example, without agricultural exports, agricultural production would have been some 45 percent lower than it actually was. Before the late 1950s domestic sales never accounted for more than half of farm cash earnings.

Another feature of Taiwan's structural transformation is the changing composition of farm demand. First, there is the predictable falling share for consumer goods and rise in production expenses, as a result of the declining share of the agricultural labor force and increased use of externally produced inputs. Allowing for wartime setbacks, production expenditures have grown faster than output, reflecting specialization and technical advances (see Chapter 2). The resource-transfer share (third row of Table 10.3) was a heavy squeeze on the Taiwanese farmer.[6]

Such large net capital transfers from agriculture were possible because the increases in farm output were achieved with relatively small increases in purchased inputs. These were only about 18 percent of the value of agricultural production in 1936–40 and a mere 13 percent in 1950–55. In both periods, this was roughly 35 percent of all purchases by farm households and was mainly on fertilizer and other variable inputs; fixed-capital spending was around 10 percent of off-farm inputs. This judicious expansion of purchased inputs, along with technological change, and fuller and more efficient use of the farm work force, made possible substantial increases in total factor productivity. Despite the resource-transfer squeeze, however, high growth of agricultural output permitted a rise in per capita rural consumption of 0.9 percent per year.[7]

Until 1940 some three-quarters of the funds transferred out of agriculture were land rents and interest payments. This fell to a quarter after the 1953 land reform, and taxes and irrigation fees rose from 20 to more than 50 percent in the 1950s. With farm household income sharply up in the 1960s,

[6] Lee's "resource transfer" overstates agricultural "savings" because of his narrow definition of agriculture (which excludes noncultivating landlords, farmers' associations, irrigation societies, traders, and all other persons in the rural economy engaged in nonfarm activity).

[7] The net outflow of capital from Taiwan's agriculture in the 1920s and 1930s was, perhaps, excessive. Rapid commercialization of agriculture associated with large exports to Japan provided a major stimulus to productivity growth in Taiwan's agriculture, but much of the huge resource transfer accrued to Japan. Hence, the effects of the net outflow in accelerating development of Taiwan's own nonfarm sectors was less than implied by the size of the resource transfer.

voluntary savings became the major route for intersectoral financial transfers, accounting for about two-thirds of the total. From 1911 to 1950 there was a moderate invisible outflow (through adverse movements in the terms of trade) from agriculture of 5 to 25 percent of the total resource transfer. After 1950 there was a dramatic change; the terms of trade turned sharply against agriculture, so that the invisible transfer exceeded the visible component by as much as 50 percent.

Agriculture's contributions to economic growth and structural transformation were significant in the 1950s and 1960s. Because of the huge increase in farm output, the absolute resources transferred in 1966–69 were higher than in 1950–55, even though the resource transfer share had declined from 22 to 14 percent. Increased output was also sufficient for rural incomes to rise, even as farming financed growth outside agriculture. Farm cash receipts more than doubled between 1950–55 and 1966–69, but the increase in off-farm income was even more significant, especially for poorer farm households (Mao 1988; Chinn 1982). Thus, agricultural productivity growth, expansion of rural nonfarm activities, and multiplication of employment opportunities outside the rural economy worked together to raise rural household income. And because of the rapid outmigration of rural labor, farm wages increased much faster than the general level of wages and prices (Wu 1988, pp. 249–50).

Macroeconomic Policy and the Role of Small and Medium Enterprises

Taiwan's macroeconomic policies departed from those of development specialists in the 1950s. Policymakers set interest rates sufficiently high in real terms to stimulate saving and encourage capital-saving, labor-using technologies and, in general, made effective use of market forces. By avoiding credit rationing from repressed interest rates, the higher rates made investment a more effective engine of growth.

Taiwan did not follow a *laissez-faire* industrial strategy even after it abandoned orthodox import-substituting industrialization (Wade 1990; Amsden 1988). The government was determined to "maintain the vigor of its guiding, pushing, and prodding activities" (Wade 1990, p. 216). Policy instruments were used *selectively* and with limited reliance on *discretionary* authority. Thus, large firms more than small ones were affected by government policies. But even for the interventions affecting large firms, "the government has not attempted to exercise anything like comprehensive influence. Nor has it, in general, tried to set prices much below market-clearing levels. If it had tried to do either to any significant degree it would have required a much larger administration and more political power, for discretionary controls tend to breed further controls which in turn need to be administered and sanctioned" (Wade 1990, p. 193).

Also, there was a continuing commitment to performance by government agencies and development-oriented institutions, such as farmers' associations and irrigation associations. "The government's use of nondiscretionary levers for guiding the behavior of most private domestic firms . . . and its restriction of discretionary techniques to a small number of specific parameters (excepting the bigger foreign investors, the big lump projects, and new projects on the technology frontier) means that it saves scarce administrative talent" (Wade 1990). Thus, strategic decisions were made by a few able people, with the resources required to perform well. Moreover, Taiwan's universities, research institutes, and consultancy firms have been involved in the policy process. There has also been skillful and selective use of foreign consultants.

In industrial strategy Taiwanese policymakers avoided macroeconomic distortions—an overvalued exchange rate, undervalued capital, government deficits, and inflation—that have such adverse effects on agricultural development. The emphasis was on export promotion initiatives for industries, which relied mainly on microeconomic incentives.

The phenomenal growth of Taiwan's manufacturing sector was, unusually, due not to growth in existing firms but to rapid growth of the number of new firms; between 1966 and 1976 they increased 2.5-fold, and the number of employees per firm rose by only 29 percent.[8] This rapid growth in the numbers of small and medium enterprises (SMEs) contributed significantly to Taiwan's decentralized industrial expansion and enhanced positive interactions between agriculture and industry (Chapter 6).

High interest rates that encouraged labor-intensive production favored employment expansion and substantially reduced income inequality by raising labor's share in the national product (Scitovsky 1985, p. 226). Taiwan's income distribution is comparable to Japan's (Amsden 1991, p. 282). The share of the top 20 percent in Taiwan exceeds the share of the poorest 20 percent by a factor of 4.3, compared to a factor of 4 in Japan and 15 in Mexico (Scitovsky 1985, p. 218; World Bank 1987b, p. 253).

Improved Living Standards

Elimination of Mass Hunger. Taiwan's expansion of agricultural production of nearly 140 percent between 1952 and 1972 coincided with a significant rise in per capita food intake (Republic of China 1985, p. 189):

	Energy (calories)	Protein (grams)
1952	2,078	49.0
1962	2,317	57.8
1972	2,738	74.6

[8] In contrast, in South Korea development took the more conventional route with the average number of employees per firm increasing by 176 percent between 1966 and 1976 while the number of firms increased by only 10 percent (Scitovsky 1985, pp. 223–24).

The 50 percent increase in per capita protein intake, compared with just over 30 percent in per capita energy (calories), reflects growing consumption of pork, poultry, and other livestock products. This follows the usual shift from starchy staples, notably rice and sweet potatoes in Taiwan, to more expensive foods—meat and dairy products and fruits and vegetables—as household incomes rise (Chapter 5). Between 1972 and 1984 there was a further increase in per capita gross national product (GNP) from 3.2 to 6.7 times the 1952 level. In 1952–72 crop production nearly doubled, and livestock production increased fourfold; in 1972–84 crop production was up by only about 5 percent, but livestock products more than doubled. There was, too, a huge expansion in animal feed imports. In 1984 maize imports alone were almost $500 million.[9] Owing to the income equality in Taiwan, most people increased food consumption, so that undernutrition has been all but eliminated as a public health problem.

Expansion of Education. Of all children of school age (6–14), 33 percent were enrolled in 1930–31, rising rapidly to 71 percent in 1943–44 (Ho 1971, p. 309). By 1960 some 95 percent of primary school age children were in school. In 1960–77 enrollment in secondary schools increased from 33 to 76 percent of the relevant age group. In higher education the increase was from 4 to 12 percent of those aged 20–24.

Education contributed not only to farmers' remarkable receptivity to agricultural innovations but also to the dynamic interactions between agricultural and industrial development. There was a strong emphasis on quality and on technical and vocational training, which received more encouragement than academic schools. In the 1960s science and engineering students accounted for more than a third of graduates from universities and other post-secondary institutions and even more in the 1970s and 1980s (Wade 1990, p. 65). That technical bias was especially pertinent to Taiwan's rapidly expanding manufacturing sector, but it also contributed to agriculture's technical progress, as well as strong backward and forward linkages.

Rural Public Health. Taiwan's agricultural development strategy and its public health initiatives were linked through the Joint Commission on Rural Reconstruction (JCRR).[10] The JCRR, which was a catalyst for increases in farm productivity, included a Rural Health Division that helped to reduce death rates, especially infant and child mortality, and to introduce family planning.

---

[9] In 1984 imports of soybeans and cotton were over $400 million each, but only soybean meal and cottonseed cake were used to feed livestock.

[10] This binational commission, made up of Chinese and Americans who had the mutual respect required for effective collaboration, exercised broad oversight over the design and implementation of agricultural and rural development policies and programs (Mao and Schive 1990, pp. 2-39–2-41; Shen 1970; Yager 1988).

During Japanese rule, the CDR in Taiwan fell from roughly 40 per thousand to an average of 18.5 for 1941–43.[11] Given the lack of resources and limited medical knowledge before World War II, that is a remarkable achievement. The means were inexpensive, rudimentary, and authoritarian: "The Japanese conducted among the Taiwanese a wide program of education and instruction . . . issued countless sanitation rules, and utilized much of their apparatus of government to enforce their observance" (Barclay 1954, pp. 138, 146).

After World War II, health programs in Taiwan became considerably more effective because of antibiotics, immunizations, malaria control, and treatment for parasites, along with continued emphasis on hygiene, sanitation, and water supply. As a result, the CDR fell from 18 per thousand in 1947 to less than 7 per thousand in 1960. With still high levels of fertility, Taiwan's rate of natural increase fluctuated between 3.2 and 3.8 percent during the 1950s (JCRR 1961, p. 50).

At that time family planning was deemed too sensitive to be promoted by government, and the conventional view was that it would probably be an embarrassing failure. Taiwanese peasants, it was thought, were too traditional to adopt a practice alien to their culture. The chief of JCRR's Rural Health Division was, however, cautiously supporting a "Pre-Pregnancy Health Program." He had come to the conclusion that the sharp decline in child mortality was creating a potential demand for limiting family size (Freedman 1987, p. 59).[12] A benchmark survey confirmed that many women preferred fewer children, but interest in methods of avoiding additional births differed among social, economic, and demographic subgroups. After a subsequent pilot study and other surveys, family planning was adapted to existing cultures by selecting target groups in a step-by-step program. The increase in the percentage of illiterate women practicing family planning was especially dramatic—from 19 to 78 percent in only 11 years (Freedman 1987, p. 69). Overall, the CBR dropped from 40 to 23 per thousand between 1960 and 1975, when the estimated total fertility rate was down to 2.8 (World Bank 1978). In Mexico, where a family planning program was not introduced until the early 1970s, the total fertility rate in 1975 was still 6.5. Mexico, too, was less successful than Taiwan in reducing infant and child mortality.

[11] Perhaps Taiwan is the only country where trends in fertility and mortality can be traced with precision from the initial stages of development. Registration of deaths in Taiwan was virtually complete by the first census in 1905; and the registration plus census data "lend themselves to a detailed test for accuracy" (Barclay 1954, pp. 140, 142).

[12] The JCRR report for 1961 avoids reference to "birth control" or "family planning." After noting that "excessive and too close pregnancies are detrimental to the health of mothers as well as of children," the report states: "Emphasis is therefore being laid on strengthening a special maternal care program by which information and knowledge concerning pregnancy and child birth are disseminated to the housewives in rural areas" (JCRR 1961, p. 56).

MEXICO: MISSED OPPORTUNITIES

By the outbreak of the Revolution in 1910, "about 90 percent of Mexico's rural families owned no land, and approximately 85 percent of the country's Indian communities had lost all their holdings" (Hansen 1971). The *hacendados* (the landholding elite) often refused to rent land to *campesinos*, Mexico's small-scale farmers. So, landowners had a local monopoly over farmland and credit, and a monopsony as employers of a labor force that was denied the alternative of subsisting on rented land.

Between one and two million Mexicans (7–13 percent of a population of about 15 million in 1910) lost their lives during the Revolution and the civil strife that persisted into the 1920s. Most deaths were from famine and disease rather than violence (Grindle 1990, p. 187). But the power of the *hacendados* was broken, creating a historic opportunity for redistribution of land that was officially recognized in 1915 and enshrined in the constitution of 1917.

Land Reform and Agrarian Structure

Mexico's redistributive land reform involved half the agricultural land and benefited two million rural households. Rights in land were allocated to groups of *ejidatarios* who comprised an *ejido*, in collective landownership by twenty or more people. *Ejidos* accounted for more than 60 percent of farms and almost half of the farmland in 1970 (Yates 1981, pp. 154, 157). Apart from a few *ejidos* that are operated collectively, cultivation is by individual family units. To prevent reconsolidation into large private holdings and fragmentation, there were restrictions on land sales. Until 1981 renting *ejido* land also was banned by law, if not in practice. This also precluded using land as collateral for loans, which shielded *ejidatarios* from eviction but also excluded them from private capital markets. In any event, the ban on land renting and sale did not maintain the intended equality. Restrictions on *ejido* land transactions and use of *ejido* land as collateral were eliminated by the Mexican Congress in 1992.

Little land was transferred to *ejidos* before 1930, at which time nearly as much land had been distributed to village *communidades* (communities), which had held land in common before the misguided reforms of the 1850s (Yates 1981, pp. 141, 154). Redistribution, especially to *ejidos*, accelerated during the administration of President Lázaro Cárdenas (1934–40) when 18 million hectares were parceled out to 810,000 people (Hamilton 1982, p. 177). This almost halved the landless in the rural population from 68 percent in 1934 to 36 percent in 1940. Cárdenas's presidency was also committed to collective farming and provision of credit, irrigation, and public services to *ejidos*, priorities that were not shared by subsequent administra-

Table 10.4. Land redistribution in Mexico by presidential period, 1915–76

Period	Total hectares	Arable hectares	Arable hectares per beneficiary
Pre-Cárdenas (1915–34)	11,244,817	1,610,561	1.7
Cárdenas (1934–40)	18,360,344	4,297,294	5.7
Avila Camancho (1940–46)	7,242,308	1,123,725	9.1
Alemán Valdés (1946–52)	4,616,352	800,996	7.4
Ruiz Cortines (1952–58)	6,182,017	1,035,665	4.6
López Mateos (1958–64)	8,845,814	1,479,747	5.1
Díaz Ordaz (1964–70)	24,729,499	2,101,534	5.6
Echeverria (1970–76)	12,742,744	925,807	4.2

Source: Grindle 1990, Table 6.2, p. 188. © 1990 Lynne Rienner Publishers, Inc. Reprinted by permission.

tions. Furthermore, although President Díaz Ordaz (1964–70) distributed the greatest area of land, Cárdenas distributed more arable land than any other president (Table 10.4).

The pattern of private, freehold landownership, especially small farms, emerged, unplanned, from agrarian reform (Figure 10.3, Panel A).[13] By 1970 about 20 percent of farms were small, private ones, under 5 hectares, accounting for around 5 percent of Mexico's arable land; 7 percent of farms were private (with 5–25 hectares) and held 11 percent of the arable land. Private farms with more than 25 hectares were about 3 percent of all farms but controlled 37 percent of the arable land.

Redistribution attenuated, but did not eliminate, Mexico's bimodal ownership structure (Figure 10.3, Panel B).[14] Of all *ejidal* units, 55 percent are small (under 5 hectares), and only 1 percent have more than 25 hectares. The 46 percent of arable land in *ejidos* adds substantially to small farms' share of area, but much of the skewness remains because *ejidos* also account for two-thirds or so of all farms. Small private holdings and *ejidos* of under 5 hectares comprise two-thirds of farms but less than one-fifth of arable land. Distribution of all agricultural land is even more biased than arable land because range and grassland is concentrated in large, private holdings (Yates 1981, p. 157).

[13] In 1930, when only about 6 percent of the land had been distributed to *ejidos*, private farms of more than 5,000 hectares accounted for less than 1 percent of holdings but controlled more than 60 percent of agricultural land (arable land plus pasture); holdings under 50 hectares included more than 86 percent of farms, but only 3 percent of the land (Simpson 1937, pp. 652, 694–95).

[14] No reliable information is available on the distribution of farm *operating* units in Mexico. Ejidatarios were prohibited from sharecropping or renting land until 1981, so these transactions do not show up in statistics. Renting out of small parcels by large landowners has been rare. They fear that renting increases the chances that land will be expropriated for redistribution. Continuing reform also made large cattle ranchers reluctant to intensify operations (Yates 1981, p. 152). The government's announcement in 1991 that there would be no further redistribution should reduce landlords' reluctance to rent out land.

Figure 10.3. Distribution of number of ownership units and of area by farm size for arable land in Mexico, 1970

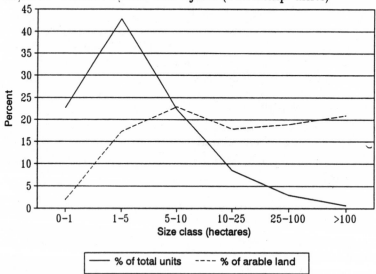

Panel A: Private Farms' Share of Total (ownership units)

Panel B: Private Farms and Ejidos (ownership units)

Source: Calculated from Yates 1981, Table 7.5, p. 157.

Notes: Percentages in panel A are based on the grand totals of ownership units and arable land in private holdings, *ejidos*, and *communidades*. As well as *ejidos* and private holdings, panel B includes *communidades*, which account for about 5 percent of farm units and 2 percent of arable land. Collectivized *ejidos* and *communidades* are excluded from both panels.

Table 10.5. Irrigated area in Mexico by region and tenure, 1930, 1950, and 1970 (in thousand acres)

	1930	1950	1970	Arable land irrigated in 1970 (%)
Northwest				
Private	712.3	948.2	1,863.1	68
Ejidal	21.6	714.4	1,411.6	38
Total North				
Private	2,072.5	2,220.9	3,325.5	40
Ejidal	220.9	1,652.7	2,552.5	24
Total Mexico				
Private	3,603.4	3,172.3	4,504.3	24
Ejidal	504.7	3,014.4	4,349.5	15

Source: Yates 1981, Table 4.1, p. 71. © 1981 University of Arizona Press. Reprinted by permission.
Notes: The Northwest includes the states of Sonora, Sinaloa, Nayarit, Baja California Norte, and Baja California Sur. The other states of the North are: Chihuahua, Durango, Coahuila, Nuevo Leon, Tamaulipas, Zacatecas, Aguascalientes, and San Luis Potosi (Yates 1981, pp. 44–45).

Public Investment in Irrigation

Mexico's National Irrigation Commission, which became a Ministry of Hydraulic Resources in 1947, initiated a program of dam construction in northern Mexico that increased the country's irrigated area from 4.5 million acres in 1940 to about 7.7 million in 1960. By 1970 the northern states accounted for two-thirds of the land served by government irrigation projects that by then covered about 9 million acres (Table 10.5).

Northern Mexico, especially northwestern states such as Sonora and Sinaloa, are the best sites for irrigation. The North's share of irrigated land is roughly the same as its share of agricultural land, and private ownership has been widespread in the arid North since before the Revolution. Because *ejidos* are most common in the humid regions of central and southern Mexico, only about 15 percent of *ejido* land was irrigated compared to almost a quarter of private land. And, in the Northwest, where larger farms are common, more than two-thirds of privately owned cropland is irrigated (Table 10.5).

Rapid expansion of irrigation in northern Mexico permitted a large increase in crop area and helped the speedy adoption of new varieties and use of chemical fertilizer. This provided a strong incentive to mechanize. Between 1940 and 1960 the number of tractors in Mexico rose from less than 5,000 to nearly 55,000, concentrated in the northern regions (Fliginger and others 1969, p. 46; see also B. Sims and others 1988). Moreover, irrigation led to a rapid rise in land values—a further incentive for those with economic and political power to extend their control over farmland.

In Mexico, as in Taiwan, research-based increases in crop yields, associated with rapid expansion in fertilizer use, have accounted for most growth in farm output.[15] The Office of Special Studies, part of the Ministry of Agriculture, was set up in 1943 as a joint venture of the Rockefeller Foundation and the Mexican government. As with Japanese researchers who laid the foundations of Taiwan's agricultural research institutions, a crucial factor was the competence and continuity among the staff of agricultural scientists, who were recruited initially in the United States and progressively augmented by Mexican agricultural scientists selected and trained as an integral part of the program.[16] One of their greatest successes was the development of high-yielding wheats, particularly short-stemmed, stiff-strawed, fertilizer-responsive varieties that have been behind the Green Revolution in other countries.[17] Yield increases were responsible for most of the threefold increase in Mexico's wheat production between the early 1950s and late 1960s (Figure 10.4).

There were great strides, too, in cotton varieties, that led to a substantial increase in yields (150 percent) and in acreage from the mid-1930s to the early 1960s, when cotton became Mexico's most important export. Much newly irrigated land was suited to cotton, and during the 1940s and 1950s the "umbrella effect" of U.S. price support policies and acreage restrictions was an incentive for U.S. firms to expand production in Mexico. Their expertise and capital eased the transfer of production technologies from the American Southwest to northern Mexico. This contributed to rapid mechanization, as happened in the American South about the same time (Chapter 3), and to increases in cotton area and yields.

Wheat and cotton are concentrated in the arid regions of northern Mexico, and expansion of output has been dependent on public investments in irri-

[15] Nitrogen fertilizer use in Mexico averaged only 10,000 nutrient tons during the years 1948–52 but reached 345,000 tons in 1968.

[16] The success of the wheat program led to the dissolution of the Office of Special Studies and the creation of a National Institute of Agricultural Research. The Rockefeller Foundation staff and some of the Mexican agricultural scientists provided the nucleus for the International Maize and Wheat Improvement Center (CIMMYT), established in 1966.

[17] The development of those higher-yielding, fertilizer-responsive varieties, which have had a profound impact on wheat production in India, Pakistan, and other countries since the late 1960s, was facilitated by the introduction of genes from high-yield, semidwarf varieties from the Pacific Northwest in the United States (see Chapter 3). As in Mexico, the spread of these high-yielding Mexican wheat varieties in the Indian Punjab depended on availability of irrigation. In the Punjab, however, small-scale farmers had much better access to credit and irrigation than their Mexican counterparts, especially the *ejidatarios*. As a result, adoption of higher-yielding wheat and application of fertilizer were comparable across farm sizes in the Punjab in 1971. Irrigation in the Indian Punjab was supplied primarily by small-scale private investment in tubewells (Nicholson 1984; Ireson 1987). In Mexico such small-scale irrigation investment has been inhibited because private farmers rarely can obtain permits to build dams or sink wells (Yates 1981, pp. 71, 85).

Figure 10.4. Yields of wheat, maize, and beans, Mexico, 1940–85

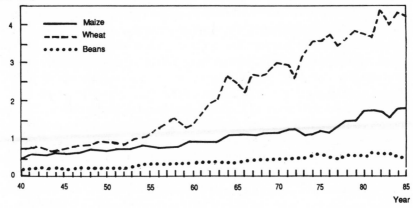

Metric Tons per Hectare

Source: Adelman and Taylor 1990, Figure 1, p. 15. © 1990 OECD. Reprinted by permission.

gation. Irrigated northwest Mexico replaced rainfed central Mexico as the main wheat producer in the 1950s and 1960s with the spread of higher-yielding varieties. This shift of wheat production toward irrigated land reinforced varietal improvements. It also meant that much productivity growth was on the large farms that had benefited from the concentration of irrigation investment, much of it public.

Maize and beans are the most important smallholder crops, and they are the staple foods of the rural population and the urban poor.[18] Maize hybrids were developed to meet the ecological requirements of different areas, and by 1960 over 300,000 hectares were planted, with an average yield roughly 75 percent higher than open-pollinated varieties. However, that was only about 6 percent of the acreage planted to ordinary maize, so, the yield differential was partly due to 32 percent of hybrids being under irrigation, compared to only 8 percent of the area planted to ordinary maize. Beans, often intercropped with maize, have received relatively little attention from agricultural researchers, and yields have grown only gradually. In the mid-1970s, only 10 to 15 percent of bean acreage was irrigated; 75 percent of Mexico's crop comes from rainfed areas (Sanderson 1986, p. 220; Byerlee and Longmire 1986, p. 24).

[18] Expenditure surveys in 1968 and 1975 show the importance of these staples in rural diets: maize and beans supplied 75 percent of calories and 80 percent of protein. Wheat played almost no role in the rural diet (Sanderson 1986, p. 221).

Mexico's large producers have good contact with agricultural research workers and, thus, prompt access to information about the new, high-yielding varieties of wheat as well as cotton. This gave them an advantage over small farmers, who suffered from the shortcomings of agricultural extension programs. The development and diffusion of innovations among Mexico's small-scale farmers was also limited by technical factors. A maize improvement program based on hybrids is more difficult to implement than one for a self-pollinating crop such as wheat. That was especially true of pure-line maize hybrids, which were location-specific.

Another complication of developing profitable innovations for small-holders is that environmental conditions of *ejidos* and small farms are highly diverse and often difficult. Some 60 percent of cultivated land in those areas has slopes in excess of 4 percent, of which about 40 percent has thin soils, vulnerable to erosion (Turrent 1987). Here, there has been little investment in irrigation. Technical progress is also difficult, because of the need to develop varieties and practices adapted to many differing local conditions. The level and seasonal distribution of rainfall are frequently inadequate; so, using chemical fertilizers is riskier.

But not all of the problems of smallholder development are due to technical difficulties and environmental adversity. Partly responsible was the poor performance of PRONASE, the parastatal organization responsible for distributing hybrid maize seed. The success of the Puebla Project, a maize improvement program, depended almost entirely on increased use of chemical fertilizers, higher plant populations, and other agronomic recommendations because scientists were unable to identify varieties that gave a significant yield increase over those already used by farmers in rainfed areas. For wheat, government policy in the 1950s and 1960s favored research on irrigated wheat; not until 1980 were new wheat varieties for rainfed areas released (Byerlee and Longmire 1986, pp. 25, 36).

Differential Impact of Incentives

Government efforts to regulate wheat prices go back to 1938, but heavy intervention began around 1960 (Sanderson 1986, p. 200). The real value of the wheat support price gradually declined from 1960 but stayed above the world price until, at least, 1971; and despite a decline in the real value of the maize support price, it, too, remained higher than world prices until the global world price spike of the 1973–74 "world food crisis" (Figure 10.5).

Thus, throughout the 1970s price policies for wheat and maize, in principle, could have benefited large and small farms alike, whether irrigated or rainfed, as long as some output was marketed. But the distribution of benefits across farms depended crucially on prices in local markets. Like investment in irrigation, public investment in transport infrastructure has

Figure 10.5. Prices of wheat and maize in Mexico, 1960–82

Panel A: Wheat Prices
(Constant 1970 Pesos)

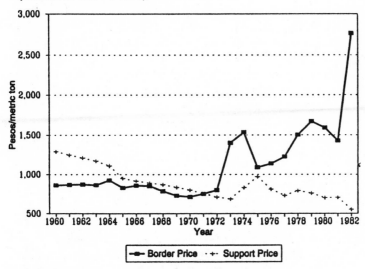

Panel B: Maize Prices
(Constant 1970 Pesos)

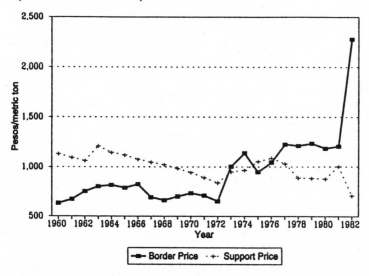

Sources: Mexican support prices: Sanderson 1986, p. 203. United States prices and producer price index: World Bank 1987–88. Exchange rates: IMF *International Financial Statistics Yearbook*, 1988 and 1989.

Notes: The "Support Price" is the government-guaranteed producer price in Mexico deflated using the implicit GNP deflator for Mexico. The "Border Price" is the f.o.b. price in U.S. ports, deflated by the U.S. producer price index and converted to pesos at the market exchange rate. The price series for wheat is for U.S. No. 1 or No. 2 Soft Red Winter wheat, f.o.b. Atlantic ports. The price series for maize is for U.S. No. 2 Yellow maize, f.o.b. Gulf ports.

favored the North. Good roads (combined with subsidies that lowered the cost of shipments of wheat to Mexico City) ensured that large farms in the Northwest received the support price for wheat. In rainfed areas of central Mexico underdeveloped transport and other marketing deficiencies meant that farmers have received prices significantly below the support prices (Byerlee and Longmire 1986).

Moreover, large producers could demand (and receive) highly favorable credit at subsidized interest rates. Small farmers, especially *ejidatarios*, had little access to institutional credit between 1940 and 1970. And, in addition to public investments in irrigation, the large private farms of the North received other substantial subsidies on water. They benefited disproportionately from subsidized hydroelectric power for pump irrigation, public investments in land leveling and drainage, and from subsidies for deep wells and diesel fuel.

Agriculture in Mexican Development, 1940–70

The rapid expansion of agricultural output in Mexico between 1940 and 1970 made vital contributions to overall economic development. Between 1950 and 1970, the population rose by 87 percent—from 25.8 million to 48.3 million. Increases in wheat production replaced imports that had accounted for half of total consumption by Mexico's exploding urban population. Moreover, since 1940 expanded exports of farm products earned much of the foreign exchange needed for economic growth. Mexico's merchandise exports increased at an average 8.5 percent a year between 1940 and 1963, with agricultural exports accounting for most of this increase (Freithaler 1968, pp. 62–65). In 1940 agricultural and forestry products were 20 percent of Mexico's commodity (mainly mineral) exports; by 1955 their share had increased to 51 percent and peaked at 68 percent in 1972 (King 1970, p. 20; Matus and Cruz Aguilar 1987, p. 134). By then, cotton and coffee were the major export commodities, and less so sugar and meat. Still more recently sales to the United States and Canada of tomatoes, fresh and frozen strawberries, and other fruits and vegetables expanded rapidly. By 1980, however, petroleum exports began to dwarf earnings from agricultural exports (Schuh 1987, p. 154; Matus and Cruz Aguilar 1987, p. 134; Mares 1987).

Intersectoral Capital Flows. Before the oil boom of the 1970s there was a net flow of resources from agriculture to the rest of the economy. It appears to have been small, however, compared to Taiwan. In terms of government expenditures and receipts, there was a net flow of funds into agriculture, mainly because of the large government-financed investments in irrigation. For 1942–61 taxes collected from agriculture fell short (by some 3 billion pesos) of the 19.1 billion pesos spent on the agricultural sector. The net flow of public resources into agriculture was especially large in the 1940s, and the acceleration in growth of agricultural output generated sufficient savings in excess of investments in agriculture so that there was a substantial net outflow of funds through financial institutions. (See Reynolds 1970, pp. 177–79; Reyes Osorio and others 1970, p. 261.)

Macroeconomic Policies

Until the 1970s Mexico, like Taiwan, avoided the most serious effects of ill-advised macroeconomic policies. Unlike other Latin American countries, inflation was under control (Solís 1980, pp. 103–10). Real interest rates remained positive in spite of interest rate ceilings. The favorable effects of price stability were reinforced by the free convertibility of the Mexican peso from 1930 until 1982 and by policies that avoided overvaluation between 1954 and the early 1970s. This, in turn, encouraged financial intermediation that helped the expansion of output in both agriculture and industry.[19] From 1955 to 1970 the Mexican miracle saw real gross domestic product (GDP) growth of 6.7 percent a year (Brothers and Solís 1966; Solís 1980; Cardoso and Levy 1988).

Oil Boom and Bust. Favorable macroeconomic policies were reversed in the 1970s, when oil discoveries led to a breakdown of the monetary and fiscal balance maintained between 1958 and 1972.[20] In the 1970s and 1980s high inflation undermined the predictability essential to investment and economic growth. Before the drastic devaluations beginning in 1982, the peso was grossly overvalued (apart from a brief period after the 1976 devaluation). The petroleum boom and its collapse resulted in a debt crisis and economic stagnation, and the cuts, necessary to restore fiscal balance, hit public investment in agriculture and social services particularly hard.

---

[19] Mexico pursued a strategy of import-substituting industrialization. However, of seven developing countries studied by the OECD, effective rates of industrial protection in the 1960s were lowest in Mexico, and Taiwan was second lowest. The figure for Taiwan is for 1965, *after* relaxation of import controls (Little, Scitovsky, and Scott 1970, p. 174). But although Taiwan moved further to scrap import substitution for export promotion, import restrictions mounted in Mexico, generating higher industrial protection through the 1960s and 1970s. Manufactured exports rarely topped 25 percent of total exports, even before the oil boom (Cardoso and Levy 1988, pp. 355–57).

[20] Harberger (1988, pp. 26–28) emphasizes that when Mexico had no oil, the authorities could deny requests by saying "we won't give you what you want because we can't." But with the arrival of the oil bonanza, instead of being able to deny excessive requests for funds because of lack of resources, the financial authorities were in the more difficult position of having to tell governors, ministers, the president, and others seeking financing for their favorite projects that they did not *choose* to finance those projects. It is not particularly surprising that in the oil boom period the Bank of Mexico and the Ministry of Finance were no longer able to maintain the monetary and fiscal balance required to avoid rapid inflation and a nonsustainable overvaluation of the peso.

Policy Initiatives of the 1970s and 1980s

Since the early 1970s government policy has given a higher priority to increased productivity and incomes of small farms in Mexico's rainfed areas. This was partly a nationalistic response to substantial imports of maize from the United States. It was also recognized that relative stagnation of productivity of the *small-scale* majority within Mexico's bimodal agrarian structure had been shaped by official policies.

PIDER, a rural development program that received loans from the World Bank and the Inter-American Bank, was launched in 1973 and emphasized investments in small-scale irrigation and other infrastructure projects. It was followed by a Rainfed Districts Program to increase research and development in previously neglected areas. The Mexican Food Systems Program (*Sistema Alimentario Mexicano*, or SAM) in the late 1970s enlarged credit for small-scale rainfed farms, put more emphasis on price incentives, and attempted to insulate farmers from risk (Cartas and Bassoco 1987). But with the end of the oil boom, a severe financial crisis, and a new presidential regime, the SAM program was abruptly terminated at the end of 1982.[21]

Social Programs and Rural Living Standards

Mexico has given less attention than Taiwan to investment in rural human capital. Education and health programs in the countryside came later, and progress was set back by the economic crisis of the 1980s. Moreover, the gaps between social programs in Mexico and Taiwan are greatest in primary education and health care, where such services count most.

Rural Education. Students registered in public primary schools increased more than fivefold between 1925 and 1960; yet, in 1960 more than 70 percent of Mexicans aged twenty-five years and over had less than four years of schooling (Reynolds 1970, pp. 290–94). In 1960–75 children of primary school age enrolled increased from about 80 percent to near-universal coverage, despite the rapid population growth. However, there has been less success in raising the quality of rural education. Moreover, in 1960 only 11 percent of the children of secondary school age were enrolled (about a third of the percentage enrolled in Taiwan), and by 1977 it had reached 30 percent (just over half the percentage in Taiwan). Only in higher education (aged 20–24) in Mexico was enrollment nearly as high as in Taiwan, 3 percent in 1960 and 10 percent in 1977 (World Bank 1980).

---

[21] A National Food Program (PRONAL) was announced in 1983. SAM's goal of self-sufficiency was transformed into the more flexible "food sovereignty" that recognizes that selective reliance on international markets can make a positive contribution to "food security" (Austin and Esteva 1987, pp. 363–71).

Table 10.6.   Infant and child mortality in Mexico and Taiwan (deaths per thousand)

Category	Mexico	Taiwan
Infants (0–1 year)		
1960	78	56
1978	60	25
Children (1–4 years)		
1960	14	8
1978	6	1

Health Services.   Medical care and health services have expanded rapidly since the Mexican Revolution. In 1960 the number of physicians per capita was slightly higher than in Taiwan and far above the average for developing countries. Moreover, health services are available through large public programs, notably the IMSS (the Mexican Institute of Social Security) and SSA (the Ministry of Health and Welfare). Even so, until recently, Mexico's rural population had limited access to health services.

With improved socioeconomic conditions and sanitation, life expectancy had reached 58 years by 1960, compared to 64 years in Taiwan. But in the next twenty years, Taiwan's rural population benefited more from advances in medical knowledge and public health techniques. The difference in increased life expectancy between 1960 and 1978 was slight, from 64 to 72 years in Taiwan, compared to Mexico's 58 to 65 years. But the widening of differentials in infant and child mortality is striking (Table 10.6).

In 1973 the Mexican government adopted a new population policy, and in the late 1970s initiated programs to reduce the bias in health care against the rural population (see Box 10.1). The emphasis was on rapid expansion of family planning services through the urban health centers and hospitals of the SSA and the IMSS, with limited effort initially to reach the rural population.[22] Even so, fertility fell by maybe 30 percent in 1970–79. The fall in the CBR was less, because the number of women of childbearing age increased rapidly in the 1970s. Reduction in the average number of children in rural families has beneficial effects on the health of mothers, as well as on that of their offspring. But Taiwan's experience also shows the longer-term importance of reduced fertility—it slows the increase in those of working age, so hastening structural transformation and raising rural wages.

[22] Once under way, these programs have been effective. By 1981 37 percent of rural women in their childbearing years had practiced contraception (Potter, Mojarro, and Nuñez 1987, p. 147). For illiterate women, the increase was particularly dramatic—from 2 percent in 1969 to 19 percent in 1981. The increase was also large for those with one to three years of schooling—from 5 to 33 percent. Prevalence rates were higher for women with four to five years of schooling or more than six years—37 and 52 percent, respectively—and since 1969 the increase has been 270 and 130 percent, although this is lower than for those with less education (Alba and Potter 1986, p. 63).

Box 10.1.   A New Direction in Rural Public Health

In 1979 the government began to expand health services in rural Mexico, especially in maternal and child care and family planning, with the so-called IMSS-COPLAMAR program. In 1978 twenty million (mostly rural) people, or 30 percent of the population, had no access to institutional health services, and the resources of SSA and IMSS were overwhelmingly in urban areas.

The new program was undertaken by COPLAMAR, created in 1977 to promote and coordinate programs for marginalized rural groups and regions. Financing was provided mainly out of funds controlled by COPLAMAR, but IMSS, a large, well-funded, and competent organization, absorbed most of the administrative expenses for the new program. The expansion of the IMSS-COPLA-MAR program between 1979 and 1982 was remarkable: 3,024 rural health posts and 71 rural hospitals were established, and by 1985 almost thirteen million people were covered (Alba and Potter 1986, p. 64; Sherraden 1989, p. 210).

The program includes family medicine, maternal and infant care, family planning, immunizations and other preventive services, detection of chronic diseases, malnutrition, health education, and promotion of environmental sanitation and community action. Village clinics are staffed by either *pasantes*, medical school graduates performing a year of required social service, or young medical doctors hired on contract. There is also a full-time and a part-time clinic aide, recruited from the community and trained by IMSS-COPLAMAR. The program has survived the debt crisis and fiscal austerity of the *sexenios* of Presidents de la Madrid and Salinas.

Between 1980 and 1986, health spending fell from 2.5 to 1.6 percent of GNP and from 5.9 to 3.7 percent of public sector spending. Decentralization of IMSS-COPLAMAR, called for in 1984, came to a halt in 1987. But the program lost only about a quarter of its clinics and hospitals, even though responsibility was decentralized in nearly half the states. Although COPLAMAR, the umbrella agency, was liquidated in 1983, the name IMSS-COPLAMAR has been retained, which lends credence to the view that IMSS-COPLAMAR survived because of "the popularity of the program among federal bureaucrats and rural beneficiaries, administrative support within IMSS, and relatively low operating costs" (Sherraden 1989, p. 136).

From Agricultural Growth to Rural Stagnation

The effects of Mexico's dualistic agricultural strategy were revealed slowly. From accelerated distribution of land to *ejidos* in 1934–40 until the late 1960s, there was a sense of notable progress. By 1970 inequality in income distribution, persistent rural poverty, unemployment, and a growing marginal population in urban slums gave rise to serious concern.

Farm output in Mexico expanded at 4.7 percent a year for 1940–53 and 3.7 percent in 1954–65 and, especially in the earlier period, was associated with rapid expansion of land, labor, capital, and other inputs. However, output growth exceeded the 3 percent growth in total inputs, implying an increase in total factor productivity of 1.7 percent a year. Expansion of crop production was almost 10 percent a year in the 1952–58 *sexenio* (the six-year period of a presidential administration). This rise was associated with a 6.3 percent increase in crop area, and employment growth was even more rapid. In the 1958–64 *sexenio*, growth in yields at 4.3 percent was impressive, but annual growth in cultivated area had declined to less than 3 percent. In 1954–65, all except the variable inputs increased at a slower rate. The annual growth in factor productivity was perhaps 1.9 percent, accounting for slightly over a half of the 3.7 percent annual rise in output (Hertford 1970, p. 99).[23] By 1970–76 the production growth was negligible, and crop area and employment both fell (see Cartas 1987, p. 113).

In the 1970s overvalued exchange rates hurt agriculture; in the 1980s it was cutbacks in public spending, which also hit the rest of the economy. Mexico's encounter with the "Dutch disease" was not as devastating for agriculture as it was as in Nigeria. But neither was it managed successfully, as in Indonesia (Box 5.4). Export crops, such as cotton, were especially vulnerable to overvalued exchange rates, which reduced peso prices and undermined production incentives; at the same time grain imports for food and feed became cheaper. There was a tendency for controlled prices of agricultural products to lag behind price increases for other products, especially as inflation accelerated in the 1970s (Cartas 1987, p. 114; Byerlee and Longmire 1986, p. 88). The increase in wage rates in the oil sector spilled over into the rural economy. Some large farms benefited from increased domestic demand for perishable goods, such as fruit, vegetables, and poultry. But the adverse effects of overvalued exchange rates and higher labor costs were concentrated in the large, export-oriented subsector that had been the engine of agricultural growth in Mexico since the 1940s. At the same time, greater profitability in construction and other nontradable activities outside agriculture led to decapitalization of the large-scale subsector. On the other hand, the lower labor costs and the flexibility of family labor meant that the small private and ejidal subsectors were more resilient (Scherr 1989).

The roots of the slowdown in agriculture run deeper than the macroeconomic mismanagement of the mid-1970s and early 1980s. In fact, the slowdown began in 1965–76. Lack of investment in smallholder development and neglect of research in rainfed areas were fundamental contributing factors. By 1970 Mexico's dualistic strategy created a rural economy in which more than 40 percent of arable land, almost half of the irrigation and of other public investment, and more than 60 percent of the higher-yielding technology and 70 percent of farm machinery was concentrated on 12 percent of Mexico's farms; moreover, these farms provided only 20 percent of agricultural jobs

[23] Solís (1971, pp. 4–5) gives higher rates of increase and estimates in Cartas (1987, p. 118) for 1952–58 and 1958–64 are much higher.

(Grindle 1990, pp. 190–91). Ironically, efforts to redress the imbalance in Mexico's agricultural strategy and in rural social services intensified in the 1970s only to be cut short by the economic collapse of the 1980s.

Persistence of Rural Poverty. Growth in Mexico's rural population has led to increasing pressure on land, especially in rainfed areas. Agriculture's share of the total labor force declined from 44 percent in 1970 to 37 percent in 1980, even though the agricultural work force rose at 2.5 percent a year because of rapid growth of the population of working age (Alexandratos 1988). And the rural labor force is likely to continue to grow until 2005.

Rural poverty is worst among the landless and the *ejidatarios* and small private farmers, who accounted for two-thirds of farms with less than 5 hectares in 1970. Land reform in the 1930s substantially reduced marginal holdings of less than 5 hectares, and there was a dramatic decline in landless households, from 1.1 million in 1910 to 200,000 in 1940. But by 1960 landless households had risen to 1.3 million. There was more land distribution during the 1960s (Table 10.4). But only a little over 10 percent of the land allocated to *ejidos* was arable (Yates 1981, p. 154).

What Opportunities Remain for Mexico? Mexico's financial and debt-servicing crisis necessitated cuts in many programs, including the SAM and the IMSS-COPLAMAR rural health programs. There could, however, be compensating benefits if this were seized as an opportunity to realign public sector priorities with emphasis on public goods, such as agricultural research and infrastructure, rather than on commercial activities.

For example, privatizing PRONASE, the parastatal for seed distribution now in liquidation, would be a step in that direction. However, such policy changes will achieve little unless there are more public efforts to increase agricultural productivity and to improve marketing of farm products, especially for the small farmer. Because private firms have been able to capture the benefits of research only for hybrid crop varieties, development of high-yielding, open-pollinated varieties has been undertaken mainly by public sector research. However, new techniques of molecular biology make it likely that the role of private companies will extend beyond hybrids, even in CARLs. Opportunities for profitable innovations suited to the small farms exist, despite the uncertainty and diversity of rainfed agriculture (Tripp and others 1990; Marsh 1991; Sims 1993).

Many small farms will be hit by trade liberalization and increased competition, as well as by the higher costs resulting from the elimination of input subsidies. However, their competitive position would benefit from the reduction of preferential treatment for large farms and from public investment in research and infrastructure. Many small farms have switched to new activities (dairying and hog rearing), but little has been done to increase productivity through research and development of more efficient linkages between crop and livestock farming (Turrent 1987). For example, small mixed farms could grow hybrid sorghums, mainly produced on large farms. Such sorghum could mean a big increase in yields and could be used for feeding hogs and other livestock. Small-farm coffee production in Chiapas, helped by an independent marketing cooperative, is another type of opportunity to be seized when the policy environment is right.

Increases in incomes of small farmers could also stimulate improvements in output and employment in rural manufacturing and service industries. Inexpensive animal-powered equipment could increase productivity and output and generate demand for implements from rural-based workshops (B. Sims and others 1988). The same applies to rural processing of agricultural products, as well as manufacture of consumer goods, including products for export now that overvaluation of the exchange rate is no longer a major problem.[24] But with agriculture's share of the labor force down to 37 percent by 1980 and, maybe, 30 percent in 1990, expansion of job opportunities in the nonfarm sectors (both rural and urban) is of greater importance than in the agricultural sector. Mexico has missed past opportunities to adopt a broad-based agricultural strategy, but economic and social reasons remain for pursuing a *parallel* strategy to expand opportunities outside agriculture while increasing the productivity and incomes of small farms which provide jobs and income for a large share of the population.

POLITICAL ECONOMY: SIMILARITIES AND CONTRASTS

Both Mexico and Taiwan have authoritarian political regimes and face domestic pressures and international tensions. Nonetheless, both maintain a reasonably stable environment for economic growth. Mexico's proximity to the United States and the U.S. government's links with Taiwan have influenced each country's opportunities and constraints. Because of the economic and political power of the United States, Mexican policymakers were concerned about protecting Mexico's industrialization. And the United States provided ready but often inappropriate mechanical technology for Mexican agriculture. Yet, although U.S. agriculture influenced the rate of technological change, choices made in Mexico led to the inappropriate bias in favor of large farms.

[24] Adelman and Taylor use the results of the SAM program between 1980 and 1982 in simulating the potential impacts of reducing the bias in favor of large farms. One result is that the more widespread increases in farm incomes "generate high linkages into demand for labor-intensive manufactures on the consumption side and for manufactured inputs on the production side" (Adelman and Taylor 1990, p. 52). Although Adelman and Taylor label this option a "unimodal agricultural strategy," it is based on reallocation of public investment in the agricultural sector along the lines of the SAM and does not involve redistribution of land to attain a unimodal agrarian structure that probably is not politically feasible in the future. See de Janvry (1981) for discussion of agriculture–industry interactions characteristic of the bimodal agrarian structure of many Latin American countries.

Taiwan's rapid economic growth since the early 1950s benefited from U.S. economic aid to the Kuomintang regime—almost $1.5 billion from 1951 to 1965, when aid was terminated. Moreover, there was an unusually effective working relationship between the AID Mission to Taiwan and the national economic planning and development authorities (Mao and Schive 1990, pp. 2-39–2-41; Shen 1970; Yager 1988). Although aid was important, Taiwan's policies and those of the Japanese colonial administration were more fundamental to its rapid growth and structural transformation.

The Kuomintang Retreat to Taiwan

Kuomintang rule began with a "chaotic interregnum" in 1945–47 when the Taiwanese people saw "mainlanders plunder and wreck their economy." Seeing their elite "systematically hunted down and murdered by the mainlanders traumatized the Taiwanese to the point that the phrase 'politics is dangerous' became a watchword etched into their collective unconscious" (Gold 1986, pp. 51, 52). Before moving his regime to Taiwan in December 1949, Chiang Kai-shek named a trusted general as Taiwan's new governor, assigned his son Chiang Ching-kuo to head the provincial party, and initiated the first land reform program (Gold 1986, p. 57). Chiang Kai-shek and other "chastened political leaders" attributed failure on the mainland largely to economic collapse and, therefore, "gave greater scope over Taiwan's economy to Western-trained experts and intervened less than they had on the mainland."

Gold and others emphasize that the state was strong and relatively autonomous in Taiwan because the majority of people had limited leverage and bargaining power. However, there was a need to maintain their support (or minimize opposition) through economic growth and outlets for their entrepreneurial talents and ambitions. This strengthened the position of those bureaucrats who advocated an expanding role for the private sector. Chinese economists, such as S. C. Tsiang, were thus able to persuade the government to adopt the 1958–60 economic reforms (of exchange rates, interest rates, and related policies) that helped the growth of private firms and provided opportunities for both Taiwanese and mainland entrepreneurs. In Taiwan this meant "selling a new policy package to the state elite rather than neutralizing the possible opposition from the society" (Cheng 1986, p. 23).

Mexico after the Revolution

Under Mexico's authoritarian regime, the president dominates both the executive and the legislative branches of government. Public policy "is an end product of elite bureaucracy and political interchange which occurs beyond the purview of the general public and the rank and file adherents to the official party" (Grindle 1977, pp. 6, 7). More generally, "the PRI [the Party of the

Institutionalized Revolution] is better conceptualized as an apparatus through which the Revolutionary Coalition controls Mexican politics than as a mechanism for representing and implementing the demands of its component interest groups" (Hansen 1971, p. 107). This is both the cause and consequence of the "personalism, patronage, corruption, and institutionalized bureaucratic politics" that are so pervasive in Mexico (Greenberg 1970, p. 138).

Even so, policymaking is constrained by reluctance to antagonize the groups that maintain the loose coalition of the PRI. In particular, the options for agricultural development are limited by the power of large farm interests that dominate the sector. Policies have also aggravated the pathological growth of Mexico City. This inhibits a dispersed pattern of industrial growth and expansion of jobs in rural areas (Chapter 6). "The active role of the state in industrial development continues to encourage location in or near Mexico City where government officials can be contacted easily, licenses acquired, special understandings arranged, and political ties maintained" (Grindle 1988, p. 72). Moreover, "The policy tools chosen by the government allowed it considerable freedom to reward and punish individual manufacturers or importers for contributing or not to national development goals" (Grindle 1988, p. 162).

Strategic Notions

Several interrelated strategic notions have had an important influence on policymaking and development strategy in Taiwan. Land reform, for example, can be explained partly by the "catastrophic learning experience" of expulsion from the Chinese Mainland and the need to maintain support of the farm population. The shift to new, remarkably successful policies following the Nationalist regime's defeat on the mainland provides an exceptional opportunity to identify the strategic notions that were key to Taiwan's success. The importance of food supply for the army and urban population and of avoiding runaway inflation stand out as two other lessons from that learning experience. Avoiding inflation became a strategic notion that explains much about the adoption of monetary and exchange rate policies that ran counter to the orthodoxy of development specialists in the 1950s. The rice-fertilizer barter scheme also helped to ensure that the Provincial Food Bureau would have enough rice to satisfy requirements and to prevent a rise in food prices. As well as concern about the economic inefficiency of import-substituting industrialization, economists favoring the reforms of 1958–60 (and the shift to export-oriented policies) were worried about "an increasingly acute problem of surplus labor" (Cheng 1986, p. 23). Export orientation would facilitate specialization, which would take advantage of abundant labor and the quality of human resources.

K. T. Li, one of the ablest of Taiwan's economic policymakers, emphasizes several other aspects of the Nationalists' policy shift. His emphasis on *prag-*

matism, which he refers to as a Chinese "cultural trait," calls attention to an attitude that appears to have been especially important in achieving a proper balance between the public and private sectors.

Li (1988, p. 151) also gives credit to the influence of Sun Yat-sen's "Principle of the People's Livelihood" on "land reform and the promotion of industries that provide for the basic needs of life—food, clothing, housing, and transportation." He then asserts that the livelihood principle translated into the operational goal of "striving for growth with equity" that embraced the agricultural sector (in which most people lived) and concurrently "promoting industries that were open to large numbers of people (that is, required little skill), all the while increasing educational opportunities for everybody." Li goes on to suggest that "in other countries a similar outlook under another name would serve the same purpose: a consensus ideology if you will, favoring growth and a generally agreed framework to achieve it."

Three features of Taiwan's experience stand out as strategic notions—essential elements in Li's "consensus ideology"—that were critical to the success achieved: (1) an *integrated perspective* was adopted, and the *organizational requirements* for rural development were met, (2) a broad-based strategy was implemented that built on and strengthened a unimodal agrarian structure, and (3) strong positive interactions between agricultural and industrial development were facilitated both by intersectoral resource flows and by rising agricultural incomes that boosted rural demand for nonfarm products.

The integrated perspective that guided Taiwan's rural development recognized the importance of concurrent progress in increasing agricultural productivity, in strengthening the rural infrastructure, and in improving human resources through investments in education and health as well as a family planning program that slowed population growth. That integrated *perspective* should not be equated with the integrated rural development programs that were fashionable in the 1970s. Taiwan's approach ensured progress in a range of activities that merited priority without attempting the impossibly difficult task of *administratively* integrating such diverse activities as agricultural research and a maternal and child health program. Taiwan, like all developing countries, was faced with the dilemma that everything cannot be done at once, especially when administrative capacity as well as funds are limited. Taiwan's response was to emphasize *sequencing* together with strengthening the capacity of local and prefectural organizations.[25] An example of sequencing is provided by the decision to start with maternal and child health programs before phasing in family planning.

---

[25] In a 1966 monograph S. C. Hsieh and T. H. Lee, who were then agricultural economists with the JCRR, asserted that "the main secret of Taiwan's development" was "her ability to meet the organizational requirements" (pp. 103, 105). In a 1990 paper reflecting on his experience with the JCRR, Hsieh stresses particularly the attention that was given to trying to achieve proper sequencing of activities and a phased approach.

A key strategic notion that influenced policymakers in Japan and Taiwan—increasing productivity of small farms—was not seen as an option in Mexico. For the Japanese administrators, it was natural to repeat in Taiwan the pattern of agricultural development that helped Japan's economic growth. That colonial pattern was a model for the Kuomintang pragmatists. But Mexico's leadership lacked such handy prototypes for small-farm development because few small farms remained in 1910. Roger Hansen suggests that Mexican "liberals had hoped to create a class of yeomen farmers" through a reform in 1856. In fact, through confiscation, debt peonage, and other processes set in motion by that reform, virtually all of Mexico's agricultural land came under the control of haciendas that were seldom less than 1,000 acres.

Another major factor in Mexico's dualistic strategy was the link between land distribution and the creation of *ejidos* to reestablish the communal landholdings of pre-Columbian Mexico and medieval Spain. Traditional tenure was deemed necessary to protect smallholders from a repeat of the concentration of land that occurred between 1856 and 1910.

Popular heroes such as Zapata were ardent advocates of agrarian reform linked to the creation of *ejidos*. But among the leaders of the Revolutionary Coalition that established the PRI, there has been "at best ambivalent commitment to the principles of agrarian reform as stated in the Mexican constitution" (Hansen 1971, p. 108). Indeed, most "political generals," many state governors, and others in the elite who dominated the Revolutionary Coalition and the PRI found ways to acquire large holdings of land. These were inclined to tout the importance of scale economies in agriculture because such notions served their private interests.

The most influential groups opposed to policies favoring large private farms were committed to a Marxist-Leninist view with its emphasis on large-scale collective farms "since the small farm could not efficiently utilize machinery and other inputs" (Hamilton 1982, p. 97). The sources of these notions "ranged from concern with Mexican traditions of communal farming in certain pre-conquest Aztec villages to influences of socialist writers and experiments in the Soviet Union" (Hamilton 1982, p. 167).[26] The socialist view of

[26] Simpson paraphrases portions of Circular 51 issued by the Agrarian Commission of 1922 as follows: "Just as the development of the technical instruments of modern industry brought to an end small industry and produced capitalism, so also, the evolution of agricultural technology tends to abolish small scale agriculture, for there is an unsurmountable incompatibility between small scale agriculture and mechanization. . . . It follows, therefore, that if Mexican rural life is to derive the greatest possible benefit from modern methods of machine production, the *ejido* villages must be organized along strictly cooperative and communal lines. . . . [Moreover,] organization of the type in question . . . must not be left to the initiative of the peasants, impoverished by prolonged exploitation, [but the National Agrarian Commission itself] must undertake to control the functioning and even to impose the installation [of cooperatives]" (Simpson 1937, p. 319). Members of the peasant league of Veracruz traveled to the USSR during the 1920s, "and the conceptualization of the collective *ejido* was influenced by the Soviet kolkhoz" (Hamilton 1982, p. 167; cf. Simpson 1937, p. 333, note 35).

rural development stressed the virtues of "cooperativism" and was hostile to individualism (for example, see Hewitt de Alcantara 1976, pp. 214–34).

Thus, there was much coalition support for collective *ejidos* and little support for a small farm development strategy. This set the stage for President Lázaro Cárdenas's attempt in the 1930s to use the collective *ejido* as the means to "combine the social goal of distributing land to those who worked it with the economic objective of maintaining economies of scale" (Hamilton 1982, p. 168):

> While previous administrations had emphasized the small productive unit, with the *ejido* seen as an intermediate stage to the small productive unit, Cárdenas stressed the *ejido*, and its collective operation, particularly for commercial crops, as necessary to maintain and increase production. . . . Since landowners and their supporters contended that expropriation would have disastrous effects on production levels, Cárdenas was determined to demonstrate that commercial production would not decline as a consequence of the transition in ownership. He proposed that the new *ejidos* be owned and operated collectively; through collective operation the *ejido* could constitute not only a means of achieving social justice for peasants and rural workers but also a model of economic efficiency. This concern was evident in his speech on delivering the land to the new *ejidatarios* on October 6, 1936: ". . . the *ejidal* institution today has a double responsibility: as a social system which liberates the rural worker from the exploitation from which he previously suffered . . . and as a system of agricultural production, with a large part of the responsibility for providing the food supplies of the country." (Hamilton 1982, pp. 165, 177)

During the Cárdenas presidency, the quantity and quality of land redistributed were high. But the majority of *ejidatarios* have not found the idea of collective *ejidos* very attractive (Freebairn 1977, pp. 219–23; Chevalier 1967, pp. 182–83). And "the Cárdenas years came to be regarded by urban elites and policy makers as a period of dangerous radicalism; the collective activities of the period considered a threat to both private property and state hegemony" (Grindle 1990, p. 189).

By the 1940s many policymakers and academics subscribed to the notion that social and economic goals required a dualistic strategy—specifically, that large farms were essential to meet production objectives whereas small farms served only social or political ends. These opinions were linked with an implicit or explicit view that distribution of land in small parcels to *campesinos* is economically inefficient. For example, Reynolds argued explicitly that dualism between large commercial farms and small ejidal units was advantageous because the redistribution of land in small parcels in *ejidos* "satisfied income security and distribution criteria essential to maintain political stability, while the policy of public investment satisfied productivity criteria designed to spur the rate of growth of agricultural production" (1970, pp. 154–55). Similarly, Edmundo Flores (1963) stressed the indirect contribution of land reform to economic growth by destroying the rural caste system, which increased mobility, and helped to stimulate road-building, investments in irrigation, and industrialization. According to Hansen (1971), both land distribution to the landless and their hope for future distributions minimized rural discontent that might have interfered with industrialization and large-scale commercial agriculture.

The tendency on the left and the right to exaggerate the importance of economies of scale derived from their low opinion of *ejidatarios* and other smallholders to competently manage their operations. *Campesinos* had been long viewed as "peon labor," and there was little confidence that they could acquire the managerial and technical skills so evident, for example, among the small-scale farmers of Taiwan and Japan. In his 1948 treatise on Mexican agriculture, Whetten notes that a *hacendado* regarded the *campesinos* who benefited from the expropriation of his land "as lazy, incompetent, and incapable of making adequate use of the land he [the *hacendado*] so badly needs." Whetten, an American agricultural specialist who carried out his study under the auspices of the U.S. Department of Agriculture, clearly shared that view to some extent. Echoing the views of the Dutch Sugar Syndicate regarding the potential of Javanese peasants, he speaks of "the culturally retarded status of the *ejidatarios*" and notes that the typical *ejidatario*'s "methods of production are backward and, without a great deal of supervision, he is likely to produce little beyond his subsistence needs" (Whetten 1948, pp. 204, 223). In a more recent book Riding (1985, p. 190) expresses the view of many intellectuals in Mexico when he says that most peasants "are functional illiterates, with neither schooling nor training to help them break out of their cycle of poverty. They therefore resist efforts to collectivize their *minifundios*, opting for security over the alien concept of efficiency."

At least until the early 1970s the prevailing view of Mexican economists was that the performance of the *ejidos* had been unsatisfactory, which reinforced the unfortunate notion that small farms could not be efficient. "Most opinions concur that the *ejido* is in crisis or stagnant and is not an institution that can provide a satisfactory solution to the agrarian problem" (Solís 1971, p. 11). Why? The inflexibility and uncertainty associated with the tenure system, the lack of credit facilities for *ejido* members (as they cannot mortgage their land), and the small plots are all factors. Some economists argue that "the small plots constitute the main problem in the agricultural sector today." They "hinder the formation of capital as well as an increase in productivity, and maintain the technological level of the rural sector as stagnant" (Solís 1971, p. 13).

Strategic Priorities and Institutional Capacities

The most important contrast between the organizational programs of Taiwan and Mexico is that, in Taiwan, they concentrated on areas where direct intervention is indispensable—notably in public goods, such as research, extension, and infrastructure. Priority was given to building institutions to supply public goods and services necessary for increases in productivity and output by millions of farms. The knowledge, capabilities, and learning capacity of small-scale farmers were recognized and appreciated.

In contrast, Derek Byerlee points out that in Mexico "no viable grass roots associations have grown up for small farmers and indeed have not been fostered by the political process" (personal communication, August 1987). Pearse and Hewitt say that disintegration of Mexico's collective *ejidos* was due to government sabotage after 1940 (Pearse 1980, p. 56). That is contradicted by other analyses, including Freebairn (1977) and Chevalier (1967), and by the failure of Soviet and Chinese collectives, despite sustained government support (Chapter 9). In each of these cases there are cogent economic and organizational reasons for the peasants' lack of enthusiasm for collective farming.

Whether collective *ejidos* in Mexico, Chinese people's communes, or Taiwanese irrigators' associations, such organizations impose substantial costs, in time and energy, on participants.[27] There are substantial benefits of collective action by, say, a local irrigators' association—economies of scale in the construction and operation of irrigation and drainage systems. However, the lack of economies of scale in agricultural production and the diseconomies of farm size (Chapter 4) mean that collective production—whether in China, Mexico, or the former USSR—does not provide sufficient benefits to attract participation.

Lin (1990) argues that an agricultural production collective can overcome the difficulty of supervising agricultural work if each member has an incentive to work hard so that other members will not withdraw. If collectives become compulsory, as in China in 1958, the option of withdrawal is eliminated and, so, too, is the mechanism that inhibits the free-rider problem. Thus, if participation is voluntary, as in Mexico, there is little incentive to join (except as a means of obtaining land); if it is compulsory, as in China, work incentives are destroyed. Furthermore, a regime with a high commitment to collectivization, as in China or the former USSR, is unlikely to maintain the voluntary nature of the movement because farmers withdraw if they can, which, according to Lin, was common in China before 1958, as it has been in Mexico. But compulsory producers' cooperatives also are burdened by the complexity of organization required to coordinate collective production in agriculture (see Box 10.2). Despite huge efforts to build the organizations and to mold members' expectations, collectives failed in China and in the Soviet Union.

---

[27] William C. Clark (Johnston and Clark 1982, pp. 173–90) has stressed three features that influence participants' willingness to invest time and energy: (1) the attractiveness of the benefits of the organization over other institutional arrangements and social techniques, (2) the simplicity of making and enforcing decisions, and (3) the composition of the organization's membership, their expectations, and the organization's capacity to meet those expectations. A crucial barrier to organizing collective action is the free-rider problem. Taiwan's irrigation associations receive high marks in relation to all three of these features.

The Problems of Communality

Organizational complexity of collective farming is only partly due to size. Trying to make the brigade the unit of management in China's communes was a disaster. Assigning managerial responsibility to the production team of thirty to forty families made control more manageable but did not eliminate obstacles to efficient production.

Simplicity also depends on what William C. Clark refers to as "communality," that is, whether participants contribute labor and other resources to a common productive activity. Problems of communality arise from inherent difficulties in assigning, legitimating, coordinating, and monitoring individual responsibilities and rewards (Johnston and Clark 1982, p. 182). Because hard work, initiative, and "on-the-spot-supervisory decisions" are so pervasive in farming, performance is better when the work force has a direct interest in the outcome. Increases in productivity may require equipment or activities with economies of scale. But commercial tractor contractors are a familiar example of a commercial solution to sharing a lumpy piece of equipment that is organizationally much less demanding than group farming. Marketing cooperatives are also likely to offer net benefits from economies of scale because, as shown by India's village producers' cooperatives for processing and distributing milk, it is feasible to establish transparent methods for ensuring that payments to producers are based on the quantity and quality of milk delivered (see Box 1.3 and Chapter 4).

Complex organizations can work, but only if they are the best means of obtaining benefits that are highly valued by participants. Since World War II local farmers' associations in Taiwan have performed many tasks well, including distribution of credit, marketing of farm products and inputs, and extension services. All involve economies of scale. Combining them in a single organization, despite its complexity, may help to minimize transaction costs for participants. However, Taiwan's associations, initially imposed by the Japanese, evolved over time. Before postwar land reform, they were dominated by landlords, but the associations' functions were still valued by owner-cultivators, tenants, and landlords. Progress in more democratic procedures and better accountability since the land reform, when the associations became self-governing, has meant more equitable distribution of benefits.

Unlike in Mexico, there was also much continuity in government support programs in Taiwan. Moreover, farmers' associations, irrigation associations, and other local organizations strengthened their competence through a learning process involving continuing interaction of farmers, government officials, and agricultural scientists. Building organizational capacity is time-consuming. Time is also critical to fostering growth in initiative and problem-solving capacities of farmers and their organizations. In Mexico there has been a lack of continuity because of the "no-reelection" rule that results in a huge staff turnover and, often, changes in organizational priorities at the end of six-year presidential terms.

Organization programs in Mexico have relied too much on centralized planning and inflexible, inappropriate blueprints for farmers and local field staff. For example, the Ejidal Bank, for many years the only source of credit for Mexico's *ejidos*, was paternalistic and tried to usurp management of the *ejidatarios* by dictating (often unprofitable) cropping (Stringer 1972, pp. 301–3). Also witness the agricultural project carried out by Mexico's Papaloapan Commission (Box 10.3) and CONASUPO (Box 5.3).

Complex organizations imposed from above, as in China and the USSR, usually fail. The colonial success in Taiwan stems in part from a lucky fit of organizations transplanted from Japan with the local conditions and farmers' needs. It is common to assume that accountability—and hence responsiveness to local needs—can be achieved only by participatory organizations. However, two essential purposes of participation—a means of *feedback* based on intimate local knowledge and a *watchdog* against abuses of power—do not depend on "participatory organizations." Provided there is competition, a market system can fulfill those functions if arbitrary interventions by government do not destroy the predictability and rationality on which economic efficiency depends (Goodell 1985). Collectivization in China and the USSR had continuity, but, aside from lack of economic advantages, these organizations also lacked channels for feedback and controls on abuses of power that would have enabled them to evolve to better serve their members.

Taiwan's success in institution building was mostly due to local organizations *and* markets playing complementary roles in providing essential linkages between individual farmers and the national economy while strengthening local initiative and problem-solving capacity. This was helped in Taiwan because resource allocation and investment decisions were guided by prices, instead of bureaucratic authority. This helped to ensure that the time-consuming process of building local organizational capacity had a cumulative effect that served local needs.

In Mexico, local political bosses called *caciques* are powerful. They profit from (and encourage) corrupt practices, including alliances with local traders whose monopoly position they help to preserve. "To a large extent," Grindle declares, "the maintenance of political stability in Mexico has been achieved through a well-controlled system of patronage, cooptation, and repression that reaches down to the most local level. . . . Support is maintained through a series of local bosses who trade allegiance to the political system in return for the economic and political benefits that ensure their continued ability to

Box 10.3.   Mexico's Uxpanapa Project

The Papaloapan Commission, established in 1947 as a semiautonomous federal authority, was modeled on the Tennessee Valley Authority in the United States. A big part of the Commission's program was an agricultural project in Uxpanapa, Vera Cruz—1,000 square miles of tropical rain forest—that was to resettle Chinantec Indian farmers. Their lands were to be flooded by a dam, which was a major element in the Commission's program "to bring the [Papaloapan] river system under control . . . and to bring the potential riches of the entire region into the national economy" (Ewell and Poleman 1979, p. 69).

The settlers were to be organized into collective *ejidos*. Central planning was supposed to ensure the efficient use of machinery and other inputs, and it was believed that technical assistance could be provided more efficiently to groups. Because of ecological problems with large-scale farming in the humid tropics, the major crops—upland rice and maize—fell short of the anticipated levels. Yields were too low to recover even the cost of fertilizers and other variable inputs. Machinery maintenance problems were severe, and, because of the heavy rains, combines were only able to harvest a fraction of the rice crop. Problems of management and incentives were severe, as is to be expected in an organization where participants contribute their labor to a common productive activity (Box 10.2).

When the collective *ejidos* failed to perform, the Papaloapan Commission increased mechanization and even decided "to plant rice itself on ejidal lands with hired labor" (Ewell and Poleman 1979, pp. 148, 152). The strategic notions related to economies of scale and farm mechanization were so strongly held that little attention was given to the option of individual farm units, ejidal or private, where family members would have a clear incentive for hard work and initiative because they are rewarded directly. Credit was only available through the Commission's paternalistic program, and the choice of "soils, varieties, planting dates, and many other technical decisions have been made contrary to the detailed empirical experience of the people, who have been growing the same crops in the tropics for years" (Ewell and Poleman 1979, p. 172).

control local clienteles" (Grindle 1988, p. 140). This may make it difficult for local organizations to emerge that serve broad interests and that cannot be subverted by the bosses. Although it may be difficult to achieve the Taiwanese agricultural associations' success in supplying credit and marketing services through local organizations, there may be other options in Mexico that can help to break down these barriers. The survival of the IMSS-COPLAMAR public health program despite funding cuts, testifies to the potential of organizational initiatives that provide public goods and services that respond to deeply felt needs (Box 10.1).

LESSONS FROM TAIWAN AND MEXICO

Taiwan and Mexico show that redistributive land reform is neither necessary nor sufficient to establish a unimodal agrarian structure or to pursue a broad-based agricultural development strategy. Land reform in Taiwan in the 1950s improved income distribution and brought other benefits. Its broad-based strategy, however, dates from the Japanese colonial period when landownership was highly skewed but the size distribution of *operational* units was unimodal because large landowners rented land in small parcels to tenants.

Taiwan's experience shows the importance of concurrent growth of farm and rural nonfarm activities in strengthening the positive interactions between agricultural and industrial development. Stalin's collectivization aimed at forcing a transfer from agriculture to finance rapid industrialization destroyed incentives and, ultimately, the social base for efficient agricultural production that was replaced by an inefficient large-scale sector that became a black hole for capital. In Taiwan sustaining production incentives that made it possible to finance industrialization while rural incomes grew depended more on technological change and investment in infrastructure than on favorable price policy. The resulting productivity increases made possible huge resource transfers from agriculture to the faster-growing nonfarm sectors.

In Mexico, despite land reform, a dualistic strategy has reinforced a bimodal agrarian structure. Productivity increases were concentrated on the large farms and had little impact on most rural people. Economic development and poverty reduction could have benefited from a unimodal structure created through land redistribution when the opportunity presented itself after the Revolution, but a new large-scale subsector was allowed to reemerge as a potent political force by 1940. The lessons of Mexico should be clear for a country such as China, where the disintegration of the Peoples' Communes is akin to the demise of collective *ejidos*: move quickly to seize and consolidate opportunities to create a unimodal agrarian structure before large-farm interests can be reestablished. Furthermore, limiting property rights—such as the restrictions on rent and sale of *ejidal* land and on private land in China—risks amplifying the farm size effects that create institutional barriers to credit for small farms (Chapter 4).

In Taiwan and Mexico there were contrasting strategic notions about the feasibility and desirability of pursuing broad-based agricultural strategies. The consequences can be summarized in terms of the "Six I's"—innovations, inputs, infrastructure, institutions, initiative, and incentives. In both Taiwan and Mexico, agricultural productivity growth benefited greatly from borrowed technology, technical assistance, and development of locally adapted innovations, notably high-yield crop varieties and fertilizers. With Mexico's dualistic strategy, however, the innovations, expanded use of inputs, and even investments in rural infrastructure gave preferential treatment to large farms, to the neglect of smallholders.

In Mexico opportunities for increasing agricultural productivity through research and technology transfer were seized mainly by large farms; in Taiwan most farms benefited from the innovations generated by agricultural research and from investments in irrigation and infrastructure. The sharpness of this contrast was also a result of many, often subtle, differences in institutions. Taiwan's success in meeting the organizational requirements of development through local organizations *and* market mechanisms provided the needed linkages between farmers and the national economy.

In Taiwan the policy environment, the local farmers' and irrigators' associations, and the response of farmers to opportunities fostered a good fit between national programs and local needs.[28] Moreover, local organizations that furthered the interests of farmers led to the strengthening of local initiative and problem-solving ability.

Fulfilling organizational requirements for agricultural development in Taiwan involved time-consuming learning. Agricultural associations created during Japanese rule were dominated by landlords and served as instruments of colonial control. However, they helped progress by diffusing technical knowledge, distributing inputs, and marketing farm products; but all this was limited, compared to the more participatory Farmers' Associations of the postwar period.

Through education and experience, members of farm households in Taiwan steadily increased knowledge and entrepreneurial capacity and became increasingly skillful in identifying and seizing new opportunities—raising mushrooms and asparagus, converting rice paddies into fish ponds for raising eels for air shipment to Japan, and many other farm and nonfarm activities.

Many factors contributed to Mexico's limited progress in broad-based increases in farm productivity and incomes. For example, its proximity to the United States and policies on both sides of the border made it easy to transfer technology and capital directly from the American Southwest to cotton growing in northern Mexico. Furthermore, the task of generating and diffusing technical innovations suited to Mexico's small farmers was more difficult than in Taiwan, because of the diverse environmental conditions of rainfed farming. These environmental constraints are not insurmountable, however. Zimbabwe and El Salvador have achieved much success in diffusing maize hybrids among smallholders. So, too, has Kenya (Chapter 11). Such efforts take time. So did development of technology suited to the farming systems in Taiwan. In Taiwan success was partly due to the sustained ef-

---

[28] See also the discussion of "Rural Programmes and Integrated Attention" in Das Gupta (1981, pp. 57ff).

fort to develop institutions and promote local organizations that could meet the needs of small-scale producers. Mexico looked to these needs only belatedly, and government initiatives have lacked continuity.

The "catastrophic learning experience" that came with their defeat on the mainland made the Kuomintang leadership especially receptive to opportunities for broad-based development in Taiwan. Mexico's policymakers attached such importance to presumed economies of scale in agriculture and had such deep doubts about the development potential of small farms that fostering widespread increases in productivity among smallholders received little attention until the economic crisis of the 1970s. By then, many of the elite were voicing concerns about the shortcomings of Mexico's agricultural stragegy, but that came thirty years late. Mexico may have missed its opportunity to pursue the broad-based agriculture-led strategy appropriate for CARLs. It transformed the structure of production and employment without dealing with the low productivity of most of its agricultural labor force. There is still scope for beneficial interactions between agriculture and the rural nonfarm sector. But with agriculture accounting for less than a third of the total work force, the economic impact of broad-based growth in agricultural productivity will be much less. Mexico must consider a wider range of interventions aimed at alleviating poverty in an economy that is no longer mainly agricultural.

Strategic notions in Mexico that exaggerated the role of government "blueprints" for direct intervention also impaired the effectiveness of agricultural development policies and programs. Investing scarce public funds and organizational capacity in paternalistic, blueprint programs such as the Uxpanapa Project contributed to the weakness of (indispensable) government programs to provide public goods, including research suited to smallholders' needs, a more equitable regional distribution of investment in infrastructure, and initiatives to promote the health and well-being of the rural population.

Taiwan and Mexico were among the first developing countries to draw on a large backlog of medical knowledge and advanced public health techniques. Thus, both were able to achieve rapid declines in mortality, especially infant and child mortality, leading to high population growth rates and, after a lag, rapid growth of the economically active population. In Taiwan the stage of the demographic transition characterized by a gap between CBRs and CDRs was cut short by the rapid spread of family planning that began in the 1950s. In Mexico the large gap between the CDR and the CBR did not begin to close until the 1970s because of the delay in adopting a population policy (Figure 10.1). This has prolonged the process of structural transformation in Mexico.

The similarities and contrasts in the fertility transition in Taiwan and China hold especially important lessons for sub-Saharan Africa. Taiwan's rate of natural increase reached 3.8 percent in 1951, similar to the extraordinarily high rates reached in the 1980s in Kenya, Tanzania, and other African countries. In the early 1960s, as noted, only a few key individuals in Taiwan perceived that the sharp decline in mortality had created a potential for limiting family size. A step-by-step family planning program, guided by survey research on cultural factors, led to a rapid decline in fertility. That experience, similar to that of Indonesia, Costa Rica, Thailand, and others, shows that population growth can be reduced rapidly without the draconian measures of China's "one-child family" policy, an approach that was not only unfortunate but unnecessary. The relevant choice for countries that have not yet entered the declining-fertility phase is not between such draconian measures and waiting for socioeconomic change to alter reproductive behavior. There is a better option: selective public health interventions and initiatives to expand family planning services can speed the decline of fertility by helping and legitimatizing parental decisions to practice contraception.

CHAPTER ELEVEN

KENYA AND
TANZANIA

D espite much in common—physical environment, socioeconomic characteristics, colonial history, and culture—Kenya and Tanzania have had widely differing stories since independence in the 1960s. Broadly, Kenya's policies have succeeded, Tanzania's have failed (although a constituency with appropriate strategic notions that is emerging in Tanzania might reverse that relative performance). Tanzania's per capita gross national product (GNP) increased at 0.9 percent a year between 1965 and 1984, to $210. In Kenya it increased by 2.3 percent annually and, at $300 in 1984, per capita GNP was well above the $220 average for twenty-five low-income countries in sub-Saharan Africa (World Bank 1986b, p. 67). More recent figures reported by the World Bank (1993, p. 238) indicate a large widening of the differential between Kenya and Tanzania because of a much lower estimate of the latter's per capita GNP. Both countries, however, exemplify the problems, as well as opportunities, facing sub-Saharan Africa.

In Kenya realistic emphasis on expanding smallholder production has been largely successful, particularly in the Central province and other so-called "high-potential areas" but less so in the semiarid regions. Farm cash incomes in those high-potential areas have risen sharply, thanks to increased production of coffee, tea, and other smallholder export crops. On top of that, there has been much investment in rural infrastructure, as well as in human capital, especially education. Farm inputs, too, have expanded and improved—for example, coffee seedlings, fertilizers, and cattle breeds.

Tanzania's policies may have been well intentioned, but they were inappropriate. Villagization and state farms have diverted scarce resources and adversely affected smallholder production through virtually all of the "Six I's" that influence agricultural performance—innovations, inputs, infrastructure, institutions, initiative, and incentives.

Yet, Tanzania and Kenya, both once British colonies, had much the same postindependence starting point in the early 1960s, although Kenya had a bigger legacy from colonial rule. The British influence in Kenya gave it a head start in manufacturing and the Empire also left behind a better transportation network. It had 2,013 kilometers of paved roads, compared to 1,300 in Tanzania; in gravel and earth roads, the contrast was even greater. In Kenya only about 2 percent of arable land is under irrigation; in Tanzania, the figure is 4 percent, the average for sub-Saharan Africa overall (Table 4.1). Moreover, in both there is a marked contrast between highland areas, with rich volcanic soils and ample rainfall, and semiarid regions with erratic rainfall, drought, and food shortages.

Tanzania's 1990 population of 24.5 million was a little larger than Kenya's 24.2 million (World Bank 1992b). With high rates of natural increase, both could reach 36 to 37 million by the year 2000 (World Bank 1987b, p. 254). In Kenya population pressure in rural areas is already a problem. There is also some pressure in Tanzania's well-endowed areas, where investments in education, infrastructure, and export crops have been concentrated.

In Kenya and Tanzania, as in most CARLs, women play an important part in the rural economy. In sub-Saharan Africa many rural households are headed by women, but in general they have access to less land and other productive resources. In Tanzania such households in 1984 had about half the acreage under crops as jointly headed households, and their annual cash income from crops was only 329 Tanzanian shillings, compared to 1,166 for the jointly headed ones (Due 1991, pp. 103, 107).

After the drought of 1973, most African countries received substantially increased foreign aid. At $24 per head in Tanzania and $19 for Kenya in 1970–84, aid was around 10 percent of GNP and an even higher share of investment. Its effectiveness has been undermined by abrupt shifts in aid policies, including the enthusiasm for "integrated rural development" and "basic needs strategies" in the 1970s and a narrow focus on policy reform in the 1980s.

Agriculture is the major foreign exchange earner in both. Its share of total exports in 1983–85 was almost 70 percent in Kenya and 80 percent in Tanzania.

Kenyan agriculture's share in gross domestic product (GDP) fell from 35 to 31 percent between 1965 and 1987, whereas in Tanzania it rose from 46 to 61 percent. Agriculture's dominance in their labor forces is pronounced; in 1985 it accounted for roughly 80 percent of the work force of both countries and could still be 70 percent in the year 2000. This slow decline is due to the rapid growth of working-age population, as well as agriculture's heavy weight in the labor force (Table 11.1).

The low levels of fertilizer use seen in Table 11.1 reflect the continuing importance of subsistence production. Even though fertilizer use in Kenya is three times the sub-Saharan average and more than five times as high as in Tanzania, the 27 kg/ha used in Kenya was only about half the average in the developing countries of Asia and Latin America (Alexandratos 1988, p. 319).

TANZANIA: HIGH HOPES, DISMAL OUTCOMES

Immediately after independence in 1961, Tanzania's agricultural performance was impressive. However, changes in agricultural and macroeconomic policies after President Nyerere's Arusha Declaration of 1967 led to an economic crisis in the 1970s that intensified in the early 1980s. These ill-advised policies and external factors, such as the cost of the war that removed Amin from power in Uganda, also had adverse effects on the rural economy. However, changes in macroeconomic and sectoral policies in 1984–87 have had big positive effects on agriculture subsequently.

Postindependence Farm Production

The 4.3 percent growth of export crop production in the 1960s was a big net addition to per capita farm incomes, particularly cash income. Exports of five of Tanzania's major export crops—coffee, cotton, cashew nuts, tea, and tobacco—grew at 8 to 13 percent per year between 1960–62 and 1966–68 (Coulson 1982, p. 145). All major export crops were grown predominantly by African smallholders, except for tea and sisal, which was the only crop to show a fall in exports in the 1960s. The size distribution of farm units and area is summarized in Figure 11.1. Agricultural exports were hugely important to Tanzania's predominantly agrarian economy, accounting for about 85 percent of the value of marketed output in the 1960s (Johnston 1989b, p. 211).

Tanzania's Five-Year Plan for 1964–69, which set ambitious targets for settlement on unoccupied lands and for spending on irrigation, earmarked most of the money (two-thirds) for the so-called transformation approach to agricultural development (Coulson 1982, p. 148). This relates to a 1961 World Bank report, *The Economic Development of Tanganyika*, which emphasized the difference between a broad-based "improvement approach"

Table 11.1. Structural and demographic characteristics of Kenya, Tanzania, and sub-Saharan Africa

Characteristics	Kenya	Tanzania	Sub-Saharan Africa
Agriculture's share in GDP (%)			
1965	35	46	43
1987	31	61	34
Agricultural labor force			
Percentage of total			
1970	85	90	81
1980	81	86	76
1985	79	83	74
2000	72	75	66
Growth rates (% per annum)			
1970–80	3.2	2.3	1.9
1980–85	3.0	2.2	1.7
1985–2000	3.1	2.3	1.8
Population growth rate (% per annum)			
1970–80	4.0	3.4	3.0
1980–85	4.2	3.6	3.1
1985–2000	4.3	3.8	3.3
Agricultural exports			
Growth rates (% per annum)			
1961–70	4.4	4.3	−2.3
1970–80	3.6	−4.4	−2.2
1980–85	4.0	−4.9	−0.4
Agriculture's share in total			
exports, 1983–85 (%)	68	79	26
Fertilizers, 1982–84 (kg/ha)	27	5	9

Source: Alexandratos 1988, Appendix Tables A.1, A.3, and A.7. Sub-Saharan Africa figures are averages for thirty-eight countries.

and a dualistic "transformation approach." The first was aimed at gradual but widespread increases of productivity and output of small-scale farmers; the second, on which, the report argued, there should be increasing emphasis, was based on large capital expenditure for mechanization and irrigation leading to "a total transformation of the agricultural systems rather than their improvement" (Coulson 1982, p. 120). This transformation approach was the justification for "the creation of settlement schemes on unoccupied land, where farmers would be given land on condition that they followed rules and regulations that define 'modern' agricultural techniques" (Coulson 1982, p. 147).

But the expansion of agricultural production in Tanzania in the 1960s, as in sub-Saharan Africa in general, actually resulted from spontaneous changes in traditional agriculture. The catalysts for change included the spread of knowledge of new crops, population growth and increased food requirements, a bigger farm work force, and better access to markets.

Figure 11.1. Distribution of operational units and of areas of farms by size, Tanzania, 1971–72

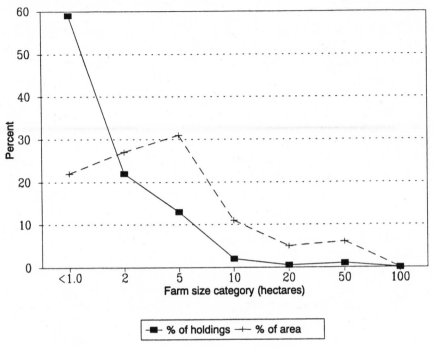

Source: FAO 1981.

One example: the Geita District. A tse-tse control program opened up new agricultural land that was filled by an influx of farm families from nearby where there was population pressure. Farm incomes rose with a 60 percent increase in cotton production between 1964 and 1967 and to a lesser extent in cassava production. Plant breeders at the Ukiriguru agricultural experiment station had produced varieties resistant to cotton jassid and bacterial blight, thus reducing yield risk.

Economic Crisis in the 1970s

A Tanzanian economist succinctly captures the economic crisis: "Since the early 1970s, Tanzania has faced difficult economic problems. Food production has not kept pace with population growth and dependence on intermittent food aid has increased. Production of agricultural exports has fallen. Severe shortage of foreign exchange and suppressed and open inflation have characterized the economy in the past decade. Production . . . of the manufacturing industry has decreased. Transport infrastructure and the provision of basic social services have deteriorated. Aggregate domestic saving has decreased and dependence on foreign aid for the functioning of the modern economy is unprecedented" (Lipumba 1986a, pp. 1–2).

Except for tea and tobacco, export crop production began to decline in the early 1970s. After increasing at 4.3 percent in the 1960s, those exports fell by 4.4 percent a year in the 1970s and at 4.9 percent in 1980–85 (Table 11.1).

The Tanzanian government blamed external forces—oil price rises (1973 and 1979), deteriorating terms of trade, breakdown of the East African Community, the Uganda War, and poor weather. However, a combination of unfortunate policies, frequent policy shifts, and changes in institutional arrangements meant that an economic crisis and difficult food situation were inevitable, regardless of external factors.

Ujamaa and Agricultural Production. President Nyerere committed Tanzania to socialism in his 1962 TANU pamphlet "*Ujamaa*—the Basis of African Socialism" and made it more emphatic in the 1967 Arusha Declaration.[1] There are three types of *ujamaa* villages.[2] There are the self-initiated villages, such as those included in the Ruvuma Development Association which began in the early 1960s (see Coulson 1982, pp. 263–71). Then there are the "signposted" villages, created overnight to enable local officials to show the growth of *ujamaa* in their areas. The third type was created in response to inducements, such as social services or grants of equipment, often tractors.

A fourth type, known officially as "development villages," were different from other *ujamaa* villages. These were founded through coercion, following a November 1973 TANU decision that all peasants should be enrolled in villages within three years. The emphasis was on resettlement, and few made any progress in collective production. Forced villagization had a direct and widespread impact on Tanzanian agriculture. Within two years, half of Tanzania's population was relocated in *ujamaa* villages; only the rural population in densely settled areas, such as the coffee/banana zone on the slopes of Mt. Kilimanjaro, were exempted from the requirement to relocate in newly established villages. Migot-Adholla (1984, p. 219) gives this summary of the villagization process: "Overzealous efforts by civil servants occurred during the course of several regional operations in which large numbers of people were summarily rounded up, at short notice, together with their belongings and trucked off to the site of their new village several miles away. In some cases, these moves were accompanied by the destruction of existing homes to insure that those moved would not return."

[1] TANU, the Tanganyika African National Union, was merged with Zanzibar's Afro-Shirazi Party in 1977 to form *Chama cha Mapinduzi* (CCM), the Party of the Revolution.
[2] This discussion is based on Migot-Adholla (1984) who attributes the typology to Philip Raikes.

How far did villagization contribute to Tanzania's food shortage of 1973–75? There was a drought in 1973–74, but Raikes (1986, p. 128) argues persuasively that villagization had adverse effects that went beyond instances where villages were poorly sited for soils and water or where main fields were distant or vulnerable to vermin. There are longer-term effects: increased traveling time to and from fields, overcultivation of fields close to the village, and greater distances for collecting firewood and drinking water.

Villagization was followed by the reintroduction of minimum acreage regulations and other paternalistic by-laws, such as compulsory growing of cassava or weeding under cashew nut trees. The effects of such arbitrary interventions were considerable. Raikes (1986, pp. 128–29) argues that with "politics in command" party and government officials with little knowledge of agriculture or economics, "felt free, indeed obliged, to issue directives, to show their commitment.... Apart from the considerable waste of time and/or energy involved in either complying with or evading directives, they appear to have contributed significantly to a decline in morale: a feeling that whatever one does to try to organize one's life sensibly, some clown in office will come along and mess it up." The point is that coercion "consistently leads to misspecified policies which have to be enforced for that very reason and obstructs criticism and revision of such policies, since the problem is defined beforehand as being one of peasant obstinacy and conservatism" (Raikes 1986, p. 133).

Disruption of Agricultural Marketing. Interventions affecting food marketing also weakened agricultural performance. Shortly after independence, the National Agricultural Products Board (NAPB) was set up with a monopoly to purchase grain, but it was limited to purchases from Cooperative Unions or local cooperative societies and sales to grain millers. In 1967 the major grain millers were nationalized, and the National Milling Corporation (NMC) was established. In 1973 the NMC assumed the activities of the NAPB; three years later, the Cooperative Unions were abolished, and the NMC was obliged to directly purchase grain from producers (Amani and others 1988, pp. 69–75).

A bureaucratic agency faces serious problems in purchasing grain from millions of scattered producers and in handling retail sales. Indeed, Tanzanian policymakers' enthusiasm for large-scale mechanized state farms was no doubt influenced by their awareness that it is easier for a bureaucratic agency, such as the NMC, to purchase grain from a state farm than to purchase the marketable surplus of many small producers. Crop authorities also were set up to market coffee, cotton, and other export crops. The decline in real prices in the 1970s applied particularly to export crops. "Real producer prices of exports declined, mainly due to the high marketing margins of official marketing agencies and an increasingly overvalued currency" (Amani and others 1988, p. 75). Except for a bit of smuggling, for example illegal sales of coffee in Kenya to finance imports of scarce consumer goods, producers of export crops felt the full disincentive effect of low official prices. However, producers of nonexport foods have been able to offset disincentives of low official prices by sales in parallel markets. From the 1970s to 1984 maybe 75 percent of marketed maize and 80 percent of rice sales were in the parallel market, whereas most wheat (mainly from large state farms) is sold through official marketing channels (Amani and others 1988, p. 87; Economic Research Bureau 1988, p. 20). Even so, returns to producers are depressed because of the risk premium collected by those who run illicit crop sales and inefficient marketing through channels are subject to police action, bribes, or punishment.

Macroeconomic Policies. Tanzania's crisis was compounded by ill-advised macroeconomic policies, the proliferation of parastatals, and distorted agricultural pricing. Particularly serious were large budget deficits, rapid inflation, unwillingness to devalue, and the sharp fall in agricultural exports, which was primarily responsible for the scarcity of foreign exchange. The decline in agricultural exports was mainly the result of a 36 percent fall in export volume in 1973–80; and in 1976–85 export earnings financed less than half of Tanzania's imports (Sharpley 1985, p. 74). The main drop in Tanzania's export volume was in 1974–77, which meant that it benefited less than Kenya from the 1976–77 boom in prices of coffee and other export crops.

Apart from the Uganda War in 1979, three things were responsible for the budget deficits and inflation in 1973–81: (1) a sharp increase in the government's industrial investment (under the Basic Industries Strategy), which rose from 2 percent of capital expenditures in the early 1970s to more than 17 percent in 1979; (2) recurrent expenditures of the central and regional government, which increased threefold between 1972–73 and 1978–79; and (3) massive financial assistance to inefficient public corporations and parastatals. Overdrafts of the ten major agricultural parastatals stood at 5.1 billion shillings in March 1981, equivalent to 37 percent of the money supply and over $600 million at the official exchange rate (Sharpley 1985, p. 82).

The impact of foreign exchange shortages on food production was grossly underestimated because of the (false) assumption that it required few imported inputs (including those manufactured domestically but with a high import content). In fact, those inputs for large-scale mechanized production of wheat and rice in 1980–81 represented a little over 60 percent of their import parity price. For sisal and tea, the figure was more than 45 percent; only for coffee and cashew nuts was it as low as 10 percent (Sharpley 1985, p. 78). For marketed maize, surprisingly, it was 45 percent, over half of which was related to transport costs inflated by pan-territorial pricing. This policy, justified by the notion of regional equalization, effectively subsidized maize in the Southern Highlands, which was the main source of official purchases. But that, naturally, involved lower prices and reduced deliveries from areas closer to Dar es Salaam (Raikes 1986, p. 123). This price distortion also weakened the incentive to expand production of high-value crops in the Southern Highlands.

Deteriorating producer incentives began in 1970, when importing, wholesaling, and exporting were nationalized under the umbrella of the State Trading Corporation (STC), a centralized parastatal. At about the same time, China began building the TAZARA rail link to Zambia, relying heavily on Tanzanian labor. Local costs were financed by importing and selling Chinese consumer goods, and, in the five years of railway building, the STC purchased many consumer goods in China, which helped to supply shops in rural areas. But by the late 1970s and early 1980s "virtually all basic household goods, including clothing, soap, edible oil, sugar, salt, matches, batteries, kerosine, corrugated iron sheets, soft drinks, beer and cigarettes had become extremely scarce (or non-existent) in rural areas" (Sharpley 1985, p. 80). This was aggravated by efforts to replace private shops with village cooperatives and measures to reduce the role of private transporters by restricting their licenses and their share of imported trucks and spare parts. The fundamental problem, however, was the sharp decline in imported and domestically manufactured consumer goods due to the acute shortages of foreign exchange and the policies that exacerbated the effects of those shortages.

Despite a big increase in investment and foreign exchange allocated to the industrial sector, domestic value added in manufacturing declined abruptly from a peak in 1978, 1051 million shillings in 1966 constant shillings. As a share of total GDP, it rose from 3.6 percent in 1961 to 10.1 percent (almost 900 million shillings) in 1973. By 1983 it had declined to only two-thirds the level of 1973 (Skarstein 1986, pp. 84–87).

The slow growth of manufacturing output since 1973 resulted from "the failure to shift the utilization of foreign exchange away from capital goods imports for capacity expansion in favor of intermediate inputs for capacity utilization" (Wangwe 1983, p. 483). Industries established under the new strategy were capital-intensive, and the heavy dependence on foreign aid gave a bias toward "projects" to build new plants in spite of a disastrous decline in imports of intermediate inputs and low utilization of existing capacity.

Tanzania's preferential treatment of industry also led to reduced expenditure on agriculture, particularly in rural transportation. In 1972 only 2 percent of government spending went to industry and 18 percent to transport. In 1980 industry received 11 percent and transport, 4 to 6 percent. Agriculture's share of government expenditure fell from 11 percent in the early 1970s to 7 percent at the end of the decade (Lele and Meyers 1987, pp. 35–37).

One of the reasons behind compulsory villagization was that the shift from dispersed homesteads to new villages with at least 300 families would allow social services to improve. Much was, indeed, achieved.

Primary Health Care. Tanzania was in the vanguard of African countries adopting rural health policies emphasizing cost-effective prevention and promotion, rather than curative care and urban hospitals. In 1982 health spending in rural areas was 65 percent of the total, compared to an average of 25 percent for less developed countries (Moris and others 1985, p. 228).

Between independence and 1980 life expectancy increased from 42 to 52 years—five years above the average for low-income countries in sub-Saharan Africa and equal to the average for the region's middle-income countries (Lele 1984, p. 171). This was due largely to declines in infant mortality, which also accounted for an increase in the population growth rate from 2.7 to 3.5 percent (World Bank 1987b, pp. 254, 256, 258). Even so, Tanzania's infant and child mortality is still high—and much higher than Kenya's.

The expansion of rural health facilities and personnel between 1961 and 1980 was remarkable (Moris and others 1985, p. 220):

	1961	1980
Rural health centers	22	239
Dispensaries	975	2,600
Medical assistants	200	1,400
Rural medical aids	380	2,310
MCH aids/village midwives	400	2,070
Health assistants	150	681

In 1981, 80 percent of Tanzania's 104 districts had a hospital. However, less than half of the divisions (that is, part of districts) had a Rural Health Center (RHC). The RHCs focused on outpatient services, including maternal/child health (MCH) clinics. Virtually all wards had outpatient dispensaries. Some RHCs and dispensaries are administered by voluntary agencies, sometimes with "grants-in-aid" from the government. However, less than 30 percent of the villages had a health post.

Water Supply. Tanzania's ambitious program to provide piped water to all of the rural population by 1981 received substantial support from external donors. In 1973 only 13 percent of the village population had a water system; by 1980 it was 34 percent. However, many systems have been plagued by maintenance problems and, probably, less than 20 percent of the rural population is regularly drawing water from improved water sources (Therkildsen 1986, p. 293).

Here, there are five significant features (Therkildsen 1986). First, providing rural water supplies as a "free" service has strong appeal to villagers (and fits well with the ideology of the Arusha Declaration). Second, water policy was also a clear example of the "we-must-run-while-others-walk" style described by Hyden (1984, p. 107): "a strong urge to do everything at once, a common tendency to make decisions without adequate knowledge of their consequences, and an unwillingness to use the past as a source of guidance for the future." Conflicts between means and ends were left unresolved until the implementation stage and allocations in yearly budgets were below those implied by bold policy statements. Third, bureaucratic and political interest began to fade as competition for limited funds intensified and as awareness grew of the cost of meeting ambitious goals. Fourth, donors tripled their contributions in the early 1970s, despite the "obvious conflict with the Party's self-reliance philosophy" (Therkildsen 1986, p. 298). Expanded funding of rural water projects fit well with donors' growing interest (then) in basic needs, the role of women in development (they haul much of the water), and in aid that involved big inputs of materials and technical assistance by the donor. Fifth, villagers were treated as "passive receivers," with donors neglecting operation and maintenance and ignoring local beneficiaries. Once completed, the water systems were the government's responsibility.

By 1982, when it became obvious that the government's targets could not be reached, there was much soul searching by the government and donors. One conclusion: "experience shows that local level involvement is absolutely necessary. Improvement of rural water supplies cannot be achieved on behalf of the villagers by the central government, the Party or the donors" (Therkildsen 1986, p. 305).

Education. The Adult Literacy Campaign has been highly successful in reaching adults with no formal schooling. Illiteracy has been reduced from an estimated 75 percent in 1962 to 27 percent in 1977 and maybe 10 percent according to some surveys (Collier, Radwan, and Wangwe 1986, p. 33; Lele 1984, p. 170).

The proportion of children of primary school age enrolled in school has risen from 32 percent in 1965 to 87 percent in 1984. And discrimination against women in access to education has been greatly reduced in both Kenya and Tanzania. However, according to official figures, the proportion of children of secondary school age enrolled was only 2 percent in 1965 and just 3 percent in 1984. How different in Kenya, where the percentage enrolled rose from 4 to 19 percent over the same period (World Bank 1987b, p. 262). It is emphasized later that a fundamental difference in educational policy accounts for that sharp contrast.

Less than half of 1 percent of the relevant age group is enrolled in the University of Dar es Salaam or other institutions of higher education. The Sokoine University of Agriculture at Morogoro comprises the former

Faculties of Agriculture, Forestry, and Veterinary Science of the University of Dar es Salaam. Its intake capacity in 1982 was 75 students in agriculture, 35 in forestry, and 25 in veterinary science. That seems hardly adequate for a country of 22 million (at that time) that is overwhelmingly dependent on agriculture, livestock, and forestry. Tanzania's limited progress in developing a national agricultural research system has been influenced by a shortage of university research scientists, both for training researchers and for planning and executing research projects (Jahnke, Kirschke, and Lagemann 1987, pp. 55–57).

Recent Reforms

Since 1985–86 the economic situation has improved, thanks partly to favorable weather but mainly to macroeconomic policy reforms together with liberalization of the marketing of agricultural products. Partial trade liberalization, which began in July 1984, was a response to "an extreme shortage of locally produced and imported goods. The economy was in a downward spiral in which scarcity of incentive goods, inputs, and transport equipment contributed to further declines in exports, which in turn gave rise to additional erosion in the capacity to import" (Economic Research Bureau 1988, p. 28).

Rapid devaluation and a crawling peg (that periodically devalued the Tanzanian shilling to adjust for inflation) reversed the serious overvaluation of the exchange rate, which was an implicit tax on agriculture. Between March and July 1986 it fell from 17 to 40 shillings to the dollar, and by July 1987 was 70 shillings. At the same time, producers were offered at least 70 percent of world prices and producer prices of maize and other staple foods were increased (Amani and others 1988, p. 93).

Producer incentives, boosted by devaluation and price adjustments, were reinforced by import liberalization, "allowing individuals with access to their own foreign exchange to import incentive goods *inter alia* and sell them at market-clearing prices in order to increase the supply of incentive goods." This meant a large implicit devaluation of the exchange rate on those imports "which significantly increased profits to owners of foreign exchange and, as a result, reversed capital flight" (Amani and others 1988, p. 92). The response was greater than expected. In fact, these "own-funded imports" accounted for about a third of imports in 1985–87 and for a 50 percent rise in imports from the 1983 low. The only plausible explanation for foreign exchange sufficient to maintain such own-funded imports is that large sums for Tanzanian exports and services (for example, payments by tourists) bypassed the official foreign exchange system.

Private traders, who flourished during liberalization, had low transportation and storage costs and could outcompete the cooperative unions and the

NMC, which thus had to operate mainly in inaccessible areas, where high costs discourage traders (Amani and Kapunda 1990, p. 77). Since July 1989, however, it has again been illegal for private traders to purchase grain directly from farmers. Presumably, the ban on direct grain purchases by private traders was to shelter the cooperative unions and the NMC from competition. These face other problems: a heavy debt burden, "diversion of funds, embezzlement/theft and buying fictitious crops," and lack of proper accounting and competent staff (Amani and Kapunda 1990, p. 87). Amani and Kapunda see the changes since 1989 as leading to a recurrence of the problems faced by producers and consumers before the 1984–87 market reforms, as well as to increased requirements for public sector credit for crop procurement.

KENYA: SUCCESS AND FAILURE

The dynamism of Kenya's rural economy has been the result of a favorable policy environment, but the impressive growth in the "high-potential" areas has been associated with limited progress in other areas.

Continuity in Agricultural Policies

Despite two world wars, the Mau Mau uprising of the 1950s, and independence in 1963, there has been much continuity of Kenya's agricultural policy in the past seventy-five years. Until the 1950s commercial agriculture was dominated by large European farms and plantations. In 1958 more than 80 percent of marketed production came from large (and exclusively European) farms. Since then, it (and subsistence production) has come to be dominated by small (some very small) African farms (Figure 11.2). In 1981 54 percent of marketed output was from small farms, and much of the remainder was from African-owned large farms (Migot-Adholla 1984, p. 208).

In 1959 colonial Britain abandoned the racial allocation of land and opened up the European Highlands to African ownership. It also provided funds for the purchase of land from Europeans, many of whom would not remain in an independent Kenya. African, and especially Kikuyu, grievances over land had been at the root of the Mau Mau uprising. The new government, formed in 1963 with Jomo Kenyatta as prime minister (later president), wanted to distribute land under both "high-density" and "low-density" settlement schemes. The most important, a so-called Million Acre Scheme, was started in 1961 and completed in 1971, with the settlement of about 35,000 families on 470,000 hectares of land (House and Killick 1986, pp. 167–69; Maitha 1976, p. 57; Smith 1976, pp. 138–43).[3] Many European mixed farms were

[3] There has been some criticism of the settlement schemes because land transfer absorbed a large part of the resources available for agricultural development (e.g., Heyer 1976, p. 2).

Figure 11.2. Distribution of operational units and of area of farms by size, Kenya, 1974

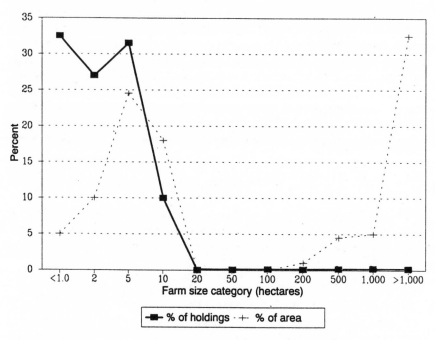

Source: FAO 1981.

transferred to influential African owners. However, mixed farming's contribution to output and agricultural exports was much less than the combined output of coffee and tea plantations in high-potential areas and sisal plantations and beef ranches in drier regions.

Kenya derived many benefits from the smooth transition to independence, which maximized the positive legacy and minimized the negative effects of colonial rule. Increases in coffee, tea, pyrethrum, and dairy production were based on knowledge acquired during the colonial period. Migot-Adholla (1984, p. 204) observes: "The expansion in small farm production of these [export] crops benefitted from many years of research that had been conducted for settler farmers in the highlands." This research, and also trial-and-error learning by settler farmers, applied to crop varieties, agronomic practices, and techniques of pest and disease control were required for success under Kenya's environmental conditions. On-the-job learning by Kenyan civil servants was also helped by good working relations with British civil servants from the colonial era. Some of those expatriates helped to set up an institutional innovation, the Kenya Tea Development Authority

(KTDA), that made possible the successful development of smallholder tea production. There was continuity, too, among Kenya's civil servants, some of whom moved on to cabinet positions.

The pragmatism of Kenyatta and of the policies adopted at independence have served Kenya well. Thus, there has been less of a tendency than elsewhere in Africa for government to interfere in productive and commercial spheres, although a grain marketing board and other parastatals have survived since colonial times. But in general, emphasis has been on the government's facilitating role so that policies are aimed realistically at "validating changes due to underlying economic forces" (Collier and Lal 1986, p. 74).[4]

Smallholder Production in High-Potential Areas

Increased agricultural output, especially exports, played an important part in the growth of per capita GDP in Kenya between 1965 and 1985—1.9 percent annually, despite population growth of about 4 percent (World Bank 1987b).

The Swynnerton Plan. Expansion of export crops by Kenya's smallholders began in 1954 with "A Plan to Intensify the Development of African Agriculture in Kenya"—the "Swynnerton Plan." It was "a counterinsurgency document and a radical departure on the colonial government's agrarian policy" (Chege 1987, p. 101). Scattered land was to be consolidated into single units and officially registered. It was to give farmers security of tenure and incentive to improve holdings through farm plans that would maintain soil fertility, avoid soil erosion, and dramatically increase farm incomes.

The "counterinsurgency" aspect of the plan was especially pertinent to the Central Province, the center of the Mau-Mau rebellion. Cash incomes for some 600,000 African farm units in the Central Province and other high-potential areas would be raised from "a mere £5 to £20 per family, to £100 a year or more" (Smith 1976, p. 126). This was to be achieved by the "radical departure" of assisting African farmers to grow coffee, tea, and other high-value cash crops. The very idea of smallholder production of tea was radical. Until the 1950s it was axiomatic that quality tea for export could be produced only on a plantation. And prior to about 1950, African farmers could not obtain a license to grow Arabica coffee.[5] This was ostensibly

---

[4] Of course, there were exceptions. Collier and Lal (1986, p. 143) argue that "the coverage of the minimum wage legislation was precisely counter to economic rationale." That is, the minimum wage legislation was applied in urban areas with a loss of employment and efficiency; but owing to the importance of monopsony power in the plantation labor market, "there was a clear case on the grounds of employment generation, efficiency, and equity" for minimum wages in plantations that were exempted from the legislation.

[5] That restriction did not apply to all of Kenya. Coffee was introduced to smallholders in Kisii District in the 1930s, but its spread was very limited until the 1950s (Uchendu and Anthony 1975, p. 92).

because of fear that the high reputation of Kenya coffee would be spoiled, but the vested interest of European settlers in having an ample supply of cheap labor was undoubtedly the main motivation. Between 1951–52 and 1959–60 Arabica coffee grown by Africans increased from a mere 83 tons to 4,607 tons (produced by 105,000 African families) (Johnston 1964, p. 172). By 1966 smallholder production (28,500 tons) had overtaken estate production (Kenya 1974, p. 64). In addition, smallholders were encouraged to keep exotic cattle, i.e. highly productive European dairy animals crossed with indigenous and disease-resistant zebu. This, also a radical departure, acknowledged that African farmers could acquire the skills required for rearing exotic cattle under difficult conditions. Moreover, a planted grass fallow (ley) would not only help to maintain fertility and prevent erosion, but also with exotic cattle it would yield a substantial cash return. This "phased development" of cash crops and milk production was in areas where research and experience had shown that these activities could be undertaken successfully. Planting material was distributed by nurseries, a strengthened extension service provided technical assistance, and marketing was helped by new cooperatives and processing plants.

With tea "the performance of a number of small, subsidized and closely-watched pilot schemes in Central Province encouraged the Department of Agriculture to make the large leap into what is now an industry of 145,000 smallholders providing green leaf to 39 factories operating without subsidy" (Howell, Hewitt, and Anthony 1988, p. 189). A Special Crops Development Authority set up in 1960 with loan finance from the Colonial (later Commonwealth) Development Corporation became the KTDA in 1964.[6] Growers' committees, which eventually will assume ownership of tea factories (built by KTDA but managed, initially, by local tea companies), helped to ensure that the parastatal was accountable to its clients. And the "tea roads" built by KTDA for collecting leaf from growers made a contribution to development that went beyond tea production.

The Dynamic Role of Smallholders. Expansion of coffee and tea has continued to be a major source of farm cash incomes and foreign exchange receipts. By 1971 coffee (£19.5 million) and tea (£12.2 million) accounted for 30 percent of exports. With the 1976–77 boom in coffee prices and increases in output, coffee exports topped £200 million in 1977 (and tea reached £71.8 million) out of total exports of £490.8 million (Hazelwood 1979, p. 109). Smallholder exports of tea in Tanzania also increased rapidly in 1970–85 (Table 11.2). However, the increase in total tea exports was much less than in Kenya, because Tanzania's smallholder production was a small fraction of total tea production (Lele 1988, p. 148). Equally im-

---

[6] A World Bank monograph by Lamb and Muller (1982) examines the reasons for KTDA's success as a parastatal.

Table 11.2. Coffee and tea exports in Kenya and Tanzania: average annual percentage growth in volume, 1970–85

	Coffee		Tea	
	Total	Smallholder	Total	Smallholder
Kenya	3.8	6.0	7.5	13.5
Tanzania	0.8	2.3	1.9	13.7

pressive has been the rapid increase in the number of smallholders producing coffee, tea, and other export crops, especially in the Central Province. There the small-farm households producing coffee increased from 16 to 45 percent of all smallholders between 1960 and 1974 and those growing tea from 3 to 18 percent (Livingstone 1986, p. 170).

Kenya has substantially enlarged its share of world coffee and tea exports—from 1.2 to 2.3 percent in coffee and from 2.6 to 9 percent in tea between 1961–63 and 1983–85. Tanzania, too, showed a significant increase in coffee exports from 0.9 percent of world exports in 1961–63 to 1.4 percent in 1971–73 and for tea from 0.6 to 1.2 percent. But between 1971–73 and 1983–85, its share of world tea exports rose only slightly to 1.3 percent, and its share of coffee exports fell to 1.2 percent (Lele 1988, pp. 150–51).

Knowledge of growing coffee, tea, pyrethrum, and other cash crops under local conditions was critical in the rapid growth of output. African farmers also had a pent-up desire to produce coffee and rear exotic cattle that had been restricted to European farmers. Innovations can be cumulative and "self-spreading" (Uchendu and Anthony 1975, pp. 89–92). Thus, pyrethrum, introduced into the Kisii highlands in 1952, was so profitable that it provided the capital for investment in tea in 1957. And, in turn, cash from tea and pyrethrum financed investments in exotic cattle in 1963. "Self-spreading" innovations, say Uchendu and Anthony, are those that are profitable, divisible, and low risk. (Divisibility means that the innovation can be adopted incrementally in small units.) But also important were tested knowledge and its diffusion by extension staff and Kenya's farmer training centers. Exotic cattle, for example, demanded a new technical competence in managing rotational grazing, purchases of feed concentrates, regular spraying against ticks, stockproof enclosures, and wells for watering stock.

The Land Reform Debate. Roger Swynnerton, Leslie Brown, and other agriculturalists who played a key role in the design of the Swynnerton plan stressed land registration and consolidation (Brown 1968, p. 44). Similarly, the *Development Plan 1974–1978* stated: "One of the requisites of successful farming is a system of land tenure which encourages investment in the land

and enables it to be used as a negotiable asset." Others, however, have been skeptical of the benefits derived from land reform.[7]

Perhaps the most that can be said is that the benefits of land registration are unlikely to exceed the costs, unless there is a demand for land titling and registration. Such a demand may have emerged in Kenya's Central Province (Bates 1989, pp. 38, 163). However, registration only restrained land seizures by the emerging rural gentry because "the colonial government administered it [land registration] in a way designed to prevent destabilizing landlessness, and so reined in the aggrandizing tendencies of the rural elites."

Cash Crops or Food? "Academic populists" criticize Kenya's agricultural strategy because, they say, its cash-crop economy has adverse effects on the nutrition of the farm population. An International Food Policy Research Institute (IFPRI) study addressed this issue, with particular reference to sugar growing. It concluded that sugar production has a positive effect on household income. However, "this benefit at the household level does not appear to influence the preschoolers' nutritional status," and, therefore, the positive effects of higher income could be increased by public health interventions (Kennedy and Cogill 1987, p. 58). Earlier studies suggested that children snacked on sugarcane, which may explain how the introduction of sugarcane had an adverse effect on children's nutritional status. Such substitution of sugar for foods of higher nutritional value can be countered by nutrition education, as part of Maternal and Child Health programs.

A more general criticism of export crops is that government emphasizes export crops and neglects food production for local consumption (see Box 1.4), but clearly, *"the choice over what to grow should be left to individual smallholders"* (Little and Horowitz 1987, p. 255, emphasis in original). Most Kenyan smallholders seem to make that decision in response to price signals and independently of government programs. Undue priority for export crops has led to neglect of government-funded research and support services for food crops. In high-potential areas, however, farm families have benefited from innovations that affect subsistence food production as well as cash crops. And as the domestic commercial market expands, the distinction between subsistence and cash crops becomes blurred. Milk is an increasingly important source of farm cash income for many smallholders, especially in the Central Province where roughly half of all farms keep cattle. Milk yields are higher with exotic cattle, which now account for about 80 percent of all cattle in the Province, and the rise in own consumption of milk has nearly matched the increase in sales (Chege 1987, p. 105).

---

[7] Controversy has not been confined to Kenya. Migot-Adholla and others (1991) have argued that the evidence supports the view "that African indigenous land rights systems have spontaneously evolved from systems of communal control towards individualized rights in response to increases in commercialization and population pressure." See also Atwood (1990), Shipton (1985), Heyer (1976), and the classic study by Boserup (1965).

During the colonial period research on maize received less attention than that on wheat and export crops. It was not until 1955 that a research officer was appointed exclusively for maize. Much progress has been made since in developing hybrid varieties that spread rapidly among smallholders and had a big yield advantage over local varieties. A survey in western Kenya showed that hybrid maize was adopted at a faster rate than by American farmers thirty years earlier; and a medium-maturity hybrid adapted to the Central Province available in 1970 spread even more rapidly (Gerhart 1975). The adoption of hybrid maize is remarkable because the seed must be replaced each year. A commercial seed company, established to produce grass seed for European farmers in the highlands, has organized production and distribution of hybrid seed to village shopkeepers, who also distribute fertilizer. Hybrids, however, have had very limited success in those areas in western Kenya where the yield advantage was too small to make adoption profitable.

Shortcomings, Failures, and Learning

Profitable innovation outside high-potential areas is a major challenge: "Kenya's rapid population growth and limited supplies of arable land pose the central dilemma for the agricultural sector's future" (World Bank 1986b, p. 176). The biggest advance outside those areas has been in sugar production—from 655,000 tons in 1965–66 to 3.9 million tons in 1984–85 (Lofchie 1989, Table 4.6). Of the output in 1984, roughly half came from smallholder outgrowers, compared to just over 7 percent in 1971 (Lele and Meyers 1986, p. V-1). Kenya's sugar industry, however, has been plagued with problems in capital-intensive sugar processing, as well as suffering from fluctuating world sugar prices.

Policies for Arid and Semiarid Lands. Some 80 percent of Kenya's population live on the 20 percent of the land with adequate and reliable rainfall. This includes high-potential areas, such as the Central Province, and densely populated farming areas in western Kenya that are not very productive. Rainfall is adequate in most years but is erratic and unevenly distributed. Furthermore, much of the poorly drained land is in western Kenya. There may be a million hectares of high- and medium-potential land with bad drainage in Kenya; drainage of valley bottomland may be a cost-effective way of expanding agricultural production (Livingstone 1986, p. 194).

The other 80 percent of Kenya's land area is either arid or semiarid. Although those areas are sparsely populated, some agricultural areas have seen population growth above the national average because of immigration (International Workshop 1988; Livingstone 1986, p. 186). Take the Machakos District. In 1932 almost 90 percent of its population was on 25 percent of the land, equally divided between high-potential hill areas (with ample and reliable rainfall) and adjacent "medium-potential" land. Annual population growth increased from 2.5 percent for 1932–48 to 2.8 percent in 1948–63 and to 3.5 percent in 1963–69. This growth has been uneven. In high-potential Machakos, there was a fall from 2.8 percent in 1932–48 to 1.6 percent in 1963–69 because of outmigration in response to increasing population densities. In the less-favored areas that have low and erratic rainfall but where land is available, population grew by nearly 14 percent a year in 1963–69 (Lynam 1978, chap. 2).

It was not until the 1970s that Kenya's arid or semiarid lands (ASALs) received serious attention, which coincided with poverty-oriented, basic needs strategies. Not surprisingly, "the ASAL districts have been treated as development hardship cases in need of special attention" (International Workshop 1988, p. 1), and some donor-funded programs have reinforced the notion that programs for the ASALs should be welfare oriented.

However, little headway will be made in semiarid areas if efforts are justified primarily as welfare programs. Because of population pressure, there is an economic justification for investments in infrastructure, innovations in crop and livestock production, and local institutions to increase productivity of the semiarid lands. Certainly, high-potential areas are losing the capacity to absorb a growing population. Although land is underutilized on some large farms, it will be politically difficult to make that land accessible to those squeezed by growing population pressure and diminishing returns to labor. Nevertheless, rapid growth of population in the semiarid areas suggests that they will have to absorb a huge increase in the rural labor force in the next few decades.

The semiarid areas are reaching the kind of population density required for economies of scale in construction and maintenance of a reasonable rural infrastructure. But development of Kenya's semiarid and arid lands is a difficult challenge. Those areas are diverse, and the constraints and opportunities for crops and livestock and water supplies differ enormously from one locality to another. The 1988 report of an International Workshop on Kenya's ASALs emphasized the need for concurrent progress in, for example, veterinary services, water supplies, market outlets, and price incentives. But increasing livestock intensifies environmental stress and exacerbates resource degradation, unless local institutions can enforce rules that avoid such degradation.[8]

Policymakers may be learning from experience. For example, the priority given to investments in irrigation has been lowered. Irrigation costs in Kenya are extremely high, partly because of limited water surplus and a lack of suitable sites for schemes. Kenya's most ambitious scheme, the Bura Irrigation Settlement Project on the Tana River, "has turned out to be a failure in

[8] The government's decentralization initiative and the strengthening of District Development Committees should facilitate the more important initiatives for higher levels of productivity in utilizing the resource potential of the ASALs.

virtually every sense" (Lele and Meyers 1986, p. V-1). The 1977 estimate of an investment cost of $13,700 per hectare was one of the highest in the world, but costs escalated to $33,000 per hectare, and the project has had a negative rate of return. Only one large project, Mwea-Tebere, has had a positive rate of return. A quarter of the budget of the Ministry of Agriculture and Livestock Development has been allocated to irrigation construction and maintenance costs (Kenya 1986). In the future priority will be given to consolidation and rehabilitation of existing schemes and to small-scale irrigation, including reclamation and drainage of water-logged lands.

Higher priority will be given to livestock, crop production, soil improvement and moisture conservation, including agroforestry. Research on drought-resistant crops also has an important contribution to make, although there are questions. For years a high priority was given to improving Katumani maize, a short-season, drought-evading composite variety. However, adoption has been limited, except as an early season crop.[9] Moreover, many specialists argue that priority should be given to sorghum, which has greater capacity to withstand periods of drought. Sorghum breeding for human consumption, however, will also require attention to consumer acceptance and adapting maize grinders for producing sorghum flour (see Box 11.1).

There may be much scope for substantial productivity increases in Kenya's semiarid areas. Australia has accumulated much knowledge about soil- and water-conserving technologies in semiarid zones. Direct transfer of those technologies is unlikely, however, because tillage techniques are by large-scale equipment—hardly fitting given Kenya's need for capital-saving, labor-using technologies. However, appropriate animal-drawn equipment innovations can accelerate increases in agricultural productivity and output by easing labor bottlenecks and helping to introduce practices such as terracing or tie-ridging. Moreover, local manufacture of such equipment fosters expanded output in rural manufacturing firms (Chapter 6).

Livestock and Animal Draft Power. Animal-powered and simple, inexpensive farm equipment have been neglected because it was thought (wrongly) that African farmers could shift directly from the machete to Massey Ferguson tractors. In fact, the profitability of investments in animal power is determined by the evolution of farming systems (Pingali, Bigot, and

---

[9] It has often been asserted that composite or synthetic varieties would be more appropriate than hybrids for small-scale farmers. Being open-pollinated varieties, they do not have the additional yield advantage of "hybrid vigor"; but neither do they experience the rapid decline in yield characteristic of hybrids. "Katumani maize" is the only composite that has been adopted at all widely in Kenya. It is a short-maturity, relatively drought-tolerant variety, developed for "medium potential" areas of fairly low and erratic rainfall. It is clear from a farm survey by Franzel (1984) that Katumani is grown almost entirely to provide farmers with early maize at a time when their supplies are likely to be exhausted. For most of their crop, they prefer to plant a variety that gives a higher yield in a year of "sufficient rainfall."

Box 11.1. Maize, Sorghum, and Science-Based Farming

Maize and sorghum, dominant in the food economies of sub-Saharan Africa, illustrate some of the key agricultural issues confronting African countries. Like sorghum (and millet), maize does well when grown under the low-input technology of a resource-based farming system. But maize also has a strong yield response to improved management and high soil fertility Moreover, maize has some drought resistance: it becomes dormant when there is no soil moisture and then resumes growth when there is. Sorghum and millet far exceed maize, however, in their ability to withstand and recover from drought. Maize is particularly vulnerable to dry heat and to water shortage before and after tasseling.

In Tanzania maize production increased from less than 400,000 tons in 1950 to about 3.2 million tons in 1989; in Kenya the increase was from less than 600,000 to 2.9 million tons. Between 1961 and 1980 maize output in sub-Saharan Africa increased by 2.7 percent annually, nearly four times the 0.7 percent for millet and sorghum. That even maize production failed to keep pace with rapid population growth in sub-Saharan Africa underscores the challenge of accelerating the growth of grain production.

Traditional farming systems embodied appropriate responses to conditions that prevailed until recently: sparse population, ample land for expanding cultivation, limited commercial demand, and lack of cash income for fertilizer and other inputs. As late as the 1960s a 1.8 percent increase in harvested areas for cereals accounted for most of the 1.9 percent annual increase in those crops (Paulino 1986, p. 28). As long as land was abundant, horizontal expansion of production was a satisfactory response to the increased demand from rapid population growth, which meant that labor was available for extending cultivation in this resource-based expansion of output.

Growing concern in the 1970s that food production in sub-Saharan Africa was not keeping pace with rapid growth of population led to cries of "bring the Green Revolution to Africa." Overoptimistic expectations of profitable technologies adapted to Africa's diverse circumstances, plus impatience for quick results, encouraged large investments by governments and donors in development programs based on "technical packages." The results have been disappointing, especially for sorghum. In part, this has been due to a misinterpretation of the Asian experience. Although the International Rice Research Institute (IRRI) and the International Maize and Wheat Improvement Center (CIMMYT) played critical roles in the development of the rice and wheat varieties at the heart of the Green Revolution, they supported and did not substitute for national agricultural research systems.

By the mid-1960s when the Green Revolution was under way Asian countries had the indigenous research capability to use imported "prototypes" of genetic material, a growing body of scientific knowledge, and effective methodologies to develop crop varieties and agronomic practices for local ecological and socioeconomic conditions. Furthermore, there were large areas in Asia that had the irrigation and other infrastructure needed to take full advantage of the yield potential of the improved seed-fertilizer combinations.

Although yield-increasing technologies for wheat and rice were immediately profitable to farmers in much of Asia, African countries, by comparison, are in varying stages of transition from land-abundant to land-scarce rural economies. Belatedly, it is recognized that there are big differences among farming areas in how much rural population growth (and other factors) have enhanced the profitability of a shift from extensive to intensive farming. "Net benefits to yield-increasing technologies are directly related to the cost of land saved and inversely related to the opportunity cost of the additional capital or labor employed" (Matlon 1990, p. 18).

In Kenya, Zimbabwe, Zambia, and Tanzania high-yield hybrid maize has spread rapidly among smallholders. In Kenya and Zambia, roughly 50 percent of the maize area was planted to hybrids in 1988, and in Zimbabwe almost all of the maize area. Moreover, in all four countries there is substantial application of chemical fertilizer to maize—50 or 60 kg of nutrients per hectare (CIMMYT/IITA 1990, pp. 45, 47).

For many years maize research programs in Zimbabwe and Kenya were biased in favor of large-scale farms. Even now, in southern and eastern Africa, "the problems associated with late planted maize, weed management and poor stand establishment remain largely untouched from a smallholder perspective" (Blackie 1990, p. 394). Still more striking, however, is the neglect of research on sorghum. In semiarid areas sorghum's comparative advantage has not been exploited because, unlike maize, the yield and other attributes have not been enhanced by years of high-quality research. In Zimbabwe, a sorghum breeding program was not established until after independence in 1980.

Binswanger 1987). Animal draft power "becomes attractive only when farming intensities increase, usually as a consequence of population growth [because] in the shift to annual cultivation [from forest- and bush-fallow systems] the demand for labor per unit of output increases faster than the supply of labor" (Pingali and others 1987, p. 25). Little attention has been given to tillage techniques and equipment to improve water use and reduce soil erosion, as well as to ease labor bottlenecks. Some research has been done to identify implements better suited to soil and moisture conservation than the ubiquitous moldboard plow, but there has been little farmer involvement.

Rural Social Services and Self-Help

Education. Both Kenya and Tanzania, and sub-Saharan Africa in general, have devoted a large chunk of government spending to education, although there has been greater expansion of secondary education in Kenya with the mushrooming of *harambee* (self-help) schools.[10] In 1972 it accounted for nearly 22 percent of Kenyan government spending; its share was around 20 percent in 1980–85 and 22 and 20 percent, respectively, in 1986 and 1991. At 17.3 percent in 1972, Tanzania's share of public expenditure in education was only a little less than Kenya's; but it had dropped to 13 percent in the early 1980s and was down to 7.4 percent in 1985, well below the 13 percent average for sub-Saharan Africa (UNDP/World Bank 1989, p. 126).

Health. Kenya has done much in health care. In 1972 a larger share of government spending went to health than in Tanzania—7.9 compared to 7.2 percent. That differential was larger in 1980—7.8 percent for Kenya and 6 percent for Tanzania (compared to an average 5.1 percent for sub-Saharan Africa). However, in 1985 Kenya fell to 6.4 percent, sharper than the decline to 5.1 percent in Tanzania and 4.9 percent for Africa (UNDP/World Bank 1989, p. 127). The Kenya Expanded Programme of Immunization in 1981, which also introduced health cards and oral rehydration therapy, has improved the health of small children. In infant mortality, the differential between Kenya and Tanzania has widened. Between 1955–60 and 1980–85 Kenya's estimated infant mortality declined from 130 to 80 per thousand; in Tanzania it was from 150 to 115 per thousand. The differential in child mortality has widened even more. In 1980–85 Kenya's estimated child mortality (that is, one-year-olds who die before age five) was 52 per thousand, only about half that of 1955–60; in Tanzania the 87 per thousand was still around 70 percent of the figure for 1955–60 (Ross and others 1988, pp. 228, 230).

Population Growth and Family Planning. Reductions in infant and child mortality have been the major reasons for the fall in Kenya's crude death rate (CDR) to 21 per thousand in 1965 and 13 per thousand in 1985. With increases in the crude birth rate (CBR) from 51 per thousand to 54 per thousand, Kenya's rate of natural increase rose from 3 percent in 1965 to 4.1 percent in 1985, making it the highest in the world (World Bank 1987b, p. 256).

A National Family Planning Program was initiated in 1967. Until recently, however, Kenya's commitment and support for family planning were limited. The estimated total fertility rate of 8.2 in 1977–78 reflected a reduction in the interval between births, resulting from weakening traditional practices, such as postpartum sexual abstinence and breastfeeding (which reduce the chance of conception).

---

[10] In 1977 there were 477 government-aided secondary schools with enrollment of 128,000, and there were 1,042 unaided secondary schools with an enrollment of 192,000 (Kenya 1979, p. 157). The aided ones include "maintained" schools that receive full government support and "assisted" schools that receive partial support, for example, salaries for teachers. Many *harambee* schools were part of a strategy of "preemptive expansion" in which schools built with local finance "were filled with students, and were presented for government support" (Court 1986, p. 287).

But Kenya has now entered the declining growth rate phase of the demographic transition: the total fertility rate fell gradually from 8.2 in 1977–78 to 7.7 in 1984, and then to 6.7 in 1989 and 6.5 in 1991 (Kelley and Nobbe 1990, p. 33; World Bank 1993). Estimates also point to significant increases in contraceptive use by married women—from 7 to 17 percent for all methods between 1978 and 1984 and then to 28 percent in 1989. For the more reliable methods, the increase was from 4 percent in 1978 to 10 percent in 1984 and 18 percent in 1989 (Kelley and Nobbe 1990, p. 58; see also W. Robinson 1990 and Kenya 1989).

Kenya's changing socioeconomic conditions and the coverage achieved by effective family planning and health programs contributed to this onset of declining fertility. Although Kenya's family planning program has been called weak, it is perhaps better assessed as "slow starting" because of the time needed for staff training and for creating the infrastructure for broad coverage (W. Robinson 1990). A National Council for Population and Development was set up in 1982 to improve coordination among government ministries, nongovernmental organizations, and donors and to overcome weaknesses in the family planning program.

Survey data indicate that in 1984–89 there was a considerable reduction in "ideal family size" (from 5.8 to 4.4) and a rise in the percentage of women who state that "they don't want more children" (from 31.5 to 49.4). In Nairobi, where the ideal family size was already small, the decline from 4.3 to 3.6 was less than half as large as in the Central and Rift provinces where the respective declines were from 5.4 to 3.8 and from 6.5 to 4.7. It seems probable that in the 1980s growing awareness of the improved child survival prospects for infants and small children was a key factor in the rapid transformation of knowledge and attitudes (see Chapter 8). Likewise, the spread of education has also been important.

Despite much attention to rural health, little has been done about family planning in Tanzania. In 1984 only about 1 percent of married women of childbearing age were practicing birth control. Estimates of contraceptive prevalence rates (CPRs) for Botswana and Zimbabwe show that they entered the second phase of the demographic transition somewhat earlier than Kenya. Botswana's CPRs in 1984 for married women of reproductive age (29 percent for all methods and 18 percent for modern methods) were almost the same as Kenya's for 1989. In Zimbabwe the 1984 CPRs (of 40 and 27 percent, respectively, for all methods and modern methods) were already considerably higher than those reached five years later in Kenya (Kelley and Nobbe 1990, p. 58).

Rural Population Pressure and Famine. Population pressure on land will be more serious in Kenya than in Tanzania. A theme of Livingstone's 1986 book *Rural Development, Employment, and Incomes in Kenya* is that its rural economy has a "sponge effect" because it can "absorb increased population as a result of the interaction between divisibility of holdings, intensification of farm output through yield increases, higher valued cash crops and livestock activities, and the development of non-farm activities." With rapid population growth, however, this "sponge" will become saturated, leading to more landless poor, spillover into marginal areas, and more pressure on the informal sector. According to Shah and Willekens (1978), Kenya's population would increase sixfold from 11 million in 1969 to 64 million in 2024 on the "most likely" estimates of changes in mortality and fertility between 1969 and 1999. On optimistic assumptions about the growth of non-farm jobs, the rural labor force would decline from 87 percent of the total in 1969 to 65 percent in 2024. Despite that decline in agriculture's share and a *sixteenfold* increase in the economically active population in urban areas, the rural labor force would increase fourfold over that fifty-five–year period (Shah and Willekens 1978, pp. 29, 38).

Arable land per capita in Kenya declined from 1.3 to 0.7 hectares in 1965–85; in Tanzania the decline was from 4.0 to 2.3 hectares (Lele 1988, p. 156). Moreover, in Kenya progress has been slow in adapting productive technologies for semiarid regions that will have to support a rapidly increasing population. But rainfall, such as it is, in these areas is so erratic that drought will be a serious problem, and the liberalization of food marketing is likely to increase hardship if crops fail. Needed are famine relief measures—for example, rural works programs that can be quickly and productively expanded when crops fail—that are within Kenya's planning and administrative capacity.

Kenya has attempted to reduce hardship from drought-induced shortages, buying all that is offered to its marketing board at its purchase price and selling all demanded at its selling price. But attempting to maintain perfectly stable official prices in this fashion is inefficient and impossible when there is a major drought. Allowing prices to vary within a band can reduce costs and increase price stability. However, also needed would be a way of modifying the official price in response to the domestic crop. And the domestic maize price should reflect changes in the world price and government stocks (see Pinckney 1988).

THE POLITICAL ECONOMY OF KENYA AND TANZANIA

Why did Kenya and Tanzania choose such diametrically opposed approaches to development? Over the past twenty-five years rural development in Kenya has been much more impressive than in Tanzania. But because of fears about long-term political stability in Kenya, it must be asked whether "the political assumptions on which it is based may prove unrealistic" (Migot-Adholla 1984, p. 227).

Equality and Economic Success

Outcomes in Kenya and Tanzania, as elsewhere, are influenced strongly by strategic notions that shaped the actions of policymakers. Their different ideas about equality, education (especially secondary education), and economic success go far toward explaining the contrasting choices in development strategies.

In his analysis of education in Tanzania and Kenya, Court (1984, p. 269) emphasizes that Tanzania's educational philosophy was influenced greatly by its ideological response to inequality; and that its official socialist ideology "denies the need for rewards and status differences, and has, as its goal, the achievement of widespread equality of material conditions." Some time prior to the Arusha Declaration of 1967 Nyerere had declared: "We have to work towards a position where each person realizes that his rights in society—above the basic needs of every human being—must come second to the overriding need of human dignity for all; and we have to establish the kind of social organization which reduces personal temptations above that level to a minimum" (as quoted in Court 1984, p. 270). Later statements by Nyerere make it clear that he views inequality as being determined in a zero-sum game. In 1976 he stated that: "At any one time there is a certain amount of wealth produced in the world. If one group of people grab an unfair share of it, there is less for the others. . . . The objective must be the eradication of poverty, and the establishment of a minimum standard of living for all people. This will involve its converse, a ceiling on wealth for individuals and nations" (as quoted in Latham 1988, p. i).

Contrasting attitudes toward equality were reflected in policies. However, outcomes have been shaped not only by social norms in official policies but also (and even more) by economic performance and the actual implementation of policies. In Tanzania, "the leadership code prevents the excesses of conspicuous consumption and conflict of interest that characterize their counterparts in Kenya" (Court 1984, p. 278). Kenyan political leaders and policymakers were not much concerned about being accused of either. Not surprising, really, as "the masses have seen the elite as people to be emulated, not chastised. In fact, farmers, rather than resenting the elite, have tended to look on them as examples of what can be attained. Much of the wealth has been amassed in a single generation, and there is hope that one's children can do as well" (Miller 1984, p. 149).

In fact, the Kenyan government went further: "The acute scarcity of top-level African managers encouraged the government to permit civil servants to engage in private enterprise. This has been widely criticized as inducing inefficiency and corruption in the public sector, which is undoubtedly the case. However, it has perhaps prevented the emergence of a bureaucratic bourgeoisie with a class interest in inhibiting enterprise" (Collier and Lal 1986, p. 168).

This raises several issues. Did that pragmatic policy foster economic growth, despite corruption and neglect due to moonlighting? Has the resulting inequality jeopardized political stability? And, finally, does economic growth benefit from preventing the emergence of such a bureaucratic bourgeoisie?

Experience suggests that despite income inequality, there was more justification for allowing civil servants to "straddle" the public and private sectors than might have been anticipated. This is partly because of the positive benefits from unleashing the energies and entrepreneurial flair of civil servants, who generally had better education and more managerial experience than the rest of the population. This was also a politically acceptable way of ensuring that Asian entrepreneurs, often "silent partners" in firms owned by African civil servants, continued to make economic contributions.

Kenya's policies, plus vigorous *harambee* action in local communities, have enormously expanded educational opportunities. The implicit "ideology of education" in Kenya is a "response to the problems of social inequality; the educational system must be part of a process that justifies the legitimacy of those differential rewards. . . . In Kenya it is assumed that inequalities are an inevitable and necessary accompaniment to rapid economic growth; and, in consequence, educational policy has emphasized the meritocratic nature of selection procedures, and the ethos of equal opportunity, so as to secure the acquiescence of the nonselected" (Court 1984, pp. 183–84).

Tanzania's educational system has been shaped by a different philosophy. Emphasis was placed on mass education, rather than on secondary and higher education. Resources were funneled into literacy campaigns and expansion of primary education. "Manpower planning" was meant to ensure that there were enough skilled people, essential for economic transformation, and progress with equity.

Kenya's expansion of secondary education was chaotic. Schools with little or no government aid accounted for most of the huge increase in enrollment. It might be expected that the importance of private schools would mean more inequality in access to secondary places. However, because of the rapid expansion of secondary schools, inequality in primary school leavers' access to education narrowed dramatically between 1960 and 1975. Knight and Sabot (1990, p. 34) emphasize that "a child of uneducated farmers was 3.5 times more likely to attend secondary school if he was born in Kenya instead of Tanzania." So, what has been seen as Kenya's "failure" to curb the expansion of secondary education has had positive effects. Differences in the quality of presecondary and the quantity and quality of secondary education have contributed to the growing differences in earnings and productivity of urban workers. It also seems likely that the higher level of cognitive skill found among Kenya's urban workers, a difference that would be equally or more evident among the rural population, would also contribute to the greater dynamism of Kenya's rural economy. Thus, the difference in educational policies reinforced the differential impact of agricultural policies in the two countries.

Class Interests and Agricultural Development

How is it that Kenya's elite pursued policies generally favorable to the agricultural sector? And why did Tanzania adopt policies that adversely affected the farm population, despite official rhetoric stressing the critical importance of agriculture and rural development?

Tanzania's "neglect of agriculture," highlighted by President Nyerere in October 1982, is seen in the ratios of prices received by producers to the world prices of coffee and other export products. Between 1972 and 1986 the Tanzanian smallholder price for coffee, cotton, and tobacco averaged less than half of the world price; coffee prices for Kenya's smallholders averaged about 90 percent of world price. These ratios are based on nominal exchange rates (Lele 1988, p. 169). Using real effective exchange rates (to allow for the differential effect of inflation in trading partners as well as the domestic effects of subsidies, tariffs, taxes, and quotas), the contrast is even sharper. Particularly during 1980–85, when the ratio of coffee prices for Tanzanian producers to international prices was about 0.5 based on the nominal exchange rate, the ratios were on the order of 0.25 using the real effective exchange rate. But in Kenya the price ratios were favorable throughout 1972–86 using nominal or real exchange rates, because the currency was not overvalued.

Part of the reason for the neglect of agriculture in Tanzania is a dominant bureaucratic class that was biased against private enterprise. The hostility was supposedly confined to a "kulak" class seen as a threat to rural equality. But the attitude toward peasant farmers, generally, was little better. Among some leaders this attitude was reinforced by Marxist views on the inefficiency of small farms and an exaggerated view of economies of scale, together with the tendency to equate economic efficiency with "modernity." (See Chapters 4 and 9.)

"Colonial rule was bureaucratic rule" (Holmquist 1984, p. 174). That fact ensured that in most countries the emerging elite were primarily conscious of "the bad side of capitalism and it is no coincidence that Africans by and large see it as the main source of evil" (Hyden 1980, p. 220). In Tanzania rural entrepreneurs were "limited due to the very poverty of the country itself and a colonial policy that had stifled the development of capitalist social relations" (Holmquist 1984, p. 176). Local manufacturing companies rose from only 137 in 1962 to a peak of 238 in 1966 and fell to 131 in 1967, after nationalization and the new code which made it illegal for government officials to own businesses. "Most private capital was in the hands of the largely Asian commercial or merchant class" (Stein 1985,

p. 114). And historical animosities between them and Africans ensured that the postindependence Asian influence would be limited.

All this has increased the tendency in Africa for the public sector to expand rapidly into productive and commercial enterprises. In Tanzania parastatals accounted for 5 percent of wage employment in the early 1960s; by 1972–73 it was 33 percent. The increase in the public sector share of employment in Kenya was only from 16 to 18 percent (Hawkins 1986, p. 298). In Tanzania "expansion and diversification of activities of the public sector have seriously overtaxed management capacities [and] overcentralization of the state and the expansion of its activities have diluted its ability to focus on priority areas" (Ndulu 1986, pp. 86, 87). Moreover, the bureaucrats have had a vested interest in enlarging control over agriculture and other sectors. Without the option of the private sector, the only path open to the ambitious was into more important government (or parastatal) jobs with greater rewards in power and perks.

Why did the new elite in Kenya differ so much from the bureaucrats that have been dominant in the rest of Africa? "Tanzania's bureaucrats have been more successful in muzzling local initiative than their counterparts in Kenya" because, in Kenya, they faced more powerful rural entrepreneurs (Holmquist 1984, p. 184). Moreover, members of Kenya's elite have a strong interest in a prosperous agricultural economy because they owned large farms in the former European Highlands and, often, enlarged farms with profitable export crops in the Central Province and elsewhere. For Kenya's elite "their own stake in the farm sector made their extraction of surplus much more modest" (Leonard 1984, p. 165).

Kenya (and Côte d'Ivoire) are exceptional in sub-Saharan Africa because their elite had interests in, and an understanding of, agriculture that encouraged them to pursue policies favorable to agriculture. Thus, "the process of class formation that led to independence in Kenya was more akin to that accompanying the rise of a gentry than that leading to the rise of a bourgeoisie. The process culminated, in the Kenyatta era, when the great landed families of Kiambu coalesced about State House. Viewing Kenya's independence coalition from this perspective helps us to understand why public policy in Kenya, unlike public policy in much of Africa, tended to treat export agriculture as a national estate: an endowment to be nurtured rather than consumed" (Bates 1989, p. 148).

Recent Developments and Future Prospects

Kenyatta was much less inclined than Nyerere to get directly involved in policymaking. Emphasis on development-oriented policies has weakened since President Daniel arap Moi succeeded Kenyatta in 1978 (Bates 1989). Personalized bureaucratic politics and patron-client ties have become more important.

Tanzania is still in flux. The impact of the policy reforms that began in 1984 was positive, although favorable weather conditions also helped. "The growth of parallel markets and corruption has, in effect, given impetus to some adjustments, eroding state control over markets" (Ndulu 1986, p. 84). More generally: "A more favorable attitude toward economic reform in Sub-Saharan Africa has resulted not only from external economic pressures, but also from perceptions of the growing costs of ineffective state control over the economy and of the detrimental effects of economic deterioration on various interest groups" (Ndulu 1986, p. 85).

In Tanzania the emergence of policy analysts at the University and in government is an encouraging development. They are examining Tanzania's economic problems seriously, systematically, competently, and with careful attention to evidence on the consequences of alternative policies. This may mean that the policy process is moving away from "platform policymaking"—that is, political leaders announcing off-the-cuff policies without analysis of feasibility or consequences. However, there is still suspicion of market forces, reinforced by Marxist ideology. Witness the reimposition of controls on Tanzania's grain traders in July 1989.

As an influential member of the Economics Department at the University of Dar es Salaam, Ndulu (1986, p. 93) could be accused of special pleading when he argues that, as well as training those responsible for economic management in Africa, "efforts should be directed at encouraging policy analyses and research in independent research institutions, including universities." But because reforms that unleash market forces adversely affect the power and vested interests of bureaucracies, independent centers for policy research and analysis are important.

Agriculture and Rural Nonfarm Activities. The lesser hold of the government bureaucracy has contributed to the greater dynamism of Kenya's economy in the past twenty years compared to Tanzania. Agricultural producers have had more incentives in the prices received for their products and the attractiveness of goods and services available for purchase (see Lele 1988, pp. 167–72; Sharpley 1985, 1986; Ellis 1983). But rural enterprises (nonfarm firms in rural areas and in towns of less than 20,000) and the microenterprises of the urban informal sector have been the most dynamic elements in Kenya's economic growth (Kilby 1987). That has been fueled by positive interactions with agricultural development, especially the growth of farm cash income.

The political power of rural entrepreneurs in Kenya encouraged a policy environment that favored positive interactions between agriculture and industry. Indeed, Hyden (1986, p. 69) regards "creative linkages between town and countryside" as more important than ideology in the differences between Kenya and Tanzania's economic performance. Since about 1980 the Kenyan government's official support for small enterprises has taken on substance, and reform of the foreign trade regime has improved the supply of raw materials and spare parts for the informal sector and rural enterprises (Kilby 1987, pp. 28–29).

Food Marketing. Marketing boards, such as Kenya's NCPB and Tanzania's NMC are bound to have problems. Without competition, they must rely on bureaucratic regulations to limit graft and corruption. Successful or not, these measures mean increased administrative costs and loss of flexibility. The efficiency of a bureaucratic institution is also reduced because of the need to obtain a marketable surplus from dispersed small farms and to meet the fluctuating food needs of rural people, as well as urban centers. Many economists stress the advantages of liberalizing food marketing in Kenya, Tanzania, and other African countries (Jones 1972, 1987). There is, however, strong resistance. Concern that Asian traders would dominate the food trade is used as a reason for continuing the statutory monopoly of a grain marketing board. There is also reluctance to dismantle an organization such as Kenya's NCPB, which has done a creditable job of distributing famine relief during drought. Most important of all, perhaps, marketing boards are a good way of distributing political patronage. However, Tanzania's performance may improve (while Kenya's deteriorates) because it may be more successful in liberalizing food marketing. The failure of Tanzania's NMC is so obvious that the need for reform is easily accepted. In Kenya shortcomings are less obvious, but inefficiency and patronage have become serious obstacles to economic growth (Bates 1989, pp. 133, 149).

WILL TANZANIA OVERTAKE KENYA?

From the late 1960s Tanzania's sectoral and macroeconomic policies began to have adverse effects on producers' incentives and initiative, and the decline in agricultural exports was a major factor in the economic crises of the 1970s and 1980s. Ideologically driven institutional innovations gave rise to big problems in marketing agricultural output, acute shortages of farm inputs, and drastically reduced consumer goods in rural areas.

Economic prospects in Kenya were more favorable at independence. The backlog of agricultural research and innovations was greater, and the rural infrastructure was superior. Moreover, farmers in Kenya's high-potential areas seized opportunities after the preindependence shift in policy that lifted the ban on smallholders growing coffee and tea. There has been much greater continuity of policy in Kenya, too; and its leaders have pursued policies more favorable to agriculture, partly because many politicians and officials had a private stake in agriculture. Most of their proagriculture policies were, fortunately, beneficial to smallholders, as well as the big farms of the elite. Some policies, for example research on wheat and credit, favored large-scale producers, but the support for smallholder production of coffee, tea, pyrethrum, and milk significantly reduced the extremely dualistic pattern of Kenya's agriculture.

In Kenya private initiatives have been jeopardized by the move in the 1980s toward personalized bureaucratic politics and patronage appointments. These changes have weakened institutions such as the KTDA—through slower payments to smallholders, deterioration of "tea roads," and delays in collection of tea leaf for factories. Kenya's increased foreign debt, budget problems, and shortages of foreign exchange in the 1980s have also caused many problems, for example, vehicles out of action because fuel or spare parts are not available. Problems of that nature have, of course, been considerably more serious in Tanzania and over a longer period.

In both countries there have been vigorous efforts to expand education. Secondary education has expanded more in Kenya, where attitudes and policies permitted more local initiative in building *harambee* schools. Public health programs and better education have helped reduce mortality, especially among infants and small children. Until recently, falls in crude death rates were not accompanied by declines in birth rates in either country, so rapid population growth compounded the problem of increasing per capita food consumption and income; and because of the rapid growth of their labor forces, the transformation of their predominantly agrarian economies will continue to be slow. Although Kenya has recently entered the second phase of the demographic transition characterized by declining fertility, that will not affect growth of the working-age population for another twenty years. Population pressure in rural areas has already become serious in Kenya, making it imperative for policymakers to give high priority to the development of strategies that increase productivity of Kenya's arid and semiarid lands.

Both Kenya and Tanzania have been hurt by their limited progress in developing strong agricultural research systems and by weaknesses in extension programs. As a result, there has been a lack of profitable and feasible innovations for rapid technological progress. Although Kenya has had a big advantage in drawing on a greater backlog of research and innovations suited to its high-potential areas, that is becoming less important with the shift in population to the semiarid zones.

In the next decade the relative performance of Tanzania and Kenya may be reversed. Tanzania may now have the domestic constituency to break with past policies detrimental to agriculture. That constituency may reshape strategic notions in such a way that macroeconomic policies and agricultural development strategy will have more positive impacts on growth and structural transformation than Kenya's policies. Because of Kenya's highly bimodal agrarian structure, political pressure may mount within the large-farm subsector and shift Kenya toward a dualistic strategy. The political economy of agricultural development in Mexico from 1940 to 1970 holds cautionary lessons for Kenyan policymakers about the pitfalls of dualism.

CHAPTER TWELVE

GETTING
PRIORITIES
RIGHT

There is no blueprint for development that fits the historical, cultural, economic, and political circumstances of all countries. Yet, the defining characteristic of the CARL—a preponderance of the work force in agriculture—means that these agrarian economies necessarily share certain *strategic priorities*. In such economies, even with rapid expansion in industrial and service jobs, the occupational composition of the labor force will change only slowly. Thus, if widespread hunger and mass poverty are to be averted, all CARLs face the need to simultaneously expand jobs and raise labor productivity in agriculture.

Marked agricultural productivity growth and economic progress in some countries shows that the structural transformation of today's CARLs can be accomplished faster than in the past, owing largely to the opportunities to draw on an extensive technological backlog. Despite progress in raising yields, however, there is no easy technological fix to increase labor productivity in agriculture. The heterogeneous physical conditions of rainfed farming, which predominates in many CARLs, complicates the transfer and adaptation of technologies to suit local conditions. Particularly for agriculture in sub-Saharan Africa, there are few technologies that can be transferred directly. Moreover, national agricultural research systems there continue to be weak. Optimism that Africa would quickly follow Asia in experiencing a Green Revolution was misplaced.

Scientific advance can be a double-edged sword, whether in agriculture, industry, or health. The dramatic lowering of the death rate with modern public health measures, for example, greatly advanced human welfare but also caused unprecedented population growth. In much of sub-Saharan Africa, in Pakistan, Nepal, and a number of other CARLs, the persistence of high fertility with declining death rates has meant a continuation of high rates of natural increase. And in most of sub-Saharan Africa and a number of other developing countries, the growth of food output failed to match rapid population growth in the 1980s.

The effectiveness of an agricultural strategy depends on the interaction of individual choices and government initiatives.[1] In the private sector, performance is influenced by incentives for individuals, their capacity for hard work, social and cultural backgrounds, and knowledge and skills. Yet, these also are influenced by macroeconomic policies, government spending on education and health, technology developed by agricultural research institutions, and public investments in infrastructure, as well as many other decisions affecting marketed output, the distribution of inputs, and access to land, water, labor, and capital. Although the purely technical difficulties of constructing all of these elements into a suitable development strategy are formidable in themselves, the task is rendered even more daunting by a variety of political conflicts. These conflicts are of two sorts, those that arise from historical inheritance and those that arise within the operations of the polity itself.

Political and social institutions do change in the process of structural transformation, but few if any clear patterns have been identified linking political development to economic change (Ruttan 1991). Actions to promote democracy and to manage political transitions are desirable. (The collapse of Communist parties in Eastern Europe in the late 1980s and in the USSR in 1991 illustrate that political change can be rapid.) Despite its social advantages, however, democracy is not a necessary condition for agricultural development. For example, although democratic institutions were well-established early in the development of the United States, emergence of similar institutions came much later in Japan. Even where democratic institutions have emerged—as in India and Sri Lanka—patronage, corruption, and factional violence are features of the political scene.

The potential for a vicious circle is obvious. Because of the unequal distribution of power in developing countries, those who bear the costs of government action (or inaction) too often are poor. These realities have led to

---

[1] Agricultural development "strategy" has many possible meanings in this context. From one narrow perspective, it is simply the mix of policies, programs, and projects that jointly influence agricultural growth. Five-year plans and political platforms contain these formal strategic statements in varying degrees of specificity. They may merit attention because they reflect the state of play at one stage in an extended process of developing a strategy. Yet, these formal strategic statements reveal little about sources of government actions or about the individual decisions that actually are carried out in the policy environment.

the popular view that an intrinsic aspect of political economy in developing countries is that policies shift benefits from the weak to the powerful and from the needy to the not-so-needy, with the net result of making the weak weaker, the poor poorer, and, ultimately, standing as an effective barrier to better agricultural development strategies. The issue is not whether this can happen—it does—but whether it is inevitable.

FORCES SHAPING STRATEGY

Whether the ruling regime is democratic or authoritarian, most governments in CARLs are politically fragile. Their survival depends to a unique degree on building political support on a narrow base. Policymakers are vulnerable to lobbying by individuals and powerful constituencies that may have but a modest interest in the social goals of development. Potential coalitions that are more broadly based—such as small-scale farmers and individuals in the informal sector—are aborted at the start because of the free-rider problem—that is, members of such a group benefit whether or not they participate. The impact of any individual will be slight, so there is little incentive to join, much less to organize such a group (Olson 1965).

Government interventions, even if intended to overcome market imperfections or to direct resource allocation toward broad social objectives, are likely to be subverted by smaller, powerful groups in this political economy.[2] Subsidized credit is the classic example of an initiative intended to help the poor but that in its execution funnels benefits to the rich.

Many examples of such subversion have been noted in earlier chapters. It is common wherever publicly supplied inputs—fertilizer, rural credit—are provided at below market-clearing prices. The stated purpose of this subsidization is to stimulate development among groups with limited ability to pay. But rent seeking emerges in response to the administrative rationing necessitated by excess demand. The result is that a substantial portion of the resources are diverted to a comparatively small number of well-to-do recipients who could easily have paid the market price.

[2] The most common approach to relating self-seeking behavior to the formulation of government policy is the influence perspective, as emphasized in the new political economy. In its purest form, the neoclassical tools of optimization are applied to the actions of interest groups as they operate in the political economy, including the "collective choice" and "public choice" schools. As such, this is a healthy reaction to the tendency of many to ignore the effect of politics on choice of development strategy or to implicitly assume that government will play the role of a neutral and benign protector of broad social interests (see Srinivasan 1985 for a review; Krueger's 1974 article on the political economy of rent seeking was a pioneering contribution). Balisacan and Roumasset (1987) and Olson (1988) develop collective choice interpretations consistent with the general pattern that agriculture tends to be taxed in low-income countries and subsidized in industrialized countries.

Why do not political leaders alter their policies in the face of these results? The answer frequently is that although these interventions requiring discretionary administrative decisions are failing to achieve their stated social or economic objectives, they are indeed achieving their intended political objectives.

A regime's leaders, whose primary objective is to retain office, may well attach more importance to the political advantages associated with arbitrary controls than to the adverse effects on efficiency and equity. Benefits can be withheld from those communities and individuals who have supported opposition candidates. The regime's own supporters can be rewarded. Preferential treatment also can secure the goodwill of large and influential farmers, who might otherwise provide leadership in championing rural interests (Bates 1981). And such policies that lower input prices (for some) rather than raise farm output prices also serve the interests of the government's urban support coalition—civil servants, the business community, and organized labor. So economic policies that are democratic in their rhetoric but elitist in their execution can be of considerable short-term advantage to an insecure political leadership.

Social Interest

Although much can be explained in terms of people acting in their own self-interest, such a narrow view of political economy cannot explain the numerous exceptions: "behavior in which calculated self-interest is not the motivating factor" (North 1981, p. 11). To focus on the pursuit of power only as a means for elites to serve their acquisitive interests (the current fashion) is as misleading as the earlier view that saw political leaders solely as disinterested servants of society. Distributional conflicts are not the entire story. Those who wield authority in CARLs, as elsewhere, combine idealism and self-interest. The agricultural development strategies of Japan and the United States reflected an activist role for government, as did elements in Taiwan's success. Sadly, even greater idealism and activism have had unintended counterproductive effects for decades for China, Mexico, and Tanzania.

It is worth recalling that between 1945 and the early 1960s, when many CARLs became independent, highly protectionist import-substitution strategies that were widely adopted were the conventional wisdom of development experts. "At the outset, few of us realized that controls could proliferate in the way they did. In the early 1950s industrial controls appeared to be sensible instruments to allocate resources in directions worked out in the Planning Commission" (Bhagwati 1988, p. 547). In the late 1950s Taiwanese policymakers faced up to the inefficiencies from excessive protection, overvalued currency, and artificially low interest rates and shifted to policies that encouraged growth and efficiency. In many CARLs import-substituting industrialization is still a factor in development strategies. Although this creates policy rents ex post, the underlying policies are not always the result of rent seeking. Indeed, ill-conceived strategic notions are often the driving force.

Even for Latin America, where development policy is often portrayed as dominated entirely by elite groups:

> It is difficult to infer domination of the state from the content or impact of the policy itself. In the agricultural sector in particular, policies to promote agrarian capitalism, agrarian reform, and rural development in Latin American countries did not consistently result from clear domination of the state by specific interests, but were influenced by the development ideologies adopted by state elites, by the leadership ("political entrepreneurship") of specific individuals, and by the political accommodations and bargains that were struck between state elites and various social groupings. (Grindle 1986b, p. 18)

Mexico's CONASUPO and Tanzania's National Milling Company and Cooperative Unions are but two examples where governments tried to displace private trade but simply created opportunities for elites to secure policy rents at the expense of most farmers. Corrupt administration was inevitable. But bad policies are not necessarily due to political influence. In Mexico and Tanzania ill-informed strategic notions about the role of private traders led to marketing initiatives that proved inefficient and corrupt. The corruption was due to bad policy, not vice versa.

Just as we observe economic policies that are inconsistent with a regime of public choice based on pure self-interest, reflection on the complexity of individual motivation suggests that there will be many occasions where individual goals and the common good meet. A growing economy is far more favorable to a regime's survival than one that is contracting. Given the significance of farming in CARLs, agricultural growth (or its absence) can affect job security and the prospects for advancement of many high officials.

More fundamentally, there is often an element of ambiguity in self-interest (March and Olsen 1976). Individuals are concerned with "how the pie is divided," but they share a collective, if more diffuse, concern with "increasing the size of the pie" (Gamson 1968). So, while influential individuals have many opportunities to pursue selfish goals, the stake they share with others in broader social and economic objectives also can motivate actions that transcend their narrow private interests.

As a case in point, President Suharto lent his influence over a prolonged period to programs aimed at raising rice output on Indonesia's small farms.[3] From whatever motive the President's concern sprang—a sense of personal

[3] In a review of President Suharto's autobiography, the *Far Eastern Economic Review* (19 January 1989, p. 17) said, "If he seems on the defensive side regarding allegations of his personal wealth, Suharto leaves the reader in no doubt about what he regards as his greatest achievement: Indonesia's self-sufficiency in rice in the mid-1980s."

accountability for economic performance, a place in history, nostalgia arising from a rural background, an altruistic concern with mass poverty—his goal of broad-based agricultural development coincided with the collective good.

Bureaucracy

In addition to the inherent technical difficulties and the many distributional conflicts, construction of an appropriate economic strategy faces one further hurdle, the nature of the agency by which economic policy is put in place. It is through public bureaucracy that policies, programs, and projects are designed, implemented, monitored, and adapted to changing circumstance.[4]

As the instrument through which policymakers carry out their work, public bureaucracy has a number of advantages. Like very large corporations, government ministries and development agencies can mobilize extensive resources, enjoy access to a wide network of specialized advisors, and in their operation realize economies of scale. Superior in some respects to private corporations, they can operate in areas where the market fails, where sales proceeds fail to cover cost. And with their customers and suppliers, they do not have to depend on voluntary cooperation based on monetary incentives; they can command compliance, either directly or through statutory monopoly.

It is advantages such as these that convinced many economists during the 1950s that parastatal enterprise had a major catalytic role to play during the early phases of structural transformation. However, this early judgment about the desirability of public sector involvement in directly productive activities has been reversed by thirty years of harsh experience. There is virtually no CARL untouched by the tidal wave of privatization.

Some of the disabilities of public bureaucracy in state enterprise apply to the area of policy as well. Government buildings in CARLs may be packed with employees, but skilled public managers and experienced policy analysts are invariably few. Moreover, salary ceilings mean that talented people are lured to more remunerative jobs outside government, often outside the country. Nurturing these key human resources can have high payoffs but takes decades. Better administrative and analytical capacity is largely an outcome of structural transformation, not a viable prescription for overcoming near-term constraints.

It is precisely this inherent shortage of administrative and analytical capacity in the public bureaucracy, combined with its comparative lack of flexibility, that makes limiting the scope of the public sector to public goods a

---

[4] The shortcomings of public bureaucracies are one reason why aid donors increasingly have turned to nongovernmental organizations (NGOs) for implementation and monitoring of certain types of projects. But some government functions—for example, setting policies on prices and exchange rates—cannot be delegated.

common strategic priority for virtually all CARLs. As discussed in Box 8.2, when the public sector in a CARL takes on responsibility for commercial activities—distributing farm inputs, marketing agricultural commodities, operating steel mills and fertilizer plants—the resulting imbalance between responsibilities and resources undermines the execution of its fundamental responsibilities to provide public goods. Unlike activities that substitute for private enterprise, agricultural research, basic education, public health, physical infrastructure, and macroeconomic stability cannot reach satisfactory levels without a preemptory claim on the use of the public sector's limited capacity for administration, policy analysis, and funding.

Political patronage and the limited stock of human resources are not the only constraints on the ability of government to accomplish what is intended. Individuals and agencies within the bureaucratic hierarchy have a certain amount of autonomy. They also have their own interests, and these may not be compatible with national development objectives. Thus, the bureaucratic politics stemming from conflicts of interests within government can further limit the range of feasible strategies. Finally, Allison (1971) and others also point out that government organizations behave according to past routines, whether or not these are appropriate to national objectives. Thus, policies, programs, and projects may resemble "a flow of decisions that is intended by no one and is not related in a direct way to anyone's desired outcomes" (March and Olsen 1976, p. 19).

Bureaucratic politics and organizational processes dictate who has access to information and what they do with it. Control over information is a major source of bureaucratic power. Information pertinent to a promising initiative may be suppressed if the benefits would accrue to a rival ministry. More in evidence are incentives for people to impede the flow of information to conceal mistakes. Such cover-ups can take on tragic proportions. Mao's "Great Leap" and rural communes disrupted agriculture in China and set the stage for the deadliest famine in history. Top policymakers were unaware as the catastrophe unfolded because local and regional bureaucrats withheld the truth in order to appear to be meeting grain production targets.

When connections between cause and effect are ambiguous—as they inevitably are regarding social, economic, and political change—even the best laid plans can fail. Authoritarian regimes—and especially the totalitarian extremes attained in Mao's China and in the USSR under Stalin—are ill-suited to processing the information necessary for effective adaptation to changing circumstances in a rural economy. Without a flow of information to decisionmakers regarding the changing policy environment and on actual outcomes, rigid strategies perpetuate failure. Under such circumstances misguided strategic notions can persist unchallenged for decades.

President Marcos's land reform while the Philippines was under martial law provides another example of the pitfalls that loom when information flow from the grassroots is obstructed both by bureaucracy *and* authoritarian rule. Marcos "unilaterally made decisions with input from close advisors who largely acted on the basis of intuition" (Godkin and Montano 1991, pp. 40–41). Under martial law, inadequate, often obsolete information that was available to insiders could not be augmented by knowledge from the press, church, and civic groups, and certainly not from a political opposition. And because the initiative was directed centrally through "letters of instruction" without a reverse flow of information, local participants were powerless to affect the reform.

The limited capacity to recognize and correct mistakes is intensified by another feature of bureaucracy, namely, its mode of decision making. Bureaucracies operate through a set of routines by which decisions are reached (Dahl and Lindblom 1953; Allison 1971). Routine behavior has its advantages. It creates reliable and predictable actions and economizes on information processing across bureaucratic levels (March and Olsen 1976). However, it also means that investment in capacity is needed to implement new activities, and it is difficult to change routines once they are established. It is not so much that bureaucracies do nothing, but that once in place, they do the same thing over and over, regardless of formal objectives (Grindle 1986a). Bureaucratic learning is a chronic blind spot of development strategy.

Changes in strategy and the implementation of new initiatives typically require new routines. The fit (or misfit) between these requirements and organizational capacity to "learn" cannot be anticipated adequately; it comes through experience. Despite its success, the People's Bank of Indonesia experienced conflicts between old and new routines for years after it began reorienting from traditional subsidized rural credit to a commercial rural bank. And a key reason for the success of Taiwan's agriculture was the development of local organizational capacities, extending back through its years as a Japanese colony. In contrast, decades were wasted in the USSR in a futile effort to collectivize agriculture. Those organizational routines will be useless in the transition from central planning to a market-oriented economy. China's communes, Mexico's attempt to institutionalize collective *ejidos*, and Tanzania's *Ujamaa* villages were other costly false starts.

STRATEGIC NOTIONS AND OPPORTUNITY SEEKING

Development failures reflect in part the limited time that a policymaker can devote to any issue. Individuals with enough clout to affect strategy rarely have the time or inclination to attend to the minutiae of implementation. But failures in development strategies are not simply an aggregate effect of individual shortcomings in collecting, collating, and interpreting information nor are they only the result of venality. As discussed in the preceding section, bureaucratic politics and processes weaken connections between policymakers' intentions and organizational actions. Concentration of local political activity at the implementation stage is another force that weakens links between the intent of policies and their outcomes (Grindle 1980). Even if change is started, the intentions of policymakers can be blocked or twisted, and the organizational routines necessary for new development initiatives may never emerge.

Prospects are dim that government actions (much less outcomes) will correspond to individual intentions or any comprehensive plan for agricultural development. So, where does individual influence and policy analysis fit in this web of uncertainty, contending political interests, and nonrational organizational behavior?

Opportunity Seeking

With a scarcity of useful information and an avalanche of fragmentary data surrounding any policy choice, policymakers often rely on rules of thumb, intuition, personal experience, analogy, anecdotes, and allegories. Furthermore, because interpretation of events is ambiguous and data contradictory, some details have a disproportionate influence on policymakers' decisions. Strategic notions can help in recognizing opportunities created by shifting circumstances and inspire decisions that match agricultural development opportunities with government actions. To the extent this occurs, well-founded strategic notions can help policymakers to make good use of limited opportunities before these disappear.

Seeking answers that are "good enough" ("satisficing") is a reasonable response to the burdens imposed on policymakers.[5] The time required to scan options must be balanced against the premium on timeliness of decisions and the limits on time available for details. Strategic notions facilitate satisficing by aiding in screening and interpreting information while economizing on a policymaker's time. Thus, decision processes following directly from strategic notions differ from the formal techniques of policy analysis (Simon 1985, p. 167; Lindblom 1959; March 1978, p. 589).

Analysis and Action for CARLs

The pressure of time and events of many strategic moments rules out comprehensive analysis of alternatives. Instead, decision making must proceed through interplay among analyses, which are constrained by capacity and limited in reliability, and action, which may be available in abundance but

[5] Simon (1985, p. 190) calls rationality "bounded" when "complexity of the environment is immensely greater than the computational powers of the adaptive system." In a complex system that has contending adaptive forces, policymakers will "satisfice," adopting the pragmatic approach of "looking for alternatives in such a way that we can generally find an acceptable one only after moderate search" (Simon 1985, p. 139).

also carries the risk of costly mistakes. Typically, policymakers must match pressing objectives with capacities available at the time (March and Olsen 1976). Many years ago, Silva Herzog captured this inevitable tension in the case of Mexico's land reform:

Land hunger was one of the causes which originated the Revolution. Upon the definite triumph of the latter, it was necessary to give land to the peasants, it was necessary to give it to them rapidly, without a definite plan, without a program, and subordinating the distribution more to the political requirements of the moment than to what science would have counselled in such a complicated problem. It was not possible to wait any longer, it was not possible to carry out investigations or to conduct a careful, complete and detailed study before making the distribution. It was necessary to give lands and they were given hurriedly, because there was no other way. Of course, grave errors were made, but to wait would have been an even more serious error. What was done, rightly or wrongly, is done, and the important thing now is to improve it. (quoted in Whetten 1948, pp. 150–51)

Strategic notions can focus policymakers' attention on implementing key programs and projects, as when President Cárdenas intervened in the crash program of land redistribution in Mexico in the 1930s. Well-founded strategic notions also can increase the effectiveness of policymakers' search for satisfactory strategies by conserving two scarce resources: policymakers' time and their advisors' capacity to produce timely analyses.

Strategic notions provide the basis for proceeding—partly by intuition, but also analysis—through the succession of policy and program opportunities. Analysis and action each can change harmful strategic notions. In particular, *catastrophic learning experiences* may force strategic notions to change. For example, the Kuomintang leadership that escaped to Taiwan in the late 1940s had shown little aptitude for economic policy. The debacle on the mainland taught Chiang Kai-shek the importance of competent economists in forming macroeconomic policies. It also taught the Kuomintang leadership the need to maintain support of the farm population after it fled to Taiwan. This created scope for policy analysts and others to identify a strategy for farm productivity increases in Taiwan, as well as a redistributive land reform. Indonesia, too, had its catastrophe. Hyperinflation, hunger, and social upheaval toward the end of President Sukarno's rule in the mid-1960s left a mark that has influenced fiscal and food policy under his successor, President Suharto.[6]

---

[6] Indonesian policymakers also have made good use of some other costly lessons. Professor Dr. Ali Wardhana, a cabinet minister for two decades and a principal architect of economic policy during Mr. Suharto's presidency, observed that "the infamous Pertamina affair of the mid-1970s [when the state oil company squandered billions in oil revenues through mismanagement and corruption and, in the meantime, incurred a massive debt] turned out to be a blessing in disguise, because it educated us on the importance of prudent borrowing and the dangers of overborrowing years before the full force of the debt crisis descended on the world" (*Jakarta Post*, 1 February 1989, p. 4).

Some leaders (Chairman Mao, President Nyerere of Tanzania, and President Sukarno) were so enamored of their strategic notions that little serious policy analysis could be done by economists and other professionals. Thus, it is not just interests that can be vested but also the strategic notions that rationalize pursuit of those political and economic interests. Selective perception of events—a close relative of satisficing—is likely to persist as long as policymakers benefit privately in ways that outweigh the personal costs of failure to serve the public.

Whatever emerges as agricultural development strategy, it will reflect a mix of interests and strategic notions from individuals' limited understanding of development strategy and available opportunities, both public and private. Strategic notions are expressed (or repressed) by political influence, bureaucratic skills and power, luck, and timing. Their outcomes will be influenced by existing administrative and political institutions and by history. For example, the success of Indonesia's rural banking reform was partly due to the foresight of policymakers to perceive this opportunity and their determination to see it through.

Shifting events can create strategic moments. Policymakers prepared to exploit these opportunities can influence strategy, but they need a deft understanding of development processes, combined with inside experience of politics, markets, and other institutions. So "opportunism" is as much a pragmatic component of good policymaking as it is an attribute of those seeking policy rents.[7] These strategic opportunities may be few and far between. But history shows that individual policymakers can make a difference by discerning opportunities, setting priorities on the opportunities to prepare for, learning from experience, and matching opportunities with action. It is this ability to recognize opportunities and act on them that really shapes the "strategy" in political economy (Simon 1985, pp. 109–10). Learning from experience is at the center of this process.

STRATEGY AND STRUCTURAL TRANSFORMATION

The shortage of physical and human capital in CARLs is associated with underdeveloped markets, with the weak capacity of government to provide services, and with the low productive efficiency of firms. Although agriculture predominates in the early stages of structural transformation, a diverse nonfarm sector also figures strongly in the unspecialized rural economy of CARLs. So, development strategies for agriculture and rural nonfarm activities are as important to CARLs as industrialization strategies are to the

---

[7] In contrast to the use of the term in game theory as unprincipled behavior to further one's interest without regard to broader consequences, we use the term in the sense of "opportune"— well timed and well adapted to existing circumstances.

newly industrialized countries (NICs) at a later stage of structural transformation. Differing natural resource endowments are one cause of different patterns of agricultural development, as seen in Japan and the United States. But their experience also shows that policy choices matter more for the growth of productivity than do endowments of land, petroleum, or whatever.

Because the evolution of markets and other economic institutions is both a cause and a consequence of structural transformation, the scope (and limits) of government policy vary throughout the long process of development. The "right" policies thus depend on the stage of structural transformation. Market imperfections and high public expectations often propel governments toward interventions. But CARLs face especially tough choices: they have the greatest need for public initiative but the least capacity to design appropriate policies and to finance and implement them. Hence, the crucial need to identify priorities.

Selective government initiatives to build key public institutions and infrastructure were decisive in the United States and Japan when they were CARLs. Building educational institutions, including rural schools, was motivated by strategic notions about the central importance of developing human resources. In the late nineteenth and early twentieth centuries, Japan began building the public capacity for agricultural research essential for the development of fertilizer-responsive seeds and farm practices, the basis for its labor-using, land-saving agricultural development. In the United States, market incentives induced private firms to produce a stream of mechanical innovations, the basis for its labor-saving, land-using pattern.

Small Farms in a Broad-Based Agricultural Strategy

The many choices for raising productivity in agriculture (evident in the contrasting patterns of productivity growth in Japan and the United States) are a potential advantage. But they also increase the risk that borrowed technologies will be ill-suited to a CARL's resource endowment. For agriculture in sub-Saharan Africa it was widely believed that because land was abundant, tractor-based technologies could be readily adopted. Such initiatives were a costly mistake. To draw maximum advantage from the technology backlog, while avoiding its pitfalls, is one of the most crucial and demanding tasks of a successful development strategy.

A risk in all CARLs is that policymakers will choose dualistic strategies— and the capital-using, labor-saving agricultural technologies used in countries that have passed their structural transformation turning point. As structural transformation proceeds and capital and job opportunities become more abundant, increases in the demand for labor will push wages up. There will then be a shift in the pattern of productivity growth toward capital-using, labor-saving technologies and faster growth in labor productivity. Such socially efficient sequences of productivity growth are likely, however, only if market prices for labor, land, and capital reflect their relative scarcities and if government initiatives create the infrastructure and institutions for agricultural research and other support services. Indeed, labor-using, capital-saving development is a window of opportunity for simultaneously increasing labor productivity and providing jobs for a growing rural work force.

The choice of agricultural development strategy is sometimes confused by emphasis on the misleading dichotomy between "efficiency" and "equity." Proponents of dualistic approaches, where a large farm subsector accounts for a major part of a country's agricultural production, often claim that a small farm development strategy is a dubious concession to equity and that only large farms can achieve the efficiency required for rapid expansion of output. The evidence in Chapters 4 and 5 however, shows that broad-based increases in the productivity of most farms (which inevitably are small) are more efficient *and* more equitable than a dualistic strategy, as long as the opportunity cost of rural labor is low.

Agricultural Strategies and Agrarian Structure

Although the average farm in CARLs is small, there is much variation of farm size around the mean. Some claim that dualistic agricultural development is inevitable without land reform. Although redistributive land reform can contribute to both economic and social goals, it is not a prerequisite for a broad-based strategy, except with extremely bimodal distributions, as in Latin America. Instead, it is the size distribution of farm operational units that is of decisive importance, especially for choice of technology and the demand for rural labor. Consequently, land tenure arrangements that permit a unimodal pattern of operational units can make it possible to pursue a broad-based strategy despite highly skewed landownership.

More generally, it is essential to consider the complex interactions among a country's agrarian structure and institutions, new technologies, and growth of economic opportunities outside agriculture. Interlinked changes in each are critical in determining whether the growth of demand for labor expands fast enough to offset the depressing effect on wages from CARLs' growing supply of rural labor.

Differentiating factors—the policy variables that favor a subset of large farms—can cause dramatic shifts toward a bimodal distribution of farms. But most policies that foster a unimodal pattern are more subtle (and slower) than redistributive land reform. Precisely because political reality typically precludes redistributive reform, it is crucial to understand the impact of policy choices on the pattern of operating units. The four pairs of case studies (Chapters 3, 9, 10, and 11) show how those choices, over decades, affect agricultural development.

The long-term results derive not from a grand strategic design but from the concrete policy choices governing our "Six I's": innovations, inputs, incentives, infrastructure, institutions, and initiative. Is agricultural research oriented toward the development of divisible *innovations*—that is, those that can be used efficiently by small-scale units to complement, rather than displace, abundant labor? Is the allocation of scarce *inputs* handled by market-clearing prices, which give producers equal access, or are they rationed administratively in a way that gives privileged access to individuals with influence and wealth? Do price and marketing policies for agricultural products provide adequate *incentives* for efficient productivity growth? Does the design of public irrigation and the layout of the road network favor large farms over small ones, as in Mexico? Or does investment in rural *infrastructure* foster broad-based growth of rural output and employment—farm and nonfarm—as in Taiwan? Are extension programs and other support *institutions* directed toward widespread adoption of innovations? Has the policy environment enabled farmers and other entrepreneurs to perceive and seize opportunities? Has government favored constructive public *initiatives*, such as the People's Bank in Indonesia? Or are they ill-advised initiatives, such as Mexico's Uxpanapa Project and elsewhere, land-rental ceilings designed to aid tenants but that encourage landlords to evict tenants and engage in mechanized cultivation of large farms?

Agriculture-Industry Interactions

The development of agriculture and its potential to increase demand for rural labor can be fully realized only with growth in other sectors of the economy. Promoting a unimodal agrarian structure can help to foster positive interactions between agricultural and industrial development to stimulate greater growth of nonfarm output and employment than can be realized through a dualistic strategy that reinforces a bimodal agrarian structure. These positive interactions occur when the pattern of rural demand for agricultural inputs, consumer goods (such as textiles and shoes), and rural services encourages the decentralized growth of small and medium-scale manufacturing firms that use labor-intensive technologies and few imported inputs. A dualistic strategy, by contrast, is associated with growth in demand for more sophisticated consumer goods and farm inputs. The resulting concentration of income gains among the few wealthy households induces demand for tractors, automobiles, and air conditioning, not for improved animal-drawn implements, bicycles, and electric fans. Even if the sophisticated items are manufactured domestically, they tend to be produced in large factories, using capital-intensive technologies and relying on imported inputs. Therefore, the expansion of such big firms is limited more by the scarcity of capital and foreign exchange than is the output of smaller ones using more labor and other indigenous resources and with lower requirements for capital and foreign exchange per unit of output—and with more job opportunities.

So, differences in the farm-size distribution that determine the agrarian structure also have a significant impact on industrial development. By shaping the distribution of rural income (both directly and through farm size effects on demand for labor), the size distribution of farms is the major determinant of the composition of intersectoral commodity flows.

The conclusion: broad-based agricultural strategies have notable advantages for CARLs, because of their impact on industrial development and their direct effects on expanded opportunities for productive employment within agriculture. With rapid growth of the rural work force, even labor-using agricultural development may merely avoid a falling rural wage. Big increases in rural wages and incomes also require faster growth in nonfarm demand for labor than can be expected with a dualistic strategy, which encourages labor-saving, capital-using technologies in (and outside) the agricultural sector.

The Six I's that are crucial to a broad-based strategy are also critical in the expansion of nonfarm rural activities. Appropriate innovations, divisible inputs that can be used efficiently by smallholders, and agricultural prices that provide incentives and rising farm profits: these provide the cash income that strengthens linkages to the nonfarm economy. Backward linkages to simple farm implements are important, but even more important is the growing demand for consumer goods that can be manufactured domestically by small and medium-size firms, employing labor-using (and capital-saving) technologies. Investments in infrastructure, so important to broad-based development, also reduce production costs and expand market opportunities for nonfarm enterprises in the rural economy. In brief, the positive interactions between broad-based agricultural development and the rural nonfarm economy are not only the keys to providing enough income-earning opportunities for the growing rural labor force. They also reinforce one another.

Fertilizer, an important farm input, is an exception to these generalizations about farm-nonfarm interactions in the rural economy (see Chapter 7). The availability of fertilizer as a divisible and low-cost input for increasing agricultural output is what is crucial. And farm productivity will be hampered if farmers are obliged to use high-priced fertilizer from an inefficient domestic industry.

Especially for nitrogen fertilizers, economies of scale are decisive: the efficient manufacture of nitrogen fertilizers means capital-using, labor-saving technologies, so investments in fertilizer plants do not expand job opportunities. A theoretical case can be made for reliance on *some* domestic manufacture of fertilizers in China and India. Because they are so large relative to the world import-export market, a large shift in their demand can have a noticeable (but transitory) effect on world prices. A stronger case can be made for large-market, low-cost natural gas exporters, such as Indonesia, who are also prepared to draw heavily on foreign technical know-how. In general, however, it is a false notion to think of the "make or buy" fertilizer decision as an issue of industrial strategy. Instead, this is one of macroeconomic management—specifically of ensuring that foreign exchange crises do not jeopardize fertilizer imports.

Macroeconomic Policies

Macroeconomic policies have an even more powerful influence on agricultural incentives than do sectoral policies. If the exchange rate is overvalued, if interest rates are artificially low, and if other key prices that guide decision makers are distorted, the transfer of inappropriate technology is the likely outcome. CARLs must avoid macroeconomic policies that have adverse effects on agriculture, and small farms in particular. This means emphasizing economic stability and predictability and permitting prices, including interest rates and the exchange rate, to reflect the scarcity value of capital and foreign exchange. Such policies encourage the allocation of resources toward their most socially efficient use, discourage investment in inappropriate, capital-intensive technologies, and minimize reliance on arbitrary controls, including the discretionary allocation of resources by administrative rationing, which will inevitably be guided by patronage and favor the wealthy and powerful.

The basic elements of good macroeconomic management are compatible with a broad-based strategy for the rural economy. Indeed, macroeconomic mismanagement will inhibit agricultural development and bias growth in favor of large farms. Moreover, control of the government budget balance is a prerequisite to adequate funding for essential government spending on rural infrastructure, agricultural research institutions, rural primary education, and selective health interventions.

Social Programs

There is general acceptance that spending on education and health contributes to economic growth, as well as being of value to the direct beneficiaries. A consensus has emerged, supported by country studies, that the social and private returns to primary education are especially high. But there is uncertainty about the other types of social programs that should be supported.

The most serious problems in priorities relate to the balance between social service programs for public health versus urban food subsidies and other food distribution programs. Because of the political influence of civil servants, the military, urban labor, and other interest groups, food subsidies can account for a large share of government outlays in CARLs. Moreover, in some countries, the explicit costs of food subsidies are reduced by holding down agricultural prices, thus transferring part of the cost to farmers, which adversely affects producer incentives. Such an urban bias is also evident in the frequent concentration of government health spending on urban hospitals and the limited access of rural households to basic health services.

Selective public health interventions, targeted at women and small children, can ease the worst effects of poverty for the most vulnerable. Experience shows that this can be done years ahead of the structural transformation necessary to eliminate mass hunger and poverty. By concentrating on cost-effective preventive and promotional activities, such as immunizations, oral rehydration therapy, and nutrition and hygiene education, these programs can dramatically reduce infant and child mortality.

These programs can also speed the demographic transition, hastening the structural transformation turning point, which eases the double bind of simultaneously increasing labor productivity and labor demand in agriculture. Witness Indonesia, which completed this transformation in only about twenty-five years. Even this rapid transformation is longer than the span of a generation and the time required to develop new agricultural techniques. Policies to moderate population growth and to raise agricultural productivity have a complementary impact on supply and demand for rural labor within this time frame. Indeed, if Indonesia had failed in either encouraging growth or lowering fertility rates, its turning point would have been delayed.

THE RIGHT PRIORITIES

The crucial requirement for agricultural development is to create a favorable environment so that many individuals and firms perceive and seize opportunities. Changing conditions mean new opportunities, but many earlier initiatives will no longer be profitable. Thus, the ability to learn from experience is crucial to avoid repeating costly mistakes and to reallocate resources to seize new opportunities.

Given the complexity of the development process, successful strategy depends on the decisions of many entrepreneurs—farm and nonfarm, small and large, male and female. Government decision making cannot substitute for the myriad decentralized decisions required to perceive and seize emerging economic opportunities. A command economy fails to allow scope for a market system to work efficiently. Markets are an economical way of transmitting information, harmonizing the decentralized decisions of producers. Competitive markets also harness the powerful motive of profit and foster continuing pressures to innovate and reduce costs. Moreover, the political system that coexists with a command economy stifles information flows, creativity, and initiative and suppresses feedback about failures. Although individual firms often try to increase profits by stifling competition and the flow of information, they rarely succeed—except when the state is "captured" sufficiently to protect the monopoly of privileged firms. With that important caveat, markets are highly efficient not only in the transmission of information but also for the *discovery* of emerging opportunities.

Even so, new opportunities depend on the supporting role of government. Experience has shown the critical importance of public goods—education, agricultural research, rural infrastructure, public health, macroeconomic stability, and prices that reflect the scarcity value of resources. But it is too easy to expand the list of essential objectives that a CARL "must" achieve. Their severe constraints mean that priority should go to elements of development strategy that are necessary either to accelerate broad-based development or to complement it, such as sound macroeconomic management and certain social programs, including primary education and selective public health interventions aimed at infants, preschool children, and their mothers. This inevitably means choosing *not* to undertake many other attractive actions. Based on our analysis, we have singled out six strategic notions that can help to guide policymakers in reaching consensus on strategic priorities in CARLs:

1. *As long as the opportunity cost of labor is low, broad-based productivity growth involving the majority of farms (which inevitably are small) is more efficient and provides more rural employment opportunities than a dualistic strategy aimed at a subsector of large farms.* A broad-based agricultural strategy has important advantages for CARLs because they need to expand jobs *and* raise labor productivity simultaneously until they reach their structural transformation turning points.

2. *The "Six I's"—innovations, inputs, incentives, infrastructure, institutions, and initiative—that are crucial to a broad-based agricultural strategy also promote expansion of rural nonfarm activities.* A successful broad-based agricultural strategy provides cash income and a pattern of demand that promotes growth in the rural nonfarm economy. Furthermore, the rural infrastructure to serve agriculture (especially roads, electric power, communication, and market places in towns of 5,000 to 30,000 inhabitants) also lowers costs and expands opportunities for rural nonfarm enterprises.

3. *Policies favoring a subset of large farms can cause dramatic shifts toward a bimodal agrarian structure. Aside from redistributive land reform, policies that favor a unimodal agrarian structure work slowly.* Thus, the advantages a unimodal agrarian structure holds for CARLs in terms of rural employment generation through mutually reinforcing agriculture-industry interactions are hard to obtain and easy to lose.

4. *Macroeconomic policies can have an even more powerful effect on agricultural incentives than do sectoral policies.* The basic elements of sound macroeconomic policy—exchange rates near equilibrium, positive real interest rates near the opportunity cost of capital, and prudent fiscal policies—are essential to creating an environment conducive to broad-based development. Overvalued exchange rates and subsidized interest rates favor large enterprises over small farms and firms. Control of the government budget is necessary to sustain funding of rural infrastructure, agricultural research, and social programs.

5. *Some direct measures to enhance rural welfare complement agricultural development and accelerate structural transformation; others do not.* Investments in human capital—especially rural primary education—have come to be regarded as important elements of successful agricultural development strategies. Selective public health interventions aimed at infants, preschool children, and their mothers can improve child survival and maternal health at very low cost. They also are associated with rapid fertility decline, thereby hastening the structural transformation turning point. Consequently, these also deserve priority. On the other hand, given the likelihood of serious imbalances between resources and responsibilities, food stamp or school lunch programs, which are highly desirable in richer countries, come at too high an opportunity cost to merit priority in CARLs.

6. *Government's comparative advantage lies in provision of essential public goods and services.* Minimizing the role of public agencies in commercial or productive activities is essential in CARLs because of the severe constraints they face. As a consequence, the first claim on scarce public finances and administrative capacities must go to those goods and services that will not be supplied adequately by the private sector. There is some scope for public sector initiative to catalyze or facilitate activities that are essentially commercial, but identifying and acting on these opportunities for public initiative is perhaps the most difficult strategic element.

The idea that development is determined by policy analysis and the projects of planners and policymakers is naive and misleading, and it engenders and reflects excessive faith in government initiatives. Policymakers do *not* begin with a clean slate. The performance of individual farmers and other entrepreneurs is decisive, and their actions depend on incentives, the capacity for hard work, knowledge and skills, and culture. But their behavior, and the outcome of their efforts, also depends on the interacting effects of their individual choices *and* government initiatives. Policymakers can and do make a difference, but mainly through preparing for strategic opportunities, discerning those opportunities, matching opportunities with action, and learning from experience. Chance will favor those policymakers who can recognize emerging opportunities—and who are prepared to act.

REFERENCES

Abdel-Fadil, Mahmoud. 1975. *Development, Income Distribution and Social Change in Rural Egypt (1952–1970): A Study of the Political Economy of Agrarian Transition*. Cambridge: Cambridge University Press.

Adams, Dale W., D. H. Graham, and J. D. Von Pischke. 1984. *Undermining Rural Development with Cheap Credit*. Boulder, Colo.: Westview.

Adelman, Irma, and J. Edward Taylor. 1990. *Changing Comparative Advantage in Food and Agriculture: Lessons from Mexico*. Paris: Development Centre Studies, Organization for Economic Cooperation and Development.

Agency for International Development (AID). 1970. *Status of Fertilizer Projects as of January 1970*, Washington, D.C.: Office of Capital Development.

——. 1989. "Development and the National Interest: A Report by the Administrator." Washington, D.C.: AID.

——. 1993. *The Substance behind the Images: A.I.D. and Development Communication*. Washington, D.C.: AID.

Agro-Chemicals News in Brief. 1990. Vol. 13, no. 3. Bangkok: United Nations.

Ahluwalia, Montek S. 1990. "Policies for Poverty Alleviation." *Asian Development Review* 8(1): 111–32.

Ahmad, Junaid, Walter P. Falcon, and C. Peter Timmer. 1989. "Fertilizer Policy for the 1990s." Paper presented at an AID Symposium on Agriculture, September 1989, mimeographed, Cambridge, Mass.: Harvard Institute for International Development.

Ahmed, Raisuddin, and M. Hossain. 1990. *Developmental Impact of Rural Infrastructure in Bangladesh*. Washington, D.C.: International Food Policy Research Institute.

Ainsworth, Martha, and Mead Over. 1994. "AIDS and African Development." *The World Bank Research Observer* 9(2): 203–40.

Aird, John S. 1986. "Coercion in Family Planning: Causes, Methods, and Consequences." In *China's Economy Looks toward the Year 2000*, vol. 1. Washington, D.C.: United States Government Printing Office.

Alba, Francisco, and J. E. Potter. 1986. "Population and Development in Mexico since 1940." *Population and Development Review* 12(1): 47–75.

Alderman, Harold. 1986. *The Effect of Food Price and Income Changes on the Acquisition of Food by Low-Income Households*. Washington, D.C.: International Food Policy Research Institute.

———. 1987. "Cooperative Dairy Development in Karnataka, India: An Assessment." Washington, D.C.: International Food Policy Research Institute.

Alderman, Harold, George Mergos, and Roger Slade. 1987. "Cooperatives and the Commercialization of Milk Production in India: A Literature Review." Working Papers on Commercialization of Agriculture and Nutrition, No. 2. Washington, D.C.: International Food Policy Research Institute.

Alexandratos, Nikos, ed. 1988. *World Agriculture: Toward 2000. An FAO Study*. New York: New York University Press.

Allison, Graham T. 1971. *Essence of Decision: Explaining the Cuban Missile Crisis*. Boston: Little, Brown.

Amani, H. K. R., and S. M. Kapunda. 1990. "Agricultural Market Reform in Tanzania: The Restriction of Private Traders and Its Impact on Food Security." In Mandivamba Rukuni, Godfrey Mudimu, and Thomas S. Jayne, eds., *Food Security Policies in the SADCC Region*. Proceedings of the Fifth Annual Conference on Food Research in Southern Africa, Oct. 16–18, 1989, pp. 75–94. Harare: University of Zimbabwe/Michigan State University Food Security Research Project.

Amani, H. K. R., S. M. Kapunda, N. H. I. Lipumba, and B. J. Ndulu. 1988. "Effects of Market Liberalization on Food Security: The Case of Tanzania." In Mandivamba Rukuni and Richard H. Bernsten, eds., *Southern Africa: Food Security Policy Options*. Proceedings of the Third Annual Conference on Food Security Research in Southern Africa, Nov. 1–5, 1987, pp. 65–100. Harare: University of Zimbabwe/Michigan State University Food Security Research Project.

Amsden, Alice H. 1988. "Taiwan's Economic History: A Case of Etatisme and a Challenge to Dependency Theory." In Robert H. Bates, ed., *Toward a Political Economy of Development: A Rational Choice Perspective*. Berkeley: University of California Press.

———. 1991. "Diffusion of Development: The Late-Industrializing Model and Greater East Asia." *American Economic Review* 81(2): 282–86.

Anderson, Kym, and Yujiro Hayami. 1986. "Introduction." In K. Anderson and Y. Hayami, eds., *The Political Economy of Agricultural Protection: East Asia in International Perspective*. Boston: Allen & Unwin.

Anderson, Kym, Yujiro Hayami, and others. 1986. *The Political Economy of Agricultural Protection*. Sydney: Allen & Unwin.

Anthony, Kenneth R. M., B. F. Johnston, W. O. Jones, and V. C. Uchendu. 1979. *Agricultural Change in Tropical Africa*. Ithaca: Cornell University Press.

Arrow, Kenneth J. 1962. "The Economic Implications of Learning by Doing." *Review of Economic Studies* 29 (June): 155–73.

Arthur, H. B., R. A. Goldberg, and K. M. Baird. 1967. *The United States Food and Fiber System in a Changing World Environment*, vol. 4. Washington, D.C.: National Advisory Commission on Food and Fiber.

Ashton, Basil, K. Hill, A. Piazza, and R. Zeitz. 1984. "Famine in China, 1958–1961." *Population and Development Review* 10(4): 613–45.

Askari, H., and J. T. Cummings. 1976. *Agricultural Supply Response: A Survey of the Econometric Evidence*. New York: Praeger.

Atwood, David A. 1990. "Land Registration in Africa: The Impact on Agricultural Production." *World Development* 18(5): 659–71.

Austin, James E., and G. Esteva. 1987. *Food Policy in Mexico: The Search for Self-Sufficiency*. Ithaca: Cornell University Press.

Balisacan, Arsenio M., and James A. Roumasset. 1987. "Public Choice of Economic Policy: The Growth of Agricultural Protection." *Weltwirtschaftliches Archiv (Review of World Economics)* 123(2): 233–45.

Bangladesh Institute of Development Studies (BIDS). 1981. "Rural Industries Study Project—Final Report." Dacca: BIDS.

Banister, Judith. 1986. "Implications of China's 1982 Census Results." In *China's Economy Looks toward the Year 2000*, vol. 1. Washington, D.C.: United States Government Printing Office.

———. 1987. *China's Changing Population*, Stanford, Calif.: Stanford University Press.

Barclay, G. W. 1954. *Colonial Development and Population in Taiwan*. Princeton: Princeton University Press.

Bardhan, Pranab K. 1973. "Size, Productivity, and Returns to Scale: An Analysis of Farm-Level Data in Indian Agriculture." *Journal of Political Economy* 81(6): 1370–86.

———. 1980. "Interlocking Factor Markets and Agrarian Development: A Review of the Issues." *Oxford Economic Papers* 32: 82–98.

———. 1984. *The Political Economy of Development in India*. Oxford: Basil Blackwell.

———. 1988. "Alternative Approaches to Development Economics." In Hollis Chenery and T. N. Srinivasan, eds., *Handbook of Development Economics*, vol. 1. Amsterdam: North-Holland.

Barkan, Joel D. 1984a. "Comparing Politics and Public Policy in Kenya and Tanzania." In *Politics and Public Policy in Kenya and Tanzania*. New York: Praeger.

———, ed. 1984b. *Politics and Public Policy in Kenya and Tanzania*, rev. ed. New York: Praeger.

Barker, Randolph, and Robert W. Herdt with Beth Rose. 1985. *The Rice Economy of Asia*. Washington, D.C.: Resources for the Future.

Barlow, Colin. 1986. "Oil Palm as a Smallholder Crop." Palm Oil Research Institute of Malaysia, Occasional Paper #21, August 1986. Kuala Lumpur: Seasons Press.

Barlow, Colin, and S. K. J. Jayasuriya, 1984a. "Bias toward the Large Farm Subsector in Agricultural Research: The Case of Malaysian Rubber." *Research and Development in Agriculture* 1(3): 153–64.

———. 1984b. "Problems of Investment for Technological Advance: The Case of Indonesian Rubber Smallholders." *Journal of Agricultural Economics* 35(1): 85–95.

Barlow, Colin, Colin Shearing, and Ridwan Dereinda. 1991. "Alternative Approaches to Smallholder Rubber Development." HIID Development Discussion Paper No. 368, January 1991. Cambridge: Harvard Institute for International Development.

Barnett, A. Doak. 1986. "China's Modernization: Development and Reform in the 1980's." In *China's Economy Looks toward the Year 2000*, vol. 1. Washington D.C.: United States Government Printing Office.

Bartlett, Peggy F. 1980. "Adaptive Strategies in Peasant Agricultural Production." *Annual Review of Anthropology* 9: 545–73.

Bates, Robert H. 1981. *Markets and States in Tropical Africa*. Berkeley: University of California Press.

——. 1984. "Some Conventional Orthodoxies in the Study of Agrarian Change." *World Politics* 36(1): 234–54.

——. 1988. "Lessons from History, or the Perfidy of English Exceptionalism and the Significance of Historical France." *World Politics* 40(4): 499–516.

——. 1989. *Beyond the Miracle of the Market: The Political Economy of Agrarian Development in Kenya*. Cambridge: Cambridge University Press.

Bautista, Romeo M. 1990. "Rapid Agricultural Growth Is Not Enough: The Philippines, 1965–80." Paper presented at the Conference on Agriculture on the Road to Industrialization. Taipei, Taiwan: Council on Agriculture and the International Food Policy Research Institute.

Behrman, Jere R., and Anil B. Deolalikar. 1987. "Will Developing Country Nutrition Improve with Income? A Case Study of Rural South India." *Journal of Political Economy* 95(3): 492–507.

——. 1988. "Health and Nutrition." In Hollis Chenery and T. N. Srinivasan, eds., *Handbook of Development Economics*, vol. 1. Amsterdam: North-Holland.

Behrman, Jere R., Anil B. Deolalikar, and Barbara L. Wolfe. 1988. "Nutrients: Impacts and Determinants." *The World Bank Economic Review* 2(3): 299–320.

Bell, Clive J. 1988. "Credit Markets and Interlinked Transactions." In Hollis Chenery and T. N. Srinivasan, eds., *Handbook of Development Economics*, vol. 1. Amsterdam: North-Holland.

Bell, Clive J., Peter Hazell, and Roger Slade. 1982. *Project Evaluation in a Regional Perspective: A Study of an Irrigation Project in Northwestern Malaysia*. Baltimore: Johns Hopkins University Press.

Bell, Clive J., and T. N. Srinivasan. 1985. "An Anatomy of Transactions in Rural Credit Markets in Andhra Pradesh, Bihar, and Punjab." Mimeograph. Washington, D.C.: The World Bank.

Bellah, Robert N., R. Madsen, W. M. Sullivan, A. Swidler, and S. M. Tipton. 1985. *Habits of the Heart: Individualism and Commitment in American Life*. Berkeley: University of California Press.

Bennett, M. K. 1954. *The World's Food*. New York: Harper.

Berry, R. Albert, and William R. Cline. 1979. *Agrarian Structure and Productivity in Developing Countries*. Baltimore: Johns Hopkins University Press.

Bevan, David, A. Bigsten, P. Collier, and J. W. Gunning. 1987. *East African Lessons on Economic Liberalization*. Thames Essay No. 48. London: Trade Policy Research Center.

Bhagwati, Jagdish N. 1982. "Directly Unproductive Profit-Seeking (DUP) Activities." *Journal of Political Economy* 90 (October): 988–1002.

——. 1988. "Poverty and Public Policy." *World Development* 16(5): 539–55.

Bhagwati, Jagdish N., and P. Desai. 1970. *India: Planning for Industrialization.* London: Oxford University Press.

Bhalla, Surjit S. 1979. "Farm Size, Productivity, and Technical Change in Indian Agriculture." In R. Albert Berry and William R. Cline, *Agrarian Structure and Productivity in Developing Countries.* Baltimore: Johns Hopkins University Press.

Bienen, Henry. 1970. *Tanzania: Party Transformation and Economic Development.* Princeton: Princeton University Press.

Biggs, Stephen D. 1989. "Resource-Poor Farmer Participation in Research: A Synthesis from Nine National Agricultural Research Systems." The Hague: International Service for National Agricultural Research.

Biggs, Stephen D., and Edward S. Clay. 1981. "Sources of Innovation in Agricultural Technology." *World Development* 9(4): 321–36.

Biggs, Tyler. 1986. "On Measuring Relative Efficiency in a Size Distribution of Firms." Employment and Enterprise Policy Analysis Discussion Paper No. 2. Cambridge, Mass.: Harvard Institute for International Development.

Bigsten, Arne. 1986. "Regional Inequality in Kenya." In Tony Killick, ed., *Papers on the Kenyan Economy: Performance, Problems, and Policies.* London: Heinemann Educational Books.

Binswanger, Hans P., and Graeme Donovan. 1987. *Agricultural Mechanization: Issues and Policies.* Washington, D.C.: World Bank.

Binswanger, Hans P., and Prabhu Pingali. 1988. "Technological Priorities for Farming in Sub-Saharan Africa." *World Bank Research Observer* 3(1): 81–98.

Binswanger, Hans P., and Mark R. Rosenzweig. 1984. "Contractual Arrangements, Employment, and Wages in Rural Labor Markets: A Critical Review." In Hans P. Binswanger and Mark R. Rosensweig, eds., *Contractual Arrangements, Employment, and Wages in Rural Labor Markets in Asia.* New Haven: Yale University Press.

——. 1986. "Behavioral and Material Determinants of Production Relations in Agriculture." *Journal of Development Studies* 22: 503–39.

Binswanger, Hans P., Vernon W. Ruttan, and others, eds. 1978. *Induced Innovation: Technology, Institutions, and Development.* Baltimore: Johns Hopkins University Press.

Birdsall, Nancy M. 1988. "Economic Approaches to Population Growth." In Hollis Chenery and T. N. Srinivasan, eds., *Handbook of Development Economics,* vol. 1. Amsterdam: North-Holland.

Birdsall, Nancy M., and Charles C. Griffin. 1988. "Fertility and Poverty in Developing Countries." *Journal of Policy Modeling* 10(1): 29–55.

Birkhaeuser, Dean, Robert E. Evenson, and Gershon Feder. 1991. "The Economic Impact of Agricultural Extension: A Review." *Economic Development and Cultural Change* 39(3): 607–50.

Blackie, Malcom J. 1990. "Maize, Food Self-Sufficiency, and Policy in East and Southern Africa." *Food Policy* 15(5): 383–94.

Boesen, Jannik, K. J. Havnevik, J. Koponen, and R. Odgaard, eds. 1986. *Tanzania: Crisis and Struggle for Survival.* Uppsala: Scandinavian Institute of African Studies.

Boisot, Max, and John Child. 1988. "The Iron Law of Fiefs: Bureaucratic Failure and the Problem of Governance in the Chinese Economic Reforms." *Administrative Science Quarterly* 33(1988): 507–27.

Bongaarts, John. 1988. "Modelling the Spread of HIV and the Demographic Impact of AIDS in Africa." Centre for Policy Studies Working Papers, No. 140. New York: The Population Council.

Bongaarts, John, W. Parker Mauldin, and James F. Phillips. 1990. "The Demographic Impact of Family Planning Programs." *Studies in Family Planning* 21(6)6: 299–310.

Bonnen, James T. 1987. "U.S. Agricultural Development: Transforming Human Capital, Technology, and Institutions." In Bruce F. Johnston, Cassio Luiselli, Celso Cartas Contreras, and Roger D. Norton, eds., *U.S.–Mexico Relations: Agriculture and Rural Development*. Stanford, Calif.: Stanford University Press.

Booth, Anne. 1979. "The Agricultural Surveys, 1970–75." *Bulletin of Indonesian Economic Studies* 15(1): 45–68.

———. 1988. *Agricultural Development in Indonesia*. Sydney: Allen & Unwin.

———. 1989. "Indonesian Agricultural Development In Comparative Perspective." *World Development* 17(8): 1235–54.

Booth, Anne, and R. M. Sundrum. 1984. *Labour Absorption in Agriculture: Theoretical Analysis and Empirical Investigations*. Delhi: Oxford University Press.

Boserup, Ester. 1965. *Conditions of Agricultural Growth*. Chicago: Aldine.

Boswell F. C., and others. 1985. "Production, Marketing, and Use of Nitrogen Fertilizers." In O. P. Engelstad, ed., *Fertilizer Technology and Use*, 3d ed. Madison, Wis.: Soil Science Society of America.

Bottrall, A. F. 1977. "Evolution of Irrigation Associations in Taiwan." *Agricultural Administration* 4: 245–50.

Bouis, Howarth E. 1991. "Commentary: The Changing Focus of Economic Research on Nutrition." *IFPRI Report* 13(2): 1, 4.

Bouis, Howarth E., and Lawrence J. Haddad. 1990. "Effects of Agricultural Commercialization on Land Tenure, Household Resource Allocation, and Nutrition in the Philippines." Research Report 79. Washington, D.C.: International Food Policy Research Institute.

Bradshaw, York W. 1990. "Perpetuating Underdevelopment in Kenya: The Link between Agriculture, Class, and State." *African Studies Review* 33(1).

Brammer, Hugh. 1980. "Some Innovations Don't Wait for Experts: A Report on Applied Research by Bangladeshi Peasants." *Ceres* 13(12): 24–28.

Braverman, Avishay, and Joseph E. Stiglitz. 1986. "Cost-Sharing Arrangements under Sharecropping: Moral Hazard, Incentive Flexibility, and Risk." *American Journal of Agricultural Economics* 68(3): 642–52.

Brewster, John M. 1950. "The Machine Process in Agriculture and Industry." *Journal of Farm Economics* 32(1): 69–81.

———. 1967. "Traditional Social Structures as Barriers to Change." In H. M. Southworth and B. F. Johnston, eds., *Agricultural Development and Economic Growth*. Ithaca: Cornell University Press.

Brooks, Karen M. 1983. "Productivity in Soviet Agriculture." In D. Gale Johnson and Karen McConnell Brooks, eds., *Prospects for Soviet Agriculture in the 1980s*. Bloomington: Indiana University Press.

———. 1990. "Agricultural Reform in the Soviet Union." In Carl K. Eicher and John M. Staatz, eds., *Agricultural Development in the Third World*, 2d ed. Baltimore: Johns Hopkins University Press.

Brooks, Karen, J. Luis Guasch, Avishay Braverman, and Csaba Csaki. 1991. "Agriculture and the Transition to the Market." *Journal of Economic Perspectives* 5(4): 149–61.

Brothers, D. S., and L. Solís. 1966. *Mexican Financial Development*. Austin: University of Texas Press.

Brown, L. H. 1968. "Agriculture Change in Kenya: 1945–1960." *Food Research Institute Studies in Agricultural Economics, Trade, and Development*, vol. 8. Stanford, Calif.: Food Research Institute.

Bruton, Henry J. 1983. "The Search for a Development Economics." Research Memorandum No. 87. Williamstown, Mass.: Center for Development Economics, Williams College.

Buchanan, James M., and G. Tullock. 1983. *The Calculus of Consent*. Ann Arbor: University of Michigan Press.

Buvinic, Mayra, and Rekha Mehra. 1990. "Women and Agricultural Development." In Carl K. Eicher and John M. Statz, eds., *Agricultural Development in the Third World*, 2d ed. Baltimore: Johns Hopkins University Press.

Byerlee, Derek. 1987. "Maintaining the Momentum in Post–Green Revolution Agriculture: A Micro-Level Perpective from Asia." MSU International Development Paper No. 10. East Lansing: Michigan State University.

Byerlee, Derek, Larry Harrington, and Donald L. Winkelmann. 1982. "Farming Systems Research: Issues in Research Strategy and Technology Design." *American Journal of Agricultural Economics* 64(5): 897–904.

Byerlee, Derek, and Edith Hesse de Polanco. 1982. "The Rate and Sequence of Adoption of Improved Cereal Technologies: The Case of Rainfed Barley in the Mexican Altiplano." CYMMYT International Maize and Wheat Improvement Center, Working Paper No. 82/4. Mexico: CIMMYT.

Byerlee, Derek, and Jim Longmire. 1986. "Comparative Advantage and Policy Incentives for Wheat Production in Rainfed and Irrigated Areas of Mexico." CIMMYT Economic Program Working Paper No. 01/86. Mexico: CIMMYT.

Byerlee, Derek, and Robert Tripp. 1988. "Strengthening Linkages in Agricultural Research through a Farming Systems Perspective: The Role of Social Scientists." *Experimental Agriculture* 24: 137–51.

Cain, Mead. 1978. "The Household Life Cycle and Economic Mobility in Rural Bangladesh." *Population and Development Review* 4(3): 421–38.

Cairncross, Sandy. 1988. "Domestic Water Supply in Rural Africa." In Douglas Rimmer, ed., *Rural Transformation in Tropical Africa*. Athens: Ohio State University Press.

Caldwell, John C. 1978. "A Theory of Fertility: From High Plateau to Destabilization." *Population and Development Review* 4(4): 553–77.

———. 1991. "The Soft Underbelly of Development: Demographic Transition in Conditions of Limited Economic Change." In Stanley Fischer, Dennis de Tray, and Shekhar Shah, eds., *Proceedings of the World Bank Annual Conference on Development Economics 1990*. Washington, D.C.: World Bank.

Caldwell, John C., and Pat Caldwell. 1988. "Is the Asian Family Planning Program Model Suited to Africa?" *Studies in Family Planning* 19(1): 19–28.

———. 1989. "Changing Health Conditions." In Michael Reich and E. Marui, eds., *International Cooperation for Health: Problems, Prospects and Priorities*. Dover, Mass.: Auburn House.

———. 1990. "High Fertility in sub-Saharan Africa." *Scientific American* (May): 118–125.

Caldwell, John C., Pat Caldwell, and Pat Quiggin. 1989. "The Social Context of AIDS in Sub-Saharan Africa." *Population and Development Review* 15 (2): 185–234.

Calloway, Doris H., Suzanne P. Murphy, George H. Beaton, and David Lein. 1993. "Estimated Vitamin Intakes of Toddlers: Predicted Prevalence of Inadequacy of Village Populations in Egypt, Kenya, and Mexico." *American Journal of Clinical Nutrition* 58: 376–84.

Cardoso, Eliana A., and Santiago Levy. 1988. "Mexico." In Rudiger Dornbusch and F. L. Helmers, eds., *The Open Economy: Tools for Policymakers in Developing Countries*. New York: Oxford University Press.

Carruthers, Ian, and Colin Clark. 1981. *The Economics of Irrigation*. Liverpool: Liverpool University Press.

Cartas Contreras, Celso. 1987. "The Agricultural Sector's Contributions to the Import-Substituting Industrialization Process in Mexico." In Bruce F. Johnston, Cassio Luiselli, Celso Cartas Contreras, and Roger D. Norton, eds., *U.S.–Mexico Relations: Agriculture and Rural Development*. Stanford, Calif.: Stanford University Press.

Cartas Contreras, Celso, and L. M. Bassoco. 1987. "The Mexican Food System (SAM): An Agricultural Production Strategy." In Bruce F. Johnston, Cassio Luiselli, Celso Cartas Contreras, and Roger D. Norton, eds., *U.S.–Mexico Relations: Agriculture and Rural Development*. Stanford, Calif.: Stanford University Press.

Carter, Michael R. 1984. "Identification of the Inverse Relationship between Farm Size and Productivity: An Empirical Analysis of Peasant Agricultural Production." *Oxford Economic Papers* 36: 131–45.

Chakravarty, Sukahamoy. 1990. "Development Strategies for Growth with Equity: The South Asian Experience." *Asian Development Review* 8(1): 133–59.

Chambers, Robert. 1983. *Rural Development: Putting the Last First*. London: Longman.

Chambers, Robert, Arnold Pacey, and Lori Ann Thrupp. 1989. *Farmer First: Farmer Innovation and Agricultural Research*. London: Intermediate Technology Publications.

Champagne, Susan. 1989. "Evading Birth Restrictions in Rural China." Unpublished ms., Food Research Institute, Stanford University.

Chaudhri, Rajiv, and C. Peter Timmer. 1986. *The Impact of Changing Affluence on Diet and Demand Patterns for Agricultural Commodities*. World Bank Staff Working Paper No. 785. Washington, D.C.: World Bank.

Chege, Michael. 1987. "The Political Economy of Agrarian Change in Central Kenya." In Michael G. Schatzberg, ed., *The Political Economy of Kenya*. New York: Praeger.

Chen, Chao-chen. 1967. "Land Reform and Agricultural Development in Taiwan." Paper presented at the Conference on Economic Development of Taiwan. Taipei, Taiwan: China Council on Sino-American Cooperation in the Humanities and Social Science.

Chen, Marty. 1989. "A Sectoral Approach to Promoting Women's Work: Lessons from India." *World Development* 17(7).

Chenery, Hollis B. 1981. "Restructuring the World Economy: Round II." *Foreign Affairs* 59(5): 1102–20.

Chenery, Hollis B., and T. N. Srinivasan, eds. 1988. *Handbook of Development Economics*, vol. 1. Amsterdam: North-Holland.

Chenery, Hollis B., and Lance Taylor. 1968. "Development Patterns: Among Countries and over Time." *Review of Economics and Statistics* 50(4): 401.

Cheng, Tun-jen. 1986. "Sequencing and Implementing Development Strategies: Korea and Taiwan." Paper prepared for a conference on Development Strategies in Latin America and East Asia: A Cross-Regional Comparison, May 4–6. San Diego: Center for U.S.–Mexican Studies, University of California, and La Jolla, Calif.: Institute of the Americas.

Cheung, Steven N. S. 1968. "Private Property Rights and Sharecropping." *Journal of Political Economy* 76(6): 1107–1122.

Chevalier, F. 1967. "The Ejido and Political Stability in Mexico." In C. Veliz, ed., *The Politics of Conformity in Latin America*. London: Oxford University Press.

Chinn, D. L. 1982. "Review Article: Growth, Equity, and Gini Coefficients: The Case of Taiwan." *Economic Development and Cultural Change* 30(4): 871–86.

Christensen, Raymond P. 1968. *Taiwan's Agricultural Development: Its Relevance for Developing Countries Today*. Economic Research Service, Foreign Agricultural Economic Report No. 39. Washington, D.C.: U.S. Department of Agriculture.

Chuta, E., and Carl Liedholm. 1979. *Rural Non-Farm Employment: A Review of the State of the Art*. MSU Rural Development Paper No. 4. East Lansing: Michigan State University.

——. 1985. *Employment and Growth in Small Industry: Empirical Evidence and Assessment from Sierra Leone*. London: Macmillan.

CIMMYT/IITA. 1990. "Realizing the Potential of Maize in Sub-Saharan Africa." In CIMMYT, *World Maize: Facts and Trends 1989/90*. Mexico City: CIMMYT (International Center for Maize and Wheat Improvement).

Cleland, John, and Christopher Wilson. 1987. "Demand Theories of the Fertility Transition: An Iconoclastic View." *Population Studies* 41: 5–30.

Cochrane, Susan H. 1991. "Comment on 'The Soft Underbelly of Development' by Caldwell." In Stanley Fischer, Dennis de Tray, and Shekhar Shah, eds., *Proceedings of the World Bank Annual Conference on Development Economics 1990*. Washington, D.C.: The World Bank.

Cochrane, Willard W. 1979. *The Development of American Agriculture: A Historical Analysis*. Minneapolis: University of Minnesota Press.

Collier, Paul. 1983. "Malfunctioning of African Rural Factor Markets: Theory and a Kenyan Example." *Oxford Bulletin of Economics and Statistics* 45(2): 141–71.

——. 1989. "Contractual Constraints on Labour Exchange in Rural Kenya." *International Labour Review* 128(6).

——. 1991. "From Critic to Secular God: The World Bank and Africa: A Commentary upon sub-Saharan Africa: From Crisis to Sustainable Growth." *African Affairs* 90: 111–17.

Collier, Paul, and Deepak Lal. 1986. *Labour and Poverty in Kenya*. Oxford: Clarendon.

Collier, Paul, S. Radwan, and S. Wangwe. 1986. *Labour and Poverty in Rural Tanzania: Ujamaa and Rural Development in the United Republic of Tanzania.* Oxford: Clarendon.

Commission on Health Research for Development. 1990. *Health Research: Essential Link to Equity in Development.* New York: Oxford University Press.

Cornia, Giovanni Andrea. 1985. "Farm Size, Land Yields, and the Agricultural Production Function: An Analysis of Fifteen Developing Countries." *World Development* 13(4): 513–34.

Cortes, M., M. A. Berry, and A. Ishag. 1985. *What Makes for Success in Small and Medium Scale Enterprises: The Evidence from Colombia.* Washington, D.C.: World Bank.

Coulson, Andrew. 1982. *Tanzania: A Political Economy.* Oxford: Clarendon.

Court, David. 1984. "The Education System as a Response to Inequality." In J. D. Barkan, ed., *Politics and Public Policy in Kenya and Tanzania,* rev. ed. New York: Praeger.

———. 1986. "The Educational System as a Response to Inequality." In Tony Killick, ed., *Papers on the Kenyan Economy: Performance, Problems, and Policies.* London: Heinemann Educational Books.

Cownie, John. 1969. "Appendix Note" to Kazushi Ohkawa and Bruce F. Johnston, "The Transferability of the Japanese Pattern of Modernizing Traditional Agriculture." In Erik Thorbecke, ed., *The Role of Agriculture in Economic Development.* New York: National Bureau of Economic Research.

Coxhead, Ian A. 1992. "Environment-Specific Rates and Biases of Technical Change in Agriculture." *American Journal of Agricultural Economics* (August): 601–3.

Dahl, Robert A., and Charles E. Lindblom. 1953. *Politics, Economics, and Welfare.* New York: Harper.

Dalrymple, Dana G. 1986a. *Development and Spread of High-Yielding Rice Varieties in Developing Countries.* Washington, D.C.: Bureau for Science and Technology, U.S. Agency for International Development (AID).

———. 1986b. *Development and Spread of High-Yielding Wheat Varieties in Developing Countries.* Washington, D.C.: Bureau of Science and Technology, U.S. Agency for International Development (AID).

Danhof, Clarence H. 1944. "Agricultural Technology to 1880." In Harold F. Williamson, ed., *The Growth of the American Economy.* New York: Prentice-Hall.

———. 1969. *Change in Agriculture: The Northern United States, 1820–1870.* Cambridge, Mass.: Harvard University Press.

Das Gupta, Jyotirindra. 1981. *Authority, Priority, and Human Development.* Delhi: Oxford University Press.

David, C. C., and R. Barker. 1978. "Modern Rice Varieties and Fertilizer Consumption." In *Economic Consequences of the New Rice Technology.* Los Banos, Philippines: International Rice Research Institute.

Day, Richard H. 1967. "The Economics of Technological Change and the Demise of the Sharecropper." *American Economic Review* 57(3): 427–49.

de Janvry, Alain. 1978. "Social Structure and Biased Technical Change in Argentine Agriculture." In Hans P. Binswanger, Vernon W. Ruttan, and others, eds., *Induced Innovation: Technology, Institutions, and Development.* Baltimore: Johns Hopkins University Press.

——. 1981. *The Agrarian Question and Reformism in Latin America*. Baltimore: Johns Hopkins University Press.

——. 1983. "Why Do Governments Do What They Do in the Case of Food Price Policy?" In D. Gale Johnson and G. Edward Schuh, eds., *The Role of Markets in the World Food Economy*. Boulder, Colo.: Westview.

de Janvry, Alain, and Jean-Jacques Dethier. 1985. *Technological Innovation in Agriculture: The Political Economy of Its Rate and Bias*. Consultative Group on International Agricultural Research, Study Paper No. 1. Washington, D.C.: World Bank.

de Janvry, Alain, and Elisabeth Sadoulet. 1989. "A Study in Resistance to Institutional Change: The Lost Game of Latin American Land Reform." *World Development* 17(9): 1397–1407.

——. 1990. "Investment Strategies to Combat Rural Poverty in Latin America." In Carl K. Eicher and John M. Staatz, eds., *Agricultural Development in the Third World*, 2d ed. Baltimore: Johns Hopkins University Press.

de Janvry, Alain, Elizabeth Sadoulet, and Marcel Fafchamps. 1989. "Agrarian Structure, Technological Innovations, and the State." In P. Bardhan, ed., *The Economic Theory of Agrarian Institutions*. Oxford: Clarendon Press.

Delgado, Christopher L. 1988. "Setting Priorities for Accelerating Food Production in sub-Saharan Africa." In *The Emerging World Food Situation and Challenges for Development Policy*. IFPRI Policy Briefs. Washington, D.C.: IFPRI.

Demeny, Paul. 1986. "Population and the Invisible Hand." *Demography* 23(4): 473–87.

Deolalikar, Anil B. 1981. "The Inverse Relationship between Productivity and Farm Size: A Test Using Regional Data from India." *American Journal of Agricultural Economics* 63(2): 275–79.

Dernberger, Robert F. 1986. "Economic Policy and Reform." In *China's Economy Looks toward the Year 2000*, vol. 1. Washington, D.C.: United States Government Printing Office.

DeVos, George A. 1965. "Achievement Orientation, Social Self-Identity, and Japanese Economic Growth." *Asian Survey* 5(12): 575–89.

Dixit, Avinash, and Barry Nalebuff. 1991. *Thinking Strategically. The Competitive Edge in Business, Politics, and Everyday Life*. New York: Norton.

Dong, Fureng. 1987. "Rural Reform, Non-Farm Development, and Rural Modernization in China." Washington, D.C.: World Bank. Paper translated for the Economic Development Institute.

Dore, R. P. 1964. "Latin America and Japan Compared." In J. J. Johnson, ed., *Continuity and Change in Latin America*. Stanford, Calif.: Stanford University Press.

——. 1965a. "The Legacy of Tokugawa Education." In M. B. Jansen, ed., *Changing Japanese Attitudes toward Modernization*. Princeton: Princeton University Press.

——. 1965b. *Education in Tokugawa Japan*. Berkeley: University of California Press.

Dorner, Peter, and William C. Thiesenhusen. 1990. "Selected Land Reforms in East and Southeast Asia: Their Origins and Impacts." *Asian-Pacific Economic Literature* 4(1): 65–95.

Dovring, Folke. 1959. "The Share of Agriculture in a Growing Population." *FAO Monthly Bulletin of Agricultural Economics and Statistics* 8(8).

Dreze, Jean, and Amartya Sen. 1989. *Hunger and Public Action*. Oxford: Clarendon.

Due, Jean M. 1991. "Policies to Overcome the Negative Effects of Structural Adjustment Programs on African Female-Headed Households." In Christina H. Gladwin, ed., *Structural Adjustment and African Women Farmers*. Gainesville: University of Florida Press.

Duff, Bart. 1987. "Changes in Small Farm Paddy Threshing Technology in Thailand and the Philippines." Unpublished manuscript.

Easterlin, R. A. 1975. "An Economic Framework for Fertility Analysis." *Studies of Family Planning* 6: 54–63.

——. 1978. "The Economics and Sociology of Fertility: A Synthesis." In C. Tilley, ed., *Historical Studies of Changing Fertility*. Princeton: Princeton University Press.

Easterlin, R. A., and E. Crimmins. 1985. *The Fertility Revolution: A Supply-Demand Analysis*. Chicago: University of Chicago Press.

Easterlin, R. A., R. A. Pollak, and M. C. Wachter. 1980. "Toward a More General Economic Model of Fertility Determination: Endogenous Preferences and Natural Fertility." In R. A. Easterlin, ed., *Population and Economic Change in Developing Countries*. Chicago: University of Chicago Press.

Eckstein, Shlomo, Gordon Donald, Douglas Horton, and Thomas Carroll. 1978. *Land Reform in Latin America: Bolivia, Chile, Mexico, Peru, and Venezuela*. Staff Working Paper No. 275. Washington, D.C.: World Bank.

Economic Research Bureau. 1988. *Tanzania Economic Trends: A Quarterly Review of the Economy*, vol. 1, no. 1. Dar es Salaam: University of Dar es Salaam and Ministry of Finance, Economic Affairs, and Planning.

Economist, The. 1987. "A Survey of China's Economy: The World Turned Upside Down." 304 (7509; August 1–7): 1–22.

——. 1991a. "The Green Counter-Revolution." 319 (7703; April 20): 85–86.

——. 1991b. "Going against the Grain in China." 319 (7711; June 15): 35.

Eicher, Carl K. 1990. "Africa's Food Battles." In Carl K. Eicher and John M. Staatz, eds., *Agricultural Development in the Third World*, 2d ed. Baltimore: Johns Hopkins University Press.

Eicher, Carl K., and John M. Staatz, eds. 1990. *Agricultural Development in the Third World*, 2d ed. Baltimore: Johns Hopkins University Press.

Ellis, Frank. 1983. "Agricultural Marketing and Peasant–State Transfers in Tanzania." *Journal of Peasant Studies* 10(4): 214–42.

——. 1988. *Peasant Economics: Farm Households and Agrarian Development*. New York: Cambridge University Press.

Elson, R. E. 1984. *Javanese Peasants and the Colonial Sugar Industry: Impact and Change in an East Java Residency, 1830–1940*. Singapore: Oxford University Press.

Engelstad, O. P., ed. 1985. *Fertilizer Technology and Use*. Madison: Soil Science Society of America.

Ericson, R. E. 1991. "The Classical Soviet-Type Economy: Nature of the System and Implications for Reform." *The Journal of Economic Perspectives* 5(4): 11–27.

Evenson, Robert E. 1978. "The Organization of Research to Improve Crops and Animals in Low Income Countries." In T. W. Schultz, ed., *Distortions of Agricultural Incentives*. Bloomington: Indiana University Press.

Ewell, Peter T., and T. T. Poleman. 1979. "Uxpanapa: Resettlement and Agricultural Development in the Mexican Tropics." Agricultural Economics Staff Paper No. 79-10. Ithaca: Department of Agricultural Economics, Cornell University.

Falcon, Walter P. 1970. "The Green Revolution: Second-Generation Problems." *American Journal of Agricultural Economics* 52: 698–710.

Farrington, John. 1988. "Farmer Participatory Research: Editorial Introduction." *Experimental Agriculture* 24(3): 269–79.

Feder, Gershon, and R. Noronha. 1987. "Land Rights Systems and Agricultural Development in sub-Saharan Africa." *World Bank Research Observer* 2(2): 143–69.

Feder, Gershon, and Tongroj Onchan. 1987. "Land Ownership Security and Farm Investment in Thailand." *American Journal of Agricultural Economics* 69(2): 311–20.

Feder, Gershon, Tongroj Onchan, Yongyuth Chalamwong, and Chira Hongladarom. 1988. *Land Policies and Farm Productivity in Thailand.* Baltimore: Johns Hopkins University Press.

Fertilizer Association of India. 1973. *Fertilizer Statistics, 1971–72.* New Delhi: Fertilizer Association of India.

Field, J. O. 1987. "Multisectoral Nutrition Planning: A Post-Mortem." *Food Policy* 12(1) (February): 15–28.

Fisseha, Y. 1982. "Management Characteristics, Practices, and Performance in the Small-Scale Manufacturing Enterprises: Jamaica Milieu." Ph.D. diss., Department of Agricultural Economics, Michigan State University.

Fliginger, C. John, E. E. Gavett, L. A. Powell, and R. P. Jenkins. 1969. *Supplying U.S. Markets with Fresh Winter Produce: Capabilities of U.S. and Mexican Production Areas.* Economic Research Service, Agricultural Economic Report No. 154. Washington, D.C.: U.S. Department of Agriculture.

Flores, Edmundo. 1963. "Land Reform and the Alliance for Progress." Center for International Studies Memorandum N. 27. Princeton: Princeton University.

Food and Agriculture Organization of the United Nations (FAO). 1978. *Annual Fertilizer Review 1977.* Rome: FAO.

——. 1981. *1970 World Census of Agriculture: Analysis and International Comparison of Results.* Rome: FAO.

——. 1986. *World-Wide Estimates and Projections of the Agricultural and Non-Agricultural Population Segments, 1950–2025.* ESS/Misc 186-2. Rome: FAO.

——. 1988. *FAO Production Yearbook 1987,* vol. 41. Rome: FAO.

——. 1989. *FAO Production Yearbook 1988,* vol. 42. Rome: FAO.

——. 1991. *FAO Production Yearbook 1990,* vol. 44. Rome: FAO.

——. 1992. *FAO Production Yearbook 1991,* vol. 45. Rome: FAO.

Forsyth, David, Norman McBain, and Robert Solomon. 1982. "Technical Rigidity and Appropriate Technology in Less Developed Countries." In F. Stewart and J. James, eds., *The Economics of New Technology in Developing Countries.* Boulder, Colo.: Westview Press.

Frank, Odile. 1987. "The Demand for Fertility Control in sub-Saharan Africa." *Studies in Family Planning* 18(4): 181–201.

Franzel, Steven C. 1984. "Modeling Farmers' Decisions in a Farming Systems Research Exercise: The Adoption of an Improved Maize Variety in Kirinyaga District, Kenya." *Human Organization* 43(3): 199–207.

Freebairn, Donald K. 1977. *Changes in Ejidal Farming in Northwest Mexico's Modernized Agriculture: The Quechehueca Collective, 1938–1968.* Ames: The Iowa State University Press.

Freedman, Ronald. 1987. "The Contribution of Social Science Research to Population Policy and Family Planning Program Effectiveness." *Studies in Family Planning* 18(2): 57–82.

Freithaler, William O. 1968. *Mexico's Foreign Trade and Economic Development.* New York: Praeger.

Friedland, William H. 1969. "A Sociological Approach to Modernization." In Chandler Morse and others, eds., *Modernization by Design.* Ithaca: Cornell University Press.

Gamson, William A. 1968. *Power and Discontent.* Homewood, Ill.: Dorsey Press.

Geertz, Clifford. 1963. *Agricultural Involution: The Processes of Ecological Change in Indonesia.* Berkeley: University of California Press.

Gelb, Alan, and Associates. 1988. *Oil Windfalls: Blessing or Curse?* New York: Oxford University Press.

George, Aurelia, and E. Saxon. 1986. "The Politics of Agricultural Protection in Japan." In K. Anderson and Y. Hayami, eds., *The Political Economy of Agricultural Protection: East Asia in International Perspective.* Sydney: Allen & Unwin.

Gerein, Nancy M., and David A. Ross. 1991. "Is Growth Monitoring Worthwhile?" *Social Science and Medicine* 32(6): 667–75.

Gerhart, John. 1975. *The Diffusion of Hybrid Maize in Western Kenya: Abridged by CIMMYT.* Mexico City: CIMMYT.

Gillis, Malcolm, Dwight Perkins, Michael Roemer, and Donald Snodgrass. 1987. *Economics of Development.* New York: Norton.

Gladwin, Christina. 1979. "Cognitive Strategies and Adoption Decisions: A Case Study of Nonadoption of an Agronomic Recommendation." *Economic Development and Cultural Change* 28(1): 155–73.

Godkin, Lynn, and Carl B. Montano. 1991. "Organizational Learning: Philippine Agrarian Reform under Martial Law." *Organization Studies* 12(1): 29–47.

Gold, Thomas B. 1986. *State and Society in the Taiwan Miracle.* Armonk, New York: M. E. Sharpe.

Goldman, Richard H., and Lyn Squire. 1982. "Technical Change, Labor Use, and Income Distribution in the Muda Irrigation Project." *Economic Development and Cultural Change* 30(4): 753–75.

Goodell, Grace E. 1985. "The Importance of Political Participation for Sustained Capitalist Development." *Archives of European Sociology* 26: 93–127.

———. 1986. *The Elementary Structures of Political Life: Rural Development in Pahlavi Iran.* New York: Oxford University Press.

Gorbachev, Mikhail. 1987. *Perestroika: New Thinking for Our Country and the World.* New York: Harper & Row.

Gotsch, Carl H. 1972. "Technical Change and the Distribution of Income in Rural Areas." *American Journal of Agricultural Economics* 54(2): 236–41 and 326–41.

Government of India. 1961. *Diesel Engines.* New Delhi: Development Commission (Small Scale Industry).

Gray, Clive, and Andre Martens. 1983. "The Political Economy of the Recurrent Cost Problem in the West African Sahel." *World Development* 11(2): 101–18.

Greenberg, M. H. 1970. *Bureaucracy and Development: A Mexican Case Study.* Lexington, Mass.: Heath.

Grindle, Merilee S. 1977. *Bureaucrats, Politicians, and Peasants in Mexico: A Case Study in Public Policy.* Berkeley: University of California Press.

———, ed. 1980. *Politics and Policy Implementation in the Third World.* Princeton: Princeton University Press.

———. 1986a. "The Question of Political Feasibility: Approaches to the Study of Policy Space." E.E.P.A. Discussion Paper No. 3. Cambridge: Harvard Institute for International Development.

———. 1986b. *State and Countryside: Development Policy and Agrarian Politics in Latin America.* Baltimore: Johns Hopkins University Press.

———. 1988. *Searching for Rural Development: Labor Migration and Employment in Mexico.* Ithaca: Cornell University Press.

———. 1990. "Agrarian Reform in Mexico: A Cautionary Tale." In Roy L. Prosterman, Mary N. Temple, and Timothy N. Hanstad, eds., *Agrarian Reform and Grassroots Development: Ten Case Studies.* Boulder, Colo.: Lynne Reinner.

———. 1991. "The New Political Economy: Positive Economics and Negative Politics." In Gerald M. Meier, ed., *Politics and Policymaking in Developing Countries.* San Francisco: ICS Press.

Hagen, E. E. 1962. *On the Theory of Social Change.* Homewood, Ill.: Dorsey Press.

Haggblade, Steven, J. Hammer, and P. Hazell. 1991. "Modelling Agricultural Growth Multipliers." *American Journal of Agricultural Economics* (May): 361–74.

Haggblade, Steven, and Peter Hazell. 1989. "Agricultural Technology and Farm-Nonfarm Growth Linkages." *Journal of Agricultural Economics* 3: 345–64.

Haggblade, Steven, Peter Hazell, and James Brown. 1989. "Farm–Nonfarm Linkages in Rural sub-Saharan Africa." *World Development* 17(8): 1173–1201.

Haggblade, Steven, and Carl Liedholm. 1992. "Agriculture, Rural Labor Markets, and the Evolution of the Rural Nonfarm Economy." In G. H. Peters, ed., *Sustainable Agricultural Development: The Role of International Cooperation.* Hants, UK: Dartmouth Publishing.

Haggblade, Steven, Carl Liedholm, and D. C. Mead. 1986. "The Effect of Policy and Policy Reforms on Non-Agricultural Enterprises and Employment in Developing Countries: A Review of Past Experiences." In "Employment and Enterprise Policy Analysis Discussion Paper #1." Cambridge: Harvard Institute for International Development.

Haile-Mariam, Teketel. 1973. "The Production, Marketing, and Economic Impact of Coffee in Ethiopia." Ph.D. diss., Stanford University.

Hamilton, Nora. 1982. *The Limits of State Autonomy: Post Revolutionary Mexico.* Princeton: Princeton University Press.

Hansen, R. D. 1971. *The Politics of Mexican Development.* Baltimore: Johns Hopkins University Press.

Harberger, A. C. 1988. "The Economist and the Real World." Remarks on the occasion of being awarded the degree of Doctor Honoris Causa, Pontifical Catholic University of Chile.

Harding, Harry. 1987. *China's Second Revolution: Reform After Mao.* Washington, D.C.: The Brookings Institution.

Harris, John. 1988. "Kenya and Tanzania: Has Ideology Made a Difference?" Draft manuscript, Boston University.

Hart, Keith. 1982. *The Political Economy of West African Agriculture.* Cambridge: Cambridge University Press.

Hawkins, A. M. 1986. "Can Africa Industrialize?" In Robert J. Berg and J. S. Whitaker, eds., *Strategies for African Development.* Berkeley: University of California Press.

Hayami, Yujiro. 1972. "Rice Policy in Japan's Economic Development." *American Journal of Agricultural Economics* 54(1): 19–31.

——. 1975. *A Century of Agricultural Growth in Japan*. Minneapolis and Tokyo: University of Minnesota Press and Tokyo University Press.

——. 1984. "Assessment of the Green Revolution." In Carl K. Eicher and John M. Staatz, eds., *Agricultural Development in the Third World*. Baltimore: Johns Hopkins University Press.

——. 1988. *Japan's Agriculture under Siege: The Political Economy of Agricultural Policies*. New York: St. Martin's Press.

——. 1991. "Land Reform." In Gerald M. Meier, ed., *Politics and Policy Making in Developing Countries*. San Francisco: ICS Press.

Hayami, Yujiro, and Masao Kikuchi. 1982. *Asian Village Economy at the Crossroads: An Economic Approach to Institutional Change*. Tokyo and Baltimore: University of Tokyo Press and Johns Hopkins University Press.

Hayami, Yujiro, Ma. Agnes R. Quisumbing, and Lourdes S. Adriano. 1990. *Toward an Alternative Land Reform Paradigm*. Manila: Ateneo de Manila University Press.

Hayami, Yujiro, and Vernon W. Ruttan. 1971. *Agricultural Development: An International Perspective*, 1st ed. Baltimore: Johns Hopkins University Press.

——. 1985. *Agricultural Development: An International Perspective*, 2d ed. Baltimore: Johns Hopkins University Press.

Hazell, Peter B. R., and C. Ramasamy. 1991. *The Green Revolution Reconsidered: The Impact of High-Yield Rice Varieties in South India*. Baltimore: Johns Hopkins University Press.

Hazell, Peter B. R., and Ailsa Roell. 1983. *Rural Growth Linkages: Household Expenditure Patterns in Malaysia and Nigeria*. Research Report 41. Washington, D.C.: International Food Policy Research Institute.

Hazelwood, Arthur. 1979. *The Economy of Kenya: The Kenyatta Era*. London: Oxford University Press.

Hemmi, Kenzo. 1969. "Primary Product Exports and Economic Development: The Case of Silk." In Kazushi Ohkawa, Bruce F. Johnston, and Hiromitsu Kaneda, eds., *Agriculture and Economic Growth: Japan's Experience*. Tokyo: Tokyo University Press.

Henderson, David. 1986. *Innocence and Design: The Influence of Economic Ideas on Policy*. New York: Basil Blackwell.

Henderson, D. R., G. R. Perkins, and D. M. Bell. 1972. *Simulating the Fertilizer Industry: Data*. Agricultural Economics Report No. 190. East Lansing: Michigan State University.

Herdt, R. W., and A. M. Mandac. 1981. "Modern Technology and Economic Efficiency of Philippine Rice Farmers." *Economic Development and Cultural Change* 29(2): 377–99.

Hertford, Reed. 1970. "Mexico: Its Sources of Increased Agricultural Output." In *Economic Progress of Agriculture in Developing Nations*. Economic Research Service, Foreign Agricultural Economic Report No. 59. Washington, D.C.: U.S. Department of Agriculture.

Hesselmark, Olof. 1975. "Appendix II. The 1974 Kenya Maize Farmers Survey." In John Gerhart, ed., *The Diffusion of Hybrid Maize in Western Kenya—Abridged by CIMMYT*. Mexico City: CIMMYT.

Hewitt de Alcantara, Cynthia. 1976. *Modernizing Mexican Agriculture: Socioeconomic Implications of Technological Change, 1940–1970*. Geneva: United Nations Research Institute for Social Development.

Heyer, Judith. 1976. "Achievements, Problems, and Prospects in the Agricultural Sector." In Judith Heyer, J. K. Maitha, and W. M. Senga, eds., *Agricultural Development in Kenya: An Economic Assessment*. London: Oxford University Press.

Heyer, Judith, J. K. Maitha, and W. M. Senga, eds. 1976. *Agricultural Development in Kenya: An Economic Assessment*. London: Oxford University Press.

Heyer, Judith, and J. K. Waweru. 1976. "The Development of the Small Farm Areas." In Judith Heyer, J. K. Maitha, and W. M. Senga, eds., *Agricultural Development in Kenya: An Economic Assessment*. London: Oxford University Press.

Hicks, Sir John R. 1932. *The Theory of Wages*. London: Macmillan.

Higgins, Benjamin. 1984. "Jan Boeke and the Doctrine of the 'Little Push'." *Bulletin of Indonesian Economic Studies* 20(3): 55–69.

Higgins, G. M., G. Fischer, and others. 1982. *Potential Population Supporting Capacities of Lands in the Developing World*. FAO, IIASA, UNFPA, Technical Report of Project INT/75/P13 "Land Resources for Populations of the Future." Rome: FAO.

Hinton, William. 1966. *Fanshen: A Documentary of Revolution in a Chinese Village*. New York and London: Monthly Review Press.

——. 1970. *Iron Oxen: A Documentary of Revolution in Chinese Farming*. New York: Vintage Books.

——. 1990. *The Great Reversal: The Privatization of China, 1978–1989*. New York: Monthly Review Press.

Hirschman, Albert O. 1967. *Development Projects Observed*. Washington, DC: The Brookings Institution.

——. 1970. *Exit, Voice and Loyalty*. Cambridge, MA: Harvard University Press.

——. 1971. *A Bias for Hope*. New Haven, CT: Yale University Press.

Hirschmeier, Johannes, and Tsunehiko Yui. 1975. *The Development of Japanese Business, 1600–1973*. London: George Allen & Unwin.

Ho, Samuel P. S. 1971. "The Development Policy of the Japanese Colonial Government in Taiwan, 1895–1945." In Gustav Ranis, ed., *Government and Economic Development*. New Haven, CT: Yale University Press.

——. 1980. "Small Scale Enterprises in Korea and Taiwan." World Bank Staff Working Paper No. 384. Washington, D.C.: World Bank.

Holmquist, Frank. 1984. "Class Structure, Peasant Participation, and Rural Self-Help." In J. D. Barkan, ed., *Politics and Public Policy in Kenya and Tanzania*, rev. ed. New York: Praeger.

Hopkins, Raymond F. 1988. "Political Calculations in Subsidizing Food." In Per Pinstrup-Andersen, ed., *Food Subsidies in Developing Countries*. Baltimore: Johns Hopkins University Press.

Hossain, Mahabub. 1977. "Farm Size, Tenancy, and Land Productivity: An Analysis of Farm-Level Data in Bangladesh Agriculture." *The Bangladesh Review of Development Studies* 5(3).

——. 1988. *Nature and Impact of the Green Revolution in Bangladesh*. Research Report 67. Washington, D.C.: International Food Policy Research Institute.

House, William F., and T. Killick. 1981. "Inequality and Poverty in the Rural Economy, and the Influence of Some Aspects of Policy." In Tony Killick, ed., *Papers on the Kenyan Economy: Performance, Problems and Policies.* London: Heinemann Educational Books.

Howell, John, A. Hewitt, and K. Anthony. 1988. *UK Agricultural Aid to Kenya, Tanzania, and Malawi.* Evaluation Report No. 388. London: Overseas Development Administration.

Hsieh, S. C. 1990. "JCRR/ADB Experience and Approaches to Economic Development in LDCS." Paper presented at a seminar held at the Department of Agricultural and Applied Economics, University of Minnesota, St. Paul, September 26.

Hsieh, S. C., and T. H. Lee. 1966. "Agricultural Development and Its Contributions to Economic Growth in Taiwan." Joint Commission on Rural Reconstruction, Economic Digest Series, No. 17. Taipei: Joint Commission on Rural Reconstruction.

Hsu, F. L. K. 1954. "Cultural Factors." In H. G. Williamson and J. A. Butterick, eds., *Economic Development, Principles and Patterns.* Englewood Cliffs, N.J.: Prentice-Hall.

Huke, Robert E. 1982. *Rice Area by Type of Culture: South, Southeast, and East Asia.* Los Banos, Philippines: International Rice Research Institute.

Hull, Terence H. 1990. "Recent Trends in Sex Ratios in China." *Population and Development Review* 16(1): 63–83.

Hyden, Goran. 1980. *Beyond Ujamaa in Tanzania: Underdevelopment and an Uncaptured Peasantry.* Berkeley: University of California Press.

——. 1983. *No Shortcuts to Progress: African Development Management in Perspective.* Berkeley: University of California Press.

——. 1984. "Administration and Public Policy." In J. D. Barkan, ed., *Politics and Public Policy in Kenya and Tanzania*, rev. ed. New York: Praeger.

——. 1986. "African Social Structure and Economic Development." In Robert J. Berg and J. S. Whitaker, eds., *Strategies for African Development.* Berkeley: University of California Press.

India. 1985. *All-India Rural Credit Survey, vols. 1–3.* Bombay: Reserve Bank of India.

International Fertilizer Development Center. 1992. *Fertilizer Situation in Developing Countries 1992.* Muscle Shoals, Ala.: TVA.

International Monetary Fund (IMF). 1982–89. *International Financial Statistics Yearbook*, vol. 42. Washington, D.C.: IMF.

——. 1986. *Government Finance Statistics Yearbook*, vol. 10. Washington, D.C.: IMF.

International Rice Research Institute (IRRI). 1986. *Small Farm Equipment for Developing Countries.* Manila. IRRI.

International Workshop. 1988. "Development in the Arid and Semi-Arid Areas of Kenya." Report of an international workshop convened at Cornell University at the request of the Government of Kenya. Ithaca: Cornell University.

Inukai, Ichirou, and A. R. Tussing. 1967. "Kogyo Iken: Japan's Ten Year Plan, 1884." *Economic Development and Cultural Change* 16(1): 51–71.

Ireson, W. R. 1987. "Landholding, Agricultural Modernization, and Income Concentration: A Mexican Example." *Economic Development and Cultural Change* 35(2): 351–66.

Jahnke, Hanse, D. Kirschke, and J. Lagemann. 1987. *The Impact of Agricultural Research in Tropical Africa: A Study of the Collaboration between the*

International and National Research Systems. CGIAR Study Paper No. 21. Washington, D.C.: World Bank.

Jakarta Post. 1989. "Oil Price Slump Prompts Economic Reforms." February 1, p. 4.

Jamison, Dean T., and Lawrence J. Lau. 1982. Farmer Education and Farm Efficiency. Baltimore: Johns Hopkins University Press.

Jamison, Dean T., and A. Piazza. 1987. "China's Food and Nutrition Planning." In J. P. Gittinger, J. Leslie, and C. Hoisington, eds., Food Policy: Integrating Supply, Distribution, and Consumption. EDI Series in Economic Development, Published for the World Bank. Baltimore: Johns Hopkins University Press.

Jamison, Dean T., W. Henry Mosely, Anthony R. Measham, and José-Luis Bobadilla, eds. 1993. Disease Control Priorities in Developing Countries. New York: Oxford University Press.

Jayasuriya, S. K., and R. T. Shand. 1986. "Technical Change and Labor Absorption in Asian Agriculture: Some Emerging Trends." World Development (14)3: 415–28.

Jodha, N. S. 1986. "Common Property Resources and Rural Poor in Dry Regions of India." Economic and Political Weekly 21(27): 1169–81.

Johansson, Sten, and Ola Nygren. 1991. "The Missing Girls of China: A New Demographic Account." Population and Development Review 17(1): 35–51.

Johnson, D. Gale. 1971. "Soviet Agriculture Revisited." American Journal of Agricultural Economics 53(2): 257–64.

———. 1983. "Part I: Policies and Performance in Soviet Agriculture" and "Conclusion: Soviet Agriculture and the Soviet Economy." In D. G. Johnson and K. Brooks, eds., Prospects for Soviet Agriculture in the 1980s. Bloomington: Indiana University Press.

———. 1987. "Agricultural Policy Reforms in the USSR and The People's Republic of China." Paper No. 87:28, Chicago: Office of Agricultural Economics Research, University of Chicago.

Johnson, Harry G. 1969. "Comparative Cost and Commercial Policy Theory in a Developing World Economy." The Pakistan Development Review (Suppl. Spring): 1–33.

Johnston, Bruce F. 1951. "Agricultural Productivity and Economic Growth." Journal of Political Economy (December): 498–513.

———. 1962. "Agricultural Development and Economic Transformation: A Comparative Study of the Japanese Experience." Food Research Institute Studies 3(3): 223–76.

———. 1964. "Changes in Agricultural Productivity and Patterns of Production in Tropical Africa." In M. Herskovits and Mitchell Harwitz, eds., Economic Transition in Africa. Evanston, Ill.: Northwestern University Press.

———. 1966. "Agriculture and Economic Development: The Relevance of the Japanese Experience." Food Research Institute Studies, 6(3): 251–312.

———. 1977. "Food, Health, and Population in Development." Journal of Economic Literature (September): 879–907.

———. 1983. "The Design and Redesign of Strategies for Agricultural Development: Mexico's Experience Revisited." In C. W. Reynolds and C. Tello, eds., U.S.–Mexico Relations: Economic and Social Aspects. Stanford, Calif.: Stanford University Press.

———. 1987. "The Implications of Rural Development for Employment and Welfare: Experience in the United States, Mexico, Japan, and Taiwan." In Bruce F.

Johnston, Cassio Luiselli, Celso Cartas Contreras, and Roger D. Norton, eds., *U.S.–Mexico Relations: Agriculture and Rural Development*. Stanford, Calif.: Stanford University Press.

——. 1989a. "The Political Economy of Agricultural Development in the Soviet Union and China." *Food Research Institute Studies* 21(2): 97–137.

——. 1989b. "The Political Economy of Agricultural Development in Kenya and Tanzania." *Food Research Institute Studies* 21(3): 205–64.

Johnston, Bruce F., and William C. Clark. 1982. *Redesigning Rural Development: A Strategic Perspective*. Baltimore: Johns Hopkins University Press.

Johnston, Bruce F., and John Cownie. 1969. "The Seed Fertilizer Revolution and Labor Force Absorption." *American Economic Review* 59(4): 569–82.

Johnston, Bruce F., A. Hoben, D. W. Dijkerman, and W. K. Jaeger. 1987. "An Assessment of A.I.D. Activities to Promote Agricultural and Rural Development in sub-Saharan Africa." Agency for International Development Evaluation Special Study No. 54. Washington, D.C.: AID.

Johnston, Bruce F., A. Hoben, and W. K. Jaeger. 1992. "United States Activities to Promote Agricultural and Rural Development in sub-Saharan Africa." In Uma Lele, ed., *Aid to African Agriculture: Lessons from Two Decades of Donors' Experience*. Baltimore: Johns Hopkins University Press.

Johnston, Bruce F., and Peter Kilby. 1975. *Agriculture and Structural Transformation: Economic Strategies in Late-Developing Countries*. London: Oxford University Press.

Johnston, Bruce F., C. Luiselli, C. Cartas Contreras, and R. D. Norton, eds. 1987. *U.S.–Mexico Relations: Agriculture and Rural Development*. Stanford, Calif.: Stanford University Press.

Johnston, Bruce F., and John W. Mellor. 1961. "The Role of Agriculture in Economic Development." *American Economic Review* 51 (September): 566–93.

Johnston, Bruce F., and Soren T. Nielsen. 1966. "Agriculture and Structural Transformation in a Developing Economy." *Economic Development and Cultural Change* 14: 279–301.

Johnston, Bruce F., and Thomas P. Tomich. 1984. "A Study of the Feasibility of Small Farm Development Strategies." Research prepared for the U.S. Agency for International Development. Washington, D.C.: AID.

——. 1985. "Agricultural Strategies and Agrarian Structure." *Asian Development Review* 3(1): 1–37.

Joint Commission on Rural Reconstruction. 1961. *Twelfth General Report*. Taipei, Taiwan: Republic of China.

——. 1966. *Taiwan Agricultural Statistics, 1901–1965*. Economic Digest Series, no. 18. Taipei, Taiwan: Republic of China.

——. 1970. *Taiwan Farm Income Survey of 1967*. Taipei, Taiwan: Republic of China.

Jones, William O. 1960. "Economic Man in Africa." *Food Research Institute Studies* 1: 107–34.

——. 1970. "Measuring the Effectiveness of Agricultural Marketing in Contributing to Economic Development: Some African Examples." *Food Research Institute Studies* 9(3): 175–96.

——. 1972. *Marketing Staple Food Crops in Tropical Africa*. Ithaca: Cornell University Press.

———. 1984. "Economic Tasks for Food Marketing Boards in Tropical Africa." *Food Research Institute Studies* 19(2): 113–38.

———. 1987. "Food-Crop Marketing Boards in Tropical Africa." *The Journal of Modern African Studies* 25(3): 375–402.

Kahan, Arcadius. 1964. "The Collective Farm System in Russia: Some Aspects of Its Contribution to Soviet Economic Development." In Carl Eicher and Lawrence Witt, eds., *Agriculture in Economic Development*. New York: McGraw-Hill.

Kanbur, S. M. Ravi. 1984. "How to Analyze Commodity Price Stabilization: A Review Article," *Oxford Economic Papers*, n.s. 36(3): 336–58.

Kaneda, Hiromitsu. 1969. "Long-Term Changes in Food Consumption Patterns in Japan." In Kazushi Ohkawa, Bruce F. Johnston, and Hiromitsu Kaneda, eds., *Agriculture and Economic Growth: Japan's Experience*. Tokyo: University of Tokyo Press.

———. 1988. "Agricultural Stagnation in the 1920s, A Macroeconomic Perspective." *Hitotsubashi Journal of Economics* 29(1): 37–57.

Karcz, Jerzy F. 1967. "Soviet Agriculture: A Balance Sheet." *Studies in the Soviet Union* 6(4).

———. 1969. "Comparative Study of Transformation of Agriculture in Centrally Planned Economies: The Soviet Union, Eastern Europe, and Mainland China." In Erik Thorbecke, ed., *The Role of Agriculture in Economic Development*. New York: National Bureau of Economic Research.

Kato, Yuzuru. 1966. "Mechanisms for the Outflow of Funds from Agriculture into Industry in Japan." *Rural Economic Problems* 3(2).

Kautsky, Karl. 1988. *The Agrarian Question*, vol. 1. London: Zwan Publications.

Kawagoe, Toshihiko, Yujiro Hayami, and Vernon W. Ruttan. 1985. "The Intercountry Agricultural Production Function and Productivity Differences Among Countries." *Journal of Development Economics* 19: 113–32.

Kelley, Allen C., and Charles E. Nobbe. 1990. "Kenya at the Demographic Turning Point? Hypotheses and a Proposed Research Agenda." World Bank Discussion Paper 107. Washington, D.C.: World Bank.

Kennedy, Eileen T. 1988. "Alternatives to Consumer-Oriented Food Subsidies for Achieving Nutritional Objectives." In Per Pinstrup-Andersen, ed., *Food Subsidies in Developing Countries*. Baltimore: Johns Hopkins University Press.

———. 1989. "The Effects of Sugarcane Production on Food Security, Health, and Nutition in Kenya: A Longitudinal Analysis." Research Report 78. Washington, D.C.: International Food Policy Research Institute.

Kennedy, Eileen T., and Bruce Cogill. 1987. "Income and Nutritional Effects of the Commercialization of Agriculture in Southwestern Kenya." Research Report 63. Washington, D.C.: International Food Policy Research Institute.

Kenya, Republic of. 1974. *Development Plan: 1974–1978, Part I*. Nairobi: Government Printer.

———. 1979. *Development Plan: 1979–1983, Part I*. Nairobi: Government Printer.

———. 1983. *Economic Survey: 1983*. Nairobi: Government Printer.

———. 1986. *Economic Management for Renewed Growth*. Sessional Paper No. 1. Nairobi: Government Printer.

———. 1989. *Demographic and Health Survey 1989*. Nairobi: National Council for Population and Development, and Columbia, Md.: Institute for Resource Development/Macro Systems.

Keuning, Steven J. 1984. "Farm Size, Land Use, and Profitability of Food Crops in Indonesia." *Bulletin of Indonesian Economic Studies* 20(1): 58–82.

Keyfitz, Nathan. 1989. "The Growing Human Population." *Scientific American* 261(3): 118–26.

Kikuchi, Baron Dairoku. 1909. *Japanese Education.* London: J. Murray.

Kilby, Peter. 1965. *African Enterprise: The Nigerian Bread Industry.* Stanford, Calif.: Stanford University Press.

———. 1969. *Industrialization in an Open Economy: Nigeria, 1945–1966.* Cambridge: Cambridge University Press.

———. 1972. "Farm and Factory: A Comparison of the Skill Requirements for the Transfer of Technology." *Journal of Development Studies* 9(1): 63–69.

———. 1986. "The Supply and Use of Agriculture Inputs—Critical Remarks on an FAO Technical Consultation." November. W/s2422. Rome: FAO.

———. 1987. "Small-Scale Manufacturing in Kenya." In World Bank, *Kenya: Industrial Sector Policies for Investment and Export Growth.* Washington, D.C.: World Bank.

Kilby, Peter, and David D'Zmura. 1985. *Searching for Benefits.* USAID Evaluation Study No. 28, Washington, D.C.: U.S. Agency for International Development.

Kilby, Peter, and Bruce F. Johnston. 1972. "The Choice of Agricultural Strategy and the Development of Manufacturing." *Food Research Institute Studies* 11(2): 155–75.

Kilby, Peter, and Carl Liedholm. 1986. "The Role of Nonfarm Activities in the Rural Economy." Employment and Enterprise Policy Analysis (EEPA) Discussion Paper No. 7. Cambridge: Harvard Institute for International Development.

Killick, Tony. 1985. "Economic Environment and Agricultural Development: The Importance of Macroeconomic Policy." *Food Policy* 10(1): 29–40.

King, R. P., and Derek Byerlee. 1978. "Factor Intensities and Locational Linkages of Rural Consumption Patterns in Sierra Leone." *American Journal of Agricultural Economics* 60: 197–206.

King, Timothy. 1970. *Mexico: Industrialization and Trade Policies Since 1940.* London: Oxford University Press.

Kirk, Dudley. 1971. "A New Demographic Transition?" In National Academy of Sciences, *Rapid Population Growth: Consequences and Policy Implications.* Baltimore: Johns Hopkins University Press.

Kislev, Yoav, and W. Peterson. 1982. "Prices, Technology, and Farm Size." *Journal of Political Economy* 90: 578–95.

Kjaerby, Finn. 1986. "The Development of Agricultural Mechanization." In Jannik Boesen, K. J. Havnevik, J. Koponen, and R. Odgaard, eds., *Tanzania: Crisis and Struggle for Survival.* Uppsala: Scandinavian Institute of African Studies.

Knight, John B., and R. H. Sabot. 1990. *Education, Productivity, Inequality: The East African Natural Experiment.* New York: Oxford University Press.

Knodel, John, and Etienne van de Walle. 1986. "Lessons from the Past: Policy Implications of Historical Fertility Studies." In Ansley J. Coale and Susan Cotts Watkins, eds., *The Decline of Fertility in Europe: The Revised Proceedings of a Conference on the Princeton European Fertility Project.* Princeton: Princeton University Press.

Kornai, Janos. 1986. "The Hungarian Reform Process: Visions, Hopes, and Reality." *Journal of Economic Literature* 24(4): 1687–1734.

Korten, David C. 1980. "Community Organization and Rural Development: A Learning Process Approach." *The Public Administration Review* 40(5): 480–511.

Krause, Kenneth R., and Leonard R. Kyle. 1970. "Economic Factors Underlying the Incidence of Large Farming Units: The Current Situation and Probable Trends." *American Journal of Agricultural Economics* 52(5): 748–61.

Kreinin, Mordechai. 1983. *International Economics*, 4th ed. New York: Harcourt Brace Jovanovich.

Krueger, Anne O. 1974. "The Political Economy of the Rent-Seeking Society." *American Economic Review* 66(3): 291–303.

Krueger, Anne O., Maurice Schiff, and Alberto Valdes. 1988. "Agricultural Incentives in Developing Countries: Measuring the Effect of Sectoral and Economywide Policies." *The World Bank Economic Review* 2(3): 255–71.

Kumar, Shubh K., and David Hotchkiss. 1988. "Consequences of Deforestation for Women's Time Allocation, Agricultural Production, and Nutrition in Hill Areas of Nepal." Research Report 69. Washington, D.C.: International Food Policy Research Institute.

Kurian, N. J. 1990. "Employment Potential in Rural India: An Analysis." *Economic and Political Weekly* 25(52): A-177–88.

Kuznets, Simon. 1966. *Modern Economic Growth*. New Haven: Yale University Press.

——. 1971. *Economic Growth of Nations: Total Output and Production Structure*. Cambridge: Harvard University Press.

Kydd, Jonathan, and Robert Christiansen. 1982. "Structural Change in Malawi since Independence: Consequences of a Development Strategy Based on Large-scale Agriculture." *World Development* 10(5): 355–75.

Laird, Roy D. 1988. "The End of Soviet Collective Farms." *The Christian Science Monitor*, October 5, p. 13.

Lamb, Geoffrey, and Linda Muller. 1982. *Control, Accountability, and Incentives in a Successful Development Institution: The Kenya Tea Development Authority*. Staff Working Paper 550. Washington, D.C.: World Bank.

Lardy, Nicholas. 1983. *Agriculture in China's Modern Economic Development*. Cambridge: Cambridge University Press.

——. 1986. "Overview: Agricultural Reform and the Rural Economy." In *China's Economy Looks toward the Year 2000*, vol. 1. Washington, D.C.: United States Government Printing Office.

Latham, Michael C. 1988. "Preface." In U. Jonsson, M. C. Latham, L. Bondestam, and R. Chorlton, eds., *Hunger and Society, vol. 3: Causes and Strategies in Tanzania*. Cornell International Nutrition Monograph Series No. 19. Ithaca: Cornell University.

Lau, Lawrence J., and Pan A. Yotopoulos. 1989. "The Meta-Production Function Approach to Technological Change in World Agriculture." *Journal of Development Economics* 31: 241–69.

Lebergott, Stanley. 1966. "Labor Force and Employment: 1880–1960." In *Output, Employment, and Productivity in the United States after 1880*. Studies in Income and Wealth, vol. 30. New York: National Bureau of Economic Research.

Lee, T. H. 1971. *Intersectoral Capital Flows in the Economic Development of Taiwan, 1895–1960*. Ithaca: Cornell University Press.

——. 1972. "Strategies for Transferring Agricultural Surplus under Different Agricultural Situations in Taiwan." In *Agriculture and Economic Development: Structural Readjustment in Asian Perspective*, vol. 2. Proceedings of conference held by Japan Economic Research Center, Sept. 1971. Tokyo: JERC.

Lele, Uma J. 1974. "The Role of Credit and Marketing in Agricultural Development." In N. Islam, ed., *Agricultural Policy in Developing Countries*. London: Macmillan.

——. 1984. "Tanzania: Phoenix or Icarus?" In Arnold C. Harberger, ed., *World Economic Growth*. San Francisco: Institute for Contemporary Studies Press.

——. 1988. "Agricultural Growth, Domestic Policies, the External Environment, and Assistance to Africa: Lessons of a Quarter Century." In Colleen Roberts, ed., *Trade, Aid, and Policy Reform: Proceedings of the Eighth Agriculture Sector Symposium*. Washington, D.C.: World Bank.

Lele, Uma, and Manmohan Agarwal. 1989. "Smallholder and Large-Scale Agriculture in Africa, Are There Trade-offs between Growth and Equity?" MADIA Discussion Paper No. 6. Washington, D.C.: World Bank.

Lele, Uma J., and Rahul Jain. 1992. "Aid to African Agriculture: Lessons from Two Decades of Donors' Experience." In Uma Lele, ed., *Aid to African Agriculture: Lessons from Two Decades of Donors' Experience*. Baltimore: John Hopkins University Press.

Lele, Uma J., and John W. Mellor. 1981. "Technological Change, Distributive Bias and Labor Transfer in a Two Sector Economy." *Oxford Economic Papers*, n.s. 33(3): 426–41.

Lele, Uma, and L. R. Meyers. 1986. "Agricultural Development and Foreign Assistance: A Review of The World Bank's Experience in Kenya: 1963–1986." MADIA Draft Paper 12/17/86. Washington, D.C.: World Bank.

——. 1987. *Growth and Structural Change in East Africa: Domestic Policies, Agricultural Performance, and World Bank Assistance, 1963–1987*, Part 1. MADIA Background Paper No. 1. Washington, D.C.: World Bank.

Leonard, David K. 1984. "Class Formation and Agricultural Development." In J. D. Barkan, ed., *Politics and Public Policy in Kenya and Tanzania*, rev. ed. New York: Praeger.

LeVine, Robert A. 1973. *Culture, Behavior, and Personality*. Chicago: Aldine.

LeVine, Robert A., Sarah E. LeVine, Amy Richman, F. Medardo Tapia Uribe, Clara Sunderland Correa, and Patrice M. Miller. 1991. "Women's Schooling and Child Care in the Demographic Transition: A Mexican Case Study." *Population and Development Review* 17(3): 459–96.

Levinthal, Daniel, and James G. March. 1981. "A Model of Adaptive Organizational Search." *Journal of Economic Behavior and Organization* 2: 307–33.

Lewin, M. 1968. *Russian Peasants and Soviet Power: A Study of Collectivization*. Evanston, Ill.: Northwestern University Press.

Lewis, Stephen R., Jr. 1973. "Agricultural Taxation and Intersectoral Resource Transfers." *Food Research Institute Studies* 12(2): 93–114.

Lewis, W. Arthur. 1954. "Economic Development with Unlimited Supplies of Labour." In A. N. Agarwala and S. P. Singh, eds., *The Economics of Underdevelopment*. NY: Oxford University Press.

——. 1988. "Reflection on Development." In Gustav Ranis and T. Paul Schultz, eds., *The State of Development Economics: Progress and Perspectives*. New York: Basil Blackwell.

Leys, Colin. 1971. "Political Perspectives." In Dudly Seers and Leonard Joy, eds., *Developing in a Divided World*. Middlesex, U.K.: Penguin Books.

——. 1982. "African Economic Development in Theory and Practice." *Daedalus* 3(2): 99–124.

Li, K. T. 1988. *The Evolution of Policy behind Taiwan's Development Success* (with introductory essays by Gustav Ranis and John C. H. Fei). New Haven: Yale University Press.

Liedholm, Carl, and Peter Kilby. 1988. "The Role of Nonfarm Activities in the Rural Economy." In Jeffrey G. Williamson and Vadiraj R. Panchamukhi, eds., *The Balance between Industry and Agriculture in Economic Development*, vol. 2. London: Macmillan.

Liedholm, Carl, and D. Mead. 1987. "Small Scale Enterprises in Developing Countries: Empirical Evidence and Policy Implications." International Development Paper No. 9. East Lansing: Michigan State University.

Lin, Justin Y. 1990. "Collectivization and China's Agricultural Crisis in 1959–61." *Journal of Political Economy* 98(6): 1228–52.

Lin, Justin Y., Xianbin Yao, and G. James Wen. 1990. "China's Agricultural Development: Recent Experience and Policy Issues." In Carl K. Eicher and John M. Staatz, eds., *Agricultural Development in the Third World*, 2d ed. Baltimore: Johns Hopkins University Press.

Lindblom, Charles E. 1959. "The Science of Muddling Through." *Public Administration Review* 19(2): 79–88.

——. 1977. *Politics and Markets: The World's Political and Economic Systems*. New York: Basic Books.

Lindblom, Charles E., and David K. Cohen. 1979. *Usable Knowledge: Social Science and Social Problem Solving*. New Haven: Yale University Press.

Lipton, Michael. 1968. "The Theory of the Optimizing Peasant." *The Journal of Development Studies* 4(3): 327–51.

——. 1977. *Why Poor People Stay Poor*. Cambridge: Harvard University Press.

——. 1989. *New Strategies and Successful Examples for Sustainable Development in the Third World*. Reprint No. 170. Washington, D.C.: International Food Policy Research Institute.

Lipton, Michael, and Richard Longhurst. 1985. "Modern Varieties, International Agricultural Research, and the Poor." Consultative Group on International Agricultural Research, Study Paper No. 2. Washington, D.C.: World Bank.

——. 1989. *New Seeds and Poor People*. London: Unwin Hyman.

Lipumba, Nguyuru Haruna Ibrahim. 1983. "Foreign Exchange and Economic Development in Tanzania." Ph.D. diss. Food Research Institute, Stanford University.

——. 1986a. *Policy Response to Economic Crisis in Tanzania*. Unpublished draft.

——. 1986b. *Reflections on Economic Development: The Tanzania Experience*. Unpublished draft.

Little, I. M. D., and J. A. Mirrlees. 1990. "Project Appraisal and Planning Twenty Years On." *Proceedings of the World Bank Annual Conference on Development Economics*. Washington, D.C.: World Bank.

Little, I. M. D., Tibor Scitovsky, and Maurice Scott. 1970. *Industry and Trade in Some Developing Countries*. London: Oxford University Press.

Little, Peter D. and M. M. Horowitz. 1987. "Subsistence Crops Are Cash Crops: Some Comments with Reference to Eastern Africa." *Human Organization* 46(3): 254–58.

Livi-Bacci, Massimo. 1993. "On the Human Costs of Collectivization in the Soviet Union." *Population and Development Review* 19(4): 743–66.

Livingstone, Ian. 1986. *Rural Development, Employment, and Incomes in Kenya*. Brookfield, Vt.: Gower Publishing.

Lockeretz, William. 1984. "Historical Insights into Contemporary Agricultural Development." *Food Policy* (May): 157–67.

Lockheed, Marlaine E., Dean T. Jamison, and Lawrence J. Lau. 1980. "Farmer Education and Farm Efficiency: A Survey." *Economic Development and Cultural Change* 29(1): 37–76.

Lockwood, W. W. 1954. *The Economic Development of Japan*. Princeton: Princeton University Press.

Lofchie, Michael F. 1989. *The Policy Factor: Agricultural Performance in Kenya and Tanzania*. Boulder, Colo.: Lynn Rienner.

Lorimer, Frank. 1946. *The Population of the Soviet Union*. Princeton: Princeton University Press.

Lynam, John K. 1978. "An Analysis of Population, Technical Change, and Risk in Peasant Semi-Arid Farming Systems: A Case Study of Machakos District, Kenya." Ph.D. diss., Stanford University.

Ma, F. C., T. Takasaka, and C. W. Yang. 1955. "A Preliminary Study of Farm Implements Used in Taiwan Province." Taipei, Taiwan: Joint Commission on Rural Reconstruction.

Mackie, J. A., and W. J. O'Malley. 1988. "Productivity Decline in the Java Sugar Industry from an Olsonian Perspective." *Comparative Studies in Society and History* 30(4): 725–49.

Maitha, J. K. 1976. "The Kenyan Economy." In Judith Heyer, J. K. Maitha, and W. M. Senga, eds., *Agricultural Development in Kenya: An Economic Assessment*. Nairobi: Oxford University Press.

Manning, Chris. 1988. "Rural Employment Creation in Java: Lessons from the Green Revolution and the Oil Boom." *Population and Development Review* 14(1): 47–80.

———. 1992. "Survey of Recent Developments." *Bulletin of Indonesian Economic Studies* 28(1): 3–38.

Mao, Yu-Kang. 1988. "Analysis of Changes in the Type of Farm Households under Rapid Economic Growth in Taiwan, R.O.C." In *Conference on Directions and Strategies of Agricultural Development in the Asia-Pacific Region (II)*. Taipei, Taiwan: Institute of Economics, Academia Sinica.

Mao, Yu-Kang, and Chi Schive. 1990. "Agricultural and Industrial Development of the Republic of China on Taiwan." Paper presented at the Conference on Agriculture on the Road to Industrialization. Taipei, Taiwan: Council of Agriculture and International Food Policy Research Institute.

March, James G. 1978. "Bounded Rationality, Ambiguity, and the Engineering of Choice." *Bell Journal of Economics* 9(2): 587–608.

March, James G., and Johan P. Olsen. 1976. *Ambiguity and Choice in Organizations*. Bergen, Norway: Universitetsforlaget.

———. 1984. "The New Institutionalism: Organizational Factors in Political Life." *American Political Science Review* 78: 734–49.

March, James G., and Herbert A. Simon. 1958. *Organizations*. New York: Wiley.

Mares, David R. 1987. "The U.S.–Mexico Winter-Vegetable Trade: Climate, Economics, and Politics." In Bruce F. Johnston, Cassio Luiselli, Celso Cartas Contreras, and Roger D. Norton, eds., *U.S.–Mexico Relations: Agriculture and Rural Development*. Stanford, Calif.: Stanford University Press.

Marris, Peter, and A. Somerset. 1971. *African Businessmen: A Study of Entrepreneurship and Development in Kenya*. Nairobi: East African Publishing House.

Marsh, Robin R. 1991. "Technology Generation and Diffusion in an Uncertain Environment: The Case of Small Maize Producers in Mexico." Ph.D. diss., Food Research Institute, Stanford University.

Martorell, Reynaldo, and Teresa Gonzalez-Cossio. 1987. "Maternal Nutrition and Birth Weight." *Yearbook of Physical Anthropology* 30: 195–220.

Matlon, Peter. 1990. "Improving Productivity in Sorghum and Pearl Millet in Semi-Arid Africa." *Food Research Institute Studies* 22(1): 1–43.

Matlon, Peter, T. Eponou, S. Franzel, D. Byerlee, and D. Baker. 1979. "Poor Rural Households, Technical Change, and Income Distribution in Developing Countries: Two Case Studies from West Africa." African Rural Economy Working Paper No. 29. East Lansing: Michigan State University.

Matus Gardea, J. A., and R. R. Cruz Aguilar. 1987. "Agricultural Policy and International Trade in Mexico, 1970–1982." In Bruce F. Johnston, Cassio Luiselli, Celso Cartas Contreras, and Roger D. Norton, eds., *U.S.–Mexico Relations: Agricultural and Rural Development*. Stanford, Calif.: Stanford University Press.

Mauldin, W. P., and Bernard Berelson. 1978. "Conditions of Fertility Decline in Developing Countries, 1965–1975." *Studies in Family Planning* 9(5): 90–147.

McKinnon, Ronald I. 1988. "Financial Liberalization in Retrospect: Interest Rate Policies in LDCs." In Gustav Ranis and T. Paul Schultz, eds., *The State of Development Economics: Progress and Perspectives*. New York: Basil Blackwell.

McNicoll, Geoffrey, and Singarimbun. 1982. "Fertility Decline in Indonesia. I. Background and Proximate Determinants", and "II. Analysis and Interpretation." Center for Policy Studies, Working Papers Nos. 92 and 93, New York: Population Council.

Meier, Gerald M. 1989. *Leading Issues in Economic Development*, 5th ed. New York: Oxford University Press.

——, ed. 1991. *Politics and Policymaking in Developing Countries*. San Francisco: ICS Press.

Mellor, John W. 1976. *The New Economics of Growth: A Strategy for India and the Developing World*. Ithaca: Cornell University Press.

——. 1986. "Agriculture on the Road to Industrialization." In John P. Lewis and Valeriana Kallab, eds., *Development Strategies Reconsidered*. U.S.–Third World Policy Perspectives No. 5. New Brunswick, N.J.: Transaction Books for the Overseas Development Council.

Mellor, John W., and Bruce F. Johnston. 1984. "The World Food Equation: Interrelationships among Development, Employment, and Food Consumption." *Journal of Economic Literature* 22: 531–74.

Mellor, John W., and Uma J. Lele. 1973. "Growth Linkages of the New Foodgrain Technologies." *Indian Journal of Agricultural Economics* 27(1): 35–55.

Merrett, Stephen. 1971. "Snares in the Labor Productivity Measure of Efficiency." *Journal of Industrial Economics* 2(1): 73–98.

——. 1972. "The Growth of Indian Nitrogen Fertilizer Manufacture: Some Lessons for Industrial Planning." *Journal of Development Studies* 8(4): 426–40.

Mexico. 1980. *Sistema Alimentario Mexicano*. Mexico City: Oficinia de Asesores.

———. 1990. *Programa Nacional de Modernizacion del Campo, 1990–1994*. Mexico City: Secretaria de Agricultura y Recursos Hidraulicos.

Migdal, Joel S. 1987. "Strong States, Weak States: Power and Accommodation." In Myron Weiner and Samuel P. Huntington, eds., *Understanding Political Development*. Boston: Little, Brown.

Migot-Adholla, Shem. 1984. "Rural Development Policy and Equality." In J. D. Barkan, ed., *Politics and Public Policy in Kenya and Tanzania*, rev. ed. New York: Praeger.

Migot-Adholla, Shem, Peter Hazell, Benoît Blarel, and Frank Place. 1991. "Indigenous Land Rights Systems in sub-Saharan Africa: A Constraint on Productivity?" *The World Bank Economic Review* 5(1): 155–75.

Millar, James R. 1970. "Soviet Rapid Development and the Agricultural Surplus Hypothesis." *Soviet Studies* 22(1).

Miller, Norman N. 1984. *Kenya: The Quest for Prosperity*. London: Westview Press.

Minami, Ryoshin. 1968. "The Supply of Farm Labor and the Turning Point in the Japanese Economy." In Kazushi Ohkawa, Bruce F. Johnston, and Hiromitsu Kaneda, eds., *Agriculture and Economic Growth: Japan's Experience*. Tokyo: Tokyo University Press.

Misawa, Takeo. 1969. "An Analysis of Part-time Farming in the Post-War Period." In Kazushi Ohkawa, Bruce F. Johnston, and Hiromitsu Kaneda, eds., *Agriculture and Economic Growth: Japan's Experience*. Tokyo: Tokyo University Press.

Mittendorf, H. J., C. Y. Lee, and H. Trupke. 1983. "Marketing Costs and Margins for Fertilizers in Developing Countries: Progress Report on Recent Surveys Conducted by FAO in Asia and Africa." *Fertilizer International*.

Mohan, C. 1986. "Establishment of the Tractor Industry in India." In *Small Farm Equipment for Developing Countries*. Manila: IRRI.

Morehouse, Ward. 1982. "Opening Pandora's Box: Technology and Social Performance in the Indian Tractor Industry." In F. Stewart and J. James, eds., *The Economics of New Technology in Developing Countries*. Boulder, Colo.: Westview.

Moris, Jon R., J. Harris, G. Honadle, C. M. Kazi, W. Mbaga, and J. Semboja. 1985. *Tanzania's Productivity Crisis: A Social and Institutional Profile*. Washington, D.C.: U.S. Agency for International Development/Tanzania.

Moris, Jon R., and D. J. Thom. 1987. *African Irrigation Overview: Main Report*. Africa/USAID Water Management Synthesis II Project, WMS Report 37. Logan: Utah State University.

Mueller, Eva. 1971. "Agricultural Change and Fertility Change: The Case of Taiwan." Mimeograph. Ann Arbor: University of Michigan.

Muhondwa, Eustace P. Y. 1989. "The Role and Impact of Foreign Aid in Tanzania's Health Development." In Michael R. Reich and E. Marui, eds., *International Cooperation for Health: Problems, Prospects, and Priorities*. Dover, Mass.: Auburn House.

Mundlak, Yair, Domingo Cavallo, and Roberto Domenech. 1989. *Agriculture and Economic Growth in Argentina, 1913–84*. Research Report No. 76. Washington, D.C. International Food Policy Research Institute.

Murphy, K. M., A. Shleifer, and R. W. Vishny. 1989a. "Industrialization and the Big Push." *Journal of Political Economy* 97(5): 1003–26.

——. 1989b. "Income Distribution, Market Size, and Industrialization." *Quarterly Journal of Economics* 3 (August): 537–64.

Musgrave, R., and P. Musgrave. 1984. *Public Finance in Theory and Practice*. New York: McGraw-Hill.

Myers, Ramon H., and A. Ching. 1964. "Agricultural Development in Taiwan under Japanese Colonial Rule." *Journal of Asian Studies* 23(4): 555–70.

Nabi, Ijaz. 1988. *Entrepreneurs and Markets in Early Industrialization: A Case Study from Pakistan*. San Francisco: Institute for Contemporary Studies.

Narongchai, A., T. Onchan, Y. Chalamwong, P. Charsombut, S. Tambunletchai, and C. Atikul. 1983. *Rural Off-Farm Employment in Thailand*. Bangkok: Industrial Management Company.

National Research Council. 1989. *Alternative Agriculture*. Washington, D.C.: National Academy Press.

Ndulu, Benno. 1986. "Governance and Economic Management." In Robert J. Berg and J. S. Whitaker, eds., *Strategies for African Development*. Berkeley: University of California Press.

Newbery, David. 1975. "The Choice of Rental Contract in Peasant Agriculture." In L. G. Reynolds, ed., *Agriculture in Development Theory*. New Haven: Yale University Press.

Newbery, David M. G., and Joseph E. Stiglitz. 1981. *The Theory of Commodity Price Stabilization: A Study in the Economics of Risk*. New York: Oxford University Press.

Nicholson, Norman K. 1984. "Landholding, Agricultural Modernization, and Local Institutions in India." *Economic Development and Cultural Change* 32(3): 569–92.

North, Douglass C. 1981. *Structure and Change in Economic History*. New York: Norton.

Nove, Alec. 1969. *The Soviet Economy*, 2d rev. ed. New York: Praeger.

——. 1971. "The Decision to Collectivize." In W. A. Douglas Jackson, ed., *Agrarian Politics and Problems in Communist and Non-Communist Countries*. Seattle: University of Washington Press.

——. 1983. *The Economics of Feasible Socialism*. London: Allen & Unwin.

Nyerere, Julius K. 1968. *Ujamaa—Essays on Socialism*. London: Oxford University Press.

Ofer, Gur. 1987. "Soviet Economic Growth: 1928–1985." *Journal of Economic Literature* 25(4): 1767–833.

Ogura, Takekazu, ed. 1963. *Agricultural Development in Modern Japan*. Tokyo: Japan FAO Association.

Ohkawa, Kazushi. 1965. "Agriculture and Turning-Points in Economic Growth." *Developing Economies* 3(4).

——. 1972. *Differential Structure and Agriculture: Essays on Dualistic Growth*. Tokyo: Kinokuniya and the Institute of Economic Research, Hitotsubashi University.

Ohkawa, Kazushi, and Yujiro Hayami. 1989. "Policy Implications of Japanese Experience in Agricultural Development." IFPRI Policy Briefs 4. Washington, D.C.: International Food Policy Research Institute.

Ohkawa, Kazushi, B. F. Johnston, and H. Kaneda, eds. 1969. *Agriculture and Economic Growth: Japan's Experience*. Tokyo: Tokyo University Press.

Ohkawa, Kazushi, and Gustav Ranis. 1985. "Introduction." In K. Ohkawa and G. Ranis, eds., with the assistance of Larry Meissner, *Japan and the Developing Countries: A Comparative Analysis of Development Experience*. New York: Basil Blackwell.

Ohkawa, Kazushi, Gustav Ranis, and John Fei. 1985. "Introduction" and "Economic Development in Historical Perspective: Japan, Korea and Taiwan." In K. Ohkawa and G. Ranis, eds., with the assistance of Larry Meissner. *Japan and the Developing Countries: A Comparative Analysis of Development Experience*, Oxford: Basil Blackwell.

Okoth-Ogendo, H. W. O. 1976. "African Land Tenure Reform." In Judith Heyer, J. K. Maitha, and W. M. Senga, eds., *Agricultural Development in Kenya: An Economic Assessment*. London: Oxford University Press.

Olmstead, Alan L., and P. Rhode. 1988. "An Overview of California Agricultural Mechanization, 1870–1930." *Agricultural History* 62(3): 86–112.

Olson, Mancur. 1965. *The Logic of Collective Action*. Cambridge: Harvard University Press.

——. 1988. "The Treatment of Agriculture in Developing and Developed Countries." *Journal of Economic Growth* 3(2): 10–15.

Organization for Economic Cooperation and Development (OECD). 1968. *Supply and Demand Prospects for Fertilizers in Developing Countries*. Paris: OECD.

Otsuka, Keijiro, H. Chuma, and Y. Hayami. 1992. "Land and Labor Contracts in Agrarian Economies: Theories and Facts." *Journal of Economic Literature* 3(4): 1965–2018.

Pack, Howard. 1972. "The Use of Labor-Intensive Techniques in Kenyan Industry." In Office of Science and Technology, *Technology and Economics in International Development*. Washington D.C.: AID.

Page, J., and W. Steel. 1984. "Small Enterprise Development: Economic Issues from African Experience." *World Bank Technical Report No. 26*. Washington, D.C.: World Bank.

Panayotou, Theodore. 1990. "The Economics of Environmental Degradation: Problems, Causes, and Responses." Development Discussion Paper No. 335. Cambridge: Harvard Institute for International Development.

Parker, William N., and J. L. V. Klein. 1966. "Productivity Growth in Grain Production in the United States, 1840–60 and 1900–10." In *Output, Employment, and Productivity*. Washington, D.C.: National Bureau of Economic Research.

Paulino, Leonardo A. 1986. *Food in the Third World: Past Trends and Projections to 2000*. Research Report 52. Washington, D.C.: International Food Policy Research Institute.

Pearse, Andrew. 1980. *Seeds of Plenty, Seeds of Want: Social and Economic Implications of the Green Revolution*. Oxford: Clarendon.

Pearson, Scott R., J. Dirck Stryker, and Charles P. Humphreys. 1981. *Rice in West Africa· Policy and Economics*. Stanford, Calif.: Stanford University Press.

Peng, T. S. 1969. "The Development of Mechanized Rice Culture in Taiwan." Mimeograph. Taipei, Taiwan: Joint Commission on Rural Reconstruction.

——. "A Survey of Utilization of Power Tillers and Mist-Blowers." Mimeograph. Taipei, Taiwan: Joint Commission on Rural Reconstruction.

——. "Present Problems and the Future of Agricultural Mechanization in Taiwan." *Industry of Free China* 35(4).

Perkins, Dwight H. 1986. *China, Asia's Next Economic Giant?* Seattle: University of Washington Press.

——. 1988. "Reforming China's Economic System." *Journal of Economic Literature* 26(2): 601–45.

Perkins, Dwight, and others. 1977. *Rural Small-Scale Industry in the People's Republic of China.* Report of The American Rural Small-Scale Industry Delegation. Berkeley: University of California Press.

Perkins, Dwight H., and S. Yusuf. 1985. *Rural Development in China.* Baltimore: Johns Hopkins University Press.

Perrin, Richard, and Donald Winkelmann. 1976. "Impediments to Technical Change on Small versus Large Farms." *American Journal of Agricultural Economics* 58(5): 888–94.

Pfeffermann, Guy P., and Charles C. Griffin. 1989. *Nutrition and Health Programs in Latin America: Targeting Social Expenditures.* Washington, D.C.: World Bank.

Phillips, James F., Ruth Simmons, Michael A. Koenig, and J. Chakraborty. 1988. "Determinants of Reproductive Change in a Traditional Society: Evidence from Matlab, Bangladesh." *Studies in Family Planning* 19(6): 313–34.

Pinckney, Thomas C. 1988. "Storage, Trade, and Price Policy under Production Instability: Maize in Kenya." Research Report No. 71. Washington, D.C.: International Food Policy Research Institute.

Pingali, Prabhu, Yves Bigot, and Hans P. Binswanger. 1987. *Agricultural Mechanization and the Evolution of Farming Systems in sub-Saharan Africa.* Washington, D.C.: World Bank.

Pinstrup-Andersen, Per. 1982. *Agricultural Research and Technology in Economic Development.* New York: Longman.

——, ed. 1988a. *Food Subsidies in Developing Countries.* Baltimore: Johns Hopkins University Press.

——. 1988b. "The Social and Economic Effects of Consumer-Oriented Food Subsidies: A Summary of Evidence." In Per Pinstrup-Andersen, ed., *Food Subsidies in Developing Countries.* Baltimore: Johns Hopkins University Press.

——. 1988c. "Some Microeconomic Policy Implications of Consumer-Oriented Subsidies." In Per Pinstrup-Andersen, ed., *Food Subsidies in Developing Countries.* Baltimore: Johns Hopkins University Press.

——, ed. 1993. *The Political Economy of Food and Nutrition Policies.* Baltimore: Johns Hopkins University Press.

Pinto, Brian. 1987. "Nigeria during and after the Oil Boom: A Policy Comparison with Indonesia." *World Bank Economic Review* 1(3): 419–45.

Poleman, Thomas T. 1981. "Quantifying the Nutrition Situation in Developing Countries." *Food Research Institute Studies* 28(1): 1–58.

Potter, Joseph E., O. Mojarro, and L. Nuñez. 1987. "The Influence of Health Care on Contraceptive Acceptance in Rural Mexico." *Studies in Family Planning* (18)3.

Pradahn, Sanjay Kumar. 1988. "Market Failures and Government Failures: Industrial Restructuring and Pricing Policy Analysis." Ph.D. diss., Harvard University.

Pratt, Cranford. 1976. *The Critical Phase in Tanzania, 1945–1968: Nyerere and the Emergence of a Socialist Strategy.* Cambridge: Cambridge University Press.

Presidential Commission on World Hunger. 1980. *Overcoming World Hunger: The Challenge Ahead.* Washington, D.C.: U.S. Government Printing Office.

Pressman, Jeffrey L., and Wildavsky, Aaron. 1984. *Implementation.* Berkeley: University of California Press.

Pyle, D. F. 1981. *From Project to Program: The Study of the Scaling-Up/ Implementation Process of a Community-Level, Integrated Health, Nutrition, Population Intervention in Maharashtra (India).* Ph.D. diss., MIT.

Quizon, Jaime B., and Hans P. Binswanger. 1983. "Income Distribution in Agriculture: A Unified Approach." *American Journal of Agricultural Economics* 65(3): 526–38.

———. 1986. "Modeling the Impact of Agricultural Growth and Government Policy on Income Distribution in India." *World Bank Economic Review* 1(1): 103–48.

Raikes, Phil. 1986. "Eating the Carrot and Wielding the Stick: The Agricultural Sector in Tanzania." In Jannik Boesen, K. J. Havnevik, J. Koponen, and R. Odgaard, eds., *Tanzania: Crisis and Struggle for Survival.* Uppsala: Scandinavian Institute of African Studies.

Ranis, Gustav. 1972. "Some Observations on the Economic Framework for Optimum LDC Utilization of Technology." In *Technology and Economics in International Development.* Washington, D.C.: Agency for International Development, Office of Science and Technology.

Ranis, Gustav, and Frances Stewart. 1987. "Rural Linkages in the Philippines and Taiwan." In Frances Stewart, ed., *Macro-Policies for Appropriate Technology in Developing Countries.* Boulder, Colo.: Westview Press.

Raup, Philip M. 1985. "Structural Change in Agriculture in the United States." Staff Papers Series No. P85-41, December. St. Paul: University of Minnesota.

Reich, Michael R., and E. Marui, eds. 1989. *International Cooperation for Health: Problems, Prospects, and Priorities.* Dover, Mass.: Auburn House.

Reischauer, Haru Matsukata. 1986. *Samurai and Silk: A Japanese and American Heritage.* Cambridge: Belknap Press of Harvard University Press.

Repetto, Robert. 1971. *Time in India's Development Programmes.* Cambridge: Harvard University Press.

———. 1986. "Skimming the Water: Rent-Seeking and the Performance of Public Irrigation Systems." Research Report No. 4. Washington, D.C.: World Resources Institute.

Republic of China. 1971. *Taiwan Statistical Data Book.* Taipei, Taiwan: Council for International Economic Cooperation and Development.

———. 1972. *Taiwan Statistical Data Book,* Taipei, Taiwan: Council for International Economic Cooperation and Development.

———. 1985. *Taiwan Statistical Data Book.* Taipei, Taiwan: Council for Economic Planning and Development.

———. 1986. "Food Balance Sheet 1986." Taipei, Taiwan: Council of Agriculture.

———. 1987. *Taiwan Statistical Yearbook.* Taipei, Taiwan: Council for Economic Planning and Development.

———. 1988. *Taiwan Statistical Yearbook, 1988.* Taipei, Taiwan: Council for Economic Planning and Development.

———. 1989a. *Industry of Free China.* Taipei, Taiwan: Council for Economic Planning and Development. Vol. 70.

———. 1989b. *Taiwan Statistical Handbook, 1989.* Taipei, Taiwan: Council for Economic Cooperation and Development.

———. 1991. *Basic Agricultural Statistics, ROC.* Taipei, Taiwan: Council of Agriculture.

———. 1992. *Taiwan Statistical Data Book.* Taipei, Taiwan: Council for Economic Planning and Development.

——. 1993. *Industry of Free China*, vol. 79. Taipei, Taiwan: Council for Economic Planning and Development.

Reyes Osorio, Sergio, Rodolfo Stavenhagen, and others. 1970. *Estructura Agraria y Desarrollo Agrícola en México*. Mexico: Centro de Investigaciones Agrarias.

Reynolds, Clark W. 1970. *The Mexican Economy: Twentieth-Century Structure and Growth*. New Haven: Yale University Press.

Ricciuti, H. N. 1979. "Malnutrition and Cognitive Development." In J. Brožek, ed., *Behavioral Effects of Energy and Protein Deficits*. NIH Publication No. 79-1906, Washington, D.C.: U.S. Government Printing Office.

Riding, Alan. 1985. *Distant Neighbors: A Portrait of the Mexicans*. New York: Knopf.

Rietveld, Piet. 1986. "Non-Agricultural Activities and Income Distribution in Rural Java." *Bulletin of Indonesian Economic Studies* 23(3): 106–17.

Robertson, A. F. 1987. *The Dynamics of Productive Relationships: African Share Contracts in Comparative Perspective*. Cambridge: Cambridge University Press.

Robinson, Marguerite S. 1988. *Local Politics: The Law of the Fishes*. Delhi: Oxford University Press.

Robinson, Warren C. 1990. "Kenya Enters the Fertility Transition." Mimeograph. Nairobi: Population Council.

Roemer, Michael. 1976. "Planning by 'Revealed Preference': An Improvement upon the Traditional Method." *World Development* 4(9): 775–83.

Rogers, Everett M. 1969. "Motivations, Values, and Attitudes of Subsistence Farmers: Toward a Subculture of Peasantry." In Clifton R. Wharton, Jr., ed., *Subsistence Agriculture and Economic Development*. Chicago: Aldine.

Roling, Niels. 1982. "Alternative Approaches to Extension." In Gwyn E. Jones and Maurice Rolls, eds., *Progress in Rural Extension and Community Development vol. 1: Extension and Relative Advantage in Rural Development*. New York: Wiley.

Romer, Paul M. 1986. "Increasing Returns and Long-Run Growth." *Journal of Political Economy* 94(5): 1002–37.

——. 1992. "Two Strategies for Economic Development: Using Ideas and Producing Ideas." In *Proceedings of the World Bank Conference on Development Economics, 1992* (Supplement to *The World Bank Economic Review* and *The World Bank Research Observer*:). Washington, D.C.: World Bank.

Rosenberg, N. 1982. *Inside the Black Box: Technologies and Economics*. Cambridge: Cambridge University Press.

Rosenzweig, Mark R. 1988. "Labor Markets in Low-Income Countries." In Hollis Chenery and T. N. Srinivasan, eds., *Handbook of Development Economics*, vol. 1. Amsterdam: North-Holland.

Rosovsky, Henry. 1959. "Japanese Capital Formation: The Role of the Public Sector." *Journal of Economic History* 19(3): 350–75.

Ross, John A., Marjorie Rich, Janet P. Molzan, and Michael Pensak. 1988. *Family Planning and Child Survival: 100 Developing Countries*. New York: Center for Population and Family Health, Columbia University.

Roumasset, James A. 1976. *Rice and Risk: Decision Making Among Low Income Farmers*. Amsterdam: North-Holland.

Roumasset, James A., and Joyotee Smith. 1981. "Population, Technological Change, and the Evolution of Labor Markets." *Population and Development Review* 7(3): 401–19.

Roy, Prannoy. 1981. "Transition in Agriculture: Empirical Indicators and Results (Evidence from Punjab, India)." *Journal of Peasant Studies* 8(2): 212–41.

Ruthenberg, Hans. 1980. *Farming Systems in the Tropics*. Oxford: Clarendon.

Ruttan, Vernon W. 1982. *Agricultural Research Policy*. Minneapolis: University of Minnesota Press.

——. 1990. "Sustainability Is Not Enough." In Carl K. Eicher and John M. Staatz, eds., *Agricultural Development in the Third World*, 2d ed. Baltimore: Johns Hopkins University Press.

——. 1991. "What Happened to Political Development?" *Economic Development and Cultural Change* 39(2): 265–86.

Ruttan, Vernon W., and Yujiro Hayami. 1990. "Induced Innovation Model of Agricultural Development." In Carl K. Eicher and John M. Staatz, eds., *Agricultural Development in the Third World*, 2d ed. Baltimore: Johns Hopkins University Press.

Sahn, David E., and Jehan Arulpragasam. 1991a. "Development through Dualism? Land Tenure, Policy, and Poverty in Malawi." Working Paper No. 9. Washington, D.C.: Cornell Food and Nutrition Policy Program.

——. 1991b. "The Stagnation of Smallholder Agriculture in Malawi: A Decade of Structural Adjustment." *Food Policy* 16(3; June): 219–34.

Sandbrook, Richard. 1986. "The State and Economic Stagnation in Tropical Africa." *World Development* 14(3): 319–32.

Sanders, John, Joseph Nagy, and Sunder Ramaswamy. 1990. "Developing New Agricultural Technologies for the Sahelian Countries: The Burkina Faso Case." *Economic Development and Cultural Change* 39(1): 1–22.

Sanders, John, and Vernon W. Ruttan. 1978. "Biased Choice of Technology in Brazilian Agriculture." In Hans P. Binswanger and V. W. Ruttan, eds., *Induced Innovation: Technology, Institutions, and Development*. Baltimore: Johns Hopkins University Press.

Sanderson, Steven E. 1986. *The Transformation of Mexican Agriculture: International Structure and the Politics of Rural Change*. Princeton: Princeton University Press.

Sansom, George Bailey. 1950. *The Western World and Japan: A Study in the Interaction of European and Asiatic Cultures*. New York: Knopf.

Sayad, Joao. 1984. "Rural Credit and Positive Real Rates of Interest: Brazil's Experience with Rapid Inflation." In Dale W. Adams, D. H. Graham, and J. D. Von Pischke, eds., *Undermining Rural Development with Cheap Credit*. Boulder, Colo.: Westview.

Scalapino, Robert A. 1953. *Democracy and the Party Movement in Prewar Japan*. Berkeley: University of California Press.

Scherr, Sara J. 1989. "Agriculture in an Export Boom Economy: A Comparative Analysis of Policy and Performance in Indonesia, Mexico, and Nigeria." *World Development* 17(4): 543–60.

Schuh, G. Edward. 1987. "Monetary Disturbances in a Changed International Economy: The Case of Mexico's Agriculture and Mexican–U.S. Trade." In Bruce F. Johnston, Cassio Luiselli, Celso Cartas Contreras, and Roger D. Norton, eds., *U.S.–Mexico Relations: Agricultural and Rural Development*. Stanford, Calif.: Stanford University Press.

Schultz, T. Paul. 1988. "Education Investments and Returns." In Hollis Chenery and T. N. Srinivasan, eds., *Handbook of Development Economics*, vol. 1. Amsterdam: North-Holland.

Schultz, Theodore W. 1964. *Transforming Traditional Agriculture*. New Haven: Yale University Press.

———. 1975. "The Value of the Ability to Deal with Disequilibria." *Journal of Economic Literature* 13(3): 827–46.

———. 1980. "Nobel Lecture: The Economics of Being Poor." *Journal of Political Economy* 88(4): 639–49.

Scitovsky, Tibor. 1985. "Economic Development in Taiwan and South Korea: 1965–1981." *Food Research Institute Studies* 19(3): 214–64.

Scobie, Grant M., and Rafael Posada T. 1984. "The Impact of Technical Change on Income Distribution: The Case of Rice in Colombia." In Carl K. Eicher and John M. Staatz, eds., *Agricultural Development in the Third World*. Baltimore: Johns Hopkins University Press.

Segura, E. L., Y. T. Shelty, and M. Nishimizu, eds. 1986. *Fertilizer Producer Pricing in Developing Countries*. Washington, D.C.: World Bank.

Sen, Amartya. 1981. "Ingredients of Famine Analysis: Availability and Entitlements." *Quarterly Journal of Economics* 96(3): 433–64.

———. 1984. *Resources, Values, and Development*. Cambridge: Harvard University Press.

Shaban, Radwan Ali. 1987. "Testing between Competing Models of Sharecropping." *Journal of Political Economy* 95(5): 893–920.

Shah, M. M., and F. Willekens. 1978. *Rural Urban Population Projections for Kenya and Implications for Development*. Laxenburg, Austria: International Institute for Applied Systems Analysis (IIASA).

Sharpley, Jennifer. 1981. "Resource Transfers between the Agricultural and Nonagricultural Sectors: 1964–77." In Tony Killick, ed., *Papers on the Kenyan Economy: Performance, Problems, and Policies*. Nairobi: Heinemann Educational.

———. 1985. "External versus Internal Factors in Tanzania's Macroeconomic Crisis: 1973–1983." *Eastern Africa Economic Review* 1(1): 71–86.

Sheldrick, William F. 1978. "World Potash Survey." World Bank Staff Working Paper No. 293. Washington, D.C.: World Bank.

———. 1984a. "Investment and Production Costs for Fertilizers." FAO Commission on Fertilizers, September. Rome: Food and Agriculture Organization.

———. 1984b. "World Fertilizer Review and the Changing Structure of the International Fertilizer Industry," Washington, D.C.: World Bank.

———. 1985. "The Economics and Outlook for Fertilizer Production." Washington, D.C.: World Bank.

———. 1987. "World Nitrogen Survey." Washington, D.C.: World Bank.

———. 1990. "Structure of the International Urea Market and the Outlook for Urea Prices and Price Fluctuations." Rome: Food and Agriculture Organization Commission on Fertilizers.

Shen, T. H. 1970. *The Sino-American Joint Commission on Rural Reconstruction: Twenty Years of Cooperation for Agricultural Development*. Ithaca: Cornell University Press.

———. 1976. *Taiwan's Family Farm during Transitional Economic Growth*. Ithaca: Cornell University Press.

Sherraden, Margaret S. 1989. *Social Policy Reform in Mexico: Rural Primary Health Services*. Doctoral diss., Washington University, St. Louis.

Shipton, Parker M. 1985. "Land, Credit, and Crop Transitions in Kenya: The Luo Response to Directed Development in Nyanza Province." Ph.D. diss., Cambridge University, United Kingdom.

Shleifer, Andrei. 1990. "Externalities as an Engine of Growth." Mimeograph. Chicago: Graduate School of Business, University of Chicago.

Siamwalla, Ammar. 1988. "Some Macroeconomic Policy Implications of Consumer-Oriented Food Subsidies." In Per Pinstrup-Andersen, ed., *Food Subsidies in Developing Countries*. Baltimore: Johns Hopkins University Press.

Sicular, Terry. 1990. "China's Agricultural Policy during the Reform Period." HIID Discussion Paper No. 1522. Cambridge: Harvard Institute for International Development.

Sidhu, Surjit S. 1974. "Economics of Technical Change in the Indian Punjab." *American Journal of Agricultural Economics* 56(2): 217–26.

Simantov, A. 1967. "The Dynamics of Growth of Agriculture." *Zeitschrift für Nationalökonomie* 27(3).

Simon, Herbert A. 1971. "Designing Organizations for an Information-Rich World." In M. Greenberger, ed., *Computers, Communications, and the Public Interest*. Baltimore: Johns Hopkins University.

———. 1977. *Models of Discovery and Other Topics in the Methods of Science*. Dordrecht, Holland: D. Reidel.

———. 1985. *The Sciences of the Artificial*. Cambridge: MIT Press.

Simpson, Eyler N. 1937. *The Ejido: Mexico's Way Out*. Chapel Hill: The University of North Carolina Press.

Sims, Brian G. 1993. "An Approach to Agricultural Engineering Research for Small Farmers in Latin America." Paper presented at the 1993 International Summer Meeting sponsored by the American Society of Agricultural Engineers and the Canadian Society of Agricultural Engineering, Spokane, Wash., June 20–23.

Sims, Brian G., B. F. Johnston, A. L. Olmstead, and S. J. Maldonado. 1988. "Animal-Drawn Implements for Small Farms in Mexico." *Food Research Institute Studies* 21(1): 69–95.

Sims, Holly. 1988. *Political Regimes, Public Policy, and Economic Development: Agricultural Performance and Rural Change in Two Punjabs*. Newbury Park, Calif: Sage.

Singh, Inderjit. 1983. "The Landless Poor in South Asia." In Allen Maunder and Kazushi Ohkawa, eds., *Growth and Equity in Agricultural Development*. Proceedings of the Eighteenth International Conference of Agricultural Economists. Aldershot and Hampshire: Gower.

———. 1990. *The Great Ascent: The Rural Poor in South Asia*. Baltimore: Johns Hopkins University Press.

Singh, Inderjit, Lyn Squire, and John Strauss. 1986. "A Survey of Agricultural Household Models: Recent Findings and Policy Implications." *World Bank Economic Review* 1(1): 149–79.

Skarstein, Rune. 1986. "Growth and Crisis in the Manufacturing Sector." In Jannik Boesen, K. J. Havnevik, J. Koponen, and R. Odgaard, eds., *Tanzania: Crisis and Struggle for Survival*. Uppsala: Scandinavian Institute of African Studies.

Slack, S. V. 1968. *Fertilizer Development and Trends*. Park Ridge, N.J.: Soil Science Society of America.

Smelser, Neil J. 1963. "Mechanisms of Change and Adjustment to Changes." In Bert F. Hoselitz and Wilbert E. Moore, eds., *Industrialization and Society*. Paris: UNESCO.

Smith, Edward. 1970. "The Diesel Engine Industry in Pakistan's Punjab." Mimeograph. Islamabad: Agency for International Development.

Smith, L. D. 1976. "An Overview of Agricultural Development Policy." In Judith Heyer, J. K. Maitha, and W. M. Senga, eds., *Agricultural Development in Kenya: An Economic Assessment*. London: Oxford University Press.

Smith, Thomas C. 1959. *The Agrarian Origins of Modern Japan*. Stanford, Calif.: Stanford University Press.

———. 1960. "Japan's Aristocratic Revolution." *Yale Review*, Spring 1960/61.

Snodgrass, Donald R., and Richard H. Patten. 1991. "Reform of Rural Credit in Indonesia: Inducing Bureaucracies to Behave Competitively." In Dwight H. Perkins and Michael Roemer, eds., *Reforming Economic Systems in Developing Countries*. Cambridge: Harvard University Press.

Solís, Leopoldo. 1971. "Mexican Economic Policy in the Post-War Period: The Views of Mexican Economists." *American Economic Review* 61(3).

———. 1980. *La Realidad Económica Mexicana: Retrovisión y Perspectivas*, 10th ed. Mexico: Siglo Veintiuno Editores.

Southworth, Herman M., and Bruce F. Johnston. 1967. *Agricultural Development and Economic Growth*. Ithaca: Cornell University Press.

Springborg, Robert. 1979. "Patrimonialism and Policy Making in Egypt: Nasser and Sadat and the Tenure Policy for Reclaimed Lands." *Middle Eastern Studies* 15(1): 49–69.

Sproat, Audrey T., and Scott, Bruce R. 1975. "Japan (A): 1853–1881: The Challenge to the Old Order. Harvard Business School Discussion Paper 375–347. Cambridge: Harvard Business School.

Srinivasan, T. N. 1985. "Neoclassical Political Economy, the State, and Economic Development." *Asian Development Review* 3(2): 38–58.

Stalin, Joseph. 1942. *Selected Writings*. New York: International Publishers.

———. 1946. "Text of Premier Stalin's Election Speech Broadcast by Moscow Radio." *New York Times*, 10 February.

Stallmann, J. 1983. "Rural Manufacturing in Three Regions of Honduras." Mimeograph. East Lansing: Michigan State University.

Starkey, Paul. 1988. *Animal-Drawn Wheeled Toolcarriers: Perfected Yet Rejected. A Cautionary Tale of Development*. Weisbaden: Vieweg.

Stein, Howard. 1985. "Theories of the State in Tanzania: A Critical Assessment." *The Journal of Modern African Studies* 23(1): 105–23.

Stigler, George J. 1951. "The Division of Labor Is Limited by the Extent of the Market." *Journal of Political Economy* 59(3; June): 185–93.

Stiglitz, Joseph E. 1986. "The New Development Economics." *World Development* 14(2): 257–65.

Stiglitz, Joseph E., and A. Weiss. 1981. "Credit Rationing in Markets with Imperfect Information." *American Economic Review* 71(3): 393–410.

Stone, Bruce. 1986. "China's Fertilizer Application in the 1980s and 1990s: Issues of Growth, Balance, Allocations, Efficiency, and Response." In *China's Economy Looks toward the Year 2000, Vol. 1*. Washington, D.C.: United States Government Printing Office.

———. 1989. "Fertilizer's Greener Pastures." *China Business Review*, September–October.

Strassmann, W. Paul. 1968. *Technological Change and Economic Development*. Ithaca: Cornell University Press.

———. 1989. "The Rise, Fall, and Transformation of Overseas Construction Contracting." *World Development* 17 (June): 783–94.

Streeten, Paul. 1981. *Development Perspectives*. London: MacMillan.

———. 1983. "Transitional Measures and Political Support for Food Price Policy Reform." Excerpted from "Food Prices as a Reflection of Political Power." *Ceres* 16(2): 16–22.

Stringer, Hugh. 1972. "Land, Farmer, and Sugarcane in Morelos, Mexico." *Land Economics* 48(3): 301–3.

Swammy-Rao, A. A. 1971. "Agricultural Machinery and Implements Industry in South East Asia." In Yoshisuke Kishida, ed., *Agricultural Mechanization in South East Asia*. Tokyo.

Syrquin, Moshe, and Hollis Chenery. 1989. "Three Decades of Industrialization." *The World Bank Economic Review* 3(2): 145–81.

Tang, Anthony M. 1967. "Agriculture in the Industrialization of Communist China and the Soviet Union." *Journal of Farm Economics* 49(5).

Tanzania, United Republic of. 1983. *The Agricultural Policy of Tanzania*. Dar es Salaam: Government Printer.

———. 1988. *Tanzania Economic Trends: A Quarterly Review of the Economy*, vol. 1, no. 1. Dar es Salaam: Ministry of Finance, Economic Affairs, and Planning in collaboration with the University of Tanzania.

Taylor, Carl E., 1977. "Nutrition and Population in Health Sector Planning." *Food Research Institute Studies* 16(2): 77–90.

Taylor, Carl E., Robert L. Parker, and Steven Jarrett, eds. 1988. "The Evolving Chinese Rural Health Care System." *Research in Human Capital Development* 5: 219–36.

Therkildsen, Ole. 1986. "State, Donors, and Villagers in Rural Water Management." In Jannik Boesen, K. J. Havnevik, J. Koponen, and R. Odgaard, eds., *Tanzania: Crisis and Struggle for Survival*. Uppsala: Scandinavian Institute of African Studies.

Thirtle, Colin G., and V. W. Ruttan. 1986. "The Role of Demand and Supply in the Generation and Diffusion of Technical Change." In Jacques Lesourne and Hugo Soneschein, eds., *Fundamentals of Pure and Applied Economics*. Minneapolis: University of Minneapolis Press.

Thomas, John W., and Merilee S. Grindle. 1990. "After the Decision: Implementing Policy Reforms in Developing Countries." *World Development* 18(8): 1163–81.

Thorbecke, Erik. 1979. "Agricultural Development." In Walter Galenson, ed., *Economic Growth and Structural Change in Taiwan*. Ithaca: Cornell University Press.

———. 1988. "The Impact of the International Economic System on Nutrition and Health." PEW/Cornell Lecture Series on Food and Nutrition Policy. Ithaca: Cornell University.

Timmer, C. Peter. 1973. "Choice of Technique in Rice Milling on Java." *Bulletin of Indonesian Economic Studies* 9(2).

———. 1976. "Food Policy in China." *Food Research Institute Studies* 15(6): 53–69.

———. 1986. *Getting Prices Right: The Scope and Limits of Agricultural Price Policy*. Ithaca: Cornell University Press.

——. 1987. "Analyzing Rice Market Interventions in Asia: Principles, Issues, Themes, and Lessons." Development Discussion Paper No. 254 AFP. Cambridge: Harvard Institute for International Development.

——. 1988. "The Agricultural Transformation." In Hollis Chenery and T. N. Srinivasan, eds., *Handbook of Development Economics*, vol. 1. Amsterdam: North-Holland.

——. 1989. "Food Price Policy, the Rationale for Government Intervention." *Food Policy* 14(1): 17–27.

Timmer, C. Peter, Walter P. Falcon, and Scott R. Pearson. 1983. *Food Policy Analysis.* Baltimore: Johns Hopkins University Press.

Tomich, Thomas P. 1984. *Private Land Reclamation in Egypt: Studies of Feasibility and Adaptive Behavior.* Ph.D. diss., Stanford University.

——. 1991a. "Comment" on Yujiro Hayami "Land Reform." In Gerald M. Meier, ed., *Politics and Policy Making in Developing Countries.* San Francisco: ICS Press.

——. 1991b. "Smallholder Rubber Development in Indonesia." In Dwight H. Perkins and Michael Roemer, eds., *Reforming Economic Systems in Developing Countries.* Cambridge: Harvard University Press.

——. 1992a. "Survey of Recent Developments." *Bulletin of Indonesian Economic Studies* 28(3): 3–39.

——. 1992b. "Sustaining Agricultural Development in Harsh Environments: Insights from Private Land Reclamation in Egypt." *World Development* 20(2): 261–74.

Travers, Lee. 1986. "Peasant Non-Agricultural Production in the People's Republic of China." In *China's Economy Looks toward the Year 2000*, vol. 1. Washington, D.C.: United States Government Printing Office.

Tripp, Robert, Ponniah Anandajayasekeram, Derek Byerlee, and Larry Harrington. 1990. "Farming Systems Research Revisited." In Carl K. Eicher and John M. Staatz, eds., *Agricultural Development in the Third World*, 2d ed. Baltimore: Johns Hopkins University Press.

Tshibaka, Tshikala B. 1989. "Food Production in a Land-Surplus, Labor-Scarce Economy: The Zairian Basin." Research Report 74. Washington D.C.: International Food Policy Research Institute.

Tsiang, S. C. 1987. "Taiwan's Economic Success Demystified." *Journal of Economic Growth* 3(1): 21–36.

Tsuchiya, Keizo. 1969. "Economics of Mechanization in Small-Scale Agriculture." In Kazushi Ohkawa, Bruce F. Johnston, and Hiromitsu Kaneda, eds., *Agriculture and Economic Growth: Japan's Experience.* Tokyo: Tokyo University Press.

Turrent Fernandez, Antonio. 1987. "Research and Technology for Mexico's Small Farmers." In Bruce F. Johnston, Cassio Luiselli, Celso Cartas Contreras, and Roger D. Norton, eds., *U.S.–Mexico Relations: Agriculture and Rural Development.* Stanford, Calif.: Stanford University.

Tussing, Arlon R. 1969. "The Labor Force in Meiji Economic Growth: A Quantitative Study of Yamanashi Prefecture." In Kazushi Ohkawa, Bruce F. Johnston, and Hiromitsu Kaneda, eds., *Agriculture and Economic Growth: Japan's Experience.* Tokyo: Tokyo University Press.

Tweeten, Luther. 1987. "Perspectives on Agricultural Development: A Review of the U.S. Experience." In Bruce F. Johnston, Cassio Luiselli, Celso Cartas Contreras, and Roger D. Norton, eds., *U.S.–Mexico Relations: Agriculture and Rural Development*. Stanford, Calif.: Stanford University Press.

Tyers, Rod, and Kym Anderson. 1992. *Disarray in World Food Markets: A Quantitative Assessment*. Cambridge: Cambridge University Press.

Uchendu, Victor C., and K. R. M. Anthony. 1974. *Agricultural Change in Geita District, Tanzania*. Nairobi: East African Literature Bureau.

——. 1975. *Agricultural Change in Kisii District, Kenya: A Study of Economic, Cultural, and Technical Determinants of Agricultural Change in Tropical Africa*. Nairobi: East African Literature Bureau.

United Nations Conference on Trade and Development (UNCTAD). 1985. *Fertilizer Supplies for Developing Countries*. New York: United Nations.

United Nations. 1967. *Demographic Yearbook, 1966*. New York: United Nations.

——. 1970. *Demographic Yearbook 1969*. New York: United Nations.

——. 1987a. *First Report on the World Nutrition Situation*. Rome: ACC/SCN Secretariat, Food and Agriculture Organization.

——. 1987b. *The Prospects of World Urbanization*. New York: United Nations.

——. 1988a. *Demographic Yearbook, 1986*. New York: United Nations.

——. 1988b. *World Demographic Estimates and Projections, 1950–2025*. ST/ESA/SER.R/79. New York: United Nations.

——. 1992. *National Accounts Statistics 1991*. New York: United Nations.

United Nations Development Programme (UNDP). 1989. "African Economic and Financial Data." Provisional document prepared by the World Bank's Trade and Finance Division, Africa Technical Department. New York: United Nations.

——. 1992. *Human Development Report, 1992*. New York: Oxford University Press.

United States Department of Agriculture. 1966. *Consumer Expenditures and Income: Rural Farm Population, United States, 1961*. Consumer Expenditure Survey Report no. 35, Washington, D.C.: Agricultural Research Service.

——. 1972. *Agricultural Statistics 1972*. Washington, D.C.: Agriculture Research Services.

United States Department of Commerce. 1902. *Twelfth Census of the United States Taken in the Year 1900, vol. V: Agriculture, Part 1*. Washington, D.C.: Bureau of the Census.

——. 1989. *Survey of Current Business* 69(7): 49. Washington, D.C.: Department of Commerce.

Valdes, Alberto. 1988. "Explicit versus Implicit Food Subsidies: Distribution of Costs." In Per Pinstrup-Andersen, ed., *Food Subsidies in Developing Countries*. Baltimore: Johns Hopkins University Press.

Van der Meer, Cornelis L. J., and Saburo Yamada. 1990. *Japanese Agriculture: A Comparative Economic Analysis*. London: Routledge.

Vatikiotis, Michael. 1989. "Summing Up: Suharto's Autobiography Defends His Years in Power." *Far Eastern Economic Review* (January 19): 16–17.

Verma, B. N., and Daniel W. Bromley. 1987. "The Political Economy of Farm Size in India: The Elusive Quest." *Economic Development and Cultural Change* 35(3): 791–808.

Vogel, Robert C. 1984. "The Effect of Subsidized Agricultural Credit on Income Distribution in Costa Rica." In Dale W. Adams, D. H. Graham, and J. D. Von Pischke, eds., *Undermining Rural Development with Cheap Credit*. Boulder, Colo.: Westview.

von Braun, Joachim, David Hotchkiss, Maarten Immink. 1989. "Nontraditional Export Crops in Guatemala: Effects on Production, Income, and Nutrition." Research Report No. 73. Washington, D.C.: International Food Policy Research Institute.

von Braun, Joachim, and Eileen Kennedy. 1986. "Commercialization of Subsistence Agriculture: Income and Nutritional Effects in Developing Countries." Working Papers on Commercialization of Agriculture and Nutrition, No. 1. Washington, D.C.: International Food Policy Research Institute.

von Braun, Joachim, Detlev Puetz, and Patrick Webb. 1989. "Irrigation Technology and Commercialization of Rice in the Gambia: Effects on Income and Nutrition." Research Report No. 75. Washington, D.C.: International Food Policy Research Institute.

von Freyhold, Michaela. 1979. *Ujamaa Villages in Tanzania: Analysis of a Social Experiment.* New York: Monthly Review Press.

Von Pischke, J. D. 1991. *Finance at the Frontier: The Role of Credit in Development of the Private Economy.* Washington, D.C.: World Bank.

Von Pischke, J. D., D. W. Adams, and Gordon Donald, eds. 1983. *Rural Financial Markets in Developing Countries: Their Use and Abuse.* EDI Series in Economic Development. Baltimore: Johns Hopkins University Press.

Vuthipongse, Prakrom. 1989. "Institutional Capacity to Address Health Problems." In Michael R. Reich and E. Marui, eds., *International Cooperation for Health: Problems, Prospects, and Priorities.* Dover, Mass.: Auburn House.

Vyas, V. S. 1979. "Some Aspects of Structural Change in Indian Agriculture." *Indian Journal of Agricultural Economics* 34(1): 1–18.

Wade, Robert. 1985. "The Market for Public Office: Why the Indian State Is Not Better at Development." *World Development* 13(4): 467–97.

———. 1987. "The Management of Common Property Resources: Finding a Cooperative Solution." *The World Bank Research Observer* 2(2): 219–32.

———. 1990. *Governing the Market.* Princeton: Princeton University Press.

Wai, U. Tun. 1977. "A Revisit to Interest Rates outside the Organized Money Markets of Underdeveloped Countries." *Banca Nazionale del Lavoro Quarterly Review* 122: 291–312.

Walker, Kenneth R. 1984. *Food Grain Procurement and Consumption in China.* Cambridge: Cambridge University Press.

Walker, Thomas S., and James G. Ryan. 1990. *Village and Household Economies in India's Semi-Arid Tropics.* Baltimore: Johns Hopkins University Press.

Walsh, Julia A., and Kenneth S. Warren. 1979. "Selective Primary Health Care: An Interim Strategy for Disease Control in Developing Countries." *The New England Journal of Medicine* 301(18): 967–74.

Wangwe, Samuel M. 1983. "Industrialization and Resource Allocation in a Developing Country: The Case of Recent Experiences in Tanzania." *World Development* 11(6): 483–92.

Warwick, Donald P. 1975. *A Theory of Public Bureaucracy: Politics, Personality, and Organization in the State Department.* Cambridge: Harvard University Press.

Welch, F. 1978. "The Role of Investments in Human Capital in Agriculture." In T. W. Schultz, ed., *Distortions of Agricultural Incentives.* Bloomington: Indian University Press.

Welsh, C. E. 1965. "The Challenge of Change: Meiji Japan and Contemporary Africa." Paper prepared for the Eighth Annual Meeting of the African Studies Association, Philadelphia, October 27–30.

Wen, Guanzhong James. 1989. "The Current Land Tenure System and Its Impact on Long-Term Performance of the Farming Sector." Ph.D. diss., University of Chicago.

Westney, D. Eleanor. 1987. *Imitation and Innovation: The Transfer of Western Organizational Patterns to Meiji, Japan.* Cambridge: Harvard University Press.

Whetten, N. L. 1948. *Rural Mexico.* Chicago: University of Chicago Press.

Wildavsky, Aaron. 1979. *Speaking Truth to Power: The Art and Craft of Policy Analysis.* Boston: Little, Brown.

Williams, W. A. 1969. *The Roots of the Modern American Empire.* New York.

Williamson, Oliver E. 1975. *Markets and Hierarchies.* New York: Free Press.

Winston, Gordon. 1971a. "Capital Utilization: Physiological Costs and Preferences for Shift Work." Research Memorandum No. 42. Mimeograph. Williamstown, Mass.: Center for Development Economics, Williams College.

——. 1971b. "Capital Utilization in Economic Development." *Economic Journal* 81(321).

Wittfogel, Karl. 1971. "Communist and Non-Communist Agrarian Systems, with Special Reference to the U.S.S.R. and Communist China: A Comparative Approach." In W. A. Douglas Jackson, ed., *Agrarian Policies and Problems in Non-Communist Countries.* Seattle: University of Washington Press.

Wong, Christine P. W. 1982. "Rural Industrialization in China." In R. Barker and R. Sinha with B. Rose, eds., *The Chinese Agricultural Economy.* Boulder, Colo.: Westview.

——. 1986a. "Intermediate Technology for Development: Small-Scale Chemical Fertilizer Plants in China." *World Development* 14(10/11).

——. 1986b. "Ownership and Control in Chinese Industry: The Maoist Legacy and Prospects for the 1980s." In *China's Economy Looks toward the Year 2000,* vol. 1. Washington, D.C.: United States Government Printing Office.

World Bank. 1961. *The Economic Development of Tanganyika.* Baltimore: Johns Hopkins University Press.

——. 1975. "Agricultural Credit." World Bank Sector Policy Paper. Washington, D.C.: World Bank.

——. 1978. *World Development Report 1978.* New York: Oxford University Press.

——. 1980. *World Development Report 1980.* New York: Oxford University Press.

——. 1981. *Accelerated Development in sub-Saharan Africa.* Washington, D.C.: World Bank.

——. 1982. *World Development Report 1982.* New York: Oxford University Press.

——. 1983a. "Tanzania Agricultural Sector Report." Report No. 4052-TA. Washington, D.C.: World Bank.

——. 1983b. *Thailand: Rural Growth and Employment* (prepared by H. P. Binswanger and others). Washington, D.C.: World Bank.

——. 1984. *World Development Report 1984.* New York: Oxford University Press.

——. 1985a. *The Assault on World Poverty: Problems of Rural Development, Education and Health.* Baltimore: Johns Hopkins University Press.

——. 1985b. Project Performance Audit Report, No. 5419. Operations Evaluation Department. Washington, D.C.: World Bank.

——. 1986a. *Sustainability of Projects: Review of Experience in the Fertilizer Subsector.* Operations Evaluation Department. Washington, D.C.: World Bank.

———. 1986b. *Financing Adjustment with Growth in sub-Saharan Africa, 1986–90.* Washington, D.C.: World Bank.

———. 1986c. "Kenya: Agricultural Sector Report," vol. 1 and 2. Report No. 4629-KE. Washington, D.C.: World Bank.

———. 1986d. *Poverty and Hunger: Issues and Options for Food Security in Developing Countries.* Washington, D.C.: World Bank.

———. 1987a. *Financing Health Services in Developing Countries: An Agenda for Reform.* Washington, D.C.: World Bank.

———. 1987b. *World Development Report 1987.* New York: Oxford University Press.

———. 1987–88. *Commodity Trade and Price Trends.* Baltimore: Johns Hopkins University Press.

———. 1988a. *Rural Development: World Bank Experience, 1965–86.* A World Bank Operations Evaluation Study. Operations Evaluation Department. Washington, D.C.: World Bank.

———. 1988b. *World Development Report 1988.* New York: Oxford University Press.

———. 1989a. *Sub-Saharan Africa from Crisis to Sustainable Growth.* Washington, D.C.: World Bank.

———. 1989b. *Thailand: Building on Recent Success,* vol. 1. Washington, D.C.: World Bank.

———. 1989c. *World Development Report 1989.* New York: Oxford University Press.

———. 1990. *World Development Report 1990.* New York: Oxford University Press.

———. 1991. *World Development Report 1991.* New York: Oxford University Press.

———. 1992a. *The World Bank Atlas: Twentyfifth Anniversary Edition.* Washington, D.C.: World Bank.

———. 1992b. *World Development Report 1992.* New York: Oxford University Press.

———. 1993. *World Development Report 1993: Investing in Health.* New York: Oxford University Press.

World Resources Institute. 1990. *World Resources, 1990–91.* New York: Oxford University Press.

———. 1992. *World Resources, 1992–93.* New York: Oxford University Press.

Wright, Gavin. 1986. *Old South, New South: Revolution in the Southern Economy Since the Civil War.* New York: Basic Books.

Wu, Torng-Chuang. 1988. "Directions and Strategies of Agricultural Development in Taiwan." In *Conference on Directions and Strategies of Agricultural Development in the Asia-Pacific Region (I).* Taipei, Taiwan: The Institute of Economics, Academia Sinica.

Yager, Joseph A. 1988. *Transforming Agriculture in Taiwan.* Ithaca: Cornell University Press.

Yates, P. L. 1981. *Mexico's Agricultural Dilemma.* Tucson: The University of Arizona Press.

Yotopoulos, Pan A. 1974. "Rationality, Efficiency, and Organizational Behavior." *Food Research Institute Studies* 8(3): 263–74.

Yotopoulos, Pan A., and Jeffrey B. Nugent. 1976. *Economics of Development: Empirical Investigations.* New York: Harper & Row.

Young, Crawford. 1982. *Ideology and Development in Africa.* New Haven: Yale University Press.

Yuan, M. H. 1964. "The Fertilizer Industry of Taiwan." *Industry of Free China* 21(1).

INDEX OF NAMES

INDEX OF SUBJECTS

Growth monitoring, Oral rehydration therapy, Breast feeding, and Immunization (GOBI), 273
"Growth-oriented" strategy, 285–87
Guatemala, landownership in, 151, 152 (figure)

Haber synthesis (of ammonia), 227
Hacendados (large landowners), 334, 355
Haiti, landownership in, 151, 152 (figure)
Harambee schools (Kenya), 388, 392, 397
Harrows, Taiwanese design for, 214–15
Health and Welfare, Ministry of (SSA) (Mexico), 345, 346
Health programs, 254, 271–72, 276–78, 414
    and child mortality, 269, 272, 273, 285–86, 362, 415
    for children, 262, 275–76, 286, 309, 389, 417
    child survival hypothesis, 278–79
    in Mexico, 345, 348, 359, 362
    and nutrition, 267–69, 273–74
    in rural China, 306–7, 308, 309
    in Taiwan, 332–33, 352, 362
    in Tanzania, 374, 388
    for women, 273, 274, 286, 309
Health Research and Development Commission, 21
High-yielding varieties (HYVs), 78, 159, 312, 323, 387
    and consumption increase, 164–65
    fertilizer needs of, 192–93, 224
    in Mexico, 338n.17, 340, 348
    and small farms, 125, 128, 129–30, 131, 132, 137, 139, 146
Homestead Act (United States), 69, 72, 91
Honduras, 151, 152 (figure), 205–6, 207 (table)
Households, rural. *See* Rural households, 262
Human resource development, 257-58, 312–13, 410, 417.
    See also Education; Social programs
Hunger, 267, 268, 269, 270, 286
    food shortages, 85, 143, 257, 400
    See also Famine
Hybrids
    of maize 339, 340, 383, 387
    of silkworms, 79
Hydrogen production, 228
HYVs. *See* High-yielding varieties

ICRISAT. *See* International Crops Research Institute for the Semi-Arid Tropics
IDC. *See* India Dairy Corporation
Idealism, in political leaders, 402
IFPRI. *See* International Food Policy Research Institute
IMF. *See* International Monetary Fund
Immunization, 275–76, 306, 308, 388
Import liberalization, in Tanzania, 376
Imports, 49
    of farm equipment, 179, 213–14
    of fertilizer, 223, 224, 245n.21, 247–51
    tariffs, 80n.5, 106, 181
Import-substitution industrialization. *See* Industrialization, import-substitution
IMSS. *See* Mexican Institute of Social Security
IMSS-COPLAMAR (Mexican health care program), 346, 348, 359
Incentives, 104, 168–72, 302, 356, 412
Income, 37, 53, 191
    distribution, 132, 155, 162–63, 259, 297
    and food expenditures, 163–64, 165, 178
    growth in China, 300, 303, 311
    rural nonfarm, 45–46, 202–6, 210, 211–12
    and structural transformation, 39, 41n.3, 60
Income, farm 45–46, 60, 213, 349n.24, 366
    in China, 300
    and disbursements, 61–63
    in India, 25 (figure)
    and the international economy, 63–65
    in Japan, 97
    in Kenya, 365, 382
    in Taiwan, 329, 330
    in Thailand, 201–2, 203
    in United States, 70, 71
India, 14, 19, 25 (figure), 164
    agricultural innovation in, 23–24, 64, 128, 338n.17
    dairy production in, 27, 165, 176
    farm equipment in, 213–14, 218–19
    farm size in, 18–19, 124, 125, 135, 136 (figure)
    fertilizer production in, 224, 232, 233 (table), 234 (table), 238–40, 242n.15, 249
    land rental in, 153, 154 (figure), 155, 157
India Dairy Corporation (IDC) (India), 27
Indonesia, 48, 161, 283, 415
    agrarian strategy in, 99, 159–60, 170–71, 181, 403–4

agricultural innovation in, 64, 128, 129 (figure), 137, 139
    banking reform in, 183, 184–85, 409
    economic policy in, 180, 181, 408n.6
    fertilizer production in, 240–41, 250, 414
Induced-innovation hypothesis, 86, 88
Industrialization, 37, 95, 243
    agriculture and, 52, 360, 412–14
    in China, 302, 303-4
    in Soviet Union, 292, 294, 295, 360
    in Taiwan, 331, 360
    in Tanzania, 372, 373
    See also Fertilizer production; Manufacturing
Industrialization, import-substitution, 64, 80n.5, 106, 179, 256, 402–3
    vs. domestic production, 222, 225–26, 250
    in Mexico and Taiwan, 330, 343n.19, 351
Infanticide, female, in China, 309
Infant mortality. *See* Child mortality
Inflation, 254, 255-56, 260, 343, 351
Infrastructure investment, 174, 258, 366, 412, 413
    and agrarian structure, 160
    in China, 292, 305, 312
    government role in, 52
    in Japan, 80, 94
    and land tenancy, 155
    for marketing, 104–5, 170, 172, 221
    in Mexico, 340, 342
    for natural resource development, 47
    rural, 208, 210, 324–25, 416
    in Soviet Union, 296
    in Tanzania, 368, 373
    in United States, 70, 91
Initiatives, public sector, 175, 394, 400, 405, 412, 417
    in Japan and United States, 104, 410
    for marketing, 176–77, 258, 371, 396, 403
    for social programs, 253–54
Innovation, 116, 146, 150
    in Africa, 140, 381, 397
    drought-resistant crops, 385, 386, 387
    induced hypothesis, 86-88
    industrial, 189, 193–96, 200–201, 229
    and inputs, 103, 166–68, 412
    in Japan, 68, 77–78, 79, 87, 103, 104
    and labor input, 132, 162–63, 193, 212
    in Mexico, 338–40, 361-62
    supply-side effects of, 211–12
    in Taiwan, 33, 319, 320, 321–23, 326–27, 361–62
    in United States, 70, 76–77, 83, 103, 104
    See also Mechanization, agricultural; Seed-fertilizer innovation
Inputs, and innovation, 103, 166–68, 412. *See also* Land-labor input ratio
Institutions
    research, 89–91, 143, 175–77, 412
    rural Mexico and Taiwan compared, 355–58, 359
    See also Research, agricultural
Integrated pest management (IPM), 32
Integrated rural development (IRD), 260, 261
Interest groups, 401n.2
Interest rates, 50, 94, 260, 343
    and financial markets, 179, 182–83
    and inflation, 256
    and rural credit programs, 184–85
    subsidies for, 417
International Crops Research Institute for the Semi-Arid Tropics (ICRISAT), 194
International economy, rural link to, 63–65, 187–88, 222
International Food Policy Research Institute (IFPRI), 31, 382
International Maize and Wheat Improvement Center (CIMMYT), 128, 145, 166, 338n.16, 386
International Monetary Fund (IMF), 257
International Rice Research Institute (IRRI), 137, 145, 194, 195, 196, 386
Intersectoral commodity flows, 187–88, 206–9, 209–10, 220–22, 413
Investment, 21, 39, 232n.4
    and financial markets, 50, 51
    foreign, 70, 159
    in human resources, 257–58, 417
    See also Infrastructure investment
Investment, agricultural, 254
    in China, 300, 303
    in Mexico, 316, 342–43
    in Nigeria and Indonesia compared, 181
    in Soviet Union, 295, 296
    in United States, 70